A Three Dimensional Approach

To

Forex Trading

Answer's the question - where is the market going next?

Using the power of relational, fundamental and technical analysis

By

Anna Coulling

www.annacoulling.com

www.quantumtrading.com

www.quantumtradingeducation.com

A Three Dimensional Approach To Forex Trading

© *2013 Anna Coulling - All rights reserved*

All rights reserved. No part of this book may be reproduced or transmitted in any form, or by any means, electronic or mechanical, including photocopying, recording, or any information storage and retrieval system, without prior permission of the Author. Your support of Author's rights is appreciated.

Disclaimer

Futures, stocks, and spot currency trading have large potential rewards, but also large potential risk. You must be aware of the risks and be willing to accept them in order to trade in the futures, stocks, and forex markets. Never trade with money you can't afford to lose. This publication is neither a solicitation nor an offer to Buy/Sell futures, stocks or forex. The information is for educational purposes only. No representation is being made that any account will or is likely to achieve profits or losses similar to those discussed in this publication. Past performance of indicators or methodology are not necessarily indicative of future results. The advice and strategies contained in this publication may not be suitable for your situation. You should consult with a professional, where appropriate. The author shall not be liable for any loss of profit, or any other commercial damages including, but not limited to special, incidental, consequential, or other damages.

Who this book is for

This book is meant, above all, for anyone whose primary goal is to become a master forex trader, written by someone with over 20 years trading experience.

If you are new to forex trading, **A Three Dimensional Approach to Forex Trading** will get you going faster than any other book on the market. If you already have some forex trading experience, this book will give you new skills and a deeper understanding of the inner workings of the forex market.

In short, this book will explain the techniques and knowledge you need to become a confident and successful forex trader.

What this book covers

A Three Dimensional Approach to Forex Trading will give you an entirely different perspective on how to trade the forex market. This book also encompasses everything you need to know about the forex market. It is the first book to comprehensively cover this market from three different angles. These are technical, fundamental and relational analysis, which when combined, provide a powerful methodology giving you unparalleled confidence in your trading decisions.

Table of Contents

Foreword 1

An introduction to the forex market and why it's all about money flow and sentiment, which can only be seen by taking a three dimensional approach. And why there are only two risks in trading.

Chapter One : Assessing Market Sentiment 9

Market sentiment is one of the keys to understanding money flow as traders and investors move between fear and greed and back again. This is revealed in the four capital markets and their relationships with the forex market at their heart. In this chapter discover how to interpret money flow for yourself, quickly and easily.

Chapter Two : Bonds & Bond Yields 17

Bonds are the least understood by forex traders and rarely, if ever watched. Yet the bond market underpins the cost of money and consequent risk appetite and is therefore vital to understanding market mood. Here you will learn about the power of bond yields and the clear message they are sending you as a forex trader.

Chapter Three : Commodity Markets Explained.................................34

Why the commodity market is the fulcrum of the financial markets. The place where real currencies are converted into real goods. It is where money meets the real world of economic supply and demand. It's a market full of clues for forex traders if you know where to look. This chapter will teach you how and where.

Chapter Four : Equity Markets Explained.. 55

Just like commodities, equities signal risk, return and money flow. It is where changes in the broader economic cycle and risk sentiment are reflected in specific currencies. As one of the few cash markets it also provides a real insight into money flow and volume.

Chapter Five : The Forex Market Revealed 63

This is the market where global politics and money collide creating a market of intrigue and political chicanery played out at the highest levels. Here you will be discover what few forex traders ever realize. This chapter alone will surprise you.

Chapter Six : The Bond & Commodity Relationship 72

One of the most complex of relationships which most traders ignore. Multi-faceted and constantly changing according to the economic cycle, this relationship reveals where we are in the economic cycle and, as a consequence, the likelihood of impending interest rate changes. Changes which will ultimately reflect interest rate differentials in currency pairs with consequent strength and weakness

Chapter Seven : Bond & Equities...80

A non linear relationship, connected to the economic cycle. But one which is also heavily influenced by sudden and unexpected market shocks. This is a pivotal relationship and one few forex traders ever appreciate.

Chapter Eight : Bonds & Currencies 85

A key 'money to money' relationship. Differential bond yields can and do cause huge shifts in money flow as central banks also indulge in the carry trade. This can result in great trends which retail forex traders can also exploit.

Chapter Nine : The US Dollar 94

The king of currencies, and still the currency of first reserve. The US dollar remains the lynchpin of the global economy. It underpins every capital market. As forex traders this is the one currency we need to understand and track. This chapter will tell you all you need to know about the US dollar.

Chapter Ten : Indices & Market Internals 103

Cross market and relational analysis can provide forex traders with some powerful insights into market sentiment, risk and money flow. The key is to know which indices and markets to follow. The price action on these instruments can help support and validate trading decisions in all time frames.

Chapter Eleven : Secondary Perspectives 122

This chapter considers aspects of relational analysis with associated analytical techniques, such as ratio analysis. This chapter also explains how to interpret the Commitment of Traders Report (COT), the Gold Oil Ratio, and how they can be used in forex trading.

Chapter Twelve : The Fundamentals of Global Economies 158

If you don't understand the economic powerhouses of the world you cannot trade forex with any degree of confidence. This chapter takes a detailed look at countries and their economies which currently dominate the forex markets and why.

Chapter Thirteen : The Next Generation 193

The economic powerhouses in waiting. The emerging powers and their associated currencies are explained in detail. After all, it's not always the majors that offer the best trading opportunities.

Chapter Fourteen : Asia Pacific Economies 223

Whilst Western economies continue to struggle, Asia Pacific booms. Once again this offers forex traders some unique opportunities, provided you understand the economies of these countries.

Chapter Fifteen : Economic Cycles & Their Drivers 257

This is the world of global market cycles, interest rates, inflation and deflation, and is the business of forecasting and managing economies around the world. Understanding the economic cycle can give some great perspectives on where and why currencies are moving.

Chapter Sixteen : Economic Indicators Explained 280

Whether we like it or not, economic releases are a fact of life and can blindside even the best technical trader. This chapter covers the most important economic indicators and fundamental news releases which drive the markets. It also explains their significance, their impact and their relevance which all depend on where we are in the economic cycle. This chapter also explains why the Rating Agencies are losing their power.

Chapter Seventeen : An Introduction to Technical Analysis 336

The third element of market analysis. This final element completes the three dimensional approach. Technical analysis is an art, not a science and in this chapter you will discover why.

Chapter Eighteen : Technical Indicators 369

One of the problems many traders face is knowing which indicators to use and when. With hundreds to choose from it can be a very difficult decision. Here we cover some of the more popular, and also explain why volume and price are the most powerful. The methods revealed will revolutionize your trading.

Chapter Nineteen : Technical Analysis Techniques 393

The most useful technical analysis techniques explained in detail and how they can be used to determine market direction.

Chapter Twenty : In The Currency Jungle 415

In the final chapter of the book, I explain the characteristics of each currency, as well as a variety of major, cross and exotic currency pairs. Just as in the jungle, there are hidden dangers awaiting, and in today's forex world, even more so. Here you will discover which currencies to consider and why, and how their personalities change, once they become a pair. In addition you will also discover the power of the currency matrix.

You will now have the skills and knowledge to become a master forex trader in your own right.

My Other Books & Acknowledgments 430

List of the chart providers used in this book along with details of free resources for forex traders.

Testimonials

Here are just one or two from the many thousands of emails I have received from traders around the world since writing this book and others in the series, and which are truly humbling.

Dear Ms Anna,

I would like to express my gratitude for taking the time and effort to write this gem. A great book, and I must admit it opened my world to another way of observing the market and the footprint of the insiders.

Anna,

Thank you so so much for your book on VPA. I could not put it down! Your book was so easy to read and understand as well! This book has changed and will continue to change my life forever. I tell people all the time how amazing it is.

Hi Anna,

I really would like to thank you for this mind blowing book.

Anna,

I've been trading for many years and just finished reading your book. It was excellent. I've always looked at volume but you have opened my eyes.

Dear Anna

I decided to re-read your book. I must say there are some important lessons to be learned from your book.

Hi Anna

I have finished your book and it is very easy to read and understand. I find the charts and explanations easy to understand too and feel confident that with practice and patience my journey into trading will be exciting and profitable........I'm glad I found you and value your honesty and insight.

And of course you an also read many of the 5 star reviews on Amazon for which I am always deeply grateful.

Foreword

[At age 106] People are always worried about the economy and the world, especially since the financial crisis of 2008 and Europe's sovereign debt crisis in 2011. I feel that people should learn to be optimistic because life goes on, and sometimes favorable surprises come out of the blue, whether due to new policies or scientific breakthroughs.

Irving Kahn (1905 - 2015)

If the marketing hype is to be believed, trading foreign exchange (forex) is not only the easiest market to trade, but is also the place which offers the fastest route to untold riches and personal financial freedom.

Open and accessible 24 hours a day, a trader only needs a laptop and internet connection to start making money with little or no effort. One email I recently received promised I could make thousands of pips by just trading a few minutes a day.

Forex is a vast market with daily volumes now approaching 6 trillion dollars. It's no wonder so many traders are drawn to it like moths to a flame. And, in many ways it is the easiest market in which to participate. Not only are there hundreds of brokers to choose from, but opening an account can be done in minutes, sometimes with just a credit card.

The trading process too is simple. All you have to decide is whether a currency pair is going up or down. What could be easier?

This is the way the forex market is promoted. A market where anyone can make a lot of money, just from working a few hours a week. It is sold as the ultimate get rich quick scheme. Open an account, start trading, and your financial troubles will be over. It can become your personal ATM machine allowing you to live your dream.

Ever since the foreign exchange markets were catapulted from relative obscurity in the late 1990's and into the public eye, they have been promoted to the mass retail market in this way. A fast way to make money. No experience required.

However, the sad fact is over 80% of trading accounts are usually in loss. These are not my figures, but from the CFTC, and more recently reported by the brokers themselves as part of the latest regulations, and so have to appear in any adverts.

The internet has also resulted in an avalanche of so called 'experts', all offering traders a promise of untold wealth by revealing some "secret" of how this market works, and usually at vast expense. Let me save you some money, right now. There are no secrets, just as there are no short cuts.

Moreover, many of these theoretical 'experts' have never traded anything in their life. In addition there has been an explosion in the numbers of forex brokers of dubious quality and murky accounting procedures.

Many of these have since moved offshore allowing them to continue their sharp practices which have blighted the industry.

The regulatory authorities have struggled to cope with the avalanche, as increasing numbers of prospective traders are lured in with the prospect of easy money, a better life for their families and a secure future. If all of this has echoes of the wild west, lawless and unregulated, this is exactly what it is. It is changing slowly, but only slowly, which is why so many traders continue to be seduced by cheap marketing gimmicks and hype.

If this sounds depressing, and you have read the first few paragraphs with a sinking feeling, don't worry. Help is at hand because I've written this book especially for you.

The purpose is to give you a detailed and deep understanding of how the forex markets really work. This book also includes my own unique trading approach based on the simple principle of combining, not just technical and fundamental analysis, but also relational analysis. In other words, it looks at related and associated markets which have a powerful effect on currencies.

This three dimensional approach is one I have used for many years, and is based on the simple principle you cannot trade successfully if you do not understand a market's true sentiment and risk profile, which in turn will identify the money flow.

As traders we just have to 'follow the money'. Armed with this knowledge, I believe it will change your approach to trading forever.

It is a book I have wanted to write for a very long time.

Furthermore, the trading techniques you will discover here are reinforced by the use of price behaviour in multiple time frames. Your trading perspective will suddenly move from a linear, one dimensional approach, to one based on three dimensions, where all the factors driving the price on your chart are revealed and the relationships and linkages become self apparent.

This will also help in your day to day trading decisions, because trading is all about money flow and sentiment, and your success will depend on whether you are trading with the money flow or against it. Furthermore, money flow reveals risk and market sentiment and traders who understand these prime market drivers can suddenly see 'inside the markets'......this alone will take your trading to a new, consistent and professional level.

From a technical perspective, price action and volume (market activity) are the only leading indicators we have for forecasting future market behaviour.

After all, the chart is the prism through which we see all three elements. The price chart contains it all, opinion from every investor, speculator, government and central bank. However, when price is coupled with volume we have the ultimate combination in forecasting future market direction. In other words, the price chart with volume, validates our relational and fundamental analysis.

Volume is pure market activity. It is the buying and the selling, the supply and the demand, being driven through the markets on a second by second basis by traders and investors. Volume is the tangible result of their hopes, fears, greed, panic and complacency. A way to imagine these emotions is what happens during an auction.

Suppose for a moment it is a wet and cold day in the middle of winter with few potential buyers in the room. The auctioneer starts with an opening price, which is quickly lowered, as no bids are forthcoming. The price is lowered again, and one bid is made. With no other interest the item is sold.

Now take another example where the auction room is full. The auctioneer opens the bidding and a bidding war begins with the price climbing very quickly, driven higher by the volume of buyers and demand for the item.

Two things are self evident from this analogy. Firstly, demand drives price, and secondly demand is revealed in terms of volume, which in the case of the auction is the number of people bidding for the item. I accept this is not a perfect analogy, but it does explain the importance of volume in trading, and why it is so powerful when read in conjunction with price.

In my three dimensional approach fundamental news is a fact of trading life, and whether we like it or not, the markets, governments and central banks all take note of this constant stream of economic releases. Much of this data is, of course, just statistics, and as the famous saying goes, ' there are lies, damned lies and statistics'.

As traders we do need to understand both the macro and micro aspects of economies, economics and why central banks and governments behave in the way they do. We need to understand the decision making processes of the central banks as they are the prime drivers of the forex market.

A classic example of this is the current bout of 'currency wars', where central banks (on behalf of their governments) around the world are actively engaged in devaluing their currency in an effort to protect struggling export markets. This competitive devaluation is being carried out by a combination of very low interest rates and deliberate market intervention. In other words, self-preservation is the name of this game.

Central bank attempts at currency manipulation simply reflect what lies at the heart of this largely speculative market, namely identifying and profiting from individual currency strength and weakness.

Having read so far, you may be wondering whether this book is for you. Perhaps you have already started to trade in this market using a short term scalping approach. So, how will this book help you?

Well, my answer is simply this....regardless of the time frame you are trading (and this applies to whatever market or instrument you are trading), if you have a deeper understanding of the technical, fundamental and relational drivers, it can only make you a better trader, since your decisions will be based on a three dimensional view and understanding, rather than on just one or two dimensions.

It doesn't matter whether you are trading on a 1 minute or a one day chart, the same principles apply. As I explained earlier the markets are all about money flow and risk sentiment, and the forex market is the perfect expression of this concept.

It is also the reason why the forex market sits at the centre of the financial markets and underpins the other three capital markets, namely commodities, bonds and equities. Every decision by every investor or speculator is about money, risk and return. The forex market is the largest of all the markets by some measure, and is unique in the sense it offers the quickest mechanism for cash conversion and asset transfer.

But this is not all you will discover in this book. You will also learn the forex market is unique. Because it is the only market where one instrument – a currency – can be bought and sold against a huge range of other currencies, adding a layer of complexity which is not found in other markets or instruments. After all, if you were trading a stock or share, all the buying and selling in the cash market is done through that instrument. So buyers and sellers in a stock such as IBM, only ever buy and sell shares in IBM. A hedge fund selling a large block of IBM shares may decide to sell these in small size orders, but ultimately there is only one market and instrument with which to sell these shares.

This is not the case for buyers and sellers of currency. A large bank who wants to trade in US dollars, can do so in a multitude of ways. First, the bank could simply sell Euros to buy US dollars. A straightforward sell on the EUR/USD. But, if the trade size were significant, the bank may decide to sell against another currency, the EUR/GBP for example, and then sell the GBP against the USD. This achieves the same result, but hides the true nature of the buying and selling from view. This is what makes the forex market both unique and complex, and why trading using one chart and one time frame can be dangerous.

If you are new to forex trading, what you have read so far may seem daunting, and at odds with how forex trading is marketed. However, once you understand the key drivers for this market it will all fall into place.

Learning to trade is like any other skill. It has to be broken down into its key components, which you learn individually, before rebuilding the whole and adding each element back into its correct place. If you think of it in much the same way as any other learning process, this will be divided into various modules, which you study, before moving on to the next one. This is the approach I advocate for all types of learning, but particularly when applied to the forex market, because of its underlying complexity.

The key is to take one small element at a time, and concentrate on this until you feel comfortable, and then to move on to the next piece of the puzzle. If you are working full time, this is even more important as your time will be limited, so you need to break the task down into small manageable topics which you can study in bite size pieces, before moving on to the next element. A few hours each evening will soon build up your knowledge.

In putting together the structure for this book I have tried to bear this in mind, and present the topic in logical sections, which can be read independently, each section building on the next. Each topic then becomes part of the complete picture as the pieces of the puzzle fit together in an ordered way.

This is what this book is all about. Helping traders acquire the right knowledge and tools which will enable them to identify the market's true sentiment. After all, markets move on sentiment, since virtually every decision in the market is about risk and return, and is made by people and their desire to either protect their assets, or increase their yield. It is this knowledge which will reduce the risk of any trade you take.

At this point, many of you may be wondering who I am and why you should believe anything in this book. So, here is a little bit about me and details of some places where you can check out my references.

I began my own trading career back in the early 1990's, before the days of the internet, and started trading index futures using price and volume. There were no online brokers and all the data came in via a satellite feed. Orders were placed by phone with the broker, and executed and filled on the floor of the exchange. It was stressful, not least because of the time delay in getting filled and when the data feed broke down.

Since those heady days I have traded virtually every market and every instrument, and indeed came to the forex market last.

This trading experience has given me the grounding I needed to succeed, which is what I want to share with you in this book.

My trading philosophy is, in essence, very simple and akin to the ubiquitous KISS, except my version is Keeping it Super Simple.

I've also found over the years the best results come from having a system that is uncomplicated, not least because the markets are complex enough. Trading may not be easy, but it is straightforward.

My trading techniques are based on chart analysis, backed by my view of the broader fundamentals and related market sentiment, which provide the framework against which the markets move each and every day. It is I who make the decision to trade, no one else.

As I stress in my forex education program and live webinars, there are only two risks in trading. The first is the financial risk and the second is the risk of the trade itself. Nothing else.

The first is easy to quantify and manage. This is pure and simple money management and which I cover in detail in Forex For Beginners. The second, the risk of the trade itself, is much more difficult to assess. This is what we need to quantify every time we open a new position or consider taking a position in the market. What is the risk on the trade? What is the probability of success? Am I taking on too much risk and how do I measure that risk?

In a nutshell, this is what I want to share with you in this book. I want to arm you with the knowledge, skills and tools so you too can become a confident, consistent and profitable trader. Like me, you will be able to make your own discretionary trading decisions based on your analysis of the price and market activity, coupled with the underlying fundamental and relational picture.

This is the approach I also use in my market analysis which is taken by a number of leading financial internet sites. I write regular market analysis and commentary on my personal site, www.annacoulling.com. You are welcome to join me in my free live webinars and all the details are on my site, along with all my latest books.

I also work closely with NinjaTrader, a company I am delighted to be associated with, as I believe they offer an excellent trading platform, and their customer support is second to none.

In addition to using the NinjaTrader platform, I also have accounts with FX brokers using the immensely popular Metatrader MT4 and MT5 platform. For more complex strategies I have an account with a large futures broker. Many of the chart examples in this book are from the NinjaTrader platform.

I would also like to express my thanks to www.investing.com for allowing me to reproduce their charts throughout this book, and without whose help, it would have been impossible to reproduce charts of the more exotic currencies and markets.

So, let's dive in and get started.

Anna

Chapter One
Assessing Market Sentiment

Remember, it [the market] is designed to fool most of the people most of the time.

Jesse Livermore (1877-1940)

In my foreword to this book I made the statement that there are only two risks in trading. The risk on the trade itself, and the financial risk we are taking in opening any new position. Of these two, it is the risk on the trade itself that is the most difficult to quantify and assess, and this is what this book is all about. I do, of course, explain everything you need to understand about money management in a separate book, but the key to success as a forex trader, and indeed any other form of trading or investing, is to assess and quantify the risk you are taking in opening a new position. In other words is this a high risk trade, a medium risk trade or a low risk trade?

The methods and techniques you will learn here will help you to understand how the markets work and how you can can assess this risk for yourself, quickly and easily. And I do this using three distinct approaches, which although very different from one another, all connect together to provide a unified picture as a result. A three dimensional picture if you like, very different from the one dimensional approach most traders adopt.

One of the reasons many traders ultimately fail is they trade in a vacuum, with little or no knowledge of the broader markets or the linkages that exist between them. This myopic approach to trading may have worked in the past, but in the last few years, with financial markets in turmoil, the rule book has been torn up, as you will discover later.

The old trading methodologies and approaches no longer work. For example, the currency markets are no longer driven simply by interest rate differentials. They are highly politicised and manipulated as individual countries attempt to protect their own export markets by competitive devaluation. Moreover, quantitative easing has now entered the trading lexicon, with central banks happily printing money, further distorting the financial markets.

To succeed as a trader now requires a much deeper understanding of market behaviour, of market sentiment, of money flow, and risk appetite, which can be achieved using a trilateral approach.

And the three elements of this approach are:

- relational
- fundamental
- technical

These are the three strands of market analysis which when combined, provide the three dimensional view of the market, which few forex traders use. Without it, failure awaits. With it, trading becomes stress free, as each trading opportunity is based on a complete view of the market, the money flow, and consequent risk.

In many ways it can be likened to the three strands of a rope. Individually they are weak, but when combined, the strength of the rope is greater than the sum of its constituent parts. This provides the framework for any trading decision across multiple time frames.

But let me start with two very simple concepts.

The first is that every decision taken by every investor, trader or speculator, in every financial market everywhere in the world is about money. Nothing else – just money.

Does this sound like an obvious statement? Perhaps it is, but it is also the single reason most forex traders lose as they sit fixated on one currency chart wondering why the pair has moved against them.

Market prices are the result of the combined decision making by investors and speculators across all markets with two objectives in mind. Either to increase their wealth or to protect what they have.

When a market participant buys a high risk asset class, they are relinquishing liquidity in return for some future gain, and prepared to take on higher risk. On the other hand, when a market participant sells a high risk asset class, they are looking for a safe haven to protect their gain, and will consequently buy a low risk asset class as a result. However, once risk appetite returns, high risk assets will be bought again.

This is the cyclical process all markets follow minute by minute and day by day, as money flows from high risk to low risk assets and back again, all driven with one thing in mind. To maximise potential returns on that money.

Every asset class in every one of the financial markets has a different risk profile and as a result, market sentiment and risk appetite ebb and flow continually. It is this constant flow of money which drives the markets. Understand the money flow, and you begin to understand market behaviour in all its forms. Consider this simply analogy of risk appetite.

Suppose you are deciding whether to buy or rent a house. If house prices are falling or perhaps just flat, your decision might be to rent. Why? Because your risk tolerance is low. You are frightened house prices may fall further, so you decide to stay liquid, and not to invest your cash in bricks and mortar. Instead you might simply decide to invest somewhere safe, but with a low return.

However, as house prices start to rise, you may decide to buy. Why? Because your risk tolerance is higher. You feel prices are likely to continue rising and are therefore prepared to relinquish your current liquidity in return for a future, and better, gain. In other words, an increase in the capital value of your house.

So how does this simple analogy play out in the financial markets? In truth, very simply, through the four principle capital markets as follows:

- Bonds
- Commodities
- Equities
- Currencies

So what is the risk profile of each of the above markets, and how does this help us to quantify risk and market sentiment? Let's start with bonds.

Bonds

Bonds are generally considered to be a safe haven asset, and are the basic ingredient of the world's debt capital markets, which in turn are the cornerstone of the world's economy. In sheer size, the bond market dwarfs the forex market, and yet all we ever hear as forex traders is how large the currency exchange market is, and how many transactions are executed each day.

Yet the bond market is almost wholly ignored by forex traders. Why? Because it is perceived as complicated, full of jargon and probably not very relevant. However, here is a market of much greater size which gives you all the signals you need about risk, money flow and market sentiment, and yet it is ignored.

In fact bonds are very simple to understand. They are simply a loan. Nothing more, nothing less.

We all borrow money in a variety of different ways, and the bond market is structured in such a way as to allow all sorts of bodies, including countries, governments, municipal authorities and private companies, to borrow money for a variety of reasons. Let's take a simple example to see how the bond market works.

Suppose you need to borrow $10,000 for a new business venture, and you have a friend who is prepared to lend you the money. He has offered to lend this to you at 5% per annum on the life of the loan, which you have agreed is ten years, as he believes it is a low risk, guaranteed return. You are the issuer of an IOU, and your friend is the buyer of the IOU. In effect he is buying your debt, and relinquishing liquidity in return for a guaranteed safe and steady return.

Now to convert this into the language of bonds, what we have actually done is to issue a bond, often referred to as a 'note' of which the $10,000 is called the coupon, and the length of the loan is the bond's maturity, which in this case is ten years. So in the language of bonds, we have sold a ten year bond, with a coupon of $10,000. Our friend has bought the bond and lent you the money for your business venture.

This leads to the next question, which is why do people buy and sell bonds, and what does this tell us about money flow? And this is where we return to the word risk.

Bonds are generally perceived as a low risk investment. Therefore, if the money flow is into bonds, and away from other markets, clearly investors and speculators are nervous, and looking for a safer haven for their money. So, in general terms, bonds are a low risk asset class which will normally see inflows of money when markets are nervous. In addition, they are also the ultimate barometer of interest rates, inflation, public sector debt and economic growth, all key measures of the flow of money and currency exchange rates as a result.

But how do we analyse this huge market to help us in our trading? The answer is yield. This simple measure gives us all the clues and signals of market sentiment, risk appetite and consequent money flow. Yield tells us whether the market is buying or selling bonds and whether the yield is therefore rising or falling. Put this on a chart and you have all your analysis for bond markets, in exactly the same way as for any other instrument.

The final point concerning bonds is to recognise that whilst they are generally considered to be extremely safe, there are some bonds which are safer than others. And you don't have to go far back in history to find some glaring examples of bonds which would once have been considered risk free.

The European debt crisis is one such example, and continues to remain so. Bonds from certain member states have now been reduced to junk status, with the market only stabilising with the intervention of the ECB standing behind them as the lender of last resort. This would have been unthinkable, even a few years ago.

Even in the US, some of the municipal bonds are no longer considered to be quite as safe as before, as governments struggle under the weight of debt.

However, there is one class of bond which are still considered to be the ultimate safe haven, and these are US Treasury bonds. US Treasuries generally fall into three broad groups, namely Treasury bills or T-bills, Treasury notes and Treasury bonds. T-bills are those with a maturity of less than one year. Treasury notes are from one to ten years and Treasury bonds are more than ten years. Each will have its own yield curve that reveals market sentiment for the short, medium and longer term. This is the benchmark bond we will use when considering bond yields and what they can tell us as forex traders.

Commodities

Just like bonds, commodities are generally ignored by the majority of forex traders, but for very different reasons. Bonds are ignored because they are considered to be complicated and confusing and of little value, an image I hope to shatter in this book.

Commodities, on the other hand, are ignored as they are seen as irrelevant. How wrong can you be, as in many ways they are even more important than bonds. As we will see later in the book, the relationship between bonds and commodities is one of the pivotal relationships in the financial markets. Why?

In simple terms, if bonds are purely about money and the cost of money, commodities markets are where real money is exchanged for real goods bought by real people to make real goods. In other words, the commodity markets play the central role of converting money into raw materials and in doing so, give us a clear insight into the fundamentals of world economics.

This relationship is the bridge if you like between the speculative world of paper based assets and the tangible world of real goods. It is the commodity markets that provide the pivotal insights into central bank policies, global economic growth and decline, currency flows and investor sentiment. A real world view where prices are largely dictated by supply and demand across continents.

Gold, of course, stands alone within the commodity sector as a unique constituent member, which is neither consumed nor used in any major industrial way, but is simply stockpiled in ever larger quantities. Its price has little to do with supply and demand, representing as it does, the ultimate safe haven hard asset and hedge against inflation. It is unique in every sense of the word, and we will look at the precious metal in detail.

Whilst commodity markets provide the real world bridge between money and goods, those same commodities in turn provide a bridge between commodities and individual currencies. A commodity based economy will sell its raw assets overseas in return for hard currency, which in turn is likely to be reflected in the currency itself.

Conversely, of course, an economy lacking in base commodities will need to import to maintain economic growth. A country such as Japan for example, has to import virtually all the base commodities such as oil, gas, and metals, a fact which is often seen in the CAD/JPY pair, which correlates relatively closely to crude oil.

All of these relationships will be explained and explored, but as a broad asset class, commodities are generally considered to be high risk, with the exception of gold. Finally, the one relationship with commodities that is pivotal, is the one with the US dollar. As all commodities are priced in US dollars, and money flows both in and out of the currency of first reserve, this is once again reflected in raw commodity prices.

Equities

The third of the four capital markets is probably one that is very familiar to you. If few forex traders ever consider the importance of bonds or commodities, fewer still look at equity markets, and the signals these markets convey. However, just like bonds and commodities, equities tell us a great deal, not least about risk appetite and market sentiment and, as you would expect, there is a strong relationship between equities and bonds. After all, equities are viewed as high risk, offering higher returns, whilst bonds are considered to be low risk with conservative returns.

As a result, there is a continuous flow of money between these two markets, with a consequent and related flow, both in and out of particular currencies and currency pairs. Equity markets provide us with a barometer of market sentiment, which in turn is reflected in the broader economy, and associated markets such as commodities.

A further facet to the relationship between currencies and equities is from an investing perspective. The best example of this is the relative strength of the Japanese yen and consequent flow into and out of the Nikkei 225. A weak yen usually results in inflows into Japanese shares from overseas investors, looking for better returns. This is a classic example of the linkages and relationships which exist at all levels and across the four capital markets, but which are rarely considered by most traders, or even investors.

Currencies

The last of our four capital markets is the forex or currency market, which is unique for a number of reasons.

First, it is the axis around which all the other markets revolve. Why? Because it is purely concerned with money and, as such, is the most liquid of all the markets. Currencies can be converted instantly – the flow is instant and immediate, allowing market participants to change direction in a flash, as risk sentiment changes on market news or economic data.

Every decision in every market, whether as an investor, speculator, government, bank or institution is about money, risk and return, which is why the forex market is the hub around which all the others rotate.

Second, it is the most complex of all four markets. Why? Because it is the market in which the central banks, governments and politicians all manipulate their home currency in one way or another, either for economic or political reasons.

Self preservation comes first in the forex market, and this aspect will continue to be a key element of price action over the next few years. The game changer for forex traders began in 2008 with the start of the financial meltdown. Since then, the rules have changed dramatically. No longer do currencies trade on simple interest rate differentials driven by inflation, growth and economic data. Now protectionist policies, market manipulation and artificial stimulus are all part of the mix.

Third, it is the only market where buying or selling of an instrument can take place against several other instruments. As mentioned in the foreword to the book, trading currencies is unlike any other. For example a bank or large hedge fund wishing to sell the US dollar can do so against a raft of other currencies using a variety of mechanisms to achieve this end. They will often do this, in order to mask their activities by constructing complex trading and hedging strategies.

Fourth, it is unique in the sense it cannot be 'pigeon holed' in terms of risk. The forex market covers every level of risk from high to low, with currencies such as the Yen and the Dollar representative of fiat based safe havens. It is truly representative of all the colours of the rainbow in terms of risk and risk appetite. This in turn is reflected in the buying or selling of particular currencies or currency pairs with consequent money flow, which brings us full circle to the other markets.

Finally, the foreign exchange market is entirely unregulated which presents opportunities for the unscrupulous, and problems for us as forex traders. With no central exchange there is no volume reporting, and as I will explain later, volume is one of the key indicators of market sentiment, whether in a cash market such as equities, or in an unregulated market such as the forex market.

So to summarise.

Markets move on risk and sentiment, which is reflected in the consequent flow of money. No market trades in isolation, and all markets are inter connected via a variety of linkages. These linkages exist in all timeframes and can be seen on every price chart, and used effectively by all types of traders, whether as an intraday scalper, or a longer term swing or trend trader.

This relational view is underpinned by the fundamental and the technical elements, which complete the picture, and provides a three dimensional view of the risk on each and every trade.

Which, when all is said and done, is the one thing we want to know before we open any new position in the market.

Chapter Two
Bonds and Bond Yields

I used to think if there was reincarnation, I wanted to come back as the president or the pope or a .400 baseball hitter. But now I want to come back as the bond market. You can intimidate everybody.

James Carville (1944 -)

Bonds are the basic ingredient of the world's debt capital markets, and is where money is borrowed by, and lent to, governments, companies, organisations and countries.

Bonds are loans, short and simple, and as such, tell us about the money flow between all the various market participants. Put simply, it is a market which not only reveals the cost of money, but also reveals a variety of deeper trends including market sentiment and risk.

Whilst bonds are loans, and similar in many ways to more traditional types of borrowing, where they differ is these loans are tradable in a secondary market.

They are often referred to as fixed income instruments or the fixed income market.

Bonds are issued in order to raise money, and the borrower is required to repay the amount borrowed, plus interest, over a specified time period, the maturity or term of the loan. So, if a loan is over a ten year period, this is the term of the loan to maturity.

In general, there are three types of bonds:

- Those with a maturity of less than a year
- Those with a maturity between one and ten years
- Those with a maturity between ten and thirty years

Bonds with a maturity of less than a year are referred to as money market debt, whilst those over one year are considered to be capital market debt.

Strictly speaking there is no difference, since money is money. This is just the way they are referred to, and in fact this has more to do with accounting terminology than anything else.

As forex traders there are really only two debt markets that interest us. Namely, bonds denominated in US dollars, and bonds denominated in so called Eurodollars. Eurodollar bonds have nothing to do with the EUR/USD currency, but is simply a shorthand way of referring to US bonds held outside the US.

The reason for focusing on the US dollar bond market is that this is the largest market by some measure, and is therefore the prime driver for money across the world.

Until recently, the primary focus of attention for analysis of market sentiment was solely on those bonds issued by the US Treasury, but in 2009, all of this changed. It has been necessary to add another group of bonds to our analysis, namely Munibonds.

Prior to 2009, the focal point was on the three types of US bonds:

- T Bills
- T Notes
- T Bonds

These bonds cover the short, medium and long term debt markets respectively.

So what changed in 2009? The answer is quantitative easing or QE, and the profound effect it has had on the bond market. QE has changed the game and the way we now interpret what the charts are telling us. We still analyse the US Treasury bonds, but now include the US Munibonds and the reasons are as follows.

Quantitative easing is a mechanism by which the central bank of a country prints its own money. It doesn't actually print this using a printing press as such, but adds this money to its own balance sheet by crediting its own account. Access your online bank account, add some more zeros and the effect would be much the same. It's that simple.

And this is what the Federal Reserve in the US and other central banks were forced to do, following the near collapse of the monetary system in the wake of the sub-prime mortgage crisis, the collapse of Lehman Brothers, Fannie May, Freddie Mac and Bear Stearns.

The logic was simple. The Central bank needed to stop the meltdown, and stabilise the financial system so it could create an environment conducive to growth. And part of this environment has been the policy of ultra low interest rates. In this way they hope to create a stable economic environment which stimulates demand, growth and employment.

However, the quantitative easing program has had two effects.

1. The first was to devalue the US currency in an effort to stimulate demand and drive inflation into the economy, in other words the desired effect.
2. The second, but unintended consequence, has been to create a distorted bond market, which could no longer be considered as the bellwether of money.

In simple terms, the US Treasury bond market has become polluted and distorted by all this additional money flow, which was then being purchased by the originator of the money, the Federal Reserve themselves.

So now, the bond market can no longer be considered a 'free' market rendering any analytical study of the US Treasury bond market unsafe as a result. Slowly, these markets are beginning to return to some normality as QE ends, and other countries begin their own tapering program.

In order to overcome this problem it has been necessary to find an alternative bond market untainted by the action of the Federal Reserve. And the answer is the so called US Unibond market.

These are bonds issued by the municipal authorities in the US, untainted by the actions of the FED and therefore more representative of a truly free market. They are also a more reliable indicator of risk and market sentiment. Equally important, however, these bonds are also considered to be extremely secure, and therefore truly reflect the cost of money along with investor appetite and risk sentiment.

This is not to say we ignore the traditional US Treasury market. We consider both, but always conscious of the fact the US bond market is distorted for the time being. And with further rounds of quantitative easing inevitable, this situation is likely to continue for years to come. Indeed with many other central banks also following this path, the situation will get worse before it gets better, and this is what I meant by tearing up the rule book.

The game has changed and is likely to stay this way for years if not decades to come. Japan has still not recovered from a similar pattern of events, first started twenty years ago.

So, how do we interpret what the bond markets are telling us? Let's look at some bond market terminology and what is meant by "yield". There are three terms which define bonds, and these are as follows:

1. Par Value – the face value of the bond. This means the face value of the bond, so a $10,000 bond has a par value of $10,000
2. Coupon – this is the interest rate and so called as bonds used to come in books of coupons
3. Maturity – the length of time before the par value has been repaid to the lender

But what is yield, what does it tell us, and where do we find this information? As always I will try to explain the yield concept using a simple analogy based on property. Not an ideal analogy, but it is a straightforward way to explain the basic concepts.

Imagine for a moment you are a property investor, and are looking to buy houses to rent to prospective tenants. You are considering two areas in which to buy. Both areas have the same average rental potential of $500 per month, but in the first area the average cost of a house is $75,000 and in the second the average cost is $50,000.

The rental yield on the first house is:

- 12 x $500 / $75,000 = 8% per annum

The rental yield on the second house is:

- 12 x $500 / $50,000 = 12% per annum

As a property investor we would choose the second area as this offers the higher yield and therefore a better return on our investment. The reason the yield is so much higher is simply because the capital cost of the property is lower. This in essence is how yield works in the bond markets.

If the underlying value of the bond falls, the yield will rise, and as the underlying value of the bond rises, yield will fall.

It is this constant price action that occurs in the bond markets every day which leads to the constant change in yields, and in turn reveals market sentiment and risk appetite.

In other words, when underlying bond prices are rising, they are in demand, their price rises and so the yield falls.

Conversely, when underlying bond prices are falling, they are not in demand and yields will be rising. In a rising interest rate environment, bond holders will see market value erosion, whilst in a declining rate environment, the market value of their bonds increases.

This is the inverse relationship which drives the bond price to bond yield linkage, which can best be explained by considering a real example.

Suppose an investor decides to buy a ten year note with a 6% coupon, when yields are at 6%. The buyer pays 100% of the par value. The rate duly rises to 7% and the buyer decides to sell, however, no-one will pay the par value as the notes are now quoted at 7%, so in order to sell, he or she has to sell at a discount price on the bond. In other words, rising rates are accompanied by a falling price.

The reverse scenario also applies. Had the rate fallen to 5% the investment yield is more than the market rate, and so the seller can offer the bond at a premium to the par value. So here, falling rates mean higher bond prices.

This is a key point that often surprises many traders and investors. Bond prices change all the time, and it is this change in the underlying price which is reflected in the yield.

So far we have discussed bonds with a fixed coupon, but in fact there are many different types of bonds, with different issuers. There are bonds with coupons which are both fixed and variable, and different terms to maturity. But of course, in comparing all the various bonds, buyers and sellers are only interested in one thing, which is yield.

The underlying price tells them nothing. It is yield that reveals everything about the bond, and the consequent returns. For us as traders, this constant change in yield tells us all about risk and market sentiment and the associated money flow to other asset classes. This tells us where the broad market sentiment is heading. Is the market looking for safe haven currencies and assets, or riskier assets with better returns, which will then be reflected in higher risk currencies.

In terms of yield, there are three types as follows:

1. Nominal yield
2. Current yield
3. Yield to maturity

It is the second and third of these which are most useful to us as forex traders.

Nominal yield is simply the interest rate on the bond, so not very helpful.

Current yield is in fact very similar to the example we used with our rental property and is simply the yield at present. So going back to our earlier example, if we had purchased a property at $50,000 with a rental of $500 giving a yield of 12%, but the property had then increased in value to $75,000, our current yield would have fallen to 8%.

The current yield is extremely helpful as it gives us an instant and visual picture of money flow second by second during the trading day, as yields fluctuate to reflect the flow of money.

These charts can be read, just like any other, using technical analysis, and technical tools and techniques, to give us a view on trends, strength and weakness, and therefore future market direction.

The time-frame chosen can be from minutes to hours, days or weeks, depending on your strategy, approach to the market, and time horizon. As an intraday scalper your focus will from minutes to hours, whilst as a longer term trend trader, this will shift from hours to days, or even weeks.

As we have already discovered, there are a huge number of US Treasuries from 30 day to 30 year, so the next question, of course, is which do we use for our analysis?

My suggestion is to use, what are generally considered to be the benchmark bonds of the 5, 10 and the 30 year giving us a good spread across the risk profile. The ticker symbols to access these charts are as follows:

- Five year US Treasury notes: FVX
- Ten year US Treasury notes: TNX
- Thirty year US Treasury bonds: TYX

Here are examples of each, using the daily chart.

Fig 2.10 Five year Treasury note – daily chart

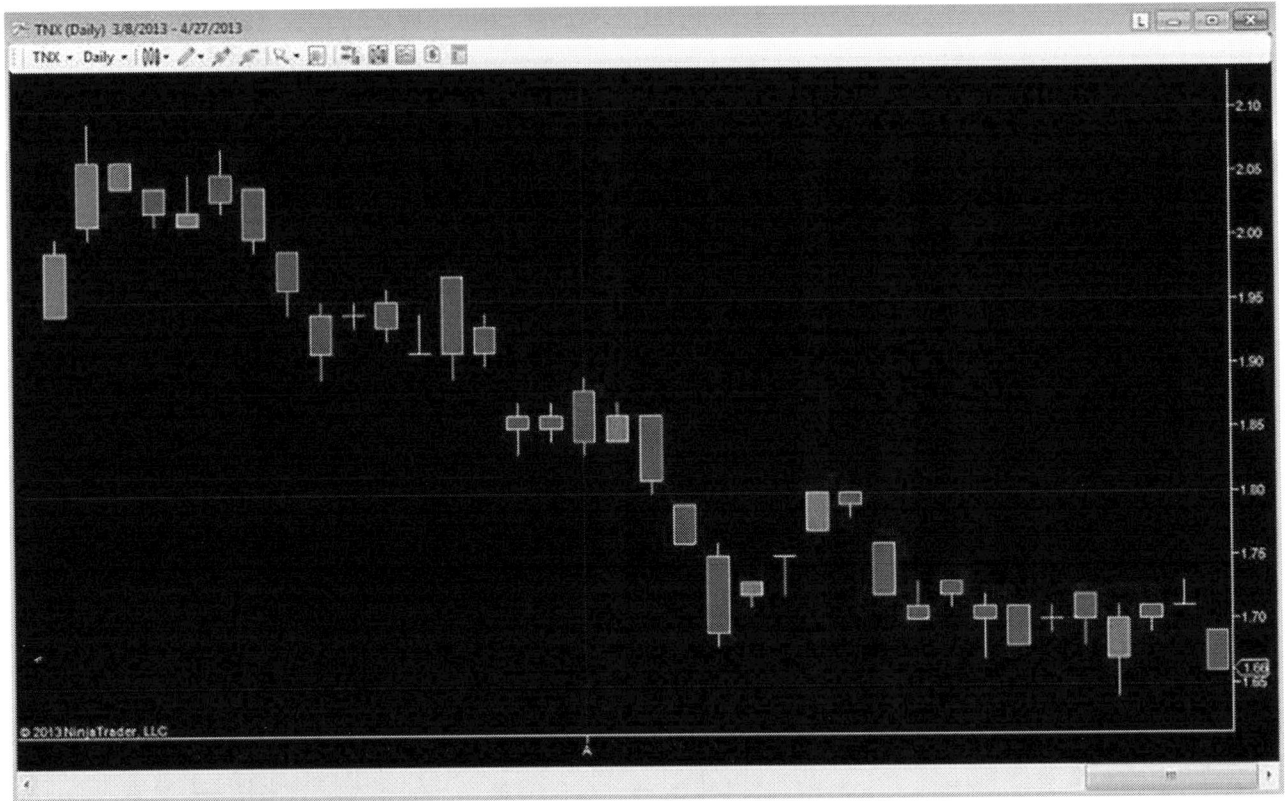

Fig 2.11 Ten year Treasury note – daily chart

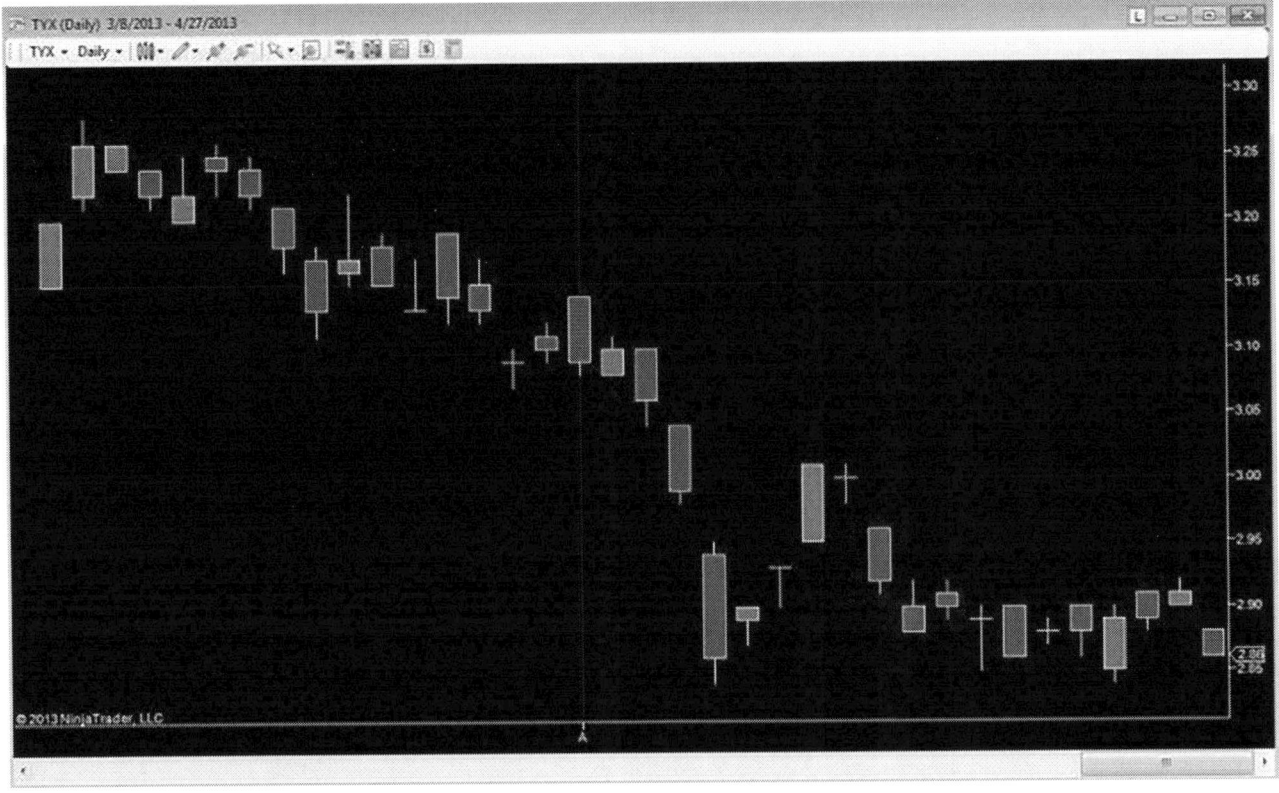

Fig 2.12 30 year Treasury bond – daily chart

These are the benchmark US Treasuries to watch and, as I mentioned earlier, one of the other key bond markets, which offers a less 'polluted' view of money, is in those bonds issued by US Municipal authorities.

The easiest place to check on the yields for this market is using an instrument referred to as an ETF or Exchange Traded Fund, which will be covered in greater detail later in the book. This is simply a fund which trades like a stock, but is based on an underlying basket of assets. In this case it is a range of municipal bonds which make up the ETF index. And one of the most popular is the S&P National Municipal Bond with the ticker symbol MUB.

Fig 2.13 is an example, once again, based on the daily chart. As with the Treasury bonds and notes the time scale you choose will vary according to your trading strategy, but in considering the Municipal bond markets in this way, you will be triangulating market sentiment using an untainted source of lending.

Fig 2.13 Municipal bonds – daily chart (MUB)

Finally, one other important point to note. As the ETF trades like a stock this also means we have volume available on the chart.

Volume is the ONLY leading indicator, and I will be covering the importance of volume in detail later. However, when read in conjunction with price action, this offers traders the ultimate in market forecasting.

Using price action with volume is not new and is what I refer to as Volume Price Analysis or VPA for short. Put simply, volume is the fuel that drives any market. If the market is rising on low volume, this is a weak move and unlikely to continue for long. Equally a move lower on low volume will fail.

For markets to move either higher or lower requires effort in the form of volume. The good news is volume and ETF's go hand in hand, in much the same way as in the cash markets for equities. For forex trading, we use a proxy which is tick volume, but again this will be covered in due course.

To summarise. When markets are risk averse money will flow into bonds as a safe haven, and the yields will fall as the underlying price of bonds rise.

When markets are risk on, and investors are prepared to take on more risk, the flow of money is out of bonds and into riskier asset classes. Therefore, the underlying price will fall, and the yield will rise as a result. This is the simple see-saw of money flow which is such a powerful analytical tool, and which works in all time frames. And regardless of whether you are a scalper or a swing trader, the bond chart will always reveal the current market sentiment to money and risk appetite.

Now we come to the most complicated aspect of yield which is the third of these, the yield to maturity. This is the yield we need to analyse when considering the bond markets over a longer period of time and is known as the yield curve. This is often simply referred to as 'yield'.

The yield curve is a graphical representation of the constantly changing relationship between the underlying bond price and the return, but viewed from the perspective of short term T Bills, right through to a thirty year bond. It is a complicated calculation and beyond the scope of this book, but there are various places to find these charts, which will be referenced shortly.

The yield curve is a snapshot of yields on bonds of similar credit quality and asset class, and the yield curve covers maturities from three months to 30 years.

As you would expect, bonds with longer maturities pay higher rates of interest. Bonds with shorter maturities pay lower rates of interest, since the owner of a longer term bond is taking a bigger risk than a holder with a shorter term bond.

The yield curve is created by joining up the various market yields at one point in time over the period of short to long term bonds, and it is the shape of this curve that tells us what the market is thinking, in terms of interest rates, risk, inflation, and of course money flow.

There are four types of yield curve all of which reflect differing views of market sentiment, risk, the economic outlook, and investors longer term appetite and anticipated returns on money. These are as follows:

1. Normal yield curve
2. Steep yield curve
3. Inverted yield curve
4. Flat or humped yield curve

As we have already discovered, all bonds have a maturity date or a time value and, as a result, bonds with longer maturities pay higher coupon rates, than bonds with shorter maturities. So in general, the rate on a 30 day T bill will be much lower than the coupon rate on a 10 year T note or a 30 year T bond. The reason is straightforward. It is because the lender or creditor is taking a much greater risk in lending for such a long period, and this in turn is reflected in the longer term yields.

The yield curve gives us a visual picture of this relationship between the short term and long term yields in one chart. The shape of the yield curve describes market sentiment, and the most common is the normal yield curve. See Fig 2.14.

This kind of yield curve is the one most often seen, and generally referred to as the normal curve. It is seen in periods of economic stability in the middle of an economic cycle. In general terms, equity markets are moving higher, the economy is growing steadily, and with normal rates of growth, the threat of inflation is being controlled. The yield curve is this shape, since short and medium term bills and notes have a lower yield, with longer term bonds offering a higher yield, but which slopes gently out to the longer term.

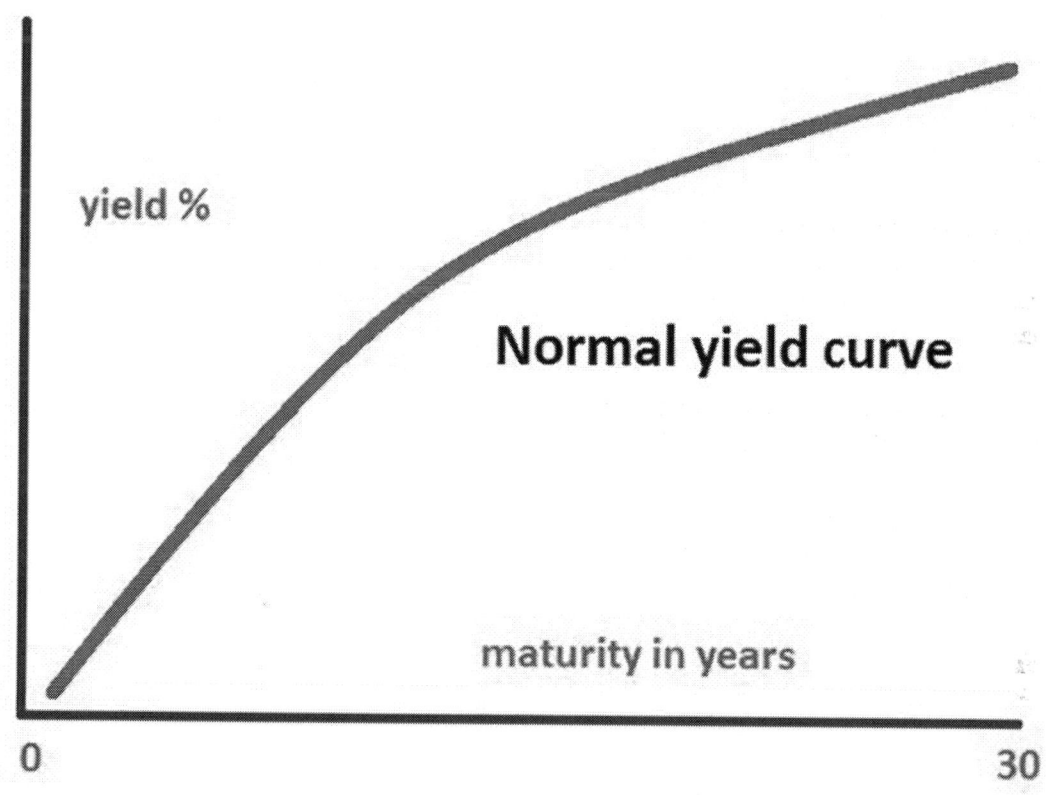

Fig 2.14 Normal Yield Curve

The second type of yield curve is one we refer to as steep as shown in Fig 2.15. Under normal circumstances, the yield on a 30 year bond is typically around 3 to 4 percentage points above the yield on three month T bills.

However, from time to time this gap increases dramatically, and the slope on the yield curve increases sharply. The message being sent here is that investors believe the economy is likely to improve quickly in the future, so typically this yield curve will be seen at the start of an economic recovery and consequent expansion. In other words, signalling the move out of recession and into the first phase of expansion. But why does the yield curve adopt this shape?

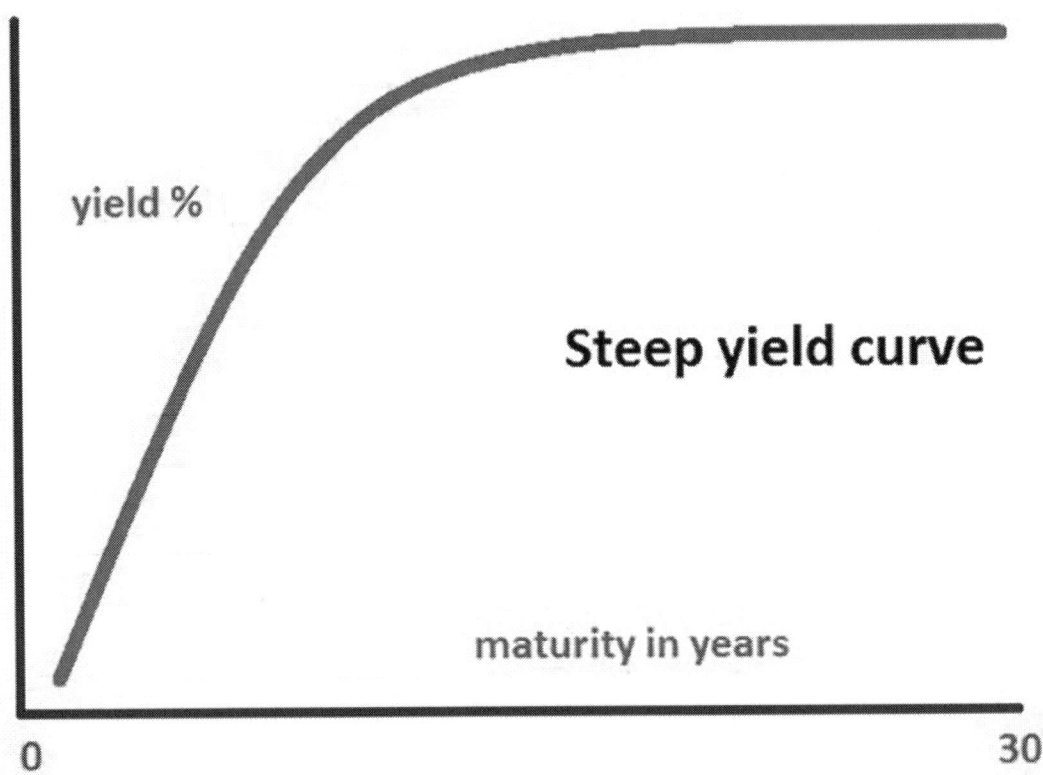

Fig 2.15 Steep Yield Curve

Up to this point, the economy has been stagnant with low short term interest rates. However, as demand for capital grows rates begin to rise, long term investors become concerned at being locked into low rates.

As a result, they demand greater compensation for taking the risk in the debt market for the longer term, when in fact they could consider moving into equities, and better returns. Longer term rates are therefore forced higher, which is reflected in an increase in the differential rates between the shorter term and longer term bond holders. So a steep yield curve sends a strong signal longer term rates are on the rise, fast, ahead of an economic recovery and expansion from recession.

The third type of yield curve is called an inverted yield curve, and at first glance may appear to be a paradox. After all, in this case longer term investors are accepting lower yields than those short term investors. Why is this?

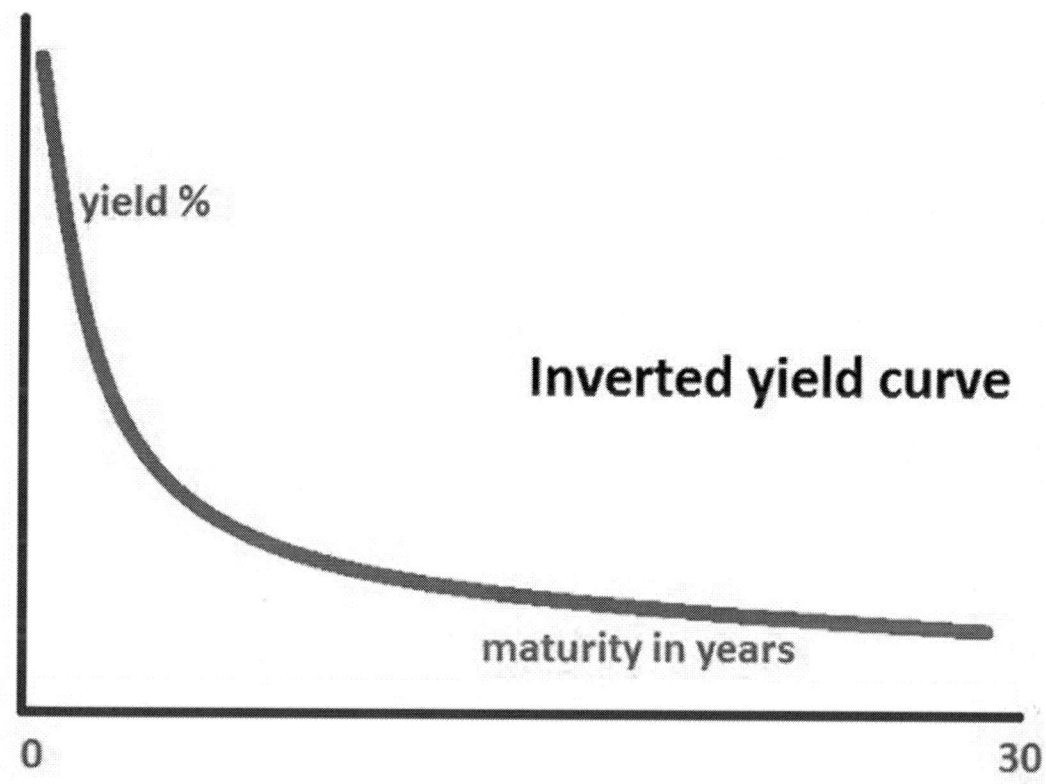

Fig 2.16 Inverted Yield Curve

In this case the long term bond holders have taken the view rates in the future are likely to be moving lower with a slowing economy, and have therefore decided locking in the current rate is a sensible decision. This type of yield curve is therefore almost always the pre-cursor to a recession, with the economy slowing and interest rates likely to fall. It is often referred to as the yield of fear.

Whilst they are rare, they are a powerful signal and should *never* be ignored, as they are always followed by an economic slowdown, or an outright recession. Lower interest rates then follow.

The final yield curve is referred to as the humped yield curve, and this may also adopt a flat shape as well as the humped version shown in Fig 2.17.

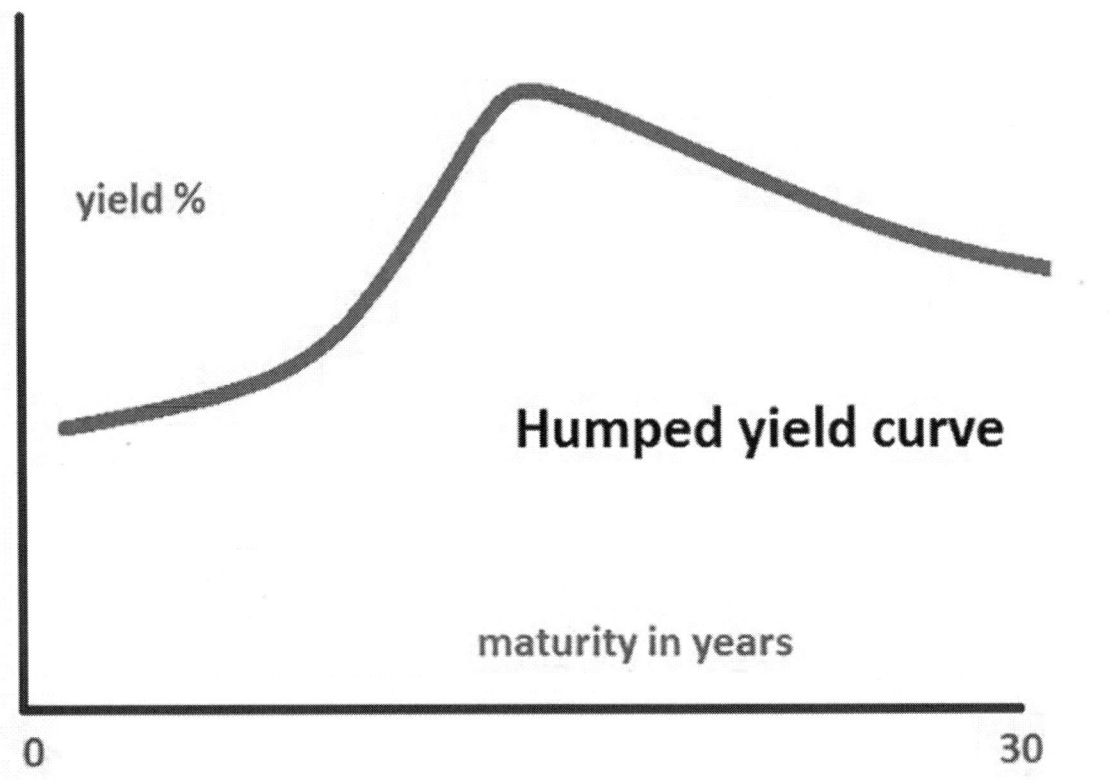

Fig 2.17 Humped Yield Curve

In order for the yield curve to take on this shape, it has to pass through a period where the long term yields are the same as short term rates. When this happens we get a flat yield curve or one that is slightly humped, generally in the middle of the curve.

Where this happens in the economic cycle, is generally, although not always, when the yield curve is moving from a normal to an inverted yield.

In other words, we are potentially seeing the economy beginning to slow, with the yield curve in transition. However, not all humped or flat yield curves make the full change to an inverted curve, but they often do, giving an excellent and early warning signal the economy is slowing and potentially moving into recession. Once again, a signal of lower interest rates.

In simple terms this is how the yield curve works, and what it reveals about the broader economy, investor sentiment, and where you are in the economic cycle.

The yield curve and yields are both powerful and relatively simple to understand, once you begin to appreciate the supply and demand within the underlying bonds themselves and the signals this price action is generating.

As I mentioned in the introduction, most forex traders never consider the bond markets as relevant, which is a great mistake.

The second reason they are ignored is simply most forex traders are short term intraday scalpers, and therefore believe the bond markets are only useful for longer term trading.

Whilst this may certainly be true when considering the yield curve, this is definitely not the case when considering the intra day price action on the Treasury Yield index charts, or indeed on the ETF MUB chart. Indeed, using price action as one of the technical tools in the traders toolbox, this is even more powerful.

Remember however, until the quantitative easing programs are finally concluded, the bond markets will remain distorted for years to come, a fact which also applies to bond yields.

Although the rule book has not been torn up completely, it has certainly been put to one side for the time being, as all market analysis, whether technical, fundamental or relational, has to be viewed in a cautious light.

True price discovery will only return to the markets once these artificial programs of economic stimulus have come to an end. Until then, we have to be cautious, be aware of the pitfalls and changes, and try to use as many analytical methods to cross check our analysis and risk assessment on each trade. Bonds are one of the cornerstones, and should be part of every forex traders armoury.

At this point, let me just say a word or two about the so called 'bond vigilantes' who you may have read about in the media. As the name implies, these are large organisations, hedge funds and bond funds, who take it upon themselves to sell large bond holdings in order to drive up yields, making borrowing more expensive as a result.

These organisations are primarily motivated by concerns over who will be the primary buyer of bonds once the FED has concluded its various QE programs. Their concern is simple. Who will buy all the devalued bonds once the FED withdraws from the market?

This is not an unreasonable view, but one which has added a further layer of abnormal and volatile price action to the US Treasuries market.

Once again, this is yet another factor which has appeared to make analysis of the markets even more complex following the financial meltdown, for traders. The message is clear and simple. Use all the markets and tools available to quantify and analysis risk.

No longer is it possible to succeed as a forex trader using one chart and one form of analysis. The odds are no longer in your favour. Hopefully this introduction to bonds will have convinced you not only is the information there, it is easily available. It simply requires some effort and a little explanation, which is what this book is all about.

Finally let me cover one of the bond markets I mentioned right at the start of this chapter which is the so called Eurodollar market, and here we turn to the futures market.

Futures will be explained in detail in another book, but this particular contract was introduced by the CME in 1981, and is now considered to be one of the fundamental building blocks of the interest rate market. Eurodollar futures are the most active short term interest rate futures contacts traded worldwide.

The contract is based on a $1million dollar face value with a three month maturity. It is a cash settled contract, with a quarterly cycle, and is traded both on the floor of the exchange and increasingly on the electronic Globex exchange, so prices are available virtually 24 hours a day.

The contract is quoted in terms of the IMM three month LIBOR index points, which is equivalent to 100 minus the yield on the security. So for example if the yield is 1.2% the index is 98.80. The minimum price fluctuation varies on the contract, with the nearest contract based on one quarter of a basis point or 0.0025%, and further contracts moving to one half of a basis point at 0.005%.

The ticker symbol for the contract on the CME for open outcry is ED and for the Globex market is GE. The chart in Fig 2.18 shows the daily price action for the contract, and again we have volume, a huge advantage to those traders who trade using price action and volume.

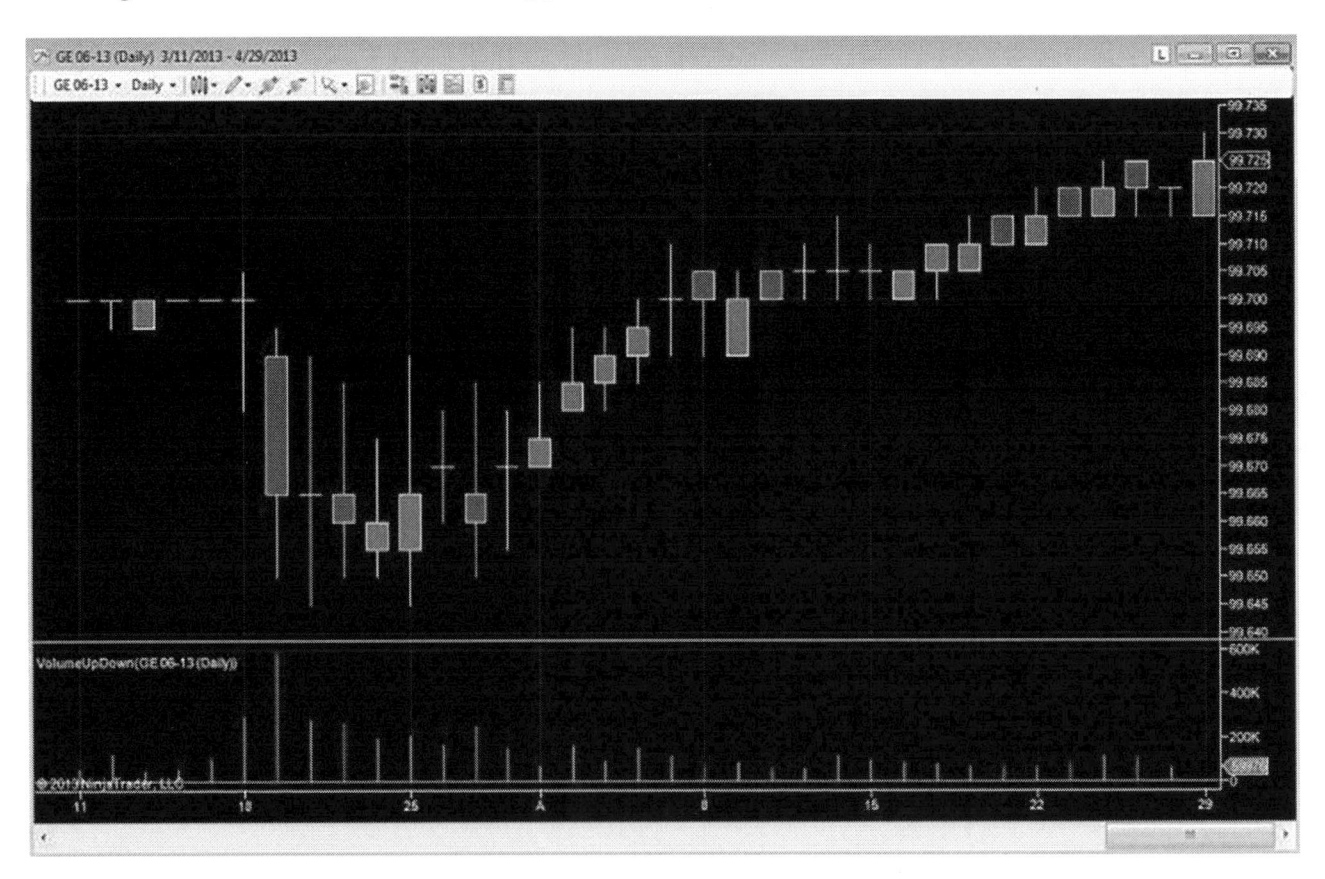

Fig 2.18 Eurodollar Future on Globex

Once again, as we saw earlier, the interest rate market gives us two views of market sentiment, money flow and risk appetite, one based on an intra day basis and the other a longer term view based on the yield curve. With Eurodollar futures we can take the same approach, coupled with volume.

Pricing patterns in the Eurodollar futures markets have a close association with money and flow, and therefore mirror the associated yield curves. Short term rates are driven fundamentally by monetary policy, whilst longer term rates are largely driven by inflationary expectations, with the yield curve reflecting these views on one chart. In simple terms, if the yield curve is steep, yields are expected to rise. If the yield is inverted or flat, yields are expected to fall.

There are many sophisticated strategies which futures traders adopt to hedge and take positions in the market, which is beyond the scope of this book.

For us as forex traders, the key point is this – short term rates are driven by the FOMC monetary policy, and as such, any comments or the release of the monthly FOMC minutes will impact the market, and seen in the price action as a result.

For intra day or short term traders this helps to establish money flow and risk appetite, which in turn will be reflected in the currency markets. Longer term rates are driven by the expectation of inflation, which is a key component of commodity markets covered in the next chapter.

By considering all three markets, the US Treasury markets, Unibond markets and Eurodollars, as a forex trader you will have a clear view, both in the short, medium and long term of risk.

Risk and return on money is what drives the markets, and if you have a clear view, this will then be reflected in the currencies you trade. No longer will you wonder why a currency is being bought or sold. You will have a clear understanding of why, and more importantly where the buying or selling is taking place.

Chapter Three
Commodity Markets Explained

The importance of money flows from it being a link between the present and the future.

John Maynard Keynes (1883-1946)

In order to understand the commodity markets, we need to step back in time a little and consider them from several different perspectives, for two reasons.

First, they are the only one of the four capital markets where real physical goods are bought and sold.

Second and, perhaps more importantly, this market has changed beyond all recognition in the last ten years, and just like the bond market, is one few forex traders ever consider.

Sadly, this again is a huge mistake and, in writing this book, is one I hope to correct, as the commodities markets play a key role.

The commodities market is the fulcrum of the financial markets because it is where real currencies are converted into real products, creating a myriad of pivotal relationships, as the world of money meets the real world of economic supply and demand in commodities.

Commodities therefore provide the bridge between global economies and the US dollar, bonds, equities, and of course currencies. Without this bridge and real global market, we would have little idea of what is actually happening in the world. Few forex traders appreciate the significance of this market, not only in terms of its position at the centre of the money flow, but also in terms of how this market is viewed, by both central banks and governments alike in their key decisions.

It is equally as important as bonds, and perhaps even more so, and this is one of the pivotal relationships I will cover in detail later in the book.

Commodities are a key component to your trading success. As traders we have to understand them, the signals they are sending regarding the economy, associated markets, and of course money flow and risk appetite.

Put simply, commodities are the shop window of the world – a trading post, a giant store where real goods are exchanged for money and money is exchanged for real goods. The ultimate warehouse on a grand scale.

The commodities market was founded on the need for farmers in the US mid West to have a fair and equitable market in which to sell their crops and livestock. From this, the futures market was born, which is why many of the largest futures exchanges, such as the CME (Chicago Mercantile Exchange) and the CBOT (Chicago Board of Trade) are still based in Chicago, with these two exchanges merging in 2007.

Whilst I will be explaining how to trade currencies using futures in another book, let me just outline the basics of a futures contract.

A futures contract is simply a contract between two parties which specifies that on a certain date in the future, the producer or holder of the contract agrees to deliver a specified quantity of the goods, at a specified time, for an agreed price.

In this way, growers and producers in the mid West were able to agree a price for crops and livestock for delivery in the future. This in turn removed the uncertainty of future price fluctuations caused by natural events, such as poor growing conditions, bad weather, natural disasters and world conflicts, allowing both parties to plan their cash flow accordingly.

Over time, the commodities market expanded to include not just the agricultural sectors, such as corn, wheat, dairy, livestock, coffee and cocoa, but into a huge variety of sectors, including metals, (precious, industrial and base), along with energy sectors, such as oil and gas, index futures such the S&P500, and other financial instruments.

Up until the late 1990's, the commodity market was considered to be a specialist one, little understood by the average trader.

Contracts were traded through the central exchange using open outcry in the pit, with the markets only trading when the exchange was physically open.

As we moved into the 21st century, everything changed with the advent of electronic trading. No longer was it necessary to call a specialist broker and instruct then to execute a buy or sell order for wheat or cotton. Now it was possible to trade online virtually 24 hours a day.

This simple innovation has changed the commodities market from one of a simple supermarket to one where commodities are now considered as an asset class, just like any other. This is also the case with currencies, which just like commodities, are bought and sold as an asset, and not purely for short term speculative gains.

One of the common misconceptions is that commodity exchanges determine or establish the prices at which commodity futures are bought and sold. This is false. Prices are determined solely by supply and demand.

If there are more buyers than sellers, the price will rise. If there are more sellers than buyers the price will fall. This is generally referred to as 'price discovery', but in simple terms all this means is that this is a free market, where prices find their natural level. This is why the commodities market is so important and why it gives us so many signals as a result.

But, why does it matter?

If I were writing this book twenty years ago, in considering this market we would be looking at two principle relationships.

The first would be with the US dollar, and this still remains an integral part of our analysis, since virtually all commodities are priced in dollars.

The second would be the economic relationship with inflation. This is a key reason why we monitor the commodities markets so closely and which also explains why there is such a close relationship with bonds.

However, we now have to add a third strand to the analysis, which is money flow, since commodities are considered to be an asset class in their own right. This means commodity futures and, in some cases, the physical asset is being bought and sold as an investment, either speculatively or for a longer term buy and hold. This is a similar approach to that in equity markets and, as a result, commodities can now tell us a great deal about risk and market sentiment.

Therefore to summarise. Any analysis of the commodity markets will tell us three key things.

First, what is happening in the global economic picture, and therefore what is likely to happen to interest rates, as inflationary pressures increase.

Second, the future direction for the US dollar.

Third, risk appetite and sentiment, and therefore money flow, as most commodities are considered to be high risk.

Later in this chapter I will be considering some of the individual commodities in detail, such as gold, oil, copper and, of course, the US dollar, but the key point to start with is this – commodities and fundamentals go hand in hand.

When interest rates rise, for example, commodities are likely to perform well. And the reason is because rising rates are likely to indicate increasing global demand, which in turn drives inflation into an economy, which is good for growth.

Commodities give us a classic view of global demand for raw goods and with their key relationship with the US dollar reveal both money flow and market sentiment. Indeed it could be argued that to be successful as a forex trader, you simply need to have a clear view on the US dollar, since every other market, from bonds, commodities, equities and currencies is US dollar centric. The dollar remains the currency of first reserve and until an alternative is found, will remain so for the foreseeable future.

Whilst forex markets underpin the other three, it is commodities which provide the real world linkage, the bridge between money and goods. They are the fuel of the economy. Japan cannot make cars without steel. Nothing moves without oil. The mobile phone market needs rare earth metals, and you cannot feed the world without wheat, corn or soybeans.

The complicating factor now, of course, is that we have to view some commodities as an asset class in their own right and therefore be careful in our conclusions and analysis. Later in this chapter we are going to consider some of the key relationships such as commodities and bonds, and commodities and the US dollar which will help in confirming any conclusions we may make. However, before doing so, I would like to spend a few moments considering the broad sectors, and some of the key commodities in each.

The Softs

In general there are three principle sectors, namely agriculture, energy and metals. Agriculture covers all the basic staple products such as wheat and corn, and soybean for which China is the largest market. There is also rice, cattle and timber along with kitchen staples such as orange juice, sugar, coffee and cocoa. All of these are basic commodities, and there is always an argument that says with an increasing world population and falling acreage, soft commodities are almost guaranteed to increase in price. After all, soft commodities are governed by supply and demand, and with increasing demand and falling supply due to a decline in arable land in emerging markets, longer term soft commodity prices look set to rise. This was reinforced recently with China's decision to begin importing corn for the first time.

However, rising commodity prices, whether in the soft or hard sector mean one thing longer term, and that's inflation. With inflation comes higher interest rates, which are then reflected in bond markets and interest rate differentials between currency pairs, with consequent money flow as a result.

Metals

In the metals sector there are three that we pay particular attention to, namely gold, silver and copper. Gold, of course is the ultimate safe haven hard asset, and whilst silver is also considered in the same vein as a precious metal, it is in fact classified as an industrial metal.

Silver's main benefit is its conductive properties, and is used in a variety of manufacturing processes and components. It's also treated as a precious metal, particularly since gold's rise to almost $2000 per ounce and now trading in the $1300 per ounce region. Finally, in the metals sector we have copper, which is considered a bellwether for the global economy, and has a close relationship to equities, as a result.

Energy

The third group is the energy sector which includes oil in all its various forms along with natural gas and electricity. Of these, oil is the key commodity, and again one we look at in detail shortly.

Finally just to round off this introduction to the commodities market, there is one further element which has changed this market dramatically in the last few years, and that's the rise in popularity of the ETF or Exchange Traded Fund.

These are investment funds traded on the stock exchange in much the same way as stocks, and generally backed by the physical asset. The rise in ETFs has been exponential in the last few years, which has led to additional buying in the base commodity, adding further demand issues to the market.

However, ETFs provide us with a rich vein of information about the commodity markets, and indeed is one of the many instruments we analyse when looking for clues and signals in related markets. To put this into context, gold and gold related ETFs now account for almost 10% of the physical bullion held, and only surpassed by the US, Germany, the IMM fund, France, Italy and Switzerland. This gives you some idea of the growing importance not only of ETFs as a trading instrument, but also of their impact on gold and gold prices in general.

Where and how do we track commodities in the market? The good news is it is possible in many different ways and all relatively easily. The most common way and, generally free is using the spot market price, for commodities such as gold, oil and silver.

Live prices for these are freely available and I have provided a resource section with this book to find all the charts and information I discuss.

The futures market is another excellent source, but remember these are prices for the commodity at some future price, and will therefore differ from the spot price which is the live current price for cash exchange in the market.

Live or slightly delayed futures prices are now becoming increasingly available and also free, so if you do not have a futures feed, or futures brokerage account, this is not a problem. Again the resources section will help you find free sources for all this data.

Finally, ETFs provide another excellent source of data and, as with futures, we have volume to help us with our analysis, making things much more straightforward.

In case you were wondering, and before we start looking at individual commodities, whether there is any direct link between commodities and currencies, the short answer is, yes. Several currencies are often referred to as commodity dollars. These are the Canadian dollar, the Australian dollar and the New Zealand dollar.

The reason is simple. These are countries whose economies and exports are closely linked to commodities due to their rich reserves of natural resources, which is yet a further reason for having a deeper understanding of commodities and the role they play.

Gold & The US Dollar

But let's start with a simple example and examine the relationship between gold and the US dollar, as this epitomises the two extremes of money.

On one side we have the ultimate hard asset precious metal, whilst on the other we have the primary soft asset of a fiat paper based currency.

Both are considered safe haven, with gold having the added benefit of being a hedge against inflation. In addition, the price of gold is also influenced by buying demand, particularly from India and China.

India has its own gold buying 'season' which typically starts in early October and runs to the end of the calendar year, which is often reflected in the price of gold. With jewellery making up almost 70% of the world's gold demand, India is at the top of the list, even more so recently with the surge in the middle classes.

China too, is adding its own weight to demand for the precious metal, and in 2012 Chinese citizens are now permitted to invest in gold directly for the first time in history. Both these countries now have a relentless appetite for gold which is increasing all the time. And China recently announced it too would be launching an ETF backed with physical gold.

The relationship between gold and the US dollar is the first we need to understand as forex traders, for two reasons.

First, this relationship is extremely sensitive, and therefore is extremely revealing.

Second, gold provides the bridge between money and all the other markets as the purest of all commodities, and it is a direct relationship, since gold, like almost all other commodities, is priced in US dollars. As a result, a trend change in one, will almost certainly have a direct and immediate trend change on the other.

When we consider other relationships between the various capital markets this is rarely the case, and we need some sort of bridge, to analyse the effects of money flow and risk. A linking mechanism if you like between two worlds. Commodity markets are one such bridge, linking the world of money with the economy and market sentiment.

Since the removal of currencies from the gold standard back in the 1970's the text book relationship between gold and the US dollar has been an inverse one, with gold rising on US dollar weakness and conversely, the US dollar strengthening as gold prices fall.

The reason for this is two fold. First, as gold is priced in US dollars, as the currency weakens the gold price rises accordingly and vice-versa. In other words, a weaker dollar allows you to buy more gold for the same number of dollars. Second, it's all to do with inflation.

Inflation is the double edged sword with which economies are managed by the central banks. It is not only a double edged sword, but also an extremely blunt instrument. Furthermore, it is the only instrument the central banks have to create relatively stable and healthy economies which are then conducive to the creation of jobs. Inflation is good, but too much is bad, and inflation is created using another blunt instrument, namely interest rates.

In many ways inflation needs to be like Goldilocks porridge, not too hot and not too cold. Too much and the economy overheats, the brakes are applied too late, and recession ensues. Too little, and no growth occurs.

Inflation also brings with it the erosion of money in real terms, which is where gold steps in as a hedge against inflation. Finally, of course, gold also serves one other purpose – it is the ultimate safe haven for money in times of economic uncertainty or turmoil in the markets.

But for the time being, let's just concentrate on the relationship between the US dollar and the price of gold. Now, wouldn't it be great if this relationship could be relied on at all times? Well, sadly it can't, and like many other cross market relationships, these can and do break down from time to time. And whilst the inverse relationship between gold and the US dollar is a strong one, it is not infallible, as is shown in Fig 3.10

Fig 3.10 Gold/US Dollar

Let's take a step back, to the start of the sub prime mortgage crisis, which saw an avalanche of banks and mortgage companies collapse, both in the US and elsewhere. This was swiftly followed by a world wide recession (if not depression), sovereign debt defaults in Europe, and historically low interest rates in most of the Western world.

Throughout this period, the gold/dollar relationship was punctuated with periods where gold and the US dollar moved higher, or both moved lower, with a consequent return to the inverse relationship shortly after. This is shown on the chart in Fig 3.11 from November 2009 to March 2011.

Fig 3.11 Gold/US Dollar

The period to consider is from February 2010 to September 2010, and plots the gold vs US dollar relationship.

As we can see, gold was rising along with the US dollar from February 2010 until June 2010, followed by two months when both gold and the US dollar fell.

In other words the relationship had moved from an inverse correlation to a direct positive correlation over this period. And the question is why, given that shortly after in September that year, the relationship reverted to normal, with gold rising and the US dollar falling, a relationship that has remained intact since.

So why did we see the pair 'decouple' from the norm? Let me explain.

Early in 2010, the sovereign debt issues in Europe began to surface. Countries such as Greece, Portugal and Ireland, and latterly Spain (all referred to as the PIGS) flagged to the markets they were in severe financial difficulty.

The prospect of default in an EU member state was a real possibility, and without support from the European Central Bank, even more likely. This was not something the EU or ECB could even consider.

The markets reacted negatively to the news, selling the Euro and buying the US dollar, the safe haven currency, and sending the US dollar higher as a result. BUT, in addition, investors also bought gold as the ultimate safe haven, pushing the price of gold higher, along with the US dollar. This buying of both assets continued into the early summer, at which point the US economic picture began to dominate, with the Federal Reserve hinting at a further round of quantitative easing.

This policy, it was hoped, would stimulate the economy by creating an environment for growth and so drive inflation into the system, but also ensure the US dollar fell, thereby making exports cheaper. Cheaper exports would help US companies with overseas operations improving their profitability as a result.

With the issues in Europe now apparently resolved, investors moved back into the Euro, a high risk currency, temporarily selling both gold and the US dollar. This continued for two months in July and August. However, once the full extent of the FED policy was unveiled, the money flow was back into gold, and away from the US dollar for two distinct reasons.

First, the threat of inflation had now been raised by the FED policy, with gold becoming the safe haven hedge. Secondly, and in tandem, the US dollar was no longer seen by the markets and investors as safe haven, given the number of dollars now being created. Gold was seen both as the safe haven and also as a hedge against the possible inflation that was likely to follow the FED policy.

The above is a very simple example of how domestic and international markets affect the flow of money between these two safe havens. More importantly, it is also an example of how a relationship between one asset and another, no matter how strong, can and does change. This does not invalidate the relationship, it is simply a recognition of the fact markets are driven by people and their money.

On this occasion, investors initially considered both the US dollar and gold as safe havens, as they moved out of the Euro and into these safer assets. Once the FED policy had been signalled to the markets, investors decided gold was the safer bet, and not the US dollar, reinstating the traditional inverse relationship once more.

This is why relational analysis is so powerful, provided you know where to look and how to analyse what the chart is saying. Key here is an understanding of the fundamental picture behind the chart, and again this is so important to understand, and will be covered in detail later in the book.

Of course, as forex traders, the US dollar is central, and if we know where the dollar is heading, this will be reflected in all the major pairs directly. Whether the money flow is in or out, whether it is safe haven buying or selling for higher risk assets, or whether it is selling to find a safer haven, as in the example above, this can all be revealed by looking at gold, and its relationship to the US dollar. Provided of course you also understand the other drivers for gold, such as inflation and safe haven status.

So where is the dollar gold relationship now?

As we can see from the chart in Fig 3.10, the relationship has now returned to the normal inverse. Gold moves higher and the US dollar moves lower, and vice-versa. But remember, there are other forces at work in this relationship which are likely to increase in importance as we begin to move out of recession and into a phase of early expansion, where inflation and interest rates will once again start to play a more dominant role.

In summary, the gold to US dollar relationship is pivotal and provides a bridge between two capital markets, linking two safe haven asset classes. It is an extremely sensitive relationship, with a change in one almost instantly reflected with a change in the other.

The relationship is normally inverse, but this can and does change for various reasons, but ultimately will revert to the traditional inverse one shown above.

But what about other currencies and their relationship to the precious metal, and the key currency here is the Australian dollar?

The Australian dollar has been underpinned by soaring prices in a variety of commodities, including gold, copper, iron ore and aluminium. In addition, and just like New Zealand, the economy is underpinned with soft commodities which have helped Australia weather the global economic storm, better than most.

With China as its largest trading partner, demand for base commodities and precious metals remains strong, despite the recent slow down, and this has all been reflected in a strong Australian currency, particularly against the US dollar and the Japanese Yen. The association with commodities is also reflected in the AUD in terms of risk appetite and, as we will see later, the AUD/USD has also seen a close correlation with equity markets as a result.

Another currency closely associated with gold is the South African Rand, and although the country remains the largest gold producer in the world, production is now falling, and the close relationship that once existed between the Rand and the price of gold is now breaking down as a result.

The problem for much of South Africa's declining industry is the shortage of power in the country, which has led to many mines simply closing or being moth balled, thus preventing exploitation of growing demand for gold. This has been reflected in the Rand which has remained weak having sold off from the highs of 2002, and in sharp contrast to the Australian dollar.

OIL

Let's turn to another key commodity and that's oil, and there are three things we can say about oil with complete confidence.

First oil will eventually run out. Second, those countries that have it will demand ever higher prices for this precious commodity. Third and, perhaps most importantly, it is the only commodity which is subject to a legal and legitimate cartel called OPEC, which controls supply in order to protect its oil rich member states.

Just as with gold, the collapse in the Bretton Woods agreement which led to the free floating currency market, also had a profound effect on oil.

Until this point the price of oil had been governed by the gold standard. At the time the price of gold was set at $35 per ounce, with oil prices stable at around $3 per barrel. However, when Richard Nixon shut the gold window, in effect refusing to pay out in gold to those countries holding the US dollar, these oil producing countries were forced to convert their excess US dollars into gold in the open market. The effect was to drive gold and oil prices higher and the US dollar lower.

This came as a shock to oil producers, who were suddenly faced with receiving a weak currency for their oil instead of gold. In two years from 1971 to 1973, the US dollar index lost almost 25% of its value, at which point OPEC was forced to act. An oil embargo was introduced against supporters of Israel during the Arab Israeli war, which sent oil prices soaring above $12 per barrel and in one short war, achieving OPEC's objective of quadrupling oil prices in two years.

In 1975 OPEC agreed to sell its oil exclusively for US dollars, in effect confirming the US dollar as the world's currency of first reserve, which is where we are today.

Now first and foremost, increasing oil prices will fuel inflation – they have to, it's as simple as that, and ultimately of course inflation will mean one thing in the longer term. Higher interest rates. However, for OPEC it's not that simple.

The group is composed of many different countries, all with different cultures, agendas and political objectives. So they rarely, if ever, agree and any production quotas which are agreed are rarely adhered to, generally to the annoyance of other OPEC members.

As a result, oil is a highly political commodity, in every sense of the word, and used by both individual OPEC members and governments to further their own agendas.

It is also the only commodity, other than gold which is unique, in that it is not governed by the simple rules of supply and demand. The supply of oil is controlled, and therefore the price of oil is not one of a free market of price discovery.

For oil producers with higher prices comes the threat of inflation and higher interest rates, which in turn may lead to a slow down in demand for oil, and coupled with erosion from inflation, leads to higher extraction and production costs.

As I mentioned at the start, the switch from the gold standard to the US dollar, left oil producers with a great deal of bad feeling towards the US government, and by extension, the US dollar.

Ever since, there has been talk of removing the US dollar and replacing it with an alternative. This now seems a real possibility following a series of secret meetings in 2009 between the Gulf states, China, Japan, Russia and Brazil. These were followed in both 2010 and 2011, with further meetings with finance ministers, to put together plans to price oil against a basket of currencies. These included the Chinese Yuan, the Japanese Yen, the Euro, and of course gold, along with a proposed 'unified' currency from the Gulf states.

Such a move would have a profound effect on world currency markets, as well as global economic stability, and it is not too fanciful to suggest we are almost sure to see an economic war in the future, between the US and China, over Middle East oil, in the next ten years.

So which countries have the largest oil reserves and how does oil impact the key currencies for us as forex traders ?

It is probably no great surprise that Saudi Arabia grabs the top spot with almost 20% of the world's supply, but the second largest may surprise you. This is Canada with almost 14%, and just like Australia, Canada's rich natural resources have helped the country to survive the worst excesses of the global meltdown.

Canada's oil resources dwarf countries such as Kuwait, the UAE and Russia, and is also ahead of both Iraq and Iran by some distance.

It is therefore no great surprise to learn that oil and the Canadian dollar have a close relationship, along with the Norwegian krona, the Russian ruble and the Mexican peso.

The Canadian dollar is generally referred to as one of a group denoted as 'commodity dollars' which include the Australian dollar and the New Zealand dollar. In terms of export market, the US is its largest and nearest trading partner, and absorbs almost 80% of its total exports, and a massive 90% of its oil.

It's no surprise therefore to see this simple relationship in action every day in the USDCAD currency pair (affectionately known as the Loonie), with rising oil prices leading to strength in the Canadian dollar and a consequent fall in the US dollar. Whilst falling oil prices lead to weakness in the Canadian dollar and a rise in the pair.

Of course, the US and Canada are neighbours and given my earlier comments about the political uncertainty in the Middle East, and a likely economic war with China, coupled with the fact the US is the world's largest consumer, importing oil from Canada seems infinitely more attractive than from the Middle East or elsewhere. It is no surprise therefore to see China also courting Canada in order to supply its own burgeoning demands.

Fig 3.12 WTI & USD/CAD

Fig 3.12 shows the daily price action for the WTI oil futures contract above, and the USD/CAD currency pair below. As you can see, as the oil price changes, either higher or lower, the USD/CAD pair moves in the opposite direction. In other words the relationship is inverse as the Canadian dollar is the counter currency, so as the oil price falls the USD/CAD rises.

Canada's oil reserves are in the region of 200 billion barrels, second only to Saudi Arabia, and representing almost 15% of the world's total reserves. Much of Canada's oil is in the form of bitumen oil, and located in the vast Alberta sands oil fields. These are now increasingly significant as the growth of alternative sources gathers momentum and begins to challenge conventional supplies, and creating yet more problems for OPEC. Keep prices low to drive out competition, and upset the members, or allow prices to climb which encourages more alternative suppliers to enter the market with lower costs of extraction.

Extraction and refining this oil is expensive but falling all the time, and as more traditional reservoirs run dry, the Alberta sands oil fields will take on ever increasing significance. All of this makes the Canadian dollar extremely sensitive to changes in the price of crude oil.

The same is also true for the Norwegian Krona (NOK). Norway is the world's third largest exporter of crude oil, behind Russia and Saudi Arabia and, in addition, also has the same ranking for natural gas.

Just like Canada, and other commodity related currency countries, Norway has weathered the financial storm extremely well, with surging oil prices helping to push up the country's trade surplus to 16% of GDP, the second highest in the industrialised world after Switzerland.

Here in Fig 3.13 we again see a similar picture to the Canadian dollar. Once again the counter currency is the Norwegian Krona, so as the price of oil rises, the USD/NOK falls, and vice-versa.

Fig 3.13 WTI & USD/NOK

The question here from a currency trading perspective is given the similarities and correlations with oil, which of the two currency pairs would you select to trade, all things being equal, based on the oil price? And the answer to this question lies in the export markets.

Canada's exports are very closely associated with its nearest neighbour, the United States. Norway's exports are dominated by the European markets, who absorb over 80% with the UK and Germany taking the lion's share. Canada's export market is primarily the US, so any economic slowdown here will be reflected more strongly in the USD/CAD.

As I mentioned earlier there are several other currencies which have a close relationship with oil. These include the Russian ruble, the Mexican peso and the Brazilian real. Of these perhaps the most interesting for the future is the last of these, the Brazilian real with not only new and exciting oil reserves being discovered, but also with a strong and growing market in ethanol extracted from sugar cane. With the world demanding ever cleaner energy sources, Brazil is well placed to benefit from this increasing demand over the next few decades.

Having considered oil producers and world oil reserves, we now need to consider the consumer end of the equation, and as you would expect, at the top of the list are the USA and China in that order. Between them they account for almost 35% of the world's total consumption of oil. In third place is Japan which, unlike

China and the US, has to import virtually all of its oil, along with every other commodity. Indeed following the tsunami which destroyed several nuclear reactors at the Fukushima plant, Japan has become even more reliant on oil as it struggles to recover, with the anti nuclear lobby now adding its own voice.

As a result, the Japanese economy and the Yen are very sensitive to changes in the price of oil, and this is reflected in the Canadian dollar, Japanese yen currency pair as shown in the chart in Fig 3.14.

Fig 3.14 WTI & CAD/JPY

In this case, the counter currency is the Japanese yen, so the CAD/JPY has a direct and positive correlation. As the price of oil rises, the CAD/JPY also rises in step, as the Canadian dollar strengthens accordingly. Conversely, any fall will see the pair sell off.

Whilst this relationship is partially driven by the Canadian dollar and the movement of the oil price, the Japanese yen is driven in this pair by the economy which is so reliant on the commodity as an import, which is therefore likely to result in higher costs and prices. This in turn drives inflation with the prospect of higher interest rates as a result.

Finally, just to round off this section on oil, let me provide a brief guide to the various oil contracts and which ones we should follow as currency traders.

Until 2009, the de facto benchmark for oil prices was the WTI or West Texas Intermediate crude oil future, which is based on the price at the physical delivery point in Cushing, the oil hub in Oklahoma.

However in the same year, the Saudis decided that they would no longer price their oil using the WTI oil contract, but instead use the ASCI which stands for the Argus Sour Crude Index. There were many reasons for this, not least because of the inventory problems at Cushing which has a huge impact on the price of oil, and this is covered later in the fundamental section of this book.

The oil fundamentals are released each week in the weekly oil inventory figures, which in simple terms show whether oil is in demand, reflected in a fall in inventories, or demand is falling with an increase in inventories.

The Saudis became frustrated at the constant price volatility each week, due to this false mechanism of measuring supply and demand, and consequently moved to the new index. This is yet another example of how political oil is as a commodity, and this has much to do with the break-even point for production. In other words the point at which oil becomes uneconomic to extract and refine.

For the Saudis, they like to see a minimum of around $88 per barrel to maintain a healthy profit. For Canada, the break-even for the Alberta Sands oil is around $60 per barrel and indeed when oil was trading at this level for some time, all extraction was suspended, and sites closed down ahead of a recovery in the price of oil.

Copper

Having looked at oil in detail let's now consider another of the key commodities, copper, and its relationship, both in the broad markets and more particularly to currencies.

If oil is one of those commodities forex traders rarely consider, copper is one they probably never even think about, and yet, just like oil, it is a bellwether commodity, which tells us a great deal about the economic picture, and therefore money flow, risk and market sentiment.

Copper is also interesting for another reason. It is an example of where one relationship which worked in the past, has since broken down, to be replaced by another. Relational analysis, like all trading is an art, not a science. Relationships do hold well for extended periods, but just as we saw with gold and the US dollar, sometimes these relationships disengage, only to re-engage later.

The key point is this. No relationship between markets can ever be considered as either guaranteed or perfect. They can and do change, and are simply there to give us an alternative view with which to quantify risk, which is what this book is all about.

So where to start with copper, or Dr Copper as it is referred to by traders, as well as being known as the red metal? If gold is the ultimate hedge against inflation, copper is the most sought after metal for all forms of economic activity as it is widely used in manufacturing, construction, and in the electrical sector, where its applications are both diverse and varied.

As a result, copper has always been considered a leading indicator of economic growth, with rising prices signalling increasing demand which in turn suggest economic growth and rising inflation.

Until 2008, the relationship all traders used to watch was between copper prices and the London Metals Exchange or the LME. Stockpile levels were monitored closely, providing traders with a view of the balance of true supply and demand, as these were held for physical delivery against futures contacts and, at the time, proved to be an extremely reliable indicator of future prices for the metal. This was largely due to the LME's ability to track the collective inventory of its global network from its warehouses on a real-time basis.

In other words, this information was up to date and not delayed and offered traders a unique fundamental view of the above ground supply of copper. Mined copper is normally shipped direct to the customer and the volumes flowing through the LME warehouses were relatively insignificant as far as global trade was concerned, but the stockpile levels played a vital role in giving traders a view on the true balance of supply and demand in the market.

Put simply, if customers couldn't get enough of the metal from their regular supplies, the LME stockpile was used to supplement this extra demand. Therefore, from a trading perspective, if the LME stockpile fell, copper prices were expected to rise and conversely, if the stockpile fell then copper prices were likely to fall.

All of this changed, suddenly and dramatically as the financial crisis exploded, when as panic engulfed the stock markets and the entire global economy, a radical shift in base metals took place. Demand growth quickly slowed and then shifted into decline and, as a result, supply quickly caught up and the supply deficient imbalance all but disappeared overnight.

The old relationship broke down completely but was replaced by a new and interesting one, this time with the S&P 500. This began in 2009 and has continued ever since. As copper prices have moved higher, so has the S&P 500, and consequently falling as the index falls. A classic example of how linkages between markets can and do change, and on this occasion the catalyst for change was the financial crisis and subsequent sell-off in the equity markets.

Fig 3.15 shows this relationship over an eighteen month period.

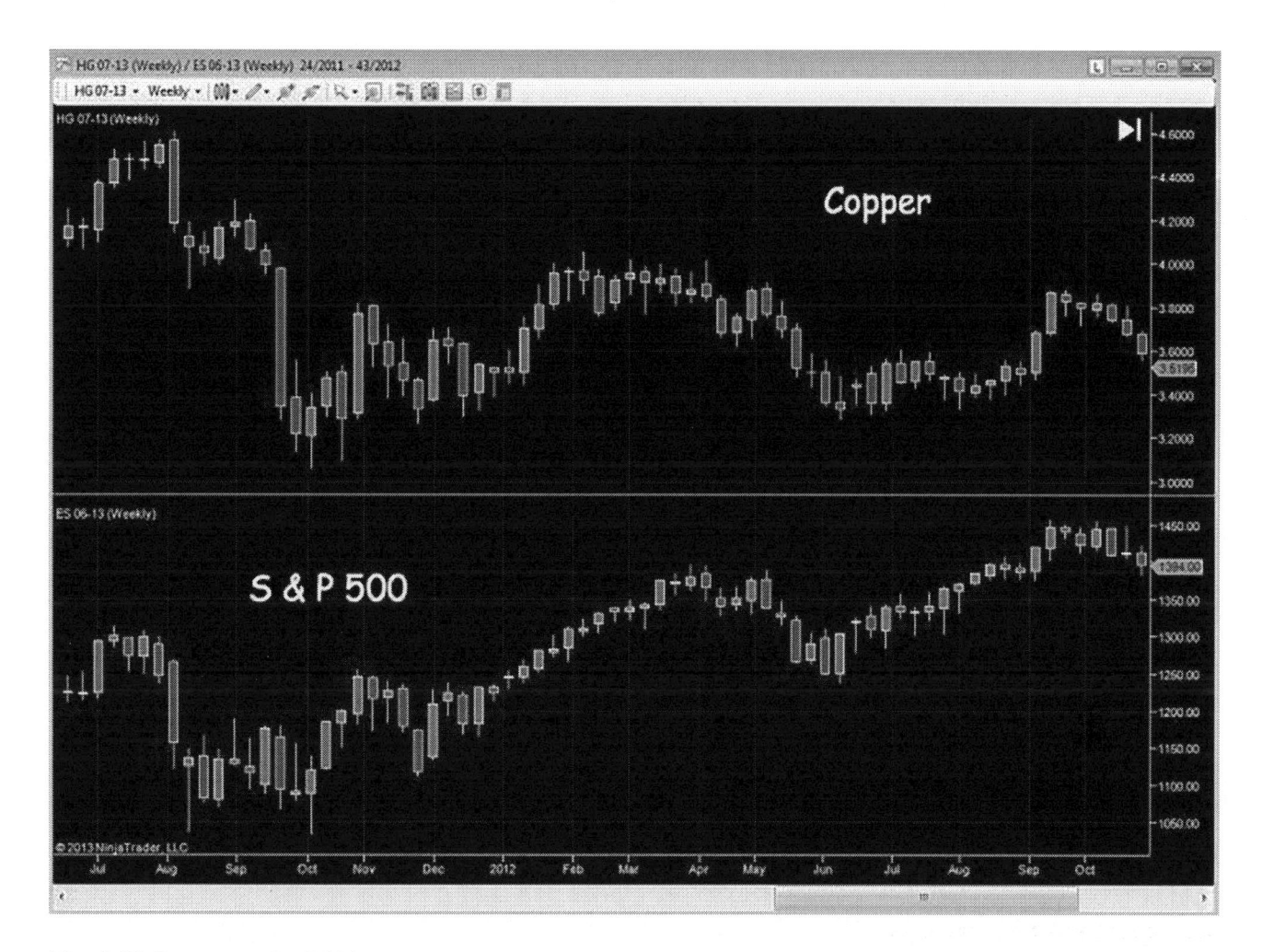

Fig 3.15 Copper & S&P500

However, there is a further factor with copper, and that is China. China is the world's largest consumer of copper and this is where we have to be careful in any analysis, for the simple reason that since 2002, China's exponential growth has masked any slowdown in the world economy.

China consumes almost one fifth of all copper mined, distorting the prices as a result and leading to some very misleading conclusions, and the problem is twofold.

First, with so much of the copper supply consumed by one country, and set to increase, this can distort the true picture. Second, over the last few years there have been continuing supply problems, particularly in Chile, the world's largest exporter of copper, which represents almost 55% of its total exports. China's domination of the commodity looks set to continue for some time to come for the following reasons.

First, China needs this commodity to build its infrastructure, particularly its aged and faltering power grid system and telecoms network. Both massive projects. Second, China is now stockpiling copper as a hedge against inflation and the damaging impact the FED is having on China's huge US dollar reserves, which will increasingly become devalued as the US dollar weakens and inflation takes hold.

Copper is seen by the Chinese as a physical hedge in much the same way as for gold or silver, and this change in dynamic is yet another reason to watch the price of copper carefully and not just as a commodity, but as a tangible asset. This is all part of the Chinese plan to move away from its dependency on US Treasuries and into more tangible assets such as copper.

In an effort to corner the market, China has been aggressively buying its own mines overseas as well as stockpiling on a grand scale. All this has driven up copper prices, but not in the conventional supply driven way.

Nevertheless, copper remains an important commodity for many reasons, not least giving us an insight into the possible future market direction for equities, risk assets, and inflation. This linkage may breakdown in the future, but for the time being it remains yet another simple and visual way to gauge money flow and risk sentiment. If copper prices are rising, risk on assets will be rising in tandem, which in turn will be reflected in risk currencies.

One of the major beneficiaries over the last few years has been the Australian dollar once again. The Australian dollar's correlation to commodity prices continues to remain strong across the board and not least as far as copper is concerned. China is Australia's largest trading partner and is responsible for more than half the country's shipments of copper, iron ore and other base metals, and should the Chinese economy slow or reverse, this will be reflected in the Australian dollar as a result. The currency can therefore be considered in two ways.

First, it can be looked at through the prism of the commodity market, and therefore as a proxy for risk, since commodities are considered to be risk assets. Second, it can be viewed in its own right as a currency driven by demand for commodities, and in particular base metals such as copper, a view which can then be validated against the US dollar.

Another currency to benefit from the last ten years in the commodity super-cycle is the Peruvian Neuvo Sol, an emerging exotic currency. Peru is the world's second largest exporter of copper, and with the Peruvian government now granting additional licences for mining, the country is set for economic growth and a strong currency based on the red metal.

As forex traders, commodities provide the bridge, with many complex linkages between the four principal capital markets. These relationships are seen in many different ways and reveal many different facets of market behaviour, from the global economic picture, to risk, to money flow, and market sentiment.

However, nothing is ever clear cut, and with the inexorable rise of China, simple analysis must always be tempered with the 'Chinese factor' upper most in our minds. China is a huge and voracious country, which not only drives explosive demand, economic growth and prices, but could also lead to equally dramatic falls in the future. All this will be played out in the commodities market, and reflected in currencies, which are the mirror against which all market behaviour is ultimately reflected.

Chapter Four
Equity Markets Explained

Bull markets are born on pessimism, grow on skepticism, mature on optimism, and die on euphoria. The time of maximum pessimism is the best time to buy, and the time of maximum optimism is the best time to sell.

Sir John Templeton (1912-2008)

Having introduced two of the least understood and rarely analysed capital markets of bonds and commodities, I'm now going to explain the third of our four markets, equities. And once again consider their role in terms of risk, money flow, and the signals they send us as forex traders.

Moreover, equities also reveal where we are in the broader economic cycle. Also in this chapter I want to consider the role of volume as a leading indicator, and its importance in revealing market reversals.

Volume in the cash markets is the only activity which the market makers are unable to hide. And when combined with price, it becomes the most powerful indicator of future market direction. The technique of analysing the market with volume and price is sometimes referred to as volume price analysis. It's a technique that can be used in all markets and in all time frames.

Originally developed from markets where true volume is reported, such as equities and futures, it can also be applied to currency markets using synthetic volumes based on tick data, and gives an excellent approximation to true volume. After all, volume is activity and activity is volume.

Equity markets are all about risk and return. Higher risk assets yield higher returns, and if there is one sacred belief in trading and investing, it is that equities are the best asset class to hold for the longer term. The mantra is simple. Buy and hold and the returns will follow.

Whilst holding cash or government bonds may offer safety in the short term, these raise the prospect of another risk – inflation, and consequent erosion of any gains in real terms. However, anyone who had invested in the Japanese stock market over the last few decades may have a different view. The principle index, the Nikkei 225 peaked at the end of 1989, and is only just regaining these levels almost 30 years later. It would be hard to find a worse example of investing for the longer term, and here's another.

Over the last 30 years up to 2010, US shares outperformed US bonds by less than 1% per year – hardly exciting, and certainly not enough to warrant the tag 'risk asset' and yet this is how equity markets are perceived, both by the markets and by investors around the world.

Therefore, until this view changes, equities will continue to be viewed as risk assets, short and simple. Investors buy equities when they are looking for better returns than in bonds or other conservative asset classes. If equity markets are rising, investors are prepared to take on more risk for 'assumed' better returns, so the money flow will be from bonds and safe haven currencies into equities and high risk currencies.

Conversely, when equity markets are falling, investors are moving into low risk asset classes and so the money flow will generally be into bonds and other low risk assets, along with safe haven currencies.

One of the key indicators used to measure and display risk, and the constant flip flop between so called 'risk on' and 'risk off' sentiment is the Volatility Index or the VIX. This is often referred to as the fear indicator, and is based on buying and selling in the options markets. I explain this in more detail later in the book.

The next issue when considering equity markets is rhetorical and it is this. Why do forex traders, rarely, if ever, look at the principle equity exchanges associated with the currency they are trading?

After all, if you are trading in a Euro pair, wouldn't you look at the main exchanges for Europe? The Euro, as we will see later, is a risk currency, so why not look at European equity markets for some clues, in a directly related risk market? This seems to makes sense to me, and yet most forex traders rarely think of this simple truism, remaining firmly glued to one screen and one instrument, oblivious to what is going on in directly related capital markets.

And when I say directly related, I am referring to the currency itself. Again, this seems to pass most traders by. For example if Japanese investors believe equity markets will offer a better return, money flow will be out of the Yen currency and into equities. The Yen will be sold, and equities bought.

Therefore, if you are trading the Yen wouldn't it make sense to know what is happening in the Japanese equity market. After all, the yen is considered to be a safe haven currency, and if the money flow is out of the yen and into risk assets, perhaps this is an important piece of information, which only takes a few minutes to establish?

Furthermore, if you are trading in the Australian dollar, wouldn't it also be prudent to consider what is happening in the Australian equity markets?

Which are the principle exchanges? Which indices do we need monitor, and what does volume tell us about the money flow?

Here is a list of the main exchanges ranked in order of size – these are the top three:

- NYSE Euronext – US equities and Europe
- NASDAQ OMX Group – US equities and Europe
- London Stock Exchange – UK equities

Then we have the following exchanges for the rest of the world:

- Tokyo stock exchange – Japanese equities
- Hong Kong stock exchange – Hong Kong equities
- Shanghai stock exchange – Chinese equities
- TMX group – Canadian equities
- Deutsche Borse – German equities
- Australian securities exchange – Australian shares
- Bombay stock exchange – Indian equities
- National stock exchange of India – Indian equities
- SIX Swiss exchange – Swiss equities

These are the major exchanges which account for around 90% of all equity transactions daily. However, when considering equity markets most traders (forex included) simply follow the ones mentioned in the media. Unfortunately, in most cases these reveal little, if anything about the economy of the country concerned.

For example in the UK the index that is always reported is the FTSE 100. What does this tell us about the UK economy? The short answer is nothing. So why is this index the one that is only ever reported?

The answer to this question is simply laziness by the media. In reality the FTSE 100 index is the least representative of the UK economy. More than 70% of the profits of companies that make up the index come from abroad, and whilst the index consists of companies quoted on the London Stock Exchange, there is nothing particularly British about any of them.

Several of the current companies such as Antofagasta, Fresnillo and Rio Tinto have no activities in the UK market whatsoever. Other more familiar companies such as Shell, BP, BAT, Unilever and Glaxo, derive most of their business and profits from overseas. When we look at other exchanges around the world we have a similar problem.

The US equity market is always quoted based on the Dow Jones Industrial Average, and yet the Dow only consists of 30 US companies, and is hardly representative of the US economy.

On the other hand, the Nikkei 225 is far more representative of the Japanese market, with almost all of the two hundred and twenty five companies being Japanese, and primarily based in Japan.

We have a similar picture in Australia with the All Ordinaries index composed principally of Australian companies.

Meanwhile in Europe the Euronext 100, is composed of European companies and therefore provides a more realistic reflection of the European economy. Canada too takes the same approach.

In summary, Australia, Canada, Japan and Europe all quote a leading index which is composed of companies with strong country specific links.

In the UK this is certainly not the case, therefore in order to gain a more balanced view of the UK economy we need to watch the FTSE 250 or even the FTSE 350. In the US, we need to watch the S&P 500, or the NASDAQ, not the Dow 30 which is far too narrow in scope.

In simple terms, equity markets serve as a basic measure of risk, whether over the longer term, where significant changes in the broad economy are reflected, or on an intraday basis, where sudden changes in sentiment are signalled in the price action, with consequent sudden changes in money flow out of risk and into safe haven assets.

The primary index to watch during the US trading session is the S&P 500 index, and with approximately 75% of companies listed having a very strong US connection, can be considered to be a good proxy for the US economy.

Once US markets have closed, equity futures then provide a view of risk, heading into the Asian session, where Japan's Nikkei 225 index becomes the standard, with the Hong Kong Hang Seng index and China's

CSI 300 providing alternative views for the Far East markets. The Australian All Ordinaries Index then takes up the baton, before moving to Europe with the DAX, the CAC 40 and finally to London.

In terms of pure currency relationships between equity markets and the associated currency, the two markets most closely watched by traders are US equities and Japanese equities. And the reason for this is very simple.

Both the currencies associated with the US and Japan, namely the US dollar and the Yen, are considered safe haven currencies. And this is something we will explore in more detail later. As a result, the associated flow of money into exchanges where these are the 'home' currency are particularly revealing when considering market sentiment.

After all, yen buyers will be buying to reduce risk with a safe haven currency. Yen sellers will be selling to increase risk by moving into equities and other risk markets.

This is revealed in the price action for the Yen against the price action for the associated index, in this case the Nikkei 225. This effect may be further magnified by effects within the currency markets themselves, where the yen is generally used as the low interest rate currency in the ever popular carry trade, of which more later.

Just as we have already seen with bonds and commodities, there are additional key relationships which exist with equities, and the one I will be covering in detail in a separate chapter is the relationship between equities and bonds.

As you would expect this is yet another of the principle relationships between capital markets, which this time defines the extremes of risk. On the one hand, we have equities, which are considered high risk, whilst on the other, we have bonds, which are considered low risk or conservative, and this is a relationship best imagined as a see-saw. Whilst the relationship is one of money flow from one to the other, it is far from straightforward, and certainly not linear as we will see.

At this stage of explaining equity markets and their importance to us as forex traders I would like to introduce two other key analytical tools. The first is sector rotation, and the second is volume. Again these are covered in more detail later in the book, but I have introduced them here for completeness. So let me begin by introducing the concept of sectors and sector rotation.

All the major exchanges around the world allocate stocks to various sectors. Just like any other asset or instrument, each sector is represented on a chart to which we can apply technical analysis techniques in order to analyse the price action, and draw conclusions about the strength or weakness of each sector. These sectors tell us a great deal about the economic cycle and current environment, as different sectors do better at different stages of the economic cycle. This is referred to as sector rotation.

For example, towards the end of an economic expansion, the energy sector and energy stocks will generally perform well, normally due to rising energy prices and a consequent build up of inflationary pressure.

In the early stages of economic recovery and expansion, as we are likely to see in the next few years, interest rate sensitive stocks are likely to perform well, with technology stocks often the first to signal a recovery from recession as companies begin to spend on capital equipment once again.

The key index here is the NASDAQ 100. This area of analysis of equity markets is one which is often overlooked, even by those trading equities. Yet it provides more clues as to the economy, the economic cycle, and in turn likely policy decisions by the central banks.

Finally in this chapter on equities, I would like to introduce another key analytical tool which we use in many ways across different markets, but particularly when analysing equities, and is what I call volume price analysis. Or VPA, for short.

I have been using this technique for many, many years not just for analysing stocks for investments, but also as a tool to help me forecast both short term and longer term turning points in equity markets, which then signal changes in the money flow to lower risk assets. This technique can be applied in any time-frame, so even if you are a scalping trader, it can be applied to a five minute chart of the S&P 500.

Let me give you a quick example of how to use this analytical tool. Suppose for a moment an item of economic data has been released, and you are watching the S&P 500 for market reaction.

On the 5 minute index chart you see huge volumes coming into the market. However, this is associated with weak price action. In other words the price is not reflecting the activity in the market. In fact, the market begins to fall on rising volume, a sure sign of short term weakness.

Simultaneously, bond yields are ticking lower as money moves into short term bonds. You can now start to look for signals in the currency markets of money flow into safe haven currencies and take advantage accordingly. Your risk assessment on a potential trade, has all stemmed from your assessment of volume in the equity markets.

As a forex trader this becomes an even more powerful tool, as we have no equivalent volume in the forex market which is one of the many reasons why trading currencies is so difficult. Therefore, let me just digress and explain about volume for a moment with regard to the forex market.

This market has no central exchange, so there is no 'real' volume reported, unlike the equity markets where volume data is collected on all transactions and reported for the cash markets, as well as in the futures market.

However, there is a solution. For the spot forex markets we use tick data as a proxy for volume, and it is generally agreed that this is a 90% approximation to true volume. Later in the book I explain tick data and how we use it in more detail, but for the time being all we need to know is we have two sources of volume data for analysis. One is based on real volume in equity markets. The other is based on synthetic volume using tick in the spot forex market, giving us two views to compare and contrast to judge risk, money flow and market sentiment.

In the cash equity markets we have volume reported second by second and minute by minute. Volume tells us a great deal as it reveals the true activity in the market and whether the market is participating in the move. In other words is the price move genuine, and if so, it will be seen in related markets. If the move is false, it is a fake move. These moves happen all the time as the market makers in equities test the market with price action, pushing indices back and forth to test support and resistance levels and to trap traders into weak positions.

The power of using volume and price (VPA) comes when we combine our analysis of the volume with the associated price action, which reveals what the market is thinking, and ultimately what is happening as a result.

Volume price analysis is equally valuable for other markets and instruments. Futures for example report true volume. ETFs, which I mentioned in an earlier chapter, report trading volumes. So it can be used in some of the ETFs we track to tell us what is happening in commodities or currencies. Or even in some of the market internal indices that are so important, and which will be covered in more detail later.

However, before moving forward let me just give you a simple example to explain the basic principles which lie at the heart of volume price analysis.

Suppose we see an equity index has reached a key technical level, but then begins to move sideways. On one particular day we see a narrow range candle, but with very high volume. What message is the price action and volume giving us?

It's a very simple message, the volume is signalling weakness because if the market were strong, the price action would have been wide and the market would have moved higher, out of congestion. Clearly the market is not interested in further buying at this level and is resistant. The buyers are moving out and have lost interest. If there were more buyers than sellers the market would have risen higher – here the sellers are selling into a market with few buyers, so the price remains in a tight range.

This is the simple concept on which volume price analysis is based. We look at the volume and then compare this with the price action on the chart which can be in any time frame. It doesn't matter whether it is ticks, minutes, hours, days or weeks.

Markets require volume (activity) to make them move, either up or down. Volume really is the fuel of the market.

If an index or ETF is moving higher on very low volume, we know it is likely to be a trap up move by the market makers, and the money flow is moving elsewhere. Similarly, if an index or ETF is moving lower on very low volume, we know this is also a false move. This is the basic principle behind VPA which I cover in more detail for you once we get to the technical section of the book.

It is an extremely powerful technique which has a host of applications, but one which is little understood or used by most traders.

Equity markets are a perfect vehicle for assessing sentiment and risk. In addition they are one of the purest markets in terms of volume. owever, we do need to ensure we are watching the most appropriate indices. And remember also, we can follow these markets 24 hours a day in two ways. First by tracking each physical exchange around the world as they open and then close several hours later. Second, we can follow the futures indices on Globex which again is virtually 24 hours a day. Here you can follow the index futures which are traded on the CME on an electronic platform, so at any time of the day or night, there is either a physical exchange open somewhere in the world, and/or the electronic markets of indices. So between the two, we have a barometer of market sentiment always available and wherever we are in the world.

Chapter Five
The Forex Market Revealed

Markets are constantly in a state of uncertainty and flux and money is made by discounting the obvious and betting on the unexpected.

George Soros (1930-)

At last we have arrived at the fourth of our major capital markets which is, forex. The markets that ultimately display the flow of money around the world.

But where to start explaining the forex market is a difficult question, and in this chapter what I do not intend to cover are the basic mechanics of exchange pairs. This is a all explained in another of my books Forex For Beginners. You can find details in the back of this book or on Amazon.

The purpose of this chapter is to try to give you a different perspective, a deeper view, an historical view, as to how this market has evolved and why. Also how it has changed over the last 50 years, and what are some of the changes we are likely to see in the future.

By doing this I hope to provide a broader perspective for you as a trader, a framework if you like, against which to trade.

The forex market is one of the most difficult both to understand and trade as it is driven by so many internal and external influences. These combine to create what appear to be random, sudden changes in price and direction. And the reasons for this are as follows.

First, the forex market is the most influenced and manipulated politically, both by governments via their central banks. This is the market where global politics meets money in one glorious melting pot. Second, it is the primary market which offers central banks a small degree of control over the economic landscape as the international powers battle for supremacy. Third, it is the market where international politics meets economics, and I cannot stress this point too strongly.

As forex traders you really do have to understand the above and the extent to which this market is subject to political intervention, coupled with false and misleading data from individual countries, all overlain with jealousy, trade wars, sanctions and political manoeuvring.

Earlier in the book I considered the relationship between the US dollar and gold and, as I stated there, as a forex trader you do have to understand the US dollar and its role as the lynch pin for the entire monetary system. Furthermore, you also have to understand how this role also impacts the currency markets.

Over the past half century, there have been a variety of attempts to control currency exchange rates, both overtly and covertly, and this is a feature of the market that will continue for decades to come, as central banks and governments set self preservation of their own markets and economies, well ahead of any concerns for any fellow members of the G7 or G20.

The principal reason for this is that there is simply too much at stake for the politically appointed officials and government representatives who put their own political appointments and opinion ratings first, and other countries second.

Central banks have a remit to provide economic stability which encourages growth, controls inflation and is a stimulus for jobs. If a country is largely dependent on exports, the central bank will do everything in its power to ensure its currency is kept artificially weak, thereby protecting its overseas markets.

In short, all the various parties involved will always do what is in the best interest for themselves, and their country, and not necessarily in that order. This is what you are confronted with as a forex trader, which is why it is such a complex but fascinating market.

Other features to consider are the issues of pegging and why it still continues today, free floating currencies, and finally intervention and why it happens. However, before looking back historically to the 1970s I want to start with 2007 and explore the ramifications of the last few years.

2007 saw the onset of the worst financial crisis in the last 100 years, probably only eclipsed by the stock market crash of 1929.

The ramifications of the near collapse of worldwide banking infrastructures, coupled with the virtual bankruptcy of entire countries will remain for years, if not decades to come. Some would argue the fractures in the credit markets may never heal, and that we could still be subject to some aftershocks, once the dust has settled.

In fact we need look no further than the so called BRIC countries of Brazil, Russia, India and of course China who having been the principle beneficiaries of the credit bubble and explosion, are now beginning to worry about the long steady decline of the US dollar.

At this point you might ask why these countries should be so worried about this decline. The reason is what is known as the "dollar peg". In simple terms this means a currency is 'pegged' to the US dollar, and does not free float like other currencies. In other words, the currency follows the US dollar as it strengthens or weakens accordingly.

Of the BRIC countries, those which have been, or indeed still are, pegged directly or indirectly to the US dollar, are the Chinese yuan, the Russian Rouble and the Indian Rupee. In addition, the currencies of the Gulf States too are pegged to the US dollar. The last of these is primarily pegged to minimise any currency fluctuations due to their dependency on selling oil, which is priced in dollars.

This list changes all the time, as countries around the world first adopt, and then modify or abandon the peg, as a mechanism for managing currency exchange rate fluctuation. But what is pegging? Why is it used? What are the advantages and disadvantages and how is the current pegging system likely to affect the currency markets in the next few years?

As rational, logical beings you would think we would learn from the lessons of history. Sadly, this is not the case, as we only have to look back to the Bretton Woods agreement and the Marshall plan of the 1950's and early 1970's. This is when the dollar was established as the 'de facto' global reserve currency, following the collapse of these agreements and the removal of the gold standard.

The gold standard was an attempt to peg currencies to gold, and on its demise ushered in the free floating currency model which has been more or less adopted across the globe.

As forex traders it's vital we understand the issues with pegging, and in particular how this mechanism affects the floating currencies, particularly when major economic nations are pegged to the dollar. For the Gulf states of course, pegging makes sense, since their primary income is derived from oil which is priced in US dollars, and as such, their oil reserves are not subject to the usual exchange rate fluctuations which would otherwise apply.

But why do countries adopt a currency peg and what are the benefits? But perhaps a supplemental question is why is this important even to a scalping forex trader? And the answer is the Euro.

When a currency is primarily pegged to the dollar, most trade and transactions are by default executed in US dollars. This is fine in a stable economic environment where currency stability is the norm.

However, in the last few years this has most certainly not been the case with central banks such as the FED creating artificial debt markets with their fiscal and monetary stimulus, whilst simultaneously creating an artificially weak dollar.

It is no surprise therefore the problems with pegging have become more exaggerated as a result. And this is precisely where we were at the start of the new decade.

In simple terms a US dollar peg does two things to those countries who have opted into this arcane system. First, the pegged countries are forced to issue new money in order to re-balance the peg which is like a see saw, so the printing presses are turned on in the base currency which in this case is the US dollar.

Second, this has the effect of driving up the cost base for manufacturers on a domestic basis and driving inflation into the economy. The side effect is monetary policy has to remain tight to combat the inflationary pressure created by the peg with the pegged currency's economy slowing as a result.

The country with the pegged economy is then locked in a no win situation unable to tackle its domestic issues or to devalue its own currency to rebalance the economy. This was the primary reason why the Bretton Woods agreement failed. The peg had the effect of stimulating inflationary pressures into the pegged currencies. This made domestic manufacturing uncompetitive in world markets and led to a protracted period of recession for the pegged currency exceeding that of the base currency.

Whilst there are parallels between the Bretton Woods collapse of forty years ago, and the pegged currencies of today there is one key difference, and it is this. Today's situation is far more dangerous for one simple reason - the US trade and budget deficits.

The FED's decision to use QE to prevent financial Armageddon has created many unforeseen and unwanted consequences. One is the creation of an artificial imbalance in the economic world, to which there is no easy answer, and until this imbalance is resolved then currency markets are likely to remain volatile and in a state of flux for years to come.

So, what has been the reaction to this problem by Russia and China, both of whom are heavily US dollar dependent with China in particular holding more reserves in dollars than Japan? The reactions have been very different. Russia started to shift away from the dollar in 2009 reducing its reserves by increasing their

Euro holding from 20% to almost 40% over a 12 month period, whilst still retaining their longer term US bonds.

China, on the other hand, appears to have been given a lifeline by the US FED via their QE programme which has allowed the Chinese to replace their long term bonds with short term holdings. This can only suggest one thing. That China is preparing, with help from the FED, to float the Chinese yuan and eventually move away from the corrosive effect of the dollar peg in favour of currency diversification.

However, at the same time neither China's currency, nor indeed any other currency, has the required liquidity to replace the US dollar as the currency of first reserve.

China's distaste for the dollar is supported by other members of BRICS, and China often uses other BRIC members as allies in its own game plan. For example, instead of buying directly from trade partners, China has set up swap agreements as a means of avoiding the US dollar completely.

So far it has set up currency swaps with Argentina, South Korea, Hong Kong, Indonesia, Malaysia and Belarus. But, more alarmingly both China and Russia have agreed to expand the use of their own currencies in bilateral trade agreements.

To add further to this cosy relationship, China is now in close talks with Brazil and, as a result, these countries can now use the Chinese yuan to buy goods and services in China, along with its close neighbours who depend on China's trade network. Think of this as a shopping club where certificates are exchanged for goods and services, a club where these certificates or coupons have replaced money. Brazil can now use its yuan to buy goods and services from, say Indonesia or Malaysia without the need to settle in dollars.

The ultimate for China would be if they could extend these swap agreements to a partner in Europe. The game for China, and it is a game, is to remove the US dollar from its position as a currency of first reserve, and to have it replaced with one which includes the yuan as part of a balanced basket of currencies.

Naturally, this would reduce the dominance of the dollar as a result and increase that of the yuan, whilst simultaneously strengthening China's trading position and providing a more controlled economic environment for growth.

Amongst all this there is a healthy dose of political rhetoric between the US and China, and whilst superficially there is a gloss of entente cordiale, beneath the surface lurks the old animosities of a communist state and the ultimate symbol of capitalism. Further reinforced with the current trade wars which have taken centre stage.

In part this can be traced back to the US policy of QE and the FED's desperate attempt to avoid a financial collapse and provide the framework for a revival of the US economy.

In addition, competitive devaluation or "the race to the bottom" by central banks desperate to protect export markets has now created a dangerous imbalance in the forex market. This market has changed beyond all recognition in the last few years as old antagonisms are resurrected and protectionist policies implemented. In simple terms we are now seeing the major economic groups fight for supremacy and their battle ground is the forex market. These economic groups fall into three broad categories.

The first group is that led by China and the BRICS, who are busy creating their own trading circle using currency swaps as a direct attack on the US dollar to weaken its position, as it continues to slide under the weight of the Federal Reserve's monetary policy.

The second group is Europe and the Euro with its political leaders desperate to salvage the euro project as they create ever larger bail out funds to avoid the embarrassment of default by an EU state. And if you are wondering if the Euro project sounds remarkably similar to a peg– you would be correct, because it is.

In forty years, no peg to any currency has ever lasted more than a few years, as it is impossible for any country to maintain its monetary policy to retain the peg. Many have tried and all have failed.

Classic failures have included Argentina and Mexico in recent years, with the former finally defaulting and creating the biggest default in history of $95 billion. This record still stands unless Greece is allowed to default.

In reality Europe and the euro project is no more than a peg between 17 countries, most of whom are now struggling to survive, with Spain, Italy Portugal and Greece teetering on the edge.

All of these countries are in effect part of what amounts to a hard currency block centred on Germany. Just as with Argentina pretending the peso was a US dollar, the fiction in Europe is Greece and Germany can operate within a common currency. Simply having a common currency does not make it a reality. It can only be so if Greece were to adopt the monetary policies of the ECB (European Central Bank) which is a proxy for the hard currency Bundesbank – something which clearly can never happen. To use a very simple analogy. This is akin to asking a spender and a saver to live in harmony together. The relationship will never survive, and this is what makes the Euro project even more risible.

To expect Greece with all its cultural and economic differences to adopt the same monetary policy as Germany, is unrealistic in the extreme. The same applies to Spain, Italy and Portugal, and it is simply a question of time before the project collapses. The project will only collapse when Germany finally throws in the towel, and with the ECB now standing as the lender of last resort, this could be some time coming.

The last rites for the Euro have been read many times, and the shorts have been squeezed, time and time again as the Euro continues to survive. Every move lower is greeted by the Euro bears as the demise of the single currency, which then promptly reverses to recover its bullish momentum.

The Euro will survive, for the time being, but like all the other 'pegs' it will ultimately collapse. It cannot survive in its present structure. One only has to look at history, and it's not a question of if, but when. Germany will return to the Deutschmark, Spain to the Peso, Italy to the Lira and Greece to the Drachma. The waters will calm and another peg failure will be added to the long and growing list.

The third group can loosely be categorised as the emerging markets of Latin America and Asia. Many of the countries within this group are major exporters within the top 20 global economies and growing fast. And their long term survival depends on having competitive export markets, but so far they have not banded together in any formal way to tackle this problem.

One reason for this is that thus far their focus has been regional rather than global. However, with many of these countries inextricably linked to the dollar through strong commodity exports, this may change in the future.

Finally, of course, we have major economies such as Japan, Canada, Australia and the UK, supportive of their own currencies, but watching Europe and the BRICS block leviathans execute their strategies to weaken the dollar and ultimately see it replaced.

For Europe this is a politically motivated strategy, whilst for China it is fuelled by trade concerns underpinned by politics. Many countries around the world see the FED policy of weakening the US dollar as simply one of self interest, and akin to a protectionist or interventionist policy commonly employed by countries such as Japan. But all these attempts to manipulate the currency markets always have two things in common.

First they always fail, and second they always cost the central bank concerned a vast amount of money in the process which is subsequently viewed as wasted. No central bank however large has the ability to reverse a currency trend no matter how much money they inject into the system. A good example is the SNB - Swiss National Bank which has spent untold millions trying to weaken the Swiss Franc and has, in effect, simply given up.

So this is the world of the forex markets which on the surface appears to be simple and straightforward. But beneath this apparent simplicity lies a complex web of politically motivated strategies coupled with long and deep seated animosities, all of which are played out in a simple exchange rate. And this is one of the many reasons trading in currencies is so difficult.

It is the market where international politics is played out on a grand scale each and every day, as these global economic powerhouses jostle for position.

Unfortunately for the US dollar, the FED is playing a very dangerous game, and it could ultimately rue the day that quantitative easing ever began should the dollar eventually be toppled from its unique position as the currency of first reserve.

Is this likely to happen? Anything is possible and if it ever did, it is debatable whether this would create a more stable environment for economic growth primarily because, as I said earlier, few currencies have the necessary liquidity to replace it.

In the meantime the IMF has also weighed in with its own proposals based on a mechanism referred to as an SDR, which stands for Special Drawing Rights. In simple terms, this would be a synthetic currency made up from a basket of currencies, primarily the US dollar, the euro, the yen and the British pound. Of course this simplistic approach has since been countered by Asian countries who want the yuan included as well as currencies from Latin America.

The IMF's view is this would create a more stable environment for world trade to thrive and negate much of the impact of the current "race to the bottom".

However, until then the US dollar will remain the lynch pin of the currency markets, and love it or loathe it, it is here to stay for the time being.

As forex traders we have to understand the underlying politics of the other major groups in the markets and my objective in this chapter has been to provide you with a deeper view of the currency markets and the powerful forces which drive it.

In the next chapter I want to explore the relationship between commodities and bonds, and the cross market relationship between these two capital markets.

Chapter Six
The Bond & Commodity Relationship

Risk comes from not knowing what you are doing

Warren Buffett (1930 -)

Having looked briefly at the four capital markets on an individual basis, I now want to look at some of the bilateral relationships between these markets. And in this chapter to focus on the relationship between commodities and bonds which is perhaps the least understood, but is one of the most important of all these cross market relationships.

Again it is one most traders ignore, either because they are so focused on their own sector of the market, or simply because they do not understand it, or even realise there is one!

However, I must stress before we go on any further, this relationship is probably the most complex to understand. But please don't worry because it will all become clear the further you read. One of the reasons this chapter may seem complicated is because the bond/commodity relationship is multi-faceted, and so can be looked at from a number of different angles.

In addition, it is not a straightforward linear relationship, and you also need to have an understanding of the factors which affect this linkage, which are also multi-faceted and constantly shifting.

Sometimes it can seem like trying to pick up a jelly. And perhaps the best way to try and visualise this relationship is to imagine it as a simple compass, with bonds at the West, commodities at the East, inflation at the North and the US dollar in the South.

What this then describes is the interplay between these four points with the compass needle moving according to where we are in the economic cycle.

Having already touched on the economic cycle in the chapter on equities, it is a topic we will be looking at in detail in a later section of the book when dealing with fundamentals. However, for the purposes of this chapter, I want to focus on the primary catalysts of economic activity, which could be inflation, deflation or even stagflation.

Again, I will explain all these terms in detail in due course. For the time being I'm going to concentrate on inflation, which, put simply, is the overall, general upward price movement of goods and services in an economy - in other words things become more expensive and the value of money is eroded, in real terms.

However, just to complicate matters, inflation is not necessarily a bad thing, it only becomes bad when it reaches a tipping point, and gets out of control. The other issue with inflation is that there are various types which will have very different effects on the bond and commodity relationship. So let me just clarify this and why as, forex traders, this is so important to understand.

It's actually very easy when you accept that whenever a government is faced by inflation it has only one, very crude and blunt weapon with which to manage its effect on the economy. In other words, interest rates. This is the tool used by all central banks to either slow down or speed up their economies. This in turn partially explains why economies in general, move in a cyclical nature, with economic growth and expansion, subsequently followed by economic contraction and finally recession.

Unlike many other financial markets, there are no direct economic charts to tell us where we are in an economic cycle, and the likelihood of inflation or deflation, which in turn could signal any likely changes in interest rates. However, in analysing the relationship between bonds and commodities some clues are revealed, as both are key indicators of inflation and hence of future changes in interest rates which are so important to us as forex traders.

Bonds and commodities tell us a great deal about inflation and deflation, as they are the principle markets used by central banks to gauge economic growth and on which interest rate decisions are therefore based. It is also the relationship where global economic demand meets the cost of money, and the currency of first reserve, i.e., the US dollar.

The principle reason we look at the relationship between bonds and commodities is their direct link to inflation, and inflation expectations in the future.

Therefore, let me start at the end, and then I'll explain how we arrive at this conclusion, and it is simply this. Whenever we see commodity prices and bond yields rising in tandem, we can expect to see inflation in the economy and a consequent change in interest rates as a result.

This is the start of our inflation expectation, from where the economic cycle begins. To try to explain this relationship I'll start with the commodities side of the equation, but first we have to remember three things about commodities.

First, all commodities are not equal.

Second, commodities are an asset class just like a stock or bond.

Third, commodity prices rise for several different reasons and not necessarily because of inflation expectations.

Starting with the first statement all commodities are not equal. By this I mean we have to be careful when simply saying commodity prices are rising and therefore we should expect inflation.

Gold, for example, is a commodity which is neither consumed nor used in industry, to any great extent, and therefore could never be considered to be representative of the commodity sector. Yet gold is also the ultimate safe haven when investors are looking for a secure asset in uncertain times. That said, gold is also a hedge against inflation.

If the price of gold is rising, one factor could the flow of money is into gold as a hedge against inflation. Therefore, in its own way gold is an indicator of potential inflation. However, it could also be attracting money flow for safe haven reasons. This generally happens on the 'faster' timeframes, but can extend into slower timeframes depending on the severity of any shock.

Silver too could be considered in much the same way, and even though silver is classed as an industrial metal, it is increasingly seen as a safe haven and a cheaper alternative to gold.

If you recall when we first began to look at commodities we looked at the three main sectors of agriculture, metals and energy. Of these, the first and perhaps easiest to understand in terms of inflation is the agriculture sector, which includes all the basic commodities grown or reared by farmers around the world, such as cereals, grains, livestock, timber and cotton.

We don't need to be an economist to realise if the price of corn and wheat is rising, basic everyday foods such as bread will also rise in price along with meat prices, since cattle feed uses both wheat and corn.

These price rises will ultimately be reflected in the economic figures for inflation, which are generally based on a standard basket of products and everyday consumables. This is why rising commodity prices are considered to be a leading indicator of inflation.

However, these prices do not usually filter through the system for at least six to nine months, and sometimes take even longer, which is an important point. These effects of inflation can take time. They do not happen immediately, and may even take between one to two years before the effects are fully reflected in any fundamental data.

Therefore, we cannot jump to the conclusion that rising commodity prices equals rising inflation with an imminent rise in interest rates. Not least because commodities have to be bought and paid for, and then converted into other goods before being bought and sold, before any inflation figures appear in the economic data.

Let's take corn as an example and consider the various factors that could influence the price, and whether we should view any price increase as a signal of future inflation, or whether the increase in price is merely a temporary factor.

Commodity prices are generally driven by supply and demand, and if a commodity is in demand, prices are likely to rise. However commodity prices could also be rising due to a lack of supply, due to growing conditions and, in the case of corn this could typically arise from weather problems such as drought or flood.

This often leads to trade embargoes with supply restrictions being imposed by governments. For example, large grain producers such as Russia will always ensure home consumption takes priority over export markets.

Finally we have the US dollar in which virtually all commodities are priced. If the US dollar is weakening commodity prices in general will rise, and conversely if the US dollar is strengthening, commodity prices are likely to fall.

Let's examine these factors in more detail.

If prices are rising due to demand this will eventually give rise to inflation, as these higher prices feed through into the system.

If prices are rising due to a supply problem, this is only likely to be a short term issue, and unlikely to cause inflationary pressure in the system.

If the US dollar is weakening, this too will cause commodity prices to rise making them more expensive and therefore driving inflation into the economic system.

The question is how do we differentiate between these three scenarios and decide whether the price of a commodity is rising due to demand, supply or weakness in the US dollar?

The last of these is easy, as we simply have to look at a chart for the US dollar to show us the trend and whether it is weak or strong. And, as a very general rule, as the dollar falls commodity prices rise and vice-versa, although not always.

The tricky part is deciding whether a rise in a commodity price has been driven by supply or demand, and in order to check this, we have to turn to the futures market and consider whether the price is in contango or backwardation.

Contango and Backwardation

These two terms are used to describe whether a commodity is being priced higher due to supply issues, or demand, and in simple terms this is how it works.

If the price of corn is in backwardation this means the futures contract closest to expiry is priced higher than one expiring at a later date. In other words, backwardation creates a downwards sloping price curve.

Backwardation tells the market there is a short term supply issue which in the case of corn could be a weather related issue.

The opposite of this is contango. This is when futures commodity prices are higher than the closest futures contract. In other words the price at a later date is higher than the current price.

This is a normal market condition, and therefore a demand led price rise. Therefore, results in an upwards sloping price curve.

This is how we tell the difference between a supply led price increase and a demand led price increase, of which the latter is signalling inflation and the former is not.

Before we move on to look at bonds in the context of inflation let's just look at the three different types of inflation and how they occur in practice. These are referred to as:

1. Demand pull
2. Cost push
3. Imported

Demand pull is the example we looked at above with corn, where demand from the market is increasing the price of the commodity.

Cost push occurs most often when salaries and wages begin to rise along with other costs of production, and this is the second clear sign of inflation.

Finally, we have imported inflation which occurs as the result of a weak currency exchange, which may be good news for exports, but not good news for net importers of goods, which increases costs driving inflation into the economy.

With the last of these, perhaps you can begin to see why as a currency trader you have to understand all these linkages and economic factors which ultimately drive the markets in their endless and often repeated cycles. So, is inflation a good thing or a bad thing? And the answer, of course, is that it depends.

Inflation is fine as long as it is under control and, if so it can be considered to be positive for the economy, as business expands and creates jobs at a measured pace. However, once inflation starts to rise and run out of control it becomes a bad thing, interest rates begin to rise causing the economy to slow and jobs are lost.

I will look at inflation in more detail in a later chapter, as well as its cousin, deflation.

But what about bonds as a measure of future inflation? If you remember in the chapter on bonds and bond yields, a bond has two elements. The underlying price of the bond, and the bond yield. As the price goes up the yield falls, and as the price of the bond falls the yield rises.

However, now let's look at a bond from an issuers point of view and assume we are a government or municipal authority who want to raise some capital for a project. We decide to issue a bond, but at what interest rate or coupon?

The first consideration is we are in competition with other organisations who also want to attract money, so we have to offer a competitive rate. For the purposes of this exercise let's assume the general borrowing rate for lending is ten percent and we decide to issue a bond with a borrowing rate of fifteen percent.

In this scenario it is not difficult to imagine there would be a queue of investors at the door desperate for this bond as we are offering a rate which is significantly higher than our competitors.

This would ensure we received our capital, but at a very high price and not in line with market rates. Equally, if we offered the bond at 5% we would have no one buying the bond. Therefore, bonds reflect market rates. They have to, otherwise no one would be interested in them.

However, back to our example. As a lender we also have to keep an eye on the economy, inflation expectations and therefore interest rates. If we believe interest rates are likely to rise in the future, either in the short term or indeed the longer term this has to be factored into the coupon rate of the bond. This is what every other bond issuer will also be considering. If we all think inflation is likely, our coupon rates will rise, as will yields, which will then be reflected in the yield curve we looked at in the chapter on bonds.

As I pointed out when we looked at commodities, rising yields are not necessarily a bad thing. We can often see the yield curve rising due to future inflation along with both commodities and equities, two risk asset classes. Rising yields and rising inflation can therefore be a positive signal of a strong economy and solid growth.

In this scenario rising yields will also be helped by the flow of money out of low risk conservative bonds, and into higher risk commodities and equities, so in any analysis of yields, we need to be careful to consider both reasons for increasing yields. Namely, is this an inflation led yield increase or a risk led increase with investors looking for higher returns, in higher risk assets, and away from bonds.

At some point, of course, investors will start to look at bonds as a better and lower risk investment than commodities or indeed equities, with a consequent flow of money into conservative bonds.

The question is where, and how, do we look for the clues and signals for such a flow of money, at this so called tipping point.

Unfortunately, there are no hard and fast rules. If it were that easy we would all be millionaires by now. However, as a rule of thumb, it is once yields on the ten year US treasury note reach 5% and beyond. Historically this has become the tipping point at which investors begin to consider moving money away from risk assets, such as commodities and equities and into safer assets such as bonds. And the question, as always, is why?

And for an answer we have to go back to inflation and it is in fact very straightforward.

The early stages of rising yields generally reflects an improving economic picture with relatively low inflation which is favourable for riskier assets such as commodities and equities.

However as bond yields rise above 5%, economic growth is accompanied by higher inflation, which is likely to threaten future growth, erode the value of future earnings and act as a drag on equities. The net result is an outflow of money from high risk assets into low risk assets, namely away from commodities and into bonds.

Whilst the bond commodity linkage can be difficult to understand it is an important one as it reveals so much about future inflation expectations and interest rates. For forex traders it can provide valuable insights into central bank thinking and future exchange rate decisions.

Chapter Seven
Bonds and Equities

The key to making money in stocks is not to get scared out of them.

Peter Lynch (1944-)

In the previous chapter we explored the complex relationship between bonds and commodities. But in this chapter I want to explain another key relationship in the capital markets, namely the one between bonds and equities (stocks).

Once again the best way to try and visualise this relationship is to imagine it as a simple compass with bonds at the west, equities at the east, yield in the north and risk in the south. What we have here is the interplay between these four points with the compass needle moving according to where we are in the economic cycle.

As I have stressed before, never ever assume a relationship, once established and identified, will always exist.

It won't, and this is true for the bonds equities relationship. This will shift according to where we are in the economic cycle as we saw in the previous chapter on bonds and commodities.

With stocks and bonds the first aspect of the relationship which is often portrayed is a very simple one, namely as a gauge of the risk tolerance of traders and investors. In other words, money flowing out of stocks and into bonds when traders and investors are fearful, and out of bonds and into stocks when happy.

Broadly speaking this is true, as stocks are considered to be a higher risk asset class and bonds a lower risk asset class.

However, it doesn't tell the whole story, and for a more complete picture we need to view bonds according to their three principle groups, namely short term T-bills, medium term T-notes and long term T-bonds. And to help us put this into context here are two simple examples.

The first is one I'm sure you are all familiar with, and typically occurs whenever bad economic news is released or there is a weak technical picture on a chart. Stock markets fall globally, and there is a so called 'flight to safety'. Sometimes also referred to as "a flight to quality paper". This 'flight' is simply a move into bonds, the US dollar and other safe haven currencies.

In this scenario, the bonds in question will be short term T-bills and generally those between thirty and ninety days, as traders and investors view this as a short term event and not a longer term change in market direction.

Nothing else has changed, other than stocks have pulled back on one item of economic news. So in this case we would see this reflected in the short term T bills, and to a much lesser extent, in the longer term bonds. The chances are on the first item of good news, these same traders and investors will simply move their money back into stocks once more.

This short term move in yields would be reflected on the intraday charts, with the percentage yield moving lower throughout the trading session with bond prices rising on buying. The yield curve for US treasuries would simply adjust slightly on the short term.

As always, we must be very precise when talking about bonds and make sure we specify yield or price when comparing money flow with another market.

The second example is one where equities have been rising steadily in a bull market, along with longer term bond yields on the ten year and thirty year US treasuries, as economic growth has been fuelled by controlled inflation and steadily rising interest rates.

In this case we can expect to see the money flow reflected in these longer term notes and bonds, as these are now signalling a longer term change in investor sentiment. Unlike the first example which was a simple knee jerk reaction to a short term market move.

Short term moves are a regular occurrence as 'risk on'/ 'risk off' sentiment see-saws daily and weekly. This is simply part of the on going price action. After all, no market ever goes up in a straight line, or down in a straight line. Instead, a market is punctuated by a series of higher highs and higher lows in an up trend, with minor pull-backs and reversals marking the way.

This is why we watch the yield curve so closely, for clues and signals as to the future economic outlook and the prospect of inflation in the longer term, leading to higher interest rates.

Moreover, bond yields rise for two reasons. First, they rise when bond prices are falling, with the money flow away from bonds and into equities. Second, bond yields also rise if interest rates rise. They have to, as bonds represent the debt market where the price of money is set.

Therefore, if we are in the early stages of an economic recovery and expansion with potential inflation on the horizon and interest rate rises as a result, when these are announced, bond yields will increase as these filter into the bond market.

Clearly we could also see a scenario where interest rates are rising in order to keep inflation under control, and as result, bond yields are also increasing. This would probably be in conjunction with a bull market in stocks, as economic growth creates jobs increasing demand and increasing corporate profits.

But, and once again it is a big but, at some point bond yields will reach a point at which corporate yields become unsustainable, and damaging to corporate profits as a result

In other words, the cost of borrowing money erodes corporate profits, and it is at this point we are likely to see money flowing into bonds and away from equities for two reasons.

First, investors can expect a better yield, and secondly, investors believe stocks pose too high a risk. Moreover, investors also believe these high yields and the cost of borrowing are unsustainable for corporate companies in the short to medium term.

Once this pattern occurs, there is only one result. A bear market begins and stocks will fall sharply.

Bonds and their yields are therefore an early warning signal of a reversal from a bull to a bear market in equities, which will also, of course, be reflected in commodities.

As I outlined in the previous chapter, when we were looking at the issue of a tipping point, anything over a five percent yield would start to flash a warning to us as forex traders that stocks were reaching an inflexion point due to the cost of money. But what happens next ?

Generally, during the bear phase for equities, there is often a disconnect between the bonds and equities relationship. As inflation begins to come under control, interest rates fall coupled with falling yields. However, with nowhere else to invest other than cash, the options for investors are extremely limited.

As a result, there tends to be no clear relationship between bonds and equities during this phase of the economic cycle. Eventually when yields start to fall money becomes cheaper once again, companies can start to borrow and expand and the whole cycle starts up again, with bonds leading the way as a leading indicator for stocks.

All of this activity is presented for us in the yield curve and it is here we find all the clues and signals as to likely changes in interest rates in the short, medium and longer term.

Coupled with an analysis of both the bond price chart, and the bond yield chart this completes the picture giving us our three dimensional view of bonds and stocks, and of course, bonds and commodities.

The relationship and link between bonds and equities is not fixed and will vary according to where we are in the economic cycle. Furthermore, the economic cycle will also dictate which bond group we should be focusing on.

Chapter Eight
Bonds and Currencies

Time is your friend; impulse is your enemy

Jack Bogle (1929-)

In this chapter, I want to examine the relationship between bonds and currencies which in many ways can be described as the meeting of the two money markets. Where the cost of borrowing is set by the bond market, and the cost of doing business is executed in the currency markets.

As we have already seen, bonds tell us about the cost of borrowing money. We watch the bond yield as it can reveal, not only risk and money flow, but it can also signal the future direction of interest rates. And it is interest rates which are usually the single most important determinant of a currency's value.

I say usually, because in the last few years the cataclysmic events which have rocked the financial world, interest rates have become significantly less important as most central banks have been forced to lower interest rates to historically low levels, where they have remained ever since.

This is one of the game changing principles which I referred to in my foreword to this book. Ten years ago, as a currency trader, interest rates would have been the most significant aspect of strength or weakness in a currency pair. Trends would have been established on interest rate differentials alone. This has all changed, and is a feature I discuss in the section on fundamental news along with its effect on the monthly economic releases.

Over the last few years and, with little prospect of interest rate changes in the short term, the forex markets have shifted their focus of attention to other market indicators, such as unemployment and housing data for a longer term view of economic activity and growth.

Lately, with rising commodity prices and the prospect of inflation and growth now on the horizon, as we start to come to the end of this long recessionary period, markets are once again starting to focus on interest rates.

Furthermore, with the slowing of the US quantitative easing programme, the bond markets will return to their natural place as the leading indicator of future interest rates which are so important to us as currency traders.

Furthermore, it is important to understand the link between interest rates and the value of a currency, is not merely the simplistic one of where they are at present. Of far greater importance is their overall direction and whether they are likely to go up or down in the future. In other words, we need to try to establish answers to the following questions:

1. Where are interest rates likely to get to in the future?
2. When are they likely to rise, i.e. the timing of any decisions?

We can tell a great deal about the future direction of interest rates from the bond markets and the bond yields we discussed earlier in the book. And the bond that is considered to be the most representative and predictive of longer term interest rates is the 10 year T bill. It is this bill which is the benchmark for our analysis. When looking at the future for interest rates in the US and the US dollar, it is the yield on the 10 year Treasury bill which should always be considered first.

The yield on the 10 year Treasury bill is the barometer, the standard against which interest rates are measured, simply because it is a time horizon most investors can comprehend. After all, trying to forecast interest rates thirty years ahead is almost impossible, and one or two years is too short a timescale to consider for longer term investments. Therefore, the ten year yield is the one to look at first.

However, let's not forget the short term yields as these will not only confirm short term interest rates, but also give an insight into the mood of the market as the money flows into and out of bonds as a result of investor sentiment. In other words, as sentiment moves from high risk to lower risk and back again.

To recap. Longer term falling bond yields generally point to a weak economic picture and therefore lower interest rates. Longer term higher bond yields generally point to a stronger economic outlook, and therefore higher interest rates, as the prospect of inflation becomes a reality.

Whilst the interest rate of a particular currency is important on its own, the key is its relationship to other currencies. It is this relationship which ultimately dictates the flow of money and causes exchange rates to rise and fall. However, this feature has been singularly lacking in the last few years, but one which will return in due course, as the present financial maelstrom passes and markets begin to return to some degree of normality.

Assuming this does eventually happen, one of the most powerful signals will be when the interest rates of two currencies begin to diverge. In other words, the gap between the interest rates on two currencies becomes wider, with one moving higher and the other moving lower.

As I have mentioned already, in the last few years interest rates have slipped in terms of market importance but they are on the way back, as the global economy begins to emerge from this long recessionary period. In addition the hugely damaging currency wars now appear to be virtually over, and we are therefore likely to see interest rates rising, fuelled by inflation and economic growth which in turn will lead to increasing differential yields between currencies resulting in increased money flow.

To consider this concept further I would like to explain the carry trade in detail at this stage, not as a trading strategy in its own right (which it is), but as one used by banks the world over, who borrow money at low interest rates, in order to fund higher yielding loans. This creates huge flows of money as a direct result of the differential yield between two currencies. This too is coupled to the outlook for interest rates in the future.

You may, of course, already be familiar with the term 'carry trade', and indeed I mentioned it in one of the earlier chapters, but you may have the mistaken impression this is a trading strategy only used by speculative retail traders in currency.

This is wrong, but is often the impression given. Therefore, let me correct this now. First, the carry trade is used in both the bond and currency markets. Second, it is used by every bank in the world to generate revenue and profit. And here's how and why.

The country with the lowest interest rates in the last twenty years has been Japan, which suffered the same collapse of its financial markets following the bursting of a credit bubble in the early 1990's.

This has many parallels to the financial crisis triggered by the US secondary mortgage market in late 2007 and onwards. Later in this book I will explain the Japanese yen in detail, but as a result of the financial collapse 20 years ago, the Japanese economy has struggled to recover.

As a result, interest rates in Japan have remained between zero and 0.5 percent ever since. This has created the perfect currency for one side of the carry trade. On the other side would be a currency with a high interest rate such as Australia, New Zealand or Canada. In the last few years we have seen interest rate differentials of five percent and higher, and for a carry trade there are always two components.

The first is the yield aspect with the interest rate differential giving the return. The second is the fluctuation in the underlying currency exchange rate which give a profit or potentially wipe out any gains from the interest rate yield. Now, stepping back several years when US interest rates were at 5% then typically this is what would happen.

An investor would borrow Japanese yen from a bank at an interest rate of say, 0.5%. They would then buy a US 10 year treasury bond in US dollars paying five percent interest. The investor stood to make 4.5 percent from the interest rate differential, but always with the underlying risk the currency exchange rate could go against the investment.

For example, if the US dollar gained by 5 percent against the Japanese yen, the investor would make 9.5 percent over the life of the bond. This is the combination of the interest yield and the underlying currency gain. However, if the dollar lost 5 percent against the yen, the investor would make a loss of 0.5 percent.

In the last few years, as the US dollar has continued to weaken interest rates in the US have fallen to historically low levels where they have remained for some time.

As a result the US dollar has now become the base currency for the carry trade, with outflows of US dollars into higher yielding bonds overseas, as investors look for carry trade yield differentials with currencies such as the Chinese yuan.

The reason here is this is one currency that is directly manipulated by the Chinese, and therefore considered to be undervalued were it ever to become a free floating currency.

This is how an interest rate differential directly affects the flow of money from one currency to another with the bond market at the centre. The reason is simple. As a retail forex trader we could take a carry trade position on a particular pair, say the Aussie dollar and the Japanese yen. To open our position we would simply place a buy order effectively buying the Aussie dollar and selling the Japanese yen.

Our carry trade is now open and we will be paid the interest rate differential every 24 hours by our broker, as well as benefit or lose from the currency movement when we close the position.

For the banks it's different, as they are generally trading in real cash so when they want to take advantage of the carry trade they have to look for investment instruments where they can place physically large amounts of cash. This is where the bond market comes into play. As a result they move money back and forth searching for the highest yields with the lowest risk.

It is these shifts in money flow, reflected in the bond yields which create the constant dynamic between one currency and another and which is why interest rates are so important to watch, analyse and understand.

There are two further key points to be aware of in the relationship between bonds and currencies and the carry trade which are as follows.

First, the carry trade is generally considered to be a longer term strategy for the banks, hedge funds, and institutional investors. And, as such, once the money flow begins, from one base currency to another, this is likely to continue for some time to come, generally creating a strong trend between the two currencies.

Second, the opposite is also true, and once this flow of money begins to unwind, it can do so very very quickly with dramatic results. Whilst all of this is very interesting, how do we, as retail forex traders take advantage of all this knowledge of money flow and interest rate differentials?

Whilst there is no holy grail in forex trading, one relationship we can study is that between interest rate differentials and currency exchange rates. The reason is because these tend to follow one another, driven by the desire of investors to benefit from the differentials in the bond yields. This creates spreads between the associated bonds of each country. And here is an example.

In November 2010 the Australian 10 year Treasury Note was trading at a yield of 5.37% whilst the equivalent US 10 year Treasury Note was trading at 2.88% giving a spread of 249 basis points – approximately 125 basis points wider than the historical norm.

At the time, the longer term prospects for both the US and Australian economies improved from November 2010 through to March 2011. Although the Federal Reserve held the Fed Funds Rate at 0.25%, markets had increasingly formed the view the US would not face any medium term threat from deflation, and by the end of the period markets could see an end to the then current QE program. The economic outlook was improving, helped by a weak currency, improved trade balance and ultra low interest rates.

By contrast, whilst the Australian economy was continuing to grow, other factors were now starting to suggest a possible slow down, not least because of a strong Australian dollar, subdued retail spending, and a possible slow down in demand from China. Over the period the RBA held interest rates at 4.75%.

By the start of 2011, with the economic recovery starting to take shape, the spread between the two bond yields narrowed considerably. By the end of March 2011, the Australian 10 year note was trading at 5.45% while the US 10 year note was trading at a yield of 3.68%. The yield spread between the two had narrowed to only 72 basis points.

So how was this reflected on the AUD/USD chart. From November 1st 2010 to April 1st 2011, the pair rose from 0.9865 to just below the 1.1000 level, a gain of more than 1000 pips. Indeed, prior to this, the pair had been rising strongly, as the spread widened in the run up to this period. The pair then topped out at the 1.1000 level before reversing lower in the following months, taking the pair back below parity once again.

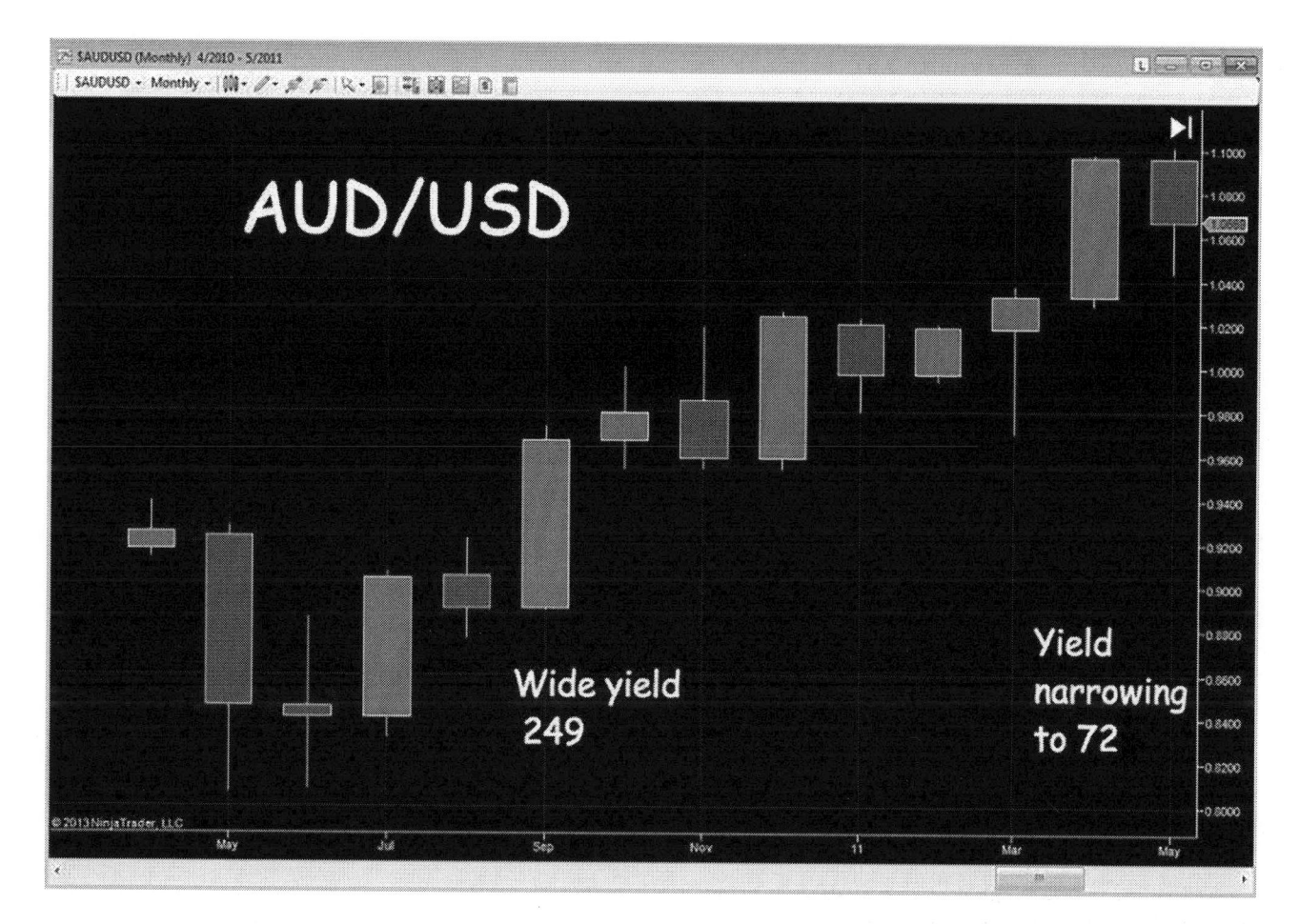

Fig 8.10 AUD/USD Monthly Chart

At this point I must make two things clear, before you run away with the idea you can make money simply by using the link between a currency pair and differential bond yields as the ultimate determinant of strength and weakness.

First, whilst differential bond yields do give us strong clues, there may be many other factors that play in any currency relationship of which this is just one. Second, the relationship between bond yields and currencies may lag as these take time to be reflected in the associated price action.

The currencies, interest rate and associated bond yield relationship is a complex one, and I don't want to give the impression this relationship will always work. This is not the case. Interest rates and bond yields move for many reasons, not least of which is risk appetite. In the last twelve months, we have also seen money flow into the Australian dollar as it is now also seen as an alternative safe haven currency. This is not surprising given the extent to which the Australian economy has been spared the worst of the ravages of the financial crisis. The same is also true of the Canadian dollar.

However, it is another weapon in our armoury and more reason not to be frightened of the bond markets as it can reveal so much about all the capital markets. A great site to follow bond prices and global bond yields is at www.investing.com.

Here you will find all the information you need. The data is live and it's free.

Remember the bond market is where the money flows, not only when markets are nervous, but also when investors are looking for better returns, and one of the ways they do this is by using the carry trade with real cash moving both in and out of bonds.

Now, let me give you another example of how we can use interest rate differentials and the bond market to give us the clues and signals we need as forex traders. As an example let's take the AUD/USD pair once again.

Suppose US bond yields rise by 5 basis points which is something we often see during the trading day, but at the same time we see Australian bond yields fall by the same amount. Again this would be normal for a trading day.

However, if we put these two events together the differential between the US dollar and the Australian dollar has widened by 10 basis points. Imagine this happened the following day again, we would have a twenty basis point differential between the two currencies. To put this into context.

If the Australian central bank cut interest rates by a quarter of one percent which is twenty five basis points move, you can guarantee one thing. The forex market would react, and fast.

This is how we have to use bonds and their unique relationship to currencies. In peering beneath the surface, the bonds reveal what the market is thinking, and what investors and speculators are doing with their money. Moreover, we use bond prices and bond yields in particular, to give us vital clues to the interest rate differentials between currencies which are ultimately one of the prime drivers of money flow.

I recommend you visit www.investing.com because, in addition to giving you all the bond prices and bond yields, there are also live charts for many of the other indices, markets and instruments I mention in this book. Finding live bond yield data for countries other than the US and US Treasuries can be difficult – this site makes it very easy. Here you can find information for all the major countries and their associated currencies. The link to the exact page is here:

http://www.investing.com/rates-bonds/world-government-bonds

Finally, as I have mentioned before, in addition to interest rate differentials, risk is also another of the primary drivers of money flow as the markets are driven by people and their money.

This is just the same in the forex market, where risk aversion is a key driver. As a result, trading strategies, such as the carry trade which is based on yields, tend to be more successful when risk appetite is high and less successful when risk appetite is low.

However, when we have rising commodities and equities because investors are taking on more risk, this is an environment when the carry trade would also do well. In this scenario traders and investors are prepared to take on the riskier currencies, which in turn offer higher interest rates to compensate for this risk.

Conversely, when risk is low and equity markets are falling, the carry trade may unwind, as traders and investors move into safer havens.

This is how the markets continually interact with one another in this constant dance of risk and return, with money flow in one reflecting movement in another.

And where do we look for market sentiment and risk? In the other capital markets and in a variety of indices which we are going to examine shortly.

Finally, of course, it goes without saying interest rates are the principle instrument most central banks have available with which to control growth, jobs, and international trade. However, their effect is rather like trying to put out a bonfire with a water pistol.

Central banks do have one or two other strategies which they can deploy and these are explained in a later chapter when we look at the central banks in detail. However, interest rates are their primary tool as they are simple to implement and have a relatively quick effect, hence they are their weapon of choice when fighting inflation, especially when it is out of control.

In reality central banks only have interest rates with which to control an economy. This makes the analysis of bond yields even more important as we try to interpret their long term monetary policy. At the same time we also have to consider the intraday movement of yields as market sentiment shifts hour by hour and day by day.

Differential bond yields can and do cause huge shifts in money flow as central banks also indulge in the carry trade. This can result in great trends which retail forex traders can also exploit.

Chapter Nine
The US Dollar

A billion dollars isn't what it used to be.

Nelson Bunker Hunt (1926-2014)

I suspect I know what you are thinking. Here is this book about forex trading and, so far little, if anything, has been written about currencies. But as Master Po used to say 'patience grasshopper'. There is a reason and all will be revealed.

I have deliberately structured this book so it starts with the three capital markets of commodities, bonds and equities as I wanted you to have a grounding in the key cross market relationships which drive the money flow from one market to another. And this would not have been possible had I started with the forex market and focused on it, in isolation.

The one currency which underpins every market and the global economy is the US dollar which we are now going to consider in detail.

It has always been my contention if traders only understood the US dollar with all its ramifications in terms of the three analytical approaches, namely technical, fundamental and relational, their chances of success would increase exponentially. And even if you stopped reading at this point I believe the information in the preceding chapters will help you in your journey as a forex trader. However, I hope you will continue to the end.

Naturally, there is a great deal more, which I cover in the remainder of this book, but as I have written on several occasions already, and will probably continue to write several times more, you have to understand the US dollar. You have to take the US dollar as your starting point and in this chapter I am going to pull together some of the strands that I have touched on in some of the earlier chapters.

These strands include the relationship of the US dollar with commodities, the US dollar and gold, the US dollar and bonds, the US dollar as currency of first reserve and finally the US as the world's largest economy.

But first a short history lesson, for which I make no apologies.

Whilst the modern foreign exchange market has its roots in the collapse of the Bretton Woods agreement of 1971, the currency market extends back to Elizabeth the First and 1560. However, I am only going back as far as 1844.

Since 1844, there have been no less than three attempts to fix currency exchange rates using gold, the so called gold standard, all of which have ultimately failed. And, the obvious question is, why have a gold standard at all? To which a simple answer would be, it is a mechanical attempt to control exchange rates.

The theory is it should introduce stability in the global economy, it makes managing inflation easier, whilst simultaneously generating a more controlled environment. One that is less susceptible to the boom and bust moves that are now commonplace.

However, the reasons each attempt has failed is simple enough. Eventually, one or more of the members who have adopted a gold standard begins to suffer, and whether from political or fiscal pressure are forced to take action in order to protect their own economy at the expense of the other participants.

A gold standard appears to be a simple solution to a complex problem, but is one that is always ultimately doomed to failure, as is a currency peg.

The first attempt was in 1844 when the United Kingdom adopted a gold standard which tied the value of notes issued by the Bank of England to gold, with the British Empire essentially adopting a gold standard as a result. Other countries followed suit, so that by 1900, the world had essentially adopted a gold standard.

Then in 1914 war broke out in Europe which led to inflation, due to the costs of war. This was followed by severe deflation in the wake of the Great Depression of 1929. This eventually led to the London conference in 1933, which saw the gold standard abandoned, with both the UK and US also being accused of trying to maintain an artificially low conversion rate for gold.

The abandonment of the gold standard led to a period of deflationary spirals, as one country attempted to devalue its currency relative to another in order to protect its economy.

Shades of what is currently happening in the forex market with many countries now actively engaged in the competitive devaluation of their home currency. So, as always there is nothing new in the world of economics and politics.

History, of course, teaches us nothing I'm afraid. The Great Depression and recovery was followed by the Second World War, which resulted in a massive depletion of the UK gold reserves which were used to fund the war effort.

This left the United Kingdom in no position to lead a revival in the gold standard. The natural successor was the United States, which emerged from the war with a huge manufacturing infrastructure.

With US output having doubled during the war it now led the world in production and exports. In addition, the US now accounted for eighty percent of the world's gold reserves. As a result, the US was positioned as the strongest nation in the world, and uniquely positioned to benefit from international trade.

With weak trading members having been devastated by the war effort, it was no surprise a gold standard was suggested once again, and in July 1944 forty four nations met in the small town of Bretton Woods to formulate a new gold standard which was eventually agreed and ratified in 1946.

This was despite two of the strongest protests coming from the UK and France who preferred to follow a protectionist policy of trade embargoes and sanctions.

However, both were eventually forced to agree to trade concessions in return for US economic aid. This is one of the reasons why there is always an underlying tension between Europe (France), and the US.

The central premise of the new gold standard was for central banks to peg their currencies at an established and fixed value within plus or minus one percent of the benchmark US dollar, with the lynch pin of the system being gold. This was fixed at a rate of thirty five US dollars per ounce.

It was at this point in history the US dollar became the world's benchmark paper currency, and the currency of first reserve. A position it has held ever since.

As the currency of first reserve it is therefore considered a safe haven currency, as it underpins virtually every aspect of world trade. Bretton Woods also saw the establishment of the International Monetary Fund or IMF. Its role was to arbitrate in disputes over the various pegs and par values of all the member currencies, as well to manage inflation by introducing controls on those member countries who could not, or would not maintain their currency rates.

This second attempt at a gold standard lasted until the end of the 1960s, when several factors combined to undermine the US dollar and ultimately see the collapse of the Bretton Woods gold standard, with the eventual collapse happening in 1971.

The first factor was the Vietnam war, coupled with President Johnston's social programme, which led to huge spending by the US government. And with tax revenues falling, this led to inflation and a reversal of the US balance of payments, resulting in a massive trade deficit. Again does this sound familiar?

As a result, the US dollar became over valued against the currencies of Europe and Japan, both of whom were happy for this to continue. Their own weaker currencies would support their export markets, making goods cheaper for their overseas buyers.

We have seen the reverse of this in the past few years where a chronically weak and artificially deflated US dollar is causing problems around the world.

However, back to our history lesson. Here the US dollar had become overvalued and strong and by 1970 with inflation soaring and unsustainable debts, countries around the world were becoming increasingly nervous in holding US dollars. They also began to doubt the US's ability to maintain the US dollar as the currency of first reserve.

This scenario suggested a possible run on gold of which the US only had approximately one third to cover all US dollar reserves overseas.

So, in 1971 Richard Nixon took the decision to close the 'gold window' which was the facility whereby holders of US dollars could redeem them in return for gold.

This was the first crack in the Bretton Woods agreement which was finally abandoned two years later, with Germany having exited shortly after the Nixon announcement.

Bretton Woods was then replaced by the Smithsonian Agreement. In this agreement the dollar gold exchange rate was moved to $38 per ounce (instead of $35) and with a wider window of plus or minus 2.25 percent.

These agreements coexisted until 1973 when, with the continued advance in gold prices, the currency market was detached from gold and world currencies were finally left to free float and settle to a market price independent of any peg to gold.

What followed for the US was a decade of high inflation and a decline in its influence around the world.

Such was the birth of the modern forex market.

This is where we are today over forty years later and, whilst there have been no new attempts to peg currencies to the price of gold (despite many news articles to the contrary), there have been other attempts to control exchange rates in other ways.

The primary one was the EMS or European Monetary System, born out of the demise of the Bretton Woods agreement.

This was an attempt by the major European nations to protect their currencies by linking them together, and so prevent exchange rate fluctuations by plus or minus 2.25 percent, using the so called ERM or exchange rate mechanism.

This collapsed in grand style in September 1992, with the British pound eventually being forced to withdraw, having come under consistent speculative attack. With George Soros being one of the principal architects of this demise in his big short of the British pound.

The ERM mechanism was finally rendered redundant with the launch of the Euro as the single currency for EU member states, or for most of them at least.

I hope the above has, at least, given you a flavour of how the US dollar arrived at its unique position, why governments and banks try to introduce artificial controls to reduce currency fluctuations, and why all ultimately fail.

It also helps to explain why countries are so desperate to manage their exchange rates, either covertly or overtly which again is something I cover in more detail shortly. This is also the reason many countries enter a currency peg, only to pay the penalty in the longer term.

In the last hundred years of currency exchange, the most dramatic change occurred on the 2nd January 2002, when the single European currency, the Euro was launched. In effect, ERM 2, replacing the old ERM system not with yet another cumbersome exchange rate peg, but this time with a real currency designed by the European powers with two simple objectives in mind.

First, to protect European member states from currency fluctuations within the Federal European state.

Second, to create a viable alternative to the US dollar as the currency of first reserve.

In other words, a politically created currency to shift the balance of power away from America and into Europe, and ultimately to create a currency for political union, as a precursor to the Euro taking on the role of currency of first reserve.

I do cover the Euro in more detail later in the book when we consider each individual currency in isolation, as we are doing here for the US dollar, but I wanted to introduce the concept of the Euro as a political currency.

As you will see the old animosity between Europe (France in particular) and the US resurfaces all the time, and indeed is ingrained into political statements both from the ECB and the EU. We only need to look at how the currency is supported when under threat from the US dollar, but more on this later.

For now, let's continue with the US dollar, and the period I would like to focus on, in particular, is that of the last fifteen years, from the end of the last century to the present day.

This period covers some of the most interesting and cataclysmic events we are ever likely to witness in the financial markets, and may have profoundly changed the role of the US dollar in the longer term as a result.

Naturally, only time will tell of course, as we rarely learn from history, and no doubt these events may be repeated once the memories fade and the cycle is repeated.

This period in history has been dominated by three major events.

First the Asian crisis which began in 1997, only to be followed by the dot com bubble bursting in 2001. Third, the near collapse of the financial world as banks and countries approached bankruptcy in 2008. But let's start with the first of these, the Asian crisis.

The catalyst for this crisis was one simple event. The decision by Thailand's authorities to decouple the Thai baht from the US dollar, and allow the currency to free float in the market.

This simple decision resulted in a collapse in the value of the Thai baht, which quickly spread to other countries in South East Asia, causing currencies to decline rapidly, and triggering stock market falls as a result, with the contagion of fear spreading around the world eventually reaching Russia and parts of Europe.

Of course, whilst it was the act of removing the dollar peg that created the catalyst for the crisis, the problem had been building for some time, with the banks providing cheap money in a boom economy creating the inevitable bubble economy. This is so reminiscent of the sub prime débâcle of the last few years, and the Japanese 'lost decade' of several years earlier. Something from which Japan has yet to recover almost twenty years later. What is deeply concerning is the present crisis could last just as long.

As the Asian crisis unfolded, fear spread around the globe and investors increasingly turned to the US dollar as a safe haven. From 1999 to 2001 the dollar gained almost 25% against a basket of major currencies, as solid economic growth, coupled with soaring equity markets and relatively weak performance abroad provided the ultimate combination of safety and growth. This saw the dollar hit an all time high in 2001 before the next major event occurred, the bursting of the dot com bubble.

In this event stock markets around the world collapsed as realism and basic economic principles finally held sway, and valueless companies, with absurd valuations, plunged. For the US dollar it was the start of a long slow decline, as the world slipped into recession between 2001 and 2002 and equity markets entered a four year bear cycle.

China meanwhile, sought to fill the void with its voracious appetite for commodities, and this proved to be a seminal period for global currencies. Whilst this was the start of the decline for the US dollar, it also marked the simultaneous emergence of the Euro which has consequently gained in strength ever since.

The falling dollar also triggered a super rally in commodities, which has extended for several years, with virtually every commodity breaking new highs on a regular basis.

But what triggered the start of this extended bearish trend for the US dollar which still continues today? As is so often the case in the forex markets, it was self preservation that was the primary driver, led by the President of the day George Bush.

As we know a strong currency makes exports increasingly expensive, with companies and products becoming uncompetitive overseas which is a problem for all major exporting nations. With the US dollar at a fifteen year high, the manufacturing sector in the US began calling on the government to act, and impose tariffs on its trading partners.

The government and the US treasury, therefore decided to adopt a policy of what can best be described as 'benign neglect'. In other words, whilst publicly stating a strong US dollar was good for the America, privately they were taking a very different approach.

And if you don't believe that currency markets are subject to political manipulation, please read the next section very carefully.

With the US dollar hitting an all time high against every other currency, in the spring of 2002, President Bush launched a trade war against steel producers overseas with two objectives in mind.

First, it was to secure a republican party victory in the Congressional elections due later in the year by winning over the key steel and manufacturing states. Second, to ensure a decline in the US dollar. This is always guaranteed, once trade sanctions were imposed.

The strategy worked, with the US dollar weakening, as selling the dollar became the de facto standard, with the Euro becoming increasingly stronger as a result, much to the delight of the Europeans.

Commodities benefited too, and we saw the start of another long bull trend as the dollar continued lower, a trend that has continued virtually unabated ever since.

And so to the last event, which is perhaps the most profound and devastating. Here we have experienced the perfect financial storm. As the debt fuelled bubble finally exploded in 2008, with banks and countries collapsing under the weight of toxic debt triggered by cheap loans made to high risk individuals with little or no prospect of repayment.

As economies ground to a halt, and recession and deflation loomed on the horizon, governments and central banks were forced to act, taking interest rates close to zero in an effort to stimulate the economies out of recession.

The problem for the world's largest economy however, was the dreaded D word, deflation, and in an attempt to prevent this the US treasury opted for two rounds of quantitative easing.

As we have already seen this has created a toxic bond market and yet further weakness in the US dollar as the currency markets have become awash with the American currency.

More subtly however, and as a direct result of this action, the US dollar has begun to lose its attraction as a safe haven currency, with investors increasingly looking elsewhere, with currencies such as the Swiss Franc, the Japanese yen and the Norwegian Krona providing alternative paper based homes for money flow. Indeed, this group of safe haven currencies has increased still further, with the Australian dollar and the

Canadian dollar now being included given the way both Australia and Canada economies have managed to weather the crisis.

This dollar weakness also helped both gold and silver make strong gains. These gains were also underpinned with safe haven buying, along with investors also seeking out the precious metals as a hedge against inflation.

The last few years has seen a seminal shift in attitude to the US dollar, and one never seen before. Only time will tell whether the FED policy has ultimately played into the hands of the Europeans with the possible replacement of the US dollar in the future by the Euro.

However, the Euro now has problems of its own with Greece, Portugal, Ireland, Spain and Italy all adding to its woes. The ECB stands as the lender of last resort, not because it believes in the currency, but because it wants to maintain the only mechanism it has to ultimately replace the US dollar.

Once again, the US authorities are being pilloried by Europe (and others) for pursuing a policy which is seen as both self serving and protectionist. Whilst this is undoubtedly true, it is also the case many other countries are also adopting the same policy, either overtly or covertly. Either via monetary policy or by outright intervention. And in Japan's case, it's both. For all countries, it is ultimately about survival and protection of their own fragile economies.

Meanwhile for the US, it is also about ensuring its exports remain competitive and jobs are protected and created. For major trading partners such as China, who continue to track the US dollar, this is where we came in with the Thai Baht.

China has seen extraordinary year on year growth fuelled by cheap credit over the past decade. Could China be the next bubble to burst, thereby triggering another Asian crisis on a grand scale? If so, this would send shock waves around the world and the US dollar soaring as a result. It is possible, and is always the big fear as China is now the world's second largest economy and set to overtake the US in the next two decades.

As I have said before, history teaches us all these lessons, but we never seem to learn. Perhaps this time it's different and we will learn but somehow I suspect not.

The US dollar is still the lynchpin of the global economy. Whether this will continue in the future remains to be seen. As forex traders this is the one currency we need to understand and track

In the chapters that follow, we are going to start looking at some of the key indices that give us strong signals of market direction in a variety of ways. I call them the market internals, and we start with the US dollar index. In many ways, the single index from which all other analysis flows.

Chapter Ten
Indices & Market Internals

Students learn more by watching than they do by listening.

Robert Kiyosaki (1944-)

In the introduction to this book, I covered some of the cross market linkages and relationships that exist between the four major capital markets. But now it's time to start looking at some of the major indices which provide us with more detailed information about these, starting with the US Dollar Index, which follows neatly on from the previous chapter.

The USD Index is perhaps the most important index of all, since if you accept the premise every market revolves around money, the principle currency has to the the currency of first reserve, namely the US dollar. It could be argued to be truly successful as a forex trader, we really only need to have a view of the USD, as every other market, instrument and flow of money centres on this currency.

Nevertheless, in this chapter we are also going to focus on several other indices which, in a variety of ways, all give us a different perspective on risk, money flow, and market sentiment. But let me begin with the USD Index.

The prime function of the Dollar Index is to reveal market sentiment towards the US dollar, crucial information to us as forex traders. And it is the one index which you should watch on an intra day basis, particularly if you are trading fast timeframes or scalping. The index should be on your screen at all times because it's so important.

By contrast you only need to watch some of the other indices detailed here on either a daily or weekly basis as they are designed to provide a longer term view.

The USD Index is so important because it reveals, on one easy to understand chart, market sentiment towards the US dollar with all the ramifications of risk and sentiment across bonds, commodities, equities as well as currencies directly.

Put simply, if the USD Index is falling, currencies quoted against the dollar are likely to be rising and vice-versa, although as you will discover later in the book, some currency pairs are not that straightforward.

The Dollar Index was created in 1973 following the move to free floating exchange rates and the collapse of the gold standard.

As the name suggests it is an index of the US dollar measured against a basket of six major currencies, which all carry varying degrees of weight according to their importance. The only change to the constituents of this basket of currencies came when the Euro was launched which has the largest percentage at 57.6%.

The other five currencies which make up the index are the Japanese yen with 13.6%, the British Pound with 11.9%, the Canadian Dollar with 9.1%, the Swedish Krona with 4.2%, and finally the Swiss Franc with 3.6%.

When the index was initially established in 1973 it began with a notional value of 100, and since then we have seen the index move to highs in the 160 region, indicating a very strong dollar, to lows in the 70 region, indicating a very weak US dollar.

The Dollar Index is available in several different forms, either as a futures contract, with both the CME and ICE exchanges who offer a dollar index futures contract, or more commonly as the spot market index. If you have a futures brokerage account and futures feed, the ticker symbol for the ICE is DX, and for the CME, a joint venture with the Dow Jones Index, is FX$INDEX.

If you are simply trading in the spot FX markets, there are two great places to find a chart. The first is an excellent site with live prices for this and many other indices and futures, at http://www.investing.com - this is one of the best free resource sites on the internet. The other site is another favourite of mine at http://www.netdania.com – again free, and furthermore you will also find charts for many other markets covered here as well.

The Dollar Index, is just like any other chart and we use exactly the same techniques of technical analysis, to forecast market direction, and consequent strength or weakness in the US dollar.

This is the primary index all forex traders should have on their screen at all times, regardless of the currency pair or time frame traded.

Fig 10.10 USD Index Chart

Fig 10.10 is a typical example. It looks much the same as any other candlestick chart. I do cover candlesticks as well as other technical indicators later in the book. Interpreting strength and weakness is identical to any other chart. We consider price patterns, candle patterns, support and resistance, trends and price breakouts.

So, are these the indices I use in my own analysis of strength or weakness in the US dollar? And the answer is a categoric, no.

Why?

In simple terms, I do not believe the above provide a balanced and realistic picture of the US dollar against the other major currencies. One only has to look at the construction of the basket of currencies for the index created in 1973. Here we now have the euro at just under 58% and with the UK pound, the two currencies constitute almost 70% of the weighting. Wholly unbalanced in my view, and the Australian dollar doesn't even feature. So in my humble opinion, far from representative of today's forex market. For me, there are better choices which are simple to understand, and more importantly provide a realistic view of the US dollar against the major currencies.

The index I use is new, and was launched in 2011 following a collaborative agreement between FXCM and S&P Dow Jones Indices. The ticker symbol is ^USDOLLAR and you can find this free on Yahoo finance. The reason I like this index is two fold.

First, it is simple to understand, and second I believe it is far more representative in it's construction. The index is quoted in terms of four base currencies, the four most liquid, namely the euro, the Japanese yen, the British pound and the Australian Dollar. The four each have an equal weighting of 25%, far more realistic in my view, with the 'European' percentage diminished, the yen weighting almost doubled, and the significance of the Australian dollar recognised. These four currencies between them account for over 80% of forex volumes daily, so to me it just makes sense.

When it was launched in 2011, the base for the index was an equivalent $10,000 long position against these four currencies, which is why the index is quoted in terms of 10,000 as the unit of measurement. So in terms of interpreting any index moves, it is very straightforward, as a 100 pip move against the underlying currencies, will then translate into a 100 point move on the index. This is one of the many reasons I now use this index exclusively. It's simple to understand, simple to interpret and provides a far more balanced and realistic view of the market in terms of US dollar strength and weakness.

Finally, there is also one other reason, and that's the fact the dollar index has a sister index for the Japanese yen. This has the ticker symbol ^DJFXJPY and once again is constructed in much the same way as the dollar index. The currencies in this case are the US dollar, the Australian dollar, the euro and the New Zealand dollar. The index was launched in 2012.

With these indices, you now have two of the most important currencies in the forex world, quoted in a clear, simple and realistic way, and which reflects the significance of the principle currencies in the market today.

In the two charts below, you can see both these indices, the first is the US dollar index in Fig 10.11, and the second is the Japanese yen index in Fig 10.12. These are from my own NinjaTrader platform, driven from the Kinetick data feed and using the tickers USDOLLAR.X and DJFXJPY.X respectively. Naturally the choice of US dollar index is yours, and indeed there are others available, and I'm sure some of you reading this may have your own favourites. These are the ones I like, and use. You may find others.

Fig 10.11 FXCM Dollar Index

Fig 10.12 FXCM Yen Index

VIX

Second in importance to the Dollar Index is the VIX and the reasons are this an indicator which can tell us so much about market sentiment and money flow. The VIX is often referred to as the investor fear gauge, as it reveals market sentiment and risk appetite in equity markets.

One question often asked by forex traders is why should we be concerned with an index which deals with equities? However, I hope the chapter on the links between equities and currencies will have given you the answer.

The VIX was originally introduced in 1993 by the CBOE (Chicago Board Options Exchange), and was named the Volatility Index, but is always shortened to the VIX. Generally this has a ticker symbol of either ^VIX or $VIX or similar, and can be a little more tricky to find.

Here are a couple of places where you can find the chart for free, albeit on a delayed feed. The alternative is to have this delivered as part of your futures feed from your broker. However, both of the following sites will give you an adequate chart for a long term perspective, but for short term intra day trading, a live feed is essential.

Fig 10.13 is a chart of the VIX, taken from my NinjaTrader platform and once again using the Kinetick data feed.

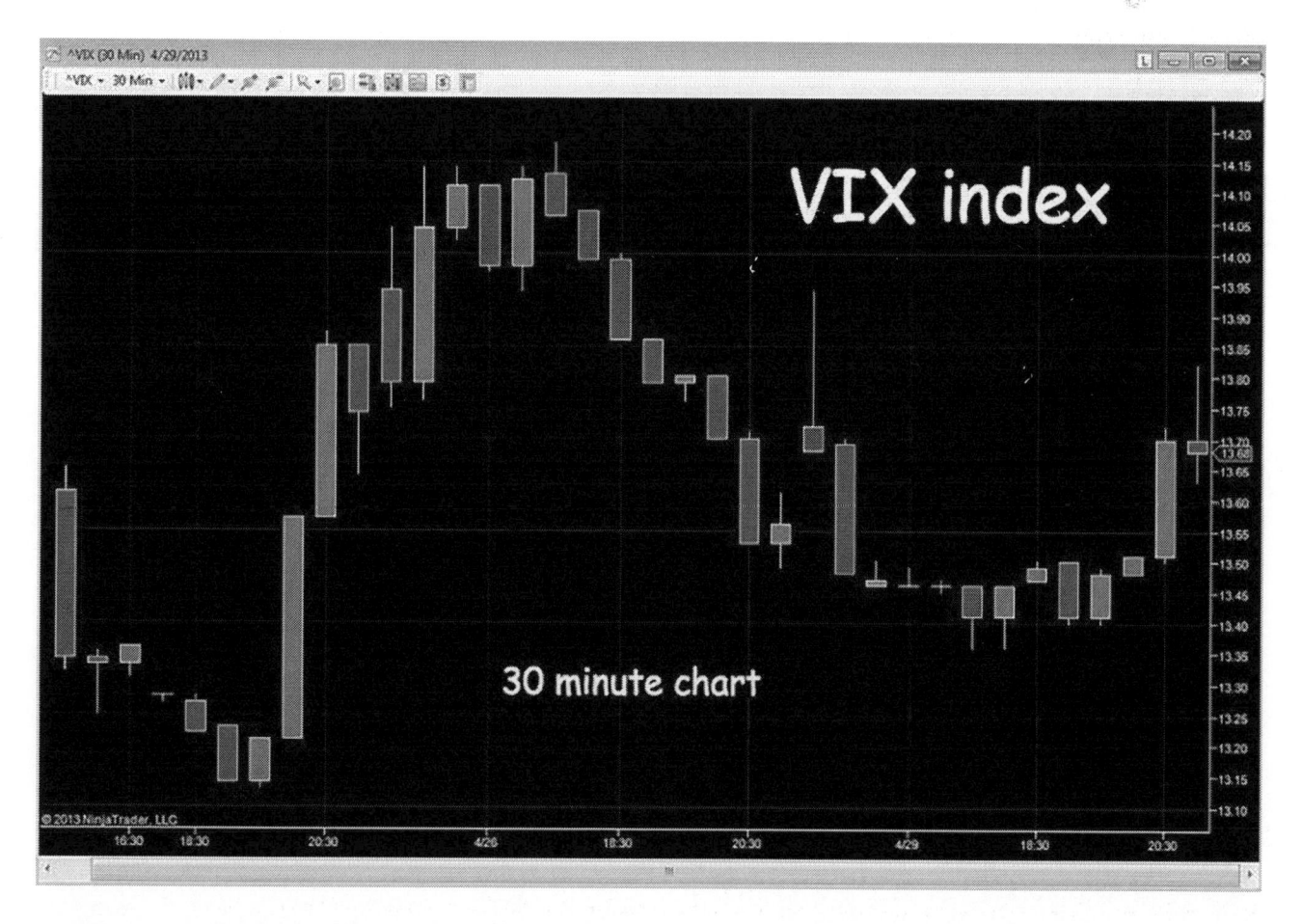

Fig 10.13 VIX 30 Minute Chart

As with the Dollar Index we looked at earlier, the chart is the same as for any other price chart.

The VIX can be found at Yahoo finance www.finance.yahoo.com and here the ticker symbol is ^VIX, and also at www.barchart.com.

But what is this index telling us, and why is it so important?

The VIX has become the benchmark for stock market volatility and, as a result, an indicator of investor fear. Volatility generally goes hand in hand with turmoil, as panic spreads amongst investors who look for safe havens once panic selling takes hold.

If the stock market is the heart, the VIX is the pulse, as it provides a measure of the mood of traders and investors using options prices from the S&P 500 companies - not all of them, but a representative sample of these large blue chip companies.

The index is constructed based on implied volatility, a term from the options market, but which essentially looks forward to the next 30 days and tries to forecast the likely volatility of the S&P 500 index.

In many ways it's not necessary to know how the index is constructed, we just have to know how to use it.

In the options market there are two instruments. Put options and call options. A put option increases in value if the underlying asset falls, whilst a call option increases in value if the underlying asset rises. As a result, if there is more put option buying, this is a signal to us as speculators, that investors are fearful and buying these options as protection against a falling market.

As a consequence the VIX will rise.

However, if more call options are being bought this is a signal investors are complacent and willing to take on more risk, so the VIX will fall. And this is the reason why the VIX is known as a contrarian indicator.

When the VIX is at a very low level this signals investors are buying equities and taking on more risk, and the further the index falls the more likely equities will reverse from an upwards trend to a downwards trend. In other words, from a bullish market to a bearish market.

Conversely, as equities tumble the VIX will move sharply higher as panic takes hold and, once at an extreme, it is at this point equities are likely to reverse once more and move from bearish to bullish.

The chart itself will typically have a scale from zero to 100, although these extremes have rarely, if ever been reached. However, there are some key numbers which will give us signals as to a likely change of direction for the equity markets, which in turn tell us about risk, money flow and market sentiment.

If we start with the VIX at a low level, if the index moves anywhere close to, or into, the 10 - 12 range, or even into single figures, investors and the market are very complacent, and happy to continue buying risk assets.

At these levels we are likely to see a change in trend in equities in due course, with the bullish trend coming to an end and transitioning to a bearish trend, with a consequent flow of money out of high risk markets and into lower risk asset classes.

At the other end of the scale, the key levels are when the VIX moves above 30 and into the 40 plus price area. In this region, investors will be starting to panic as equity markets begin to fall. Anywhere beyond 50, everyone is selling, but at this point we also start to look for a major reversal and for the bearish trend to end and the start of a new bull trend. This is why it is called a contrarian indicator.

When everyone is selling, we are looking for the markets to turn higher, and when everyone is buying we are looking for the markets to turn lower.

To put this into context for you, since the VIX was introduced, the highest reading it has ever recorded was in 2008 during the dark days of the financial crisis when markets went into free fall and the index touched 89.53. However, the average trading range is between 50 and 10 and a lowest reading of 9.39 posted in 2006.

The VIX is all about risk, fear and market sentiment, and as such, reveals what investors are thinking as well as telling us where the money flow is likely to move in the future.

Along with the US dollar index the VIX is an extremely important index to watch all the time and, one which also has a strong relationship with the Dollar Yen currency pair for reasons I will explain later in the book.

The VIX can be analysed in two ways. First, we look to see the level of where we are on the index itself, which tells us whether we are close to a major turning point, simply by whether the VIX is low or high. And the way to remember this is with a simple rhyme which is as follows:

When the VIX is low it's time to go - in other words sell.

When the VIX is high it's time to buy - in other words the bear market is over and likely to reverse soon.

Easy to remember.

The second way to analyse the VIX is to treat it just like any other chart. We analyse the candles in exactly the same way, except with this chart we are also looking at the level of the VIX itself. So we have two analytical approaches which help to reinforce one another.

For example, if we see a strong reversal candle signal which is coupled with the VIX at a significant low or high point, this reinforces our analysis of a potential turning point in the equity market. Therefore, we can expect a consequent change in market sentiment and risk.

This is the power of the VIX and is yet another of the premier indices you need to watch closely in order to trade in the forex markets successfully.

The time frame you choose will, of course, reflect your trading strategy, and this applies to all the major market internals. If your approach to the forex markets is as an intra day trader or scalper, perhaps only holding positions for a few minutes at a time, a live feed for these indices is essential.

Having watched many professional traders from the futures markets, this is perhaps one of the major differences between retail traders and full time traders.

A scalping trader on tick charts or fast time based charts, will almost certainly have the tick or time equivalent charts for the VIX and the US Index, since the moves in both will reflect the constant ebb and flow of sentiment and money, throughout the trading session.

Imagine this like the swell of a big sea, constantly moving, constantly changing. And if there is a strong reversal pattern or signal on the price chart for the USD index, and the VIX, then both are confirming a change in market sentiment. This change may only be for a few minutes, or perhaps for a few hours, but it will give you the confidence to take the trade in your chosen currency pair, provided this reinforces your analysis.

What we are actually doing here is very simple. We are quantifying risk by analysing associated market price action – in this case in market internal indices, but the principle is the same. We can then reinforce the analysis by considering the price action in multiple time frames. Another key approach.

Using multiple time frame analysis to assess the risk of the trade makes trading less stressful and increases the probability of success. For example, if the VIX appears to be moving higher in the 1 min chart, but is still bearish in the 5 and 15 minutes, the risk assessment is simple. The move in the 1 min may only be a short term pull back and any trade taken will be short and be against the dominant trend.

This principle applies to all charts, whether on the instrument itself, or an associated index. It is an immensely powerful technique, and when coupled with the knowledge of relational analysis, becomes yet another weapon in the arsenal of the forex trader.

Commodity Indices

Now let's focus on the next key index, this time for commodities, which just like the Dollar index and VIX, is another important chart giving us a view of what I call market internals.

This index is denoted as the CRB, for short, which stands for the Commodity Research Bureau, originally created in 1957, in an effort to implement a benchmark index for the commodities markets.

It was originally devised and introduced by the CRB, the world's oldest and leading commodities and futures analysis organisation.

Since then, it has undergone many changes and amendments, but it still remains the de facto standard for commodity prices. It is the standard, not only for speculators and investors, but also for Governments and Central Banks who pay very close attention, for obvious reasons. Commodities and commodity prices are the cornerstone of markets and a key measure of growth, inflation and economic prosperity.

Like all financial indices, the constituents and weightings of the CRB index have changed several times over the last 60 years, with lard, potatoes, onions and rye, amongst the first constituents of the index. And, believe it or not, there were no energy or metals in the first index.

The first metals to be introduced were platinum and silver in the 1971 revision, with gold only being added in 1983, almost a decade after it became legal to own in the US. Crude oil was added at the same time.

The first index had a total of 28 constituent commodities and this number continued, more or less unchanged, until the 1987 revision when it was reduced to 21. Finally in 1995 it was further reduced to seventeen, with this number increasing to nineteen during the last and most recent revision in 2005.

Whilst the index is generally known as the CRB, it is also referred to as the Thomson Reuters Jeffries CRB index, as first Reuters and Jeffries Financial products combined to maintain the index, with the Thomson corporation adding further resources. This was reflected in the name being changed in 2008 to the current one, and you will often see it referred to as the TR/J CRB.

The official ticker symbol for this index is $CRB, and this is where it gets a little more complicated.

As you can appreciate, even from the above brief overview, this is an index which represents a constantly changing market, and as a result, ever since its introduction there have been endless changes, amendments updates along with changes in focus in an attempt to derive an index everyone agrees is representative of the commodity markets in general.

Whilst the CRB index has generally been considered the de facto standard, there has always been a second index running in parallel, denoted as the CCI or Continuous Commodity Index. The idea here was to try to create a more balanced commodity index, which more closely reflected commodity prices in general, and one less weighted in terms of constituent commodities.

In order to provide a more meaningful index, the CCI includes only 17 commodities, and these are continuously rebalanced and are equally weighted.

Whilst the CRB and other commodity indices tend to have overweighting in certain sectors, in particular oil, the CCI index provides (in my view at any rate) a more meaningful exposure to all four principle commodity groups. The seventeen components are then rebalanced to maintain an equal weight of 5.88%. Even more recently further changes have been announced to the CCI, with a move towards an arithmetic formula instead of geometric calculations in the daily rebalancing of the index.

As the CCI components are **equally weighted** they distribute more evenly into the major sectors with energy at 17.65%, metals at 23.53%, softs at 29.41% and agriculture also at 29.41%. While other commodity indices tend to have overweighting in certain sectors (in particular energy), the CCI provides a more meaningful exposure to all four commodity subgroups. The 17 components of the CCI are continuously rebalanced to maintain the equal weight of 5.88%.

When a future reaches the first notice day or it matures, it is not considered in any calculation. A future is only eligible for inclusion when it has 6 months to maturity, and no more than 5 futures can be included for any commodity.

To summarise the primary differences – here we have two commodity indices, both owned by the same company, but using very different approaches to generate the index.

In the CRB index, energy is weighted heavily, whilst in the CCI index a more balanced approach is taken. Put simply, it is equal weighting vs different weightings.

Whilst there is nothing wrong with the CRB index, it was designed to take account of the importance of energy, my own view is that in using this index, it provides a rather unbalanced view of the real world, and in particular when considering inflationary pressure in the market.

The choice of index, of course, is a personal one, but my own view is the CCI is more truly representative and gives a more 'real world' view of the commodities markets. Finally, and if this weren't confusing enough, the primary exchange which lists the futures for these contracts, (ICE) has since decided to de-list these indices owing to a lack of market volumes.

A rather confusing picture all round, but I hope the above explanation has at least clarified some of the issues when searching for this index. If you're not sure which index you are looking at on a chart, the CCI normally trades over 200 points higher than the CRB.

There are several places to find the CCI chart, and my favourite at present is on http://www.netdania.com which actually lists the chart as the CRB index, but which in fact is the CCI index (so yet more confusion)

Nevertheless, this is one place to find the CCI chart. Another is on http://www.barchart.com where the chart is listed as the CRB CCI Index Cash.

Finally if you do prefer to follow the CRB index this can be found on Bloomberg at http://www.bloomberg.com under the ticker symbol CRY:IND and is commonly referred to as the CRY index for obvious reasons.

If all this sounds a little confusing, there are some easier ways to follow these two indices, and of course the choice is a personal one. All I have given here are my own personal thoughts. As with many indices, you can now find the equivalent in the ETF market, and this is true for both the CCI and the CRB, and in addition they both report volume, so another reason to follow them using this instrument.

The ticker for the CRB is CRBQ and for the CCI is GCC and I have included both instruments here, once again from my NinjaTrader platform and using the Kinetick data feed. The GCC is the Greenhaven Continuous Commodity fund, based on the CCI, and the CRBQ fund is based on the CRB.

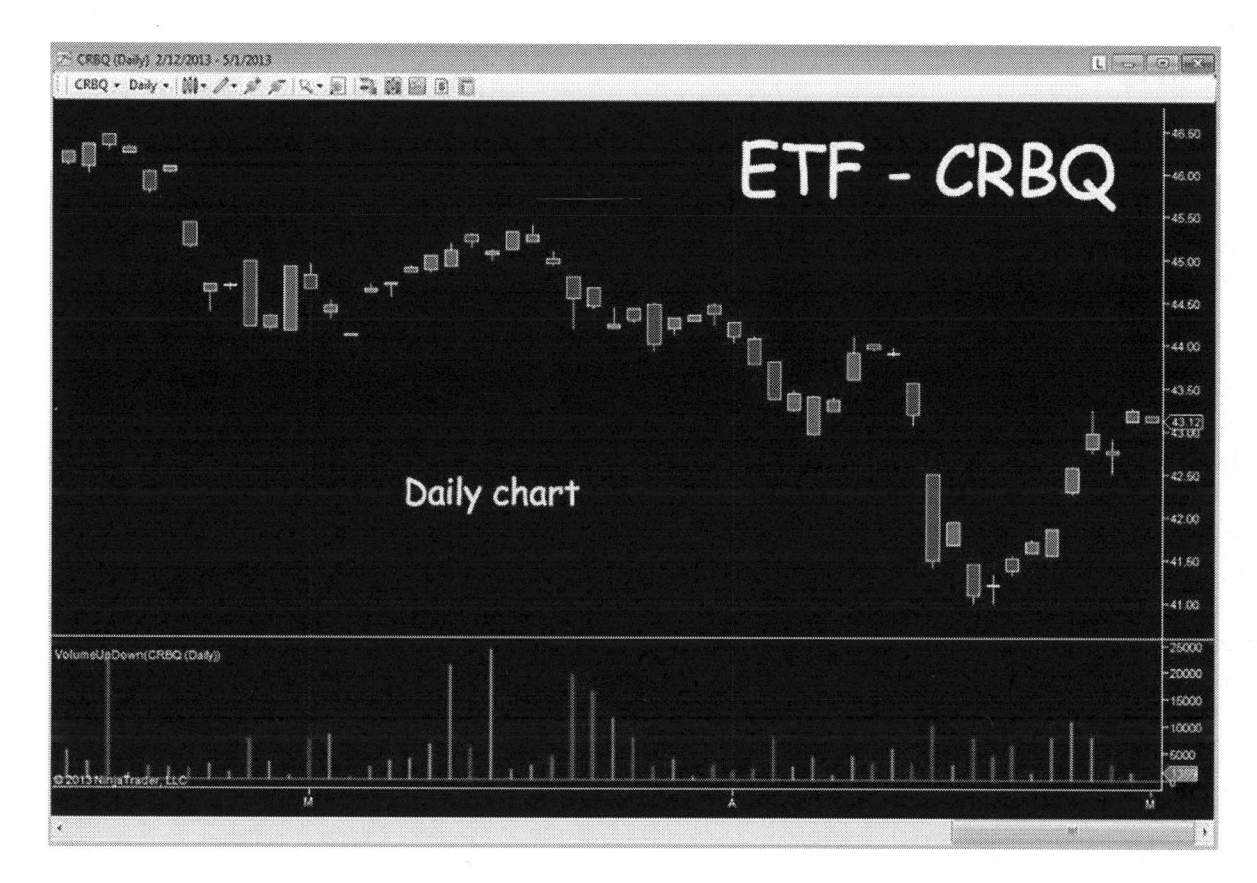

Fig 10.14 ETF For The CRB Index

Fig 10.15 ETF For The CCI Index

How to interpret the data from these indices is relatively straightforward. First, commodities and the US dollar generally move inversely, although not always, so this gives us an alternative view on the US dollar index chart we considered earlier.

As a rule of thumb, as one is falling so the other should be rising, and vice-versa, although, as I have stressed previously, any cross market or relational analysis is not a science and correlations do break down for various reasons. For example it is perfectly possible to have a risk asset class falling, and a safe haven currency falling in lock-step.

There can be many reasons for this, but the most likely is investors are seeing better returns in other markets, which in turn would suggest risk appetite is strong. After all, if the money flow is away from commodities, which are a risk asset in their own right, this money must be going somewhere, and clearly not into a safe haven currency, such as the US dollar.

In addition, US dollars are also being sold, with a consequent flow away from this safe haven. Could this flow be into bonds? The answer is no, because bonds are yet another safe haven.

The only conclusion we can draw is investors are seeing higher returns in risk assets such as equities, and high risk currencies. Voilà. We have arrived at our conclusion based on two index charts. This may seem overly simplistic perhaps, but I hope you can start to see how powerful this analysis can be in revealing the interplay within the financial markets.

Furthermore, please don't assume this analysis only applies to longer term swing or trend traders, it doesn't. These flows are happening second by second throughout the trading session, and these indices can be viewed and applied to all time frames.

But how else can we use this knowledge to help us make better informed trading decisions?

Once again by focusing on the charts on their own and applying classic technical analysis techniques to determine market direction for the longer term. Or, as is the case for the VIX and USD Index, using live intraday charts to confirm moves in associated markets, which validate our analysis in the currency pair we are considering.

Finally, a commodities index will tend to rise as commodity prices rise. In other words there is a direct relationship, and in this case, we would expect to see associated strength in commodity related currencies such as the Australian Dollar, the Canadian Dollar and the New Zealand Dollar.

From one simple index, we can glean a wealth of information. It is so powerful, and yet so simple, once you know where to look.

However, I would be the first to admit the commodities indices are subject to more change than most, and that no-one has yet delivered the 'gold standard'. No doubt there will be further changes and further attempts to standardise on a methodology, but until then, we have to try to make the best of what we have, which in my humble opinion, is the CCI index.

The Baltic Dry

I would now like to take a look at another index to watch, the curiously titled Baltic Dry Index which, like the VIX, is another volatility index, but this time one which is linked to commodities.

The Baltic Dry Index, gives us a measure of the cost of moving commodities by sea and as result, just like the price of the commodity itself, the index gives us a real world view of physically shipping commodities from one place to another.

It is therefore a key economic indicator, and a leading indicator of demand for commodities around the world.

In simple terms, the cost of moving commodities by sea is extremely volatile as the physical supply of ships is not an elastic relationship. In other words, if there is a shortage of ships, it is not possible to simply meet demand by building new ships which generally take between two and three years to build.

If there is a lack of ships, the cost of shipping will rise quickly. Equally, if there is an over supply of ships, the costs of shipping will fall just as quickly. It is a constant see-saw, and very logical when you consider it in this way.

In other words, a small change in demand will be reflected in a relatively large change in price, either up or down, depending on whether there is an excess, or shortage of ships. This in essence is what the Baltic Dry Index tells us in two distinct ways.

First, as a leading economic indicator of demand. A rising index is sending a clear signal of higher prices, increasing demand, inflation and therefore higher interest rates.

On the other hand, a falling index signals weak demand and a slow down in the world economy.

Second it gives us this information in a pure and untainted way as there is no speculation on the index and, in addition, and perhaps more importantly with no government or central bank manipulation or massaging of the data.

Indeed this is one of the oldest indices, having originally been founded in the mid eighteenth century as much of the sea trade at the time was between London and the Baltic States around Germany.

The ticker for the BDI chart is bdiy:ind and the site I use to find this chart is Bloomberg at http://www.bloomberg.com

The BDI index has only one value, which is issued each day at around 1300 GMT, and it is the price in US dollars for shipping raw commodities by the twenty six largest shipping companies in the world.

It is important to realise that just as a weak US currency will have a direct impact on commodity prices the same applies to the Baltic Dry Index, so when the dollar is weak, the index will rise as a result, in much the same way as for commodity prices in general.

This is not a chart you check daily, but merely an index to provide a backdrop for longer term trading and analysis.

Given the chart is subject to the movements in the US dollar, we have to be careful in drawing any conclusions from the chart. Nevertheless, in general terms the relationship between the BDI index and the CRB or CCI index is a direct one.

A rising BDI index will generally indicate rising demand for commodities and economic expansion, whilst an index that's bearish, suggests falling demand for commodities and an economic slowdown. In addition the BDI gives us an excellent clue to any likely trend in commodity prices, which in turn signal investor sentiment and attitude to risk, but and it is a big but, always remember the Baltic Dry Index is quoted in US dollars.

So if the US dollar is falling the BDI index will tend to rise, and if the dollar is rising the index will fall.

It is also important to realise that, just like commodity prices themselves, there is always a time lag. Things do not happen immediately, but instead give us an early warning signal, and is therefore an excellent index for the longer term trends which we can follow in the currency markets, with the Baltic Dry Index, generally leading commodity prices.

As we will see shortly in ratio analysis, an overlay of the Baltic Dry Index against the CCI index we looked at earlier, is a classic relationship to watch.

Equally, if the Baltic Dry Index is falling, and a commodity such as copper is rising in price, this starts to set the alarm bells ringing, as this could be an early warning of a reversal in the the commodity itself or more broadly of the commodity sector in general. Commodities lead us to risk, which is linked to currencies, with the additional link to commodity currencies. I hope you can now begin to see how the pieces of this particular jigsaw fit together to form the complete picture.

As a forex trader you may surprised to be learning about shipping costs as part of your forex trading education, but I hope I've proved this is one of the few economic indicators we can watch which is both pure and untainted, and gives us a real world view of the financial markets by considering sea shipping costs.

This is the power of relational analysis at work, allowing us to make our trading decisions on the real economic costs of shipping commodities by sea. This is not an index you would watch daily, but certainly one to consider on a weekly basis, and particularly for longer term trend trading strategies.

Whilst the Baltic Dry is one index to watch for the cost of shipping, there are others, and indeed as we saw earlier, once again we can also find this index represented with an ETF, which in this case has the ticker SEA, (very appropriate). This ETF is derived from the Dow Jones Global Shipping Index, and whilst it is not a perfect correlation with the Baltic Dry, because the SEA is weighted to shipping related to energy, it gives us another view into the 'real world'. Both are good indicators of shipping costs, and for oil traders the SEA gives some excellent clues to the longer term direction for crude oil prices.

Fig 10.16 ETF For The DJGS Index

To round off this chapter on important and related indices, I make no apology for mentioning the obvious, as I want to reinforce the point you must watch the major stock indices around the world for two reasons.

First, they will give you a perspective on risk appetite in the currencies of a particular country and the consequent money flow. This was the case in point above with the USD index and the CCI indices both falling.

Second, they provide us with the one indicator that is missing from our spot forex charts which is true volume. This is a theme I am going to continue in the next chapter which covers ETFs and the weekly CFTC COT report, both areas where we can find further information on volume to help us in our analysis of the forex markets. I will also be explaining how to interpret the price volume relationship in a later chapter.

The Indices

The major indices we should watch are these. In London it's either the FTSE 250 or the FTSE 350. The FTSE 100 is simply not representative of the UK economy if we are trading the British pound, as the companies are primarily international with most of their revenues earned overseas.

The FTSE 250 or 350 include a far more representative sample of UK companies across all sectors.

In the US, the same applies, and we do not watch the Dow Jones index as this only contains 30 companies. Rather, take the S&P 500 as your barometer of risk appetite. The other, is the NASDAQ 100, but remember this can lead during recovery phases of the economic cycle.

This S&P 500 index is based on the 500 largest US companies and therefore gives us an excellent view on market sentiment, money flow and economic outlook for the US economy. The other index which is also a good barometer is the Russell 3000, which is based on the 3000 largest US companies and again an excellent index to watch.

If we are trading the Japanese yen, the index to watch is the Nikkei 225 index, the primary index quoted, and in this case does truly represent the Japanese economy, and therefore risk, sentiment and money flow. If the Nikkei 225 is rising, the yen is generally falling and vice-versa because of the carry trade with flows away from safe haven and into risk.

For the Australian dollar, we look at the S&P ASX 200 which covers the 200 largest companies in Australia. For China we watch the SSE composite which is the principle index of all listed stocks at the Shanghai Stock Exchange, and includes both A and B shares.

In Hong Kong, we watch the Hang Seng Composite Index which covers around 95% of the total market capitalisation of companies listed on the main board of the Hong Kong Stock Exchange.

In India, we watch the S&P CNX Nifty also known as the 'nifty fifty' which is the index for the 50 largest companies listed on the National Stock Exchange of India.

In Canada, it is another of the S&P indices, and in this case it is the S&P TSX composite, an index of the stock prices of the largest companies on the Toronto Stock Exchange.

Finally, for Europe, we watch three separate market indices. The first is the CAC 40 in France which contains 40 stocks of the top 100 market capitalisation and the most active stocks listed on Euronext Paris, now part of the NYSE.

Secondly, for Germany it's the DAX, which measures the performance of the Prime Standard's 30 largest German companies in terms of order book volume and market capitalisation.

Third and last for a general European perspective we check on another of the Standard and Poors indices which in this case is the S&P Europe 350, a free float market cap weighted index which covers at least 70% of European equity market capitalisation - so a solid index to watch for market sentiment, risk appetite and money flow and consequent appetite for the euro.

Whilst in general, all major stock indices around the world will tend to follow similar trends as risk sentiment ebbs and flows, this is not always the case so we look at equity markets in three distinct ways.

First, from a broad fundamental perspective.

Second, using a technical approach based on candlestick analysis.

Third and last, using volume which is always available for all of the major stock indices, and this is where volume analysis becomes such a powerful analytical tool for us as forex traders. All are covered for you in detail in a later section.

The reason I have included all of the above is because many forex traders simply ignore, or simply don't understand the importance of equity markets and the ones detailed above are those to consider. It's one of the many reasons traders require such a large number of screens.

Cross market and relational analysis can provide forex traders with some powerful insights into market sentiment, risk and money flow. The key is to know which indices and markets to follow. The price action on these instruments can help to support and validate trading decisions in all time frames.

In the next chapter I want to consider a group of instruments, analytical techniques and market information which can also provide us with yet another method of assessing risk, sentiment and money flow.

Chapter Eleven
Secondary Perspectives

One reason why financially educated people want to keep their money moving is because if they park their money in one asset class, as many amateur investors do, they may lose their money when cash flows out of that asset class.

Robert Kiyosaki (1944-)

I have called this chapter, Secondary Perspectives, as I would like to introduce some of the more sophisticated approaches to market analysis, which combine aspects of relational analysis, with associated analytical techniques, such as ratio analysis.

Ratio analysis is an approach widely used when analysing companies and their performance, and can be applied in a similar way to gauge market performance using indices.

In this chapter I also want to consider the CFTC data, which gives us a complementary view of the market, and round off by looking at a particular set of instruments, namely ETFs, which are increasing in popularity, and once again provide us with an alternative way to analyse the market using volume.

The first ratio I would like to introduce is known as the TED spread. The TED spread is all about risk, and although it is in fact a ratio between two instruments, it does appear on a single chart.

TED & TIPS

The TED spread gives us a view on the credit markets or the cost of money, and the reason it's called the TED spread is because it was originally established as a measure of the difference between interest rates on 3 month T bills and the 3 month Eurodollar contracts with identical expiration months. The T comes from the T of T-bills, whilst the ED is the ticker symbol for the Eurodollar futures contract on the CME, so the two were simply joined together to come up with the TED.

Today, the TED spread measures the difference between the interest rates on a 3 month T-Bill measured against the 3 month LIBOR rate. LIBOR is the London Interbank Offered Rate. It is a very simple calculation. For example, if the LIBOR rate is 2.75% and the equivalent rate on the T-bill is 1.75%, the TED spread is the difference between the two, in other words 1%. This is normally expressed in basis points so the difference is simply multiplied by 100, However, charts do vary. Some record in this format, whilst others present the spread in the true percentage difference.

The question of course is, what does the TED spread chart tell us?

Despite the financial crisis of the last few years T-bills are universally perceived as risk free, whilst LIBOR on the other hand reflects the interest rates banks are prepared to lend money to one another. Wholesale lending if you like.

The TED spread reflects the difference between the rates at which lenders are prepared to lend money to the US government and what banks are likely to charge each other. So, it is an excellent proxy for credit risk.

Typically, the spread is represented in basis points so a 0.25 percentage difference would be appear as a 25 basis point spread; a 0.50 percentage difference would appear as a 50 basis point spread and so on. On the chart the spread will be appear as a simple number somewhere between zero and 500. But as I said earlier, this does vary from one chart to another.

The highest number ever recorded was 463 in mid 2008 when the financial crisis was at its peak. This meant at this point there would have been a 4.63% difference in interest rates between the Libor rate and the US 3 month T-bills.

But, how do we read the TED spread chart?

Put simply, as the TED index rises it is denoting a widening spread, which signals increasing concerns about credit risk for two reasons. First, it could be as a result of banks becoming increasingly nervous about lending to one another. Or second, it signals investors are flocking to safe haven investments such as US treasuries. In other words, LIBOR rates are rising and the yield on Treasuries is falling.

A TED spread that is falling denotes a narrowing of the spread and tells us credit markets are functioning. In this case, the LIBOR rate is falling, so risk is considered to be low in the wholesale banking market, and in addition, investors are more willing to accept risk by selling T-Bills, with a consequent rise in yields.

If the spread is widening and the index on the chart is moving higher, we can assume the market is not in the mood for risk. In order words it is a 'risk off' environment. Money flow is likely to be into safe haven assets and safe haven currencies and away from risk assets such as equities, commodities and risk currencies.

Investors are moving into T-Bills as they believe stock markets are likely to fall, with the spread increasing and the index rising.

A widening spread can also be an indication the credit markets are not functioning correctly, and can therefore be a potential sign of economic contraction, because if people cannot obtain credit the economy is unlikely to expand.

What if the TED spread is falling or the spread is decreasing with the index falling? In this case it tells us the opposite of the above.

There is a lower risk of default, so wholesale interest rates between banks will be lower, investors are selling bonds and T-Bills as they believe they will obtain a better return in the stock market and from higher risk asset classes. Finally, with credit markets working normally, we can expect to see economic expansion as a result. At first glance this can appear a complex index to follow. In reality it isn't, and whilst it is not one you are going to watch every day, you do need to consult it periodically to check for any clues or signals of what is going on in the money markets. And, in particular, watch for any signs of changes in risk appetite and market sentiment.

Until recently it was relatively easy to find a chart for the TED spread. It used to be freely available at Bloomberg as part of the charting options. However, Bloomberg recently decided to withdraw the chart of this index, so the place to go now is to head over to http://www.stockcharts.com and enter the ticker symbol $TED which will bring up the respective chart.

As I said earlier, this is not a chart to watch on an intraday basis, but rather on a daily or weekly basis. This will give you an alternative perspective on risk and risk appetite as measured using the ever changing spread in this relationship.

Just like the VIX in the previous chapter, which is the premier fear indicator, the TED index works inversely with equity markets. In other words, if equity markets are rising the TED index will be falling, and conversely when stock markets are falling, the TED index will start to rise. Anything about 100 or 1% will set the alarm bells clanging, while a move below 50 or 0.5% is where markets are complacent and risk appetite it rising.

You can find an alternative to the TED spread index by visiting the Federal Reserve Bank of St Louis, and creating your own chart, which is shown below. I show you how to do this in the next section when we look at the TIPS spread.

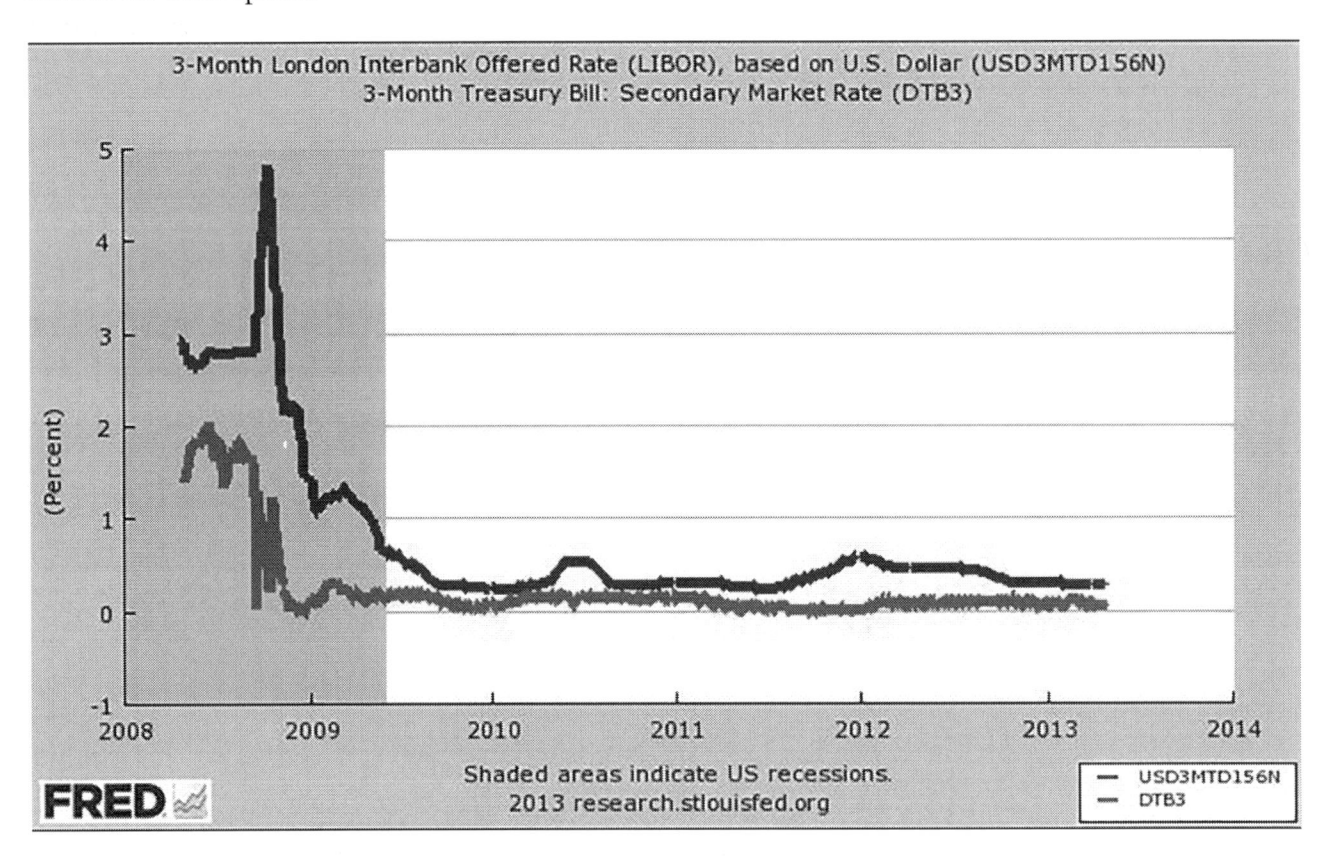

Fig 11.10 TED Spread - Courtesy of the Federal Reserve Bank of St Louis

Another important secondary index is the TIPS spread. Like the TED spread this one is not really an index at all, but a measure of the variation between two interest rates, but I've included it here, so the TED and TIPS sit together in the same place within the book.

The TIPS spread is a little more difficult to construct, as we have to create the chart ourselves using two different instruments, but it is yet another important economic indicator which this time tells us about inflation.

Like the TED index, this is not a chart we look at constantly, but simply one to refer to now and again, for a longer term perspective on the economy and the prospects for inflation.

The good news is it is very simple to understand as the chart is a simple comparison between the yield of TIPS which are **T**reasury **I**nflation **P**rotection **S**ecurities, hence the acronym TIPS, and our old friend the conventional US Treasury with the same maturity date.

The reason the TIPS spread is so important is that the payments for TIPS adjust for inflation, whereas the simple Treasury note or bill does not. This gives us a direct and simple view on the prospects for future inflation.

The TIPS spread is one of the few market based measures of inflation expectation, and the spread is therefore the difference between a normal bond, usually the ten year Treasury bond and an inflation index bond of the same maturity. Moreover, the principle reason for watching the TIPS is that inflation index bonds are benchmarked using the CPI, the Consumer Prices Index, a term I will explain in the next section of the book.

In plain English, the wider the spread between the two yields the higher investors' expectations are of inflation, whilst the narrower the spread between the two yields the lower investors' expectations. If the spread is widening, traders and investors are expecting inflation, and conversely if the spread is narrowing, inflation expectations are declining. This is another key measure used by central banks to gauge the current inflationary pressures in the economy and whether to manage this through the interest rate mechanism.

I hope, by now, you are beginning to see how powerful related markets and analysis of these relationships can be in providing a fully formed view of the market. Perhaps, you can also begin to see why so many forex traders fail. However, I do understand some of this can seem overwhelming when you first start, but you must remember some of these charts and indices are only checked occasionally, not every minute of the day.

Furthermore, whilst there appears to be a lot to do each day, once you have a routine, it will only take a few minutes to check the latest charts to see what these indices are telling you. This quick check is something you should do before going on to your detailed analysis of the particular currency pair you are thinking of trading.

Constructing the chart for the TIPS can be a little complicated as there are only a few places on the internet which have this chart, but you can find it here : https://research.stlouisfed.org

Click on the Data Tools tab and from the drop down box select the 'create your own graphs' option. This will open your FRED graph where you can create your own TIPS spread chart. To do this, enter the following ticker – DGS10 - in the Add Data Series box. This is the 10 year Treasury Constant Maturity Note.

Once done, click on the Add Data Series below to add your second instrument which in this case is – DFII10 – this is the 10 year Inflation Indexed Linked Note.

Select the same time period of 5 years or 1 year below for each instrument, and click the redraw graph button at the bottom of the screen.

You should now have a chart with two lines which converge and diverge. You now have your own TIPS spread and a personal view on inflation. Remember this is not a chart to check daily, but will help to frame some of the economic data releases, in particular when we begin to look at fundamental analysis in the next section of the book. When the Federal Reserve release their monthly statements on the economy and possible changes in interest rates in the future, this chart will help you understand why.

Your chart should now look something like the one in Fig 11.11

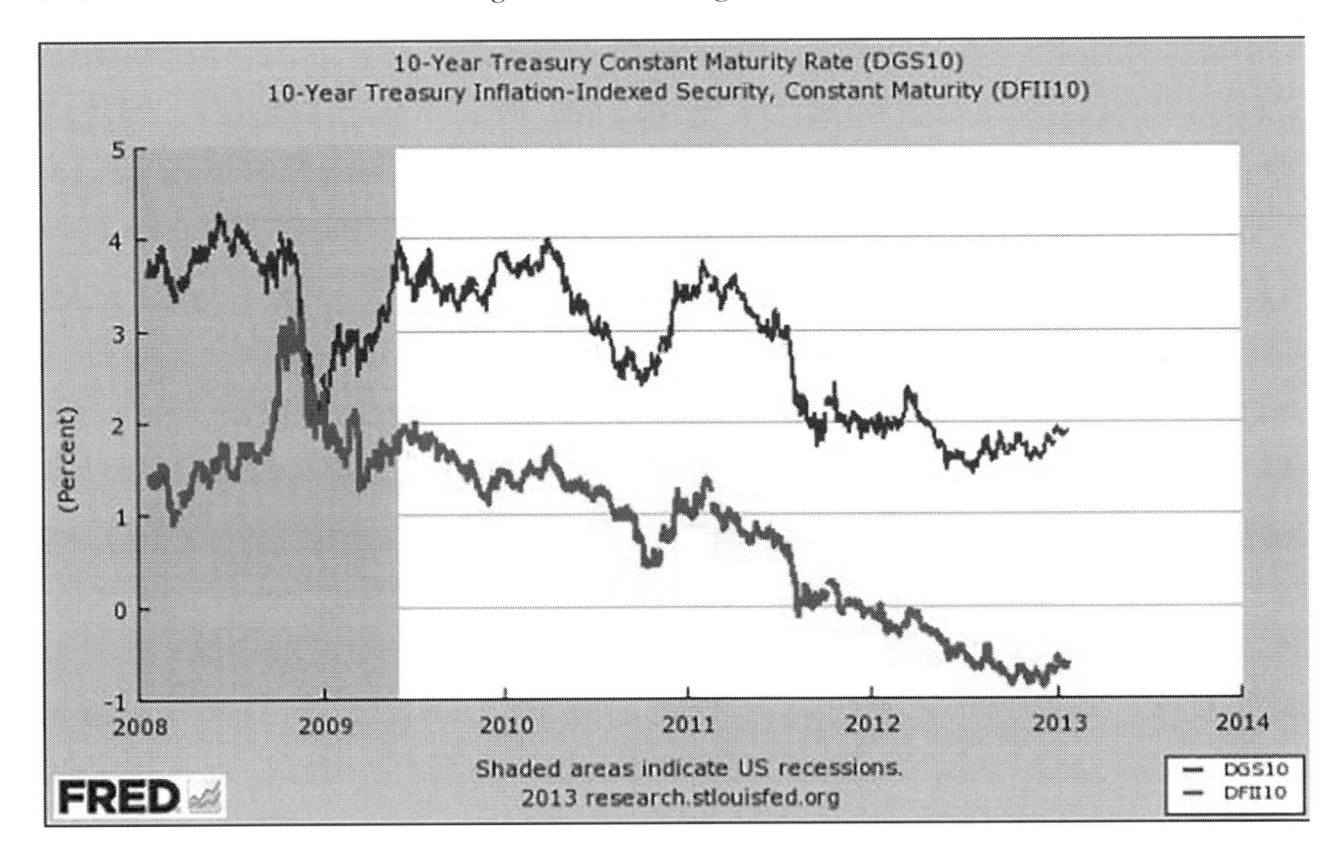

Fig 11.11 TIPS Courtesy of the Federal Reserve Bank of St Louis

In the previous two chapters we looked at several of the major indices which reveal different aspects of these underlying relationships. This all helps to give us a view of the markets and, as forex traders a deeper insight into what is actually happening, and more importantly, what is likely to happen in the future.

This is still a relatively one dimensional view. After all an index is just an index, so in order to try to give us a more descriptive three dimensional view, we use a technique called ratio analysis.

Ratio Analysis

Ratio analysis is a technique where we compare one index with another, in order to arrive at a deeper analysis. In some ways it is similar to the TIPS and TED spreads where two instruments are compared to reveal market sentiment or economic activity.

The simplest analogy I can think of to explain ratio analysis is if we were to look at a chart for the the price of petrol, which would probably only tell us petrol prices were rising or falling. However, if we were to compare the price of petrol with the price of oil this might tell us a little more, and may even surprise us.

So ratio analysis at its simplest level is comparing one price chart or index with a related or tangential market which, as a result, reveals deeper market information for us as traders.

These markets or indices are rarely directly related but it is this cross market analysis that can be so revealing.

Here are some examples of ratio analysis which have a direct impact on currencies.

In many ways we have already touched on ratio analysis by looking at relationships such as gold and the US dollar where I introduced you to some of the basic concepts of relational analysis. A good place to start is with gold as we consider some of the simple relationships and ratios that work in the currency markets.

Fig 11.12 is the weekly chart for gold using the ETF with the ticker GLD.

Fig 11.12 Gold Weekly Chart

Now compare this with the Australian Dollar US Dollar weekly chart in Fig 11.13 over the same period.

Fig 11.13 AUD/USD Weekly Chart

Australia is one of the worlds largest gold producers, and is currently ranked third in the world in terms of production. The Australian dollar is therefore sensitive to the price of gold and the pair, which are quoted with the Australian dollar first as the primary currency, will tend to move in step. Therefore, as the price of gold rises, this is likely to be reflected in strength for the Australian dollar, and likewise, a fall in the price of gold may see the Australian dollar weaken.

The gold effect is also seen in some of the other commodity currencies such as the New Zealand dollar and the Canadian dollar. In the case of the Canadian dollar this is quoted as the counter currency, so as the USD/CAD falls, this is reflecting strength in the Canadian dollar and the price of gold, (and other commodities) will be rising.

Whilst New Zealand is a much smaller producer it still ranks twenty fifth in the world, so movements in gold will be reflected in the New Zealand dollar too. The NZD also has other major influences such as interest rate differentials and the carry trade, as do other high yielding currencies such as the Australian Dollar, so please don't run away with the idea this is the only relationship that influences the pair. It isn't, there are many others, and this is just one, with gold.

Fig 11.14 is the weekly chart for the Canadian dollar vs the US dollar (USD/CAD) which reflects this inverse relationship.

Staying with gold, the next one may surprise you a little but the Euro also tends to rise when gold rises as both are considered as alternatives to the dollar, gold as a safe haven and the Euro as the first reserve currency 'in waiting'.

Fig 11.14 USD/CAD Weekly Chart

Now whilst all of the above are conditional on changes in the price of gold, all of these are underpinned by the generally inverse relationship between gold and the US dollar, so as gold prices rise the US dollar tends to fall, a relationship we studied earlier in the book. This is one of the complex issues we face as forex traders, which is this.

When considering a currency pair, what are the factors driving the pair? For example, with the Euro vs US dollar, is it strength in the Euro, or is it weakness in the US dollar? What impact are commodity prices having on the currencies which make up the pair? Is the driver due solely to the direction of the US dollar, or are other factors playing a part?

Learn to identify and unravel these factors and your trading success will increase exponentially. After all, if we can identify why a currency is strong or weak, we can track this in different pairs and in different ways, using all the techniques and analytical tools you will discover as we move deeper into the subject.

The final currency pair which has a strong association with gold is the Swiss Franc, and there are two reasons for this.

First, the Swiss banking system holds almost thirty percent of its reserves in gold, and therefore any change in the price of gold is likely to be reflected in the currency. Second, the Swiss Franc is also seen as a safe haven currency, partly due to the underlying gold in the banking system, and partly because Switzerland is seen as a safe and stable country. Furthermore, Switzerland likes to protect its banking clients from the prying eyes of the tax authorities.

The most popular currency pair is the USD/CHF (Fig 11.15) with the Swiss Franc as the counter currency against the US dollar. So just as with the USD/CAD we considered earlier, this pair too has an inverse relationship with the price of gold.

The USD/CHF pair will fall as gold rises and vice versa, just as with the USD/CAD.

Fig 11.15 USD/CHF Weekly Chart

Finally and, staying with the commodity theme, I have introduced this one before, but as oil prices rise and fall, the impact of this price action will be seen in several pairs featuring the Canadian Dollar, primarily against the US dollar and the Japanese Yen.

Fig 11.16 is a weekly chart for WTI oil, followed by the equivalent charts for the Canadian Dollar against the US dollar and the Japanese Yen.

Fig 11.16 WTI Crude Oil Weekly Chart Over 12 Months

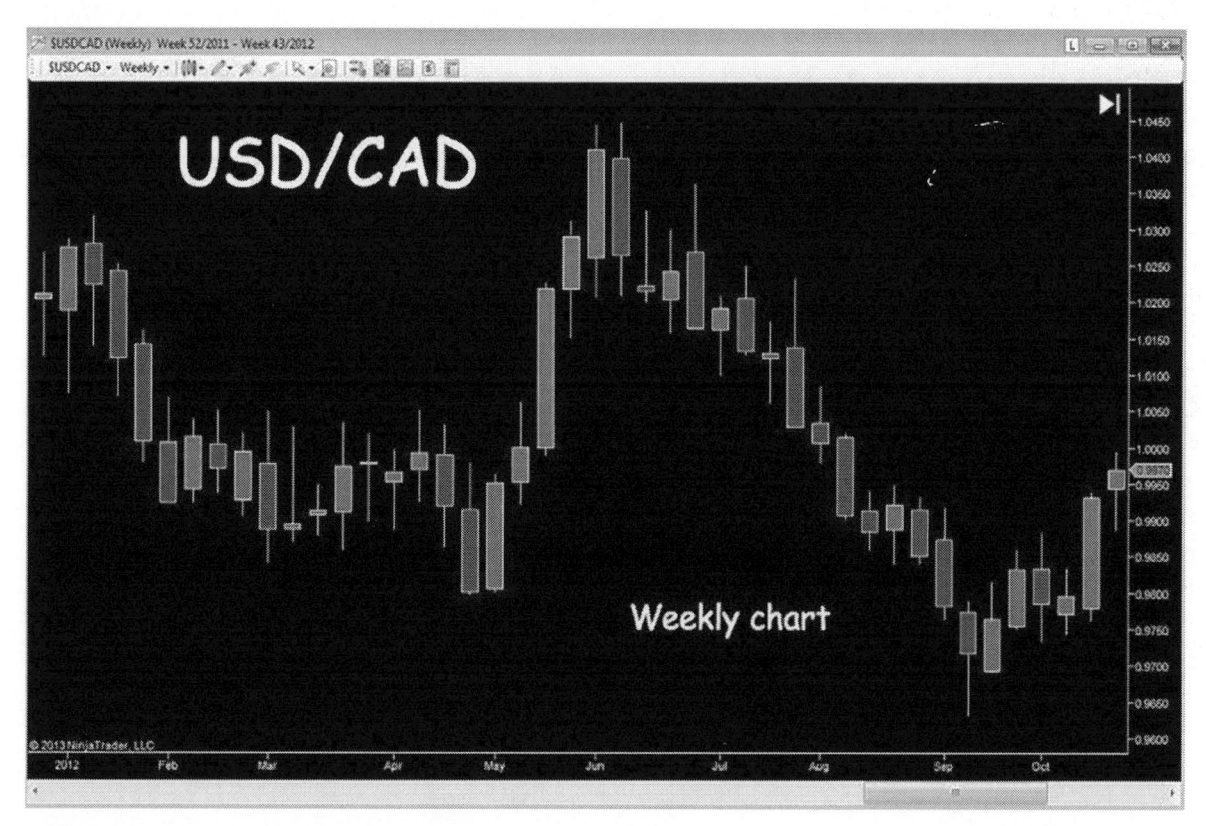

Fig 11.17 USD/CAD - Weekly Chart Over 12 Months

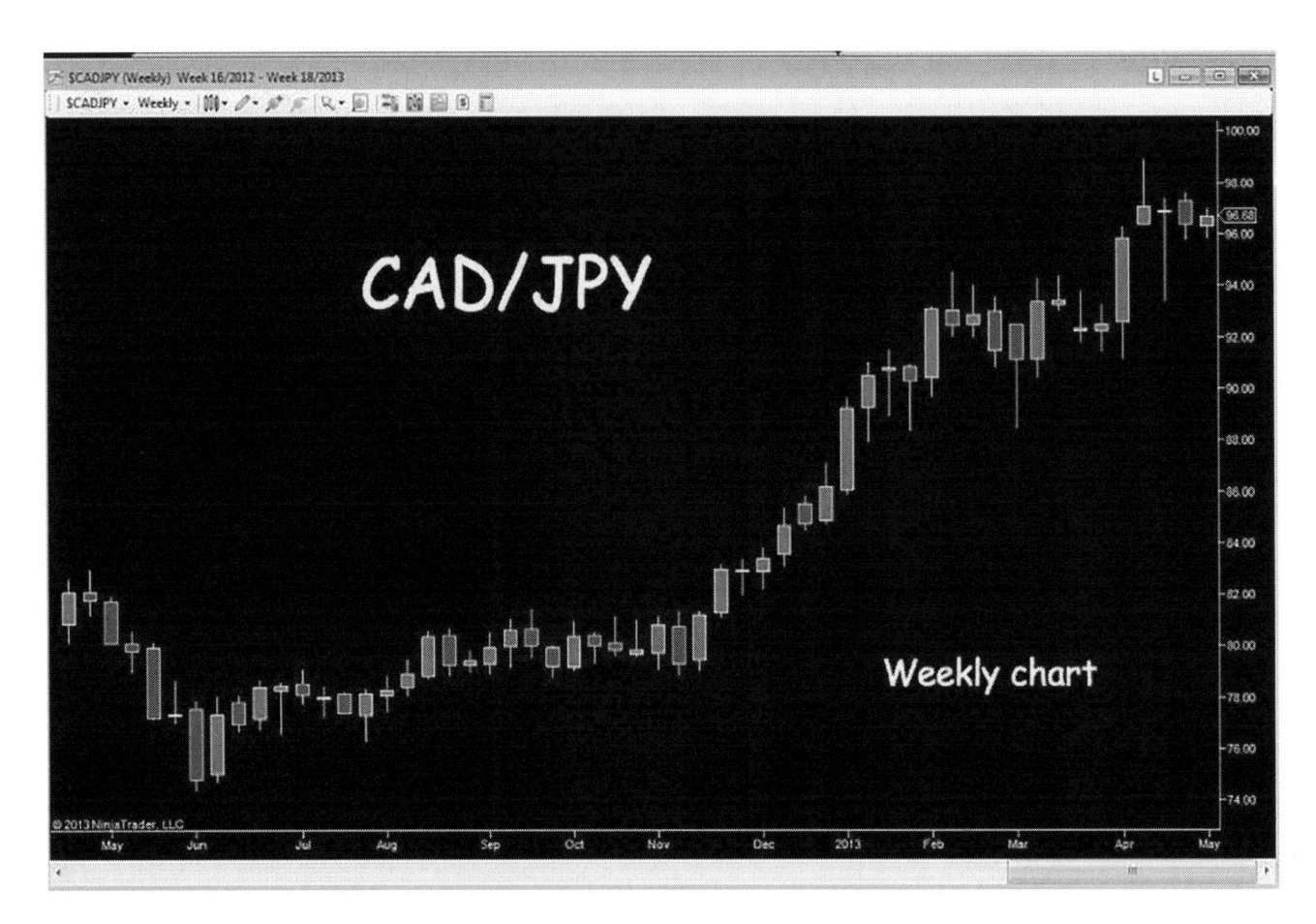

Fig 11.18 CAD/JPY – Weekly Chart Over 12 Months

However, before moving to consider more complex studies, let's look at a couple of examples of equities and currencies and, in this case it is the Nikkei 225, the primary Japanese equity index and the US Dollar vs Japanese Yen pair (USDJPY), which tend to move in the same direction for the simple reason the Yen is also considered to be a so called safe haven currency. Therefore, if Japanese stock markets are falling, investors will move from a risky asset class such as equities into a safe haven currency such as the Japanese Yen.

As the Nikkei 225 falls, the USD/JPY pair are also likely to fall.

In addition, this relationship is further reinforced since selling of Japanese equities, is reflected in the consequent buying of Yen denominated safe haven assets such as bonds. However, as always this view has to be tempered by the fact the US dollar is also a safe haven currency, and once again it is a question of understanding and unravelling whether price movement in the pair is being driven by the US dollar, or the Japanese Yen. This is always the conundrum, and is one of the many reasons why looking at these relationships using relational analysis, can give us the clues and signals which will help us solve this problem.

Fig 11.19 Nikkei 225 – Weekly Chart Over 9 Months

Fig 11.20 USD/JPY – Weekly Chart Over 9 Months

One other relationship that stands out between currencies and equities is that between the Euro Yen pair (EURJPY), and the US S&P 500 index. Here again it is the risk aspect which drives the money flow, so if investors are nervous, they will move out of equities and into safe haven currencies such as the Yen.

In this case, the Euro Yen currency pair will fall as the S&P falls and rise as the index rises Fig 11.21 and Fig 11.22 are both weekly charts over a 3 month period.

Fig 11.21 EUR/JPY

Fig 11.22 S&P500 Weekly

Finally to conclude this section let's take a look at one of the key relationships between markets of the same asset class. So far we have looked at money flow between assets, but what about money flow as reflected in markets with the same risk profile? And here the same principles apply.

The two indices to watch are in the Nikkei 225 and the S&P 500, which will almost always move in the same direction given the close relationship between the two economies. Therefore, if you are trading in the London session as the European and UK markets get underway, always check the Nikkei 225 for a view on overnight market sentiment, which will provide clues to trading sentiment in London and the US sessions.

Fig 11.23 Nikkei 225 – Daily Chart Over 3 Months

Fig 11.24 S&P 500 – Daily Chart Over 3 Months

Having covered some of the basic relationships let me move up to the next level and consider more complex relationships and ratios which give us a little more than just a simple direct comparison.

I also want to make the point you don't need to check these every day. Some are long term ratios, such as with the TED and TIPS spreads. They are useful because they give us a mental picture of where we are in the longer term cycle, whilst others will be shorter term and more relevant for intraday traders. And this is particularly true when we look at bonds.

However, as a general rule of thumb this type of analysis is an analytical tool designed to provide a framework against which to trade. It is an overview, a birds eye view, as we survey the financial landscape for clues and signals as to the broader economic outlook. This overview will reveal trends in inflation as well as potential turning points in related markets which, in turn will reveal money flow, risk and market sentiment.

In the above examples where we have considered commodities and currency pairs, an intraday trader would almost certainly have live charts, along with bond yields, major indices and the sentiment indicators such as the VIX. All would be telling the market's story in their own unique, yet interrelated way. Add to this analysis the power of technical price action coupled with volume and backed by an understanding of the fundamentals driving the markets, and you have the complete picture.

These are the insights and tools I am trying to deliver in this book. The tools which allow you to see the whole picture and not simply one simple price chart for one simple currency pair. The forex market is far more complex than this, and is one of the reasons why it is the most difficult market to comprehend and trade.

However, to return to gold, but this time to consider the gold oil ratio which has a strong inverse relationship to stocks and market sentiment. This simply means as stocks rise this ratio will fall and vice versa.

Fig 11.25 is a simple chart showing this ratio over an approximate 12 month period.

The Gold To Oil Ratio

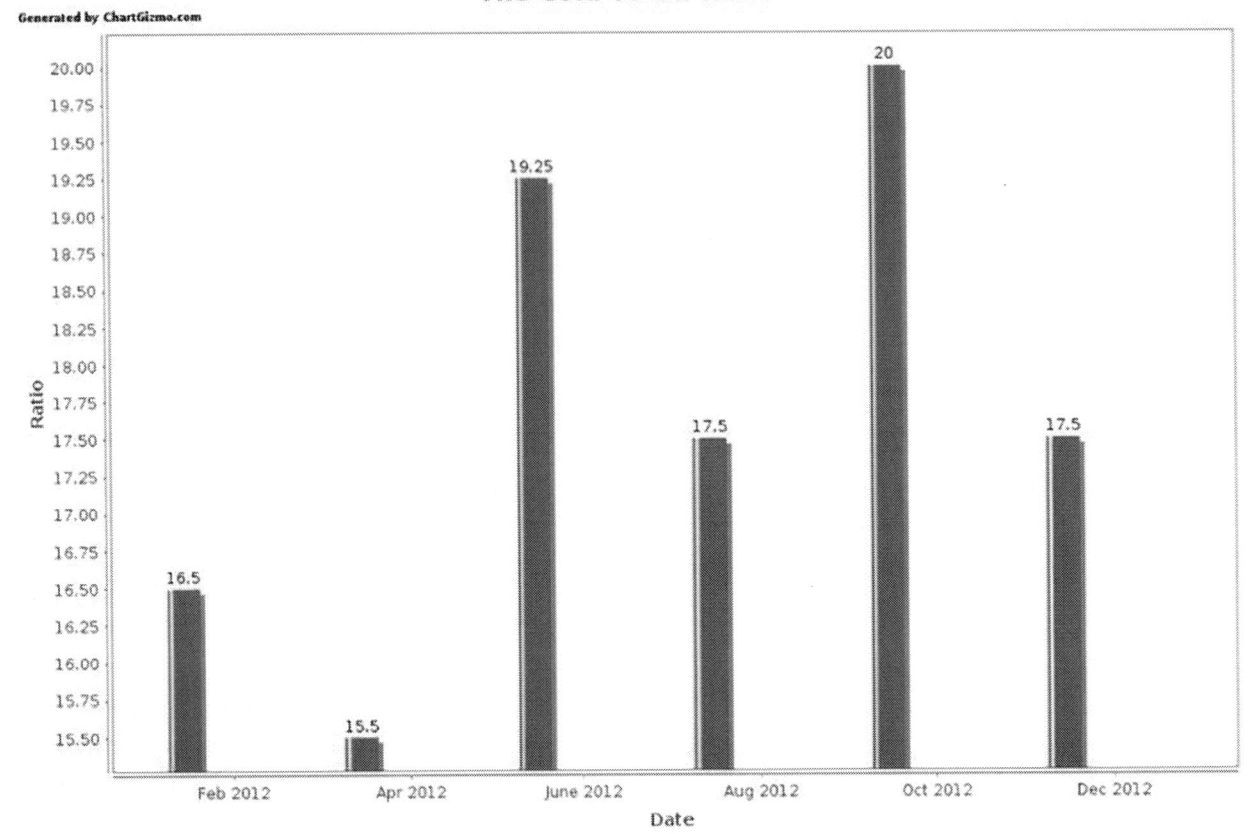

Fig 11.25 Gold/Oil Ratio

What does this chart and ratio reveal about risk and related markets? In simple terms, a falling Gold to Oil ratio, as we can see here in the last few weeks on the right hand side of the chart, suggests a stabilisation in oil, which is usually accompanied by a rise in risk appetite for equities and energy currencies in particular. The associated fall in the price of gold, is suggesting an increase in bond yields as money flows from bonds and into equities. In addition, there is also the simple logic, that as the ratio begins to fall, this is a signal of possible rising energy prices which generally lead stocks higher, particularly when an economy is moving from a recessionary period into the early expansion phase.

This ratio is expressed mathematically as the per ounce price of gold, divided by the cost of a barrel of crude oil, and therefore tells us how many ounces of gold it takes to buy a barrel of oil.

What makes this ratio more meaningful is the lack of correlation between these two commodities, both of which are considered (in different ways) to be bellwethers of inflation. This can lead to large differences, with the ratio varying widely over time. For example, since 2001, one ounce of gold could have bought between 6 and 24 barrels of oil at various times.

In the middle of 2008, as the price of oil surged, the ratio fell to an historic low of 6, before climbing back fast to 24 following a sharp decline in oil when the price fell back below $100 per barrel.

This ratio is also considered to be one of the bellwether ratios for the US economy with the norm considered to be around the one to fifteen level. In other words, if a barrel of oil is $100 dollars and gold is $1500 per ounce this is the median point for the ratio.

How do we use the gold oil ratio?

The ratio can be used in as many ways you can think of. It can be used as a 'reality check'. It can be used to draw conclusions as to whether oil or gold is over or under-priced, and from there to consider the impact on the economy and, perhaps more importantly, on oil or commodity related currencies.

When the ratio fell to an historic low of 6 in 2008, as the oil price peaked at $147 per barrel we could have had three outcomes to bring the ratio back to its median of 15.

First, oil prices could have stayed at this level, and gold would then have had to rise to over $2200 per ounce. Second, gold could have stayed at its then current price at just under $900 per ounce, with oil falling to $58 per barrel. Third, oil prices could have fallen and been matched with a rise in the price of gold.

The principle idea behind the ratio is that it is premised on the fact crude oil prices are one of the main contributory factors to inflation.Increasing oil prices signify an increase in prices at the pumps. The cost of manufacturing and transporting goods also increases, all adding to inflation. Inflation is linked to commodities, and precious metals will then appreciate in such an inflationary environment due to demand. If both oil and gold are rising the ratio may remain flat and settle at the median level. This conclusion has, of course, to be validated by our analysis in other markets such as bonds and equities and further reinforced by our technical analysis of the price charts for both commodities.

However, the ratio should not be viewed as a chart in isolation, but rather as a way of giving you an alternative perspective on the price of both commodities. In addition, the ratio will also give you a view on inflation and the prospect of inflationary pressure. Your analysis will also encompass many of the fundamental topics in the next section of the book, which will combine to give you a feel for the economic cycle in the short to medium term.

Another ratio we look at regularly is the S&P 500 against the VIX both, of course, equity related, but nevertheless an excellent ratio, which when plotted gives us a technical view of risk and fear and therefore market sentiment. As a result, this provides us with a strong visual picture of potential tops and bottoms in the risk markets of equities and commodities, with consequent money flow into bonds and away from risk currencies. Fig 11.26 reveals the power of this relationship which is almost perfectly inverse.

As the VIX falls the S&P 500 rises, and vice versa. The key here is the VIX. Once we see the index trading down to low levels, and into single figures, this is the first warning of danger, of a potential change in longer term risk sentiment in the market. There is no guarantee this will happen quickly, as markets can stay at these extremes for some time, but we know it will happen, it's just a question of when.

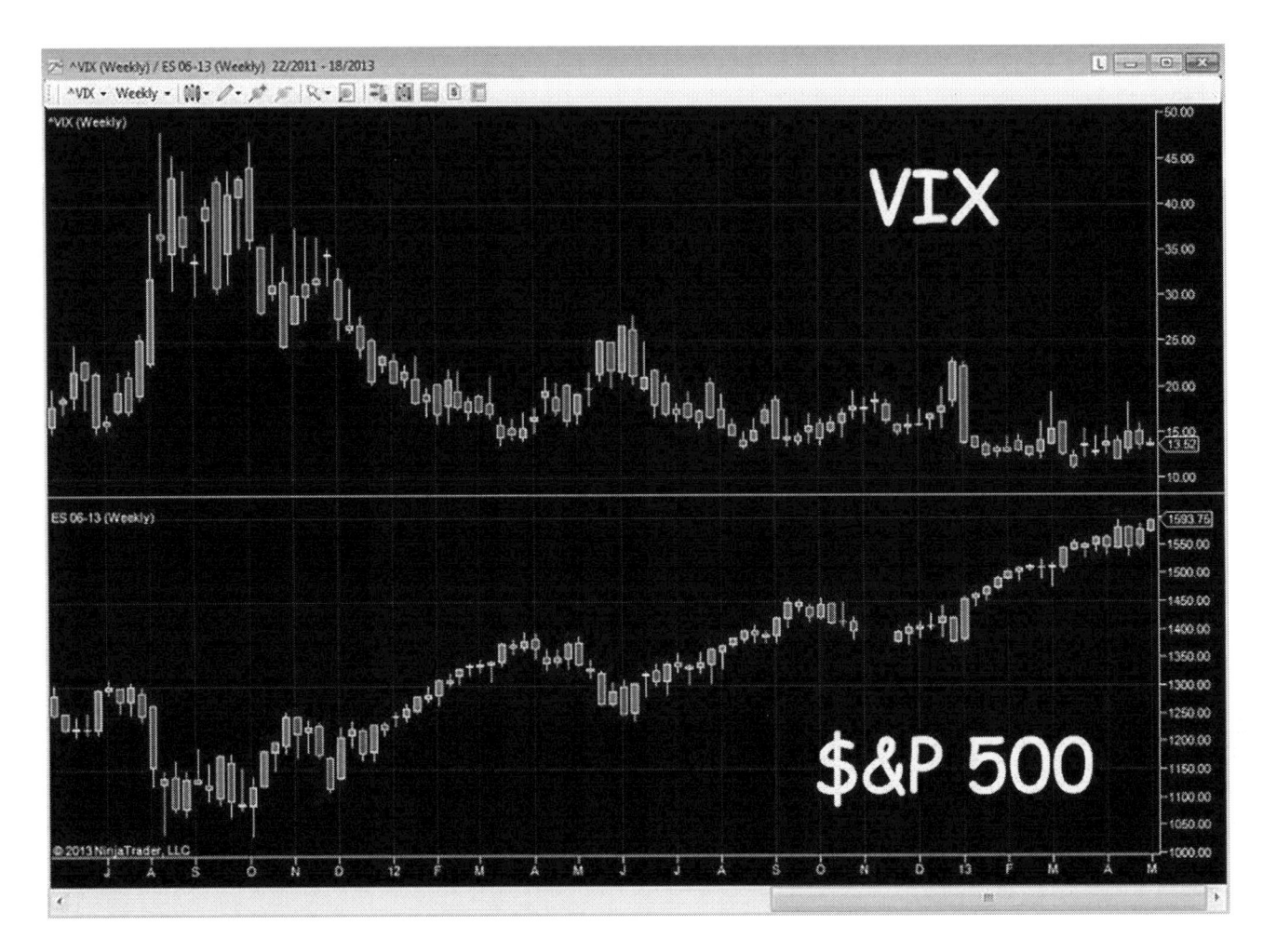

Fig 11.26 VIX/S&P500

Gold DOW Ratio

Finally in equities we look at the gold Dow ratio which measures the value of all the Dow 30 constituent companies priced in gold. In other words how much gold would it take to buy each individual stock in the Dow 30?

Looking at a ten year period between 2000 and 2010 at the start of the decade it would have taken 41.7 ounces of gold to buy one stock from each company. Ten years later it took just 9.4 ounces, a simple but stark message for stock investors the value of these stocks had plunged in the last ten years relative to gold

If this trend continues we could see these stocks move towards one ounce, only seen three times in the last century and all precursors to a long bear market. However, whilst this is a longer term ratio is does provide us with an interesting link between the ultimate safe haven and hedge against inflation (gold) against the returns on risk based assets such as equities.

Dow To Gold Ratio

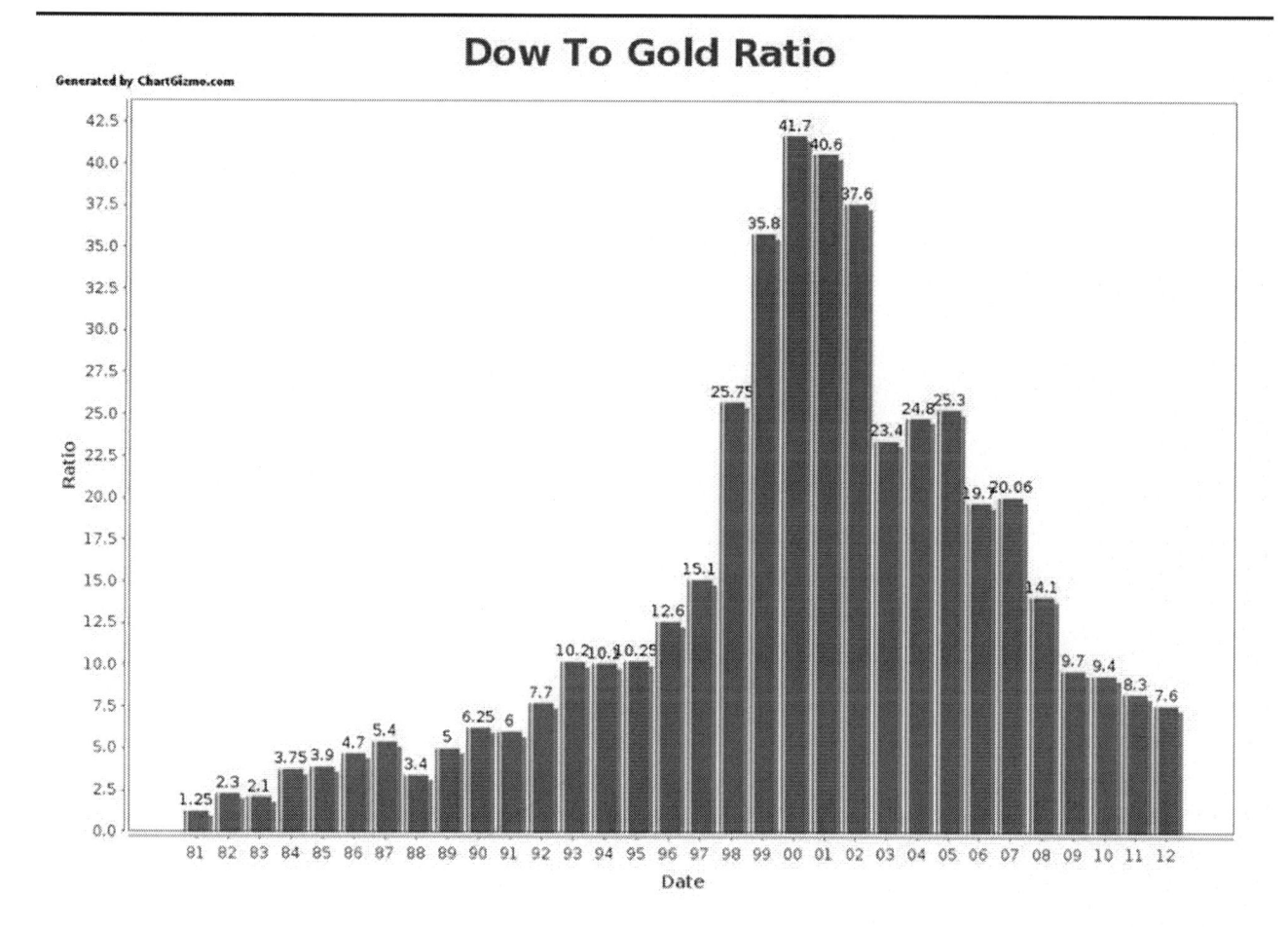

Fig 11.27 Dow/Gold Ratio Chart

Commodities & the US Dollar

Finally, I would like to move to one of the most important indices we looked at previously, the CRB or CCI index, and here I would like to consider three ratios or relationships in detail.

The first is with the US dollar and, as you would expect, this is broadly inverse and what we should expect to see as virtually all commodities are priced in the US dollar. However, we keep an eye on this relationship just to see if it is holding firm, as any breakdown could provide clues as to changes in sentiment or risk.

Fig 11.28 and Fig 11.29 show two charts, one for the CCI and the USD index respectively, over the same three month period and based on daily price action. And the important point to note here is that whilst the relationship was as expected during November, it broke down into December and for parts of January. The reason, as explained earlier, was largely due to surges in equities, which saw a consequent flow of money out of safe haven coupled with a rush to high returns in stocks as investors moved fast into risk assets. Stocks were seen as offering better returns than commodities, and hence the breakdown in the relationship.

However, this breakdown was also reflected in the next relationship. The CRB and 10 year T-note. As the king pin of the markets, the US dollar, also fell out of step which I explain next.

Fig 11.28 CCI - ETF GCC Daily Chart

Fig 11.29 US Dollar Index Daily Chart

CCI (CRB) & Bonds

The next relationship is the CCI or CRB with bonds and, in particular with US treasuries which is yet another of our key relationship. What does the CRB or CCI vs US bonds relationship tell us?

First, there is generally a positive relationship where higher commodity prices will see bond yields rise and bond prices fall, reflecting risk appetite and rising inflation as investors seek higher returns in riskier asset classes.

The second reason is one we touched on previously, which is the leading aspect of commodity prices. As commodity prices tend to lead inflation they can often signal likely changes in interest rates, moving forward. The reason for this is that it takes time for higher commodity prices to filter through into the economic system and ultimately be reflected in the data and statistics produced by governments and central banks. Statistics such as the CPI and PPI numbers, which we're going to look at in the next section of the book.

Therefore, in comparing the Commodity Index with the yield on the 10 year US Treasury note, gives us a unique view on the potential for interest rate rises and, of course the corollary, falls in interest rates, which are equally important.

Ultimately, rises in interest rates drive an economy back into recession with the Commodity Index falling as bond yields fall, as money flows back into bonds and away from riskier assets.

Unfortunately, in the last few years the US bond market has become distorted by the action of the US Federal Reserve in its attempts to weaken the US dollar severely by printing money. In addition, the currency wars continue unabated as central banks around the world desperately pursue measures to ensure a triple dip recession is avoided. No one wants a strong currency which is leading to distortions in all of these once key relationships.

Whilst writing this book, we have had a situation with a falling US dollar and falling commodities. The relationship has broken down temporarily, and is a stark reminder no relationship, no matter how solid in the past can be guaranteed in the future. This has been proven many times in the last few years, with markets distorted by so much money. And, as I said earlier in the book, the rule book has been torn up. So, it's just as important to understand this fact as it is to understand these relationships.

In this example we have the CCI and the 10 Year US T-Note yield over a three month period and what we expect to see is as follows.1

If commodity prices are rising, and the CCI is rising, this signals positive risk sentiment, which should be reflected in the yields on US T- notes (and others) in rising yields, as money flows from bonds and into risk assets. In other words, this is a positive direct relationship.

Equally if yields are falling the CCI or CRB should be falling as well, reflecting money flow into safe haven and away from risk.

But as you can see from the charts in Fig 11.30 and Fig 11.31 almost the exact opposite is happening.

Yields through December rose, yet the CCI index fell. Finally, in January the relationship stepped back into line with rising yields and a rising CCI index. But not for long, breaking down again in the last few days of January with an inverse relationship back in place.

Fig 11.30 GCC - ETF Daily Chart

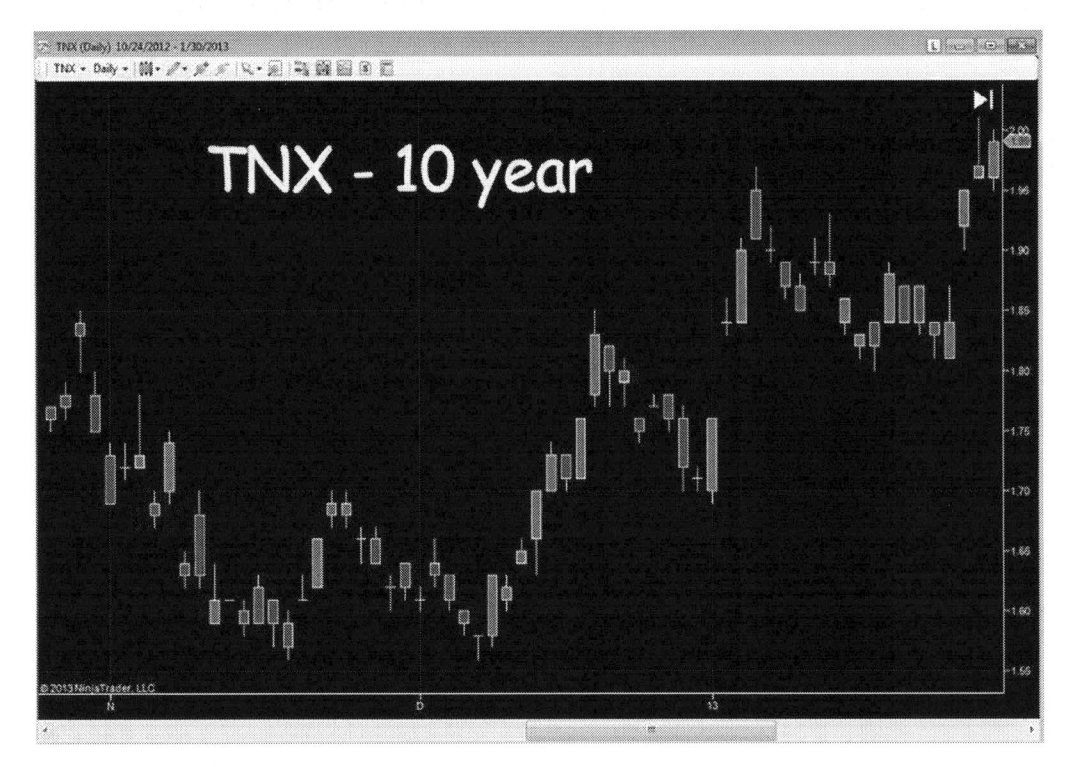

Fig 11.31 10 Year TNX

And the reason has to do with the US dollar. If the US dollar relationship, which underpins all others, falls out of kilter, this will also be reflected in all these secondary relationships and ratios which are underpinned by the first.

As we saw earlier, in November we had a falling CCI index and a falling US dollar index which is an anomaly, and largely triggered as a result of a headlong rush back into risk assets. This was triggered by benchmark stock markets moving higher very quickly and through some key technical price levels, having broken out of an extended period of sideways price action.

Furthermore, this behaviour also has to be seen against the backdrop of the last few years, with investors constantly fearful as one financial crisis has followed another, with safe havens being sought out in both paper and hard assets.

The move higher in 2013 was much the same as a dam bursting, with a flood of money into risk as investors, fund managers and hedge funds scrambled onto the fast moving train, selling anything and everything in an effort not to miss out. Commodities were no longer in demand as the key risk asset, and consequently fell with the US dollar index. Bond yields rose as expected, but with the underlying distortion of the US dollar selling off, these once reliable index relationships stalled, and reversed.

Market behaviour over the last few years, and probably for the next few, is likely to be characterised in this way. This is part and parcel of understanding how the markets work, and in their own way give us another important signal – an anomaly of what we would normally expect to see. This in turn makes us ask the question, why? Which hopefully will lead us to a common sense conclusion based on sound market analysis and understanding market behaviour at that point in history.

A valuable lesson learnt and one I cannot stress too strongly so let me just recap on the above.

Normally when the USD index falls, the CRB or CCI would rise because it is an inverse relationship.

As the USD index falls, bond yields rise, as money is flowing out of safe havens and into riskier assets.

From the above we should expect to see the CRB or CCI rise with bond yields in a positive relationship.

In other words one relationship, CRB/USD is inverse, whilst the CRB/T-note yield is positive.

All these relationships do fall out from time to time and the key is to understanding first, what they should be, all things being equal. Second, if they have fallen out, to ask why?

ETFs

Moving on to consider some of the other 'secondary' relationships that can help us to understand and answer this question, as well as others, let's move to exchange traded funds or ETFs.

These are a relatively new instrument, having originally been introduced to the US markets in the early 1990s, the first being a fund which tracked the performance of the S&P 500 index.

Since then, the market for these instruments has grown exponentially and they are now widely available in all markets.

They are traded on most of the international exchanges, and just like any other stock or share, their price changes second by second during the trading session as the underlying asset or index moves accordingly.

In other words, they are derivatives or derived from an underlying asset, which for the purposes of this book are currencies, all of which are quoted against the US dollar.

There are different types of ETFs. Some work inversely. In other words, they rise as the market falls. However, for the purposes of this book I am only going to focus on those ETFs which track their underlying asset.

One final point. The fund which underpins the ETF holds the physical currency or a futures contract to buy the currency, so in buying or selling these instruments, you are actually holding the physical currency at the face value of the ETF.

In many ways this is a classic example of how currencies have moved from pure speculation to one where they are considered to be an asset class in their own right.

However, as forex traders why should we be interested in ETFs?

First, it's possible to trade forex markets using these instruments and, just like a stock or share, they can be bought and sold in a regulated exchange.

Second, the reason they are important to us is that, just like a stock or share, these instruments report volume, because they are bought and sold through the exchange. And, as I have said many times before, volume and price are vital in forecasting future market direction. With ETFs we have true reported volume associated with a currency.

The question, is who is buying or selling? In this case it is hedge funds, private individuals and speculators, but predominantly hedge funds as a hedge against currency movements in large portfolios. It is primarily the professional money.

This is important when we start analysing volume. As traders we want to make sure any analysis is based on following the professional (the insiders) money. We don't want to follow the retail traders who are generally on the wrong side of the market.

Richard Wyckoff, one of the great iconic traders of the past who understood the power of volume said there were: "*usually one or more large operators working in every stock. Sometimes there are many*". His purpose in studying the charts was to uncover their motives, their 'game plan' and in doing so would ensure he was trading with them and not against them.

In many ways this is the main purpose of this book. It is to explain how you too can learn to trade with the professionals, the insiders, the 'large operators' and not be crushed by them.

Finally all the ETFs I mention here are plain, vanilla and not leveraged. There are a huge number, and many of them have hidden dangers. Some are **very** highly leveraged to gear up profits fast, but equally losses can grow just as quickly. Some work inversely to the underlying market, so as the market rises, the ETF falls. So you have been warned.

The following is a list of ETFs to watch which can give a different perspective on the currency under investigation. As always we start with the US dollar and I'm going to list all the tickers here for you, and then tell you where you can find live prices, which is free.

UUP : US Dollar

FXA : Australian Dollar

FXB : British Pound

FXC : Canadian Dollar

FXE : Euro

FXY : Yen

FXF : Swiss Franc

FXM : Mexican Peso

XRU : Russian Rouble

FXS : Swedish Krona

BZF : Brazilian Real

CYB : Chinese Yuan

ICN : Indian Rupee

BNZ : New Zealand Dollar

SZR : South African Rand

What we have in effect is a chart for each currency, with exchange volume. And the best place to get live data, for free, on all the above ETFs is at: http://www.freestockcharts.com/

You will need to download the software onto your own pc, but it's excellent and provides a great free resource for watching the ETF market.

The ones I suggest you follow from this list are the UUP, which is the biggest ETF by market capitalisation. The UUP tracks the US dollar index, so once again this gives us an alternative perspective on the US dollar, coupled in this case with volume. The UUP has a simple direct relationship, so as the US dollar index rises, so will the UUP and vice versa.

Next in terms of size comes the FXA with the Australian dollar, which confirms the importance of this currency, followed by the Canadian dollar, the Swiss Franc the Euro and the Yen.

It's interesting the commodity currencies have larger market capitalisation than the Euro and the British pound. The British pound fund, by the way, comes after the Yen. As you would expect, the larger the market capitalisation, the more liquid the pair and the more volume activity you will see.

Some of the smaller ETFs above may move very slowly, so my advice is to focus on the larger ones highlighted above.

Finally, a word of warning. PLEASE, stay away from some of the exotic leveraged ETFs and inverse ETFs. Over the years I have received many emails from traders who failed to understand how they worked. One in particular was very sad where the person concerned had lost over 70% of their pension in one such fund, so please be careful. They are, a valid way to trade and have many advantages and we will return to them again later in the book.

COT Data

To round off this chapter I'm going to explain one of the more intricate pieces of relational data we can use in analysing the currency markets. And this is the COT report, which stands for the Commitment of Traders report.

This report is issued each week by the CFTC, the Commodity Futures Trading Commission which is the financial regulatory body in the US, responsible for administering and regulating all trading in US markets.

Every Friday afternoon, the CFTC issues a report which provides a wealth of information about the futures markets, and in particular, the changes in trading volumes across a huge range of commodities, currencies and treasuries. Buried within this report is the information we use as forex traders to give us yet another perspective, from a secondary piece of market information. However, there are two problems with this report.

First, it is extremely long, complicated and full of jargon, and it is not presented in an easily digestible format.

Second, it is based on data, up to and including the previous Tuesday, so by the time it is published it is always three days out of date. Nevertheless, it is another useful piece of the jigsaw and one which gives us an insight into the weight of money in the market, and where it is for each of the major currencies. Yet another view of market sentiment for each currency and another view which is based on volume.

The best way to use this data is to keep it very simple. But the data can be used in many different ways. The explanation here is based on my own interpretation.

Every Friday afternoon at 15.30 EST, the CFTC releases all the data covering the previous week's trading in futures and options, in a series of consolidated reports from all the major exchanges covering the four capital markets.

The data is based on figures to the previous Tuesday which are then consolidated into the report released three days later on the Friday.

Until recently, the CFTC only produced this data in one format. However, in 2009 this all changed. A more detailed report was devised which reported the figures in a revised format.

In theory, the logic was to provide more transparency for everyone. Unfortunately the exact opposite appears to have happened resulting in the CFTC producing even more complex and jargon filled reports.

Fortunately for us, the CFTC does still produce the old report in its simple format, and this is the one I prefer to use. This version of the report gives me all the information I need in a quick and relatively easy way and this what I want to share with you here.

I'm going to show you where to find the information, what to look for, and then I'll explain how to use the data in the reports.

The weekly data is issued on the CFTC site at http://www.cftc.org/ and on the home page we look for the market reports tab at the top of the page.

Fig 11.32 Market Reports

Hover over this tab, and a drop down menu will appear, and from this menu click on the first which is 'Commitments of Traders' which will open the page shown in Fig 11.33:

Fig 11.33

Scroll down the page and ignore everything including 'disaggregated reports' and look for the following as shown in the image. The 'disaggregated reports' are the new style format, and very confusing in my opinion, so please ignore them. Instead what you are looking for are the current legacy reports which appear lower down this page and appear as shown in Fig 11.34.

Current legacy reports simply means the old style reports which are the ones we want. Next look for the CME which is the largest exchange, and so called 'long format' report and futures only which is in the left hand column. Fig 11.34. Click on this and it will open the report for the latest week.

CURRENT LEGACY REPORTS:				
	Futures Only		**Futures-and-Options-Combined**	
			Long Format	Short Format
Chicago Board of Trade	Long Format	Short Format	Long Format	Short Format
Chicago Mercantile Exchange	Long Format	Short Format	Long Format	Short Format
Chicago Board Options Exchange	Long Format	Short Format	Long Format	Short Format
Chicago Climate Futures Exchange	Long Format			
Kansas City Board of Trade	Long Format			
Minneapolis Grain Exchange	Long Format			
Commodity Exchange Incorporated	Long Format	Short Format	Long Format	Short Format
ICE Futures U.S.	Long Format	Short Format	Long Format	Short Format
ICE Futures Europe	Long Format	Short Format	Long Format	Short Format
ICE – Futures Energy	Long Format	Short Format	Long Format	Short Format
New York Mercantile Exchange	Long Format	Short Format	Long Format	Short Format
NYSE Liffe	Long Format	Short Format	Long Format	Short Format
New York Portfolio Clearing	Long Format	Short Format	Long Format	Short Format
Supplemental Commodity Index			CIT Report	

Just look for the CME Long Format - ONLY

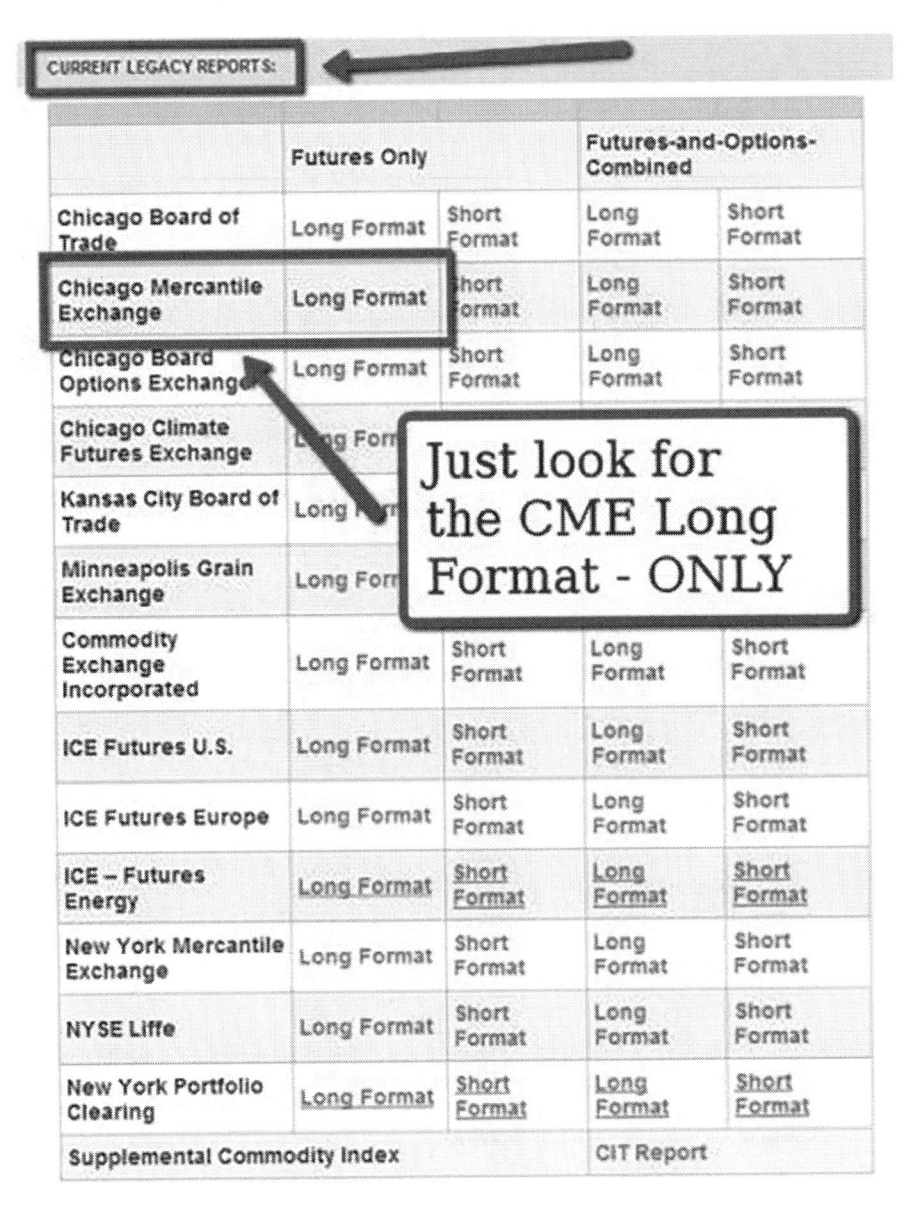

Fig 11.34

As you will see when you start to do this analysis for yourselves the report covers a wide range of commodities as well as currencies, and the CME report always starts with milk. As shown in Fig 11.35.

```
MILK, Class III - CHICAGO MERCANTILE EXCHANGE
Commitments of Traders - Futures Only, January 22, 2013
--------------------------------------------------------------------------
         :   Total    :                    Reportable Positions
         :------------:--------------------------------------------------
         :   Open     :        Non-Commercial        :    Commercial
         : Interest   :   Long  :  Short  : Spreading:   Long  :  Short   :
--------------------------------------------------------------------------
         :            : (CONTRACTS OF 200,000 POUNDS)
         :            :
All      :  19,909:     2,984      3,472       729     13,369    11,681
Old      :  19,909:     2,984      3,472       729     13,369    11,681
Other:          0:         0          0         0          0         0
```

Fig 11.35

Therefore, we need to scroll down the report in order to find the section on currencies. This section begins with the Russian ruble, followed by the Canadian dollar, Swiss franc, Mexican peso, British pound, the Japanese yen, the Euro, the Brazilian real, the New Zealand dollar, and finally a little further down the report comes the Australian dollar.

Let's take a closer look at one of these reports before moving on to how to find the other data we need on the same site.

In this case I've taken the Australian Dollar (Fig 11.36) as an example, but all the other currencies will be presented in exactly the same way. I apologise for the poor quality of the image, but this is taken directly from the CFTC site where as you will see, the quality of text is poor.

```
AUSTRALIAN DOLLAR - CHICAGO MERCANTILE EXCHANGE          AUD on the CME
Commitments of Traders - Futures Only, January 22, 2013  for 22/01/13
--------------------------------------------------------------------------
         :   Total    :   Total open interest    Reportable Positions
         :------------:--------------------------------------------------
         :   Open     :        Non-Commercial        :    Commercial
         : Interest   :   Long  :  Short  : Spreading:   Long  :  Short   :
--------------------------------------------------------------------------
         :            : (CONTRACTS OF AUD 100,000)
         :            :
All      : 208,776:    143,776    46,765       618     21,291   141,610
Old      : 208,776:    143,776    46,765       618     21,291   141,610
Other:          0:         0          0         0          0         0
```

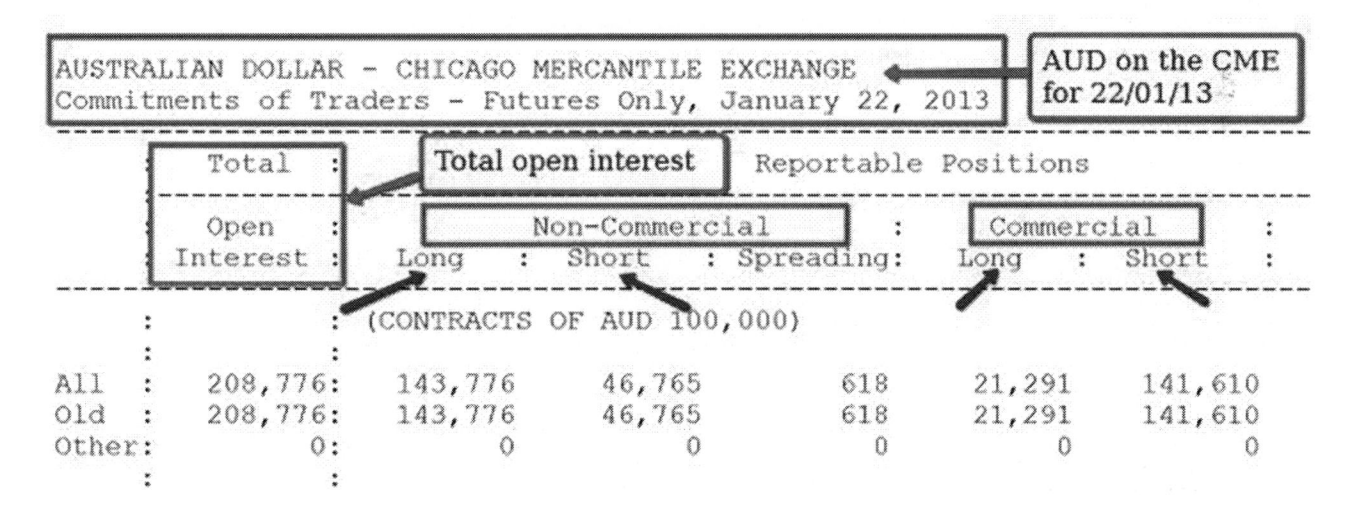

Fig 11.36 Australian dollar

The top line tells us it is the report for the Australian Dollar and the CME and below we can see we are looking at the futures only for the date.

The first piece of data we want to focus on is on the left hand side of the table, and in the second column where we have the word **Total**. Immediately below its says **Open Interest**.

What we are looking at here is the total number of futures contracts on the Australian Dollar which were open when the data was recorded the previous Tuesday. Open interest simply means contracts that are open or live.

In this case we can see that on the 22nd January 2013 there were **208,776** open interest contracts on the Australian Dollar at the CME on this date. Immediately to the right of the words 'open interest' we have two headings. The first says **non commercial** and the second **commercial** and beneath these headings we have the words 'long' and 'short'.

Please **IGNORE** the heading entitled 'spreading'.

Below the long and short headings are the numbers, and in this case we have **143,776** and **46,765** for the non commercial, and **21,291** and **141,610** for the commercial respectively.

The terms 'Commercial' and 'Non Commercial' refer to the broad class of futures traders, with non commercial simply meaning those large speculators and commercial hedge funds who hold positions in the futures market for themselves or their clients.

The commercial group would be the banks who are holding positions for their clients, generally as a hedge against future currency transfers for goods and services and therefore not buying or selling as a speculative trader. They are there simply to hedge their clients against currency risk. For me, this latter group is of no interest, as the contracts have been placed with a neutral view of the market and with no bias whatsoever.

Finally, on this line we also have the 'non reportable' grouping which is the small retail traders who are generally wrong and are sometimes used as a contrarian indicator as a result.

In my opinion the only group to watch is the non commercial group as this is the group that buys and sells on a purely speculative basis. These are large professional groups trading large contract sizes.

Therefore, the only data that is of interest to us in each report and for each currency is as follows:

1. The Total for Open Interest which in this case is 208,776
2. The Non Commercial Long – in this case 143,776
3. The Non Commercial Short – in this case 46,765

These numbers on their own tell us very little, but the key point here is to compare them with the previous week's figures, and against the figures for the weeks further back. This exercise allows us to build up a picture of the changes, week by week.

The total open interest figure is telling us whether futures trading in the Australian dollar is rising or falling, in other words it is a measure of volume.

For example, if the Australian dollar is rising strongly on falling futures volumes, clearly this is an anomaly and we need to look elsewhere for an explanation.

Alternatively, we may see a large build up in open interest with very little price movement, possibly telling us the market is weak at this level.

This rise and fall in volume in the futures markets for the currency, will then be a function of our volume analysis on the chart.

Next we consider the difference between the long and the short position, which in this case would be 143,776 – 46,775. In other words, the market at the moment is heavily long the Australian dollar, net long 97,001 contracts. This is often the figure you will see reported in the financial press, where a currency is net long or net short. This is generally the figure being referenced

Over time you will start to build a weekly picture of this difference, which in turn will also tell you whether this is a high medium or low figure. In other words, where the currency is in relation to an extreme in the futures market. If the currency is strong and this is an extreme net difference, this could be signalling a turning point in the market. The same would be true at the bottom of the market where the difference would be net short.

Moreover, the reverse is also true. If the net difference is low there is no market bias, and the currency may be set for a period of consolidation. In other words, the professional money is neutral on the currency. However, once this starts to shift, either to the long side or the short side, this is signalling the sentiment of the professional money, information we would be foolish to ignore.

Therefore, each week we look at all our currencies and pick off the weekly figures to check two things. First, the sentiment for the currency as shown by the non commercials and, second whether there has been any significant shift in sentiment, as indicated by a shift in the net long or short position.

If there has been a significant shift from net long to net short, we ask ourselves – why? Then check our price charts and our other indicators for market sentiment and analysis. If there has been a shift from long to short, has net sentiment increased in one direction dramatically or stayed much the same? Again, we check our price charts to confirm.

Finally, is the open interest volume rising or falling and how does this compare to the price action on the chart? Does it confirm the price action or is there an anomaly?

For new traders this may seem a little overwhelming, but in fact all you are looking for is three numbers:

1. The total Open Interest
2. The Long numbers for the Non Commercial group
3. The Short numbers for the Non Commercial group

From there you simply do this for each currency and it's done. It takes a few minutes on a Friday evening as you wind down at the end of the week.

You will need to build up some historic data as you construct your own simple spreadsheet of figures and these can be found as follows:

Simply scroll back up the page, and in the left hand sidebar you will find a secondary menu below the first, with a tab called 'Historical Viewable' (Fig 11.37) . Click on this menu link and you will find the legacy reports going back several years.

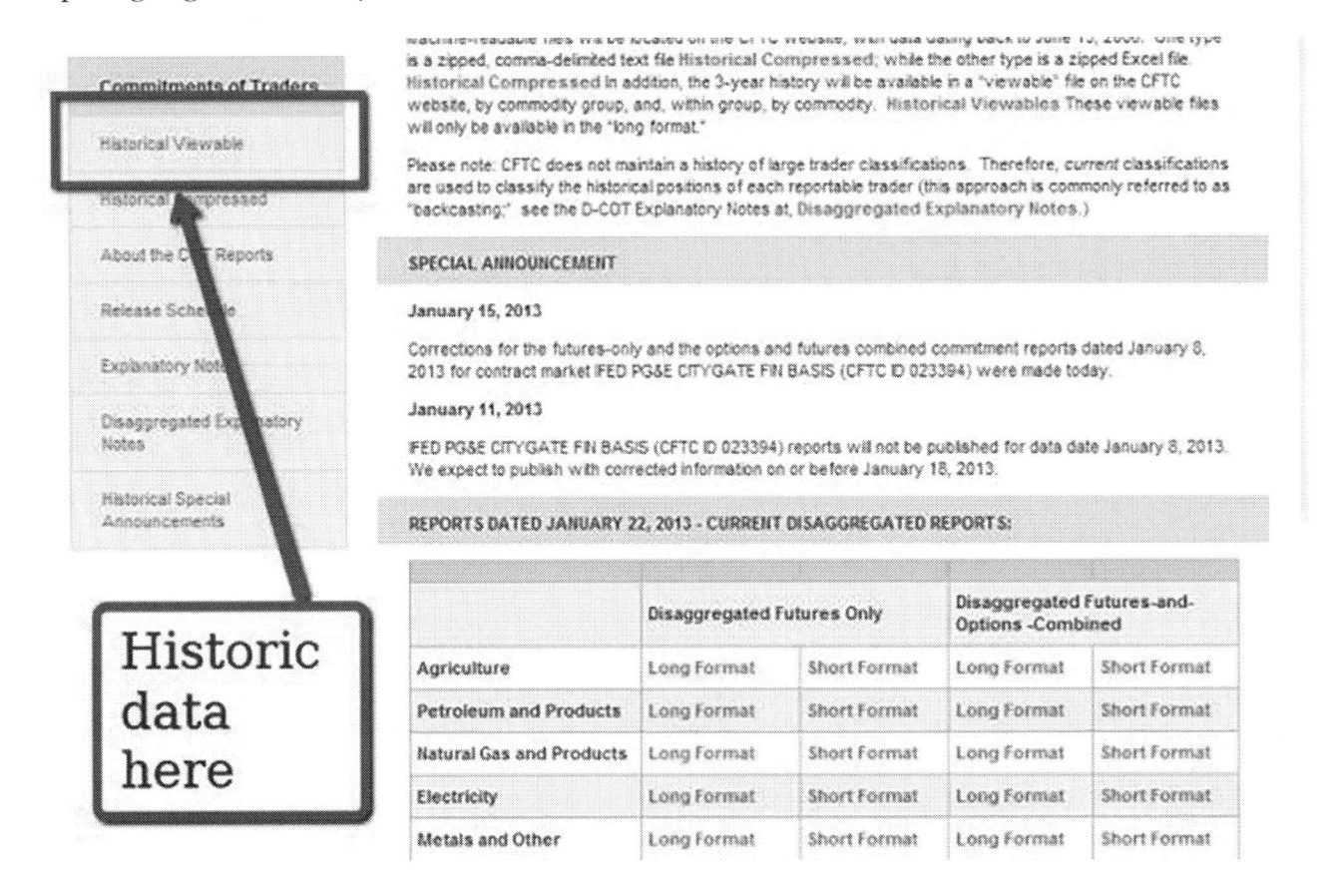

Fig 11.37

If you think this analysis is only for longer term traders, think again. What this data is giving you is market sentiment for a hugely influential group of traders. And if they are net long, then as an intraday trader, would it not be better to be trading with them or against them? Provided all your other analysis suggests the same.

I cannot stress this too strongly. Trading is all about quantifying risk, and if this simple piece of analysis helps to reduce the risk on a trade - great. For longer term traders it is self evident. This is a powerful item of data to use.

However, the COT report is far from perfect, and has many critics. These critics argue it is worthless as it is always out of date by at least 3 days. My own view is different.

I accept its imperfections and would never make any trading decisions based purely on what it is telling me. Rather, it is a simple piece of analysis which I do each week, as it builds into a longer term picture.

The COT report does not give buy and sell signals, but like many of the other techniques and principles I have explained in this chapter, provides a framework against which we can assess market sentiment.

With the COT report, with all its flaws, we at least have a mechanism for seeing the professional money flow in a pure market. Whether they are right or wrong is, of course, a point for debate.

Nevertheless, this is the professional money we are watching, and is more likely to be on the right side of the market than the small non reportable positions of the retail traders. However, this is a conclusion you have to reach yourself. All I can do here is put forward the case and explain how to find and use the information which I believe is relevant, to both intra day and longer term traders.

In the next section of the book we are going to move away from relational analysis and focus on the fundamentals and economics that drive the global economies and currency markets.

Chapter Twelve
The Fundamentals of Global Economies

Change is the investor's only certainty.

Thomas Rowe Price Jr (1898-1983)

In the first section of this book we considered many of the key relationships and secondary market linkages that reveal so much about sentiment, risk and money flow. And in the first few chapters I laid down the basis of the first strand to analysing market behaviour using relational techniques.

This was the first element of my three pillars to trading success based on using relational, fundamental and technical approaches which combine to form a powerful three dimensional view of the financial markets.

The second pillar I now want to examine, and present are the fundamentals of market economics, which provide the foundation of Central Bank and government policies. In addition in this chapter I also want to introduce the world's four powerhouse trading blocks.

These are China, the USA, Japan and finally Europe. In doing so this will provide the foundation to move on to the specific fundamental releases and consider each of these in turn and how they impact the markets. In the following chapters we are going to consider the global picture, the big picture if you like at the macro level, before moving to the micro level of country specific fundamental news releases and how they affect the currency markets.

I am going to start with China and the reason is simply that in the next decade, China is forecast to overtake the US as the world's largest economy. Therefore, as forex traders, we have to understand China, not least because the Chinese economy will slowly and surely begin to dictate world economic cycles, in much the same way as the US economy has done for much of the last century.

Furthermore, as China's growth continues, its economic impact will also increase. We do not have to look far for evidence of this already taking place. Five years ago you would have been hard put to find Chinese data in any economic calendar. Today every economic release is reported in detail. And the reason is because Chinese data now has the ability to move markets dramatically.

Some years ago it would have been solely the US. Now it is also China. A poor number from China can rock the markets, due to the impact this data has on world demand. No market escapes, and no country has more power at present to move every market with one economic release. This is the power of China at present. A feature for many years to come, and likely to be replicated in the emerging nations in due course.

When considering China it can be difficult to know where to start as the statistics are on a truly gargantuan scale. However, there is really only one thing you need to understand about this extraordinary country, which is that it operates its own brand of capitalism, often referred to as state run capitalism. This is the ultimate paradox of a communist country grappling with the apparent transition from that of a closed State run economy to one of a consumer orientated Western economy with all the problems this entails.

I use the word 'apparent' deliberately, since China is, and always will be, a communist country at its core for the simple reason it has no democracy, as power is transferred from one dynasty to another in a preordained way, laid down years in advance.

The latest group to gain control in 2012 are the so called Princelings, the children of communist revolutionaries who are now in line to to take over from the current leadership. While writing this book this has occurred with Xi Jinping installed as President for the next 10 years. However, his appointment was decided more than five years ago and merely consecrated by the country's ceremonial legislature. He was the only candidate for the role of President garnering 2952 votes of support from the National People's Congress. Although apparently there was one vote against him and three abstentions.

In addition to being President, Xi Jingping has also been appointed General Secretary of the Communist Party and Chairman of the Central Military Commission.

The question now is whether this regime change will see China return to greater state controls on the back of nostalgia for the Mao era. Or whether China continues with its capitalist model with a gradual move towards greater monetary liberalisation. Only time will tell.

The dramatic growth in China over the last few years has been fuelled for one reason, and one reason only. To ensure the political elite running the country keep the vast population employed, happy, and above all, under the illusion they are, to all intents and purposes, a Western economy.

At present, China's economy is approximately one third that of the US, but the gap is closing quickly, as its share of the global economy is expected to grow from 14 to 18 percent in the next five years, whilst the US share is expected to fall to 17.7%.

But the Chinese authorities are gambling, and in gambling they are likely to create exactly the same problems that saw the Japanese economy disintegrate in the early 1990's, and more recently, the virtual collapse of the world banking system in 2008 and onwards. And the catalyst for a repeat of these problems is cheap money. Precisely the same catalyst which caused so many problems for Japan and has been responsible for the current crisis.

In creating the feel good factor for the Chinese people, the Communist State has also created two further major problems which need to be resolved. And quickly if we are not to see yet another global crisis which would trigger a further deep recession.

The first problem is the credit bubble which has now been created, with cheap money. This has fuelled a housing boom as the population moves en masse from the country into ever expanding cities. To give you an idea of the scale, it is thought that over 500 hundred million people will migrate, leaving their once traditional farming communities to join the growing throng of city workers producing cheap goods for overseas markets.

However, with inflation now rising, and rising fast, cheap credit will cease and rising prices will start to bite deep into an economic bubble created on this mountain of debt. A mountain of debt which, it has to be said, has been gratefully embraced by the Chinese people, as the brave new face of a Western economy.

The second and, perhaps even bigger problem, is that of the economy itself, which is now so heavily dependent on exports.

The Chinese export market has been built on the simple concept of a cheap, plentiful and almost endless supply of workers.

To convert the Chinese economy from one based on manufacturing and export led, to a more balanced one based on increasing demand from the Chinese themselves is unlikely, if not impossible in the short or even medium term and the reasons are as follows.

Increases in labour costs will make Chinese goods uncompetitive in overseas markets and, in addition, as Japan knows all too well, when the home currency strengthens goods and services become more expensive for overseas buyers.

In other words, the Chinese authorities are now wrestling with the problem of attempting to rebalance the economy by giving economic power to a wider consumer class. The Central Government is targeting an increase in minimum wages of 13 percent per year until 2015 as well as increasing per capita household income by seven per cent per year in real terms.

Before the recent transfer of power ex-Premier Wen Jiabao had also pledged to improve social security and health care for lower income households, all in an effort to give the country's 1.3bn people greater spending power.

This is the goal. But no one has any idea of how it will be achieved, and this essentially highlights the dilemma for the Chinese authorities as they continue to cling to their core principles of communism, whilst attempting to embrace the new order of a Western economy.

Indeed the next few years could see dramatic repercussions in world markets, should the Chinese leaders fail to manage their economy correctly. But what does this mean for us as forex traders?

As I mentioned at the start of this chapter, it means China will dominate world economic events over the next few years in several key areas.

First, we have the yuan US dollar currency peg, which we have already examined in an earlier chapter, and is now being managed by the Chinese.

Second, is the continuing and ever increasing demand for base commodities, which is likely to drive future prices provided China's economic growth continues, with Australia one of the key trading partners likely to benefit the most from this demand. And the corollary is Australia is also likely to suffer the most in any slowdown. One reason why the Australian dollar is so closely linked to the Chinese bubble.

Third, we have the traditional loathing of the US by China which has fuelled the development of the BRICS, with China leading the way in establishing a series of closed trading relationship with these partners. China's goal? To conduct international business in the Chinese currency of the yuan, rather than the US dollar.

Finally, we have the issue of US Treasury debt, with the Chinese now holding in excess of $1.2 trillion in US treasuries, and with the FED continuing to print money at an alarming rate, China is rightly concerned over the value of this paper.

But how does all this play out on the global stage, and what do we need to consider when watching the latest fundamental news release for China? Also what do we need to consider during the latest round of talks between the US and China over unfair trade practices?

First and foremost to watch the monthly and quarterly releases of figures for the Trade Surplus, Consumer Price Index and Gross Domestic Product, (all of which will be explained in the section on the fundamentals) for the simple reason inflation in China is now rising, and rising fast.

If the Chinese economy crash lands, as some experts are predicting, we can forget any economic recovery in the short term, with the world being plunged into a deep double dip recession. This is the power of China and Chinese data which you simply cannot ignore or any of the major economic releases from China given their huge influence.

In 2010, China's inflation was already running at 5.5 percent, well ahead of virtually every other economy, with the Peoples Bank of China duly forced to raise interest rates on four successive occasions. Thus far this has failed to halt its upwards rise, and the economy is now beginning to overheat with money flowing into the country faster than it's flowing out, with the whole economy fuelled further by cheap credit.

The only way this credit flow will slow down is if the authorities are able to turn the ship around and rebalance the economy with imports and exports broadly matched, which seems highly unlikely at present. This can *only* be achieved if the Chinese achieve their goal of becoming an innovative technology led economy.

Currencies, of course, play a key role in achieving this goal. With the Chinese increasingly worried about the US policy of printing further US dollars, thereby potentially devaluing China's huge holding of US treasuries, a fact it makes perfectly clear in all its statements on US policy.

The US, for its part, makes it perfectly clear in its replies that the Chinese authorities are deliberately maintaining a weak currency in order to support their exports. No surprise, and a similar policy to virtually every other economy around the world at present. This is seen as undermining US jobs, and this aspect alone has the potential to develop into a dramatic and damaging trade war between the world's two largest economies.

The main economic goal for the US has not changed for the last few years, as the US continues in its attempts to force China to move faster in allowing the Chinese yuan to rise in value against the US dollar. This would make Chinese products more expensive in the US and in turn make US exports cheaper in China. It would also help to narrow the US trade deficit with China. The largest the US has with any country.

The ongoing currency issues between China and the US will continue to dominate for years to come, if and until the Chinese loosen their US dollar peg, or ultimately allow a free floating currency, which is unlikely at present.

Moving away from currencies, commodities will also play a pivotal role in the next decade, and any commodity trade war is also likely to emanate from China. This has already begun with rare earth metals, of which China controls around 95% of the world's supply. Although rare earth metals are in fact quite abundant, China is the only place that currently has the capability to produce them in large quantities. These are the metals you would not recognise immediately, yet they are crucial in the future development of many technology and green products such as high power batteries for cars, solar panels and alternative energies.

In a deliberate attempt to manipulate prices China reduced its rare earth export quota by 75% in 2010, which sent prices soaring and sparking a war of words between China and Japan as a result. China followed up this action with an export tariff which added between fifteen and twenty five percent to the already inflated prices.

Whilst China controls its own commodities closely, it is also a major importer from Australia, its fifth largest trading partner. China imports over forty percent of Australia's iron ore as well as being a major importer of coal.

This key relationship is one we will cover in detail when we look at the Australian dollar in the next section of the book and the effect China has on this particular currency.

If we had to sum up China in one word, that word would be, control, which takes us back to where we started, with the Communist authorities desperate to control their people, their economy, their currency and their supply of raw materials.

It is almost inevitable that, at some point, one of these factors will trigger a breakdown in control, with a consequent tsunami in the currency markets as a result. The bottom line is China is big and getting bigger every year, and its growth can no longer be ignored, especially given its long term investment potential if, and it's a big if, it is able to avoid an economic trauma in the next five years. If it does, ultimately it will overtake the US as the worlds largest economy.

In the short term, not only do we have to understand the importance of the country, but also the underlying psyche of the Chinese authorities, as they wrestle with their communist roots in an increasingly Westernised economy. And, ironically this could be their ultimate downfall.

I hope in this short introduction to China, I have given you a thumbnail of this fascinating and increasingly important country. Make no mistake, the fundamental news and economic picture of China will dominate the currency markets for years to come, and to make sense of the market reactions to any news you have to understand a little of its background and history, which I've covered here.

USA

If China is Emperor Elect, the USA still sits on the throne. And to understand the US dollar it's not only essential but also fundamental you understand a little of the US economy and how it works. This will give you a complete understanding of the currency of first reserve. Unless and until it is replaced by the Chinese yuan or even the euro.

To understand the US economy, you also have to understand the role of the Federal Reserve which is the central bank of the USA, and though many speak and write about the US economy, few understand how the FED really works.

In this short introduction, I'm going to try, once again, to give you a thumbnail sketch of the worlds largest economy. And here I would like to begin with the Federal Reserve which many people mistakenly believe is part of the US government. In fact, it is not and never has been.

The Federal Reserve is an independent bank created as a private corporation. It is in effect a cartel of private banks of which the Bank of New York is the most powerful and influential.

If this comes as a surprise, it certainly is to most forex traders. But let's just think about the logic of this. The US economy, which is the world's largest, is effectively controlled by one private organisation owned by a handful of the worlds largest banks. This is why in 1916, three years after its inception, the then President of the United States, Woodrow Wilson, denounced the Federal Reserve in the following terms:

'I am a most unhappy man', *he said.*

'I have unwittingly ruined my country. A great industrial nation is controlled by its system of credit. Our system of credit is concentrated. The growth of the nation therefore, and all our activities are in the hands of a few men. We have come to be one of the worst ruled one of the most completely controlled and dominated governments in the civilised world.

No longer a government by free opinion, no longer a government by conviction and the vote of the majority, but a government by the opinion and duress of a small group of dominant men'.

Remember, this is the President of the United States writing at the time following the creation of the Federal Reserve. In effect an institutionalised monopoly of the US dollar, which was created in 1913 by the United States Government. With the creation of the Federal Reserve the Government gave up its right to coin money, and so regulate its value. Instead it passed this right to a private corporation owned by the Federal Reserve.

This single move resulted in the massive accumulation of wealth by a small number of people, companies and corporations whose combined power gave them almost total control over both the US and world economy. And this has continued to the present day.

The Federal Reserve controls the US economy by virtue of the rights bestowed upon it in 1913. And with its immense power, controls the lives of every American citizen living and working in the United States. Therefore, the largest economy in the world is, in fact, run by the Federal Reserve Bank of New York, the most powerful and profitable bank in the world.

You may be wondering how on earth the largest economy in the world is now run by a group of private banks operating as a cartel. The answer is simple, but we have to step back to the turn of the nineteenth century to find the answer.

At the time, pressure was building for a US central bank to provide some stability to an increasingly unstable US dollar. The President, Theodore Roosevelt was also petitioned and the leading banks of the day decided to support this idea, but they had a separate and clear private agenda.

This agenda was to ensure any central bank would be run by the private banks. It was therefore no surprise when the commission was set up to consider the options, the chairman was none other than senator Nelson Aldrich, a high profile banker whose daughter was married to John D Rockefeller Jr. His grandson became Governor of New York and Gerald Ford's Vice President.

His great grandson John Davidson Rockefeller IV, became Senator of West Virginia in 1985.

When the commission duly reported, it decided to name the central bank the 'Federal Reserve' in part to hide its real identity, but also because the term 'central bank' was not a popular one. This arrangement was given an air of respectability by placing it under the supposed control of a board appointed by the US

President, who was also responsible for appointing the chairman for a fourteen year term. A policy that has remained in place to this day.

The Board of Governors of the Federal Reserve is a seven member group. Each of the governors is appointed by the President and the appointment has to be confirmed by the Senate. Once appointed each member serves a fourteen year term. The banks which make up the Federal Reserve are divided across the US into twelve 'districts', each of which has its own Federal Reserve Bank which is responsible for overseeing member banks in its district.

Finally we come to the FOMC or Federal Open Market Committee, a euphemism if ever there was one, which is the group responsible for determining the Fed Funds rate and interest rate decisions.

This group consists of twelve members. Seven are from the Board of Governors, four are rotated from the district Federal Banks, and one is a permanent position. No prizes for guessing who holds the permanent position. This position is always held by the President of the Federal Reserve Bank of New York.

This is the composition of the most powerful financial cartel in the world. It meets eight times a year to decide the fate of the US, and by default the global economy.

To date the FED's most notorious contribution to world economic history came during the Wall Street crash and the Great Depression of the nineteen twenties and early nineteen thirties. The events leading up to the Great Depression have many parallels to the ones of the last few years. And could also be likened to China's current dilemma with cheap credit creating a debt bubble.

This was essentially the root cause of the Wall Street crash, with cheap money flowing into equity markets. When the inevitable bubble finally imploded it resulted in the Great Depression.

The response from the Federal Reserve was to do nothing. It simply sat back and watched.

The greed which had fuelled the debt bubble was ultimately paid for by the borrowers. It was they who bore the brunt. Banks which had been eager to lend simply foreclosed picking up property and assets at bargain prices.

You might ask why I have included this background in this book, and you may also think I am anti the banks. I am not. The reason for explaining this is, first to make you aware the FED is not what you think. Second, I am not suggesting the Federal banks manipulate the economy to meet their own ends, this would be too obvious, but any organisation set up in this way can only have one ultimate aim. And that is its own, and its members' self interest.

This knowledge will also make you realise most of what is presented in the financial press and elsewhere is largely rubbish. The press has little understanding or interest in history, and little time to present anything other than headline numbers – a headline for a headline sake, before it moves on to the next topic.

In many ways, this is akin to how the market makers operate in the equity markets, as they push and pull the market around according to the news flow which allows them to further cement their direct influence over the market.

As you read this book I want you to understand the motivation of the key players, of which the Federal Reserve is the biggest. If you understand their agenda, at least you will be able to make more sense of their regular statements and releases. You will be able to read between the lines looking for the clues as to what they are actually thinking, rather than what they are saying.

It is ironic to think the two largest economies in the world are run by just a handful of people, both with similar agendas. In the case of China it is the elite of the Communist party who are desperate to retain control and whose greatest fear is social unrest and public protests.

In the US it is the elite of a banking cartel who are equally desperate to retain control.

Enough of history as we now examine what the FED has been up to in the latest financial crisis, a crisis of its own making and which started under the chairmanship of Alan Greenspan.

Once again this crisis has its roots in cheap money with loans and mortgages given to all and sundry. The only criteria for qualifying for a loan appeared to be having a pulse. This led directly to the housing market bubble and its subsequent collapse and it was left to Ben Bernanke, followed by Janet Yellen, to clear up the mess.

Bernanke's solution was to create even bigger bubbles in other asset classes, such as in commodities along with the continued and unrelenting creation of bonds and consequent weakening of the US dollar.

However, times are changing for the Federal Reserve, with many now starting to openly question the institution itself, as it is increasingly seen as insular, secretive, self interested, and self motivated with little or no interest in the lives of the average US citizen or indeed anyone else.

Evan as the crisis subsides, the pain of the recent financial crisis continues to bite deep into the American psyche, many are now waking up to the realisation the FED is no better, if not worse than all the banks it represents.

In response to a rising tide of criticism and outright hostility which now threatens this private organisation, on Wednesday the 27th April 2011, the Federal Reserve took the unprecedented step of issuing its first press release, something it had never done before in its ninety seven year history.

As the FED declines in popularity, so the international community continues to press for a replacement for the currency of first reserve, as the global financial system continues to stagger from crisis to crisis with the US dollar and the FED at the heart of the problem. A currency, after all, that is derived from a country with negative real interest rates, negative savings rates and a dubious commitment to price stability.

If you recall when we looked at the US dollar and the Bretton Woods agreement which saw currencies pegged to gold, the reality was currencies were in fact pegged to the dollar, since it was only foreign central banks who were able to convert their dollars into gold.

Following the collapse of the agreement many expected this to signal the demise of the dollar as a reserve currency. In fact the reverse occurred and it wasn't long before the share of foreign reserves in dollars actually increased during the 1970's, with currency instability during the Asian crisis in 1997 increasing demand for the dollar, as a result.

Today, the percentage of reserves held in dollars is greater than under Bretton Woods and there are now more than 50 countries pegged to the dollar. So what does all this mean for the US economy and the Federal Reserve?

The best quote came from the French president in the late 1960's who said:

"the trouble is that America has abused this exorbitant privilege".

Which has given the US and the US economy a free lunch if you like with over 500 billion US dollars in circulation outside the country.

Strong demand for US assets has resulted in lower long term rates whilst America also earns a higher rate of return on its overseas assets than it pays to foreign holders of US assets. In turn this strong demand has allowed the US to run massive trade deficits, with lower long term rates helping to fuel the credit bubble and weaken the economy further. The FED's response to the current crisis, like many others, is to print further dollars in an effort to kick start the economy back to life.

Ironically this recent and artificially created weakness in the dollar, coupled with ultra low interest rates, has created further demand for dollar denominated assets, some of which has come from the many dollar pegged countries who have been forced to buy dollars in order to prevent their own currencies appreciating.

In addition, since the collapse of Lehman Brothers, global foreign exchange reserves have increased by over forty percent adding further demand for dollar denominated securities.

Across Asia, many countries are now exhibiting the first signs of a housing bubble. Credit growth in countries such as India, Indonesia, Hong Kong, Thailand and China are all growing at an increasingly fast pace, with some markets now expanding at twenty per cent per annum. Finally, in Latin America foreign exchange reserves are exploding along with strong credit growth, and it therefore comes as no surprise the calls for the Federal Reserve to be replaced are increasing, not only in the US but from around the globe, as the US dollar and its privileged position are likely to wreak a further round of economic havoc.

But the beneficiaries once again.....the banking cartel which sits at the heart of the US economy, the Federal Reserve Bank of America.

Perhaps you can now begin to understand and appreciate the mistrust and dislike beginning to build globally towards the FED and the US authorities. As with its twin privileges of holding the currency of first reserve, coupled with its unique position as a global banking cartel, it is able to both create and destroy, governments, currencies and economies all from its base in New York.

Whether the FED survives, remains to be seen. However, one thing is for sure, the US economy will always be at the mercy of, and dictated to, by the actions of the Federal Reserve. As forex traders this is what we have to understand.

We have to recognise the FED and its agenda for what it is. Then interpret its decisions and future statements with this knowledge clear in our minds. Only then can we begin to understand the logic, the rationale of the Federal Reserve and why the US economy, the US dollar and the Federal Reserve are so inextricably interlinked as a result.

I hope it has made you realise the financial markets can be a very unethical world. The FED is perhaps one of the worst examples, but there are many others. What many find so objectionable is the thin veneer of credibility the FED is given by appearing to be a governmental or quasi governmental body, with responsibility for monetary and economic policy. Sadly, nothing could be further from the truth.

JAPAN

So where does Japan fit into all this as the world's third largest economy, having only recently been surpassed by China? And to understand Japan we need to understand its economy, the Bank of Japan, the Japanese Yen, and the lessons of the so called lost decade when the miracle of its post war revival all came to a shuddering halt.

Up until the second half of the nineteenth century, Japan's economy was largely agricultural. Japan only developed into an industrial nation in the first decade of the twentieth century, thereby enabling it to emerge as an expanding global power in the 1930's, before war destroyed virtually all of its industrial base.

Following support from the US during the post war occupation, Japan slowly restored its free enterprise economy, expanding dramatically and developing quickly as an innovative, technology led economy in much the same way that China is now looking to replicate.

Indeed, there are many similarities, with a workforce quickly migrating from agriculture to industry and developing innovative products. Japan has a highly skilled and educated workforce, all underpinned by an ethic of hard work.

This ethic led to Japan dominating the world as an export driven economy, with cars and technology leading the way. Whilst exports were, and still remain, the driving force of the economy, imports are the Achilles heel for Japan. Virtually everything from food to raw materials and base commodities has to be imported, given the almost complete lack of space and any natural resources with which to fuel economic growth.

As you would expect, all the major commodity producers are only too well aware of this fact, and whilst countries such as Australia and Canada are happy to benefit accordingly, China takes a different view, jealously protecting its own vast resources, and manipulating prices accordingly.

Japan's annual GDP remained steady from the mid 1950's until the 1970's, resulting in Japan often being referred to as an economic miracle, having risen in a quarter of a century from the ashes of a world war to become the second largest economy in the world by the 1980's.

This decade was one of unparalleled prosperity for the Japanese, characterised by opulence, corruption, extravagance and waste.

The economic expansion was also fuelled by cheap money leading to house prices rising alarmingly resulting in a housing market bubble.

Personal spending soared out of control, sending the Nikkei 225 to an all time high of just below 40,000 at 39,915 on the 29th December 1989, with Japanese companies embarking on a wild spending spree as the weak dollar made foreign assets cheap. Everything had a price, including the Rockefeller Centre in New York.

If all this sounds familiar, then it should. However, the simple truth is everyone forgets and the same will apply to the current crisis, which will dim with memory, as the banks look for innovative ways to make money once more from an ever gullible public.

The Japanese party had to come to an end and did so in spectacular fashion early in 1990, leading to what has been called the lost decade. This extended from 1990 until early in the new millennium, with the Nikkei plunging in value as investors panicked, and banks teetered on collapse, only surviving with intervention from the Bank of Japan and taxpayers money.

The housing bubble duly burst, companies went bust, credit dried up and the Japanese people stopped spending. The carnage lasted for over ten years, despite the Bank of Japan pumping trillions of yen into the system in increasingly futile attempts to stimulate the economy, with interest rates reduced to zero.

A recovery was only triggered, as a result of the dramatic growth in its near neighbour China.

But what were the causes, what are the changes that have been triggered, and what is the situation in Japan now?

Most economic historians agree the foundation for this disaster was laid in September 1985, when Japan and five other nations signed the Plaza Accord in New York.

This was an agreement that called for a depreciation of the US dollar against the Japanese yen in an effort to increase US exports by making them cheaper.

Unfortunately, it had the opposite effect, and Japanese companies went on a buying spree overseas. At the same time, the cheap US dollar coincided with dramatic growth in the Japanese economy.

With the Japanese, having substantial and unparalleled levels of disposable income, the Bank of Japan simultaneously lowered interest rates from five percent in 1985 to two and a half percent in 1987 with the banks jumping onto the credit bandwagon and offering cheap loans to anyone and everyone.

The country went on a massive spending spree buying anything and everything they could. Prices soared accordingly while the banks never stopped to wonder how all this debt would be repaid. For many, it was one long party with the Imperial Palace at one point reported to be worth more than the entire state of California. Then the party ended with a bang from which Japan is only just starting to recover, almost thirty years later.

What are the legacies of the lost decade and what has been its longer term impact on the people, the currency, and the economy?

In the aftermath of the crisis, political attention and pressure focused on the Ministry of Finance. However, in an attempt to deflect criticism and blame for the crash it was the Bank of Japan (BOJ) which was offered as the scapegoat for reform.

The bank was given more independence. Prior to this, the Bank of Japan under the 1942 Bank of Japan law, had been placed under the supervision of the Finance Minister, who had the power to order the bank to act according to any instructions it issued or conversely, did not issue.

In other words the bank had very little power to act on its own account. It was essentially simply taking instructions from the Finance Minster who had instructed the bank at the height of the crisis to reduce interest rates, as the threat of a slowdown and possible recession loomed.

Some commentators have suggested the bank took this action on its own, worried about an increasingly strong yen, something we will come to in a minute, and an increasingly weak dollar.

Whichever is true, the Bank of Japan was finally granted independence from the Finance Ministry in 1997 with responsibility for monetary policy, issuing bank notes, and the management of a stable economy.

As a result of these actions is this bank truly independent? The answer, I am afraid is not, it is not, and never will be, as the BOJ always buckles to political pressures exerted by either the Finance Ministry or the public. All remember the dark days of the lost decade which heaped so much shame on the nation and brought the economic miracle to an abrupt end.

Exports are the life blood of the Japanese economy, and in the last decade the Japanese Yen has been strengthening against the US dollar moving from an all time high of 263.12 in 1984, to an all time low in of 76.67 in 2011. A strong yen makes exports increasingly expensive for overseas buyers, creating the possibility of a fall in demand for Japanese products with a consequent slide into recession.

As a result the Bank of Japan is always acutely aware of the yen exchange rate, particularly against the US dollar and is therefore openly supportive of its currency. It is the most interventionist of all the central banks, stepping in to support the currency when it feels adverse pressures are being applied to artificially weaken the yen.

These interventions rarely succeed in turning the tide or reversing the trend of the market and simply result in a short term change in direction for the currency. Furthermore, these interventions are often perceived by the markets as a political response by the bank, as it bows to pressure from the Finance Ministry and the Government.

One of the classic examples of this came in 2007 when the bank, having set up the markets for the second instalment of an interest rates rise, the BOJ buckled under political pressure and instead elected to keep the rate unchanged at 0.25%.

Independence for the Bank of Japan does not mean political independence, and political pressure has continued to increase on the bank in the last few years as the US policy of artificially weakening the dollar has impacted the Japanese yen further. This has prompted the Japanese to add their own voice to the growing demands globally for an alternative currency.

In the case of Japan, the relationship of the yen to the dollar is crucial to their longer term recovery, and a return to more normal economic conditions, making the BOJ extremely sensitive to any external pressures which are seen as anti competitive or anti trade.

Moreover, the BOJ bank has a further problem with its dollar dependency.

Japan is hugely dependent on importing all its raw materials and commodities which are priced in dollars. Rising raw material and commodity prices, mean rising inflation and increasing costs of production, which in turn are likely to lead to a fall in exports. So, once again the BOJ is extremely sensitive to rising commodity prices which have been on a long bull run for some time, partly as a result of the artificially weak dollar created by our old friend the FED.

This in turn has made the yen very sensitive to rising commodity prices and, in particular, the price of oil. Rising oil prices will generally be bad news for the Japanese yen and vice versa, which is one reason why the CAD/JPY is an excellent pair to view against the price of crude oil. Stronger oil prices are generally reflected in Canadian Dollar, and with Japan being a net importer of oil, along with other commodities, the pair correlate relatively closely with the price of crude oil.

To complete our brief look at the Japanese economy and its impact and relationship with the yen, we also need to look briefly at two other peculiarities.

The first is how Japanese companies invoice their goods and services and their accounting periods. And the second is the carry trade, which continues to remain popular owing to the interest rate differential with Japan's remaining ultra low since the bursting of the economic bubble in the early 1990's.

The first of these issues concerns the way Japanese exporters invoice their goods, which is odd to say the least. Most large companies do not invoice in yen, as you might expect, but in fact in the currency of the country of delivery.

For example, where a Japanese company is delivering to the US markets it will generally invoice in US dollars, even if those goods are manufactured outside of Japan rather than yen, or euros or pounds, in effect taking on currency risk as part of the invoicing procedure.

This is a further reason why the BOJ keeps a constant watch on the foreign exchange markets, and intervenes so often. Clearly, if these companies are receiving foreign currency, at some point they have to sell these currencies and convert them back into Japanese Yen. In other words buy the yen and, this is something we often forget as forex traders. The forex market is where real companies have to exchange real money in the markets every single day.

However, with these monolithic Japanese organisations, the volumes are huge and easily capable of moving the exchange rates on their own, further adding to the problem of a strengthening yen, particularly against major export countries such as the US and Europe.

Why do Japanese companies work in this way? In many ways it is cultural. However, it is also an effort to control the currency risk as each year budgets are set for an exchange rate against various currencies, particularly against the US dollar. These budgets are monitored on a half yearly basis and amended accordingly.

In 2010, for example, most large corporations such as Honda and Toyota set their half year targets at Y85 to the dollar which was adjusted later in the year to Y80. What happens is that as the exchange rate approaches these levels, the accumulated reserves of dollars and other principle currencies are sold and yen repatriated.

As forex traders this is important to understand and goes some way to explaining the long term down trend for the yen against most major currencies. To put this into very basic terms. If the Japanese economy is booming, exports will be rising and the inflow of major currencies will be increasing dramatically, which at some point will have to be converted back to yen, strengthening the currency accordingly.

This is one reason why the USD/JPY pair has been falling for many years, and particularly since the recovery from the lost decade.

As well as the currency flows caused by this curious invoicing procedure which is partly historical and partly tradition, there is yet another factor which affects the yen dramatically at certain times of the year as a result of Japan's export led economy, and this is called repatriation.

This occurs twice a year causing spikes in late summer, generally between August and September, just prior to the accounting half year end on September 30th. This effect is then repeated between February and March leading up to the fiscal year end on March 31st.

The primary reason this is done is as window dressing on the company balance sheet, but also for tax reasons. These periods are also characterised by market volatility as major currencies are sold and yen bought, repatriating the income back to the home currency of the yen. This results in relatively predictable movements in the exchange rates.

Those traders who understand the reasons are happy to trade accordingly. The Japanese are creatures of habit, discipline and procedure and these events occur year in, year out as a result. Therefore, if you are trading the major yen based pairs at these well defined times of the year, expect to see this price action develop.

Finally, to round off this section on Japan and its unique economy, there are two other factors that play out in the currency and the economy.

These are the well known carry trade, and the yen as a safe haven status currency. The first of these I will explain in more detail when we look at the yen currency pairs, but in simple terms this trade has been created by virtue of Japan's ultra low interest rates, allowing traders and investors to benefit from the interest rate differential between the low interest rate of the yen against a higher bearing currency such as the New Zealand dollar or the Australian dollar.

The final aspect of the yen is its status as a safe haven currency which places it in direct competition to the US dollar in this respect. However, given the parlous state of the Japanese economy over the last two decades you may well be wondering why. And again the answer lies in the carry trade.

When the carry trade is in favour, traders are selling yen and buying higher yielding currencies as they take on this risky trade. If we put the 'risk' element to one side, just like a rise in equities, traders are feeling confident. So selling the Japanese yen becomes a sign of confidence. Money flow is out of the yen and into other assets and currencies.

However, when these same traders and investors begin to panic and start unwinding their positions, they begin buying the yen and selling the counter party currencies and risk instruments, so the yen is perceived as a safe haven, but not in quite the same way as the US dollar.

The 'safe haven' is the result of carry trade speculators wanting to reduce risk and close their positions. This is a subtle but important difference, and is what makes trading the USD/JPY such a difficult pair. Traders are faced with the Bank of Japan, the peculiarities of the Japanese invoicing system, the carry trade, and the 'safe haven' status of the Japanese yen. This is counterbalanced by the US dollar on the other side which in itself is the ultimate safe haven currency.

In the current environment of global ultra low interest rates, even the US dollar has been considered to be a funding currency for the carry trade, adding a further layer of complication to this most complex of countries and currencies, although this is changing as US interest rates begin to rise.

This is Japan and I hope you are beginning to appreciate the complexity behind the yen, and, as a result why it can be a very tricky currency trade without the knowledge I have outlined here.

EUROPE

Where do we start? And perhaps the most obvious place is at the end, rather than the beginning, by starting with the euro, the most recent addition to the world order of currencies.

However, before proceeding, remember this statement throughout the remainder of this chapter.

All currencies, no matter wherever they are in the world, must have three central tenets to survive. These tenets underpin all aspects of the currency, and for a currency to be viable it ***must have all three***.

These three tenets are:

- political union
- economic union
- monetary union

In the case of the euro, it has only one of these, namely monetary union, and in the history of money, no currency has ever survived in the long run without having all these three basic and fundamental principles in place.

Longer term therefore, the euro is unlikely to survive unless the other two tenets are put into place. It is as simple as that, so for the time being the euro is simply a monetary union of expediency, with no immediate prospect of ever achieving political or economic union.

In a political union there is a central budget and a pot of money accessible in times of crisis. This mechanism is completely absent in the case of the euro. Instead, when a crisis starts individual governments first begin arguing, apportioning blame, with all the old grudges, animosities and political in fighting coming to the fore. In addition, and adding to the above problems, there is a fundamental contradiction at the heart of the euro which is simply this.

Whilst the Eurozone (euro) has a Central Bank in the form of the ECB (European Central Bank), each member state has its own Central Bank and is free to set its own monetary policy accordingly, ignoring any fiscal rules as each follows their own path driven by their own tax and spending plans.

This makes it impossible to impose fiscal discipline on a rag bag of unruly member states created in one union and motivated purely by politics.

In short, the euro is a currency looking for a state, unlike the yuan which is a currency with too much state, and indeed even the profoundly uninspiring, unelected and incredibly un-dynamic President of Europe, Herman Von Rompuy, was forced to admit in a recent statement:

"we are clearly confronted with a tension within the system. The dilemma of being a monetary union and not a fully fledged economic and political union"

This tension has been there since the single currency was created. Some would say it was deliberately created this way, and at the time of its creation the general public was not really made aware of these crucial flaws.

Therefore, how has the Eurozone arrived at this sorry situation? A Eurozone now mired in political in fighting, as the euro project stumbles and stutters from one crisis to another. The short answer is given the lessons from Japan, the euro crisis looks set to continue to stumble and stutter for many years to come as one country after another teeters on the brink of collapse. Financial bankruptcy has only been avoided by the intervention of the European Central Bank, whose president was famously quoted as saying

"Within our mandate, the ECB is ready to do whatever it takes to preserve the Euro – and believe me, it will be enough"

Thus far, it has been enough to prevent a collapse of the euro, and prevent the exit of some of its high profile casualties such as Greece, Spain, Italy Portugal and Ireland. But for how much longer and at what price?

As always, it is easier to understand if we take a step back, and look at the key stages in the creation of the European state, its roots, the collapse of communism, and what this all means for the future both economically and politically. And for the single currency which sits at its heart.

The European Union really began life following the second world war, and was in fact a treaty designed to provide the framework for an economic recovery around the core industries of coal and steel as the shattered and war torn countries of Europe attempted to rebuild their infrastructures and economies.

The original treaty signed in 1951 was called the European Coal and Steel Community or ECSC, with the six founder members of Belgium, West Germany, Luxembourg, France, Italy and the Netherlands, and in 1957 these six countries duly signed the Treaty of Rome.

This, in effect, was the creation of the European Economic Community or the EEC, along with the curiously named Atomic Energy Community, all of which had been created in an attempt to remove trade barriers and form a 'common market'.

The three institutions of the EEC, the AEC and the original ECSC, were ultimately merged in 1967 creating a single commission and a single council of ministers. The first assembly met in Strasbourg on the 19th March 1958 as the European Parliamentary Assembly and changed its name to the European Parliament on 30th March 1962, but it was not until 1979 the first direct elections were held to appoint members directly using the novel and rather democratic system of a vote.

During the 1960's and early 1970's, the economy in Europe, boomed helped by the elimination of custom duties on trading between EEC member countries, and during this period the CAP or Common Agriculture Policy was also introduced. This was an agreement which had been designed to help poorer countries compete by providing food subsidies and aid.

However, the net result of the CAP was the creation of mountains of surplus food no one wanted including butter mountains, and wine lakes.

On the first of January 1973 three new members joined the EEC with the United Kingdom, Denmark and Ireland creating a union of nine members, followed during the late 1970's and 1980's by Greece, Spain and Portugal with the single European Act of 1987. This act attempted to harmonise laws and policies, effectively removing all the remaining trade barriers and thus creating the European single market which has since become the European Union.

The next major world event was the collapse of communism, symbolised by the removal of the Berlin wall separating East and West Germany, coupled with the collapse of the old Soviet Union. In 1993 the single market was completed creating one trading block with the free movement of goods, services, people and money between the various member states with the Treaty of Maastricht formally establishing the European Union.

In 1995 Austria, Finland and Sweden joined with only the Norwegians having the sense and foresight to tell the Europeans what to do with their project, rejecting EU membership with a resounding no vote.

Five years later in 1998 the most important piece of legislation was ushered in namely the Treaty of Amsterdam. And it was this treaty which established the ECB, the European Central Bank as the arbiter of monetary policy for EU member states, adding the final plank to this political monolith. With a 'so called' parliament and a 'Central Bank' the stranglehold on Europe was now complete.

The final nail in the coffin was the introduction of the euro on the 1st January 1999 which was released for public use on the 1st January 2002.

With the collapse of communism the clamour to join the European Union increased, with ten new countries joining in 2004, and a steady stream joining, which has taken the total to 27 at the time of writing.

Of the twenty seven member countries only seventeen currently use the euro, with notable exceptions being the United Kingdom, Denmark and Sweden who have all vetoed the currency in favour of retaining their own. Something which many other countries are wishing they had had both the wisdom and foresight to do.

There we have it. What started as a simple idea to foster trade in the EU has morphed into a rag bag coalition of disparate countries each with different agendas, cultures, objectives, and perhaps most importantly, long standing grudges.

Technically the EU is supposed to be led by the President of Europe, but in reality it is Germany with France who wield the power.

Other than giving you a brief history lesson on the creation of the European Union, what else can we learn about this trading block and, in particular, the fallout from the financial crisis that continues to reverberate around Europe and the euro?

The place to start is with the powerhouse of Europe which is Germany.

In the last twenty years, Germany has undergone two traumatic events. The first a massive downturn in the economy in the late 1990's. Second, and perhaps even more searing, was the unification between the East and West which caused mass unemployment, cultural change on an epic scale, and massive spending on infrastructure and welfare as the Germanys were reunited.

More remarkable, is following all these problems the German people were then able to regain the lost momentum with a return to economic prosperity, driven by a vibrant and powerful export market for its products and services. All very reminiscent of the Japanese recovery.

Given the above it is perhaps not surprising Germans feel little, or no sympathy for the plight of countries such as Greece, Spain or Portugal.

Germans believe they suffered the pain of reunification in silence, survived and recovered to become an even stronger nation as a result.

The cultural divide between Germany and these Club Med countries has never been wider and is what is causing so much friction and animosity. And here I write from personal experience. I am from Southern Europe myself. My parents left Italy to settle in the United Kingdom, so I understand both sides. However, the views I express here are my own and based on my own personal knowledge and experience.

Among the many differences between Germany and the Northern Europeans and the Latin Bloc is one of tax, or perhaps more specifically the attitude to tax collection. In general, Southern Europeans take a very different view of tax to their northern counterparts. Put simply, they will try to avoid paying it at any cost.

Southern Europeans are also seen as, how can I put this politely, not quite so hard working as their Northern friends. Hardly any wonder the Germans are less than enthusiastic when it comes to agreeing on any further bail outs for the Club Med group of countries.

The problem is these cultural differences are impossible to ignore when considering the EU as a whole. With more countries waiting to join the EU these differences will continue to cause friction. The cultural issues cover every facet of life, from working practices and family life to tax and the fundamental issues of saving and spending.

It has taken the recent financial crisis to shine a light on these differences and reveal in stark detail just how flawed the entire EU/euro concept has become. And the prospect of the euro replacing the dollar as the currency of first reserve is now risible.

Whilst the original aims of the European Union were laudable and honourable, as a treaty between nations to help one another after a long and destructive war, the project has long since descended into one of political nepotism, incompetence, fraud and above all a never ending gravy train for the incompetent and narcissistic. Polemic over.

However, as forex traders we cannot allow our prejudices to interfere with our judgement. Yes, we read about the problems in Europe. Yes, we read one of the member countries may reject the Euro and return to its home currency. Yes, we read the Euro will never replace the dollar, which is true. Yes, we read commentaries of how the Euro may one day die and be replaced.

But, there is one reason the Euro will survive, at least for the time being, and that is because its political lords and masters in Europe, **cannot**, indeed **will** not let it fail. There are simply too many egos and reputations at stake to allow this to happen. And, as I wrote earlier, it may be the originators of the project deliberately created the project in such a way to ensure its ultimate survival.

This current crisis may simply be the prelude to the imposition of the remaining tenets needed to create a solid, viable currency, namely political and economic union. But for the time being here are the words of Mario Draghi, current ECB President:

"People underestimate the amount of political capital that European leaders have invested in the Europe."

So, when the ECB president speaks, he will always be supportive and protective of the euro. Any problems in the union will be glossed over and the cracks papered over.

The problem for us, as traders, is we have to ignore our own prejudices and trade what we see on the chart using our own analysis, and *not* trade with an opinion, which is fatal. Never ever trade with an opinion. It flies in the face of all your own analysis, but this can be a problem in trading the euro.

You **have** to put whatever you believe or have read about the currency to one side, and simply trade what you see on your price chart, taking account of the fundamental news, using relational analysis, and take positions accordingly.

In the last few years, many, many traders have lost money betting the euro will fail. Huge short positions have been taken in the futures market. Euro shorts and bears squeezed until the pips squeaked. The euro is structurally flawed and euro bears are correct in their analysis. However, for the time being it will survive and the euro should be traded without an opinion. Indeed, to hold an opinion in trading is extremely dangerous. With the euro it's a fatal mistake to make.

Let's move to the ECB, its mandate and how it attempts to manage this ever growing group of member states along with the broad economies that drive this trading block.

The mandate for the ECB is, in fact, simple. It is tasked with maintaining price stability which, in simple terms, means keeping inflation under control. This is interpreted as keeping harmonised inflation over the medium term, below two percent.

It also has a second mandate, which can only be fulfilled once the first has been met, and it is to support the general economic policies of the community. It is important to realise the formation of the ECB involved a huge concentration of power being devolved to form the Central Bank, with twelve national banks, small central banks if you like, being collapsed into the one. This created both a highly political organisation, as well as one that is more interested in its perception and reputation in the financial markets than in making difficult and potentially unpopular decisions which could damage its reputation in the longer term.

As we now begin to emerge from the wreckage of the financial crisis, the ECB is caught between a rock and a hard place in terms of its mandate. Does it raise interest rates in line with its remit of maintaining price stability and keeping inflation in check? However, the effect of this decision is likely to kill off any economic recovery in the weaker member states as well as tip them either into bankruptcy or add further to the mountain of debt currently being underwritten by the ECB and the IMF. In addition, it would also increase the feelings of anger and resentment from taxpayers in the Northern European base.

Alternatively, does the ECB cling to the old ideals of the German Bundesbank which is simply that growth in Europe is best achieved by higher investment in industry, which in turn requires low and stable long term interest rates, the German model if you like.

When faced with this dilemma the ECB usually reacts in two ways. First, it generally does nothing, and hopes the problem will simply resolve itself. Or, there is a knee jerk response which is often followed by a complete U turn, making it almost impossible for traders to know what they are likely to do next.

The bank's decisions are often idiosyncratic and unpredictable, and more to do with image and perception than with dealing with the real issues in Europe head on. Every interest decision is also accompanied by a press statement immediately afterward, and it is in these sessions that we have to read between the lines to understand the logic and reasoning behind any decisions.

There is also a further problem. The euro, and as I mentioned earlier the ECB, just like its political masters, are desperate to ensure the currency survives and prospers. So, decisions are made not necessarily from an economic standpoint, but to ensure the euro continues as the primary currency within the union. Even to the extent of propping up bankrupt countries such as Greece, to ensure they do not leave the EU and the euro, potentially triggering a domino effect with other countries then abandoning the euro to its fate. This is the danger of taking the ECB at face value. There are so many political and personal influences it almost becomes impossible to make any sense of their role.

In 2011 Jean Claude Trichet was replaced by Mario Draghi, who was personally endorsed by Angela Merkel the German Chancellor. Draghi was backed as he is perceived as the most 'German' in outlook. In other words, Draghi is seen as hawkish.

This is good news for us as forex traders as we have a clear expectation of how he is likely to act. Even more importantly he has also made it public knowledge he will have no problem in dismantling the ECB stabilisation fund at the earliest opportunity, sending a clear and unequivocal signal to the markets that weak member states will be sacrificed, if necessary, and for the greater good of the longer term survival of both the EU and the euro.

With this appointment a much clearer picture appears to have emerged from the ECB with a more hawkish tone and clearer decision making as a result. If the weaker countries are indeed sacrificed in the interest of the stronger Northern European economies, this may ultimately provide the foundation of the future of the European union in an export led recovery.

Europe is a complex mix, made even more difficult with the financial problems which still continue today. Ireland has already requested and agreed a bail out package, Greece is likely to be next. If either Spain or Portugal collapse, this will send a shock wave through the markets. And yet despite all this doom and gloom the euro continues to survive and flourish, which is why we have to try to set aside all the media comments along with our own personal views of what you think *should* happen.

It is pointless believing the euro can ever go down on bad news. It is not that simple, as I hope I have proved. There are too many political and personal interests at work to view this as a straightforward currency. I could, in fact, spend several more chapters, just writing about Europe and the role of the ECB. After all, when member states signed up to the euro, they were supposed to abide by a set of rules for spending and borrowing. Few did of course so the rules were relaxed to make it easier for countries to comply. Needless to say some still don't.

A further classic example of how rules originally enshrined in a treaty are circumvented by simply amending the treaty. This is what happened in order to set up the bail out fund. In this case the Treaty of Lisbon was amended to allow this to happen. The reason why is very straightforward. The EU is a politically created trading block which must be protected at all times, and if one or other of its members are likely to fail on a particular test or rule, simply change the rules or amend the treaty.

Since I started writing this book the latest calamity to befall the euro is the banking crisis in Cyprus. The difference here is that, for the first time, it is bank's account holders who are being asked to forfeit their savings to bail out the banks. This has never happened before and is a precedent which has worrying consequences for the future. And more recently, we now have Italy and the Italian banking system which continues to creak and groan. This is potentially far more serious as Italy is a net contributor to the EU.

We will come back to the euro in a later chapter, but for now I want move on to consider the commodity currency countries of Australia, Canada, New Zealand and Norway. In the next chapter I will also be looking at some of the other major commodity producers including Africa, the Middle East and South America.

Australia

Blessed with a wealth of natural resources Australia has always had a reputation for having a strong economy, and is one of the few global economies to emerge relatively unscathed from the recent financial crisis.

Whilst other economies collapsed, Australia has continued to grow at just over 3 percent per annum, largely as a result of its strong links with the Asian markets and, in particular China.

Australia's top five commodity exports are iron ore, coal, gold, crude oil and liquefied natural gas, with Japan being the major customer for oil and gas, coal, aluminium and copper. China is the largest importer of iron ore, with the UK retaining its position as the largest market for gold.

Whilst strong export demand for commodities provided the platform for stability in the economy, it has been underpinned by the Central Bank of Australia the RBA (Reserve Bank of Australia) which has always laid down strict lending criteria for Australian banks. Most of whom have therefore avoided the excesses suffered by the rest of the world.

There are two primary factors which drive the Australian Dollar, both of which are related to the economy, but in different ways.

The first is due to the relatively high interest rates which makes the Australian Dollar an ideal candidate for the carry trade, and it is the counter party currency to the Japanese yen which has ultra low interest rates. Interest rates in Australia have rarely fallen to the levels of Europe or the US, only touching a low of three percent for much of 2009. Since then, rates have fallen further along with the rest of the world and are now stable at 1.5%. Even at this low level they are considerably higher than for many other countries.

As a result, the Australian dollar is an ideal high yielding currency for the carry trade, along with Australian denominated assets.

The second effect follows from the first, as traders take on more risk with the carry trade, the Australian dollar will tend to strengthen when markets generally are prepared to take on more risk. In other words, the Australian dollar is a gauge of risk tolerance. Stock markets will be rising, along with rising commodity prices, which in turn will tend to pull the Aussie dollar higher as export demand increases.

In many ways, the Australian economy and the Australian dollar are very straightforward, (unlike the Euro) and perhaps reflect the Australian character. What you see is what you get and, with the RBA running a tight ship, Australia has duly weathered the financial maelstrom which has engulfed virtually every other economy around the world.

The RBA was established in 1960 to carry out central banking functions of setting monetary policy to ensure currency stability, maintenance of full employment, and economic prosperity and welfare for the people of Australia. The RBA make a point of saying that since 1993 these objectives have found practical expression in a target for consumer price inflation of 2 to 3 per cent per annum.

In the bank's view, controlling inflation, preserves the value of money and, in the long run, this is the principle way in which monetary policy can help to form a sound basis for long term growth in the economy.

This is where the linkage between interest rates and commodity prices become key and, why generally speaking, rates will always be higher than in other countries around the world.

The RBA is non political. It is not privately owned, and acts quickly to take the necessary action when required. It takes no direction from the politicians whatsoever, a refreshing change from the central banks in Europe and the US.

As a major commodity exporting country, whilst rising commodity prices are good, too much can also be damaging. Whilst other countries will be driving inflation into their economies to stimulate demand, Australia will always be aware of the other side of this equation, and keeping a watchful eye in order to ensure inflation is not running away and out of control. At the first sign of a commodity market that is out of control, and probably well before, interest rates will rise. This in turn will create a further imbalance in the carry trade, with risk hunting traders, buying the Australian dollar against the yen.

The AUD/JPY (aussie yen) pair is therefore a good indicator of risk tolerance across the markets, since money flowing into the Aussie dollar is taking on more risk, and in selling the yen, risk is reducing. The mistake many traders make is to believe this is something unique to the currency markets. It is not. We are talking about risk here, and money flow is not simply the buying and selling of individual currencies, but also includes buying and selling assets denominated in these currencies, which could be bonds, equities or commodities. We will return to the AUD/JPY in more detail later, but as a proxy for risk sentiment, this is one of the best currency pairs to watch in any time frame.

CANADA

In many ways the Canadian economy is very similar to that of Australia. Canada is recognised as one of the wealthiest nations in the world, both financially and in terms of natural resources, and often referred to as mixed economy, with its exports dominated by commodities.

The Canadian prairies are one of the largest producers of wheat and grain, whilst the four major provinces which bound the Atlantic coast are a vast natural resource of gas and oil along with zinc, nickel, lead, uranium and gold, with British Columbia famous for timber.

Whilst Australia has managed to weather the financial storm relatively unscathed, Canada has not been so lucky and, in 2009 the country recorded its first ever fiscal deficit. In simple terms, the government's spending exceeded its income, the first time this had ever happened, which gives you some idea of how well the country is managed and run, both by the Government and the Central Bank, which in this case is the Bank of Canada.

The only reason Canada has fared less well than Australia during the crisis, has nothing to do with any change in economic policy, but simply due to its exports markets, as Canada, unlike Australia, is primarily dependent on one country, namely the USA. Canada's nearest neighbour absorbs almost 80 per cent of Canada's exports, and with the US economy hitting the buffers, Canada felt the effect more than most.

As expected, commodities are the cornerstone of Canada's export market, with energy dominating in terms of conventional and unconventional oil deposits, the second of which are huge. These are deposits in the Alberta sands which are essentially grains of sand coated in bitumen. Venezuela has similar resources, and between the two countries, these reserves are considered to be greater than the world's total reserves of conventional oil.

With conventional oil deposits and reserves in other countries eventually coming to an end, we are likely to see the Canadian economy remain strong for decades to come.

In terms of exports, Canada produces around 3.4 million barrels of oil per day, whilst Canadians themselves consume around 2.3 million barrels per day, leaving exports of around 1.1 million barrels, most of which goes to the USA.

The Canadian dollar therefore has a close relationship with the price of oil with the raw commodity converted to US dollars which flows into the country. So, the higher the price of oil, the more US dollars flow into Canada which are then converted into Canadian dollars. In other words US dollars are sold and Canadian dollars are bought.

In addition, oil is priced in dollars so this effect will be further reinforced, especially if rising oil prices are also the result of a weak US dollar, as has been the case in the recent bullish run for commodities. As a general rule, any rise in the price of oil is likely to see the Canadian dollar strengthening, a relationship that seems to remain relatively stable over the longer term time frames.

The other relationship to watch and already mentioned, is the one between Canada as an oil exporter, and Japan as a major oil importer. Here the currency pair that reflects this relationship is the CAD/JPY which also tends to follow the price of oil, so is a good pair to trade in place of oil. However, as forex traders, oil futures or spot oil prices are the place to start when considering any of the Canadian dollar pairs.

Canada's central bank is the Bank of Canada, founded in 1934 as a privately owned corporation, but subsequently becoming a Crown Corporation in 1938, since when the Minister of Finance has held the entire share capital issued by the bank. In effect, the bank is owned by the Canadian people.

The bank is not a government department, as the governor and deputy governor are appointed by the bank. Although not political, the Deputy Minister of Finance does sit on the board of the bank, but he or she has no vote. Furthermore, the bank's accounts are audited externally and not by the Auditor General of Canada.

Much like Australia, the bank is independent, free of political coercion, and therefore able to make balanced and impartial decisions on the economy of which, like many others, price stability forms the central plank, with inflation as the key measure.

In other words, the BOC has a clear structure of central bank independence with a currency that also has clear and well defined attributes in the currency markets.

New Zealand

Staying with the commodity currencies, although New Zealand is a relatively small country, it retains a strong and vibrant export market.

Hard commodities such as gold and coal form the core, with other metals also mined including platinum and tungsten, but the bulk of New Zealand's export market is composed of dairy products, soft commodities and timber. Australia is New Zealand's largest export customer, followed by China, Japan and the USA. Just like Australia and Canada, New Zealand has emerged relatively unscathed from the financial turmoil, thanks largely to its close relationship with Australia which hardly missed a beat as countries around the world headed deep into recession.

One of the idiosyncrasies of New Zealand and New Zealanders in particular is that, as a nation they have a strong preference for property investments, rather than investments which are likely to increase business, exports or jobs. In many ways they are similar in this respect to the British, who are obsessed with owning property as an investment. Therefore, interest rates play a large part in the New Zealand economy.

The New Zealand dollar is yet another of those currencies which is heavily influenced by inflows of cash due to high interest rates. It is another carry trade candidate as interest rates in New Zealand have been high for the last two decades. In fact, substantially higher than most other countries, rising from 4.5% in 2000, to a high of 8.25% in 2008, before finally falling with the rest of the world to more normal levels. At time of writing they stand at 1.75% but, will no doubt, begin to rise once global demand resumes.

One of the reasons they are higher than the rest of the world is due to country's low rate of savings, relative to investment. This forces the central bank, the Reserve Bank of New Zealand, to raise interest rates in order to keep inflation under control. This increase attracts yet more inflows. In other words, it is a vicious cycle where the currency and currency based assets are constantly being purchased, as the other side of the carry trade, resulting in New Zealand dollars flowing into the country. This in turn puts pressure on the exchange rate, with this extra spending power adding inflationary pressure into the economy.

This pressure forces the central bank to act by raising rates, which adds further to the carry trade differential. It is a tricky balance which the RBNZ constantly struggles to manage. To make matters worse, when this relationship unwinds it does so very quickly, with rapid reversals in the price trends.

This is the dominating factor for the New Zealand currency and its central bank. A central bank which has no shareholders and is in fact owned 100% by the New Zealand government. However, whilst it is owned by the government, it is entirely independent when making monetary policy decisions, of which inflation is the key priority for the bank.

The currency pair that attracts the most attention from investors is, of course, the rate against the Japanese yen (NZD/JPY). Once New Zealand rates begin to rise, the currency will be driven higher as speculators buy the currency to take advantage of the interest rate differentials once more, thereby perpetuating the cycle.

Finally, in this section on mainstream commodity currencies, let me introduce you to a currency many forex traders either ignore, or have little or no knowledge of . It is a valuable currency to have in your armoury and is closely associated with oil.

NORWAY

Norway has many similarities to Switzerland, in the sense that the standard of living is extremely high, as is the cost of living. In fact the cost of living in Norway is one of the highest in the world. It could be argued Norway has more money than any other equivalent nation. The value of its sovereign wealth fund stands, at time of writing, at a truly staggering $710 billion. Known as the 'oil fund' the money is invested overseas and really tells the story of the country and its wealth.

Norway is a country whose wealth is inextricably linked to oil and gas, and it currently ranks as the world's fifth largest oil exporter, and the eleventh largest producer. Since the early 1970's, North Sea oil has provided the country with a rich source of income which has been invested wisely, with successive governments only allowed to spend a maximum of 4%, with the remainder invested overseas. One reason why Norway, along with Australia and Canada, has been almost immune from the ravages of the financial crisis.

Norway's petroleum industries, which include oil and gas, account for almost 25% of GDP and approaching 50% of their export market. And, as you would expect, the Norwegian Krona is another of those currencies which could be classified as a commodity currency since, like the Canadian dollar, the price of oil will tend to be reflected in the Krona.

The first Norwegian oil field was Ekofisk, which first started production in the late 1970's, since when, large reserves of natural gas have added to Norway's rich resources. With hindsight, Norway's decision in 1972 to stay out of the EU appears to have been a wise one.Notwithstanding, Norway's trade policies were aligned with harmonising its industrial and trade policy with the EU. A further referendum in 1994 produced the same result as in 1972, and Norway remains one of only two Nordic countries outside the EU, the other being Iceland.

In hindsight a very shrewd move and one which has allowed subsequent governments to invest the oil revenues overseas in its own sovereign wealth fund. Furthermore, the Norwegian government is one of the few in the world to own its own oil company, Statoil, which awards drilling and productions rights to various companies.

An astute move with the company now ranked as Europe's second largest natural gas supplier, and is in the world's top ten of oil companies. In the last few years Statoil has moved into the markets of other major producers such as Canada, where it now works in some of the largest fields, using leading edge technology to extract oil from the Alberta sands reserves, amongst others.

One of the ironies of Norway is, whilst the oil boom has brought enormous wealth to the country which has been wisely invested, along with a high standard of living, over the years there has been little incentive by the various governments to invest in any other technologies or markets. Or even to help develop the labour force. Furthermore, it is strange that in a country with such a healthy bank balance, little investment has been made in infrastructure, transportation or hospitals which, whilst adequate, are nowhere near the standards of other oil rich countries in the Middle East.

Norway's central bank is the Norges Bank and, in common with many other central banks, has a very simple and clear mandate, namely financial stability coupled with price stability. However, the bank is also responsible for 'added value in investment management'. In other words, economic stability to encourage growth in a non inflationary environment. Norges Bank has executive and advisory responsibilities in the area of monetary policy and is responsible for promoting robust and efficient payment systems and financial markets. Norges Bank also manages Norway's foreign exchange reserves and the Government Pension Fund, all of which are massive and growing, as oil revenues continue to flow into the country.

Historically, from 1991 until 2012, interest rates averaged 4.8 % reaching an all time high of 11% in September of 1992 and a record low of 1.3 % in June of 2009. Most recently interest rates have moved below 1% and aligned with European rates.

But what of the Norwegian Krona? As I mentioned earlier, historically it has relatively strong links to the price of oil and the traditional pair to trade in this respect is the USD/NOK. This is a positive relationship with the Krona strengthening with rising oil prices. This adds the same dynamic as with other commodity currencies, where the effect on the direction of the pair may either be reinforced or counterbalanced. In other words, is the effect on the exchange rate, US dollar strength or weakness, oil price strength based on US dollar weakness, or Krona strength based on fundamental news for Norway, of which the two largest are GDP and debt figures. With interest rate differentials and quantitative easing also playing their part.

However, there are risks in trading the Norwegian Krona, and the biggest of these is market volatility. The currency is relatively thinly traded, and therefore illiquid. This can result in spiky price action and for new traders this is perhaps one to watch rather than trade. Secondly, the Norwegian economy is currently on the brink of a housing bubble collapse, which could trigger a similar situation to that seen in Europe and the US, with banks under pressure and collapsing. Whilst this has not happened yet, it is a possibility and one the central bank is attempting to combat at the time of writing.

If the currency is too strong exports are penalised, so it would not come as a great surprise to see the Norges Bank intervene at some stage to protect their market. However, it is very difficult for the bank to combat the twin problems of a housing market that is over heating whilst simultaneously trying to manage a strong currency. Raising interest rates would help to stem the housing bubble, but it would also help to strengthen the Krona further. In this case the expression a 'rock and a hard place' come to mind.

This is the conundrum for Norway at present and, rather like the shipwrecked sailor, there is plenty of water and none to drink. It is perhaps the irony of Norway that, despite all the wealth, the resources and the cautious saving over the last few decades, they ultimately still face the same issues as every other nation of managing their economy and currency in an attempt to achieve long term stability. Something which appears almost impossible to achieve.

UNITED KINGDOM

Staying in the Northern Hemisphere I would now like to consider two more EU 'refusniks', the United Kingdom and Switzerland, starting with the British pound, also referred to as Sterling, and its relationship to the UK economy.

It may come as surprise, but once upon a time the British pound was the currency of first reserve. In fact this was the case for much of the 20th century, and was only replaced in the latter half due to economic weakness, before being replaced by the US dollar.

Sterling still constitutes a significant percentage of bank reserves and is the third most widely held currency after the US dollar and the euro. In the last few years, with the continuing weakness of the US currency and the financial crisis in Europe, the British pound has increased in popularity as a result with an ever increasing number of banks holding sterling as one of their reserve currencies. This has been given further impetus following Brexit, as the currency is now seen as independent, safe, outside Europe, and backed by the most prestigious bank of all, the Bank of England.

The importance of this knowledge to us as traders is if other banks are buying the British pound as a reserve currency we are likely to see the currency move higher, all things being equal, particularly whilst problems remain in Europe, and once an agreement is finally reached with Brussels.

However, in these difficult times even the British pound has come under pressure with ratings agencies suggesting the UK may lose its AAA rating – unthinkable even a few years ago. And since writing the first draft of this book the UK has in fact suffered a downgrade. More on the dreaded ratings agencies later.

Many once 'safe' currencies, are now under threat, and this is a new feature in the currency markets. By contrast currencies such as the Australian and Canadian dollar, are increasingly perceived as 'safe', primarily as a result of the way their economies have been managed during the current financial maelstrom.

For the British pound, the single biggest factor which affects demand for sterling is the health of the UK economy, or rather how the markets expect the economy to perform in the near future.

And, like many other economies around the world, other then Australia and Canada, the UK has been teetering on the brink of a triple dip recession for some time, and not helped by uncertainty over Brexit and future trading agreements.

A combination of weak fundamental data, high unemployment and a lack of consumer demand have all added to the problems for the world's seventh largest economy. In the last forty years the British economy has undergone a painful transition from one underpinned by manufacturing to one dominated by financial services.

Unlike Norway, who established their own sovereign fund from their oil wealth, the UK did nothing and, as a result has wasted all the North sea oil reserves which are now running out.

London, of course, represents the financial capital of the world where much of the new wealth is now based, and which helps to reinforce the view of the UK pound as a safe currency, backed of course by the Bank of England the central bank for the UK. The BOE was originally a private bank and only nationalised in 1946 when ownership passed to the UK government.

The biggest change for the BOE came in 1997 when the bank was given complete independence from the government with total responsibility for monetary policy, and free from political intervention. The BOE resembles virtually every other central bank in that their mandate is twofold; to provide, monetary and financial stability. The first is achieved by the setting of interest rates and the second by using its regulatory powers to ensure the financial crisis which started in 2007 is not repeated.

Although the BOE is not interventionist, it is not against making comments and observations about the relative strength or weakness of sterling. Such comments are generally made by the Governor of the BOE who, in the last few years has suggested a weak currency would be helpful to an economy struggling to recover from both a financial crisis and economic recession. Again since writing the first draft of this book the British pound has had a torrid time in the markets, selling off over 6% between January and March 2013, followed by the extreme price action, post Brexit.

The BOE tone is one which many other central banks have also adopted as something of a mantra, in order to protect their export markets. Competitive devaluation, the 'currency wars', the 'race to the bottom' all terms used to describe the systematic weakening of a currency in order to protect and stimulate a country's economy.

SWITZERLAND

Hop across the English channel, drive through France and we come to Switzerland which, geographically, sits at the heart of Europe yet it is not part of the European Union. Having remained fiercely independent from Europe, it has also remained neutral in any conflicts, although it does have a standing army which is only deployed in peace keeping missions around the world. Therefore, unlike virtually every other nation, Switzerland only spends a limited amount of its income on military assets and personnel with revenues reinvested within the country instead.

It is no surprise therefore, to find the Swiss have one of the highest standards of living in the world. The Swiss economy is based on two primary sectors, banking and tourism, of which the banking services are world renowned, largely due to the privacy laws which protect clients with Swiss bank accounts from the prying eyes of tax, and other authorities. However, this exclusivity and privacy has recently undergone a degree of reform.

The currency of Switzerland is the Swiss franc and the central bank is the Swiss National Bank (SNB). As you would expect, with banking at its core the SNB holds the seventh largest reserves of gold in the world which underpin the banking system. And which only means one thing for investors – safety.

With a high standard of living, political neutrality, huge reserves of gold, a world renowned banking system and its own currency, Switzerland stands for one thing in the currency markets and that is a safe haven in times of turmoil, and this is reflected in two ways in the Swiss franc.

First, the Swiss franc is seen as a safe haven currency. In the last ten years it has been strengthening consistently, as the US dollar has declined, with inflows into the currency accelerating dramatically as the current financial crisis has deepened. It has also seen a dramatic rise against the euro in the wake of the ongoing crisis in the Eurozone.

In times of market turmoil and uncertainty we can expect to see the Swiss franc strengthen against most other currencies. Equally, when markets are bullish and offering better returns in higher risk assets, we can expect to see the Swiss franc weaken as investors and speculators look for better returns elsewhere.

With such a strong association with gold the Swiss franc also tends to trade positively with the gold price. If the price of gold is rising expect to see the Swiss franc strengthen, partly due to the fact both are seen as safe haven assets. Gold prices may also be rising for other reasons, perhaps as the result of a weak US dollar. However, the Swiss franc may also rise because of the sheer quantity of gold in its reserves.

This situation however, does give the Swiss National Bank a huge headache. With the Swiss franc constantly strengthening for over a decade, it has made Switzerland very expensive for tourists as well as for its well developed export market in high tech machinery, electronics, chemicals and pharmaceutical products.

Furthermore, with little in the way of natural resources virtually all raw materials and base commodities have to be imported and, with over fifty percent of corporate earnings coming from exports, the strength of the Swiss franc has given the Swiss authorities a big problem. As a result the SNB is one of the most interventionist central banks in the world. Despite repeated failures to halt the remorseless upwards trend for the currency, this does not appear to deter them, just like the Bank of Japan.

However, unlike the BOJ who deny any knowledge of such actions, the SNB are quite open about their interventions.

Even the IMF, which is charged with ensuring stability of the international monetary system, has made several public statements to the effect that the SNB should intervene in the currency market in order to smooth disorderly currency movements. This is an instruction the SNB always follows.

However, each attempt at intervention by the SNB over the last few years has failed spectacularly with the only effect resulting in a sharp and temporary pull back for the Swiss franc; a spike in the markets and an expensive way to achieve very little. But, like the Bank of Japan, this is done more as a PR exercise than with any real expectation of a reversal in the longer term trend for the currency. It is also proof that even a central bank cannot stop the tide of money moving a currency in one or other direction. The only time a trend change occurs is where there is a real change in sentiment towards the currency or there is a real interest rate differential, which then makes the currency either attractive or unattractive to investors.

The most dramatic change made by the SNB in recent times was the removal of the cap against the euro in January 2015. Until then, markets had believed this was a cornerstone of SNB policy. On 16th January 2015, this all changed. The cap was removed and the Swiss franc soared almost 30% in value against the euro causing market turmoil. Brokers collapsed and customers lost billions as the tsunami swept through global markets.

Coupled with this cataclysmic event, the SNB also introduced negative interest rates in an attempt to deter investors from moving funds into Swiss francs, a policy which has remained in place since, despite an economy which is now booming. And as you can appreciate, offering an alternative to the yen for the carry trade which many consider is now the superior choice.

These two events are often referred to as 'Frankenschock'.

THE BRICS

This section would not be complete without a look at some of the emerging nations, often grouped together as the BRICs which includes China where we started. Here we need to consider the remaining members, namely Brazil, Russia and India.

During the first decade of the 21st century the BRICs group contributed over one third to world GDP growth. In the next decade Brazil's economy will be larger than Italy. India and Russia will individually be greater than Spain, Canada or Italy.

By the end of the decade these countries will probably contribute more than 50% to world GDP which is extraordinary and these countries will be dominating world economics for decades to come.

Brazil

Brazil and the Brazilian real is a relatively new currency only adopted in 1994 following a series of disastrous changes in currency with no less than eight between 1942 and 1994. The constant change of currency was mostly due to rampant inflation and, until 1999, Brazil's currency was pegged to the US dollar on a one to one rate.

It was then uncoupled and left to float freely in the exchange markets and is a classic example of zero to hero, with the country having recovered from a deep and damaging recession which had been triggered by the default of close neighbour Argentina in 2001. This, in turn, caused a debt crisis in Brazil from which it slowly recovered throughout the remainder of the decade, as tight monetary policies and strict credit control allowed it to emerge as one of the powerhouse nations in Latin America.

As a country Brazil has the largest economy in Latin America, but economic stability has not been easy, as it had an economy often characterised by high inflation. Inflation which has finally been brought under control using tight monetary policies and more market based economic strategies.

The cost of reducing inflation however, also led to a deep recession during the early part of the decade. Since when Brazil has become the star of the region, with a booming economy which continues to grow bringing wealth to the people of Brazil and moving millions out of poverty.

In terms of the economy, agriculture forms a major part of its exports as it is the largest producer in the world of many of the so called soft commodities such as sugar cane, coffee, tropical fruits and orange juice. In addition, Brazil also has the largest commercial herd of cattle. It is also a major producer of corn, cotton, cocoa and tobacco, along with soybeans and is second only to the US in terms of production of this increasingly valuable commodity.

With over half of the country covered in forest, timber products too also form a major part of the Brazilian export economy and therefore, just like Canada, Australia and New Zealand, the Brazilian real is classified as a commodity currency. But, in this case, one associated with the soft commodity sector.

There is, naturally, a strong and positive relationship between the Brazilian real and the US dollar, given Brazil's commodity based economy, so as commodity prices rise the Brazilian real tends to strengthen against the US dollar. This also helps to explain in part the dramatic economic expansion of the last few years as commodity prices have soared on an extended bull run.

Furthermore, rising demand from Brazil's largest export market China which, like Brazil continues to expand at an ever increasing rate, continues to increase demand for both hard and soft commodities. Monetary policy is set and managed by the Central Bank of Brazil, a relatively new bank having only been established in 1964. The bank has been given the responsibility for both monetary policy and the setting of interest rates to manage inflation, which is a key priority. Inflation has been rising in the last few years requiring a consequent increase in interest rates as a result.

This has led to the bank raising rates on a regular basis to control consumer spending as the nation has become wealthier. Interest rates in Brazil even rose to an eye watering 26.5% in 2003 but, at the time of writing, have settled back to 6.5% thereby making the Brazilian real a target for the carry trade.

However, unlike the Australian or New Zealand dollar, there are pitfalls in trading this strategy using the real because no matter how attractive the rate differential, the usual risks still apply. For example, lower commodity prices or a sudden change in risk sentiment. However, the biggest drawback to trading the Brazilian real is the lack of liquidity.

It is a lightly traded currency, with extremely small volumes on the futures market, which makes it difficult to exit when markets are volatile. Nevertheless, it is well worth considering provided you are aware and understand the risks involved.

Brazil is a fascinating and dynamic economy which has not just survived, but has become one of the star performers of this emerging market group.

Russia

Russia, just like Brazil has an economy dominated by commodities and, also like Brazil, has seen dramatic changes in the last 25 years. Russia has had to deal with the dissolution of the old Soviet Union and consequent collapse of communism. This was followed by a traumatic move towards a free market economy in the late 1990's after years of state control before Russia was finally accepted as a member of the International Monetary Fund in 1992.

Not long after however, Russia suffered its own financial crisis in 1998 with the Russian currency, the ruble declining by almost sixty percent overnight. This plunged Russia into an economic spiral of inflation and economic decline which it only survived through tight fiscal policy.In much the same way as Brazil has done.

At the time of the crisis the Russian government had the foresight to create a stabilisation fund which, by 2007, had grown to 127 billion dollars. With the largest foreign exchange reserves in the world, the Russian government has also attempted to protect the economy from sudden changes in commodity prices as commodities have been at the heart of Russia's recent rapid expansion while they continue to develop a market driven economy.

Whilst energy commodities such as oil and natural gas are the life blood in this vast country rich in natural resources, Russia is also a major exporter of soft commodities, particularly in the grains market and was an indirect contributor to the recent bullish trend in this market sector. Grain prices soared due to a damaging and lasting drought which forced Russia to implement an export ban on its grains. This in turn sent prices sharply higher in the short term.

In the last few years the economy has moved rapidly, with growth rates in excess of between 7% and 8% per annum. Much of this growth has been due, once again, to rising commodity prices in both oil and gas, which have boosted revenue flows into the country as a result. These inflows have created a strong trade balance with a massive build up in currency reserves.

The central bank in Russia is the CBR, the Central Bank of the Russian Federation. It was formed in 1990 following the collapse of the Soviet Union and the bank likes to maintain a tight grip on the Russian ruble. Much like the SNB the CBR too is quick to intervene to prevent the ruble becoming too strong.

As a result, the bank uses the exchange rate mechanism to control the value of the ruble, in particular against the US dollar which has been weakening as the Federal Reserve pursues its policy of quantitative easing. The CBR has the same problem as many other Central Banks, namely inflation.

However, unlike Western economies it has been a continuous struggle for the CRB to bring inflation under control. In the last twenty years the CBR has only managed to bring this down to single figures twice, but still well above those of most Western economies. In addition, the CBR has had one other major problem to deal with, namely the currency peg, which still remains in place. The Russian ruble is managed against a basket of two currencies, the euro and the US dollar, in the ratio 55% to 45% respectively.

Over the years the CBR has reiterated its desire to see a free floating currency, but as each year passes, this objective becomes less and less likely. The bank has an inherent fear of a free floating exchange rate, particularly given their strong relationship to volatile prices in the oil market, which are then reflected in the currency. As the oil price increases, so the ruble strengthens and the bank intervenes. It has also intervened when it considered the currency too weak. Despite making the right noises the bank has yet to make the psychological jump to a free market in foreign exchange.

This is now becoming an increasingly difficult problem for the bank. The dilemma is whether to focus on trying to control inflation, which is difficult when Russia's export market is so dominated by commodities, in particular oil and its close relationship to the dollar. Alternatively, should the bank continue to control the exchange rate mechanism using the peg.

This problem was finally resolved in 2017, when the currency was unpegged from the US dollar and the euro and allowed to free float, and so adding another strong commodity currency to the trading armoury.

India

Our final BRICSs country is India.

With a population of just over one billion people, it is the world's largest democracy and, in the last decade, just like the other BRICs, has seen its economy grow at an ever increasing rate, propelling the country to become the world's tenth largest economy and third largest in Asia.

Again India's currency, the rupee, could be considered another commodity currency, since the country is rich in both base minerals, such as iron ore, manganese and bauxite, but also agriculture which forms the core of its export markets, along with textiles.

However the economy is gradually changing. Increasingly, India is seen as a leader in high tech industries in the computer industry as well as developing one of the fastest growing car manufacturing sectors in the world.

With a diverse and extremely well educated population, coupled with low labour costs, the country is able to provide a range of outsourcing solutions for companies around the world. This is likely to be a continuing theme over the next decade, as the Indian economy expands and develops from its traditional base.

However, just like many other economies, India has struggled to keep inflation in check with consumer spending rising fast, particularly on high tech goods and services. In addition, increases in commodities has meant the Indian authorities, in the form of the central bank (the Reserve Bank of India) have struggled to keep inflation below ten percent. The same dilemma suffered by both Russia and Brazil.

The bank has been forced to act quickly in the last few years raising interest rates from a low of 3.25 percent in 2009 to 7.75% in 2013, and more recently 6.5% in 2018.

The currency of India, the Indian rupee is also a pegged currency. However, the rupee has been pegged in a variety of ways throughout its chequered career. From 1950 until 1975 the currency was pegged to the British pound, at which point it was decoupled following the collapse of the gold standard.

It was then linked to a basket of currencies, primarily those of its major trading partners. However, following a long period of devaluation the currency was then switched to a 'managed float' regime. In theory, this means it is a free floating currency which is only managed in times of volatility, or when economic conditions dictate an intervention and adjustment of the exchange rate.

This system seems likely to continue for some years to come given India's strong growth which is fuelling consumer spending. This in turn is leading to rising inflation as commodity prices continue to soar, a common theme for all the BRICs. Rapid expansion brings an explosion in the middle classes with rising consumer spending, inflation, and the associated problems of currency management.

Most books on forex usually stop at this point, but in the next chapter I'm going to focus on three distinct geographical regions, which deserve a section of their own. These are Africa, the Middle East and South America. They are all hugely important in different ways, but with a common theme - commodities.

Chapter Thirteen
The Next Generation

The market can move for irrational reasons, and you have to be prepared for that...you need to make big bets when the odds are in your favour..not big enough to ruin you, but big enough to make a difference.

Bill Gross (1944-)

If China is the Emperor elect in the world order, who will be the successors in the world order in the next decade, and what opportunities will this present in the foreign exchange markets?

In this chapter I'm going to consider the continents of Africa and Latin America, as well as the Middle East, three geographic regions which have one thing in common, namely commodities.

Africa

Africa is a complex continent, not only in its chequered history of currencies, but also in terms of growth over the last decade, where it is unmatched, except by China. With average annual growth rates of 5% year on year and poverty falling, Africans are now joining the consuming classes in much the same ways as on the Indian sub continent. However, the staggering fact is this – by 2035 it is forecast Africa's labour force will be greater than that of any individual country in the world. Whether this forecast will be achieved will largely depend on the implementation of sweeping and dramatic reforms, which would lift millions of Africans out of poverty and in turn create a middle class, both employed and affluent. This would create stability and the springboard for sustained growth and job creation.

Ironically, the problem for Africa is similar in many ways to that of Norway, whose enormous wealth is underpinned by the boom in commodities, which has led to successive governments focusing almost entirely on one sector of the economy, namely petrochemicals. This has resulted in a lack of government focus in developing and educating their workforce in other sectors.

Africa, of course, is one of the world's richest continents in terms of natural resources, with both soft and hard commodities a key component of GDP. However, from an employment perspective, this sector employs less that 1% of the current workforce, making it even more imperative that changes happen and, happen fast, if the continent is to succeed in developing further and able to compete in world markets.

In the soft commodity sector, Africa has approximately 60% of world acreage for growing crops of all kinds and, with such vast resources, has the potential to dramatically develop new and exciting export markets. But, this requires change, education and money. This is possible and indeed Mali is a classic example, which has managed to increase its mango export market by 600% into the European Union. This was achieved following an extensive project which focused on improving road, rail and sea links, allowing refrigerated fruit to be exported quickly and efficiently.

Whilst infrastructure is one issue, the second is in providing growers and producers with the education and finance to develop large scale farming projects, coupled with a move to more advanced production techniques. These techniques include the development of higher yielding crops, particularly in new and developing markets such as ethanol production. All major car manufactures have now developed engines which can run on a blend of fuels to include ethanol. With green issues likely to dominate over the next decade, and the development of further 'flexible fuel' vehicles, Africa is well placed to take advantage.

There is further potential for Africa with the so called 'Cinderella crop' - soybean - as huge and growing demand from China will drive prices for this commodity ever higher. Advances in locally adapted GM varieties as well as increasing mechanisation in soybean production have made this a relatively easy crop for African growers and once again education is the key, coupled with modernisation and scaling up of production.

Mining, oil and gas are the most significant contributors to Africa's GDP, but for sustained growth and longer term prosperity, Africa needs a jobs strategy and not just a growth strategy. And here Morocco is an excellent example, with cars underpinning the success story. Today, this sector employs more that 70,000 people and more recently Renault opened its first plant in this region.

This is the success that awaits other African nations, and it is one of the greatest ironies, that a country so rich in natural resources has so many poor.

In the past decade, growth has been faster than that seen in Asia, and Latin America, earning Africa the title of the Lion Markets. The World Bank recently reported the economies of the sub Saharan African countries were growing at a faster rate than worldwide.

But, what is the composition of Africa, who are the main players and, more importantly, what are the tradable currencies? How are these currencies influenced in the foreign exchange markets, and what is on the horizon as the Lion Markets develop and grow?

Africa is the world's second largest continent and second most populated. It has a total of 54 fully recognised sovereign states, 9 territories and three 'de facto' states with limited recognition. Virtually all of these states are rich in commodities, but it is Nigeria that stands head and shoulders above the rest.

With a maximum crude oil production capacity of 2.5 million barrels per day, Nigeria ranks as Africa's largest producer of oil and the sixth largest oil producing country in the world. The crude oil of Nigeria is divided into two classes, namely sweet and light. Both extremely high quality and, within the OPEC group, Nigeria is the biggest producer of the so called 'light sweet crude' which carries the highest premium in the market due to its low sulphur content and consequent lower costs of refining.

As you would expect it is the USA which is the largest importer of crude oil from Nigeria, and Nigeria supplies around 10% of all oil imported.

Nigeria, however, is not the only country with large oil reserves, with many other countries in the top twenty of world producers, including Algeria, Angola, and Egypt.

The second commodity associated with Africa is gold, with many traders wrongly assuming South Africa is the largest gold producer in the world. In fact China is the world's largest, with South Africa currently ranking 5th in the world order and Ghana 8th.

Whilst South Africa holds over 35% of global gold reserves and exports virtually all of its output, gold production has been falling fast, particularly in the last decade, due to rising costs of extraction coupled with rising labour costs. To put this into context, an ounce of South African gold currently costs over $250 per ounce to extract, whilst the equivalent in the US is $190 per ounce and in Canada even lower at $170 per ounce. In an effort to bring costs under control and reverse this decline, several of South Africa's major gold producers including AngloGold and Gold Fields, two of the countries major producers, have gone through some significant restructuring in order to arrest this worrying trend.

Other countries who are increasingly significant in the gold market are Ghana, Zimbabwe, Tanzania, Guinea, and Mali. Of these both Tanzania and Mali are rapidly becoming major gold producers in their own right.

South Africa is the largest economy of Africa and accounts for almost 25% of the continent's GDP, with mining its most recognised industry. However, it's not just gold and gemstones that are mined, but other base commodities such as coal, iron ore and chromium. South Africa is also a major supplier of platinum, producing almost three quarters of the world's consumption of this precious metal.

However, it is in the rare earth metals that the true wealth of Africa's commodities may be buried, as I explained earlier when we looked at the economy of China. As one of the world's largest resources of rare earth metals, China is already exploiting this market, both by stockpiling its own reserves whilst simultaneously driving prices higher using trade embargoes. This group of commodities is the most sought after for an increasing variety of lifestyle gadgets such as mobile phones, flat screen TVs and tablets and, with a limited number of countries with sufficient supplies of these, the race is on to find alternative sources. And Africa is top of this list.

With China continuing to tighten its stranglehold on this market, Africa is seen as holding the key for the future, and it's not difficult to see why as the consensus view is the continent has more than 50% of the total deposits worldwide of carbonatities, a particular rock formation which is seen as a primary source for rare earth metals.

These formations are found in most African countries and the race is on to discover and extract sufficient quantities. This would provide an alternative source to those of China, who currently control around 95% of the world's supply. Should Africa ultimately provide the solution to this problem, this will add a further chapter to the story of Africa. A story which is inextricably linked to commodities and, much like the other players in the rare earth metals markets, namely Australia and Canada, their currencies will also reflect this in any future exchange rate mechanisms.

Before turning to the currencies of Africa, it is perhaps one of the ironies of this unique and fascinating continent that, just like Europe in the 1990's, there is only one topic of conversation currently dominating the hearts and minds of the great and the good. And that topic is whether Africa should have its own single currency.

Despite all the problems with the Euro, the structural flaws of the EU, the issues with sovereign debt, the issues of culture, of work ethic, and of political and monetary union, Africa is considering the prospect of a single currency. We never seem to learn from history and perhaps Africa seems determined to follow a similar path.

Given the number of African states and the wide diversity in cultures, wealth and history, it comes as no surprise to learn there is also a huge variety of currencies used throughout the continent and, as such, impossible to include all in this short introduction.

Therefore, in order to narrow these down I am only going to focus on the following groups. The CFA, which breaks down into the West African Franc, the Central African Franc, the Naira, which is the currency of Nigeria, and finally the South African Rand. However, before examining these in detail we need to step back in history. But only very briefly.

In 2010, a total of fourteen African states celebrated 50 years of independence, finally breaking free from their French colonial ruler, whilst Nigeria and Somalia also achieved independence in the same year, 1960, from Britain.

However, the legacy of France still remains firmly in place and, nowhere more so than in the currency markets, where the CFA franc remains and, indeed is, a currency still guaranteed by the French Treasury. What is even more ironic is that it is pegged to the Euro. By the way CFA stands for Communaute Financiere Africaine which translates as the African Financial Community – one could say an African version of the EU.

The CFA Franc is now the currency of 14 countries of which 12 were former French colonies. The currency was created on the 26th December 1945 following the Bretton Woods agreement in an attempt to protect the colonies from any devaluation.

Today, there are two separate CFA francs in circulation in Africa. The first is that used by the West African Economic and Monetary Union (WAEMU) which is made up of eight countries including Benin, Burkina Faso, Guinea-Bissau, Ivory Coast, Mali, Niger, Senegal and Togo. The second group is composed of six countries, namely Cameroon, Central African Republic, Chad, Republic of Congo, Equatorial Guinea and Gabon, and collectively known as CEMAC. Each of these two groups issues its own CFA franc, the West African CFA franc and the Central African CFA franc which, whilst separate, are in essence interchangeable.

The CFA franc follows the same monetary polices laid down by the ECB, with these policies executed by the respective central banks for both regions, the Central Bank of West African States and the Bank of Central African States. Both banks extend their credit facilities to other financial institutions as well as to other members' states Governments, with the CFA franc guaranteed by the French Treasury.

However, what's strange, is whilst the two CFA banks are African in name, they have no monetary policies of their own, and indeed have no idea of how much of the pool of foreign reserves held on their behalf by the French Treasury, actually belongs to the group itself. The reason is simple. The accounting procedures of the French Treasury are entirely hidden from view, making it impossible for these banks to establish any clear idea of profitability on their assets.

This shroud of secrecy, which has become a fact of life for many African nations, makes it impossible for African members to regulate their own monetary policies. It is a bizarre and arcane situation, in which the French Treasury controls virtually every aspect of life, rendering any political changes virtually worthless.

Government officials simply come and go and, whilst many may wish for change, it is impossible to implement these changes without the full support and knowledge of the fundamental economic data, so vital to managing economic growth. With all this information effectively kept secret, politicians and governors are effectively powerless to make decisions or implement change. With many African states increasingly vulnerable due to economic and inflationary pressures, this is putting several at risk and is one of the many drivers towards the dream of a single currency.

The biggest problem for Africa with the CFA currency is devaluation and, since its inception, has only been devalued once in 1994. This created shock waves throughout the region as overnight, 1 French franc which had been worth 50 CFA was suddenly worth 100 CFA, with a consequent huge rise in the price of imported foodstuffs.

More recently in 2012, with the Eurozone in crisis and the possible collapse of the euro, to which the CFA currency is pegged, rumours began to circulate a further devaluation was on the way. The irony is not lost on the African people. After all, France has run out of money, has massive public and bank debt, and has one of the largest exposures to both Greek and Italian debt. Furthermore, France has recently lost its AAA credit rating.

One possible solution to these problems? Devalue the CFA and release funds to the French Treasury. In effect Africa paying for the Euro crisis. Ironic to think Africa is even considering a single currency based on the European model. A model which is proving to be so corrosive.

Rumours still continue but, for the time being the two currencies which make up the CFA remain pegged to the Euro. This peg replaced that of the Franc on the introduction of the Euro on the 1st January 1999 and was fixed at 1:100 rate. At the time of writing the exchange rate is 655.70 CFA to one euro.

Nigeria

Moving to Nigeria and here the situation is a little less complicated, but only just. The Nigerian currency is the Naira, and is issued and managed by the Central Bank of Nigeria. The currency was introduced on the 1st January 1973 and replaced the British pound at a fixed rate of 2:1 with Nigeria being the last country to abandon the old 'pre decimal' pounds, shillings and pence. This fixed rate has remained in place ever since, but again, as with the CFA there was a rumour of a move to a 1:1 rate in 2008, but this never materialised.

The overriding problems for Nigeria and its currency are much the same as for the CFA, namely devaluation, which is once again on the horizon with the Bank of Nigeria threatening to introduce a 5000 Naira note.

As a currency, the Naira is a managed float against the US dollar by the Central Bank of Nigeria, which buys or sells US dollars twice a week on a Monday and Wednesday to keep the currency peg in a tight range. Over recent years this has been set at N150 before moving higher to N155, with the exchange rate then maintained in a range of plus or minus 3%. In effect, the Naira now floats in a range approximately between N155 and N160 to the US dollar.

As a result, the Naira and the Nigerian economy are almost entirely dependent on two things. First, the price of oil, and second, the strength or weakness of the US dollar, both of which are inextricably linked. And herein lies the paradox. As one of the world's leading oil producing countries, and sitting on some of the largest reserves of light sweet crude, rising oil prices are good for exports. However, rising oil prices are generally the result of a weak US dollar and, this in turn, is reflected in Naira strength.

A strong Naira imports inflation, which is reflected in the rising price of imports such as food on which Nigeria is hugely reliant. In other words, as the price of oil rises Nigeria receives more US dollars per barrel, but if this increase is based on a weak US dollar, this is reflected in strength in the Nigerian currency.

The Central Bank of Nigeria then steps in using the twice weekly auction to manage the exchange rate and, in this scenario would need to buy US dollars to weaken the Naira accordingly. A difficult and ongoing balancing act for Nigeria and its currency, and one which is not going to change in the short term.

However, where Nigeria's relationship to its currency could change is in acting as the catalyst for a single currency, which has long been muted but, as yet shows little sign of becoming a reality. Meanwhile, Nigeria is the only country with the experience, financial weight and economic expertise to manage an independent currency with a central bank. Furthermore, one which is a commodity based currency, referenced against a commodity index or basket of commodities.

In this scenario, if commodity prices fell, the currency would be devalued automatically and export revenues in the national currency would not be affected. All of this remains an aspiration for the time being and, until then, the US dollar, oil and the Naira, will continue their dance, with the Central Bank of Nigeria conducting the orchestra twice a week.

South Africa

Before moving to consider the broader FX markets in Africa let me just finish with a free floating African currency which is the South African rand. And with the recent growth in many African nations over the last decade and, with poor returns on both the euro and the US dollar, speculators and investors are increasingly considering more of the exotic currencies. As a result, trading volumes in the South African rand reflect this view with Reuters confirming daily transactions passed the $18 billion level in 2017. Furthermore, the rand has been one of the best performing currencies out of 20 other emerging markets.

To put this into context, the daily volumes on the Egyptian foreign exchange markets were approximately $200 to $400 million per day, with Nigeria and Kenya even smaller at $100 to $200 million a day.

Today the majority of African currencies are freely exchangeable, for example those of Ghana, Kenya, Nigeria (with the Naira we looked at earlier), Uganda and Zambia, although many of these countries have imposed some restrictions to avoid excessive currency speculation.

Many of these self imposed restrictions apply to the related bond markets, although in 2011 Nigeria did relax the rules on overseas buying of local government bonds, thereby allowing speculators to trade strength and weakness on the Naira directly. Whilst Nigeria has relaxed its restrictions in recent years, other countries have not, with both Kenya and Uganda maintaining strict rules on overseas speculative investments in local bond markets.

But what about the South African Rand, which is normally classified as an 'exotic' currency?

A general principle that can be applied to many of the 'exotic currency pairs is they tend to correlate with underlying market forces. For South Africa this means only one thing, the price of gold. As I explained earlier, although in the last decade gold production has been falling for a variety of reasons, South Africa still retains its pre-eminence in terms of gold reserves. Therefore, the South African Rand generally has a positive relationship with the precious metal. However, as with all cross market relationships these can and do change for many reasons but, any longer term move in the price of gold, will usually be reflected in the South African rand.

As an example, the charts in Fig 13.10 and Fig 13.11 show the last two years of price action on a monthly time frame for the USD/ZAR and the spot price of gold and, whilst the relationship is far from perfect, it does, nevertheless, show the linkage between the rand and gold.

Fig 13.10 USD/ZAR Monthly Chart

Fig 13.11 Spot Gold Price - Monthly Chart

However, there are several issues we need to be aware of when trading any of these high risk exotic currency pairs.

The first point concerns volatility. Exotic currencies are generally thinly traded, with low volumes when compared to other currencies. One consequence of this can be seen in the wide spreads, and is certainly the case with the South African rand. A large spread requires more margin and, in addition, bigger moves are required to take positions out of negative territory and into positive territory. Price action on the day can be both volatile and wide, so the average price range on an intra day basis for a currency such as the rand will be greater than the equivalent of a mainstream major pair. With the USD/ZAR for example, the pair can move between 800 and 2000 pips on the day, and one reason why speculative traders are attracted to these markets.

With such wide ranging moves big gains are possible along with equally big losses. Taken with the wide spread an opening position in the USD/ZAR could be negative between 80 to 100 pips. So not a pair for novice forex traders.

In addition, there are also optimum times to trade the USD/ZAR. As South Africa is only one hour ahead of London, volatility is generally high as the European session gets underway. Furthermore, any move in the gold market will also impact the South African rand along with the US dollar and USD index.

In general, exotic currencies require more of everything. More time for the trade to develop, more patience to wait for the right trading opportunity and, more time for the trade to play out in the market. But, provided you have the experience and the necessary funds the rand certainly offers some unique trading opportunities from a country that is diverse, fascinating and set to become a star of the world stage in the next decade.

So, be warned the 'Lion markets' are preparing to roar.

Latin America

If the Lion markets have yet to roar, the Latin American resurgence is well under way, once again fuelled by increasing and rising world wide demand for commodities. However, in the second decade of the 21st century it is currency markets which are set to dominate. And the problem for many central banks will be in managing the fine balance between interest rates, economic growth, and inflation, along with the ongoing protection of their export markets in the face of an onslaught from investors and speculators. This will not be an easy task.

However, what exactly is the problem for the major commodity countries in the region such as Brazil, Chile, Peru, Mexico, Argentina as well as all the other large exporters? It is a complex problem grounded in simple economics, and one which will have a huge impact for the region's two largest economies, Brazil and Mexico and their respective currencies, the Brazilian real and the Mexican peso.

The problem starts with interest rates and, as we emerge from the wreckage of the economic tsunami of the last few years, the problem for many emerging economies in Latin America is in stemming the flood of money seeking a higher return. This flood threatens to engulf these countries and, others like them, forcing their currencies ever higher.

These economies are suffering the consequences of the last few years, which has seen the major economic blocks involved in an ongoing and ever more brutal game of competitive devaluation of their currencies, by fair means or foul. The only country with the motto 'a strong currency is a good currency' ironically is Germany, where the memory of the rampant inflation suffered during the Weimar Republic still runs deep.

As a result, and with the prospect of risk appetite returning, investors and speculators will be out in force looking to move away from the low yield markets of Europe, the USA and Japan. Instead these investors will be hunting out high yielding currencies such as the Brazilian real and the Mexican peso.

Interest rates in Brazil hit an all time low in 2013 of 7.25%, a level of yield unachievable elsewhere in the world at the time, whilst in Mexico, rates of 7.75% now appear very attractive. With high interest rates comes increasing demand from yield hungry investors and, with economies slowly emerging from a long and damaging recession, demand for commodities will once again start to increase, adding a further level of pressure to these currencies.

Oil is one of the stars of the region and with over 20% of the world's oil reserves held in Latin America between Venezuela, Brazil and Mexico, rising oil prices can only add further pressure. Whilst rising commodity prices would normally be welcomed by a large net exporter, with a strong currency comes rising prices of imports and a higher cost of living.

The problem for Latin America is it is uncomfortably dependent on base commodities and in the first decade of the 21st century, this asset class accounted for almost 53% of the region's exports, according to a report from the World Bank. By contrast this is dramatically lower than the 85% of the 1970's. Nevertheless, over 90% of Latin Americans live in a country whose revenues are reliant on commodities.

In terms of oil, it is Venezuela which dominates and holds approximately 85% of the regions reserves and, in terms of production, the three countries of Venezuela, Brazil and Mexico are responsible for 80%, with Colombia, Ecuador and Argentina making up the balance.

In general, much of this so called 'hot money' seeking a higher return goes into equity markets and bonds. This effect was seen in the Brazilian real between 2010 and 2011, when the currency gained 12% against the US dollar, driven higher by 'hot money' inflows, an effect clearly seen in the Fig 13.12 chart.

Fig 13.12 Brazilian Real/USD

This was promptly followed by an equally significant reversal through the latter part of 2011 and into 2012, which leads to the next problem for many of the currencies associated with these countries, namely volatility. This has been a problem which has bedeviled the New Zealand dollar over the years, which has always attracted hot money owing to its standing as the currency of choice for the carry trade. Whilst the carry trade in itself is a high risk strategy, using this strategy with one of the many exotic currencies, such as the Brazilian real, or the Mexican peso, adds a further layer of risk. This is yet another factor that increases volatility. Not only do speculators move fast to reverse positions in and out of these currencies in line with risk sentiment, this underlying volatility is also driven by the price movements in the commodities themselves, as they are risk assets in their own right. What we have therefore is a risk multiplier in trading these currencies.

This creates a massive headache for the Central banks of the region. Exporters with large manufacturing bases can generally rely on relatively stable prices from month to month, which is also reflected in raw material import prices, leading to an economy which is measured and, which by using the blunt instrument of interest rates, can be managed with some degree of success. Whilst these manufacturing based economies can and do overheat, it is a relatively straightforward process to manage inflation and control the currency as a result.

For commodity based economies such as Brazil, this is a real and constant problem. Until 1999 the currency was pegged to the US dollar. However, following its de-pegging, the real suffered a massive devaluation with the currency falling to a rate of 2:1 against the US dollar This is the problem for all central banks and, in an effort to control its currency exchange rate, the Central Bank of Brazil has recently opted to revert to the so called 'dirty float' exchange rate regime, in an attempt to protect the currency from any excessive volatility.

At the same time the bank has also handed control to the government, which now has a mandate to restrict the movement of the Brazilian real to a tight range against the US dollar, currently set (in 2013) between R$ 2 and 2.10 or 0.50 to 0.475. This decision was prompted by the strength of the currency, clearly evident on the chart and, just like the rest of the world, the Brazilian authorities have decided a strong currency is something which is not to be welcomed right now. What is acceptable for developed economies, is also acceptable for emerging economies.

However, a strong currency is not all bad news for countries and economies such as Brazil but, is a dilemma for managing the economy in turbulent times. After all, a strong Brazilian real would certainly be good for its export markets, its soft commodities, oil and raw materials, whilst also helping to control inflation. In addition and, perhaps more importantly, a strong currency would provide some much needed price stability leading to economic stability, provided inflation can be managed in an orderly fashion.

This is the dilemma and the paradox for Brazil. It is this constant problem that Brazil, and many other commodity currencies face in the region, and is likely to continue to do so for years ahead. The problem is almost insoluble, given the current global crisis and is further exacerbated by the twin effects of commodity markets and hot money.

In addition to oil, Brazil is the world's largest exporter of ethanol and soybeans which are becoming increasingly important in world markets. Increasing concerns over environmental issues have dramatically increased demand for ethanol, which is derived from two primary sources, corn and sugar. Of these, sugar cane based ethanol is cheaper and more energy efficient than corn based ethanol produced in the United States. This has made Brazil the primary supplier worldwide, However, in an attempt to protect their home markets for ethanol, the USA and Europe have both recently imposed trade tariffs, a move that has not been warmly welcomed.

The soybean market is another where the US and Brazil lock horns, with both competing for the number one slot as China becomes one of the fasted growing markets for this product. Whilst there is no direct correlation between the Brazilian real and the soft commodities such as soybean, nevertheless, strong trends in these markets, and in particular in soybean futures, will always have an impact not least for two reasons. First, trends in commodities will always be reflective of underlying strength or weakness in the US dollar, and second, strong trends in commodities will in turn signal possible rising inflation, a positive sign of economic growth and economic expansion, provided economies do not overheat and run out of control.

Mexico

Moving to another key currency in the region, namely the Mexican peso. This is one of the oldest currencies of North America and which underpins an economy which is changing, and changing, fast.

Mexico has the second largest economy in Latin America and like Brazil is also a major oil producer and exporter. And like Brazil, Mexico is rich in natural resources and minerals.

Economically however, this is where the similarities end, as in the last decade, Mexico's oil production has started to decline as has its position as a net exporter to the USA, its largest and nearest neighbour. In addition, and perhaps even more ironic, is the fact that Mexico is now a net importer of natural gas, and the reason is as follows.

Over the past decade and, certainly since the start of the 21st century, Mexico has slowly but surely been changing its DNA, by moving from an economy based on commodities and exports to a more stable and manageable one, based on high tech manufacturing, even beginning to challenge China. Mexico has also been simultaneously gaining market share, moving away from its traditional dependency on its nearest neighbour and increasingly expanding away from the region, and taking market share from China.

A decade ago approximately 90% of Mexico's exports went to the USA. By the start of the second decade of the 21st century this had fallen to below 80% but, at the same time managing to increase market share in the USA at the expense of China. Furthermore, Mexico is increasingly seen as providing a stable, economic environment for investment, with a motivated, young and educated workforce. All underpinned with a relatively low cost base for production. In addition, Mexico also has one other major advantage – proximity of delivery to local markets in both North and South America.

Goods exported from China to the US typically take between 20 and 40 days to arrive in the US. From Mexico, with its well developed road and rail links, delivery times are usually just a few days. Many of the major car manufactures are now investing in plants and assembly lines and what would have seemed a fantasy just a few years ago, is now a reality. The ultimate paradox is Mexico is now manufacturing both parts and complete cars for the Chinese markets – unthinkable when China first exploded onto the world economic stage at the start of the century.

Suddenly it seems Mexico has become the country of manufacturing choice by large multinational companies, all looking to supply the region and, increasingly overseas. Today, Mexico exports more manufactured products than the rest of Latin America put together. This is an extraordinary transition in such as short period of time. Made in Mexico is now becoming the standard and slowly but surely impacting the de facto standard for overseas manufacturing, the 'made in China' label.

As a result, Mexico has grown to become the 13th largest economy in the world and much of this success can be traced back to the North American Free Trade agreement, which was critical to integrating Mexico back into the global economy. What the agreement provided was the basis for reform, both in terms of infrastructure and also perhaps, more importantly, in trade agreements.

This fundamental shift in the economic landscape for Mexico is reflected in the peso and in particular, against the currency of its nearest neighbour the US dollar. And here again, Mexico is very different from Brazil, with the Mexican authorities taking a 'hands off' approach to managing the currency itself. Whilst Brazil and Mexico are the two largest economies and both therefore likely to attract significant inflows of currencies, the reasons are very different. For Brazil, it's the hot money looking for better yields and better returns.

But for Mexico, it is principally investment dollars looking for longer term growth and capital returns. As a result, Mexico's central bank has a much easier task than its counterpart in Brazil, with the Mexican peso left to float relatively freely in the foreign exchange markets.

However, this was not always the case. Over the last 50 or 60 years, Mexico has tried virtually every form of currency exchange model in an attempt to manage its currency including: 'fixed rates', 'dual rates', 'multiple rates', 'exchange bands' and 'a regulated float'. All ultimately failed with perhaps the most spectacular being the collapse of the peso in 1994 where a combination of factors, including rising US interest rates, finally saw Mexico's central bank, the Banco de Mexico move to the current model, a free floating exchange rate which was introduced on December 19th 1994.

This has been in place ever since, with interest rates managed in the usual way and, akin to other Western economies, creating the unusual combination of an 'exotic currency' with a free floating mechanism, all underpinned by a non interventionist central bank.

This has led to sustained economic stability for Mexico, with volatile currency movements almost relegated to history, as the country and its currency emerge from the shadows to become yet another winner from the increasing band of emerging nations.

The first thing to remember is that from a trading perspective the Mexican peso is still labelled an exotic currency with the same characteristics of the South African rand. The peso can present some interesting opportunities but, like the rand, needs to be approached with care.

The first point to note is the peso can be considered a 'commodity currency' in spite of the dramatic and lasting changes which Mexico is now making to it economy. Therefore, the currency will still reflect the underlying general trends in crude oil, and for evidence of this relationship, we need look no further than the daily charts.

In the first chart we have the MXN/USD (Fig 13.13) and in the second chart the daily spot price for WTI oil (Fig 13.14).

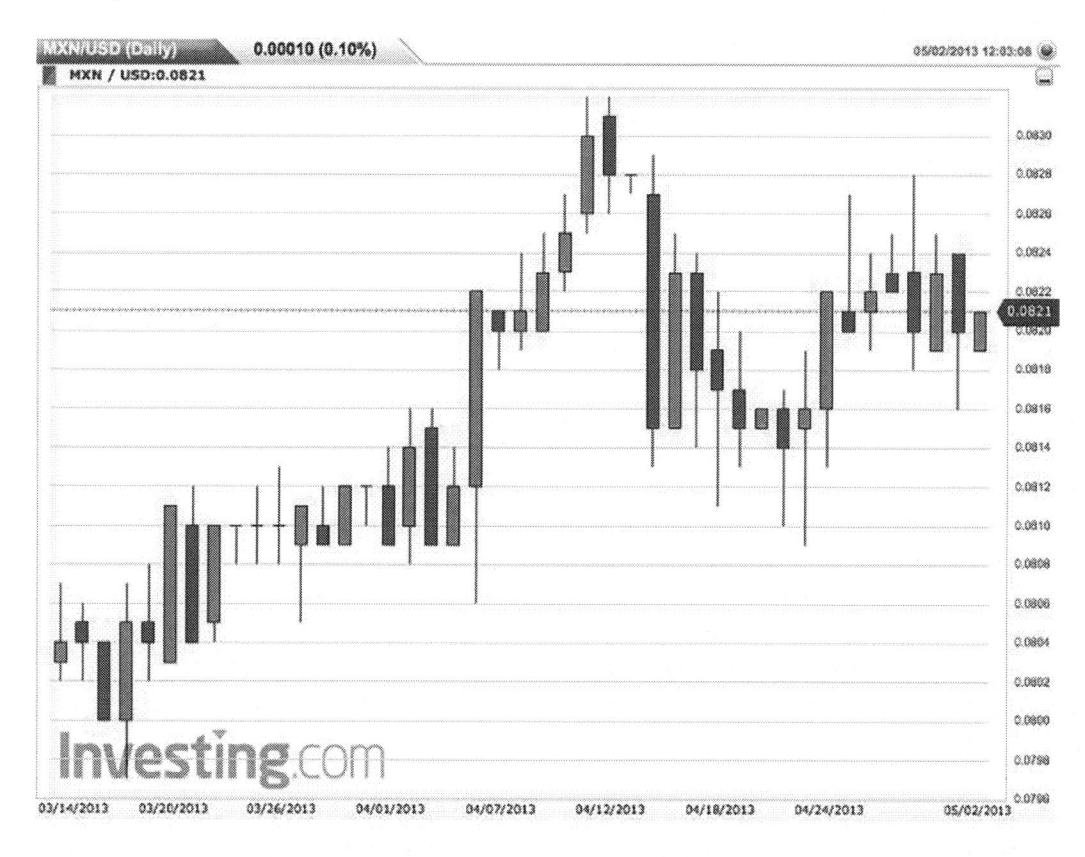

Fig 13.13 Mexican Peso/USD

Fig 13.14 WTI Crude Oil

As you would expect with a commodity currency, the effects are twofold with the price of the commodity also being driven by underlying strength and weakness in the US dollar.

For the Mexican peso, there is also the additional element of the economy of its largest neighbour. And here the peso has many similarities to the Canadian dollar. Both are commodity currencies, both are large oil exporters and, both are major exporters to the US markets which have a huge influence.

Therefore, if the US economy slows down or reverses, this will be reflected in trade and ultimately in the currency.

In the next few years, the Mexican peso is likely to be one of the major beneficiaries of the move away from the so called 'major currencies', as emerging 'exotic' currencies become increasingly in demand. This is particularly true in Asia where this trend has already started, with investors and speculators searching out higher yields in currencies such as the Korean won, to which can be added the Russian ruble, the South African rand and the Mexican peso.

And with yields now higher than the Brazilian real, it is Mexico's currency which is seen as increasingly attractive for investors. In addition, with a free floating currency and a non-interventionist central bank, these are all additional benefits for investors.

The characteristics that investors look for in currencies are that they are liquid, they have a good yield differential and a central bank policy which is not overtly geared towards currency devaluation. This is certainly the case in Mexico and similar in many ways to the South African rand which we considered earlier.

However, despite its growing popularity, the peso, as with other currencies in the region, will always be at the mercy of a shock to the global economy. And, as always, the reason is very straightforward. It is the US dollar.

The collapse of Lehman Brothers, saw the Mexican peso, the Brazilian real and also the Chilean peso suffer badly as a result. The problem stems from one of rapid changes in market sentiment, with speculators and investors all selling high yielding, high risk currencies, in favour of safe haven assets of which the US dollar is one.

This results in sudden spikes in the US dollar, with the double effect of currency outflows and weakening commodity markets. A double whammy if you like. This is the risk all currency investors and speculators accept when trading in these currencies and ultimately is a question of quantifying risk. After all, the higher the risk the higher the returns, but the opposite is also true. Falls, when they come are fast and spectacular which is what makes managing both the economy and the currency so difficult for the central bank.

In the case of Mexico, the balance is about right. But Brazil has some way to go to reach that happy median.

Argentina

Whilst Brazil and Mexico are the success stories of Latin America, having made a transition to a more stable economic landscape and currency, the same cannot be said of the third largest economy in the region, namely Argentina.

Argentina continues to struggle with a variety of issues, many of which are self inflicted. Sadly, Argentina has yet to learn the lessons from its own volatile history, and in the next few years could again be faced with yet another currency crisis which have so bedeviled this country.

A recent incident neatly encapsulates Argentina's past problems. In 2012 hedge fund billionaire Paul Singer obtained a court order to seize the classic three masted Argentinian frigate, the ARA Libertad while it was moored in Accra and effectively holding it to ransom. The ransom he demanded was $1.6 billion, money which was owed to him by the Argentine government. This action stemmed from Argentina's default in 2001.

For a wealthy country, looking to expand into international markets, the above is not the image to portray. And when added to the problems of civil unrest, coupled with a deeply unpopular president, Argentina seems once again on the verge of collapse.

The question is, how has Argentina arrived at this sorry state and where does it go next? As we have seen, Brazil and Mexico have already made the transition to a stable economy, with Mexico in particular, supplanting its dependency on commodities with a growing reputation for manufacturing and industry.

The answer, as always, lies in the history. Over the last two centuries there have been few countries in the world which have suffered as many booms and busts as Argentina. There is an old saying in Argentina which is often quoted:

"wages go up in stairs, and prices in escalators."

And which in many ways sums up the roller coaster ride of this rich, varied but highly volatile country.

Difficult to believe, but at one time, Argentina was the richest country in the world which is reflected in the grandiose architecture of Buenos Aires. However, the period following the second world war was marked by political instability and military dictatorships, with Juan Peron at the helm on three occasions. First in 1946, again in 1952 and, finally in 1973.

During this time, economic policy became increasingly socialist in sentiment and even more importantly, inward looking, underpinned with increasingly bizarre laws, some of which are still in place today.

Political instability followed and reached a peak in 2001, when five presidents were elected and promptly replaced in a period of just two weeks. In the same year Argentina became infamous for the biggest sovereign debt default in history of almost $100 billion. Three years later the Government offered its creditors 30 cents in the dollar, most of whom accepted this as settlement of the debt, except Paul Singer, hence his action against the frigate.

The run up to this period of extreme volatility, a collapse of the financial systems, riots on the streets and rampant inflation, can all be traced back to one simple linkage. The currency peg of the US dollar and the Argentinian peso, introduced in 1991 by a so called 'currency board'.

Between 1975 and 1990, Argentina had experienced crippling hyperinflation averaging over 300% a year before finally peaking in 1989 at an astonishing 5,000%, largely driven by unsustainable money supply to finance government debt which had grown under successive governments. Tax evasion and losses in state enterprises were the main culprits and, in order to control inflation and pull the country back from the brink, the government was faced with three choices in terms of currency exchange.

First, to introduce a floating exchange rate. Second, to introduce a currency board. Third, to introduce some sort of hybrid. The decision was taken to introduce a currency board which was established in April 1991 with a fixed peg of one peso to one dollar.

The role of any currency board is very different from that of a central bank in several key ways. Firstly, it is not the lender of last resort. Secondly, it does not have powers to affect monetary policy. Third, it has no mandate to manage interest rates. Fourth, it has to ensure there are sufficient foreign reserves so all holders of the home currency can convert into the reserve currency, if required. Finally, a currency board only earns interest on its reserves, not on speculative currency transactions.

Whilst the initial effects were positive, with inflation falling from 3000% to just over 3.5% by 1994, the longer term effects were far more damaging and the peg was doomed from the start. In many ways Argentina's experience can be likened to the situation with the Eurozone at present.

Any marriage of currencies is also a marriage of countries, cultures and underlying fundamental economics, but to peg with the US dollar was foolhardy in the extreme for many reasons. The most significant in any currency board is the renunciation of both the exchange rate policy and monetary policy for the country, with interest rates, in effect, being set by the Federal Reserve in the United States.

As such, the Argentinian government was left with few instruments with which to control its own destiny. The first sign of trouble came in 1995 when Mexico was forced to devalue the peso, with investors in Argentina reacting swiftly by withdrawing their reserves, resulting in the collapse of many banks. The government responded by tightening banking regulation and capital requirements, in an effort to prevent a total collapse in the banking system.

However, shortly after, four major shocks drove the nails into the coffin of the currency board. First, commodity prices stopped rising and began to fall. Second, the cost of money began to rise for emerging economies. Third, the US dollar began to appreciate against other currencies. Fourth and last, Brazil, one of Argentina's largest trading partners devalued.

The currency board, much like the band on the Titanic, continued to play on, ignoring what was happening around them, and refusing to accept the economy was in crisis. By 1998 Argentina was in recession, with the currency board maintaining the economy would grow by 6%.

Finally, three years later, with the country mired in debt, the country defaulted. In January 2002, after almost ten years, the currency board was abandoned, with the peso losing quickly, with a provisional rate of 1.4 pesos to the US dollar introduced as an interim 'floating exchange rate'. Whilst the peso continued to weaken, with the abandonment of the currency board, the country finally moved towards a recognisable model of the developed economies. Fiscal policy was no longer dictated by US dollars, whilst interest rate management became the responsibility of the central bank.

In 2003, commodity markets, which had been one of the catalysts for the collapse in the late 1990's, came to the rescue and, with booming export markets and rising demand coupled with expansionary government policies, the economy started to grow once more, moving out of bust and back into boom again. But the question now is for how long? And with the global economy in recession, in the second decade of the 21st century, the outlook for Argentina is looking bleak.

Once more it is a combination of rising commodity prices and currency weakness which lie at the heart of the problem. With inflation running at 25% and rising, and a peso that is depreciating fast, the government is implementing punitive exchange controls, which have merely exacerbated the problem. With Argentinian nationals no longer allowed to travel freely overseas, and with the government clearly signalling its concerns by rationing US dollars, investors are moving their money out as fast as possible pushing the currency into crisis once more. So much so, that there is now a secondary and informal black market in US dollars which, unlike the real economy, is booming. The streets of Buenos Aires are once again bustling with money changers, reminiscent of the 1980's.

Companies have also joined this secondary market, adding further pressure, using a mechanism called blue chip swaps, which were used in a similar way in Brazil in the 1990's.

In simple terms this financial mechanism allows a company to purchase a foreign asset, such as a US dollar denominated bond in pesos, and then transfer those assets to the US where the bond is then sold.

Perhaps commodities will come to the rescue once again. Like Brazil, Argentina is a significant exporter of soft commodities which remain the mainstay of the economy, with soybeans leading the way. Add to this, key commodities such as copper and gold, along with lead, tin, iron and manganese, and it's sometimes difficult to understand the paradox that is Argentina.

The country is rich in both human and natural resources and indeed it has nurtured its people by implementing policies of social inclusion. As a result, it is one of the most literate nations in the world and, provided it has the political will, the country and its people should be able to engineer a recovery and regain its prominence as a leading G20 nation.

Finally, just to round off this overview of Argentina, its history, economy and its currency, let's take a look at a monthly chart of the Argentinian Peso against the US dollar. Bear in mind this is a monthly time frame so you are looking at almost three years of price action here. An extraordinary chart, and one which neatly encapsulates the boom to bust nature of Argentina, and its roller-coaster ride.

Fig 13.15 Argentine Peso/USD

Chile and Peru

Finally, before we leave Latin America I would like to take a very quick look at two other countries, both linked by one principle commodity, which is copper. The two countries are Chile and Peru who between them account for over 40% of the total reserves of the red metal. A metal so precious to China and other expanding economies.

Chile is the world's largest exporter of copper and accounts for almost 60% of its exports, which is why the Chilean peso is often referred to as the copper currency. Indeed, if there is one statement guaranteed to strike terror into the heart of any Chilean politician, it is that the copper super-cycle has come to an end.

In the first decade of the 21st century, copper has been on an extended bullish trend which has seen the metal climb from $2,000 per tonne at the start of the new century, to over $8,000 per tonne twelve years later, and more recently to just over $6,000 per tonne.

One of the peculiarities of copper is the various prices it is quoted in on futures exchanges and also in the media. Dollars per tonne is popular, however it is also quoted in dollars per pound and dollars per ton, so comparing prices can be confusing as it is quoted not only in different unit sizes, but also in both metric and imperial measures. The chart in Fig 13.16 shows copper quoted in US dollars per pound which is the measure primarily used in the futures markets. The chart shows monthly candles over a seven year period.

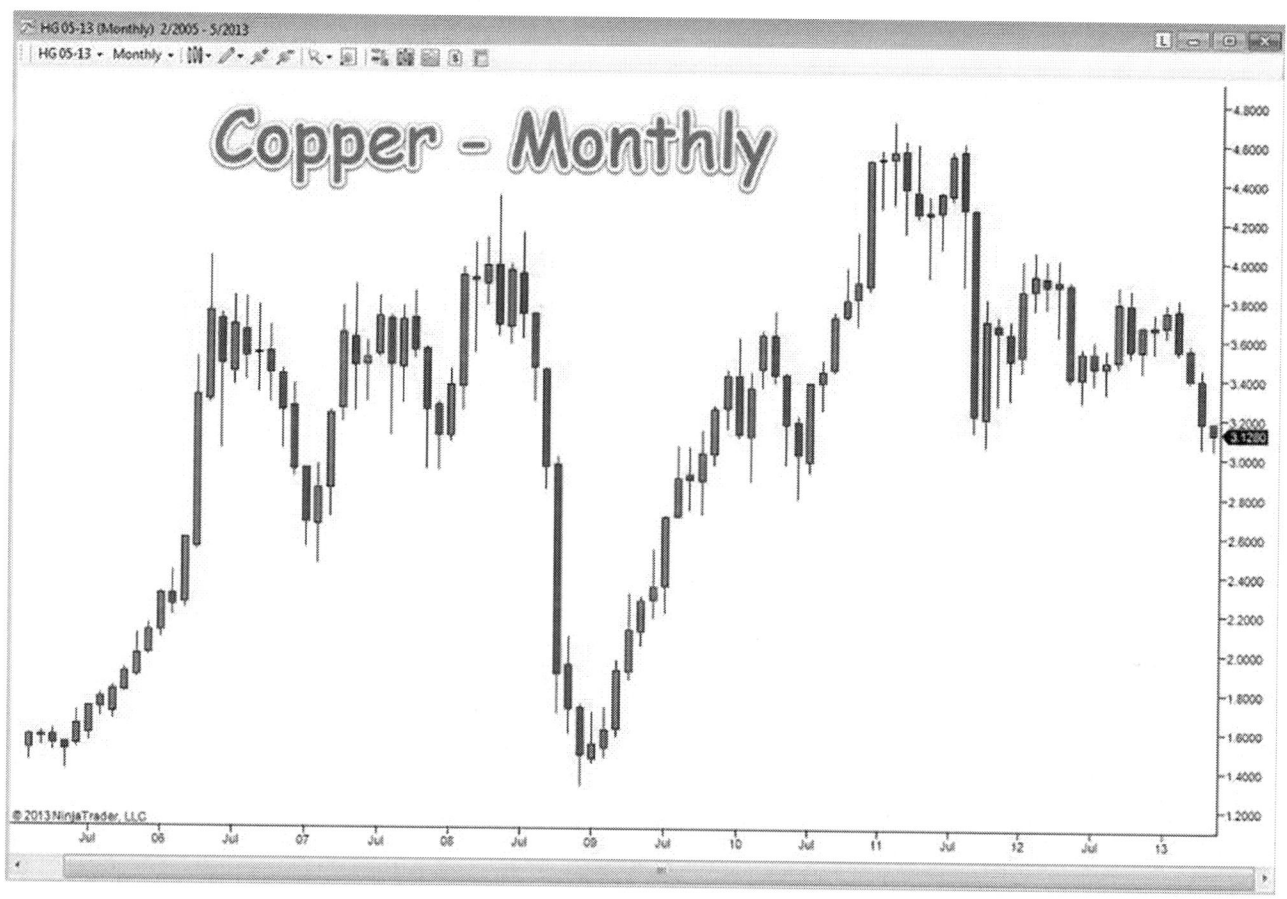

Fig 13.16 Copper Monthly Chart

Peru too has enjoyed a long period of sustained prosperity, with the economy growing an average of 6.5% per year since 2002, and looking at the price chart for copper, it is not difficult to see why.

Despite the sharp fall in the commodity at the start of the financial crisis, growth has remained firmly positive. In addition and, unlike many other Latin American countries, inflation has remained firmly under control in Peru, remaining in a relatively tight range between the 1% to 3% target set by the central bank, and only recently rising marginally above this in 2011 to 3.4%.

However, as with all commodity dependent countries, the volatility of the market and demand for base commodities remains the underlying problem. The close relationship between the currency and the commodity are never far away and below in Fig 13.17 is the monthly chart for the Peruvian New Sol (PEN) against the US dollar.

Fig 13.17 USD/Peruvian New Sol

As copper prices recovered from the sharp move lower in 2008 and moved into a bullish phase from 2009 through to 2012, so the currency strengthened in step, and whilst no relationship is ever perfect, it does demonstrate the issues for the central bank in dealing with the volatile price action in the commodity markets, which is then reflected in the exchange rate for the home currency.

Whilst the 21st century has been good to both Chile and Peru, with the industrial force of China keeping demand high, the supply equation of copper has been less straightforward and, in some respects, the ever rising price of copper is far from a true market of price discovery, driven by the balance of supply and demand.

And the reason for this is that, to date, it has been the supply side of the equation which has been the primary driver, and whilst the demand side has been important with China leading the way, the lack of supply has been the principle reason for the super-cycle in copper in the 21st century from which countries such as Peru and Chile have benefited. The danger is that copper is about to return to a more balanced state, which in turn will be reflected in the price and the currencies of these countries.

The supply problems so far have been concentrated in two areas. First, the inability of existing mining operations in both Chile and Peru to keep pace with supply, driving the price of copper higher. These problems have primarily centred around strikes, a common feature in the region. The strikes are generally short, but they are intermittent, so disrupt supply which causes supply chain issues further downstream. Second, water, or the lack of water is a major problem, and here the issue is threefold.

First, there is the difficulty and cost in supplying sufficient water supplies to the mines as these are generally located in remote and arid regions.

Second, with limited water resources the governments of both countries are constantly having to balance the water resource demands for other markets, in particular agriculture and domestic demand.

Third and finally, there is an increasingly vocal and growing lobby opposed to expanding the copper mining industry and, in particular the effects that this is having from an environmental perspective. Pollution from copper excavations is a constant and growing problem, which increasingly the Chilean and Peruvian public are no longer willing to accept.

The second supply problem has been created by China itself.

China's demand for the metal is driven by two factors. Infrastructure demands and export demands. China has an ageing and crumbling telecoms network which requires massive investment if it is to sustain its current rate of growth and keep pace with other developed economies in the 21st century. Second, China's export market demands ever rising supplies of copper for a vast array of components.

As a result, China has created a supply shortage by stockpiling and continues to do so on a regular basis, building ever larger reserves.

The reasons for stockpiling are twofold. First, China has its own significant resources of copper and other base metals, and therefore has a vested interest in maintaining a high price for the commodity. Second, China sees copper and many other commodities, such as the rare earth metals, as an investment asset class, and not so much as a commodity. Therefore, stockpiling makes sense as a longer term investment on two levels, artificially driving the price higher. A win/win situation for China. On the downside, this makes manufacturing and finished goods more expensive, but this is a price the Chinese are prepared to pay.

All of these elements combine to make the price of copper anything but a true reflection of the supply demand relationship. Whilst the price of copper is generally considered to be a bellwether of the global economy, it is also wise to remember the supply side is far from perfect and, with China dominating both sides of the equation, not only as the world's largest market, but also as the world's largest stockpiler, the red metal can no longer be considered in quite the same way as in the past.

Finally, if this weren't enough there are always continual rumours of individual companies and hedge funds stockpiling copper themselves, with a recent report suggesting one company now holds 85% of all the copper currently sitting in the London Metal Exchange warehouses.

For countries such as Chile and Peru, this is the ongoing problem, but despite this both have survived and prospered and continue to do so, with stable economies, relatively low inflation, and a well managed monetary policy run by their respective central banks. The GDP for Chile is the highest in Latin America, and the World Bank classifies the country as an upper income economy. The currency, the Chilean peso is not pegged and is allowed to free float in the foreign exchange markets, and whilst copper is a dominant export, increasingly wine and fish products, particularly salmon are developing export markets, along with soft commodities.

Peru, on the other hand, is still classified as a developing economy, but one characterised by stability, with the Peruvian Neuvo Sol (to give it its correct title) one of the more steady and reliable currencies in the region. Peru's principal exports are copper, zinc and soft commodities and, once again the central bank has managed to maintain a framework of the economy, more familiar to developed economies, with controlled and low inflation, modest interest rates and a policy designed to stimulate growth in a managed way.

These then are just some of the principal economies and countries of Latin America. It is a continent in a process of change, a process mirrored in many other parts of the world, and one where commodities will always play a dominant role. Whilst many of the Latin American currencies could be classified as exotic, they are increasingly moving into the mainstream of foreign exchange markets and, provided the underlying risks are clearly understood, they do offer many opportunities to more experienced traders and investors.

In many ways it could be argued that, unlike the Euro, the daily price action of these currencies does at least represent the true dynamic of the market. Volatile they may be, but that volatility is based on related market activity and not on the whim of a politician or government official.

MENA

Moving around the globe to another major economic block, namely the MENA group and, whilst there is no definitive agreement on the countries in this group, for the purposes of this book, I am going to suggest it broadly covers the Middle East states plus Yemen, Morocco and Egypt.

If there are two common threads which tie this large and diverse group together, it is oil coupled with the legacy of economic and international politics which have influenced the region so heavily.

A feature of the MENA group is that it is extremely diverse and, when considering such a group, it can be difficult to know where to start. Perhaps the best place is with a recent statement made during a World Economic forum by the Minister of Economy and Finance for Morocco who said:

"the importance of the region is enhanced by its exceptional location. It acts as a bridge between vibrant Asian economies, European and Mediterranean partnership opportunities, and Africa's significant potential for development. "

In a sense this does sum up the opportunities for the region and, almost like the old trading routes, stands as a portal for international trade.

The simplest way to deal with MENA is to divide the countries into two broad groups based on oil and whether the country is a net exporter or net importer of crude oil.

Net exporters includes the countries of Bahrain, Kuwait, Qatar, Oman, Saudia Arabia and the UAE, (collectively grouped under the GCC banner of Gulf Cooperation Council members) along with Algeria, Libya, Iraq and Iran. Net importers are Egypt, Jordan, Lebanon, Morocco, Syria and Tunisia.

In terms of these countries and their currencies, most are either pegged to the US dollar, for obvious reasons, or in some cases pegged to a basket of other currencies, leaving little leeway for monetary policy to play any part in the associated exchange rates.

This in turn leaves little opportunity for currency speculation in the region, for the time being but, as with many other parts of the world, change is everywhere, with one topic the centre of debate. Namely, what is the correct exchange rate regime for emerging economies? And, as I will explain shortly, the region covers virtually every type from a currency board, to hard pegs, free floating and hybrid regimes which incorporate various elements of each.

Given the problems in the Eurozone it is ironic this group is even considering monetary union, yet this is an idea which is gathering momentum, with the suggestion being an implementation of the Gulf Dinar for the member states.

This is something that has been mooted for many years as protection against the constant volatility of oil prices and the US dollar. In any such system there are advantages and disadvantages and, even as discussions continue, one member state has already expressed a view it will not join. The reason is partly as a result of the location of the proposed Central Bank, which was not going to be based in the country concerned. That country is the UAE, the second largest economy, and gives some idea of the stresses and strains monetary union can bring. If countries cannot even agree on the location of the central bank, there is little hope of an integrated monetary and fiscal policy based on a single currency.

With such a sizeable member already expressing their view to stay out, benefits to members on the inside would be limited and weakened as a result. What is perhaps more interesting in the case of the GCC is that one of the big disadvantages with such a scheme, namely the loss of monetary and exchange rate policies, would have less impact, because as I outlined at the start, most of these countries are pegged to the US dollar anyway, effectively relinquishing control of these matters to the Federal Reserve.

The problem for the GCC is the political relationship or lack of it, between the UAE and Saudi Arabia, which may well decide whether this particular monetary scheme ever sees the light of day.

It goes without saying the MENA group is dominated by oil in every way, and to put the size of this group into context, if we take the GCC and add Iran and Iraq, between them these eight countries hold approximately 55% of the total proven world oil reserves and 40% of the world's total proven gas reserves respectively. Commodities and commodity prices therefore dominate this economic block.

As a result, one would imagine that as major oil producers all the GCC and other members of OPEC others would want is ever higher prices for crude oil. However, this is not the case at all.

For an answer to this paradox let's consider oil and the economic concept of price elasticity. Most markets operate on a relatively simple principle. This principle is if something rises in price it is likely demand will fall and, conversely if the price falls demand will rise – all things being more or less equal. This simple relationship which drives many markets is called price elasticity and works at all levels in all markets. If the supermarket reduces the price of an item, sales are likely to increase. If the same item is increased in price, sales are likely to fall.

However, the problem for oil producers is more complex for several reasons, both culturally and economically.

The first problem is the cost of extraction is rising all the time and, whilst new reserves are being discovered, these are increasingly being found at deeper levels or in more inhospitable regions. For example, the Alberta oil sands in Canada, the deep sea reserves off the Gulf of Mexico, and the giant pre-salt fields in Brazil.

These are all examples of future oil reserves with great potential, but which are more expensive to extract and process. If the cost of extraction is rising, the cost of refined products have to increase in order to make the extraction economically viable, so prices have to rise. This is what makes Light Sweet Crude oil a premium product and why Nigeria's oil reserves are so valuable.

However, rising prices have two effects. First, there is an initial fall in demand and, second there is a potential longer term shift, away from oil and into alternative energy sources.

As individuals we can all make personal choices about how much petrol or gas we consume, which may affect demand in the short term, but there is very little else we can do in the longer term, unless we are fortunate and have the land to move to alternative wind or solar sources. For the less well off this is simply not an option. Governments, on the other hand, do have the option to fund environmental projects to develop greener energy sources and this is already being seen in the production of ethanol, which is seen as a green source for the future. Electric cars are increasingly commonplace too.

So, the GCC and OPEC have to tread a fine line, between raising oil prices to a profitable level for all their members, but not so high developing countries are priced out of the market, or are forced to develop alternative sources which would damage the oil revenues for oil producers in the longer term.

And here we come to the cultural and social problem. The West and developed economies could easily stand higher oil prices, and pay accordingly. The emerging and developing nations cannot, and herein lies the cultural problem. With demand from emerging nations in Asia growing as well as in the Middle East and MENA itself, any dramatic increase in price could force some of these developing nations to explore alternative options with more speed. In addition, these same nations could suffer economically as a result, something the oil producers would not wish to see.

So the GCC and members of OPEC constantly tread a fine line between maintaining an economic price for themselves, whilst also ensuring prices do not rise too quickly. It is a difficult balance and each year the GCC sets its budget for the year ahead, based on what it considers to be a 'fair price' for a barrel of oil.

In 2009 it was considered to be $70-$80 per barrel. In 2012 it had risen to around $90 per barrel, but there is no question in the near future, this will climb again to $100 per barrel and beyond. It has to, since the supply side of oil is forcing up the costs of extraction all the time, and there is only a certain percentage of these increases that the GCC and others will be prepared to absorb.

In addition, finding and extracting oil is becoming more difficult, not easier. In other words, the elasticity of oil supply is falling and in the future oil demand will have to adjust accordingly.

What the GCC and others hope is that in managing oil supply and price accordingly it, and others, can manage their way through, ensuring continuing profitability for themselves, whilst maintaining a fair price for all consumers in the market. This is the balancing act all oil cartels are faced with, which is why oil is yet another commodity which can be extremely volatile. And with further complexities added, as alternative sources begin to impact traditional suppliers.

In this respect, the US dollar peg does, at least, provide some stability and is, perhaps, one of the many reasons the GCC is dragging its heels in moving towards any form of currency union. However, not everything in the garden is rosy with the dollar peg, as rising inflation in the region, coupled with a weak

US dollar, has led to increasing pressure for an upward revaluation, or even a possible move away from the peg to some form of hybrid system.

The most credible suggestion gaining some traction, is the suggestion of a peg underpinned by a basket of currencies, principally the US dollar and the euro, as these are the two currencies which account for the greatest share of international trade for economies in the GCC.

Time will tell and, before then, there is that small matter of agreeing to the location of any central bank.

EGYPT

The second group in MENA are those countries who are net importers of oil and, for this section, I want to examine briefly the exchange rate regime and history of one country, namely Egypt which is both fascinating and sad.

The choice of which exchange rate regime to select always involves a trade off. The primary reason for maintaining a fixed peg regime, as is the case in most Arab countries, is it maintains investor confidence in the region and in the currency, reducing exchange rate risks as a result. The net result domestically is that it encourages savings and investments and discourages currency outflows from the country.

Furthermore, a fixed rate regime also reduces inflationary pressures and provides an anchor of non inflationary monetary policy. So, plenty of reasons to maintain a fixed peg regime. However, it is not all good news. The downside is that countries have no ability to react to global changes; they have no control on monetary policy and no control on the rate itself. Furthermore, fixed pegs can and do come under attack from speculators from time to time.

However, some countries in MENA have taken the bold step to move away from such a regime and one such is Egypt. But, it has not been an easy path to take. In considering Egypt in more detail it also highlights the problems for currency traders in establishing the type of currency regime which is in operation, as it is often unclear to the casual observer, which is the case with Egypt.

So let's take a closer look at the currency and economy of this fascinating country, the currency history and its relationships in the region and internationally, and the problems it is now facing as a result.

The official currency of Egypt is the Egyptian Pound (EGP) and until the first world war was based on the gold standard, before moving shortly afterward to the British Pound until 1962. At this point the currency was moved to a peg against the US dollar.

The UK sterling peg was reinstated in 1973, and remained in place for many years before the US dollar peg was once again re-established.

This remained in place until 2001, with the currency trading in a tight and managed range around 3.45 pounds to the US dollar.

However, the currency then came under speculative pressure at the start of the 21st century, and in August 2001 a crawling peg was introduced based around the 4.5 Egyptian pounds to one US dollar rate, with a 3% leeway.

Finally in 2003 the Egyptian government, to the surprise of many in the region, introduced a 'floating' exchange rate policy on the 29th January 2003 which immediately triggered a move lower to 6.0, from where it moved to 6.7 pounds to the US dollar, before finally settling in this region.

As I mentioned earlier, to the casual observer, the Egyptian pound would appear to be a free floating currency, but the reality is the exchange rate has been tightly managed by the Central Bank of Egypt, using various mechanisms such as capital controls and trading in foreign currencies. For evidence of this one only needs to look at a chart of the Egyptian pound against the US dollar.

The weekly chart in Fig 13.18 for the pair covering just over a year from the start of 2012 into the 2013, show an interesting phase, with the sudden sharp sell off taking the pair back down to the initial float levels of 6.7 and beyond. The reason for this is that the last two years have seen the country in turmoil once again following the Arab Spring, with the central bank now struggling to maintain the exchange rate as its currency reserves collapse, forcing the currency ever lower, as a result.

Fig 13.18 Egyptian Pound/USD

Whilst writing this section the Egyptian Central Bank has been forced to intervene announcing the introduction of US dollar currency auctions in an attempt to prop up the ever weakening Egyptian pound.

In just ten years, what started so well now seems be ending in chaos and collapse.

Following the introduction of the 'floating exchange' in 2003, everything seemed to be going well. Fiscal and monetary policies were implemented, new business legislation helped the economy grow slowly, moving the country to a more market orientated culture. With the reforms came economic growth which averaged 5% per annum. However, what the Egyptian government failed to do was ensure this increasing wealth filtered down to the Egyptian people. Instead, only the upper classes and government officials were seen as benefiting. Unrest followed with the Arab Spring and President Mubarak was forced to step down early in 2011.

With increasing instability in the country, the currency itself has also become increasingly volatile and difficult to manage, with the CBE forced to step in to prop it up, thereby reducing still further its dwindling reserves of US dollars.

For much of 2012 these reserves have been falling at over $2billion per month with the result that they are now at dangerously low levels.

As with all interventions, there seems little that can stop the downwards spiral and many analysts are now forecasting a drop to the 9.0 level or much lower in the medium term, a disastrous level for the economy which is so reliant on imports.

The outlook for Egypt now looks bleak. As the currency weakens further the price of staple goods is set to rise further, with prices of vegetables, coffee and, most importantly, bread, all rising fast.

As the world's largest importer of wheat, this is having a major impact on the Egyptian people, which in turn is adding to the instability. In an effort to control public opinion, the government has been forced to introduce food aid and, in addition has increased the subsidies for energy which many Egyptians struggle to afford.

With the CBE now increasingly desperate and rapidly running out of US dollars, there is only one way out for the Egyptian pound, and that is to call in the IMF. The IMF is now waiting in the wings, to provide a conditional bailout to support Egypt.

This downward spiral of the Egyptian economy is reflected in virtually every economic indicator, with rising unemployment and rising inflation which has jumped to over 10%. Moreover, overseas investment has fallen as the CBE currency reserves continue to drain away.

The number of Egyptians now classified as poor is also rising fast, government subsidies are increasing to maintain some sort of living standard and tourism has collapsed. In simple terms, every economic indicator is moving in the wrong direction.

This is the nightmare scenario facing the Egyptian authorities in the post Mubarak era. Once again, it is currency markets which lie at the heart of the problem. They may not be the causal link, but they are certainly one of the many drivers. It is a complex issue and, as a net importer the situation is not the same as for net exporters. Furthermore, with the economic, political and social elements now combining in an explosive mix, the outcome for Egypt is very uncertain.

In one decade the country has gone from a new beginning and stable growth, to instability and possible bankruptcy. All that one can say is the Egyptians were brave enough to try.

In the next chapter, just to round off on the major economies and currencies I am going to examine several countries in the Asia Pacific region.

Chapter Fourteen
Asia Pacific Economies

Emerging markets possess a greater upside in the long term because of their strong economic growth.

Dr Joseph Mark Mobius (1936-)

This is the chapter in which I want to focus on several countries in the Asia Pacific region. A region often ignored by currency speculators and investors. However, in these times of changing global dynamics, there are some very interesting opportunities on the horizon. And the place I would like to start is Hong Kong, which needs little introduction. It is now part of China but, until 1997, was a British Colonial territory before it was handed back.

Hong Kong is one of the most advanced economies in Asia and is renowned for its open approach to business. Strategically placed at the heart of Asia it offers a unique environment of freedom and stability, yet is in close proximity to the largest trading nations in the world. It is the ultimate springboard for companies of all sizes to launch their products and services into Asia and mainland China.

The economic landscape of Hong Kong is dominated by the services sector, which represents approximately 90% of GDP, of which financial services form a significant percentage, as most manufacturers have now moved their operations to mainland China.

The currency of Hong Kong is the Hong Kong dollar and is one that is tightly managed by the Hong Kong Monetary Authority, to the extent that since 1983 it has been contained in a tight range against the US dollar, trading between 7.75 and 7.85 HKD to the USD. This type of exchange rate regime is often referred to as a 'linked exchange rate' and ensures the band the currency trades in remains narrow.

The HKMA is, in effect, a currency board and central banking authority, but is also a government body with no remit to manage monetary policy. Its remit is to maintain the currency in a narrow range and to ensure it has sufficient foreign reserves to allow exchange for all holders of the home currency. All of this is reflected in the chart in Fig 14.10 which is perhaps not the most exciting if you're a currency speculator.

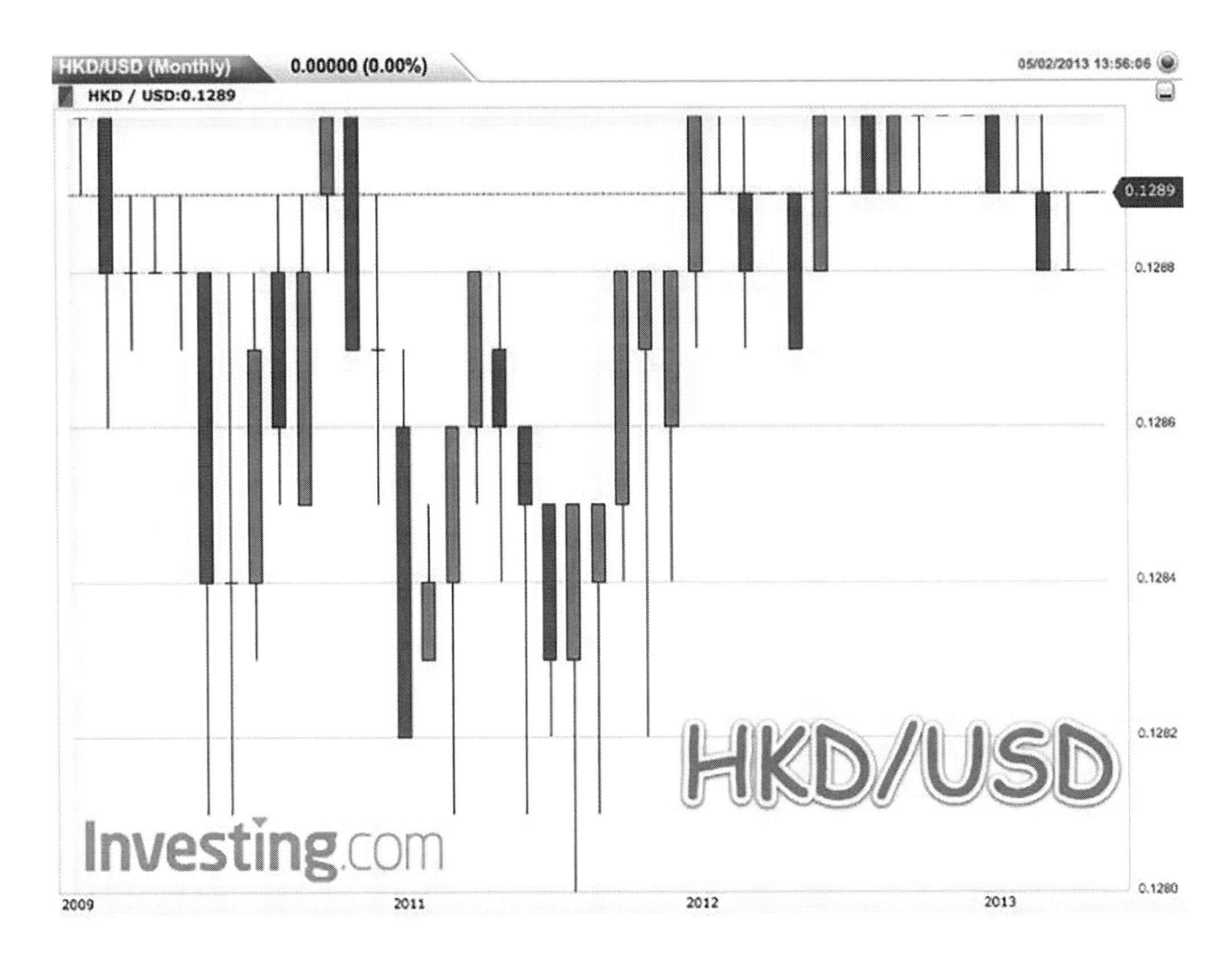

Fig 14.10 HKD/USD

But times 'they are a'changing' for the Hong Kong dollar, as the issue for the HKMA and other currencies pegged in the same way, is the two speed economies that are now increasingly a feature of the global economic landscape. With Asia growing, and growing fast, while the US economy stagnates and only recently has begun to show signs of life.

In this scenario the FED is keen to maintain low interest rates, backed with sustained quantitative easing programs which help to support a weak dollar. Through the currency board, the HKMA has to maintain the peg within the range specified, ignoring (for the time being) the effects this is now starting to have on inflation and a potential housing bubble, all by products of 'so called', imported inflation.

Furthermore, Asian currencies have been strengthening, forcing the HKMA to intervene in order to defend the currency peg. This, in turn, has added further fuel to the fire of inflation which has now started to become an issue for the Hong Kong authorities who are increasingly locked in a cycle of repeated interventions and rising inflation.

Weakness in the Hong Kong Dollar has also been reflected in consequent strength of several Asian currencies, not least against the yuan and, with over 45% of imports coming from mainland China, this is also fuelling inflation as the cost of imported goods rises.

Finally, with low interest rates and cheap money, the Chinese are increasingly becoming property speculators in Hong Kong, driving prices higher, thus creating the classic conditions for a housing bubble. And one which has many parallels with the Japanese bubble of the late 1980's and early 1990's. To put this into context, property prices rose by 23% in 2012 in a country which already has some of the world's most expensive real estate.

Against this backdrop what options are available to the HKMA who are becoming increasingly frustrated by the actions of the Federal Reserve?

The first option is to free float, but this is unlikely. The second option is a widening of the band, which is possible. The third option, and one which is increasingly gaining some traction, is a re-peg to the yuan. This is under serious consideration, given the increasing importance the yuan is now taking on the world stage.

Of all the options the last is perhaps the most realistic, tying together Hong Kong and mainland China in a currency peg two neighbouring economies moving at the same speed, with close trading relationships. This may also trigger the ultimate demise of the Hong Kong Dollar. Whilst it is unlikely the Chinese will ever succumb to pressure from the West to allow their currency to float in a free exchange regime, there will inevitably come a point when the Hong Kong Dollar becomes redundant and is ultimately absorbed into the Chinese currency, and disappears from sight altogether.

Singapore

Singapore is a small but strategically placed city island nation with the Singapore dollar as its currency. With its unique location on the major sea route between India and China, it is one of the smallest, yet most successful economies in the world.

Singapore is one of the great success stories of Asia, of which there will be many more in the next few decades, as in one generation Singapore has managed to transform itself from a developing country to a leading industrial economy at the heart of the Asian tiger economies.

This is very different from where it was in the 1960's and, in many ways difficult to believe. In the 1960's Singapore was struggling with the problems of high unemployment and an inability to sustain the economy.

This changed once there was a major restructuring of the education system. This has resulted in a highly skilled and educated workforce with an emphasis on mathematics and the core skills required in industry. Indeed, if the Asian success story could be encapsulated it would almost certainly include the emphasis on education and the thirst for knowledge, coupled with a personal desire to achieve a better standard of living.

This drive and motivation is further reinforced by 'Tiger Mothers' who push their children to achieve, and has been one of the key factors in the extraordinary transformation that is Singapore.

Whilst Singapore's economic transformation has been one of the iconic examples of the last century, the country has not been immune from global economic shocks, as in the late 1990's, Singapore, along with Hong Kong, saw their GDP growth drop from 4.5% in 1997 to -3.5% in 1998, as the effects of a sudden spike in oil prices took their toll. At the time this period was dubbed the 'Asian flu'.

This period recorded Asia's first drop in demand for crude oil since the early 1980's and was coupled with sudden currency depreciation and rising interest rates. What had begun as an attack on local Asian currencies, quickly escalated into a lack of confidence in the monetary systems, debt defaults and a freeze on foreign capital. All of this was reflected in the price of oil which fell sharply, as the twin effects of a reversal in growth in Asia, coincided with an increase in the oil supply from Iraq. At this point the oil price dropped to an unbelievable $12 per barrel at the end of 1998. A huge fall from the highs of mid 1997 which had seen oil prices test $21 per barrel.

The Singapore dollar is 'supervised' by the Monetary Authority of Singapore. The currency is managed against a trade weighted basket of other currencies of Singapore's major trading partners. The composition of this basket is always kept secret, and revised periodically to take into account changes in global economics and associated exchange rates.

Moreover, the band within which the rate is allowed to float is also kept secret. Here we have one of the more unusual exchange rate mechanisms. The Singapore dollar is allowed to float, but only within a range which is never disclosed and the underlying basket of currencies and their weighting is also never disclosed. So is there anything we do know about this currency which is shrouded in secrecy and mystery?

For an answer let's consider the chart in Fig 14.11 for the SGD against the USD which is a monthly chart and two elements are perhaps striking.

Fig 14.11 USD/Singapore Dollar

The first is the continued strength of the currency, at a time when every other country around the world (almost without exception) is looking for a weak currency, not only to protect their export markets, but also to drive some much needed inflationary pressure and growth into their economies. Singapore and the MAS, on the other hand, are happy to maintain a strong currency. Maintaining a strong currency appears to be their intent, preferring to keep inflation in check, to see import prices rise, and maintain a stable but healthy economy. This policy was recently further reinforced by the Trade and Industry minister who said:

"The strengthening of the Singapore dollar is a key macro-economic policy tool to keep inflation in check over the medium term,"

"The MAS recognises the need to strike the right balance between ensuring exporters are not unduly hurt by a stronger currency in the short term, and capping underlying price and cost pressures in the economy."

This is the balance the MAS is looking to maintain in its secretive policy of currency management.

The second point to note from the above chart is that it gives us clues on the bands the MAS are currently using. This can provide some perspective on whether, as a speculative trader, we can take advantage and what is clear from the above is currently the 1.2200 level appears to be the lower limit. The currency was allowed through this level briefly in 2011, before the MAS intervened.

This technical picture, notwithstanding, one of the characteristics of the Singapore dollar is that it is generally considered to be a safe haven currency. However, when investors and speculators are looking for better returns the Singapore dollar becomes a less attractive proposition, given the ultra low interest rates in Singapore.

Singapore does not have a central bank. Instead the MAS is tasked with controlling inflation and the economy through the exchange rate basket.

Interest rates are set by the local banks themselves using two widely used benchmarks as reference points. These are the Sibor or Singapore Interbank Offered Rate, and the Swap Offer Rate known as the SOR. Both of these rates are fixed by the Association of Banks of Singapore on a daily basis, and the Libor rate is just like any other – it is the rate at which banks lend to each other. The SOR on the other hand is effectively a measure of interest rates for commercial lending. It is these rates that form the basis for all other lending.

The Singapore dollar is also considered an 'exotic' currency, and therefore has many of the characteristics of other exotic currencies. Price action can be both relatively spiky and sluggish, with sudden moves occurring whenever the MAS step in to the market, which they do frequently.

The spread against the US dollar, which is one of the more liquid pairs, can be relatively wide, therefore the Singapore dollar is more appropriate for longer term swing or trend trading. The general bias for the pair is to the short side of the market, and the question with any managed pair, made more difficult with the Singapore dollar, is where the targets for the currency have been set in the short and medium term. This downside momentum is also helped by US dollar weakness which has been a feature of the last few years.

Finally the Singapore dollar can also be considered as a proxy for the Chinese yuan and the reasons are as follows.

First trading the US dollar yuan directly is almost impossible given the way the Chinese currency is managed and the pair is also highly illiquid. Therefore, for traders who want to take advantage of Chinese data, one option is to trade the currency of a country with a close relationship with China such as Singapore. Moreover, the consensus view (at least in the US) is that the yuan is under valued against the US dollar so buying a yuan proxy is one way to exploit this opinion.

Other yuan proxy currencies include the Malaysian ringett, the Korean won and the Taiwanese dollar.

Taiwan

This brings us neatly to the next country in our whistle stop tour of Asia Pacific, which is Taiwan and to examine how its economy and its currency fits within the Asian tiger economies. Just like Singapore, Taiwan has transformed its economy in the space of four decades to become the 19th largest in the world in terms of GDP.

To put this into context, in the early 1950's almost one third of Taiwan's output was from agriculture. In the second decade of the 21st century this is now below 3%.

Taiwan is now the place for leading edge manufacturing for high tech electronic goods. These now dominate Taiwan's export dependent economy, as much of its more traditional manufacturing of clothes and shoes has moved to mainland China.

This change of emphasis in its economy has not only led to an increase in living standards but also to an increase in overheads which is why many of these businesses moved to China, where manufacturing costs are lower.

Like other economies in the region, Taiwan was not immune from the Asian crisis of 1997, but in Taiwan's case the effects were far less dramatic. For Taiwan, the crisis was little more than a pause point, where the economy drew breath, before moving on once the storm had passed. By contrast, Indonesia suffered badly with a 14% fall in output. However, in Taiwan, business continued much as before, with unemployment remaining low and, with significantly lower debts than some of its nearest neighbours, Taiwan remained in surplus throughout this period. This is testament to the banking system and an economy focused on exports.

However, Taiwan is not without its problems, some cultural and some economic. The cultural problems are well documented and revolve around its relationship with China. Whilst this relationship has improved, tensions still exist. Indeed China and Taiwan are often referred to as the 'two Chinas', with China believing Taiwan is still part of its territories. This in turn creates problems internationally both diplomatically and in terms of trading agreements. Ironically, it was China that provided the strong demand that offset a fall in demand from the US.

The second problem for Taiwan is a lack of natural resources and, in many ways, the economic profile of Taiwan is similar to that of Japan. Taiwan's economic growth has been based on exports. It is one of the world's most export dependent economies, with Western consumers its major targets. As a result, in the financial storm that has engulfed the world in the first decade of the twenty first century, Taiwan has not managed to escape.

Not only has demand from the West fallen sharply, but exports to China also slumped, as Taiwan's export markets suffered a double blow. This has put pressure on consumer spending. In tandem with falling exports, rising commodity prices in particular oil, has resulted in imported inflation, which has become a major issue for the Central Bank, which has been forced to cut interest rates.

Finally, the strength of the Taiwan currency, the New Taiwan dollar, in particular against the South Korean Won, has impacted exports making Taiwan less competitive in the region. A heady cocktail which is an ongoing issue several years into this crisis, as the Taiwanese economy struggles to cope with the global slump in demand both from its nearest neighbours and from the West.

And now for a little background on the New Taiwan dollar, the economy and how the exchange rate is managed.

Although the currency of Taiwan is referred to as the 'New' Taiwan dollar this is something of a misnomer as the currency was actually introduced in 1949. It is the official currency of Taiwan which (just to confuse) is referred to in many places as the Republic of China or the ROC.

The central bank is also denoted in this same way, and has the title of, The Central Bank of the Republic of China. Like all central banks it is responsible for managing the Taiwanese economy, primarily through the use of interest rates, although the bank is another with an interventionist policy, much like the Bank of Japan.

In the last ten years, central bank interest rates have remained relatively low, moving higher in 2007 to a peak of 3.38%, before falling as the effects of the global slowdown took hold, to settle at 1.87%.

As we have already seen, the countries of East Asia have adopted a variety of exchange rate policies, with Hong Kong adopting the currency board, Japan a free float, China a crawling peg, and the Singapore dollar a tightly managed float. The Taiwan New dollar can be considered as a free float although, as outlined earlier, the central bank will step in as necessary should the currency strengthen too much.

Such action is not restricted to Taiwan with many other countries in the region taking similar steps.

This is now increasingly becoming a bone of contention with the US starting to suggest major exporters such as Taiwan, Japan and China, are deliberately keeping their currencies undervalued, to protect their economies from the worst of the economic collapse. Furthermore, these actions now constitute 'currency manipulation' and violate some of the principle Articles of Agreement within the IMF.

Moreover and, perhaps even more interestingly, the US has also suggested the East Asia 'economic block' has entered into an unwritten agreement to maintain relative exchange rates in the region. A pact of exporters if you like, where one currency is not allowed to strengthen too much against another within the East Asian region, thereby ensuring exporters are able to compete on an equal footing, and one country does not suffer through the interventionist actions of another trading partner.

The fear in East Asia is deep seated and stems from the damage done during the Asian crisis of the late 1990's, and although Taiwan did weather the storm better than most, the fear of the consequences of a free floating exchange rate still remains. This is a common view in East Asia and, whilst many currencies in the region are classified as 'free float', they are in effect managed through an interventionist policy operated by the central bank.

This is certainly true with the New Taiwan dollar which is generally quoted against the US dollar as in the chart in Fig 14.12 which shows the monthly exchange rate movements over an approximate four year period.

Fig 14.12 USD/New Taiwan Dollar

The first point to note is that just as with the Japanese Yen and other major exporters, US dollar weakness is not something which is welcomed in the region, as it drives strength into the home currency. Indeed, the sudden volatile move lower in early 2012, was promptly supported with several interventions by the central bank, which helped to move the rate firmly from the $25.50 region and back towards a more comfortable $29.50.

This price level was duly maintained for the remainder of 2012 and into 2013. Whilst this is the exchange rate most often quoted and traded, this relationship is slowly changing, in part due to the changing dynamics of Taiwan's export markets. The US market was once the principle consumer of Taiwanese goods with over 50% of Taiwan's manufacturing output going there. However, this has fallen sharply in the second decade of the 21st century to just over 10%, with China absorbing the slack.

As a result, the Taiwanese central bank has now shifted its focus for intervention away from the US dollar and onto the Chinese yuan, which has long been seen by Taiwan and other East Asian countries as the universal gear lever for the region. Or a speed governor if you prefer. As outlined when I covered China in detail, the tensions between China and the US are well documented in terms of their respective currencies, with the US authorities firmly believing the Chinese currency is deliberately undervalued to protect China's export markets.

With Taiwan's changing shift in export markets, China is now seen as far more significant and, in addition, it also gives Taiwan two further side benefits. First, the central bank policy of intervention is less aggressive, given the 'unwritten agreements' that exist between the East Asian countries and which bind them together both economically and socially. Second, this economic relationship helps to provide a bridge between the deeper social and historical divide between the two countries.

In this case, the implications for forex traders and speculators are very clear. The focus for this currency should be its connection to the yuan and not the US dollar. Moreover, as long as the Chinese currency continues to appreciate gradually, the New Taiwanese dollar is likely to follow suit. This broad principal can be applied to the other currencies in the region and, as competitive devaluation becomes ever more destructive, it will be more and more the case that countries will close ranks and protect themselves as a block, rather than be left to fight in the markets alone.

The region is a variant of the Eurozone if you like, where underlying social and historical differences have been put to one side, in an effort to protect business in the region as a whole. How long this 'entente cordial' will last is anyone's guess, but the motto at present is 'safety in numbers'. Whether the West likes it or not, the East Asian countries are closing ranks and acting in unison. With the memories of the Asian crisis still fresh in their minds, overt intervention coupled with loose currency pegs are the order of the day, and are likely to stay that way in the years ahead.

Indonesia

If there is one word which could be said to define the currency of Indonesia, that word would be volatile. Over the past few decades the currency of Indonesia, the rupiah, has crashed, recovered, been devalued, and even re-denominated. And yet, the country and its resilient people have somehow survived. But, moving to examine the currency to see what opportunities it presents for forex traders and speculators, let's take a brief look at Indonesia its history and economy.

In many different ways, Indonesia is an extraordinary country, not least in its economic history which has been turbulent, to say the least. However, in the second decade of the 21st century, the economy is once again leading the way in South East Asia, challenging the view that, over the last few decades, it has been described as 'the land of missed opportunities'.

By contrast, mid way through the second decade of the 21st century, the country has finally established itself as the largest economy in the region and, despite the growing pains associated with success and growth, Indonesia is now poised to take its rightful place on the world stage. Indeed, stability which is increasingly a feature of the economic landscape in the country, was reinforced in 2012 with both Moody and Fitch raising their credit rating for Indonesia to Ba1 from Baa3, investment grade. This is the same grade as for India.

This is the seal of approval Indonesia has sought for so long and with it will come prosperity, growth and foreign investment, which will all create further growing pains. However, they are a measure of the remarkable transformation from the catastrophic effects of the 1997 Asian crisis, which decimated the economy in two short years. This is sometimes referred to as the Second Great Depression, since the effects in Asia were just as dramatic and devastating as the Great Depression in the US in the early 1930's.

However, to step back in history for a moment. It was following the second World War the economy of Indonesia started the long process of recovery. But with little foreign investment, progress was slow, as recession followed recession.

A significant change came in 1967 when Suharto was elected acting President and the following year in 1968 became President, a position he held for 31 years, until forced to resign under a tide of rising opposition following the Asian crisis.

Whilst the debate about his presidency continues today, what is hard to argue is Suharto did achieve economic growth, political and economic stability and, perhaps most importantly, brought discipline to the economy. He restored the inflows of Western capital which provided the basis for industrial expansion. As a country with a vast wealth of natural resources, including coal, oil and tin, exports rose, bringing wealth to the country as oil and commodity prices rose throughout the 1970's and 1980's.

However, as with other commodity based economies, Suharto was keenly aware of the dangers of relying on commodities, which at the time accounted for over 60% of earnings from overseas. The dangers also included the associated price volatility and consequent impact on the currency and economy.

Economic reforms were therefore introduced and designed to stimulate investment and growth in non-commodity based markets, including the financial services sector which until the early 1980's had been heavily regulated. Deregulation began in 1983, allowing for greater freedom for private banks, who since then had been tightly regulated in the control of lending and competitive credit.

With cheap money came prosperity and economic growth, but it also laid the foundations for the Asian crisis. Superficially the banking system appeared controlled and regulated but, beneath the surface, corruption was rife at every level, with the flaws duly exposed as the crisis hit the country.

Whilst some countries such as Taiwan weathered the storm in 1997 and 1998, Indonesia's economy collapsed, along with its corruption riddled banking and financial infrastructures. Contagion from Thailand soon spread in the region as panic stricken investors tried to sell currencies in favour of the US dollar. The devaluation of the Thai baht, which had triggered the collapse, meant that Thailand's exports were suddenly cheap, forcing other countries in the region to devalue to keep pace.

Indonesia's currency, the rupiah, was badly hit and eventually the authorities were forced to devalue by almost 90% in a matter of months, a devastating move. The effect on the economy was savage and in 1998 the economy shrank by almost 14%. The timing of events could not have been worse with the rupiah having just been floated on the foreign exchange markets a few weeks after the initial problems in Thailand began to unfold. Until that point the currency had been pegged to the US dollar.

Over the following two years the currency plunged from the float value of 2,700 to the US dollar, to an exchange rate of almost 16,000 to the US dollar towards the end of 1998, as the crisis finally started to abate.

Meanwhile, international confidence in the country and the currency evaporated, along with the public who abandoned the banking sector. Export markets ground to a halt, owing to lack of credit, and overseas customers cancelled orders as confidence in the country collapsed. The final nail in the coffin was a downgrade from the rating agency Standard and Poors who moved Indonesia to a CCC rating, followed in 2002 by a further move lower to 'selective default'.

There were several reasons why Indonesia was hit harder than most but, looking back, the crisis was not only a defining period for the country, but also in many ways created the platform and springboard for its eventual sustained recovery and move to a stable and economic powerhouse of South East Asia.

The primary reasons for the collapse were largely the failure of both the political and financial systems. Moreover, the recent economic reforms that had been put in place, also played their part and, whilst these caused immense pain to the country in the short term, in the longer term they provided the cornerstones of Indonesia's economic success.

The reforms which were implemented at the time of the crisis included government policies designed to encourage structural changes in the way Indonesians viewed the world and business opportunities.

The policies were essentially created to develop an export driven economy and reduce dependency on imports. An improvement in productivity was also targeted so that competitive and market led products could be sold to overseas customers. In addition, the chief aim of the reforms was to reduce Indonesia's dependency on commodities as a primary source of overseas earnings.

The timing of these changes could not have been worse, as they were coupled with the float of the currency. This left Indonesia completely exposed to the full force of the Asian Crisis which crippled the economy for several years, battering it with soaring inflation and rising unemployment.

However, from the ashes that remained, Indonesia rose phoenix like, with a strong and stable political system, a disciplined and regulated financial market, a motivated and dynamic workforce and an environment which encouraged business to develop overseas markets. The major changes were in the banking and political areas, but the legal structure was also radically amended and updated, with the banking sector in particular made more transparent and accountable.

But, it has to be said all of this would not have been accomplished without help from the IMF, which provided the necessary funds to keep the country afloat. In return for the bailout package Indonesia implemented the above changes, along with other reforms. These included trade reforms in the wholesale and retail sectors, which were opened up to foreign investors. Investment restrictions in the palm oil industry were lifted and government contracts opened up to overseas bidders. Restrictive marketing arrangements in both the manufacturing and agricultural sectors were also removed.

These changes provided the foundations for recovery, which has now seen Indonesia become a shining star in the region, with economic GDP growth running at between 4% and 6% per annum. In the first decade of the 21st century Indonesia's growth was the third fastest behind only China and India in the G20. Now, with an investment grade credit rating, the country is poised to lead the world.

As mentioned, the Indonesian currency is the rupiah which has been a free floating currency since 1998. The currency is managed by the Central Bank of the Republic of Indonesia in a traditional role.

Where the bank is perhaps less traditional is in its intervention, which is frequent and clear. The problem for the bank however, like many others around the world, is in balancing economic stability with controlled inflation in the face of increasing capital flows from overseas driven by exports and investment.

This, in turn, is reflected in the management of the economy where the blunt instrument of interest rates is used once again. In the case of Indonesia this instrument is a double edged sword.

In raising rates to control inflation, this only attracts speculators to the currency seeking out higher yields and, just like other commodity currencies such as Australia and New Zealand, this is one of the constant battles the central bank has to fight. In other words, the carry trade is always an ever present threat.

In the period from 2005 to 2013, interest rates had fallen from a high of 12.75% to the current level of 5.75% and, even at this low level, still represents a very attractive rate to yield starved investors from overseas. This rate is also highly attractive to the ever present currency speculators keen on searching out currencies for trading the carry trade.

And herein lies the problem for Indonesia and other countries in Asia and Latin America. Whilst inflows of overseas currencies are generally seen as a positive sign for the economy and was one of the principle drivers of the economic changes following the crisis of 1997, these same flows can move out just as quickly, making the currency extremely volatile.

In addition, these sudden surges are not conducive to a stable economy, and evidence of this can be found in the Indonesian government bond market where ownership of these bonds has doubled in the last few years, with over 30% now held by overseas investors, keen to take advantage of the higher returns.

The problem for the central bank, is that in raising interest rates to control inflation, will only lead to yet more inflows, adding further upwards pressure to the rupiah. More pressure will trigger further rises in interest rates, and further inflows. This in turn makes exports increasingly expensive and uncompetitive.

A vicious circle which can be explained as follows.

Strong capital inflows from overseas are welcome. They raise the levels of investment in the country and encourage economic growth, so are considered a positive benefit for the country. However, one of the unwelcome side effects is that these inflows tend to strengthen the home currency. The inflows from overseas lead to a build up of foreign exchange reserves as these are used to buy the home currency. The domestic base expands accordingly, but without any corresponding increase in production.

In other words, there is an excess of money chasing too few goods and services and a bubble is created. This adds further pressure on the home currency which adds to inflationary pressures. This in turn puts pressure on the bank to control inflation by raising interest rates. Higher interest rates attracts more inflows of overseas money thereby creating an upwards cycle which is difficult to control. And, whilst there are ways to control this cycle, in practice these measures often result in further upwards pressure on the home currency.

In the case of Indonesia, the approach taken by the central bank is to intervene, and to intervene regularly, selling the rupiah for US dollars to prevent it rising too quickly, in order to protect its exporters from a strengthening currency. If this all sounds very familiar it should, since the same approach is taken by Japan, China and many other countries in an effort to protect their export markets. However, for countries such as Indonesia the problem is even more tricky.

Not only is the Bank trying to protect Indonesia's export markets, but they are also trying to keep inflation under control. Keeping inflation under control means higher interest rates which, in turn, simply results in additional flows of overseas money.

However, the bank has now intervened so heavily in the past few years there are growing concerns the bank itself may need an injection of capital from the government to prop up its balance sheet.

All of this is summed up rather neatly in the chart in Fig 14.13 which again is a monthly chart over a four year period from 2009 into 2013.

Fig 14.13 USD/Indonesian Rupiah

Throughout 2009, 2010 and for much of 2011, investors and speculators were bullish on the rupiah, buying and investing for better returns and yield. Then towards the middle of 2011, sentiment changed towards the currency, triggered by concerns the central bank would be looking to cut interest rates.

Initially, there were two rate cuts, the first from 6.75% to 6.5%, followed by a second and deeper cut in November 2011, which saw the rate fall to 6.00%. A further cut followed shortly after in 2012, to 5.75%.

This action neatly encapsulates the problems for the central bank which is constantly walking a tightrope of trying to support exports, deliver a stable economy and a stable currency whilst simultaneously keeping inflation in check and trying to protect the currency from attack by currency speculators.

It is a fine balance to strike and, for forex traders, the issue is whether interest rates are likely to rise in the medium term, attracting money flows back into the country with a consequent reversal in the current downwards trend against the US dollar.

Much will depend on whether there is an escalation in competitive devaluation (aka currency wars) and, in an increasingly competitive world, central banks are constantly under pressure to protect their home markets. Japan and China are classic examples, Indonesia is now another. If it is to maintain growth and remain competitive with its nearest neighbours, the bank has little room for manoeuvre.

The problem is made worse for the bank with Indonesia's huge market share for base commodities such as coal and tin, along with palm oil. Indonesia dominates the market for thermal coal supplying over 30% of world demand and since the accident at the Japanese nuclear plant, demand for coal is set to increase in the short term, as many governments delay plans to implement nuclear fuel as an energy solution.

Indonesia's market share for tin is even higher at almost 40% of world demand, an extraordinary percentage. The country is also rich in bauxite, copper, gold and silver. The problem with coal and tin, is that it is difficult to increase these markets in any meaningful way, given the dominant market share already commanded. This simply adds to the problems for the bank. Whilst rising commodity prices are good for major exporters such as Indonesia, this is reflected in inflation and, whilst the country is a net exporter of base commodities including oil (although now in decline), it is a net importer of basic soft commodities such as rice, and other staple foods. It is these prices which feed through into inflation, so starting the cycle once again.

This then is Indonesia – a fascinating country in every respect and the key to trading its currency is to understand the complex relationship between the central bank, inflation, interest rates, its export driven economy which is underpinned by commodities, along with the sentiment of the carry trade speculators. As always, with an 'exotic' currency, there are plenty of opportunities, but like many others, the moves in the currency can be volatile. Profitable positions can change quickly, and losses mount up fast.

One solution is to try to understand the broader economic picture and from the price chart determine a view on the bank's future policy. It's not easy, but I hope the above has at least provided a flavour of the country and its currency.

Malaysia

In many ways Malaysia is similar to Indonesia in terms of its rich natural resources, and also in the economic transformation the country has made since the Asian crisis of 1997. Once again, this is a country that has weathered the current storm and is now another star performer in South East Asia. However, the question many are asking is for how long, as Malaysia has a cloud on the horizon, which could potentially see this Asian tiger stumble.

Over the last decade domestic demand and government spending on large capital projects, such as the new transit system which links Kuala Lumpur and Iskandar, one of the country's largest industrial zones, have been the primary drivers of growth.

However, government spending on these major projects has come at a price, and it is a price yet to be paid, as the government's deficit grows larger each year. This structural deficit has the potential to undermine further growth. So much so that in 2011, Fitch, one of several credit ratings agencies, cut the country's rating from A plus to A. The cut was over concerns the deficit is likely to continue and, taken together with the longer term view, with falling exports, the deficit may just run out of control. At 52% of GDP it is currently one of the highest in Asia after India and Pakistan.

Furthermore, whilst Malaysia has revolutionised its economy, in much the same way as Indonesia, it still retains a valuable and important export market in soft commodities. Palm oil, a valuable resource is now grown in an increasingly sustainable way, with Malaysia the world's largest exporter and Indonesia running it a close second. Whilst the economy has undoubtedly been transformed, palm oil and other commodities including oil and rubber still underpin the export market with all the associated volatility this brings to the economy, the country and its currency.

Unlike Indonesia, the success story that is Malaysia has been based on some very simple principles and, as a result, it has managed to survive the Asian crisis better than most. It has weathered the storm, rebuilding and moving forward. As a country, it has one of the most open economies in the world, with very few barriers to doing business internationally, and it was only as the crisis took hold that temporary exchange controls were introduced. These controls were subsequently removed once the storm had passed. This philosophy of openness also applies to Malaysia itself which has a diverse mix of cultures and religions, all of whom coexist, enjoying the economic prosperity that growth and stability has brought to the country.

Second, the transportation and infrastructure in the country is world class, with the government spending heavily on airports, roads, rail and ports. Whilst this has had a direct impact on growth and local employment, the deficit is now approaching unmanageable proportions. This massive spending spree was one of the catalysts of growth in the 21st century, as the country emerged from the crisis.

Third and, perhaps most importantly, the country has managed to avoid many of the volatile currency flows suffered by other Asian countries, as inflation has generally remained low and within a defined range. This is reflected in interest rates which, in the last ten years, have moved between 3.5% and 2%, thereby avoiding many of the problems associated with high interest rates that are an ongoing problem for Indonesia and others in the region.

Moreover, Malaysia has never suffered a balance of payments crisis in its history. Even at the height of the Asian crisis, Malaysia was one of the few countries to reject help from the International Monetary Fund and, despite seeing a sharp contraction in GDP in 1998 of almost 8%, the country bounced back in 1999 with GDP growing by almost 6%.

Finally and, perhaps in sharp contrast to Indonesia, the political and financial systems were tightly regulated and controlled, which is reflected in the economy and which, for the most part, has been stable and well managed.

But, as I said earlier, the wind of change is now blowing through the country and, whilst the first decade has been good with GDP growth strong year on year, unlike other economies in the region, Malaysia has yet to make some of the changes necessary to continue to sustain this growth in the longer term.

As a country, Malaysia is rich in natural resources. These resources have been well managed, with palm oil and rubber two of the key exports and, to a lesser extent oil and natural gas. Like Indonesia the country has developed an alternative export market based on electronics. However, one of the problems for the country now, is that with an increasingly wealthy population, and labour costs rising, it is becoming difficult for Malaysia to compete with lower labour cost economies in the region and elsewhere.

This is an issue seen in the flow of workers between Indonesia and Malaysia, as Indonesians now enjoy their own prosperity with the numbers of migrant workers falling sharply. This has added to the problems for Malaysia's manufacturing sector. However, the government is now taking action, by dramatically increasing its spending on research and development, along with building the educational programs to ensure Malaysia has a highly skilled labour force capable of competing and attracting foreign investment.

One of the most significant changes in the last decade has been the introduction of the ETP or Economic Transformation Program, This was introduced in September 2010, and is a plan designed to help the country become a high income nation by 2020. One of the key sectors in the plan is managing and developing the palm oil sector, with major improvements in both the production and onward processing, whilst also focusing on growing the crop in a sustainable way for the future.

These are some of the challenges facing Malaysia in the next decade, and to this list we could also add the share of exports that go to the stagnant US and European markets. However, the problem that dwarfs all others in the next few years is the government deficit which is now massive and fast growing. This is the price that has had to be paid to develop country.

Furthermore, as successive governments come and go, spending continues to maintain growth and prosperity in the country. But, at some point, this deficit will have to be addressed before it becomes an unmanageable problem for the country. Only in 2012 the government announced the launch of the Tun Razak Exchange, a vast project which is designed to replace and expand the Kuala Lumpur financial district, which on its own is expected to generate over half a million new jobs once the project begins.

This is a massive project which will propel the financial district onto the world stage and make a bold statement that Malaysia has arrived. Put alongside the equally impressive projects of the Petronas refinery, Menara Warisan, Petrochemical Integrated Development and, of course, the Mass Transit Railway, it is easy to see the statement that Malaysia is making to the rest of the world.

The question, of course, is whether the economy can sustain such massive government spending, and whether the deficit now being built will eventually prove too much to bear.

The currency of Malaysia is the ringgit which, up until the Asian crisis, was in fact a free floating currency. The year that everything changed for the currency was 1997 and, like many other Asian currencies, it was speculative pressure driving the currency lower which was the problem. Foreign investors took fright, moving their money out with the ringgit dropping sharply in value against the US dollar, and moving from a rate of 2.50 to a low of 4.80.

Bank Negara, the central bank was forced to step in, and duly imposed capital controls to stem this flow whilst simultaneously pegging the ringgit to the US dollar at a rate of 3.80, which remained in place until the peg was finally removed in July 2005. The move was triggered by China removing its own dollar peg, with Malaysia following suit just hours later.

Since then the currency has been run under a 'managed float' regime by the bank, with the government stating that 'the ringgit will be internationalized once it is ready'.

The managed float is against a basket of currencies and, just like Singapore, the constituents which make up the basket are **always** kept secret and never revealed leaving traders and speculators to guess at where or when the bank will intervene. This quote from the Bank Negara website reveals little :

"The ringgit will be allowed to operate in a managed float, with its value being determined by economic fundamentals. Bank Negara will monitor the exchange rate against a currency basket to ensure it remains close to fair value."

Therefore, as currency traders and speculators what conclusions can we draw from the above, using our knowledge of the economy, the management of the currency and the broader global picture?

The first thing to note about the Malaysian economy and, as a consequence the ringgit, is that unlike many other currencies in the region and similar countries in Latin America, the word stable really does sum up Malaysia.

The economy has not been subject to violent swings, other than during the Asian crisis, and growth has been steady and built on changes in market focus, excellent management of existing resources, and considerable and ongoing investment in the country.

Inflation has been benign over the last two decades and, as a consequence, interest rates have remained within a relatively tight range, and are certainly not high enough to attract speculative attacks from the carry trade. This picture of a stable economic environment looks set to continue, and the only major questions for Malaysia are the deficit and its dependency on US and European markets which remain sluggish.

Fig 14.14 is the monthly chart for the ringgit against the US dollar for a view as to where the currency may be heading in the short to medium term. As we can see from the chart, between 2009 and 2011, the ringgit strengthened against the US dollar as the US currency weakened with quantitative easing helping to drive the pair lower. Since then the pair has traded in a narrow range moving between 2.9000 to the downside and 3.2000 to the upside, with the pair trading at 3.0936 at the time of writing. But where next for the ringgit?

Fig 14.14 USD/Ringgit

First, I expect to see the currency appreciate against the US dollar in the longer term for several reasons. First, and by no means least, is the investment now going into major infrastructure projects which will provide positive support for the economy as well as a possible buffer against any short term shocks in the market.

Second, the economy is well managed and growing at a steady pace with both internal and external growth.

Third, with the government's commitment to spending, plus its longer term outlook for change and development of its natural resources, the home consumer market is likely to remain buoyant.

Short term, the ringgit may come under selling pressure due to the potential exit of hot money. A view backed in a recent research note from Alliance which said:

"With the steady rise in the foreign holdings of equity and governments' debts post global financial crisis, any negative shocks such as political uncertainty, Euro debt crisis and US fiscal cliff may trigger risk aversion, leading to sudden outflow of funds,"

Finally, of course with interest rates in the US likely to remain ultra low for some years yet, this can only help to provide some upwards momentum to the ringgit.

Moving forward, I believe we can expect to see the currency continue to trade in the current range, but with an upwards bias, probably back towards the 2.9200 region and perhaps a little lower.

Remember, that on the chart the ringgit is quoted as the counter currency, so when the ringgit is strengthening, then the currency pair (USD/MYR) will be moving lower.

Much will depend on any intervention from the central bank, who will be keen to maintain the currency in the current range, as the bank continues to create an environment for growth in a stable and well managed economy. Inflation is expected to remain between 2% and 3%, with interest rates in a similar range between 2.5% and 3.5%, so unless there is some unexpected shock to the market, or a sudden change in investor sentiment, the outlook for Malaysia and the ringgit looks rosy.

But, and it is a big but, as the deficit grows ever larger, how long before the elephant in the room can no longer be ignored, and this could ultimately signal longer term weakness in the currency as we move towards the end of the second decade of the 21st century.

Philippines

The Philippines is another fascinating and beautiful country in South East Asia, which has suffered at the hands of both external and internal forces, but has somehow managed to survive, prosper and grow, along with the other countries in South East Asia.

The Filipinos are nothing if not resilient, taking everything that is thrown at them, in their stride, and fighting back, stronger and more determined to succeed. This resilience is now starting to pay off, with the country poised to move dramatically up the league table of world economies. And, if the current trend of economic growth continues, according to Goldman Sachs, the Philippines is forecast to be the 14th largest economy in the world by 2050. This is a staggering statistic given the recent history which has seen the country crippled by corruption, internal conflicts and economic instability. Despite these destructive forces the country has survived and rebuilt its economy. There is still a long way to go, and problems still lie ahead but, as we will see shortly, the foundations are slowly being put in place to provide the springboard which will propel the country into the top 20 economies in the world.

In terms of geography, the Philippines is an archipelago of over 7,000 islands, lying on the fringe of the South China Sea. Pristine and idyllic, it is divided into three main island groups, Luzon, Mindanao and the Visayas. And herein lies one of the many problems for the country – the region is volcanic in origin and therefore always subject to natural disasters, including earthquakes, floods and hurricanes all of which are part and parcel of daily life.

Historically, the Philippines has had many masters over the centuries. First came the Spanish in the 16th century, followed by the United States three centuries later whose occupation lasted until independence in 1946 leaving the country with a US style constitution. Prosperity followed with sustained economic growth until the imposition of martial law in the early 1970's under President Marcos.

His corrupt and repressive regime led the country into a long and painful period of economic stagnation, and ultimately into a deep and damaging recession during the 1980's. The term that was coined at the time was 'crony capitalism', with Marcos at the centre of a spider's web of nepotism, raping the country of resources and wealth. This despotic president was finally replaced by President Aquino who started the rebuilding process. Aquino was followed by President Ramos, who is now widely regarded as the catalyst for the change having laid the foundations for the economic success that is finally coming to the Philippines. His presidency lasted from 1992 to 1998 and, during that time he was responsible for eradicating corruption in many areas of political and administrative life, the deregulation of many of the major industries, opened up competition, and reformed tax collection.

At the heart of this rejuvenation of the country lay the Philippines 2000 program, which was the cornerstone of the Ramos philosophy and is seen as the greatest legacy of his time in office. Privatisation lay at the heart of the plan, with monolithic and bloated state owned enterprises moving out of public hands. These included Philippines Airlines, the Philippines Long Distance Telephone Company, and several large power plants. Coupled with this, the government began investing in major construction projects, creating jobs, growth and attracting overseas investors to the country. At the same time VAT reforms were introduced, raising the rates from 4% to 10%. Finally, and perhaps most importantly, peace and stability were finally achieved on the island of Mindanao.

The Philippines 2000 plan helped to kick start the economy back into life, with rapid growth following between 1994 and 1997, ahead of the Asian crisis. It was largely as a result of the Ramos changes, that the country was able to emerge relatively unscathed from the crisis. Like Malaysia, the Philippines too was able to avoid the crippling effects of the Asian crisis and for very similar reasons.

Whether by luck, planning or simply fate both countries had been involved in restructuring their economies and in a sustained period of reform prior to the crisis which helped to lessen its impact.

Nevertheless, shortly after the collapse of the Thai baht, the trigger for the Asian crisis, the Philippine peso also came under pressure against the US dollar, falling from a rate of 26 at the start of the crisis in 1997 to 38 by mid 1999, continuing lower at the start of the 21st century, before moving to 54 by 2001. Initially, the Philippine central bank attempted to defend its currency by raising interest rates and pumping $1.5 billion of foreign reserves into the system. However, on July 11th the bank threw in the towel, and like other Asian countries left the peso to float free, whilst simultaneously tightening monetary policy, and strengthening the banking system to ride out the storm.

A further factor which also helped to buffer the Philippines came from its own people. The Filipinos are a migrant workforce and, if the latest figures are to be believed, almost 30,000 a day leave their homeland to work overseas in a variety of markets.

Once overseas these workers remit their earnings back home, generating their own source of overseas earnings for the country. Latest estimates suggest this revenue is as high as 10% of GDP, an astonishing figure. It also goes some way to explain why the Philippines was better placed than most to weather the storm of the Asian crisis.

Unlike many other Asian countries, its overseas income was not the 'hot money' of investors seeking out high yielding assets before leaving equally quickly, nor was this money investment dollars. Instead, this was revenue from real Filipinos, simply sending money home to their families which, as a consequence, helped to support their country at a time of crisis.

This remains a unique feature of the currency and its strength or weakness in relation to the US dollar, which we will examine shortly. No other country in the world has this 'home grown' pipeline of overseas earnings. In addition, these earnings are not subject to vagaries in export markets, nor are they subject to pressure from competitive markets, or changes in the economy. Instead, it is a guaranteed source of overseas earnings which is stable and consistent. And will remain so until the dynamic changes, which is entirely possible, over the next decade.

For the time being, however, it is one of the unique benefits to the economy which has helped to propel the Philippines back onto the road to recovery, assisted by the government which is also developing and delivering the policies and plans of President Ramos.

Whilst GPD declined to 0.6% in 1998, the economy bounced back in 1999, growing by 3.4% and into the first decade of the 21st century, with year on year growth steady and rising between 4% and 5% per annum. Indeed, as the global financial crisis of 2008 took hold, it was once again the overseas income from Filipino workers which came to the rescue, with growth slowing to just over 1%, before bouncing back once again in 2010 to 7.3%, a 34 year high in the economic history of the Philippines. Since then, the country has gone from strength to strength, building on the strong platforms put in place almost 20 years ago.

In July 2012, the Standard and Poors ratings agency lifted the country's debt rating to just below investment grade, an extraordinary achievement when one considers it was only thirty years since the worst excesses of the Marcos regime. This rating is now at its highest level since 2003. But there's more good news.

In the first quarter of 2012, according to the central bank, the GDP growth rate was 6.4%, outperforming every country in the region, other than China. What is perhaps even more extraordinary, given the history and what this nation has had to suffer over the decades, is that in 2012, the Philippines pledged $1billion to the IMF bailout fund for Europe. An ironic twist, given the IMF helped to bailout the Philippines in the 1980's. However, what this also demonstrates is the strength and stability that has been built by the central bank which now has over $70 billion in reserves.

However, is this growth sustainable and, if so, what impact will it have on the currency? How will the central bank and government create the economic environment which will allow the Philippines to move into the top 20 economies by 2050?

The good news for the government is that once again the solution is likely to come from its own people. Not only is the Philippines diaspora remitting ever increasing sums back to the country from overseas, the population at home is also increasing fast. And it is this combination of the overseas and domestic economies which are seen as the drivers for future growth.

By contrast, many countries in Asia have a working age population which is declining in number, which will present huge problems in the future, as these countries will be forced to attract workers from overseas. For the Philippines this is not an issue, as it has over 60% of the population in the 15 – 64 age group.

Furthermore, with the birth rate rising, it has a pool of workers able to sustain the current growth levels in the future. Indeed, with one of the highest birth rates in Asia, current forecasts suggest the population could double within three decades.

As always the danger is that should the dynamic growth suddenly stall, this could leave the country with a huge problem in the future. However, the advantages are clear – as other countries see their own labour costs rising, the Philippines will remain extremely competitive due to the sheer number of workers joining the labour market.

The key for the government and the central bank is to ensure all these workers have jobs in the future, and benefit from the wealth and increasing standards of living which will come as a result. This will be a fine balancing act, as the country already has the highest unemployment in South East Asia. And is one of the reasons the workforce is a migrant one and leaving to look for work.

However, whilst the rate is relatively high at over 7%, it is in fact at a record low for the country, and the lowest for over 30 years. The challenge now, with an increasing birth rate, is to ensure economic growth continues at the current pace to ensure that unemployment rates are maintained at low levels in the future.

To see how the government, its central bank and currency are likely to respond to this challenge it may be useful to consider the Philippines current markets together with what is on the horizon.

At present, the key markets for the Philippines is in commodities and, in particular agriculture, which has been the backbone of the export markets for many decades. However, this sector has always under performed in terms of GDP, despite employing over 35% of the workforce it only contributes around 13% to GDP and the reasons for this are twofold.

First, a lack of investment in the infrastructure and irrigation to support this key sector of the economy, and second, many of these markets are essentially labour intensive, so the key for the future is to scale up these operations and to add value by converting the basic foodstuffs into an alternative product. The Philippines is currently the world's largest exporter of pineapples and coconuts, and whilst rice is an important crop, ironically the country is a net importer.

The Philippines is also rich in minerals and geothermal energy sources, along with natural gas but, once again it is the lack of investment in infrastructure which has seen this export market under perform. Exports of minerals have remained flat for the last decade, largely due to legal issues surrounding the overseas ownerships of mines, coupled with concerns over environmental issues. In a recent court case, the law was upheld which should allow the Philippines to see inward investing in its mining infrastructure and a growth in its export markets for base commodities in the next few years.

Under Benigno Aquino's leadership the Philippines in now starting on an ambitious plan, in much the same way as Malaysia has done in the last decade. Since the start of his presidency the government has committed to major capital investment programs in all areas, including mass transportation, water supply systems, improved roads, upgrading of ports, so important to the country's ship building industry and, of course schools, to educate the workforce of the future. Spending on these projects is expected to be in the region of $5 billion a year through the remainder of his term, which will then provide the foundations for growth, along with a vibrant domestic economy coupled with strong employment prospects.

To cater for the growing tourism industry and business travel, the government is also proposing to spend heavily on its airports, either upgrading or building new, and in the last few months two major projects have already gone to tender to develop the Bicol and Central Mindanao airports. Three other projects also in the pipeline include the New Panglaro airport, the Mactan-Cebu International Airport Passenger terminal building and the NAIA Expressway project Phase 2.

Whilst capital projects are visible and high profile, other sectors of the market are also receiving attention with the services sector top of the list. This has been one of the major success stories of the Philippines of the last decade. Overseas companies have increasingly been outsourcing their call centre operations, and one of the primary beneficiaries has been the Philippines. With a highly educated, reliable and skilled workforce with excellent language skills, the market has been growing exponentially, and is now a key part of future growth for the country. This sector has grown rapidly and is often referred to as BPO or Business Processing Outsourcing.

The government is also relaxing many of the rules concerning the gaming industry which is one of the fastest growing sectors in Asia, and has recently awarded licences to overseas operators for four major new casinos in the Manila bay area.

All this growth could not have been achieved without stability. Economic stability and currency stability are in place, and with the recent Standard and Poors rating approval, this can only help to attract further investment from overseas, to a country which is increasingly seen as a safe and secure place to do business, which brings us to the central bank and the currency.

The central bank for the Philippines is the Bangkok Sentral ng Pilipinas, and is responsible for delivering a stable economic environment for growth, using the primary tool of interest rates to control inflation, currency flows and money supply. Over the last twenty years, the economy and its associated economic indicators, has been transformed from highly volatile in the late 1980's and early 1990's to one that is benign, stable and manageable.

For evidence of this we need look no further than interest rates. In December 1990, the interest rate reached an eye watering all time high of 56.6% in just twelve months from 8.6%, before falling just as fast the following year. Since then the rate has fallen consistently lower and, in the last ten years, rates have continued to decline from a high of 7.5% to a modest 3.5%, a record low for the country.

This picture of stability is also reflected in inflation with the headline rate falling year on year, despite a spike in 2008, is now running at a modest 3% in 2013, which is at the low end of the Government's inflation target range of between 3% and 5%. In fact, the forecast rate for the next 3 years is 4%.

The problem for the bank, as with many others in the region, is once again walking the tightrope of inflation, exports, interest rates and currency flows and, in the last few months the bank, along with others in the region, has been forced to introduce currency controls on some of the more sophisticated instruments, namely currency forwards, where currency prices are agreed on futures contracts.

Currency forwards are simply agreements to buy or sell an asset, in this case a currency contract, at a set price at an agreed future date. These are cash settled in dollars and are favoured by many investors as the funds don't have to be deposited or registered locally. The Philippine central bank is not the only Asian country to impose these regulations with the Koreans also adopting a similar policy.

And the principal reason for this is currency strength in the Philippine peso.

Since the Asian crisis of 1997, the Philippine peso has been allowed to free float against the US dollar, one of the Philippines primary export markets, but the history of the currency against the dollar can be summed up in one word. Weakness. Through the decades the rate has gradually broken 10, then 20, and during the Asian crisis, it weakened again moving above 40, before finally peaking at 56 at the start of the 21st century.

Since then the pair has been on a reverse journey, with the peso gaining in strength against the dollar, and as we can see in Fig 14.15 is now starting to test the 40 level once again.

Fig 14.15 USD/Philippine Peso

Strength in the peso is now becoming an increasing concern for the central bank and, in particular, the risks this poses to the export markets which are now delicately poised to benefit from the massive government spending.

Further development of exports, is a key plank of future growth, and inflows of overseas capital are helping to strengthen the peso. In addition, the continued remittances from Filipinos working overseas is also adding to the problem, which can be clearly seen here in the chart.

The problem for the central bank is also the continued and sustained weakness of the US dollar. With US interest rates set to remain low, and quantitative easing also playing its part as major exporters look to protect their home markets with a weak currency, this is simply adding to the problem.

But that's not all. With low interest rates and confidence rising, the property market in the Philippines has been booming in the last few years in both the private and commercial sectors, raising the spectre of a housing bubble fuelled by cheap money.

The good news for the bank is that with currency reserves at a record high and with the ratings agencies all giving their seal of approval, the outlook is extremely positive.

The bad news however, is that with a strong or strengthening currency come a variety of other problems. But why is the peso getting stronger and how is the central bank likely to react?

The first, and perhaps, most obvious reason, is continued weakness in the US dollar. Whether overt or covert, deliberate or otherwise, the US has a weak currency at the moment and, like many other countries, will want the currency to remain weak for the foreseeable future. The second reason is the continued and relentless funds from overseas Filipino workers which continue to grow year on year, and constitute a significant share of GDP.

Third, GDP is strong and growing fast, and through the end of the first decade of the 21st century was running at between 3% & 5%, with astonishing growth in 2012.

Next comes the ratings agency 'seal of approval' which will attract further overseas investors and foreign earnings, adding to current inflows. The bank is also adding its own fuel to the fire with the large foreign reserves it has built up itself, and additionally is also in the habit of 'making the most' of any economic fundamentals which point to growth and prosperity. This is not to say they are untrue, but perhaps are given a little extra gloss from time to time.

Finally, low inflation, whilst welcome, also plays its part.

In addition, to the above elements there is also a further dynamic which plays in the Philippine peso and that's the state of the US economy. Unlike many other Asian countries, the Philippine's largest trading partner (and also their largest investor) is the US and not China which currently ranks third. Therefore, if the US economy is weak with low interest rates, money tends to flow into higher yielding assets such as the peso. Conversely, if the US economy is doing well then demand for exports grows, fuelling inflation and raising interest rates with a similar effect. So, a double whammy if you like.

All of these effects are compounded by the unrelenting flow of money from overseas Filipino workers remitting their hard earned incomes home. Whilst this continuous flow is an ever present driver of peso strength, it is also recognised by everyone, including the central bank, that without it, the country would almost certainly not have survived. Indeed, these workers are often referred to as the Philippine's economic savours.

Of course, for the bank, and private companies, there are benefits in a strong peso, which makes paying off the debts from foreign investors significantly cheaper. Imports too become cheaper, but all of this has to be balanced against the effects of a strong currency on exports and the inflow of overseas currencies from Filipino workers. A strong peso makes it more expensive for these workers to support the families left behind, which is why the bank pays such close attention to this phenomenon. It cannot afford to damage its valuable export markets, nor drive up the costs of supporting the families left behind by their overseas workers, and the reason for this is very simple.

Whilst the Philippines is booming and looks set to become one of the rising stars of the region, it still has one major problem, namely poverty. Recent reports suggest between 30% to 35% of the population live below the poverty line, with a further 15% only marginally above this level. This is a frightening figure which belies the wealth of the country and apparent success, and is the conundrum the government now faces and will have to address. Therefore, the government and the central bank not only have the current high poverty levels to address, but also the future impact of a birth rate that is likely to accelerate. And herein lies the problem.

If the economic growth that is planned is unable to keep pace with the birth rate and absorb an increasingly skilled workforce, this could increase poverty levels still further. This is the danger the authorities in the Philippines now face. The bank and the government both seem to have the will to succeed, and are investing in the capital projects, infrastructure and education that will create the basis for future growth and prosperity of the country.

The problem, of course, is the peso and the global economy. The Philippines has many different drivers which will then all play out in the peso. Managing these sometimes conflicting forces is not easy, so the central bank is constantly vigilant. At the current level of 40 pesos to the USD and below, expect to see the bank intervene to prevent further strength in the short term, and avoid the problems such strength will bring. In the last few years the currency has moved from 50 down to 40, but any further strength is likely to set the alarm bells ringing at the bank. With their reserve coffers full, they certainly have the fire power to intervene but, as always, it is a tightrope they and other banks have to walk. But in the longer term, ironically it may be renewed strength in the US dollar which ultimately drives the pair higher.

With the Philippines the stage is now set, and the benefits that have flowed to so many other countries now look set to flow here. The bad times appear to be over as the country prepares to take centre stage in a new world order, something which its long suffering people will welcome with open arms.

South Korea

The final country I would like to consider in South East Asia is South Korea, which is yet another of those countries which has transformed itself in the last 50 years, and now ranks in the top 12 of economies in the world.

It is one of the starkest reminders, if any were needed, that whilst South Korea has been been transformed into an industrial powerhouse of the world, and continues to remain so, its nearest neighbour North Korea has descended into totalitarianism and poverty. However, it is impossible to consider South Korea without mentioning North Korea since their relationship continues to impact the currency markets.

Again we need a short history lesson which starts with the invasion of South Korea by the North which led to a damaging and destructive war, leaving several million dead. Following the signing of the armistice in 1953, both countries rebuilt, and ironically, in the short term, the North was more successful than the South largely due to support from Soviet Russia. And, it wasn't until the 1960's the South, supported by the USA, began to develop more quickly, with GDP growing fast in the 1970's and 80's.

Despite the fact the country was not a democracy, the changes implemented were both sweeping and fundamental, and laid the foundation stones for South Korea's continued and unrelenting growth in the second decade of the 21st century.

Under the then government led by Park Chung Hee, exports were hailed as the future for the country, and today the country is one of the world's leading export driven economies. In the 1970's currency reforms were introduced, along with changes to the banking and financial systems to underpin growth with policy changes directed at the promotion of heavy industries, chemicals, consumer electronics and cars.

With the changes in the banking and financial sectors, the manufacturing sector grew rapidly as South Korea began to dominate all sectors of the market, becoming increasingly reliant on exports for the economic miracle to continue.

Whilst South Korea had chosen a more liberal approach, true democracy was not achieved until 1987, finally replacing the military with a democratic system with the driving forces being the new, young middle classes of the country, whose prosperity had its roots in the economic revolution of the 70's and 80's. The democracy was further cemented in place with the appointment of Kim Dae Jung to the presidency in 1997, a defining year which coincided with the Asian crisis.

For the North, the contrast could not be more extreme. With the collapse of the old Soviet Union, economic collapse has followed and, coupled with natural disasters, lack of investment and a country ravaged by a corrupt and increasingly isolated dictatorship, North Korea's decline has continued ever since.

But how did South Korea fare as the Asian crisis took hold? The short answer is that initially, better than most, at least superficially. However, it is at this point that the concept of the 'Chaebol' came into play, and what had apparently seemed to be growth built on solid foundations was suddenly revealed to have been built on sand, with a consequent collapse in business, the economy and the currency.

As in any successful economy there are always large and successful international companies run by powerful family groups or as they known in South Korea 'Chaebol'. These are often seen as a key part of a country's success. Consider Fiat for example in Italy, Walmart in the US, the Tata group and Marriott Hotels. All still owned and run by family members. These companies are so large and so iconic they become an integral part of the culture as well as the economy of the country. In the case of South Korea, however, from the 1960's to the start of the Asian crisis, the chaebol was a lot more, and in many ways was an accident waiting to happen. One classic example was Daewoo.

Daewoo was founded in the early 1960's, as indeed many of these companies were, as the country struggled to recover from the rubble and destruction of the Korean war. But from humble beginnings in textiles, Daewoo grew to become one of Korea's many iconic companies.

From this small start, the company expanded and grew through the 70's, 80's and 90's adding shipyards, car plants and electronics manufacturing to its rapidly expanding empire. However, following the Asian crisis the company went bust, spectacularly, owing over $80 billion dollars.

The founder, fled the country but was later arrested. A fate other business owners also suffered. Some survived, but many failed, and it took the Asian crisis to bring down the pack of cards which revealed for all to see, the extent of corruption and financial mismanagement that had allowed these companies to become so large, so quickly.

At the heart of the problem was the willingness of each government to lend vast amounts of money to these companies, on extremely favourable terms and with virtually no guarantees. This was done, in general, for political or other favours. These loans were made from state owned banks and to companies that were seen as the future of Korea.

To compound the problems, no formal accounting was ever requested with double booking of orders a common practice in order to inflate company values and turnover. Profits were over stated, costs under stated and, in addition, the chaebols helped each other to falsify values by the interlocking of shareholdings and false invoicing between themselves, all under pinned by vast loans of cheap money provided by the state.

Corruption was endemic, fraud the standard, and transparency was a word no one understood or could even spell. Then came the Asian crisis which exposed all the corruption, the falsified accounts and the over extended borrowing that had created the illusion of success. In creating the illusion overseas investors had also been sucked in, investing billions of dollars in what was considered to be financially strong, dynamic and well managed organisations diversifying and expanding into ever more broader markets.

The first to fall was Hanbo Steel followed soon after by Sammi Steel, then Jinro Group and, in the summer of 1997, the Kia Group which collapsed with debts of almost $400 million. As panic ensued, international investors tried to move their money out fast, but with a currency that was collapsing like many others in the region, this put an impossible strain on the banking system and bankruptcies followed.

The banks refused to renew loans, and with the major banks running short of foreign reserves, further pressure was applied as the Korean currency followed the downwards spiral of all the other Asian currencies, which up until late 1997 it had managed to avoid. As a result, whilst other currencies weakened dramatically, the won only fell marginally and, in relative terms to others in the region, was in fact appreciating, and impacting exports.

However, the won could not avoid the inevitable, and duly succumbed, falling heavily towards the end of 1997. Finally, to add further to the maelstrom, a presidential election was in progress at the same time, with the front runner, Kim Dae Jung sending confusing messages to investors on economic and fiscal policy and merely adding to the panic.

As the won tumbled, so pressure increased before finally on the 18th December 1997, the IMF agreed a bailout package of $60 billion. However, the bailout came with some very tight strings. At the time of the bailout foreign currency was leaving the country at a staggering $1 billion per day. Korea came close to default and had this happened, the shock waves would have reverberated around the globe.

However, what is perhaps even more extraordinary is the IMF debt was repaid in just three years, and three years ahead of schedule, a remarkable achievement given the financial state of the country in late 1997. Like many other Asian countries caught up in the storm, rapid changes were implemented and in Korea, as with many others, it was the financial sector that saw the most radical changes, with the country forced to implement the conditional changes of the IMF bailout fund.

However, for Korea and Koreans, the crisis changed many things for ever. Prior to the crisis and its devastating effect, unemployment had been almost unknown, running at just under 2%. Jobs were plentiful and one of the complaints from industry prior to the crisis was the problems it had in finding more workers to meet demand. In addition, many of these jobs came with a complete package of benefits, including housing and education. The culture was one of cradle to grave employment and care. All of this changed as the storm of the crisis took hold and jobs, which were once plentiful, became scarce. Those Koreans with jobs were considered to be lucky, even though salaries were cut and benefits removed. Nevertheless, the crisis hit Korea hard, and yet somehow it survived and recovered, with growth returning to an astonishing 10% in 1999 and 9% in 2000.

Following the implementation of the IMF reforms, coupled with credit and import restrictions, and with the government promoting the import of raw materials and technology in place of consumer goods, Koreans were encouraged to save rather than spend in the first few years of the 21st century. This is one of the many legacy sentiments from the crisis. Growth steadied at around 4% annually and in 2004 the country joined that elite group of economies which exceed a trillion dollars. A transformation of staggering proportions and an extraordinary testament to the South Korean people.

Since these torrid times the economy has grown steadily and, despite a contraction in 2008, has continued to grow to propel the country ever higher up the list of world economies. However, the country is not without its problems.

The Chaebol companies still dominate the country, its economics and its politics, and as each election comes and goes, the old rivalries and animosities are ignited once again. Companies such as Samsung, Hyundai, and LG generate around 50% of GDP, with critics suggesting these state endorsed giants are not good news for the country longer term, as they squeeze the small to medium size companies out of business.

Indeed, these companies are also seen as fanning the flames of inequality, which is increasing the divide between rich and poor. However, what is interesting is that for many Koreans, these companies are no longer seen as the shining stars of the country and its export driven market, but as elitist, inward looking, self indulgent and self serving. Furthermore, redistribution of wealth back to Koreans who are helping to build these companies, does not seem to be part of their longer term plans, so Korea now seems increasingly divided. And, with a rapidly ageing population, these companies need to reassess their attitude to their workers. Korea is in stark contrast to the Philippines, which has a rapidly growing birth rate and a bright future. By contrast, Korea has a labour market rapidly running out of workers, and this is one of the major challenges the country faces for the future.

So, having considered the background and underlying issues of the country and its history, how does all of this play out economically and, more importantly, with the South Korean currency, the won.

South Korea, like Japan, is an export dominated economy, with the same problems as Japan and the same view, namely currency strength or currency weakness will always be viewed in the light of the export market. Just like the Japanese yen, a strong Korean won will make exports more expensive overseas, as well as making goods less competitive against the other major competitors in the region.

Furthermore, just like Japan, the country is reliant on imports of base commodities, in particular crude oil and rare earth metals. Rising commodity prices are reflected in rising prices which adds to inflation, in the longer term. This is the battle the central bank of South Korea (Bank of Korea) faces on a regular basis.

As the world's fifth largest importer of crude oil, Korea's economy is extremely sensitive to changes in the price of oil. Rare earth metal prices are also extremely important as they are used in a wide variety of exported goods from cars to consumer electronics, and with China now effectively controlling this market, and driving prices higher through supply restrictions, this is likely to hurt Korea in the medium term, and certainly not engender any warm feelings towards China.

But what of the South Korean won, a currency which can best be summed up in one word – volatile. Indeed the currency has recently been described as the VIX currency, an association with the Volatility Index which is well deserved, and the question therefore we need to address is, why is it so volatile?

However, first things first. The won was free floated in December 1997, following the IMF bailout as this was one of the conditions of the loan. The currency had to be allowed to float in the market, along with other currencies in the region, and has remained so ever since. The central bank does intervene in the market from time to time, but no more than the Bank of Japan, or any other central bank.

However, the currency itself has some peculiar characteristics all of its own. The first of these is its extreme volatility, a volatility usually associated with an exotic currency. And not one representative of an export led economy of the stature of Korea.

The second characteristic is that it behaves in an inverse way to the Japanese yen in terms of changes in the global economy. When the economy is weak and demand is sluggish, as has been the case in the last few years, the Korean won tends to weaken. This is good news for the country and, in particular for the Bank of Korea, as no intervention is required to weaken the currency in order to maintain a competitive edge. This is very different to the Japanese yen, which works in the opposite way, growing stronger when economies are struggling and weaker when markets are buoyant. Needless to say the Japanese find this extremely annoying, that whilst the Bank of Japan has to intervene constantly, the Bank of Korea does nothing and simply waits for its currency to weaken automatically. And the reason for this quirk is interest rates.

Whilst interest rates in Japan have effectively remained at zero for the last 15 years, those in South Korea have varied between 5.25% and 2% and currently sit at 1.5%. As a result, South Korea is a magnet for overseas investors and speculators with huge inflows of currency into the country when the economy is strong, and equally large outflows when global economies are weak. Good returns in a stable and safe economy are sought out with money pouring into the bond markets from overseas as a result. This is something the Japanese cannot offer and, whilst their economies are equivalent in terms of strength and export led, the Japanese have no such returns to offer, with their own currency seen as either safe haven, or as a funding mechanism for the carry trade.

However, it is not all good news for the Bank of Korea, as this constant ebb and flow of massive currency reserves not only gives the won its 'volatility' tag, it also leads to higher inflation in terms of imports, with imported inflation. Therefore, if the currency weakens too far the bank intervenes. And it has plenty of cash with which to do so, with a reported $300 billion plus to play with.

The volatility for the won (KRW) is clearly evident on the weekly chart in Fig 14.16 which is against the US dollar.

Fig 14.16 USD/Korean Won

Therefore, whilst weakness in the currency is welcomed it is limited by intervention. So too is currency strength and, in the early part of the second decade of the 21st century, this is now the issue the central bank is facing, as global markets slowly recover. The primary drivers once again being investor speculation of an economic recovery with inward flows into the country as a result.

Like other countries in the region, currency derivatives are the issue, and the Bank of Korea has recently suggested restrictions may be imposed on currency forwards, to prevent further speculation.

And herein lies the problem for the Korean authorities and its currency. First there is the volatility issue which remains an ever present threat. In the last ten years, the won has seen some extremely volatile price moves, first in 1997, then again in 2008, and followed by a third bout in 2011, all driven by speculative investment flows. Moreover, volatility has also increased further by the quantitative easing of both Japan and the US, with US dollar weakness driving the pair lower, and the won strengthening as a result. This makes the won extremely sensitive to shifts in market sentiment and this is also reflected in the principle stock exchange the KOSPI – Korea Stock Exchange, which is equally sensitive and volatile.

Second, is the protection of the precious export markets which are the cornerstone of the economy. Whilst a weak won is good news for the ship builders, the technology companies and car manufacturers, if it is too weak imported inflation becomes the issue. Rising inflation leads to higher interest rates with consequent inflows of capital raising the prospect of volatility in any sudden changes or market shocks. Conversely, a strong won is unwelcome for exports.

Finally, it's not just about remaining competitive in the global markets, it is also about managing the won against the other Asian currencies. This was a feature at the start of the Asian crisis. As near neighbour currencies weakened, the won held firm, in other words strengthening in real terms, thereby making Korean exports less competitive against those of Japan, China and other major exporters.

Whilst currency controls provide some answers to the problems for the Bank of Korea, they are not the complete answer, and intervention and interest rates remain the key 'levers' of currency management. However, the characteristic of the Korean won is well entrenched and unlikely to change soon, so the term the 'VIX currency' looks set to remain a feature for some years to come.

For the Korean people, the past two decades have seen many changes, with many more likely to come. It is the social and cultural changes where the real stresses and strains lie in the future.

The country has transformed itself from an autocracy to a democracy, from war to peace, and from poverty to wealth. It is a country that has arrived on the world stage and, whatever obstacles it may face in the future, is likely to remain there for decades to come.

Chapter Fifteen
Economic Cycles & Their Drivers

Don't panic. Panic...is an irrational visceral response to a sense of powerlessness and helplessness, which often comes from a lack of understanding of the actual circumstances.

Dr Joseph Mark Mobius (1936-)

In the previous chapters we looked at some of the world's largest economies, their history, their culture and their currencies with the focus on the 'big picture' economic factors which underpin these countries and their relationship to one another. This provides the framework against which we can now consider the micro economic data, which is released in a never ending stream, and which provides a snapshot of an economy and its performance against the market's expectations.

Economic data and news releases are a fact of life for traders and, they are important, not simply in the messages they convey to the market, but also because these are the numbers all central banks and policy makers watch for the signs and signals which will shape future economic policy. These are the numbers that form the basis of government policy and central bank decisions. They cannot be ignored and, the key for us is not so much to understand them from an economic perspective, but much more importantly to try to understand and interpret the likely market reaction to the release. This may seem straightforward, but unfortunately it's not quite that simple.

The issue is all to do with the market's expectation, and is one of the reasons markets go up on bad news and fall on good news. In addition, economic data has to be viewed in the context of a trend rather than as a number in isolation. Market sentiment rarely, if ever, reverses a longer term price trend based on one single piece of economic data. There may be a period of volatility immediately following the news, and perhaps for some hours after, but in general the longer term price trend will remain in place.

For example, suppose unemployment is rising month on month, but the latest data shows a fall. The markets may react positively to the news, but this one piece of data is not signalling a change in the unemployment trend, and would certainly not form the basis of any policy decision by a central bank. After all, the fall could be seasonal, or simply be a statistical blip and, until the fall is confirmed by falls in subsequent months, market sentiment for the time being would remain unchanged. The reason for this is straightforward. Markets are perfectly aware that 'one swallow does not make a summer' – in other words, one isolated economic release, no matter how positive, does not necessarily signal a change in a longer term trend.

The second reason forecasting market reaction to an economic release is so difficult, is in judging the data against the markets expectation as each economic release is associated with a forecast of what the market is expecting. Hence, if the market is expecting bad news, and the number is not quite as bad as expected, the market may rise on the news. Equally, if the market is expecting good news, and the number falls short, but is still positive, the market may fall. It is all about market expectation which leads to the third reason, which is shock.

The markets do not like surprises or shocks which come in all sorts of ways. The first and most obvious, is the shock piece of economic data which can be extremely good or extremely bad. The second is a release which was unexpected or unplanned which is generally the precursor to a shock piece of news, otherwise it would have been planned. The third is from comments or statements (intended or otherwise) from senior policy makers. These are sometimes intended to shock in order to prompt a sharp response from the market. Finally, of course, there is always the shock which comes from natural disasters, war, and weather.

The question you may be asking yourself, is whether you need to be an economist to understand how to interpret fundamental data, and the answer is a categoric, no. Whilst fundamental news releases do have a jargon all of their own, the language of economic data is relatively straightforward, and I hope from the explanations here, you will soon see that in most cases their meaning and significance is surprisingly obvious. Moreover, never forget the media is a voracious beast with a very short attention span, and the markets even more so, and it is generally the simple so called 'headline' number which grabs the attention of the markets, rather than any detailed analysis of figures which lie buried in the depths of the release.

However, before we consider all the various economic releases in detail, we need to start with a macro view of the world, and the context in which central banks make their decisions. This is the world of global market cycles, interest rates, inflation and deflation, and is the business of forecasting and managing economies around the world.

A central bank is rather like a greenhouse. Its function is to create the perfect conditions for an economy to grow at a steady pace and, just like plants in a greenhouse, too much water or too little is equally bad. Likewise, too much heat and the plants die. In the case of the bank, this is akin to the economy overheating, which is generally the precursor to a recession or slump, since unlike our greenhouse analogy, the instruments that central banks have at their disposal are limited and blunt to say the least. In addition, and also unlike our greenhouse, when the water is turned on, it may take months to appear.

To use another analogy, the economy is like an oil tanker – once it is moving at full speed it takes many miles to slow down and stop. This is the reason most central banks fail to act at the correct time. As a result, economies are doomed to constantly move from boom to bust and back again since no one is able to forecast, with any degree of accuracy, where the economy is at any particular time, and therefore when or indeed how much pressure to apply or release. This is the ultimate problem all central banks face, so let's start here before moving on to consider the big picture of cycles, as well as examining individual economic releases in more detail.

However, I just want to explore further the role of the central banks, the tools they have available, how they communicate with the currency markets and their relationships with government.

As you now know the Federal Reserve is the only privately owned central bank in the world and any decision it makes will always be made with half an eye on its own shareholders. The ECB is a political bank, in every sense of the word, and will do its utmost to ensure the euro survives, even to the point of crass stupidity. This is their unwritten remit, so do not expect rationality or logic to enter their decision making process.

The Bank of Japan is only concerned about Japan and the yen and is one of the most interventionist banks of the major currencies. If the yen strengthens, expect the BOJ to step into the currency market to weaken the currency, if possible.

The Bank of Canada, the Reserve Bank of Australia, and the Bank of England are fairly straightforward, rarely intervene and remain independent and balanced in their decisions.

At the other end of the spectrum there is the Swiss National Bank, the most interventionist in the world. They make no secret of the fact and are often encouraged to do so by the IMF to take action whenever the Swiss Franc becomes too strong owing to its safe haven status.

In between all of these we have central banks who manage a float, a dirty float or have their currencies pegged, or who are simply the mouthpiece of the government. Over the last few years competitive devaluation, aka the currency wars, have taken centre stage with each country desperately protecting its own markets. For the Asian markets, in particular, this has been a sensitive issue, further compounded by sustained US dollar weakness. In addition, with so many exporters competing from this region, as we saw with the Korean won, relative strength and weakness between local currencies is also an issue, and once again an issue for the central bank.

Finally, there are always the issues of speculative attacks, managing foreign currency reserves, volatility, and interest rate differentials, all of which play a part in the bank's decision making process.

However, the number one issue all central banks worry about more than anything is inflation which, I'm going to cover shortly in more detail. However, in simple terms, inflation occurs when an economy is growing, the central banks have three weapons at their disposal to manage the growth. Furthermore, we also need to remember inflation can be both a good thing and a bad thing. Too much and an economy overheats and tips into recession. Too little, and an economy remains flat and stagnant.

The banks have three simple tools to manage inflation. The first tool is interest rates, which they can raise and is a very visible signal for us as traders. This is nearly always the preferred course of action since it is the simplest, and generally the quickest, and its effects filters through almost immediately into the lending market, increasing costs of mortgages and loans in general.

As a result, consumers feel the pinch and begin to slow their spending. Again, I am going to cover interest rates shortly in this chapter but, in general, as interest rates rise demand for the currency will also tend to rise as the interest rate differential increases between countries and pairs.

The second tool is increasing the reserve requirements for commercial banks within the country. In simple terms, this means they have to hold higher reserves of cash, thereby reducing the amount of money they have available to lend. This, in turn results in lower consumer spending and achieves, more or less the same result as increasing interest rates. Indeed this is a preferred mechanism used by the People's Bank of China with its pegged currency and, whilst it is effective, it is slower than the more straightforward method of simply raising interest rates. The level of reserves required to be held are generally referred to as the reserve ratio and, if and when a central bank changes this ratio, you can guarantee inflation is on the horizon with the prospect of higher interest rates to follow

Third, the central banks operate what is known as 'open market operations', (bond buying and selling to you and me), in order to regulate money supply and ultimately control consumer inflation. They do this using their inter-market dealers, generally on very short term bonds such as T-bills in the case of the Federal Reserve, either to temporarily reduce or increase the supply of money.

In simple terms, if the central banks are buying bonds they are putting money into the system and increasing money supply. Conversely, if the central banks are selling bonds they are reducing money supply which will be the case when inflation is on the horizon, and this is likely to lead to higher interest rates, which is the objective of the strategy

Finally, we have currency appreciation as a tool to fight rising prices and inflation. This strategy is typically used only where the currency is pegged, simply because the bank can effectively control the currency's exchange rate as it is not free floating. For example in the following scenario.

Suppose crude oil is trading at $100 per barrel and the exchange rate between the Chinese yuan and the US dollar is six, a barrel of oil will cost the Chinese six hundred yuan.

However, if the yuan is strengthened, using the peg to the dollar, and now trades at three, this makes the cost of a barrel of oil three hundred yuan instead. This effectively means a barrel of oil now only costs fifty dollars, and many currency traders and investors will see this as an opportunity, as this strategy is likely to continue for some time with the currency strengthening further.

A classic example is Singapore which has adopted this approach to managing inflation over the last few years with the Singapore dollar rising dramatically against the US dollar as a result.

So these are the tools the central banks use to combat inflation and we should also include quantitative easing here, as it is now widely used as a mechanism for stimulating demand, driving inflation into the economy and weakening a currency.

Quantitative easing (or QE) has been widely adopted by the Federal Reserve, the Bank of England and the Bank of Japan but with mixed results to date. No one is sure whether this strategy will work, or even what the consequences, longer term, are likely to be. No doubt we will discover in the next decade.

The next issue is how and when central banks make these decisions and, as a general rule of thumb, most central banks will report interest rate decisions monthly, at times and dates advertised well in advance. These are easily found on many of the economic calendars freely available on the internet.

The only bank that tends to differ is the Bank of Canada which meets eight times a year, as opposed to twelve which tends to be the norm.

Whilst interest rate decisions are widely reported with the dates and times of any announcement known well in advance, other actions may be less well reported, such as open market operations or changes in the reserve ratio. These decisions are more likely to be reported on a live or delayed news feed which may come as part of any brokerage account. However, these news items are important, but few traders have an understanding of what they signify or their importance to the currency concerned.

In terms of interest rate decisions, each central bank has its own way of reporting this information to the markets. The rate itself will be a simple number which is either held, increased or decreased. However, many banks will now issue a statement associated with the rate decision and, it is often the statement that follows the actual announcement that creates volatility in the market.

The reason is the statement will always contain more information, particularly if you know how to read between the lines of the statement and understand the context of what is being said and why. This is why I have tried to analyse each bank in terms of any underlying or hidden agenda that may not be obvious, at first glance.

The banks' statements are often accompanied by question and answer sessions from the financial press and, it is during these unscripted sessions the governor or president of the bank may give clues, either intentionally or by mistake, of future bank policy.

This can also be a problem for us as traders since one word or phrase can send the markets suddenly higher or lower, with the interbank market taking full advantage and whip sawing prices around in the aftermath of any comment. So it is important to check to see if any interest rate decision is accompanied by a statement.

The Bank of England and the Federal Reserve do not hold press conferences following a rate announcement. Neither do the Reserve Bank of Australia, nor the Bank of Canada, who all issue statements around a week later. The ECB however does hold a press conference, for reasons of image and PR. These sessions allows the ECB to raise the profile of both the bank and its President.

The ECB press conference currently takes place 45 minutes after the rate announcement. The Bank of Japan follow the ECB model, although their press conference is often shown as tentative for reasons which are never clear.

Naturally, the problem with any communication from any central bank is in trying to interpret what the bank is actually saying, and who is saying it. And here we need to be aware of two important aspects that are part and parcel of any statement. First is the hierarchy within the bank and, second is the concept of doves and hawks. Hierarchy is key.

Most central banks will have a committee responsible for setting interest rates, which is often referred to as the MPC or Monetary Policy Committee. Generally these committees operate on a simple one member/one vote system, but not always. The FOMC which is the Federal Reserve's equivalent, has a rotating system with both voting and non voting members. Any comments from non voting members will therefore carry less weight in the market than comments from voting members.

With regard to any statement following a rate decision, this is usually delivered by the President or Chairman, as he or she is seen as representative of the committee. Any variation in policy or hints at changes therefore carry more weight when delivered by the Chairman or President of the committee, and the same applies to comments made during non scheduled announcements or in parliamentary or congressional evidential meetings.

Next, we have the issue of hawks and doves, and the markets are keenly aware of who is who within the bank. A hawk is a member who favours an aggressive approach to fighting inflation, and therefore any comments will be viewed by the market as a potential signal of an interest rate rise. Hawks consider inflation must always be brought under control, even if this means damaging the economy.

Doves, on the other hand are more, well, dovish. Their view of the world is that the economy, growth and jobs are more important than managing inflation, so will tend to avoid raising interest rates for as long as possible. In simple terms, hawks focus on inflation, whilst doves focus on growth and jobs.

The issue for the markets and, for us as forex traders is this, and it is back to the issue of a surprise or shock. If a hawk issues a hawkish statement, this comes as no surprise to the markets, and reaction may be negligible. However, if a hawk makes a dovish statement this is a surprise and markets will react accordingly.

So, a hawkish member who suggests inflation may be less of an issue than previously thought, will send a strong signal to the market.

Conversely, if a dovish member hints or suggests inflation is becoming an issue, again the markets will react sharply to these comments as they carry significantly more weight.

The central banks and the committee members are always keenly aware of the impact their comments have on the markets, and will make every effort to convey a precise message, either overtly or covertly. There is also a trend, which is becoming increasingly common, whereby the members like to give advance warning to the markets in terms of timings in any changes to policy or interest rates.

This is now commonplace and the difficulty here is knowing whether, in a month's time or later, the initial hint of an impending change has already been factored into the market, and if so, by how much. The rationale behind this approach is to reduce market volatility on any statement and avoid surprising or shocking the markets. The logic here is to prepare the markets for future changes by giving hints and clues via statements and press releases ahead of the actual release date.

This is a relatively new phenomenon, but one which is growing in popularity amongst the central banks. Timing is everything and, generally the central banks get it wrong, for the simple reason as I mentioned earlier, the economy is like a tanker and can take months (if not years) to change course.

Therefore, any changes the bank may make, will take time to work their way through the system and for the desired effect to take hold, by which time it's usually too late.

The dilemma all central banks face is, apply the changes too early in an economy that is expanding fast and the bank runs the real risk of pushing the economy into reverse, and killing off longer term growth. If the bank waits too long, the economy overheats, so the consequent actions required to apply the brakes fast are likely to be harsh and can send the economy spiralling into recession. To try and smooth out some of the more volatile price swings, each central bank now tries to signal its intentions to the markets well in advance, which then acts as a gauge for the bank as to the likely reception of the news, when it does finally arrive.

In some cases when changes are made, these are simply ignored and interest rates are a case in point. Interest rates are a blunt instrument with which to manage a complex economy and currency, and do not always have the desired effect. Whilst the central bank sets the base rate, it is the retail banks who set the rates for commercial and residential lending and their views may differ. The central bank may wish to lower lending rates, to stimulate demand, but the retail lenders may keep rates high if they feel the longer term outlook is weak.

Conversely, the central bank may push interest rates higher, but the high street lenders may have plenty of cash which they wish to lend and will therefore reduce their rates to encourage further borrowing. The direct relationship therefore between the central bank and the 'real world' does not always work as a simple 'push me, pull you' arrangement, a further example of the difficulties all central banks face.

If the central bank signals a likely rate increase, for whatever reason, and the financial markets subsequently respond in the way the bank is expecting, this confirms to the bank the message has been received. Moreover, when the news is officially released, the central bank can be fairly certain the market will react in the way it wants and expects. Central banks do not like to be embarrassed and, in the above example, this would then become a waiting game for both parties.

Moving on from interest rates to another aspect of financial management by the central banks (and governments) which is the topic of currency reserves, which we touched on several times when looking at some of the Asian countries and how they coped during the Asian crisis.

As we saw when looking at countries such as the Philippines and South Korea, foreign currency reserves can be both a blessing and a curse. For the Philippines it is the constant flow of money from Filipino workers overseas which has been its saviour in difficult times.

Meanwhile, for South Korea it is in managing the constant volatile flows both in and out of the Korean won which almost saw the country bankrupt in 1997. With central banks now increasingly and routinely intervening in the forex markets to manipulate exchange rates, either in free floats or in managed pegs, currency reserves have even greater significance today.

Almost every country in the world holds foreign currency reserves and these are generally acquired through overseas trading, so countries which are large exporters will build up equally large foreign currency reserves. Generally, these are primarily in the US dollar as the currency of first reserve, followed by the euro and the yen. Foreign exchange reserves held by the central bank are a major national asset and a primary tool of monetary and exchange rate policy.

Foreign currency reserves make up $11 trillion of capital and the country with the largest reserves in the world is China, which puts it in an enviable position when it comes to the management of its currency in the market. We saw a classic example of this in 2011, when the People's Bank of China took action to support its own currency, the yuan. However, the downside is the PBoC is also a massive holder of US Treasuries, which is a huge dilemma.

Foreign currency reserves are generally seen as a positive for the country and its central bank, as the norm is usually a lack of adequate reserves. However, for China, massive reserves are a double edged sword, as the country has primarily invested in long term US Treasury bonds, along with other government backed securities. These holdings are now so large (although no one is quite sure how large) that if the China attempted to diversify its holding, it could trigger a catastrophic collapse in the US dollar coupled with a rise in inflation in the US, whilst simultaneously lowering China's own assets reserves. As a result, the PBoC has to move extremely slowly, gradually selling its US dollars and diversifying into the euro and other assets. It is estimated China's reserves of euro are now so large it could absorb all of the Eurozone debt and still have plenty left to spare.

To round off this introduction to global fundamentals we cannot move on without considering the relationship between these custodians of monetary policy, and their respective governments. And the question here is whether any of the Central Banks are truly independent? The short answer is no and it would be naive to think otherwise.

Historically, central banks have often taken a subordinate role to governments, but all this changed in the 1970's when the oil price shocks ushered in a new era and one with a simple message. The prime role of any central bank was to control inflation and maintain price stability in an economy. This became the overriding aim for virtually every central bank around the world, and independence from political pressure was seen as the pre requisite for achieving this objective.

New Zealand was the first country to implement these changes, with every other central bank eventually following suit, and inflation has remained virtually the sole focus of attention ever since. This begs another question. Why did none of the central banks foresee the current financial crisis? Why didn't the Federal Reserve and its counterparts in Europe, UK and elsewhere, learn the lessons from those central banks in Asia, where lending is now tightly controlled with sensible equity to loan ratios for home buyers? This approach alone would have reduced the impact of the sub prime debacle. Such a policy may soon become part of central bank responsibility. However, with any expansion of remit for central banks comes the need for increased transparency and accountability to the people, the markets and politicians.

Governments and central banks do meet, and meet regularly with the president or governor usually attending a weekly or monthly meeting. In the UK, for example, the Governor of the Bank of England appears before the parliamentary Treasury Committee, giving parliament the opportunity to grill the governor on policy and the financial issues of the day.

In the US, the Federal Reserve chairman appears before several senate committees to routinely answer questions on a range of financial matters. In Europe there is no formal mechanism for communication between the ECB and the European parliament, so can we assume there is no link? Absolutely not.

The truth is central banking is, by nature, highly political. It functions within a political environment, and no matter how independent the bank may appear, it is impossible for those running the bank to ignore the social and political mood of the country. Furthermore, most of the central bank appointments are in fact made by a government, with honours and rewards used as a means of ensuring compliance. It takes a strong character to forgo such riches and rewards and to take a stand on principle.

For the Federal Reserve, their lords and masters are the banks that make up the system and from whose ranks the top positions are filled. So perhaps the ultimate irony is that the Federal Reserve, as the only privately owned central bank, is perhaps the least manipulated or influenced by government. Why? Because it is they who are the manipulators.

At the other end of the spectrum sits the European Central Bank whose remit is vague, and run by politically motivated men keen to advance their careers as part of the European project and determined to ensure its continuation and the survival of the euro 'at all cost'.

One only has to consider the future appointment of the next ECB president and the level of lobbying which takes place around member states to realise politics and the central banks are more closely entwined than ever.

It would be naive to think otherwise. One only has to look at examples such as South Korea, Japan, China, and many others to realise the two are inextricably linked.

However, never forget, whatever we may think of these people individually, they all have one thing in common. All of them have the power to move the markets with a single word or phrase, often in code, but which is sufficient to send a strong signal to the market. Some of their comments are part of prepared statements, others are off the cuff remarks at public account committees or senate hearings or simply at a press conference.

As traders, we not only need to understand how central banks work, but we do need to recognise the key people and their motivations. When governors or presidents change, the markets will watch for changes in mood or style. Will the new governor be more hawkish or dovish than his predecessor? Are they likely to be more communicative or more transparent? All these things matter, and are all part of the mix of following the fundamental news which emanates daily from the central banks around the world, and which constantly impacts on exchange rates on a daily basis.

Moving on from the central banks let us now consider one of the broader economic concepts which also plays a large part in their decision making, is what I refer to as global market cycles.

In the earlier chapters of this book we spent a great deal of time considering the capital markets and the relational aspects of stocks, commodities bonds and currencies. We considered some of the complex and intricate relationships that exist and which tell us so much about the money flow from one market to another.

In this section I want to explore this aspect in more detail. In particular I want to examine how the performance of a particular market can give us clues as to where we are in the global economic cycle, thereby giving us further insight into the money flow and the future direction of interest rates, which are so critical to us in the currency markets.

I want to start by considering the economic or business cycle, but not in terms of the time each cycle may take to unfold, since this is almost impossible to predict and never follows a regular pattern. Instead, to focus on what actually happens during each cycle. We all know instinctively economies throughout the world move from boom to bust and back again, with interest rates rising and falling accordingly.

This is the global picture all central banks monitor, using all the economic data that streams out daily in an attempt to determine the true state of the economy, and to implement the correct monetary policy as a result. But how is this done?

Traditionally, the 'boom to bust' cycles are well defined and relatively easy to identify. They are usually denoted in the following way. Late expansion, early recession, late recession and finally early expansion.

Whilst these terms are more or less self explanatory let me explain them briefly.

In late expansion the economy is still strong with relatively high interest rates and plenty of credit available. Unemployment is low, but inflation is rising with interest rates.

Sooner or later, the economy begins to tip into early recession. As the economy starts to cool, unemployment begins to rise, and rising interest rates begin to have an effect on inflation and consumer spending. The number of new jobs created begins to fall, as does demand from consumers for imports and luxury goods.

The economy continues to move lower and reaches the bottom in late recession. At this stage, interest rates have fallen sharply as the economy has slowed. Unemployment has been rising fast and consumer spending has all but stopped, other than for essential goods and services. Property prices may also fall with repossessions and defaults.

Finally, the economy begins to recover once more, moving into early expansion. In this phase, unemployment begins to fall and new jobs are created as the economy starts to recover. Interest rates begin to rise as the economy shows signs of expansion.

This continues until inflation becomes too high and interest rates are increased once more. Consumer spending increases with cheap credit, and so the cycle begins once more.

Although this is a simplified version of the economic cycle, it typically reveals how economies move between the phases of growth and prosperity when the economy is doing well, to phases of shrinkage and hardship in recession.

However, how does market behaviour and sentiment fit into these cycles?

Prior to early expansion central banks would begin reducing interest rates as inflation would be under control. This is generally accompanied by an increase in state spending as the euphemistic 'green shoots' of a recovery begin to appear. Unemployment begins to fall and consumers start to spend again.

During early expansion commodities and equities tend to do well for the simple reason investors are anticipating a rise in economic activity and therefore risk appetite is rising on the expectation of better returns from these two asset classes. Bonds, on the other hand, are generally performing badly, with poor returns particularly in long term bonds which, on average, may only return somewhere between two percent and three percent with flat yields.

From early expansion the cycle gradually moves into late expansion as the economy expands, consumer confidence is high, unemployment is falling, short term interest rates are rising as the threat from inflation appears on the horizon. During this phase bond yields and equities are generally rising, with commodities continuing to do well. Profit expectations are high as stock markets continue to rise, and although credit is easily available, it is becoming increasingly expensive.

During late expansion, energy and metals will outperform other commodities. However, the economy gradually begins to slow as the central banks continue to restrict the money supply to the markets. As interest rates continue to rise, consumer confidence begins to fall, unemployment increases as late expansion begins to enter the early recession phase.

Early recession is characterised by declining confidence and a reduction in risk appetite. Stock markets are falling, but inflation is still rising on the back of the bullish run for commodities. Short term interest rates are generally at a peak, and bond yields will also have peaked at this point. However, they too will start to fall, as the money flow moves back into the bond market as risk appetite declines and commodity prices fall.

Finally, the economy slows, and may even grind to a halt, as central bank pressure on money supply finally takes effect, and inflation begins to fall along with interest rates.

Risk appetite and consumer confidence drains away, with unemployment rising fast as companies cut back on production and output. Bond yields are likely to be falling as the money flows back into bonds. Stock markets will also be falling as investor confidence wanes, with commodities moving lower as risk appetite fades, although commodity staples such as maize, soybean and sugar may perform well as people still need to eat in a recession. Gold may also do well during this phase as investors seek safe havens for their money.

This is only a general and stylised view of how the economic cycle works, but I am sure you can recognise all the various elements and, as I said earlier, it is impossible to put any time to each of these phases as they always vary. However, by considering the various capital markets it does give us a broad view of where we are and also helps to give some perspective when looking at the fine detail on our daily or weekly charts of the forex markets.

Therefore, let me try to summarise this for you into the principle markets, and their likely performance during the various phases of each cycle.

Equity markets tend to do well during the expansion phases of the cycle, when economic conditions are improving and revenues are rising, but will tend to be at their most volatile during the peak phase when the economy is about to turn from expansion into recession. At this point, equities will generally be falling as we move into the recession phase of each cycle.

Commodities generally do well during the early and late expansion phase of the cycle, with corporate demand increasing and risk appetite rising, with precious metals performing well and being purchased as a hedge against inflation. Precious metals often fall during the run into early recession on the prospect of falling inflation, but other commodity sectors such as grains may continue to perform well.

Finally, bonds tend to do well during the late recession phase when both short and long term interest rates tend to decline, with bond yields falling and bond prices rising.

Conversely bonds perform poorly during the late expansion phase when both short and long term interest rates are rising, with the money flowing into riskier asset classes and bond prices falling.

Another way of gaining an insight as to where we are in the economic landscape is by using equity markets. Just as the broader capital markets can give us clues, so too can the various sectors which help to identify where we are in the economic cycle.

The reason for this is that in each phase of the cycle, certain sectors of the economy will perform better and others perform poorly, depending on where we are.

I'm sure you are familiar with the principal indices I covered in one of the earlier chapters in the book, but all equity markets are also broken down or sub divided into sectors. For example, the energy sector is where we may find oil and energy related stocks, such as gas and refined products and services. The technology sector for IT equipment and services. Another sector might be basic materials for base commodities. There are many others, ranging from financial sectors to industrial sectors, health care, telecommunications, consumer staples and utilities.

These sectors will vary from stock exchange to stock exchange and often the sectors are also broken down into smaller groupings. For example a primary sector may be sub divided several times. However, for our purpose the broad sectors are fine for whichever country's index you are following.

The broad sector groups are generally common to all exchanges, although they may be named differently. There is no need to worry about finding exact matches as this is a 'broad brush' approach to tell us where we are in the economic cycle.

As each sector will generally be presented as a chart, it is easy to see which sectors are performing well and which are weak and looking at sector charts for a particular stock index should only take a few minutes each week.

To recap, the four stages of our economic cycles are: early expansion, late expansion, early recession and late recession and the principal sectors fit into these stages as follows.

In early expansion, the sectors of the market that do well are technology and telecommunications and the reason is fairly straightforward. As the economy emerges from the dark days of recession and begins to pick up pace, companies need to invest in new technology and infrastructure as they prepare to expand and begin to recruit. So these sectors will generally lead the way with the basic materials sector following behind as economic recovery builds. This is often reflected in the performance of the NASDAQ 100.

Another sector that will start to perform well is the consumer discretionary, which includes companies and services which are a discretionary purchase by consumers. This sector typically includes companies such as hotels, retail clothing, consumer goods, and restaurants. In other words, markets where consumers spend when they have some disposable income on non essential goods and services.

When the economy starts to move into the late expansion phase, here we are likely to see basic materials continue to do well, as industrial demand increases along with the industrial sector. Corporate profits begin to increase with the energy sector also doing well from additional demand. This demand is also likely to be reflected in the transportation sector as more goods are shipped locally and worldwide.

In late expansion, financials will also be doing well, having picked up through the early expansion phase. Money supply has been increasing and demand for financial products and services grows as consumer confidence and lending returns to the market. The discretionary sector also does well as consumer spending increases on the back of employment and wealth creation.

In the early recession phase, sectors that perform well are generally consumer staples, as even in a recession people still have to eat, along with the utilities sector. Stocks in this sector are traditionally classified as a buy and the reason for this is interest rates. As these companies have such huge capital investment programmes, any reduction in their debt financing is seen as a benefit to their overall profitability which is in addition to their constant and continuous revenue stream. This sector is also considered one of the bellwether sectors to watch for any downturn in an economy into recession.

Finally, in late recession the utilities sector is likely to perform well along with consumer staples and health care. Just like food, people still need health care and related products and services, even in a recession. So the stocks in these sectors are likely to hold up well.

Sector analysis is an analytical tool that can provide us with some perspective on where the broader economy is heading. As an approach it can provide that perspective against which the currency markets move, and so give us a more complete picture.

Nothing is perfect, but this analysis will help to reinforce the picture from your analysis of the principal capital markets, a triangulation if you like on the bigger picture.

Once we have a broad idea of where we are in the economic cycle, we can begin to consider, and put into context, all the fundamental news and data we need to understand and interpret as forex traders. Therefore, I want to start with interest rates, the Federal Reserve and the US dollar, before moving onto inflation and deflation, before finally considering the economic releases themselves.

For central banks, interest rates are the primary tool they use to control the money supply in an economy. In the case of the Federal Reserve there are two interest rates we have to watch, the FED Funds Rate and the Discount Rate. It is generally the first of these which is reported in any scheduled release.

The Fed Funds Rate is the lever by which the FED manages the reserves held by the commercial banks in the US, and acts like a sluice gate on a dam which is moved up and down to control the amount of water in a reservoir. The sluice gate controls the flow of water as demand increases or falls.

In the case of the FED Funds Rate, the rate is raised when the FED wants to decrease the amount of money in the system, and lowered when it wants to increase the money flow. So how does this work?

Well very simply, since interest rates are dictated by the supply and demand of money. In other words, if there is plenty of money in the system, interest rates will generally start to fall, and if there is too little, interest rates will rise. It's a very simple commercial market, with banks borrowing and lending between themselves. In other words, this is price discovery at work but for interest rates. The 'governor' for all this is the reserve ratio. So how does this work?

Every evening, the banks look at their reserve ratio, and check whether they are above or below the minimum set by the Federal Reserve. If they are above the threshold, the bank will contact other banks who are below the threshold, and therefore need to borrow, to top up their reserves. Bank A, with too much money, then lends to Bank B, who has too little. Bank A is now earning interest on this 'spare' money, whilst Bank B is fulfilling it's obligations of maintaining the reserve ratio. The interest rate which the banks use as their 'guide' is the 'target' benchmark of the Fed Funds Rate, which acts as a governor on wholesale banking. So the reserve ratio is the sluice gate for wholesale banking if you like, and is raised or lowered to encourage or discourage the overall money supply, and in turn wholesale interest rates.

The Discount Rate sits above the Fed Funds Rate as the interest rate at which any bank which cannot borrow from another bank at the wholesale level to meet its obligations, then has to borrow from the Federal Reserve itself, at a higher and less competitive rate.

The entire process is one of a 'free market' where the wholesale interest rate will settle according to the amount of money available in the system. If there is an over supply, interest rates will be lower, as there is too much money chasing too few potential borrowers. After all, no bank is going to pay more than is dictated by market forces. If there is an under supply, interest rates will move higher driven by the simple economics of supply and demand.

Finally, and in addition, the Federal Reserve also increases or decreases the amount of money in the system, by either buying bonds, and creating additional dollars, or removing money by selling bonds. This is generally reported as Open Market Operations.

The flow of money is either increased or decreased with this mechanism. Banks who are short of reserves can borrow from banks with an excess of reserves on the overnight market. Conversely, those with an excess of reserves lend to those with a shortage.

The FED Funds Rate is the interest rate the banks use as the basis for agreeing borrowing and lending amongst themselves.

The second interest rate tool the Federal Reserve uses is the Discount Rate. This is set at something called the discount window, and is the interest rate charged to commercial banks on loans from the Federal Reserve itself.

The Discount Rate is just like any other interest rate, although in this case it is the Federal Reserve lending money to commercial banks. However, it works in exactly the same way as any other interest rate and it simply governs the cost of borrowing from the FED.

Therefore, when the Federal Reserve wants to see more money in the system it lowers the discount rate by encouraging the banks to borrow money from them. This money is then passed into the market as commercial loans. Conversely, when the Federal Reserve wants less money in the system it simply raises the discount rate to discourage borrowing.

As a general rule the Discount Rate is normally higher than the FED Funds Rate as the Federal Reserve wants to encourage the banks to lend to one another rather than borrow from the FED itself.

These interest rate decisions are usually made at the monthly FOMC meetings. These meetings are scheduled and publicised in advance, but these rates can be changed at any time should circumstances dictate.

In addition, the rates themselves will also vary slightly from day to day. In fact, the only rate the FED actually sets is the Discount Rate as the FED Funds Rate is only ever given as a target rate and banks are left to negotiate amongst themselves on any borrowings.

So how does knowing this help us as forex traders? And the best way to answer this is with an example.

On the 18th February 2010, the FED, at its monthly meeting surprised the currency markets by raising the Discount Rate from 0.50% to 0.75%. This was the first rise in three years following a long period of ultra low interest rates. At the same time the FED kept the FED Funds Rate unchanged.

In the aftermath of this decision the US dollar immediately strengthened against all major currencies and continued to do so until early in 2011, for the following reasons.

First, the FED was sending a message to the markets that interest rates were likely to rise in due course. Second, it was also suggesting the FED was concerned about inflation, and looking to control money supply in the system using the Discount Rate.

Finally, in increasing the spread between the Discount Rate and the Fed Funds Rate it wanted to encourage the banks to lend amongst themselves, rather than borrow from the Federal Reserve which could then see the FED being forced to take action on rates in general.

The forex markets took this as a clear signal of a tightening in monetary policy by the Federal Reserve and therefore good news for the US dollar. The move was seen as signalling a possible end to ultra low interest rates and increasing investment potential for dollar investors. It also reduced interest rate differentials against other major currencies.

In this particular instance dollar strength only continued for a few weeks, but it was more than enough to take some profitable trades. This is why it is so important to understand the simple headline rate, which in the case of the Federal Reserve is the FED Funds Rate on which all the commercial and retail rates are based, but also the Discount Rate which is equally important.

It is also important to realise these rates are set or targeted by the FED and, as traders, we simply have to wait and watch for these announcements and then draw our own conclusions accordingly.

In the case of the FED Funds Rate there is a futures contract quoted on the Chicago Mercantile Exchange and this can be extremely useful in giving us a clue as to market expectations for the longer term trend.

The contract is called the 30 day Federal funds futures contract. To find it simply visit the CME site at http://www.cmegroup.com.

This futures contract is priced in a slightly confusing way with 100 at the top of the chart, which in fact is zero so as the FED Funds Rate increases, the price will move lower on the chart. When the Fed Funds rate is five percent then the interest rate would be at 95 and if the rate falls to 4% then the price on the chart will move to 96 and so on.

It is important to realise the FED funds futures chart is showing us what traders think is likely in the future, and not what is happening right now. This is the markets' or traders' views of where the FED Funds Rate is moving in the next thirty days. When the markets are expecting an imminent change in monetary policy from the Federal Reserve then it will be reflected in the FED funds rate chart.

It is not the prettiest of charts, but nevertheless one which reveals the markets' view on the rate, in the future. See Fig 15.10.

Fig 15.10 Fed Funds Chart - Courtesy of the CME

In addition to this contract the CME also offer another quick reference point at http://www.cmegroup.com/trading/interest-rates/fed-funds.html

This is referred to as the CME Group FedWatch, and provides a snapshot of market sentiment and likely changes in the rates for future rounds of the FOMC meetings. See Fig 15.11

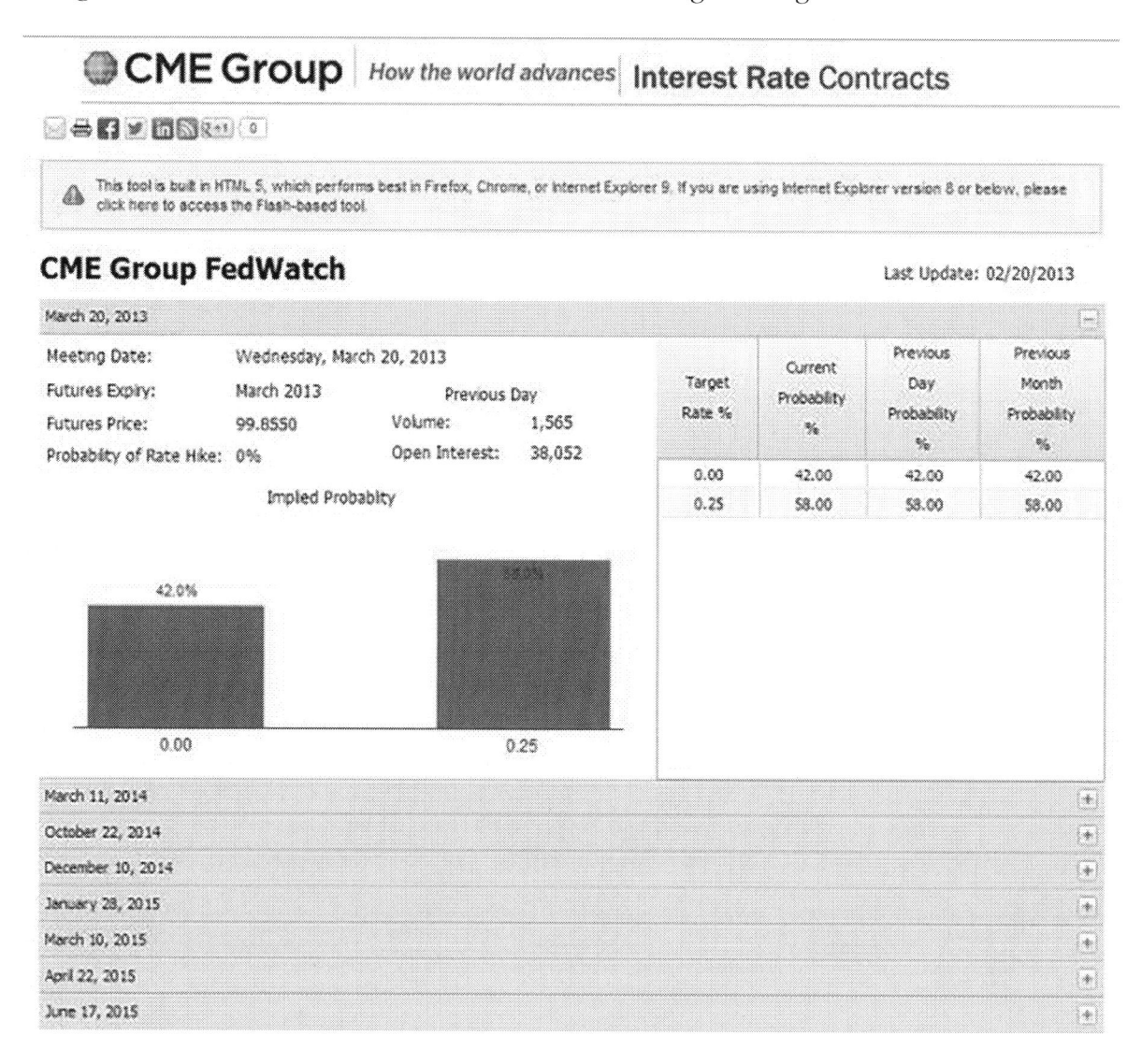

Fig 15.11 CME Group Fed Watch Chart - Courtesy of the CME

Here, the FOMC meetings are matched with the corresponding 30 day FED funds futures contract. This is where you will find the probability of any change to FED rates.

If traders are expecting interest rates to rise soon, this will be reflected in a falling price on the futures chart. Conversely, if they are expecting interest rates to fall soon, this will be reflected in a rising chart. This is giving us an early warning of possible changes in monetary policy with a consequent change in interest rates and money supply as a result.

UK and Europe

In the UK and Europe interest rate decisions are handled slightly differently. In the UK these are announced at the monthly meeting of the Bank of England (BOE). The interest rate quoted is the Official Bank Rate and it is the rate at which banks can borrow from the BOE.

LIBOR is the equivalent of the FED Funds Rate and it is the interest rate banks use to lend to one another. However, LIBOR is constructed in a very different way as it is not set or targeted by the Bank of England.

Every morning at 11 am the LIBOR rate is announced in London and is calculated following a survey of sixteen major banks. The survey asks the banks for details of the interest rates they have been charging each other to borrow money. The list is then compiled. The top and bottom four rates are excluded with the mean taken of the remaining eight. This is then published as the LIBOR rate which tells us two things.

If LIBOR is rising, interest rates are also rising, with the prospect of an increase by the Bank of England in the Official Bank Rate. This could also imply banks are nervous of lending to one another and therefore unwilling to take risks.

Alternatively, if LIBOR is falling, this implies interest rates may fall or that banks are becoming less risk averse and prepared to lend to one another.

You can track the LIBOR rate and the daily changes at a dedicated site run by the Intercontinental Exchange which is now the body responsible, having taken over from the BBA.

https://www.theice.com/iba/libor/

Finally to Europe, and here we have the European Central Bank (ECB) reporting the Minimum Bid Rate at a monthly meeting. The Minimum Bid Rate is the equivalent mechanism the ECB uses and, like the Bank of England, the ECB also have an interbank lending rate known as EURIBOR.

The EURIBOR rate is calculated every day by Reuters in much the same way as for the LIBOR rates and published at the same time, 11 am London time. In the case of EURIBOR, it is a panel of European banks who submit their overnight lending rates. Reuters then eliminates the top and bottom 15 per cent and produces an unweighted average which is published as the EURIBOR rate for overnight lending.

To find the latest EURIBOR rates visit the following site where you will find charts, from one month to twelve months: http://www.euribor-rates.eu/euribor-charts.asp

Whilst the LIBOR rate is quoted in London, it is one of the most widely followed and watched rates and used in several other countries as a benchmark, including Switzerland, Canada and also the US. By contrast the EURIBOR rate is predominantly used in the European banking system.

Although I have only covered three countries in this section, most central banks will be structured in a similar way with interest rates at the heart of their monetary policy allied to inflation control mechanisms.

Professional traders will always watch the Discount Rate in the US, the FED Funds Futures Rate and London LIBOR interbank rates for clues and signals as to how the central banks may react at their next meeting.

So far in this book I have only focused on inflation and its significance in the economic cycle. And the reason is primarily because everyone watches the economic releases for evidence of inflationary pressure in the economy. Inflation can be both good and bad. Too much, and the economy runs out of control and overheats, usually leading to a major crash. Too little, and the economy never gets going. It could remain stagnant or even fall into deflation. Deflation is inflation's evil twin which I will explain later.

This is the perennial problem for governments and central banks around the world, and one to which they have never really had an answer, as they only have limited tools with which to manage an economy. This is one of the reasons why an economy just moves from boom to bust because, just like an oil tanker, it can take a long time to get going, and an equally long time to stop. An economy usually hits the buffers and it is almost impossible for central banks to engineer a 'soft landing'. Instead an economy generally crash lands.

Inflation is often described as a general rise in prices measured by one of the economic indicators we're going to look at shortly. However, many people often confuse the cause of inflation with its effect. A simple definition of inflation is a persistent increase in the level of consumer prices or a persistent decline in the purchasing power of money.

In other words, the effect of inflation is goods and services become more expensive, and the cost of living rising as a result. However, the cause of inflation is due to an increase in available currency and credit, beyond the proportion of available goods and services. In other words, too much money chasing too few goods.

Put simply, when most people speak about inflation they are really referring to price inflation, prices are going up. Whereas the actual cause is monetary inflation which is the tool most central banks use to both accelerate and decelerate the inflationary pressure in an economy, using the fairly crude levers and principles we discussed earlier.

Monetary inflation drives price inflation and, over the last few years, we have seen this principle in action around the world.

Central banks such as the Federal Reserve, the Bank of England, the Bank of Japan and many others have increased the money supply in the system, and once the money supply increases faster than the quantity of goods increases then we get inflation.

A further misconception is that prices rise due to businesses taking advantage of a rising market, but this is simply not the case. In a price sensitive economy customers would simply buy elsewhere, assuming the same quality of goods and services were available, as we live in a competitive world. What actually happens is that because each pound, dollar or euro is worth less, because the money supply has increased, so businesses are forced to increase prices in order to get the same value for their products.

Looked at another way, the value of money has decreased and as inflation rises the pound or dollar or euro in your pocket buys you less of the same goods and services.

The dilemma for all central banks is to try and control inflation as best they can in the cyclical battle. This is normally done with some predefined target range. The first objective is to increase inflation to a certain level, then to maintain it at that level, and finally to stop it running out of control above this level. This is the ideal scenario, and one which most central banks fail to achieve, hence the reason why the economic cycle described earlier keeps repeating itself.

High inflation is harmful to an economy. It is viewed as unsustainable by companies and business in general, and the inevitable consequence from a boom to a bust. Second, if inflation is rising faster than in other countries this makes companies uncompetitive in overseas markets.

But perhaps most importantly, from a consumer perspective, inflation erodes the value of money and therefore of savings.

This is one of the reasons investors rush to gold and other tangible assets when inflation starts to run out of control as they are seen as a hedge, and a way of protecting monetary wealth as paper based currencies and assets decrease in value.

Finally, of course, the standard of living of anyone on a fixed income declines.

It is generally accepted inflation comes in two forms. Demand pull and cost push and, if you recall in the earlier chapter on commodities, this is much the same effect, with demand led inflation resulting from too much money chasing after too few goods, whilst cost push inflation comes from an increase in raw goods and materials, such as commodities.

There is no clear definition of how inflation is broken down between these two elements, but in general it is normally a complex combination of the two working together which drives inflation higher. For major exporters this is the perennial problem, and for the central bank in managing its monetary policy, to create the right environment for sustained, but steady growth.

Whilst a weak currency may be good for exports, it is not so good for imports which will cost more and result in imported inflation. Rising inflation may signal economic health, but may also lead to inflows from overseas, strengthening the home currency. This results in the prospect of rising interest rates which attracts yet more inflows (the 'hot money'), which will ultimately damage exports.

These are the reasons why so many people from governments to central banks and economists focus on the headline inflation rate, which is quoted in a variety of economic indicators we consider in the next chapter.

It is also why it plays such an important role within the early expansion and late expansion phases of the economic cycle.

This is when inflation is rising along with interest rates and is the point at which markets are focused on watching for the tipping point.

The tipping point at which the economic cycle moves from late expansion and into early recession. This is when inflation starts to fall, along with interest rates, with the markets shifting their attention to other economic indicators.

As a forex trader, inflation is one of the primary economic indicators to watch and there are many pieces of fundamental data which are released which reflect inflation or inflationary related pressures.

It is the economic principle which guides monetary policy, and consequently interest rate decisions. It is the obsession of hawks and matched by indifference from the doves. However, whichever side of the fence they sit, it cannot be ignored. In the public's eyes, government success or failure is judged by the performance of the economy, and in the government's handling of it. If the public 'feel well off', they will continue to support the government of the day. If, and when, those feelings change, so too will the government regardless of whether it is their fault or not.

Whilst monetary policy is generally set by the central bank, governments have a vested (personal) interest in ensuring that headline inflation is kept under control and managed effectively, at least while they are in power. This is for many different reasons, but primarily so that any 'feel good factor' remains in place for as long as possible, or at least until the next bust or election.

As mentioned earlier, inflation's evil twin is deflation, which sits on the opposite side of the economic balance.

Deflation, unlike inflation which can sometimes be a good thing, is always very bad and is something governments and central banks want to avoid at all costs.

On the surface, this seems counter-intuitive because if inflation is about rising prices then its opposite deflation should be welcomed.

However, it's not that simple. As we saw earlier, when demand is greater than the supply of goods and services then prices rise, and similarly when demand is weaker with an over supply of goods and services, prices will fall.

Falling prices are a signal the economy is weak which in turn is bad news for companies and businesses. Falling prices lead to falling profits which inevitably result in companies reducing costs. Cost cutting includes redundancies so unemployment will rise. This puts pressure on household incomes and budgets which leads to falling consumer demand and confidence.

In a property centric economy there is also the added pain of property repossessions and foreclosures with an increase in property coming onto the market. House values are therefore likely to fall, adding further to the downwards spiral.

Anyone with money to spare will be reluctant to spend and frightened of taking any risk. Rising unemployment will also feed into this fear and, as consumer confidence continues to fall, the economy finally comes to a dead stop.

This is precisely what happened to Japan during the economic crisis at the end of the 20th century.

The Great Depression of the late 1920's and early 1930's followed a similar pattern, and this is why central banks are so terrified of deflation as it is the precursor to an economic slump.

It is the natural extension of an inflationary period that slows too quickly, sending the economy into a deflationary spiral, as a result.

This is why governments around the world have attempted to spend their way out of the current financial crisis, in effect replacing business and retail spending with government spending.

Central banks have played their part by reducing interest rates to ultra low levels in an attempt to stimulate the economy and encourage spending. At the same time, central banks are increasing the money supply to try and inject some inflationary pressure into the economic landscape.

The deflation spiral starts when buying stops which in turn leads to growing levels of debt as everyone struggles to survive with wages and salaries falling.

In summary, deflation is defined as negative inflation. Once the annual inflation rate falls to 0%, we are approaching a deflationary period which will once again be signalled in the economic releases.

This is why it is feared so much. For us as forex traders it simply means interest rates for that country and currency are likely to remain low for some time to come. It is also confirming a very weak economy and, as a result, helping to identify which currencies are likely to be weak or strong and for how long they are likely to remain so. This in turn helps to define the length of any consequent trend.

Finally, there is also a third type of inflation known as stagflation, which is a hybrid mix of inflation and deflation. In this scenario we have rising prices, which should signal rising interest rates, but instead we have an economy which is in decline or is stagnant.

Despite this being an unusual combination it does happen and remains a grave threat as we start to emerge from this current crisis.

With stagflation prices are rising and consumers are spending with the increased money supply, but something in the economy causes businesses to see a fall in profits, not an increase. This leads to cost cutting and a loss of jobs. The trigger in the early 1970's was a rapid rise in crude oil prices.

The problem with stagflation is the central bank is trying to fight two diametrically opposing problems using the same tool, namely interest rates.

On the one hand, it is trying to slow inflation by increasing interest rates, while on the other it is trying to stimulate the economy by lowering interest rates. This is why stagflation is such a problem to which there is no real solution. And the reason why it is dreaded by central banks the world over.

It can also be very confusing for us as traders. When we are in an inflationary or deflationary period, we know exactly how the central bank is likely to react. When we are in a stagflation period, it is far more difficult to predict as we have no idea of how they will manage the problem. Therefore, inflation and deflation are easy to identify and trade accordingly. Stagflation is extremely difficult, but the good news is it is a very rare occurrence.

In the next chapter I want to examine, in detail, the economic data that is released and what the numbers reveal. And how banks and governments are likely to react, as a result.

Chapter Sixteen
Economic Indicators Explained

Prepare for bad times and you will only know good times.

Robert Kiyosaki (1947-)

In this chapter we're going to explore the fundamental news flow that shapes the currency moves we see each and every day. And in particular, to examine how these moves are driven by the constant stream of economic indicators which are derived from the underlying fundamental data.

And in order to do so, we need to understand what we mean by an economic indicator, as well as define the attributes and characteristics of economic indicators in general. The chapter will cover this in three areas as follows.

First, to look at how economic indicators can be grouped into three broad types.

Second, to consider how the importance and relevance of an economic indicator changes, depending on where we are in the economic cycle.

Third and finally to explore their relationship to market expectations, once the data has been released.

First and foremost, an economic indicator is simply an economic statistic based on data which indicates how well or how badly an economy is performing. Based on this release, the market and policy makers then decide how it is likely to perform in the future. And, as we all know there are statistics and there are damn lies. But more on that later.

In terms of the groups into which economic indicators can be classified, these are cyclical, counter cyclical, or pro cyclical.

A counter cyclical economic indicator is one that moves in the opposite direction to the economy, so for example if the economy is doing well, unemployment will be falling.

A pro cyclical indicator is one that moves with the economy, and GDP is an example of a pro cyclical indicator.

Finally, a cyclical indicator is one that may rise or fall as the economy expands and contracts and therefore has no direct correlation. In terms of timing, economic indicators fall into three broad categories namely leading, lagging and coincident.

Leading indicators are those that signal a change to the economy, before it happens and are therefore the most useful. They give us strong clues as to the future direction for the economy particularly on interest rates and inflation.

Two examples from this group would be building permits and consumer sentiment.

Lagging indicators are those that take time to filter through to the economy, and typically here we would include unemployment or employment data.

Finally, we have coincident indicators. These are indicators which track the economy and would include personal income and retail sales.

In this introduction to fundamental data and economic indicators I also thought it would be appropriate to cover an issue which is rarely explained. Namely, that much like the economic cycle, fundamental news releases also have a cyclical relationship depending on where we are within the cycle.

But let me explain this in more detail, taking interest rates as an example as these are probably the simplest and easiest to understand.

As a general rule of thumb, whenever a piece of fundamental news or data is released the markets will consider it from two perspectives. First, its relevance to the economic cycle and any changes in monetary policy that may follow as a result. Second, how close the numbers are to the market's expectations.

In the last few years, as the financial crisis has enveloped the globe, interest rates, by and large, have all fallen to ultra low levels and some into negative territory, and as such have become of relatively low interest to the market as a whole. The reason for this is with inflation threatening to roll over into deflation, the prospect of any change to interest rates in the short, or even medium term, is almost nil.

As a result, the monthly interest rate announcements from the various central banks have became an irrelevance as it has been clear to everyone there is little prospect of interest rates changing. These releases are perceived by the markets as unimportant, as there is nothing in either the rate decision or in any accompanying statement to surprise or startle the markets. In other words, the 'no change' decision has already been factored in.

With little prospect of any changes in interest rates for months or even years, the markets have moved their attention to other data, focusing instead on unemployment, followed by manufacturing, housing data, and retail sales figures.

The reason for focusing on those releases is they are the ones which might show the first signs of any recovery, as economies begin their slow journey into an expansion phase. This is yet a further reason why we need to understand where we are in the economic cycle, as the impact of any fundamental news release will vary according to which phase we are going through at any particular time.

For example, as the economy moves from late recession and into early expansion, this is when inflation data begins to take on an increasingly important role, along with the number of jobs created and data concerning output and production.

By contrast, interest rates begin to take on increasing importance as the economy moves from early expansion into late expansion, with inflation related data now dominating the releases as the markets become increasingly concerned over a slow down in the economy and a potential crash landing.

The slowdown arrives in due course with interest rates falling along with inflation. At this point, the markets concentrate on unemployment data and manufacturing output, as well as market sentiment, to try to gauge the depth and length of any recession. Interest rates have fallen in terms of importance.

Finally, the economy enters late recession with interest rates flat and therefore of little interest and market focus is once again on unemployment, and so the cycle comes full circle.

As mentioned earlier, every economic indicator or fundamental data release will have a market expectation number attached. This is generally from a poll of economists, so every release will have an associated forecast. It doesn't matter whether you believe the forecast or not, the market will consider the release in the context of the forecast and this is one of the reasons why a currency may decline on good news and go up on bad news.

For example, if the news is good, but not as good as the forecast, a currency may decline, and similarly if the news is bad, but not as bad as expected a currency may rise. This is a fact of forex trading and something we all have to accept.

It doesn't matter if a forecast is right or wrong. Nor does it matter where the forecast came from. All economic releases have a forecast attached, and the market will judge the data against this forecast and react accordingly.

As I wrote at the beginning of this chapter there are 'lies, damned lies and statistics' and when it comes to fundamental news and economic indicators, we really do need to keep this quote in mind at all times.

This is one of the reasons I have developed my own three dimensional approach to the market, combining relational, fundamental and technical analysis. It is simply not possible to rely on the fundamental data alone. It may not even be valid as there are so many reasons for it to be 'massaged' or modified so it can be presented in the best possible light to all concerned.

This is an important point and one I want you to remember throughout the remainder of this chapter as we look at the economic numbers in more detail. Just remember who is presenting these numbers and why.

As an example, let's take unemployment, which is probably one of the most manipulated and misleading group of economic indicators. And here we need look no further than the official US unemployment figures issued by the Department of Labor and, one would imagine, an august and trustworthy body.

However, like most statistical offices who issue economic data, they are part of the government and, as such, run by civil servants. Civil servants who are no doubt keen on developing their careers and therefore likely to do as they are told by their lords and masters, namely the politicians. Politicians who, unsurprisingly, are also only interested in themselves, their re-election or future career in high office.

I make no apology if this sounds a little cynical. I would say it is realistic and a plain fact of life. In some ways it is partly our own fault and our inability to absorb complex data in a fast moving, 24 hour media world where everything is conveyed either in a short headline or is broken into sound bites. Once a number has been released the media circus simply moves onto the next item. Governments are perfectly aware of this and so take full advantage, knowing that by the time any data has been analysed the media's focus has moved on to the next item of news.

In March 2011 the Department of Labor issued its monthly report, which suggested the headline rate of unemployment had in fact fallen from the previous month's figure of 8.9%, to record a further fall to 8.8%, thereby suggesting the US economy was starting to pick up.

However, the true figure is actually more than double this figure at almost 20%, but the government figure is intentionally carefully crafted to underestimate the actual unemployment rates, which would shock the public and ensure the politicians of the day were never re-elected.

The unemployment figures are massaged in a very simple way. First, the data is collected by conducting a small survey. It's small because it is simply too expensive to do it in any other way. Second, the survey only includes people who are claiming unemployment benefits, which is only paid for a limited time anyway. Third, the survey does not include anyone out of work and not claiming benefits. It does not include people actively seeking work or those who have simply given up looking. In addition the survey also assumes those claiming unemployment have found a job after six months, and are therefore excluded from the survey result. But it gets worse.

In order to be counted as unemployed, claimants have to confirm they are looking for work, so the unemployment rate didn't fall because the unemployed had found jobs, it fell because people had simply given up looking for work. Only in Washington could this be hailed as good news.

In reality, instead of there being approximately 14 million unemployed in the US, there are in fact close to 28 million, a truly shocking figure.

The same misleading method is used when presenting data on job creation in the US. In this case the government uses a model known as the birth death model. This model has nothing to do with the births and deaths of actual people. Instead, it is a statistical model for the births and deaths of companies and it has been constructed in such a way as to over estimate the number of jobs created when a new company starts up. Furthermore, the data does not then subtract the number of employees who lose their jobs, when a company ceases trading or goes out of business. It is only the jobs created by new company start ups which form the basis of the 'monthly jobs created' release and this number simply gives the number who have entered the jobs market each month.

In one month recently, the government reported a gain of 100,000 jobs, but their own birth death model suggested that 175,000 should have been created. In other words, instead of jobs being created, the true result was a loss of jobs.

This sort of data manipulation which ranges from minor window dressing, to outright fabrication and lies, goes on in every single government department responsible for statistical data around the world.

And here I am not simply attacking the US. This occurs everywhere, with very few exceptions, and across all the economic indicators, with unemployment, inflation and job creation the top three as these are the most politically sensitive. These releases are also highly visible and are a direct measure of a government's performance in handling the economy.

Inflation data is another classic target. Here you will find the goods and services used to gauge inflation will change all the time, as will the basis of measurement. Economic indicators and indices will come and go as governments find increasingly confusing and elaborate ways to baffle the public, safe in the knowledge the financial markets have little time to absorb or analyse the data in any detail.

Moreover, many of the numbers reported are subsequently revised or corrected and brought up to date with the latest figures, but these are rarely reported and hardly mentioned in the financial press. You will see this pattern a great deal once you begin to follow the economic calendar releases on a daily basis, with reports being updated or released as 'revised'. However, by this time no one really cares, as the markets have moved on and long since forgotten the original release.

The US unemployment data is a classic for this, as is the inflation data, and you will often see an update issued maybe a week later with so called 'corrected figures'.

There we have it. The economic data we are about to consider is all manipulated in some way. It is a fact of life and there is nothing we can do about it. In some ways we could say that since we are all looking at the same data, does it really matter if it is true or not? And the short answer is no. However, it is the market's perception we need to understand.

It is also important to remember that professional traders, and more importantly the interbank market which controls the market, will certainly be aware of the truth, so to blindly accept the data as fact is dangerous in the extreme.

Your success will depend on independent thinking. Never take anything at face value, particularly if it involves information from a government body where politicians are involved.

The question to ask yourself is this? What is the game plan? For example, why is the US dollar and US economy managed by a banking cartel? And whose interests are being protected and advanced?

Therefore, when you are trading and looking at economic data, as we are going to do in the remainder of this chapter, stop and ask yourself these questions. Does the release make sense? Does the release align with what I am seeing in the real world? Can I cross check the validity of this number or data set? This is how you have to think when faced with the constant stream of fundamental news and economic releases which cross your screens on a daily basis.

However, before moving onto the economic indicators themselves, let me touch on one common aspect which applies to all of them.

All these indicators are imperfect. They are all flawed. I could write a small treatise on each economic indicator and explain these flaws. But, just like data massage, this is a fact of life. Some of these indicators have been around for many years, and in some cases decades. To date, they are the best the markets have of gauging economic health. Some are more representative than others and one thing is for sure, they are ranked by the markets in order of importance.

Some indicators are extremely important whilst others less. Therefore, I have tried to rank them in order of importance as well. As you will appreciate it's very difficult to cover every indicator for every country. Fortunately, some are 'generic', such as GDP which makes things easier.

However, a GDP figure from China, the US, Japan or a top ten country, is always going to carry substantially more weight in the market than the equivalent number from a smaller economic power. In other words, an important number from a heavyweight economy will move the markets dramatically.

Some economic releases are country specific, such as the Tankan survey in Japan, the KOF in Switzerland or the ZEW in Germany, but regardless of how the data is structured or released, the underlying principles will be the same. Economic data is economic data.

The primary economic calendar I use is free and available from www.forexfactory.com as it is reliable, comprehensive, and reflective of how things have changed in terms of the types of data which is now reported.

For example, five years ago, the calendar would not have included any Chinese data. Neither would the calendar have included any releases relating to bond auctions. This is an example of how the markets have changed and shifted their focus and how the importance of economic data changes with the times. China's dominance is now recognised, so their data ranks alongside that of the US.

Bond auctions are now also important as they reveal underlying issues with sovereign debt, particularly in Europe. A further example of the economic cycle changing over time.

Two final points before we move on. First, when considering any release, always check the historical data which appears to the right of the release, using the chart graphic. This will display the last 12 or 18 months of data. This is the trend, which will put the latest release into context for you. This is important. Always view the release in the context of the trend over the previous 12 months.

Second, all releases are colour coded. The red releases are high impact, and will almost certainly move the markets. The orange are medium impact, whilst the yellow are low impact. The releases covered here are all high impact, tier one releases.

GDP - Gross Domestic Product

I want to start with GDP which is one of the 'big' numbers all markets consider to be extremely important.

Of all the economic indicators we are going to examine in the rest of this chapter, GDP or gross domestic product is perhaps one of the most important, as it tries to provide a snapshot of the economy in one simple number.

GDP is widely used by virtually every bank and government as a key indicator. Governments will base their tax and spending plans on this figure. It is a figure which is closely watched by all the central banks, the IMF and the World Bank.

Central banks and governments also use this data as a benchmark for where the economy is heading.

In order to explain GDP I have taken the UK model, but most economies around the world all use a similar method. It is the number that matters, not its calculation. What is important is its relationship to market expectation, and to the previous number to see if there is a trend developing in the economy. In other words, how the release is likely to affect the currency which I will explain shortly.

GDP tells us whether the economy is growing or shrinking, and is generally based over the previous three months, therefore released quarterly.

If the number is positive the economy is expanding and if it is negative the economy is contracting. It is a complex number to calculate, and is generally measured in one of three ways, namely as output, expenditure or income.

Output measures the total value of goods and services produced across all sectors from agriculture to financial services and everything in between. In simple terms, imagine the country as a company and output is really everything it sells which produces income for the company or country.

Expenditure measures what everyone buys, you, me, the government, business etc., and again covers everything but also includes the value of exports minus imports.

The income method measures and calculates the income generated in terms of profits and wages.

In theory these three approaches should produce more or less the same number, but they rarely do and, in addition, each method of calculation becomes progressively more complicated. The output measure is the least complicated, as it involves surveying around 50,000 companies which is then augmented with additional economic data. Typically, this calculation will only have around 40% of the data required to provide the complete picture, but if the authorities waited until the figure had been calculated using both expenditure and income, the release would be so out of date as to be almost meaningless as an indicator of the economy.

Furthermore, the data is based on the previous three months, and by the time of first release the data is almost four months old, which is why it is considered a lagging indicator, albeit an important one.

There are ways around this problem, and in the UK the issuing authority is the Office of National Statistics, which like many other issuing bodies around the world, take the following approach, issuing the GDP in three phases.

The first phase is often called 'preliminary' and based on the simplest approach to calculating GDP, namely using the output data, which is a rough and ready guide. This is the release which generally causes most volatility in the market.

Some weeks later a revised GDP figure is released using a more rigorous approach based on expenditure, before finally a few weeks after, the final GDP figure is released.

This is the approach taken by virtually every other country. First there is the preliminary or flash GDP number, followed by the revised figure before the final GDP number is released. And each time giving the market a different number.

The interim and final release numbers tend to have less impact as the markets will have already factored in the news from the first release, so unless there is a major change, which is very unlikely, the impact of the interim and final numbers will be muted.

GDP numbers are quoted as a simple percentage, such as +1.5% or +3.2% or -0.6%. A positive number suggests the economy is growing while a negative figure tells us the economy is shrinking. Furthermore, whenever a number is released, whether GDP or any other release, there are three things we need to consider.

First, the number itself, is it negative, positive or flat and what is this saying about the economy. Second, how does the number relate to market expectation - is it better than expected, worse then expected or in line with market expectation.

Third, we need to see the trend for the data and consider the following. Is the economy growing steadily or perhaps too fast? Is the economy shrinking? Is the number a blip in a recent trend or could it be the first sign of a change in the economy? Is it much as expected and simply a continuation of the trend?

All these factors are extremely important and we need to check each one as the data is released.

In general terms a positive GDP figure will almost always be good for the currency of the country, as it indicates growth, a strong economy and the prospect of rising interest rates, thereby making the currency more attractive to investors.

But, as always it does depend on the figure. If the figure is good but perhaps not quite as good as expected, the currency may move lower temporarily as the market reacts. Perhaps the figure is good, but not as good as last time, and therefore could be the first signal the economy is slowing down.

The figure could be too good, and suggest an economy that is out of control, and therefore one that could potentially be over heating with a consequent crash landing resulting in a sudden reduction in interest rates. All these factors will play out on any release but particularly one as important as GDP.

If the GPD data is positive, in line with expectation, and generally in line with the current trend for the release, this should not surprise the markets. But, if better than expected, this is normally good news for the currency which should strengthen as a result.

Of the three GDP releases, the one that has the most impact is normally the first as it is 'fresh news' and can therefore surprise the markets, particularly the forex market. The second release is simply a revised version of the first, so is much less of a surprise, and finally the third is simply yet another revision of the first two, so it tends to have the least impact of the three.

As explained earlier, this is a generic indicator with all countries reporting GDP in much the same way. However, there is one country which stands out from the rest in their presentation of GDP which is Canada.

Canada is unique, in that it presents GDP on a monthly basis, instead of quarterly, which is the norm for everyone else. Canada does release a quarterly figure, but this is simply a summary of the previous three months data.

The net result is that for Canada each GDP release has the ability to surprise the markets, an important point to note when trading the Canadian dollar. So whilst GDP is a lagging indicator for most countries, for Canada it could almost be considered to be a leading indicator.

CPI : Consumer Price Index

The CPI (Consumer Price Index), is a key economic indicator and measure of inflation and, just like GDP, one that is watched by all central banks and governments for signs as to the level of inflation in the economy, and is therefore a guide to future interest rates.

In simple terms the CPI is an economic indicator which attempts to show the changes in consumer prices over a given period, and all governments measure these in their own idiosyncratic way.

The data is generally based on a 'basket of goods' which are supposed to represent a cross section of goods and services, consumed or used by households in their normal daily lives. This basket of goods is created to signal whether prices are rising, falling or remaining flat and hence to be an indicator of inflation.

In the US, the CPI data is based on a basket of over eighty thousand goods and services which are then divided up into eight broad categories

- food and beverages
- housing
- apparel
- transportation
- medical care
- recreation
- education and communication
- other goods and services

The above list also includes some taxes, but ignores others. Each item in the basket is then weighted according to its importance and finally prices are averaged, based on this weighting. Just like any other index, such as an equity index, CPI is calculated using a base number, generally 100, fixed at a point back in time, which is then used as the reference point for all future calculations.

For example, if the index was established in 1984 (taking 100 as a base) and the index in 2010 is now at 250, then prices have risen by one hundred and fifty percent in that period.

So how is CPI reported around the world and what do we need to look for in this release?

First, virtually every leading economy in the world publishes their CPI data on a monthly basis. Second, this is generally reported in two ways. The first is called CPI, and the second is usually referred to as 'core CPI'.

Of the two, core CPI is generally considered to be the more important, and is normally shown in red on the economic calendar. The reason for this is the markets consider this number to be a more representative measure of inflation. This version of the CPI data typically ignores items such as food and energy as these prices can be very volatile and so distort the true picture of longer term inflation.

This number is therefore considered to be more accurate and the one policy makers consider more relevant.

So, when the CPI data is released, it normally comes in two versions, CPI and core CPI, of which core CPI is the one to watch.

Third, the CPI number is released as a percentage and not as an index number, so if it appears as 0.5% percent this means prices have risen 0.5% since the last release.

Fourth, some CPI releases are based on a month by month comparison, whilst others, such as China's are based on a year on year comparison and this will be shown alongside the economic release, where it will say either m/m, meaning month on month, or y/y meaning year on year.

CPI is interpreted in much the same way as GDP and in much the same way as all the other economic indicators we are going to cover.

The first thing to note is whether the number is positive or negative? If it is positive then consumer prices are rising, and if negative then they are falling. If consumer prices are rising this is a good signal, as long as they are not rising too fast, which would suggest an economy running out of control with a possible slowdown and collapse into recession in the future. So a positive number for CPI is generally good for the currency, as long as it's not too high, with the currency strengthening as a result.

Conversely, if consumer prices are falling, the question is whether we entering a recessionary period with falling interest rates which would be negative for the currency, and generally weaken as a result.

The next step is to check to see how the CPI fits into the overall trend against previous releases and, provided the number is in step, this too is a good sign. Finally, we check the number against market expectation to see whether it is better than, worse than or in line with what the market expected.

Provided it is as expectation or better, then this is usually good news for the currency, as higher interest rates are likely to follow in due course.

But, as always, too much inflationary pressure will be considered as negative by the markets. In addition, market reactions to these numbers, and indeed many others, is based on the market's perception of how the data will be interpreted by policymakers. In other words, the direction the currency moves, will be partly based on the data, but also partly based on how the markets believe that data will be interpreted.

To complete the picture for CPI, there is one oddity which is the UK, which uses both CPI and RPI (Retail Prices Index) which are reported at the same time.

Of the two, CPI remains the more important and, is considered a better gauge of consumer prices and inflation, as RPI only measures goods and services bought for the purpose of consumption, although it does also includes housing costs, which are excluded from the CPI data.

Therefore, if you are trading the British pound the number to watch is always the CPI release, as the RPI number is always higher.

As you might expect, CPI data is considered a lagging indicator.

Employment Data

The next group of indicators are all based on employment data.

On the first Friday of every month in the US, at 8.30 am EST, comes the release of the most anticipated economic indicator. This is the big one, the Non Farm Payroll release or the NFP, issued by the US Department of Labor and gives the markets a snapshot of the jobs market (excluding the agricultural sector) for the biggest economy in the world. Furthermore, it is the one economic release which causes more volatility than any other. And it is the big one for several reasons.

First, it is an economic indicator for the largest employment market in the world.

Second, it is considered to be a leading indicator of the world's largest economy as it is released monthly and therefore considered to be up to date. For example, the report in the first week in January is reporting the employment market for December and therefore gives a very close view of the current situation.

Third, it comprises four economic indicators in one release, so takes on added significance as a result.

Finally, jobs are the backbone of any economy and being the largest in the world the release takes on an increased significance, affecting as it does not only the US market but also the remainder of the world. As the saying goes, when America sneezes, the rest of the world catches a cold.

In other words, if the largest economy is not creating new jobs, ultimately this will affect the rest of the world, with a global slow down virtually guaranteed in the near future.

The NFP release is therefore extremely important and, as mentioned, comprises four economic indicators in one, with each piece of data related to unemployment or the jobs market in some way.

Of these four elements it is normally only two that are announced in the release as these are easy to absorb for the markets which react immediately.

These are the headline unemployment rate, and the number of jobs created or lost in the month. The headline unemployment rate is reported as a simple percentage, and is the total number of people who are currently deemed unemployed divided by the total workforce in the US. But, as I said earlier, whether this is true or not is questionable.

The first number to watch is the unemployment rate which will be quoted as a percentage and, as always we need to compare this against the forecast. Is it better or worse than expected or in line with expectations? Like all markets, the forex markets does not like surprises, so any dramatic change can create very strong moves in the US dollar.

Then we need to see how the numbers fit with the previous month's data, whether it is better or worse and also whether it is following the longer term trend over the last six to twelve months. If the headline rate in unemployment is falling, this is signalling an economy that is growing with jobs being created. If it is rising this is bad news for the economy with jobs being lost and a potential slow down in growth.

In the US, consumer spending makes up around 70% of the US economy and therefore the jobs market is central to growth, affecting consumer confidence as a result.

As in any economy, if people feel confident and have security of employment, they will spend and the economy will grow. Conversely, if people feel insecure consumer confidence falls and the economy slows, and indeed consumer confidence surveys are yet another of the key economic indicators we watch.

The second big employment number reported, and probably the most closely watched, is the number of jobs created or lost since the previous month. This is reported as either a negative or positive number. For example, we could see a number of say 128,000 which is the number of new jobs created in the previous month. Alternatively, if the number is reported as -128,000 this would be the number of jobs lost in the previous month.

However, once again these numbers have to be judged against the forecast and the longer term trend so they can be put into context.

These are the two numbers that receive the most attention from the media and which are widely reported. However, beneath these two headline grabbing numbers there is a wealth of other data. This describes in detail how the jobs market has changed over the last month and these details take time to absorb and digest. This is usually the excuse given for the schizophrenic reaction in the forex markets where the US dollar will first move sharply in one direction, before reversing within the first 10 or 15 minutes of the announcement.

At the time of the NFP release, if the longer term trend for the dollar is down, the market is likely to move sharply higher on the news, only to reverse some minutes later. Conversely, if the longer term trend for the dollar is up, the market is likely to move sharply lower on the news, then reverse and resume the original trend once the dust has settled.

This type of reaction does not happen all the time, but once you become familiar with the NFP you will soon see it happens on a very regular basis. For intraday traders it presents plenty of trading opportunities.

The excuse given for the drama, is that the headline numbers causes the knee jerk reaction, while the second and subsequent response follows once the underlying numbers have been considered and digested, which may or may not be true.

The real reason is that this is one of the premier releases the interbank market makers use to trap traders into weak positions. For them it is just too good an opportunity to miss and indulge in a spot of stop hunting.

There are in fact four key pieces of data in this release and the remaining two are average hourly wages or earnings and the average work week. Both of these are extremely important, but receive much less attention as they require some effort to find within the report as they appear in tabular form. Earnings, of course, can be an extremely important indicator as this tells us whether families and households are likely to have more to spend, or less. In addition, it also signals if the economy is in an inflationary cycle with hourly wages rising, or is in a deflationary cycle with hourly wages falling. This information will have a direct impact on the prospects for interest rates since wages are one of the primary drivers of inflation.

The key here is the trend and, whether we are in a rising trend, a falling trend or whether the trend is just flat because it is a stagnant economy.

Finally, we have the average work week, which tells us whether people are working longer or shorter hours. And here, longer hours represent a growing economy with people working overtime whilst shorter hours worked represents a shrinking economy as demand falls.

Within the report there is the option to dig down and look at market sectors. However, for forex traders I would suggest the above numbers are sufficient and my top four within the NFP release. If you do have the time, the overtime hours can be an excellent indicator of future employment and likely GDP trends. Typically, overtime tends to fluctuate between four and five hours a week on average across industry sectors. If this is consistently above above 4.5 to 5.0, this is sending a strong signal of growth, job creation and strength in the economy.

In the last few years employment data, including NFP, has been the indicator most closely watched. Much more so than interest rates as employment (or lack of it) is considered the leading indicator for the health of the US economy. Therefore, with little prospect of interest rates changing, even in the medium term, jobs and unemployment have become the focus of attention for the markets.

As we discovered earlier, the importance and relevance of economic data will tend to ebb and flow. With the world still recovering from the financial crisis of the first decade of the 21st century, interest rate statements and decisions are currently no longer the most important item of fundamental news. Jobs have taken the top spot. Without job creation, nothing moves, and until the trend begins to rise, and rise significantly, interest rates will remain a low priority release.

For the time being NFP is the number one 'jobs' report in the world and its effect on the US dollar is as follows.

Under 'normal' circumstances, a strong report should drive interest rates higher, if part of a longer term trend upwards, which in turn would make the US dollar more attractive to foreign investors. These investors would get a better return on US Treasuries in the future, something China would welcome.

By contrast, a weak NFP release is likely to have the opposite effect, possibly signalling lower rates in the future, and making the US dollar less attractive for longer term investments to overseas holders of bonds and US stocks.

The second major report on employment in the US is the ADP. This is data collected from the payroll records of a private company called Advanced Data Processing, which is responsible for processing over 500,000 payrolls in the US, covering over 450,000 separate business entities and over twenty three million employees.

The payroll data it collects is used by the US Bureau of Labor to compile an employment report. This report is released monthly, and perhaps more importantly, is released two days before the Non Farm Payroll, so always appears on the Wednesday prior to the NFP data on Friday.

The ADP is therefore watched extremely carefully as it can provide clues to the more significant release two days later, and the reason for this is simple. The data in the ADP is based on actual payroll figures. In other words these numbers should more accurately reflect the state of the employment market, as Advanced Data Processing runs the payroll services for so many large organisations in the USA.

The ADP is just one number and represents the change in the number of employed people during the previous month, excluding farming and public sector jobs. As with all the other employment reports, a positive number indicates an employment market that is increasing with jobs being added thereby suggesting a stronger economy, whilst a negative number indicates jobs lost and a weaker economy.

The question about the ADP is whether it is a reliable predictor for the NFP data two days later and this is always a hotly contested point. My own opinion is as follows.

First, the ADP data is heavily biased towards private sector jobs, which make up just over 80 per cent of the data sample. NFP data on the other hand is based on a survey of business and includes government employees.

Second, the ADP release uses the US Labor Department data as a base line benchmark, who then adjust their numbers accordingly. Estimates are based on a statistical comparison of ADP growth rates to the Bureau of Labor payroll employment growth rates, whilst the Labor Department adjusts its numbers to account for new businesses that are not yet included in the survey, along with businesses that may have gone bust.

So both sets of data are far from perfect, but then we knew that anyway. In addition, both sets of data are then revised, sometimes weeks later.

In general terms, the relationship between the two is rather shaky and, having looked at the data over the last few years there appears to be around a sixty per cent correlation between the two.

As a very rough rule of thumb the NFP data is generally more accurate than the ADP, so if the numbers from the ADP are bad, we might expect the NFP data to be 'less bad'.

Equally if ADP numbers are good, we may expect the NFP numbers to be better.

To summarise. In my opinion, the best way to consider these two economic indicators is to view them in isolation and not to try to use the ADP report as a predictor of the NFP. Instead, consider the ADP indicator as more representative of private sector job creation and therefore a much better predictor of the true state of the economy.

Whilst the NFP release creates huge interest and volatility, it is in fact, more of a mix, a broad brush of the jobs market as it includes both the private and public sectors in equal measure.

To put this into context. In a recent release the ADP data reported gains of 368,000 jobs, whilst two days later, the NFP report came in with only 107,000. And, over the last two years there have been discrepancies of more than 200,000 on seven different occasions.

So ADP may be saying one thing, but it cannot be relied on to be an accurate barometer for the more significant release two days later. Given the discrepancies why is the ADP reported at all? The simple answer is that it was introduced to create an alternative subscription service paid report, which would then be used by professional traders and investors to forecast the NFP. However, to date this has failed to materialise and it remains a rather curious and isolated economic indicator.

Nevertheless, the numbers should still be watched and noted, but we cannot assume they will be an accurate reflection of the NFP two days later and may not even come close.

Next we have the unemployment claims, which is a weekly jobs report, once again in the US. This reports the number of new claimants who registered for unemployment insurance during the previous week, so this number will always be a positive one. The number simply reflects whether the trend in people registering for unemployment is rising or falling.

In general terms if the number is better than expected, in other words, lower than the forecast, this is generally good for the currency so the dollar should strengthen as a result. The reason is this suggests the economy is growing with the number of people registering for unemployment falling. Conversely, if the number is worse than expected this is usually bad for the currency as it suggests the economy may be running into difficulties, with the number of unemployed increasing as a result. As always, the number has to be considered in the context of the trend.

Having mentioned the ADP indicator earlier and its reliability, or otherwise, as a guide to the NFP data, the weekly unemployment claims are my preferred economic indicator to use for an insight into NFP, for several reasons.

First, they are produced by the Department of Labor and therefore use similar statistical methods to the NFP release.

Second, the unemployment claims are produced weekly and therefore prior to the NFP release we have a four week trend to consider in the run up to the release.

Third, and perhaps most importantly, they are seasonally adjusted which means they do provide a more accurate reflection of what is actually happening in the real word of employment in the US.

There is, of course, employment data congestion in the first week of any new month for the dollar, with the ADP release on the Wednesday, followed by the weekly unemployment claims often on Thursday, finally followed by the NFP on the Friday, so a plethora of unemployment news in three days.

To summarise. My advice is to use this report as your guide to the unemployment levels in the economy and to watch in particular, the overall trend.

There are, of course, employment indicators for other countries and currencies which mirror the NFP data. These are usually referred to as 'employment change' and here are the examples for Canada, Australia and New Zealand.

The Canadian equivalent is released early in the month approximately eight working days after month end, so the timing of the release will vary from month to month. Other than this the employment data the report contains is very similar to Non Farm Payroll, and again the two numbers to watch are the unemployment rate and the employment change.

Just as for the US employment data, the unemployment rate will be a percentage and reflect the percentage of the population out of work, and is therefore a key indicator of falling or rising employment. The second is the employment change which will be either positive if the number of jobs created has increased over the month, or negative if the number of jobs has decreased.

This is a big release for the Canadian dollar and, when it coincides with the NFP there is even more volatility for both the US and Canadian dollars. However, other than this, the same analysis applies for this economic indicator.

If jobs are being created at a steady pace and the unemployment rate is falling steadily, the economy is growing and interest rates are likely to rise in due course.

Any shortfall against the forecast or a sudden and dramatic change in the longer term trend may surprise the market and cause a temporary pullback in the trend. However, as a general rule if the data is better then expected this is generally good for the Canadian dollar, all things being equal.

As always with these numbers, job creation is a key indicator of the economic health of a country since consumer spending represents such a large proportion of Gross Domestic Product.

An alternative interpretation of the Canadian data is as an indicator for the US jobs market, given the strong relationship between the two countries in terms of exports. If Canadian growth is strong, this should be reflected in the US market and in the employment data. So always keep an eye on Canadian data as an early warning of changes in the US markets.

The Australian equivalent for unemployment and job creation is exactly the same as the Canadian model, the only difference being it is generally released around ten days after the month end.

Once again it follows the same model with the headline unemployment rate and the jobs created or lost being the two big numbers the markets watch.

Finally, we have New Zealand in this group which uses the same terminology for its release, only in this case New Zealand releases its data on a quarterly basis. Moreover, it does not release this data for a further thirty to forty days after the end of the quarter. So, compared with other countries, the data has to be considered a lagging indicator as it is almost four months old by the time the numbers reach the market.

Generally speaking, employment data is a lagging indicator, although it could be considered to be coincident, where the numbers are reported weekly. However, as always, the key is in the trend. No self respecting policy maker would consider a few weeks of falling employment claims as sufficient evidence of an improvement in the economy. Any falls may simply be for seasonal reasons and temporary, thereby masking the reality of the situation.

The last in this short list of employment relates to the UK, and here it is the National Statistics Office who produce the data and release a report called the Claimant Count Change. This is published on the second Thursday of every month. The data comes from a body known as Job Seekers Allowance, a government agency responsible for managing and paying benefits to people out of work, with the Claimant Count Change simply recording whether the number of people claiming benefits has gone up or down from the previous month.

Whilst this count is a useful economic indicator of one aspect of what is happening in the jobs market, it is far from being a comprehensive employment indicator as it simply measures the change in people claiming unemployment benefit.

Therefore, the data is a simple number, either positive or negative. If it is positive the number of people claiming benefits has gone up on the previous month. This is generally considered bad news for the UK economy and the British pound as it suggests a weak economy, low inflation and low interest rates.

A negative number confirms the number of claimants has fallen, and therefore the economy may be stronger with an increased chance of an interest rate rise in the medium term.

As always, the number has to be considered, not only against the market forecast, but also against the overall trend. So, if the longer term trend is falling and the number is simply following the trend, this is good news for the economy.

Similarly, if the longer term trend is rising and the number adds to the rising trend this is bad news longer term. In addition, there is always the chance the markets will be surprised with a number that is well above or below expectation, or well above or below the previous month's figures.

A quirk of UK employment data is that details of the headline unemployment rate and the number of jobs created are not released in tandem with the Claimant Count. These numbers can be found, but only by visiting the National Statistics Office website.

This reporting method is odd, to say the least, and can best be described as the government's attempts to manage market reaction.

This may change in the future, but this is the way it is as the moment. Furthermore, the reporting mechanism is out of step with other countries and currencies.

PPI

The Producer Price Index or PPI is another key measure of inflation in the economy, only this time one that is designed to measure from a seller's perspective, rather than from a consumer perspective.

The CPI (Consumer Prices Index) economic indicator gives us a view of inflation and the economy from the consumer's point of view in terms of rising prices, whilst the PPI aims to give a view from the manufacturer's perspective, as it tries to measure the change in the selling prices for finished goods. This is also sometimes referred to as the Wholesale Price Index. In other words, PPI is all about the wholesale price for goods and services. And, whether the cost of raw materials are rising or falling in price which in turn are passed on to the consumer in due course.

The PPI data is usually presented as a simple percentage. For example, if the number is shown as +0.8% then prices of finished goods have risen by this amount over the month, whilst a negative number indicates they have fallen.

This economic indicator is therefore a strong barometer for inflation and deflation, as well as a good indicator for the broader economy. Rising wholesale prices suggest a strong and growing economy, provided rising prices are demand led. Remember they could also be supply driven. Meanwhile, falling prices would suggest a weak economy, with demand and inflation falling as a result leading to lower interest rates in due course.

As always, we need to consider three things. The actual number versus the forecast and whether it is on target, better than expected, or worse than expected. Furthermore, has the number surprised the market either by coming in much higher or much lower than expected. And finally, how does the number fit into the longer term trend.

As a general rule, if the number is better (higher) than expected, we should see the currency strengthen as a result, as this would suggest higher interest rates in due course to keep any inflation under control. A worse (or lower) than expected number is likely to weaken the currency, although if the longer term trend for the currency is higher this could simply result in a short term pull back.

The PPI figure quoted is often referred to as the core number, since food and energy prices are removed from the calculation. This is the same reason they are removed from the CPI release as food and energy prices can be volatile.

The reason the PPI release is considered a 'red flag' release, is that it is an excellent companion to the equally important CPI number. This is watched even more closely than the PPI, because it is assumed any increase in prices within the PPI index will automatically be passed on to the consumer and eventually be reflected in the consumer price index. Therefore, if the PPI in any country is announced in advance of the CPI data, this can offer an excellent opportunity to prepare a trading position based on the PPI data. So, a release to watch very carefully.

In the US and Australia, this economic indicator is simply called PPI, whilst in New Zealand and the UK it's called PPI Input, and the only other thing to be aware of is the frequency of these releases.

In the US and UK the releases are monthly, whilst in New Zealand and Australia they are quarterly.

The major economic indicators examined so far are all based on simple numbers and percentages, so therefore easy to understand in the context of the release. However, I now want to turn to those indicators which are referred to as a diffusion index.

The PMI (Purchasing Managers Index) release is the first example of a diffusion index. A diffusion index is generally based on a survey, and in simple terms it measures the degree to which a change is 'spread out or diffused' in a particular group or sample.

The survey sample is asked if something has changed and, if so in which direction, allowing the survey group to answer in one of three ways. Things have got better, have got worse or have stayed the same.

In other words, the survey tries to establish if business conditions in a certain market have improved, declined or stayed the same over the previous month. The survey only ever has three possible answers which are, better, worse or the same.

A diffusion index is calculated by taking the percentage of respondents who reported better conditions than the previous month. To this is added 50% of the respondents who reported 'no change', and adding this number to the total. This is reported as an index figure between zero and one hundred. An index result which reports as fifty is saying an equal number of the survey said better, and an equal number said worse. The respondents who reported worse are not included in the equation.

Here is the formula used to calculate the index.

$$\text{Index} = (A*1)+(B*0.5)+(C*0)$$

A = percentage number better than previous month

B = percentage number no change from previous month

C = percentage number worse than previous month

Taking some hypothetical numbers the following could result:

Index = 10 + (60*0.5)+0 = 40

The magic number for a diffusion index is 50 which is seen as the fulcrum. At this number the survey is balanced with no bias either way. If it were at say, 75, this indicates a strong bias of the sample with a 'better' response. Conversely, if it were at 40 (as in our example above) the index is indicating the survey has largely replied with a 'worse' response.

If the index is looking at economic growth, any number above fifty would indicate an economy in expansion and below fifty an economy in contraction. 50 is therefore considered the tipping point.

A diffusion index will always register a number between zero and 100 and, just as with other releases, the trend is important. If the trend has been below the tipping point of 50, and starts to climb above this number, the index has changed from one reporting negative sentiment to one reporting positive sentiment (or whatever the index may be measuring). In general, diffusion indices are set up in this way, with above the line suggesting positive responses, and below the line suggesting negative responses.

In summary, those economic indicators which are classified as a diffusion index are used to determine the turning points in an economic or business cycle. The tipping point is the fulcrum which is the median point, reflecting changes in survey responses from positive to negative and back again.

Moving back to the PMI this is a barometer of the manufacturing sector of the economy.

The PMI or Purchasing Manager's Index is another key economic indicator, which in this case gives us clues as to the broader economy. The index is focused on the manufacturing sector of the economy, and is constructed from a large survey of purchasing managers working in manufacturing companies.

In the US, the PMI is released by the Institute of Supply Management, and every month the ISM polls approximately 400 of its members and covers a variety of industries. The purchasing managers are asked for their opinion on whether activity in their industry is unchanged, rising or falling. The assessment is based on a number of questions covering all aspects of manufacturing.

For example, the questionnaire asks the purchasing managers about new orders, output, hiring levels, exports and imports, prices for raw materials and supplies, supplier performance, and backlog of orders yet to be completed. In other words, all aspects of manufacturing from supplies and raw materials in, to finished goods out of the factory gate and on to customers. The index is then compiled from these responses and, of course, weighted. New orders carry the most weighting at 30%, down to inventories at 10%.

All the responses are then compiled to produce the PMI report and the level above or below 50 is the the key.

One of the many reasons this report is so closely watched is that the Federal Reserve is given access to the data, prior to its release. This tells us just how seriously this data is taken, although some traders consider it a low level release. It most certainly is not.

Second, the PMI in the US is released on the first business day of each month, so it sets the tone on how the manufacturing sector has performed over the previous month.

For major exporters and manufactures such as the US, China, Japan, Germany and many other countries in South East Asia and Latin America, this is a very important release, since exports are the building blocks of their economies.

In the US, a second and associated release comes two days later with the equivalent for the services sector which is the ISM's non manufacturing report. However, it is the manufacturing report which is the focus, for policy makers, traders and investors.

The next question is what are the levels that are considered to be 'defining' as far as the markets are concerned. And in essence there are three.

The first is any number above 50. Here we have evidence of manufacturing and the economy expanding, so anything above the fulcrum is all good news. The further we move away from 50 the stronger this sentiment becomes. Above 60 and the economy is expanding fast, but also in danger of running out of control.

It is at this point the Federal Reverse in the US would consider raising interest rates.

Below 50, the key number is around 42. If the release is between 42 and 50 we can assume whilst manufacturing may be weakening, the broader economy may still be growing, but perhaps not quite as fast as before. It could also be a possible signal of a slow down in due course. Remember the economy is like the oil tanker – it takes time to slow down and speed up. The monthly PMI will reflect the more subtle changes much more quickly as it based on 'the shop floor' – real numbers from real people.

Once we move below 42, it is likely that both manufacturing and the economy are contracting with a possible move deeper into recession. It is at this point the Federal Reserve would need to take action and reduce interest rates in an attempt to stimulate the economy once again.

The key point, as always, is that 'one swallow does not make a summer'. The release has to be seen in the context of the trend of the previous 6 to 9 months. A sudden surge above 60 is not necessarily going to trigger action by the Federal Reserve. However, if the index stayed above this level for an extended period, and the more sustained the trend, the more likely the FED will take action. The same philosophy applies when the index falls to 42 and below.

To put this report in context and its significance, the Federal Reserve always reference this release in their reports and updates on the state of the economy, as the effects and changes in this sector will ultimately filter through into all parts of the economy.

The central banks of Japan, China and other leading manufacturing countries also use this data as a key plank of their monetary policy decision making. Therefore, it is a very important number, and one which most countries release monthly. It is also closely watched by the bond markets for signs of inflation or deflation and associated changes in interest rates.

To recap, the non-manufacturing PMI which is released two days later, does not carry the same weight, but nevertheless is still one to watch and to take note of.

China, the world's second largest economy, releases its PMI report on the same day as the US, and on the first working day of the month. So, this can be a volatile phase for currency markets.

Canada releases its PMI report around five days after month end and is known as the IVEY PMI as the data is compiled by the Richard Ivey School of Business.

Meanwhile, in the UK, the PMI report is released in three versions, often over three consecutive days, with manufacturing PMI coming out first, followed by construction PMI, and finally services PMI.

With regard to the UK it could be argued, that with a manufacturing industry in decline, construction PMI and services PMI might be more important. This may be the case for the UK, but elsewhere in the world the PMI data is a crucial number as it leads the way to GDP. So, please watch this report carefully and always check the longer term trend.

For the US any reaction in the US dollar depends on the trend. For example, any number over 50 should see the US dollar move higher, but only if it is part of a consistent trend. Any number below 50 and moving towards 42 should see the currency weaken as this may be signalling a possible slow down with traders and investors selling the dollar on the prospect of lower interest rates in the medium term.

Naturally, much will depend on where the economy is in terms of the broader cycle. An early expansion phase, coupled with a series of strong PMI releases, will simply reinforce the view the economy is picking up and expanding fast. Equally, if the market is moving into recession, and the PMI is moving to 42 and below, again on a consistent basis, the prospect of interest rate changes are greatly increased, and the reaction in the currency markets will be proportionately more volatile.

Japan varies from the rest of the world, as here the PMI data is released in a report called the Tankan survey, which is slightly different, so let me explain it in more detail.

The Tankan economic indicator is released by the Bank of Japan on a quarterly basis and is the equivalent of the PMI, but is reported in a slightly different way. For yen traders the Tankan is the indicator to watch for three reasons.

First, it is produced by the BOJ and therefore carries additional weight as it underpins the BOJ's thinking on the economy.

Second, as Japan is such a dominant global force in manufacturing, this is a core release.

Third, it will indicate whether the BOJ is likely to intervene in the forex market to weaken the Japanese yen in order to protect their export market should the report suggest a weak, or weakening economy.

In addition, this report is also watched closely by businesses considering investing in Japan requiring yen investments, adding more reasons to buy yen, thereby pushing the currency higher as a result.

The Tankan report, now referred to as the Tankan Manufacturing Index and, prior to that as the Tankan Survey, reports both the manufacturing and non-manufacturing sectors. However, the one that is always watched is the manufacturing sector which is further sub divided into small, medium and large companies. However, the headline number is for large manufacturing enterprises which covers the conglomerate companies that make up the core of Japan's economy.

The report is constructed in much the same way as for PMI data in other parts of the world. In the report a large number of manufacturing and non manufacturing companies are surveyed and asked to rate the economy as better than, the same as, or worse than, over the preceding quarter to produce the diffusion index.

However, in this case the fulcrum point is zero, and we therefore have both negative and positive numbers. So above zero is positive for the economy with a positive number, whilst below zero and a negative number, is not good news for the economy and longer term outlook.

Although the Tankan is a quarterly report and not monthly, it is hugely influential, not only on the yen, but also on the global economy. In addition, it guides BOJ economic policy and potential interventions.

One final point. If the BOJ is responsible for preparing the report, is it possible companies complete their returns in such a way as to influence the bank and its monetary policy, for their own advantage? An interesting question, and one which is open to debate.

The Tankan has the highest return rate of all the diffusion indices at an amazing 98%. Is it fear of upsetting the Bank of Japan, or eagerness to ensure monetary policy is in line with what the companies themselves want?

Continuing with the manufacturing theme I now want to take a brief look at two other economic indicators, namely the 'Philly Fed' and the Core Durable Goods, both released in the US.

The 'Philly FED' manufacturing index, is another diffusion index which is released monthly, and compiled from a survey of purchasing managers from manufacturing companies in the Philadelphia region of the United States. However, unlike the other diffusion indices we looked at earlier, this one is reported in a 'Tankan style' index. There are both positive and negative numbers, with the tipping point being zero. Anything above zero is positive suggestive of an expanding economy, whilst below zero and a negative number is a contracting or stagnant economy.

As with many other of these types of indicators, if the data is better than expected and the trend is positive, this is likely to be positive for the currency, which in this case is the US dollar. Higher interest rates are also likely in the near future. Conversely, a poor release is likely to have the opposite effect on the currency with interest rates potentially falling in the future as the economy stalls.

Whilst the Philly Fed release is unique to the US market, it nevertheless carries a surprising amount of weight in the markets, despite representing a relatively small sample of the US manufacturing market. In addition, some of the sub indices within the report can also provide some insight into commodity prices, as do many of the other manufacturing reports giving us further clues to inflation and therefore interest rates.

The bond markets are also highly sensitive to both the PMI and the Philly Fed which is usually released in the middle of the month, so can either be seen as confirming the earlier PMI release or forecasting the next.

The last economic indicator on the manufacturing theme is another index, Core Durable Goods. This release tries to measure the change in the total value of new orders placed with manufacturers for 'durable goods'. These are generally considered to be those goods expected to last at least three years or more. The index excludes the transportation sector as this tends to distort the results.

This index is therefore looking at relatively high capital value items which is significant, since high value purchases are often the first items to be cut from budgets in any economic slow down. Therefore, this index is not just an economic indicator, but also gives us a feel for the strength of the economy based on these high value ticket items.

The data is reported as a simple percentage and therefore indicates whether orders have risen or fallen over the period of one month. A rising index indicates strength in the US economy with growing demand and increasing employment and with it the prospect of a rise in interest rates. Any positive number in a rising trend is generally dollar positive. Equally, if the index is falling with a negative number this is normally bad news for the dollar which may weaken on the news.

Trade Balance

Now, let's move away from manufacturing to the economic indicator which every country reports, namely the Trade Balance Figures which relate to imports and exports.

The Trade Balance economic indicator is another of those economic releases which can have a significant impact on a country's currency. Furthermore, it is also a universal indicator which you will find reported around the globe, generally on a monthly or quarterly basis. And, it is one of those big numbers in every sense of the word.

However, what is a Trade Balance and what is the likely impact of such a release on the home currency? In simple terms, the Trade Balance is the difference between the value of goods a country exports, and the value of the goods it imports. If a country exports more than it imports it has a trade surplus, which is positive. But if a country imports more than it exports it has a trade deficit, which is negative. This is how the figures are reported when the data is released.

The release is presented either as a negative number to indicate a trade deficit or a positive number to indicate a trade surplus. And again there are three questions we need to consider.

1. Why is this important?
2. What is it telling us?
3. How is it likely to affect the currency, as a result?

The trade balance is important because when the economy is in recession exports are likely to be down so countries will try to export more in order to try to reduce the deficit. More exports generally means lower unemployment. In theory, when a country is importing heavily it is not creating employment, so changes in the trade deficit can reveal what is going on in the economy. In particular, if the country in question moves from being a net exporter to a net importer.

This is an issue that has come to the fore during this financial crisis and is the prime feature in competitive devaluation. Or, what the press call 'currency wars' or 'the race to the bottom'.

While writing this book this is still ongoing, and shows no sign of abating. This is one of the ongoing features of the US and Chinese relationship with China refusing to strengthen the yuan, and the US authorities in return weakening the US dollar via quantitative easing. Therefore, the trade balance figures have a direct relationship to an individual currency's strength or weakness.

There is also a further reason. If there is a trade surplus, or at least a trend to a decreasing trade deficit from the previous month, those countries buying products must convert their own currency to that of the exporter. This increases the demand for the exporter currency, thereby increasing its value. In other words the currency of the exporter country will strengthen in the currency markets.

Conversely, where there is an trade deficit or a trend to a decreasing trade surplus from the previous month, there is an increased supply of the domestic currency, which could in turn cause the currency to weaken.

Therefore, the Trade Balance Figures can give us an insight into the potential demand for the domestic currency, particularly where we see longer term trends changing from positive to negative, or vice versa.

In summary, the Trade Balance Figures can also give traders a valuable view on the economy of a particular country. Many countries with strong export markets, such as Japan, Germany, and China will always have a trade surplus.

However, this in itself is not necessarily a sign of a strong economy, as it is all relative to the trend. Moreover, the Trade Balance Figures can also be misleading, since it is the difference between exports and imports, so if both are rising the deficit or surplus will remain the same and the same would apply if both are falling. In either case we would see no change.

The key is to look at the trends and to try to draw conclusions based on the data in the following way. First, does the number reveal anything about the economy which might suggest a change? This could be signalled by a change from a surplus to a deficit, or from deficit to a surplus. Such a change would almost certainly surprise the currency markets, particularly if that country was normally a strong exporter. For example, Australia where the export market dominates and underpins the economy, which is relatively small. Therefore, a trade surplus is expected and is the norm. It does vary, but is generally positive.

However, if a trade deficit were to be reported for Australia, this would have a significant impact on the Australian dollar, since this would not only be a shock, but also signal an economy in trouble, with reduced demand for the currency as a result. This has occurred several times in recent years and in 2015 hit a record low of - 4214AUD million, before recovering into positive territory with a record high in 2016 of 4510 AUD million. Huge swings and reflected in the Australian dollar as you might expect.

The same effect would be seen in New Zealand for the same reasons. Another economy supported by a strong export market, so any trend of declining trade surplus, would start to send alarm signals to the markets.

However, any sudden shock may only be a temporary blip and, as always we have to view the data against both the forecast, the previous month's figure and the longer term trend. Nevertheless, the Trade Balance Figure is one traders simply cannot ignore as its sends out so many signals regarding the health of the economy.

Virtually every major country releases their Trade Balance Figures on a monthly basis, with strong exporters such as China, Australia, Canada and Japan all running consistent and strong trade surpluses. As a general rule, countries with a strong trade surplus tend to have lower unemployment as export demand creates jobs and employment opportunities. By contrast, countries with a large trade deficit such as the United States and the United Kingdom, tend to have higher rates of unemployment.

Furthermore, countries with a consistently strong trade surplus will usually see their currencies strengthen as the currency is in demand by overseas buyers of their exports. Conversely, countries who run a trade deficit which may be increasing, are likely to see their currency weaken, relative to other currencies, since it will not be in such great demand.

This is the problem that faces the central banks of major exporting nations. This constant battle to maintain a weak or competitive currency which is driven higher by the natural flows of currency from overseas buyers. For some countries, such as Japan, intervention remains one of the key tools of currency management. For others, such as China, it is in maintaining a weak currency through the peg.

I now want to move away from the 'big' economic numbers and look at those which look more closely at specific sectors of the market, which provide more of a 'macro economic' view of the economy as a whole.

Retail sales

The first of these are Core Retail Sales, and Retail Sales which go to the heart of consumer spending.

As I mentioned earlier, in the US economy consumer spending constitutes somewhere between 70% and 80% of GDP and, in simple terms if the consumer stops spending the economy goes into reverse.

This is what has happened during this financial crisis, so any economic indicator which measures consumer spending is a key measure. As the names suggests Core Retail Sales and Retail Sales measure the spending of consumers at the retail level and the difference between the two is quite simple. Retail sales includes all consumer spending, whilst Core Retail Sales excludes the sales of cars, since this can represent a large percentage of consumer spending and, being a volatile sector, can also distort the numbers.

As a general rule, Core Retail Sales will tend to have a greater impact on the currency markets, as it reveals in one number how consumers are feeling about the economy as reflected in their spending habits. This is then reported as a percentage increase or percentage decrease.

For example, we might see the number reported as 0.8% which shows consumer spending having risen by this amount over the period. Conversely, a negative figure indicates a drop in consumer spending. Naturally, a positive number is usually good news for the economy and for the currency it represents which should strengthen, as a result. A negative number is usually bad news for the currency, as it suggests a slow down in spending which is likely to be reflected in the GDP figures.

This is why these numbers are so important and considered to be leading indicators of the economy. These numbers can also be an excellent guide to the big GDP release which usually follows this economic release.

A further reason this release is significant, particularly the core figure, is that once again, like many of these economic indicators, it is one of the numbers used by governments and central banks to formulate both economic and fiscal policy, revealing as its does consumer spending patterns and therefore the health of the economy.

The US and Canada for example present the release as Retail and Core Retail Sales. Others simply release their retail sales without this refinement.

This doesn't really matter in terms of the numbers but, where the release is not split out this way, the numbers tend to have a lower impact. Also Core Retail Sales are usually given a red flag. In other words, they are likely to have a high impact on the markets.

However, as always, the devil is in the detail, the trend, and the market's expectation. Once again, I cannot emphasize enough the importance of this release. Many currency traders simply ignore it, failing to recognise its significance.

It is only when traders begin to appreciate the extent to which consumer spending dominates the economy and ultimately GDP data do they begin to realise the significance of this release.

Once consumers stop spending, for whatever reason, the economy will grind to a halt, stop and fall into recession, with all the implications on interest rates, money flow and currencies as a result. Please watch these numbers carefully. They are not just another number. They are the key numbers for consumer spending in every country around the world.

Housing Data

The next data set is one related to housing, of which there are several each month in the US.

Again many traders and investors ignore housing data, deeming it boring, dull, and generally of little use to the markets. This is wrong. If I were asked which numbers had the most relevance in forecasting the future for the economy I would say housing data. It is the one group of indicators which have the power to provide an insight into the broader economy and the reasons are as follows.

The housing market is crucial to every aspect of our lives and the economy. If house prices are rising, consumers feel confident. They spend more and they are also more likely to move, adding some churn to the housing market.

This activity is reflected throughout the economy. It is reflected in every sector and every area of the economy, from commodities, to jobs, to services, and to goods. If the economy is growing and healthy, the construction industry will be creating jobs to meet demand for new homes. Basic materials will be in demand, skilled labour will be required, and the pull through effect is seen rippling across all the other sectors of the market, as consumers spend with every sector from financial services to white goods feeling the effect.

So, the housing sector is a strong sentiment indicator. But, what really keeps housing and housing data so far ahead of the economy is the sensitivity of the market to changes in interest rates. After all, this is the first pinch point that hits consumers first. When interest rates rise or fall, this is normally reflected very quickly as residential mortgage rates change fast, either increasing or decreasing within weeks of any changes from the central banks.

If rates rise consumers start to feel this directly in higher monthly outgoings and sentiment can change very quickly. Equally, falling interest rates stimulate demand and sentiment changes and this is when the house builders start to return, releasing land and funding construction with cheap loans as interest in the housing market returns.

In many ways housing is similar and, indeed reflects the economic cycles we considered earlier in the book. Most housing markets around the world will go from 'boom to bust' and back again, generally leading the economy owing to their sensitivity to interest rates. Whilst some of the following releases are more significant than others, I hope I have made the point that housing and housing data is pivotal. NFP does grab all the headlines, but trends in housing can reveal just as much, if not more about the economy, and will also reveal changes in trend earlier and in many different ways.

The first indicator in our tranche of housing data is the New Home Sales, released monthly in the US market. It is generally considered to be a leading indicator of the housing sector, providing as it does, information on new homes sold in the period.

However, before considering this release in detail I just want to explain a little about housing data in general terms, because it is so influential and can have a dramatic effect on a currency when released.

The impact of housing data, when house prices are rising in a strong housing market, results in consumers feeling better off. They are likely to spend more, not only on the necessities of life, but also on discretionary goods and luxury items. This is all good news for the economy provided it isn't being fuelled on a credit bubble.

Second, if the housing market is strong, this will create a pull through effect in other market sectors, not least in construction, but also in the financial services sector with lending increasing. This then filters through into the home renovation and DIY markets, and on into white goods, furniture and furnishings.

These sectors all help to create a strong demand for goods and services which all underpin the economy, supported by consumer confidence and spending, and jobs.

A strong housing market also tells us about consumer confidence, which in turn is all about jobs. If people feel secure in their job, demand for houses will increase with a consequent increase in house prices which continues to fuel spending, so is a cyclical event.

However, problems start when it all comes to a shuddering halt, as witnessed with the sub prime mortgage débâcle which was the catalyst for the current global recession, from which we are only just emerging.

Moreover, economic indicators in the housing sector can reveal both longer term problems in the economy as well as pick up signs of growth, as demand picks up on the back of increased demand for houses or mortgages.

The first housing indicator I would like to consider is the New Home Sales, which is collected by the US Census Bureau and, as the name suggests, is based on the sale of new homes. However, what is interesting about this data is the criteria for what constitutes the sale of a new home.

In this case it is when the sales contract has been signed or a deposit accepted whilst the house itself can be at any stage of construction, from being off plan (not yet started) to complete and ready to move in. However, for the purposes of the report it is generally agreed around 25% are complete and ready to move in whilst the other 75% in the report are in various stages of completion. In simple terms this indicator is one of 'intent to buy' a new house, with the sales contract used as the determinant.

If the above figures are correct, New Home Sales should be a good indicator of economic growth in the future, and an equally good indicator of any slow down in the economy since the basis of the data is on the sales contract not on the construction itself.

When consumers are confident, the trend will be rising along with the economy, and when consumers are worried the trend will be falling. In simple terms, we don't need to see house prices necessarily rising to have a strong economy. However, we do need to have activity in the market and this is what the data is telling us, with this activity being converted into sales and increasing demand moving forward across sectors, from construction to finance and furnishings.

Although the number released is a monthly one, it is then annualised. This is a common practice with many economic releases, and simply means it is multiplied by twelve. So the number released for the US market is anywhere between 200,000 as a low, to 1.5 million at a peak but, as always it is the trend that matters as well as the number itself and its relation to the previous month.

Furthermore, this indicator is all about the trend, as the longer term trend more closely mirrors the longer term ups and downs of the economy. As a result, once the trend starts picking up, with any number coming in better than expected, this will be seen as positive for the US dollar. Equally, a poor number will tend to be bad news for the currency which may weaken as a result.

In a nutshell, a strong number gives the markets and administrators many clues about consumer spending, consumer confidence, and the longer term outlook for the broader economy.

US Pending Home Sales

The second of our housing economic indicators in the US is Pending Home Sales, which in this case is prepared and released by the National Association of Realtors, and is published on a monthly basis for the US market. This release generally appears towards the end of each month.

Once again it is the longer term trend here that is important as this release is also a leading indicator of activity in the housing market. This in turn is likely to translate into economic growth as the ripples from activity in housing move out into a wide number of market sectors.

This release measures contract activity in the existing home sales market, as opposed to new home sales. Therefore, these are sales of existing, preowned homes. The data here is reported as the change in the number of pending home sales and appears as a percentage change, so we may see a figure of −2.2% with sales falling during the month, or +3.1% representing an increase in sales during the month. As always, it is the trend that matters and the question is which of these two reports carries more weight.

This is a difficult question to answer since both New Home Sales and Pending Home Sales are leading indicators of the economy.

However, of the two I would suggest New Home Sales is probably more important since this encompasses the construction industry and all the ancillary services that are part and parcel of house building.

After all, activity in the existing home market can often be stimulated by cheap money. Furthermore, activity in the new homes market also reflects corporate activity from major house builders and developers and these companies are unlikely to be building new homes for speculation.

Therefore, construction in new homes carries more corporate significance than in pending home sales, which may be based on pure speculation and not economic growth. This, in my view, is an important distinction.

However, the important point to note about all housing data, wherever it is reported around the world and in whatever format, is this. Housing data is really a production figure and, by that I mean it tells us more about business confidence and how the house building sector is viewing the future. Existing home sales are more a measure of sentiment. If consumers are happy to move home, generally this is due to a rising market, with security of employment, and rising house prices driving the desire to move. However, the impact of these moves is relatively limited on the overall economy. What the data reveals is sentiment.

On the other hand, New Home Sales are more a measure of confidence by the major house builders, who never build speculatively. This release could be viewed as a 'manufacturing index' for houses, which will ultimately have greater significance and impact on the economy. After all, they also generate jobs,

The effects of housing data on any currency are relatively muted and, as a general rule, should be viewed as longer term indicators of changes in underlying economic trends, and signs of potential reversals from boom to bust and back again.

Building Permits

The next indicator in this section is Building Permits which is released both in the US and Canada on a monthly basis, although the data formats are slightly different.

Building Permits is an important release as regardless of where we are in the world no building can be constructed, legally at any rate, without formal approval from the regulatory planning authorities. In the US and Canada these are referred to as Building Permits, and the data released relates to residential permits only, so excludes commercial data.

A Building Permit is the first step in any construction process before the first trench can be dug or brick laid on site. In the context of the economy, if New Home Sales was an important indicator, Building Permits is even more significant as nothing can start without one.

If the number of Building Permits are rising month on month this is a clear signal the first stage in an economic recovery is under way, or simply a confirmation of a strong economy with a boom in house construction.

Therefore, a great leading indicator of the longer term economic outlook. If this number is falling or is weak, clearly the economic outlook is weak and it is not good news for the currency, as a result. If the number is strong with a positive trend upwards this is an excellent signal and on release, the currency should strengthen as a result.

As I mentioned, these indicators are released in both the US and Canada. In Canada they are released in terms of the value of Building Permits issued during the month which are then converted to a percentage. For example, the Canadian authorities might issue permits with a value of 5.8 billion Canadian dollars which is converted to a percentage change, so a simple positive or negative percentage change will be reported.

In the US the equivalent indicator is released as a number which is annualised in much the same way as for New Home Sales. In other words, multiplied by twelve, Here we will see a number from 200,000 up to 2 million and beyond, when construction and the economy are booming.

As always, it is the trend that matters here and, if we have a nicely rising trend with good figures, the currency should strengthen as a result. Conversely, a falling trend with poor figures indicates a weak economy and weak corporate picture which is generally negative for the currency.

A sudden change can also surprise the markets although they will generally revert back to the trend once the news release is over.

In Canada the Housing Starts are the equivalent to the US New Homes Sales. This figure represents the number of new residential houses started in the previous month. Once again this figure is reported in an annualised format. A single figure is therefore reported and confirms the number of new houses under construction. Just like the US data it is extremely important to the Canadian economy and, of course the Canadian dollar.

If the economy is doing well the trend in Housing Starts is likely to be rising and, provided the release is in line with the trend, the Canadian dollar should strengthen, particularly if the number is better than expected. Equally if the number is bad and continues a trend lower this is signalling a weak economy and therefore is not such good news for the Canadian dollar.

The Housing Starts is considered a leading indicator of the Canadian economy. It is an indicator which is carefully watched by both the central bank and the government and is widely used in both fiscal and monetary policy decision making as a result.

Moving to Australia it is the Building Approvals which gives us an excellent guide to the Australian economy. This data provides us with another leading indicator for residential housing construction with the planning application and approval, the first step in any new house building projects.

Strong growth in new approvals is an excellent guide to both the current and future economic outlook. Construction in housing leads the way and ripples through into many other sectors of the economy, from construction to home furnishings, as well as financial services, which in turn leads to strong consumer spending.

The Australian data is presented as a percentage change of total approvals given for the month, so we get both positive and negative numbers depending on whether the trend is rising or falling. A positive and rising trend is always a good signal to the longer term economy and if the number is better than expected the Australian dollar should strengthen on the prospect of rising consumer spending and an increase in interest rates in due course.

Conversely, if the trend is falling this could be indicative of a weakening economy. An economy which is likely to slow resulting in lower consumer spending, falling inflation and lower interest rates as a result.

The headline number which is reported for Building Approvals is the seasonally adjusted percentage change in new building approvals from the previous month. It is usually released around 40 days after month end by the Australian Bureau of Statistics so always runs a little behind the others, but nevertheless is one to check and monitor.

The equivalent in New Zealand is called Building Consents, and this is another great economic indicator of strength or weakness in the economy with construction leading the way as new building consents are approved for new build projects.

Like the Australian data, the New Zealand number is released monthly, after month end, but takes between thirty and thirty five days to be appear. Nevertheless it is another excellent guide to the underlying economy and future outlook for growth and consumer spending.

Once again the trend is everything, so provided the number is good and the trend is rising, the New Zealand dollar should strengthen on the release.

Equally, a weak number or shock in a falling trend is likely to weaken the New Zealand dollar on the prospect of a slowing economy and falling interest rates in due course.

Once again the Building Consents number is reported as a simple percentage change and is therefore either positive or negative.

Finally in this section on housing indicators I would like to mention data which is related to the housing sector, namely some of the economic indicators related to loans and mortgages.

Loans & Mortgage Data

This associated housing data in the form of loans and mortgages is where the current financial crisis first started. It was the problems in the US sub prime market (high risk loans) which was the trigger. It is the fallout from these instruments which is still causing so many problems to the global economy.

Credit bubbles and defaults are nothing new. Japan's problems all stemmed from cheap money fuelling a debt and housing bubble. These same problems are appearing in some of the powerhouse economies with China a classic example. Here too low cost loans are fuelling a property bubble.

The easy availability of relatively cheap loans and mortgages can be a double edged sword. On the one hand they will help to drive a positive trend in economic prosperity, consumer confidence and activity in the housing market, which filters through into all other sectors. However, this can create a bubble and what is never known is when this bubble will burst.

In the UK one of the economic indicators to watch is the Nationwide HPI release. This is a monthly report which looks at the change in house prices, but which is based on mortgages provided by one of the largest providers, the Nationwide Building Society, and is referred to as the House Price Index or HPI.

In general terms, rising house prices suggest a strong economy with consumers feeling better off and therefore prepared to spend more to keep the economy moving. However, falling or stagnant house prices will indicate the reverse and, as such, any movement in house prices is generally considered to be a leading indicator of the broader economy.

Higher house prices nearly always suggest an expanding economy, while falling house prices are suggestive of an economy in contraction. House prices can therefore be a good early indicator of inflationary pressure which could lead the Bank of England to raise interest rates in order to ensure inflation is kept in check.

The headline number reported is a simple percentage increase or decrease in the monthly house price index and, if the number is better than expected and is in a rising trend, this is generally good for the British pound which should strengthen. Conversely, if the number is worse than expected and in a falling trend, this is likely to be seen as bad news for the economy and inflation, with a consequent weakening of sterling.

In the last few years in the UK, house prices have been stagnant or falling with the monthly report coming in with numbers both above and below the median level at zero and therefore this indicator has tended to have little impact recently. This is a perfect example of how the weight of an economic indicator can change depending on the economic cycle.

The reason is simple enough. We are in a recessionary period so no one expects house prices to rise and, certainly not develop a trend in the short term, and coupled with uncertainty over Brexit. Therefore, the impact of this indicator will be muted as the market's focus is on shorter term leading indicators such as the jobs market and any agreement with the EU.

However, once a recovery gets under way this report and others reporting house prices and lending will increase in importance, in much the same way as interest rates themselves which increase and decrease in importance within the economic cycle.

So the Nationwide HPI report is one to watch when trading the UK pound, but it can have a reduced impact depending on where we are in the economic cycle.

The Halifax HPI is another house price for the UK housing market, only this time released by the Halifax Building Society.

Like the Nationwide it is based on house price data from their own lending over the last month and in many ways confirms the Nationwide HPI index.

The two reports are both released monthly and generally appear within a few days of one another so whichever comes second is likely to have less impact than the first as they are both essentially reporting the same economic news i.e. house prices, but just using different sources of data.

Therefore, unless there is a huge discrepancy the markets will generally not react strongly to the second release as both companies are large lenders and therefore their statistics and results should be similar. Once again this is considered to be a leading indicator and is reported as a monthly percentage change which will be either a negative or positive figure. As always with house prices and housing data it is the trend which is important and the best way to view this release is merely as a confirmation of the Nationwide HPI, or vice versa whichever comes first.

The Home Loans Report from Australia is another key economic indicator for the housing market and the release reports the change in the number of new loans for residential properties during the month. Once again it is considered to be a leading indicator of the Australian economy and is released by the Australian Bureau of Statistics. It is an extremely important release since it is closely watched by the central bank, the RBA, for signals on the economy and therefore future decisions on monetary policy and interest rates. As a result this release always produces a strong move in the Australian dollar.

The number released is once again the change in the number of new loans issued for owner occupiers in Australia and is therefore reported as a simple percentage either as a negative or positive number every month.

Therefore, a positive number indicates a rise in the number of loans approved and a negative number indicates a fall in the number of loans approved. As always, it is the trend which is important, and this is what the RBA will also be watching to guide their decisions on any future interest rate decisions.

If the number is better than expected and is in a rising trend, this will generally be positive for the Australian dollar. Conversely, a poor number or, a worse than expected number, will tend to weaken the home currency, as this is suggesting a slowing economy and the likelihood of falling interest rates.

Composite Indices

I would now like to move on and explain a type of index known as a composite index. Earlier in this chapter we looked at data based on a diffusion index, those types of economic indicators which have been designed to show us potential turning points in the economy moving above and below a tipping point at fifty.

By contrast, a composite index is a release which provides a quantitative measurement of economic strength or weakness and, as such a composite index differentiates between small and large overall movements. They are often referred to as volume indicators in terms of economic activity as the data is presented in a bar chart format so we see both volume by the highs and lows on the chart, as well as the trends in economic cycles with peaks and troughs as these highs and lows form. Therefore, in a composite index the data is presented from a baseline of zero with a bar, unlike the diffusion index which oscillates around the tipping point of fifty. In other words a composite index is presented as an histogram.

The main aim of a composite index is to measure the tempo and magnitude of economic fluctuations, and here are some of the more important composite economic indicators starting with the CB Consumer Confidence Index which appears on the US economic calendar.

This is the first of our composite economic indicators and the reason I have chosen this one is that it is simply one of the most important. Having said that, like all economic releases their impact will vary according to where we are in the broad economic cycle.

The CB Consumer Confidence Index is released by a private non profit making company called the Conference Board on a monthly basis in the US. This is a company that specialises in a range of business data for members and, with almost half the fortune 500 companies now subscribing to their services, this is a highly respected and regarded economic release for three reasons.

First it is released monthly, so is considered to be a leading indicator of the economy. Second it is based on real responses by real people and is all about consumer confidence. Put simply, if consumers aren't confident, they won't spend and if they won't spend the economy eventually slows and grinds to a halt. So once again the trend is important with this indicator.

Finally, this indicator is also closely watched by the Federal Reserve. It is an indicator which they use to formulate monetary policy so is hugely important and demands close attention.

The CB Consumer Confidence report is released monthly in the US on the last Tuesday of each month. It is one of the most watched indicators of this type, as it provides a clear view of the US citizens' attitudes to current and future economic conditions. But, what does it measure and how is it constructed?

The survey is derived from a survey of over five thousand households and is designed to determine the financial health, spending power and confidence of the average American consumer. In essence, the survey aims to discover how consumers feel about jobs, the economy and spending.

These responses are compiled and translated into a single figure which is released as the index figure of the month. When the American consumer is feeling ultra confident about the future and happy to spend, the index is likely to rise well above 100. For example in early 2000 the index reached a high of 144, before falling to a low of 25 in 2009 with confidence and spending at an all time low as the US economy ground to a halt.

The strength of this type of index is that, not only do we get a headline number to compare to the forecast and previous month figure, but there is also a trend which is seen on the histogram. The histogram gives us the economic highs and lows in a vivid and visual way.

To summarise. The CB Consumer Confidence report is a very important leading indicator of what the average Joe in the US is thinking and doing with their money. It reveals confidence (or lack of) in the future and therefore future spending plans.

Whilst the headline number is important, it must be considered in the context of what has gone before and where it is in the cycle. Consequently, if the index is giving a reading in the mid fifties or low sixties but trending up, and in the past we have seen highs of well over a hundred, we can assume the economy is recovering, but has a long way to go. In this scenario, interest rates are unlikely to rise in the short term.

Conversely, once the index reaches an extreme this can signal the end of a growth phase in the economy with interest rates high and likely to fall as the economy and consumer spending slowing, as a result. An economy in boom, but now preparing to burst.

However, as the economy strengthens, with the index moving higher, expectation of an interest rate rise will also increase. In addition, if the trend on the index is also rising and a good number is released, which is better than forecast or even surprises the market, this should be good news for the dollar with strength in the currency as a result.

Equally if the trend is rising and a poor number is released this is likely to be seen as bad news deferring any interest rate increases and sending the dollar lower as a result.

However, this release has many detractors and reasons include that the response rate is thought to be poor, with on average around only half of the survey responding within the required time. Indeed, a month or so later, a revision is published which includes those respondents who failed to meet the deadline, but there is rarely any significant difference between the two.

Second, and perhaps more importantly, there is always an ongoing debate about the accuracy and relevancy of such indices. Indeed, when two similar reports are released, they often vary enormously. The reason for this is survey respondents vary in lifestyle and income, so surveys place different emphasis on certain questions. Finally, survey groups are often quite small, which also begs the question of why anyone would want to be in a survey anyway? Do surveys attract a certain type of person with a certain type of character? This leads to the issue of bias, so these types of releases are far from perfect.

Notwithstanding, the CB Conference Board is one of the more respected, having been issuing this data since 1967.

Our second example in this category is the UoM (University of Michigan) consumer sentiment report, another of our composite economic indicators which ranks alongside the CB index. It is another of the economic indicators which gives us a view on how consumers in the US are feeling with regard to their future spending plans and their outlook on the economy in general.

Once again this report is produced monthly but, in this case we get two bites at the cherry, with a preliminary number which is released around the middle of the month, followed by a revision which comes out two weeks later. However, as you would expect it is the preliminary number that carries more weight and has more impact.

The report is prepared by the University of Michigan and has been around since 1946. This survey is based on a much smaller sample of consumers, generally around five hundred, so is a tenth the size of the more significant CB Consumer Index which is based on around five thousand. However, many market experts believe the UoM is a more accurate predictor of sentiment than the CB index. The reason for this is the sampling method used by the index which is based on a rotating system whereby every month 60% of survey respondents are new, whilst only 40% are included twice. The UoM also carries the label of being provided by an academic and august organisation.

Whatever the views, the UoM is an important release, and the data is presented in the same way with a headline number which reflects the level of the sentiment and presented as a bar chart. This gives us a view on the economic trend and where we are in the cycle as viewed by consumers and their willingness to spend, or otherwise.

As always, it is the trend that matters and the CB index coupled with the UoM index, should correlate positively. However, there can be a variation between the two. So if the CB comes out first with a good number that sends the US dollar higher, then the UoM should confirm this view and reinforce this dollar strength provided there are no shocks or surprises. Once again, the index is viewed as a leading indicator of consumer sentiment, and therefore a guide to future interest rates, inflation and the broader economy as a result.

If the number is better than expected we should see the dollar strengthen on the news, provided this is in a rising trend and in line with the trend. Conversely, if the index comes in worse than expected the dollar should fall, particularly if the trend is lower.

Moving to Europe and here the most important economic indicators are those which relate to Germany. Not only does Germany sit at the heart of Europe, but its industrial strength and strong export driven economy is currently propping up the euro and the entire Eurozone.

As far as key economic indicators for Germany it is the IFO Business Climate Index which is the one to watch as it carries considerable weight, for a number of reasons.

First, it is produced by the Institute for Economic Research and therefore carries the stamp of authority from a learned body.

Second, as an indicator for German business if the economy in Germany begins to struggle, the rest of Europe will be in recession. It's that simple.

Third, the index is based on a large sample size of over seven thousand businesses and is therefore a comprehensive survey.

Finally, this is one of the economic indicators most closely watched by the ECB and used by them as part of their decision making process for monetary policy in Europe. So, a key number which always moves the euro.

The IFO indicator is released monthly and the survey encompasses businesses across the entire market and business sector, including manufacturers, wholesalers and retailers, so is thoroughly representative.

In the survey, respondents are asked to rate the outlook for their businesses over the next six months, so is an excellent guide to the future of the economy. This is the reason why it is considered to be a leading indicator and therefore carefully watched by the ECB.

However, we need to be careful in making comparisons over the longer term historical trend, because the base year for the index, which was originally 2000, was changed in 2011 to a base year of 2005.

In other words, instead of the year 2000 being the base index of 100, 2005 is now the base index year. The consequence of this change is the headline number for the index has increased by around five points on a monthly basis. This has to be kept in mind when making comparisons.

The IFO is normally released around three weeks after the month end and, as mentioned earlier, is the one indicator that will always have a big impact on the euro. If the number is good and confirms a rising trend this is signalling positive confidence in the business sector. The market can expect increasing consumer demand, with the possibility of rising inflation and consequently the prospect of higher interest rates in the future.

However, one of the main problems for the ECB is in trying to keep inflation under control by raising interest rates, they do not strengthen the euro as a result and choke off the German export machine. An export machine which is so critical to the European project, and to the survival of the euro, overall.

This factor is always an ongoing problem for the ECB. However, it should also be noted Germany is one of the few countries in the world which has always welcomed a strong currency.

If the IFO number is worse than expected, or surprises the market by coming in weak, expect to see the euro fall, as a result. However, if this is just a blip in an otherwise strong trend higher, this may simply cause a short term reaction in the euro before the trend is re-established once again.

As an aside, you may find it strange that in all the red flag economic indicators we have covered so far in this chapter, this is the first one for the euro. In many ways, this is symptomatic of the euro and the Eurozone, which in reality is no more than a loose collective of nations with no unified approach other than in a variety of treaties and agreements. It is therefore no surprise none of the many country specific economic indicators are considered important enough to warrant a red notification in the calendar. This is why there are so few economic indicators considered important enough to have a direct impact on the euro. However, the section on second tier indicators (coded orange on the Forex Factory website), is where we find a whole clutch for the EU and covering all aspects of the European economy.

France is the only other country with sufficient mass of both population and economy to have an effect on the euro or ECB economic policy.

The German IFO release is one of the most anticipated pieces of economic data to be released in Europe, as the German economy is seen as the bellwether for the rest of the EU. One of the reasons this release is so keenly awaited is the speed with which the data is collected and reported. The data is released in the same month the survey is conducted. Therefore, a true leading indicator in every sense of the word.

What is also interesting about this indicator is that over the years it has shown a close correlation with the equivalent ISM report from the US, with the two generally reporting similar trends and numbers.

As a speculative trader it is always worth bearing this in mind, as one report is likely to give you a 'heads up' on the associated release later in the month. The German IFO release generally appears around 3 weeks into the month.

Moving to Switzerland and the Swiss franc where, once again, there is an important composite index which is a hybrid indicator. It is a composite of various economic indicators, but one which is based on an amalgam of data from both business and the consumer. This is then combined into a single headline number which is reported in a diffusion format, with the indicator reporting either a positive or negative number.

In the case of this indicator the tipping point is zero (not 50), and the reason this economic indicator is so important for the Swiss franc is twofold.

First, it is prepared and released by the KOF, an economic research establishment in Switzerland and, second it is used by the Swiss National Bank in decisions on economic policy, so it is an important indicator.

The KOF has been designed to forecast economic growth over the next six to nine months with the index created from surveys across all business sectors, and it also includes consumer confidence and housing data.

In many ways the KOF is an odd index, but in terms of its relationship to the currency the reaction is as expected. If the number is better than expected and in a rising trend of optimism, this is likely to be bullish for the Swiss franc but if the number is worse than expected and in a pessimistic trend, this is likely to be bearish for the Swiss franc.

The second German indicator to consider is the ZEW economic sentiment indicator which delivers another key number for the euro.

The ZEW provides further data on the German economy and is released monthly. This economic indicator is another from the diffusion index stable, and is based on a survey of both institutional investors and analysts. The survey covers all areas of the economy including exchange rates, stock markets and inflation.

Like the IFO, this is a highly respected indicator, as the index is prepared and released by the centre for European Economic Research and is based on a large sample of over three hundred and fifty respondents. The respondents are asked to rate the economy and their outlook for the next six months.

It is considered to be a leading indicator for the Germany economy, the most important in Europe. The survey data is converted into a diffusion index which, in this case, has a tipping point of zero, with above the line representing optimism and below the line representing pessimism.

The index is reported as a single headline number which is either positive or negative and which can be anywhere between minus fifty or sixty to plus seventy to eighty depending on the economic outlook of the analysts.

The investors and analysts may of course be wrong in their view, but they are given credence by virtue of their experience and knowledge of the markets. Therefore, the sentiment for the economy expressed in this index carries a lot of weight in the market.

In general, if the number is better than expected and in a rising trend above the zero line the euro is likely to strengthen, and if the number is weak and falling or even below the zero line the euro is likely to weaken. However, as always with the euro, traders are at the mercy of the ECB and its political masters.

Moving back to the US and to a curious economic indicator known as the TIC long term purchases. The relationship this economic indicator has with the US dollar is not straightforward. At times, it can spark a strong reaction in the dollar, while at other times the release passes by unnoticed by the markets as they wait for the next item of news. Despite this behaviour it is still considered a tier one or red flag item of news on the economic calendar.

TIC stands for Treasury International Capital and this indicator measures whether there has been a net outflow of US dollars, or net inflow into the country. As result, it should logically affect the strength or weakness of the US dollar. Moreover, the indicator is also making a statement about overseas confidence in the US dollar as well as giving information about longer term investment returns.

Here is an example of the data which is incorporated into the TIC. When a non US citizen wants to buy US shares or bonds, the home currency has to be converted and US dollars bought. Conversely, when a US citizen wants to buy foreign securities US dollars have to be sold and converted.

It is these transactions which the TIC is measuring on a monthly basis and presenting the difference between the two. In effect, if more dollars are bought than sold, this is bullish. Whereas, if more dollars are sold then this is bearish for the currency.

The headline figure which is reported can be either positive or negative, depending on whether there has been more overseas buying from US investors, or from overseas investors buying in the US. Generally however, this number is positive as there are usually more investors buying US dollars than selling, but negative numbers have been recorded from time to time.

Therefore, the headline number presented in the release, such as +140.5 billion is the value of US dollar assets bought by overseas investors during the month. A positive number, signals more capital is coming into the country than is flowing out. In other words, demand for US assets from overseas buyers was strong, and outweighed the counterbalance effect of US buying in overseas markets. This sends several signals to the market, not least of which is the fact that confidence in the US dollar remains strong and returns on these investments are seen as positive in the longer term. This, in turn, is seen as dollar positive and the currency should strengthen as a result.

If the number is negative, which has happened from time to time, this is signalling a lack of demand for US dollar assets, with US buying overseas outweighing overseas buyers of US assets.

This is likely to see the US dollar weaken as it is suggesting a lack of interest in these assets and consequently weaker demand for the currency.

The report is published by the US Department of the Treasury and, as mentioned earlier, this release can have a mixed reaction in the dollar. Normally, if the figure is positive and high this should see the dollar strengthen, whilst a weaker figure may see the dollar decline. However, this is a difficult indicator to read as it lacks any consistent and logical market reaction. Part of the reason for this lies in the balance and make up of the various overseas investors.

The report actually distinguishes between the various types of buyers of US assets and whether they are governments and financial organisations, or private investors. Of course, some of the largest overseas investors are The People's Bank of China and the Bank of Japan, to name just two.

China on its own could move the market in US Treasuries as its holdings are so large. This is one of the reasons it is so difficult to forecast and interpret the monthly release, since a small change by the Chinese, either buying or selling, would have an enormous impact on the data and send it rocketing one way or the other.

As a general rule, the markets like to see a strongly positive figure, which is signalling confidence in the US dollar, particularly where the bulk of the investment has come from central banks and governments. In addition, this is also a measure of the US's ability to cover the monthly trade deficit and the logic here is that if this is the case, there is no need to weaken the dollar on the release.

So far in this chapter I have concentrated on those releases which are considered to be tier one or 'red flag' announcements. In other words, those which are likely to have a significant impact on the market. However, at this point I would like to stress the following.

First, although I have concentrated on the US markets, every country around the world will have its own releases, which will follow the same principles and have the same reaction in the market, and my purpose here has been to give you the insights into the various types of releases, and their associated market reaction.

Although this can then be applied to other regions around the world, do bear in mind when considering the release for a particular country it may have more or less relevance depending on the economic characteristics of the country in question.

Second, as I have already mentioned, economic indicators are cyclical, and therefore their relevance and impact will change as the economic cycle changes. In addition, during extreme periods, other economic data may be introduced to try to provide an enhanced view of the economy, and a classic example here is the release of bond auction data, a relatively new phenomenon.

The result of a country's bond auctions have only recently started to appear in the economic calendar as a consequence of the economic crisis of the last few years. The focus of the auctions is usually with the struggling economies of the PIGS (Portugal, Italy, Greece and Spain). But France too has now been added to this list, given the parlous state of its economy.

For the time being, these releases are considered a 'red flag' release. However, in the next few years, as the recovery begins in ernest, interest in the bond auctions will wane with market focus moving away from sovereign debt and back to interest rates and more 'mainstream' economic data. Data which has been the mainstay in the past few decades.

New Zealand

In this section I want to mention some of the more important economic indicators for New Zealand and the New Zealand dollar. The reason for devoting a section to the New Zealand is the unique role it plays in the carry trade strategy.

This is all the more reason to focus on those indicators which will signal the start of any possible rise in interest rates.

The first of these indicators is the NZIER Business Confidence economic indicator, a quarterly index prepared and released by the New Zealand Institute of Economic Research. This is a highly respected index which is based on a large sample of over three and a half thousand so an important release and one to watch carefully when trading the kiwi currency.

It is a diffusion index and the respondents are from all sectors of business including manufacturing, wholesalers and retailers, so represents a good balance of economic opinion. In this case, the index is based around zero as the tipping point with optimism moving the index above and pessimism below. A single headline number is reported quarterly and generally moves within a range of approximately minus 60 and plus 60, above and below the fulcrum.

As a highly respected release it is therefore considered to be a leading indicator of the New Zealand economy and also a release closely watched by the Reserve Bank of New Zealand as part of their decision making process for monetary policy.

Once again it is the trend that matters. A rising trend with a good number which is better than the forecast is likely to see the New Zealand dollar strengthen, and conversely a falling trend with a bad number is likely to see it fall.

But, and it is a big but, when trading in these high yielding currencies we always have to bear in mind the effect of the carry trade, not always an easy reaction to forecast, so avoid jumping to any quick conclusions.

The second of our New Zealand economic indicators is almost identical to the previous one, and really only differs in the timing and the sample size. Like the NZIER release, the ANZ Business Confidence (sometimes referred to as the NBNZ Business Confidence) too is highly respected and, perhaps even more so as it comes from the National Bank of New Zealand. It's released monthly and based on a survey size of fifteen hundred businesses across all the sectors, which is consolidated into a diffusion index.

The tipping point is zero and the index is considered to be a leading indicator of the economy and of future interest rates. Strangely this indicator only appears eleven times a year as it is not released in January. As always, it is the trend that matters, with a better then expected number helping to lift the New Zealand dollar in an up trend and to weaken it if the number is bad and in a down trend.

The Labor Cost Index is another from New Zealand, released quarterly by Statistics New Zealand, a government body. This index is designed to measure changes in the cost of labor and is therefore a key measure of inflation in the New Zealand economy. The cost of labour is one of the largest contributors to inflationary pressure, as they are always ultimately passed on to consumers in the form of higher prices.

The index is usually released around one month after the end of the quarter, so it can be a little out of date. Nevertheless, it is still considered a leading indicator of the economy and an excellent guide to inflation and the prospects for an increase or decrease in interest rates. The indicator is released as a simple percentage increase or decrease and, if the number is better than expected and in a rising trend, this is generally good news for the New Zealand Dollar which should strengthen on the news. Conversely, if the number is lower than expected this reduces the prospects for the economy and there is less chance of a short term rise in interest rates.

As always, any conclusions must be drawn against the ever present influence and effect of the carry trade.

The Inflation Expectation economic indicator is a relatively new addition to indicators for the New Zealand economy, and important for two reasons. First, it is a survey conducted and released by the central bank, the Reserve Bank of New Zealand so carries a great deal of weight in the market. Second, it is a key measure of inflation, which the bank itself uses as part of its own monetary policy decision making.

This indicator too is released quarterly and is based on a survey of managers across a wide range of business sectors. The managers are asked to provide forecasts as to the likely changes in the price of goods and services annually over the next two years. This is released as the headline figure for the indicator. Despite being relatively new, this is a release which is growing in importance as the data builds into meaningful trends.

If a better than expected figure is posted in a rising trend this should be good for the kiwi, as it is signalling the possibility of rising inflation and therefore an increase in interest rates. Equally, a poor number in a falling trend signals a weak economy with rising unemployment and falling inflation with the prospect of lower interest rates to come

So, between these indicators we have some excellent leading information on future interest rates for the New Zealand economy, vital to all forex traders, but particularly so for traders of the carry trade strategy.

Second Tier

So far in this chapter I have focused primarily on tier one or 'red flag' economic indicators, but there are also many second tier releases which can and do move markets. These too can be useful to us as forex traders and here the one I want to start with is from Canada and is the BOC (Bank of Canada) Business Outlook Survey.

The BOC Business Outlook Survey is unusual in that it is conducted and released by the Bank of Canada on a quarterly basis. It therefore carries a significant amount of weight in the market as it is coming directly from the central bank itself.

However, sadly for us as traders this report is not converted to a simple index with a headline number. Instead, it is uploaded in great detail to the Bank of Canada website and it can take time to absorb and evaluate.

Nevertheless, the markets take this report very seriously, and an interesting aspect of this indicator is that since it does not have a simple headline number the Canadian dollar may be slow to react to the release. Perhaps this is a deliberate policy by the BOC?

The survey itself is actually quite small scale and restricted to around one hundred or so companies who are asked to rate economic conditions, the outlook for sales growth, spending on plant and equipment. They are also asked whether the company plans to increase or decrease staff numbers, along with their views on likely changes in both input and output prices as well as inflation. The information is then displayed on the BOC web site as soon as the report is compiled.

The results are displayed either in the diffusion index format with zero representing the change from positive to negative sentiment, or as simple histograms or bar charts as in the composite index format.

For traders of the Canadian dollar this release is important, and worth studying. It only takes a few minutes to check each chart and see the trends for the indicator. It's not complicated and although a relatively small sample, the data comes from a highly respected source, the central Bank of Canada which has a good reputation in the markets.

An interesting second tier economic indicator I would like to mention here is in Australia and is the ANZ Job Advertisements Report from the Australian and New Zealand Banking Group in Australia. This tracks the change in the number of advertised jobs, both in the newspapers and also online, which is reported as the percentage change on a monthly basis. It is considered to be a leading indicator of the economy, and I've included it for two reasons.

First, it is an example of how diverse the field of economic indicators can be, and second to demonstrate how simple second tier indicators can be highly predictive and effective. In many ways it it often the simple signs that are overlooked in the tidal wave of economic data and releases which arrive each day.

This is why housing is so important because it represents what is going on in everyday life and can therefore tell us more about the economy than complicated dry statistics.

The ANZ Job Advertisement report is another such indicator and it's very straightforward. It is premised on the fact if the number of jobs advertised is rising the economy is in a growth phase. Conversely, if the number of jobs advertised is falling the economy may be weakening.

A rise in adverts suggests a likely rise in interest rates with a consequent strengthening of the Australian dollar. Whereas a fall in adverts suggests a likely fall in interest rates with the Australian dollar likely to weaken, as a result. A simple and uncomplicated way of gauging whether the economy is strong or weak.

Another second tier indicator which can also move the Australian dollar is the Private Capital Expenditure release which is a quarterly measure of economic activity for the country. It is published by the Australian Bureau of Statistics and measures the alteration in the overall inflation amended values. In other words, the real value of new capital investments from private companies. It is considered a leading indicator for the economy because it is measuring the confidence of business by the amount of capital they are prepared to invest in their own companies.

This is really a confidence indicator but in a different guise. Private sector investments are a key measure of economic confidence and activity, and the indicator is reported as a simple percentage change on a quarterly basis. So a strong number in a rising trend, which comes in better than expected is likely to be good news for the Australian dollar which should strengthen as a result. A strong number is suggesting economic activity and therefore higher interest rates in due course.

A poor number, which is below the forecast will have the opposite effect with the Australian dollar weakening on the news.

An important second tier release for the UK and sterling, is the Public Sector Net Borrowing release which too can affect the British pound.

This release tells us the financial health of the UK and how much the government needs to borrow in order to meet its spending requirements. In other words, how much the government needs to borrow from international investors to fill any shortfall from tax revenues. Therefore, if tax revenues are low the government has to borrow more, or cut its spending which is what has been happening in the last few years in an attempt to cut the UK deficit.

This is no different to you or I balancing our income and spending and perhaps using our credit card when we are short of cash while we wait for our next pay check or salary. The UK government (and many others) are no different, the numbers are just bigger. This economic indicator simply tells us how much the UK government is borrowing.

This report is released by the National Statistics Office on a monthly basis, around twenty days after the month end and is delivered as a headline figure of how much has been borrowed. A positive number indicates a budget deficit, whilst a negative number indicates a budget surplus. Since the start of the financial crisis borrowing for the UK government and other governments has been rising at an alarming rate, forcing spending cuts on public services in order to keep borrowing under control.

However, borrowing looks set to continue rising for several years as the UK government pays for the bank bail outs which almost bankrupted the country. As a consequence, this is an indicator where bad news is expected by the markets so any figure which is slightly better than expected and lower than the previous month will be considered as good news and should be positive for the British pound. Any figure which comes in worse than expected, reporting higher borrowings will not generally surprise the markets.

Under normal circumstances this would be a 'red flag' release, but in the current economic environment its importance has slipped down to the lower levels of news. However, once markets return to something approaching normality, this economic indicator will once again rise up the rankings to the 'red flag' list. It is an important number, but one the forex market tends to take in its stride and is likely to do so for some time to come.

As we start to come to the end of this chapter I want to round off by covering some of the statements, comments and news flow that comes from the central banks, week in and week out.

Virtually all of this news is classified as 'red flag'. In other words any statement, comment or release from a central bank is considered important enough to move the markets.

The problem, however, is that some comments are made 'off the cuff' and are not necessarily intentional. Most of the time comments and statements are well rehearsed and prepared in advance. Furthermore, senior bank officials will often test the market with some well chosen words in order to gain some insight into the likely reaction to a proposed change in policy.

Alternatively, comments may be deliberately made in order to signal a change in policy and to prepare the markets accordingly. It is often difficult to distinguish the two, but generally prepared releases are easier to interpret, it is the unprompted remarks made during press conferences following interest rate statements that are harder to predict.

The good news with this information is that all the central banks use the same coded language and most of the time seem to follow the same script. The reason is because, as guardians and custodians of their home economy and currency, they all face the same challenges and problems.

There have even been press reports that maybe the traditional role of the central banks may now be coming to an end. And that as an institution they may not even be around in a few years time. Given their track record in the run up to the financial crisis this may not be so far fetched.

The best way to approach these comments, statements and releases is in the context of the economic indicators and the politics and how these affect the home currency.

For central banks the most important economic indicator is the interest rate decision. All the banks have their own name for this indicator. In the US it is the Fed Funds Rate. In Canada it is the Overnight Rate. In Australia it is the Cash Rate. In New Zealand it is the Official Cash Rate.

Meanwhile in Europe it is the Minimum Bid Rate. In Japan it's known as the Overnight Call Rate and in the UK it's The Official Bank Rate.

Once an interest rate decision has been made most of the central banks, but not all, will also release a statement to support and explain their decision. And, in some cases the accompanying statement may, in fact, be more important than the rate decision itself. The reason is that it is a simple way for the bank to communicate to the markets. Therefore, the language used is important and significant.

A word or phrase here or there can send a message about monetary policy in the future so it pays to read these statements for any clues as to the future. As most are now streamed live I would urge you to watch one, and note the spikes in price action on a fast chart as words or phrases are used. You will be amazed.

In Australia, New Zealand and Canada these statements are released immediately, whereas the Federal Reserve and the Bank of England release theirs a few days later, thereby creating another 'red flag' item of news as the content of these statements will be scoured for meaning by the markets.

The ECB have no statement but instead hold a press conference shortly after the release. The Bank of Japan also holds a press conference and, more recently even the Federal Reserve, in a PR effort to improve their battered image has taken to airways and held a press conference. This was the first time in their 100 year history.

Although, the pattern for interest rate decisions and subsequent statements is very regular and easy to follow, what is perhaps more difficult to follow are the speeches and comments from key central bank figures. These can happen in a variety of ways. These can occur when senior figures are called upon to report or testify before their political masters. This is a frequent occurrence in both the US and the UK. It is at these events many unscripted and 'off the cuff' comments are made.

Other speeches are usually well prepared and given at a variety of functions, whilst other comments may appear in newspaper and magazine articles, and are usually carefully crafted to communicate particular messages to the markets.

If I were asked to bracket the central banks in order of transparency, ambiguity or self interest I would suggest the following.

The most straightforward of the central banks are Canada, Australia, New Zealand and the UK. Next would come Japan who can be misleading given their self interest in the yen, followed by the US Federal Reserve who are highly self interested. As ex Chairman Alan Greenspan once said:

"I guess I should warn you if I turn out to be particularly clear then you've probably misunderstood what I've said." Last, but not least, the ECB and the euro, of whom Greenspan also famously said:

"I've consistently said the Euro should die, but [it] will be saved by a bunch of ego-maniacal politicians" which really sums up the ECB in one statement.

Finally, of course we have the Jackson Hole symposium. For symposium read 'junket', where the central banks have their annual 'love in' in the shadows of the Teton mountain range.

In addition to central banks muddying the waters, we also have the politicians and in particular the finance ministers, who meet at both scheduled and unscheduled meetings to discuss world financial affairs and generally in two forms. Namely the G7 and the G20.

The G7 was the first to be formed and meets several times a year and includes France, Germany, Italy, Japan, the UK, the US and Canada. More recently, this was expanded to the G20 to include several of the tiger economies from the emerging markets.

Both G7 and G20 meetings are scheduled well in advance so you will find them in the economic calendar and they are important as they do issue press statements and releases both during and after the event. These often come on a Sunday night as many of these events run from a Friday to a Sunday.

For traders who keep overnight or weekend positions, it is imperative to keep a note of these events as their statements can cause volatility when the forex market re-opens.

The G7 meetings are regular and frequent whilst the G20 tend to be twice a year and have less impact. The G20 meetings generally focus on third world issues, whereas the G7 meetings tend to focus on trade and economic matters and are likely to be of more interest to the currency markets.

Finance ministers, particularly in Europe, are also not averse to commenting on monetary policy when it suits them, so once again comments in print or on the TV are always of interest and the euro will react accordingly. Comments which allude to the ECB will always cause a reaction.

In the last few years we have also seen a plethora of bi-lateral meetings between finance ministers, particularly in Europe and, often at short notice. These meetings are usually convened to deal with the latest crisis to befall the Eurozone. To date they involved most of the Club Med countries and usually revolve around the issue of debt and the need for another bail out. Markets always react nervously but generally subside after a couple of days.

At the time of writing this book the latest crisis involves Cyprus and its banks which are, once again, teetering on the point of bankruptcy. More recently Italy is now presenting yet another threat to the Eurozone.

The Rating Agencies

So far we've looked at many of the factors which influence price, from external forces to internal forces, and to market manipulation, both overt and covert. However, there is one group which has the potential to move the markets more significantly, and more dramatically than all of these forces combined, and that's the ratings agencies. Universally loathed and despised by most in the financial world, they sit in judgement as the ultimate arbiters of risk, handing out their judgements with reference to no-one. They have the power to create, and the power to destroy which they use with equal measure. They are judge, jury and executioner rolled into one. Their power is unlimited and frightening, and with a single release, they can wreak havoc in the market.

Yet, all of these companies are privately owned, and worse still, paid for by the very banks and organisations which they are supposed to rate on an objective basis.

So, who are the major credit ratings agencies, what do they do, how do they operate, and why do the markets react in the way they do when a statement is made by one of the 'so called' big three?

There are three major ratings agencies the market watch above all others, and these are Standard and Poors, Moody and finally Fitch. Of these, Standard and Poors is the oldest by some distance and originally founded in 1860 by Henry Poor, with the 'Standard' added in 1940 when Poors and the Standards Statistics Bureau were merged into one company. Moody began life in 1909 and was founded by John Moody whilst the last of the big three, Fitch, was formed four years after Moody by another John, John Fitch, in 1913. There are of course, many others, but these are the three that dominate the markets and their purpose is two fold.

First, to offer an assessment of risk by those organisations, financial institutions banks and companies offering bonds, a rating, which is supposed to give lenders a standard or benchmark against which to judge the bond issuer. And secondly, to make as much money for themselves in providing these ratings.

Does this sound like a conflict of interest? The simple answer, of course, is that it is, but as always in the financial markets, when there are huge sums involved no one is going to kill the goose that lays the golden egg. Each of these companies makes several hundred million dollars a year in fees for their services, and their power and influence extends to the very top of governments, central banks and beyond.

However, whilst traders investors and speculators around the world have had to tolerate the existence of these self appointed dictators, in the last few years their influence and power has finally started to wane. And the catalyst for this turnaround in their fortunes, was ironically the financial crisis of 2007, which all of these agencies somehow managed to fail to forecast. Here was a situation where the markets were awash with securities backed by worthless mortgages never likely to be repaid, and yet the so called 'experts' failed to raise a signal or warning of any kind. Of course no one else did any better, but then these companies were supposed to know what they were doing, unlike the Federal regulators who just pretend to know what they are doing. Indeed Lehman Brothers was given a AAA rating, just before it went bust.

Not only did this raise questions about the value of such agencies, it also had much deeper ramifications.

In Europe, for example, the Parliament was so concerned at the prospect of a possible downgrade from one of the big three that laws were passed restricting the number of releases from these agencies to a maximum of three a year, and only after the close of the main financial markets. Other countries have followed suit and many advised their major banks and commercial organisations to do their own ratings assessments.

More recently some of these agencies are now facing lengthy legal proceedings as ex employees are increasingly speaking out, about the culture of intimidation and harassment which existed in these companies in order to ensure the companies' clients would be given favourable ratings.

Had I been writing this book ten years ago, I would have been explaining the power of the ratings agencies, and how a downgrade or an upgrade could affect a country's economy and its currency overnight. After all a rating from one of these company's was seen as a seal of approval from a respected source. In the normal course of events a downgrade to a country would have meant the cost of borrowing went up. This has all changed since 2007, and the reason is simple. The power of these companies is waning and waning fast. The SEC (Securities and Exchange Commission in the US) is taking its usual approach, which is to say much and do nothing, whilst the markets have delivered their own verdict, which was exemplified when the US received it's own downgrade in 2011. The cost of borrowing actually went down on the news and not up.

This is how life is changing and has changed forever with the ratings agencies. Yes, it is true to say they still have the power to move the markets, but that power has been dramatically reduced in the last few years. Their credibility was blown apart as the sub prime saga exploded onto the markets. Since then, their importance has declined. This is not to say they can be ignored, they cannot, and for many countries, particularly those in the Far East and Asia, they represent a key catalyst for growth, but for those developed economies, their power has been dramatically reduced, and for that we can all be eternally grateful. It is one less thing we have to worry about from a fundamental perspective.

Having examined the most important economic indicators and how they impact the currency market, I would now like to consider some currency specific economic indicators. In other words, those releases which can move a currency and currency pair. Whilst most of these will also be 'red flag' or tier one releases, I have also included a number of tier two news items which can also have an effect. These latter releases are usually coloured orange on the forex factory calendar.

The Euro

Although the euro has the least number of tier one (red flag) indicators it does have a very long list of orange (tier 2) indicators which are primarily country specific. Often, the same release appears twice, one for the Eurozone followed by the country specific version. In most cases the country will be Germany and, on occasions France.

The reason Germany's data is treated as a separate entry is simply a reflection of the power and importance of the German economy in the Eurozone. The tier 2 economic indicators which relate directly to Germany include the monthly Preliminary CPI numbers; the month on month unemployment changes; month on month factory orders; the monthly production figures; German consumer sentiment along with German retail sales, and flash manufacturing PPI. 'Flash' simply means 'a quick overview', a snapshot or the latest news.

As the second largest economy, France comes next with around half the number of German releases and here the list includes: industrial production; PMI data for manufacturing and services; preliminary GDP for the quarter along with consumer spending and employment data, both of which are released monthly.

So between them, Germany and France constitute virtually all the economic reports at this level for Europe on an individual country basis.

Europe denominated data is shown as EUR and covers all the countries using the euro. For example, retail sales in Europe will be shown as EUR Retail Sales m/m. On the other hand German retail sales will be shown as EUR German retail sales m/m. Again the reason for this additional release is that any drop in German retail sales is likely to have more impact due to the strength of the German economy. A drop in Italian retail sales is hardly worth a mention (despite my own best endeavours) and not significant enough, even though Italy is the third largest economy in the Eurozone in terms of GDP.

Furthermore, even an EUR consolidated number will often have less of an impact than the equivalent German figure.

In this group there are also several economic releases for Europe. These include the unemployment rate reported as the headline rate; industrial production figures; monthly CPI and core CPI percentages. Again this consolidated data will have a relatively muted effect, as it generally follows the German equivalent.

Other releases include the GDP figures along with M3 money supply figures and the ECB monthly bulletin. Of these it is odd the M3 money supply release is classified as a tier 2 indicator release, given that M3 measures the amount of currency in circulation and is therefore a direct indicator for inflation. It is also one of the measures the ECB uses in its monthly interest rate decision. M3 is also important because in the early part of an economic recovery an increase in the money supply indicates a growing economy with increased spending and investment, whilst later in the economic cycle it leads to inflation and higher interest rates. So, if this number is better than expected it is generally good for the euro, as long as inflation is under control.

The ECB monthly bulletin which appears about a week after the rate decision fleshes out the criteria for the decision, coupled with a look ahead to the future for the economy. Once again it is strange this does not have more impact on the markets given the volatility created by its equivalent from the Federal Reserve, namely the FOMC minutes.

Finally, for the euro what has never been made clear is why there are quite so many releases. However, it may simply be an attempt to portray the Eurozone as one, united entity hence the need for so much data.

The US Dollar

Among the tier 2 indicators for the US dollar the first one to note is the weekly Crude Oil Inventories. This release is unusual in that it can have an equal impact on the Canadian dollar, for obvious reasons. Moreover, it is the only oil specific release and, in my view very important, particularly if you are trading the Canadian dollar.

The indicator reports the oil inventory at Cushing in the USA. Cushing is a major oil supply hub and the inventory figures confirm whether there has been a build in the oil reserves or a draw. The significance of these figures is fairly straightforward. A build in the oil reserves represents an increase in the oil inventories which suggests a fall in demand. Conversely, a draw is a decrease, suggesting an increase in demand.

These numbers are presented as either positive or negative. A positive figure represents a build while a negative one indicates a draw. As a rule of thumb, a draw or reduction in the inventory is generally positive for the Canadian dollar, as it suggests an increase in demand and higher oil prices likely to follow. Conversely, a rise in the inventory is not such good news for the Canadian dollar as it suggests a fall in oil prices in the short term. Remember however this is reported weekly, so more of an intraday trading indicator.

Another economic indicator that appears in the orange tier is the quaintly named, Beige Book which appears eight times a year. There is divided opinion on this release with some traders believing it should be considered a tier one release, whilst others (myself included) believe its impact is muted. In addition, this type of release can often move the markets simply when there is no other news.

The Beige Book is, in essence a collection of anecdotal evidence and information gathered from senior employees from member banks within the Federal Reserve network of banks. It consists of their thoughts and comments on the current economic climate. Its use is in giving traders some clues to the market and how the Federal Reserve is likely to react in the future. It is generally released around 2 weeks prior to the FOMC meeting itself and FED watchers pick through every comment and word to try to interpret any likely changes in future monetary policy.

The principal reason why I do not advocate its use is that the FED also has two other books, one Green and one Blue. However, as neither is made public it does rather beg the question as to the validity of the information in the Beige book.

In addition to the above orange group of releases in the US, the markets are also subjected to an endless round of statements and speeches from FOMC members. Impact is generally muted as these events are a means of reiterating current FED policy. The only exception will be speeches and statements from the FED Chairman himself.

Of the next set of orange flag indicators, namely Core PPI, Durable Goods Orders, Revised UoM Consumer Sentiment, the Advance GDP Price Index and the Employment Cost Index, only the last two, I believe, are deserving of a higher rating.

Even though the US GDP figure is usually well known in advance, any GDP related release is always important, particularly for the world's largest economy so should, in my view, take a higher priority.

Similarly with the Employment Cost Index which is released quarterly and measures the percentage increase in wages and salaries over the period. This is a key measure of inflation and interest rates with any increase suggesting higher interest rates and therefore highly US dollar positive. A fall in this number suggests a weakening economy and lower interest rates likely to follow, with consequent US dollar weakness.

In the last clutch of tier two releases for the US, the two most important include The Empire State Manufacturing Index and Core PCE.

Core PCE is an interesting indicator, standing as it does for Personal Consumption Expenditure and measures consumer spending on goods and services by individuals. It is important because many believe the Federal Reserve keep a sharp eye on consumer spending patterns for clues as to the economy and inflation.

The headline figure is a simple percentage. If the number is positive and moving higher it is signalling that consumers are happy to spend and the economy is likely to be expanding. An expanding economy signals higher interest rates to follow and again is generally US dollar positive. If a negative number is reported which is also in a falling trend, expect the dollar to weaken as a result

The Empire State Index, is a monthly release and is a diffusion index based on manufacturers in New York State and, despite only having a survey size of approximately two hundred, it is nevertheless a widely regarded index. The tipping point for the index is zero so anything above the line is positive and below is negative. A good number coming in better than expected is usually good news for the dollar, and a bad number should see the dollar decline.

One reason for mentioning the Empire State Index is to highlight the fact other cities also produce similar survey based releases. For example, the Chicago PMI is another diffusion index based on surveys in the Chicago area. What makes this release particularly interesting is that it is released 3 minutes earlier to paid subscribers allowing them to take market positions, as a result. The Chicago PMI is also interesting as the private subscribers can sometimes impact the market and the US dollar.

Finally, in this round up of releases and indicators for the US markets, the twice yearly Treasury Currency Report produced by the Department of Treasury deserves a special mention.

The report itself does not always appear as scheduled in the economic calendar. This is because it is subject to heavy, last minute revisions so the release date and time can be a movable feast.

However, it is worth the wait, not least because it details the views of the US Treasury on economic conditions, foreign exchange rates and currency manipulation around the world.

The immediate impact of the release on the currency markets can be variable. However, its importance is in revealing which countries the Treasury believe are manipulating their currencies. In addition, it also gives traders some excellent background reading on the US Treasury's views of the currency markets themselves.

The Japanese Yen

In this section are some of the indicators to consider in relation to the Japanese Yen.

The first is the Bank of Japan's monthly report which provides details of the Bank's view of the longer term economic outlook, as well as the economic data used for the latest interest rate decision. Despite Japan's rates having remained low for a decade or more, the report still makes interesting reading. However, the report lacks market impact for this reason.

The same reason applies to the BOJ meeting minutes. These are released around a week after the interest rate decision and this is the reason they are here, since the minutes are unlikely to reveal any surprises for the time being. However, at some point in the future this will change.

Japan too has city specific economic indicators of which the Tokyo Core CPI Index is the most important. The index is the same as for the Japanese CPI Index and only includes consumer data from Tokyo. What is useful about this report is that it is released a month before the figure for the whole of Japan, and can be an excellent guide for the national release. In my view, it is an extremely important release since Tokyo is the largest city in Japan and therefore an excellent guide to the national trend.

The Tokyo Core CPI is a monthly report and, just like its bigger brother, is a leading indicator of inflation which is reported either as a negative or positive percentage.

In addition to the Tokyo CPI there are several other indicators which are also important for the Japanese economy and the yen. These include Retail Sales, Preliminary Industrial Production, Core Machinery Orders, Household Spending, Preliminary GDP Price Index and Final GDP.

However, what is perhaps surprising is that for such an important economy the Trade Balance Figures, the Tertiary Industry Activity and the All Industries Activity releases are all classified as second tier. Tertiary Industry simply means the third industry sector, and in this case refers to the services sector of the market, in particular services purchased by businesses. The figures are released monthly and are considered a leading indicator. Therefore, if the actual is better than forecast this is usually good news for the yen thereby making it an essential release for traders involved in the carry trade, particularly in the NZD/JPY.

In this group of economic indicators for the Japanese yen is a subsidiary of the Tankan Survey, namely the Tankan Non Manufacturing Index. This is released with the main Tankan Survey and is a diffusion index based on a survey from non manufacturing companies. Although not as important as the one for the manufacturing sector, this release is nevertheless worth watching, as it can reinforce the main report with additional information on the Japanese economy.

The British Pound

Tier two economic indicators for the British pound which deserve some attention include the Trade Balance figures and the Construction PMI data, a key leading indicator for economic growth fuelled by the construction industry.

The Retail Price Index release now appears in this group having been replaced by the Consumer Price Index. This was a political decision in order to show a lower figure when calculating pensions and state benefits. However, the RPI is still reported and is released at the same time as the CPI.

There are also two mortgage approval releases which come into this category. The first is Preliminary Mortgage Approvals, a leading indicator of the economy, which confirm the number of new housing loans approved during the month. The second is the BBA Mortgage Approvals, from the British Bankers Association which reports the same thing, so one confirms the other. The important point to note here is how the number relates to past levels of lending and, whilst the number may be better than expected and suggest a pick up in demand for mortgages, if the numbers are extremely low compared to three or four years ago, clearly the economy is a long way from the peak of a cycle. Therefore, always check against the historical data and where the lending level is in relation to the past.

This group also includes a couple of consumer sentiment indicators in the form of the Nationwide Consumer Confidence and GFK Consumer Confidence. Once again leading indicators of the economy, but classified as second tier data.

Finally, to round off the UK, there is the NIESR GDP estimate indicator, an important release which attempts to forecast the UK GDP figures on a monthly basis. The reason for watching this indicator is that it is released by the National Institute of Economic and Social Research, a learned body, with a good track record in forecasting GDP data.

The Yuan

As mentioned earlier in this chapter, economic releases for China are now the norm and vital for all traders. As the world's second largest and fastest growing economy all Chinese data will cause markets to react and have particular impact in the currency market.

In the orange group (tier two releases) there are six economic indicators to consider. These are, HSBC Final Manufacturing PMI, HSBC Flash Manufacturing PMI, New Loans, Fixed Asset Investment, Industrial Production and finally, and surprisingly, the PPI indicator.

The first two economic indicators are prepared and released by the Hong Kong and Shanghai Bank and, of these the Flash Manufacturing is the more important as it is released first. Both indicators are diffusion based with a tipping point at fifty, so any number above fifty indicates the Chinese economy is in expansion, and below fifty in contraction. Flash Manufacturing is the more important as it is released approximately one week before the final and therefore has more impact across the forex markets, as a result.

Both these reports are released monthly and, if they come in better than expected then this is good news for the world's second largest economy, and should provide a boost to both currencies and commodities.

The New Loans data too is monthly and released by the central bank (PBoC). The release provides details of new loans denominated in Chinese yuan and can be a good indicator of consumer and business confidence in China, with a positive figure providing a good news story for the global economy. However, this is the release which can highlight how the Chinese also appear to be creating a credit bubble similar to the one responsible for the current financial crisis.

The Fixed Asset Investment release is a measure of capital spending by the Chinese in major infrastructure and new projects. It is reported monthly by the National Bureau of Statistics as a simple percentage, so an increase is good news and seen as increasing demand for base commodities and confirming economic growth, whilst a decrease suggests a slow down and reduction in spending as a result.

Chinese data is important but is often reported at odd times, including weekends so may impact any open positions. Five years ago Chinese data rarely appeared on economic calendars, but now it moves markets. The same will happen as many Asian countries, Mexico and Brazil, continue to grow and begin to influence global growth. China is simply the first of many.

Finally, here are some tier two releases for Australia, Canada and New Zealand. As this is quite an extensive list I have only included the indicators which, I believe, carry the most weight in the market.

Australian, Canadian and New Zealand Dollar

In New Zealand the ones to watch are the Trade Balance, Building Consents, and the REINZ HPI indicator, with the last two providing views of the housing market, so leading indicators. However, as always these releases can and do impact all carry strategies.

For Canada the CPI is the most important in this group. In many ways this release should be classed as tier one given its importance as a leading indicator of inflation and therefore interest rates. The CPI is a monthly release from Statistics Canada. CPI should always be read in conjunction with Wholesale Sales, Retail Sales and Manufacturing Sales, all of which provide data on the the three primary sectors of the economy in terms of sales revenues.

These sales indicators are all leading indicators and reported as simple percentages of change, so easy to check and monitor both on the trend and also against the release. As always, positive numbers are perceived as good news for the Canadian dollar, provided they fit within a rising trend.

Finally, for Australia there are over twenty tier two releases but the most significant are as follows. The first is the Commodity Price Index which tracks the prices of commodities on a monthly basis and, not a surprise given the strength of the Australian export market. This index is usually released on the first business day after month end. The index is reported as a simple percentage change in price. Any increase is generally seen as good news for the economy and the Australian dollar. However, any increase can also signal inflation and higher interest rates elsewhere in the world. Therefore a vitally important release for all currencies.

Next is the Westpac Consumer Sentiment release. This is a diffusion index published monthly and based on a relatively large sample size. The Westpac is generally read in conjunction with the business confidence index published by National Australia Bank. Again the tipping point for these indices are zero.

In this group are several other indicators including the Wage Price Index. This is a quarterly indicator produced by the Australian Bureau of Statistics and tracks labour costs, one of the key ingredients of inflation. Therefore, an important number and the reason why it has been included here. The release is reported as a simple percentage change and if the trend is rising with positive increases in wages and salaries, expect the central bank to be watching, and interest rates likely to rise as a result. Conversely, a fall is likely to signal a weak economy with a consequent fall in interest rates.

The second inflation indicator is the MI or Melbourne Institute Index which is, in fact, a report that forecasts future inflation. The report is released around the middle of the month and is reported as a simple percentage figure.

Finally for Australia, two sales related indicators, the HIA New Home Sales and New Vehicle Sales data, both of which can give the markets strong signals as to consumer confidence in these sectors.

If you have read to the end of this chapter – many congratulations. It has been a long trek but one which I hope has proved to you understanding these indicators is not difficult. I also hope it has proved the importance of these indicators.

There are, of course, many more whose significance will depend on the economic cycle. In addition, economic indicators, like football teams, move up and down a league. One day they may be in the Premier Division and, on another be relegated and languishing in a lower league. These indicators are not static, they are fluid as central banks and their political masters use (and abuse) them in an effort to drive and control their economies as well as their own political ambitions. Remember also, how they are constructed does change, so always check for any changes in methodology or approach.

Finally just to round off this chapter, let me briefly recommend the calendar I use, which is from http://www.forexfactory.com.

This is the most popular calendar available, and is where all the releases mentioned can be found. All are coded in the way I have described in red, orange or yellow. I have deliberately excluded the yellow set as this would make this chapter three times as long. The one thing I would urge you to do when checking any release is to click on the chart icon on the right hand side of the screen, which will reveal the trend for the release over the previous months, which is so important.

This concludes the fundamental section of the book and in the next few chapters we're going to look at the third and final element of my three dimensional approach to forex trading, namely technical analysis.

Chapter Seventeen
An Introduction to Technical Analysis

So simple in concept. So difficult in execution.

Sir John Templeton (1912-2008)

In the first half of this book I covered two of the three elements of my own personal trading approach to the forex markets, namely relational and fundamental analysis. Now, I would like to bring in the third strand which is technical analysis. This final element completes the three dimensional approach which, I believe, delivers a true understanding of market behaviour. From this all trading and investing decisions then flow.

This is the principal reason I wrote this book, to share this trading approach with you. It is the one I believe will offer you the tools and techniques to succeed in this market.

However, I do accept it is possible to trade using just one of the elements in isolation. Moreover, many new and existing traders do just that, with the majority focusing on technical analysis alone. In addition, there are many successful fundamental traders. However, once traders begin to realise the forex market in particular is the most complex of all the capital markets, any single linear approach may simply not be enough to ensure long term, consistent profits.

This is the realisation I arrived at some years ago, since when I have been using this three dimensional approach, of which technical analysis is the third and final aspect. However, please don't misunderstand, appearances can be deceptive, the foreign exchange market is the most multi layered of all the four capital markets. It is also driven by powerful, self interested forces whose sole motivation is survival. It is Darwinian in nature and very much red in tooth and claw.

There is a great deal to learn, but in reading this book I believe you will have the foundation in place to build your own successful trading career.

But, what is technical analysis, and how does it fit within this three dimensional trading model? The explanation generally given is technical analysis is based on the underlying philosophy that all market sentiment is contained within a simple price chart. That a price chart encapsulates the views of every market participant at a given point in time. Moreover, technical analysis is simply price analysis, and that traders can forecast the future direction of price by analysing and studying where it has been in the past.

This is the core belief of traders who use a purely technical approach to forex trading, and is the explanation most often used. However, I find this view very misleading and will give you my own definition shortly. However, regardless of the definition used, analysing a chart in isolation without any reference to the complex web of fundamental and relational issues which may also be influencing and affecting the price, is both blinkered and restrictive. Furthermore, I hope from reading thus far, you can understand why. The forex market is the most manipulated of all the markets, and this is something we always have to bear in mind, particularly when considering price and price behaviour.

The simple truth is this. If we accept the forex market is manipulated in many different ways, how can we be sure any price move is valid? It is validation of price that holds the key to success in forex trading, more than in any other market. Yes, other markets are manipulated as well, but not by so many diverse and disparate elements. This is what makes price action on a forex chart stand apart from all the other markets, and why I believe validation of price is the lynchpin of trading success in the forex world. In other words, the price action is meaningless without validation.

As a methodology, technical analysis is perfectly genuine, and most traders start with a price chart as their only form of analysis. However, in isolation a price chart cannot make sense of the underlying forces which drive forex and other markets. Fundamental analysis too is a perfectly valid methodology, with many traders taking this approach to trade currencies. However, my belief is that only by using all three elements of market analysis can traders gain a true perspective of what is really driving the price action. After all, the information is there, and if we can understand and interpret it, then why not use it? And as the saying goes: 'the whole is greater than the sum of its parts'.

Furthermore, as I have already stated: there are only two risks in trading. The first is the financial risk, which is easy to define, quantify and manage, but the second, which is much more difficult to assess and quantify, is the risk on the trade itself. In other words, it is the question traders ask themselves each time they place a trade (or should ask themselves). Is this trade a high, medium or a low risk? Predictably, the answer to this question can be answered in different ways, not least by considering the fundamental and relational aspects, coupled with the price action on the chart. Furthermore, there are various techniques in trading which help reduce the risk still further, which I will be covering in other books which deal with trading strategies, but this is the starting point, the top level for assessing risk. So, to use any of the three approaches in isolation is simply foolhardy. If the information is there, as we have seen in previous chapters, why ignore it?

Nevertheless, I do accept there are many traders who only look at the technical picture when trading, and I hope they are successful. However, I do have my doubts since two traders can look at the same chart and reach very different conclusions about the future direction of the price. Furthermore, both could also be right in their analysis and trade.

This brings me to the issue of time, which again I will cover in more detail later, but let me give you a quick example of what I mean here. Imagine we have two forex traders looking at a chart, one of whom is an intraday scalping trader and the other a longer term trend or swing trader. The scalping trader believes a currency pair is bullish, and likely to move higher, whilst the swing trader believes the currency pair is bearish and moving lower. Both are proved right and take successful trades.

The reason this is possible is very straightforward. In the case of the intraday trader the currency pair moves higher in a matter hours so the scalping trader makes a profit and closes his or her position later in the day. At this stage, the swing trader has a potential loss. However, over the next few days the currency pair moves lower and the trend trader closes his or her position at a profit. So, both traders are right and both have made a profit on the trade. It has simply been a question of the time, and in the case of the swing trader also requires sufficient trading capital to hold the position open long enough for the trade to develop. In any case, unlike a stock, a currency pair never goes to zero, and will eventually turn. The turn could even take several years to move from loss to profit, but it will eventually happen, it is just a question of time (and money). So, in many ways with forex trading, if you have enough money you can never be wrong.

In reality, no one trades this way. I simply wanted to make the point that two traders looking at the same chart can have very different views and both take successful trades. It's simply a question of time and timing. The perspective or time horizon if you like.

Taking these examples it could be said technical analysis is about price action over time, and what it can tell traders about the future price action, over time. Now, in the introduction to the book I explained how the markets are driven by people and money. In technical analysis it is the people element which is the focus, and provides the core belief system on which technical analysis is built, but there is a twofold argument for this belief system.

The first argument is this:- if people have behaved in a certain way in the past, they are likely to behave in same way in the future. The second argument is:- if all traders are looking at the same chart, then technical analysis could be considered to be a self fulfilling prophecy. And, if most are using a purely technical approach, the market is likely to react accordingly, thereby reinforcing the reaction further.

But just how true are these arguments? Well, like many things in trading they are both true and false.

First, as we have already seen, two traders can look at the same chart and arrive at very different conclusions, depending on their time horizons. Second and perhaps more importantly, the market has seen a huge rise in high frequency, computer driven trading where trading decisions are entirely automated, using pre-set levels and price pattern recognition. These robots trade in the markets thousands of times a minute, and with no human intervention whatsoever, are becoming an increasing problem in all aspects of trading, not just forex. Indeed, the regulatory authorities are now considering putting a speed limit on this type of trading.

As a result, the concept of traders making discretionary trading decisions on a price chart are outdated with small retail traders very much in the minority, in this respect. Perhaps not so much in terms of the numbers of traders, but certainly in terms of the percentage of trades executed manually, as opposed to software generated trades based on sophisticated algorithms trading billions of dollars every week.

This reason alone makes it even more crucial you consider taking a three dimensional approach to the market, and not rely on just one method of analysis.

This issue notwithstanding, technical analysis is perfectly valid, and when we start to explore the power of candlesticks and candlestick patterns, even more so. However, when it is used in conjunction with both relational and fundamental techniques it becomes all the more powerful. But, and this is a big but, only when the price action is validated. After all, if the price is moving higher on the chart, how can we be sure this a true move higher, or a false one? Is this price move being driven by the market, or by external forces? In other words, is the price move genuine or false.

As I said earlier, this is the one question we simply have to answer when using technical analysis in this market. Without it, the approach is flawed, but don't worry, I do explain how shortly. In addition, I have also recently written another book on the subject, which explains this approach in more detail and exclusively for trading forex, so help is at hand.

In many ways technical analysis is the glue which binds the other two analytical approaches together. Whilst fundamental and relational analysis are perhaps more 'scientific', technical analysis is much more of an 'art than a science'. It takes practice to develop the skills needed, but once learnt they are never forgotten.

As technical trading continues to grow in popularity so do the number of indicators and analytical techniques, thereby making this branch of analysis very confusing for the novice or inexperienced trader.

My task here is to try to point you in the right direction, and highlight what I believe are the strengths and weaknesses of each. But I do have some strong views.

At this point let me just try to summarise where we are.

Technical trading is based on the principle future price trends can be forecast by looking at previous price action on a price time chart. Onto this simple display, traders can then add an array of technical indicators which can help to identify patterns, trends and turning points on the chart.

However, technical indicators are nothing more than tools for traders to use. They have not been designed to give entry and exit signals. Instead, they should be viewed as providing traders with information which would otherwise be difficult, if not impossible, to calculate manually and quickly. The analogy I use here is from the DIY market, and it is this – drilling a hole in a wall is easier and faster with an electric drill than doing the same job with an old fashioned manual drill. Both tools achieve the same result, a hole in the wall, but the electric drill just makes it easier, and a great deal quicker.

This is my philosophy in using technical indicators in trading. Almost all could be replaced with a manual system, but it would be slow, laborious and time consuming, even though we would arrive at the same conclusion, eventually. However, by the time all the calculations have been done the market would have probably moved on and any trading opportunities lost.

My philosophy is this. In viewing technical indicators, if they can reveal something of value quickly, they are worth using, but as a tool to provide information that would be impossible to produce as fast using manual methods. In the end, all a technical indicator is doing is completing some complex calculations and then presenting the result in an easy, visual format on a chart.

This is all they are, tools to help traders analyse the markets quickly, whilst giving detailed information and perspectives which would be impossible to achieve in the same time using manual methods.

Technical indicators are also there to give traders the confidence to take the plunge. They are like the water wings and floats which are used to teach someone to swim. Eventually, they become redundant, and for traders this will mean using price action with just one or two key tools. As technical analysis becomes ever more popular, so do the number of indicators and analytical approaches that are developed and applied, all promising to provide traders with the magic bullet to trading success.

The key is to keep things as simple as possible. The risk with not keeping it simple is traders end up with cluttered charts and 'analysis paralysis'. In other words, there is too much information so traders are unable to make a decision. This is the curse many traders ultimately suffer, believing that having 'more is better' will help them in their decision making.

As a methodology, technical analysis can be broken down into three broad categories. First, there is simple chart analysis, used to identify various price trends in various time scales. Second, there is pattern recognition, which is the study of different price patterns on a chart which are often repeated and can represent significant price levels.

Finally, there is momentum and trend analysis which looks at the rate of change of prices for clues as to changes in market sentiment. It is within these three broad groupings traders can find a plethora of technical indicators, graphical price presentation methods and techniques, all of which have their own advocates and passionate followers.

However, this raises three questions in relation to the forex markets.

First, is a technical trading approach valid for the forex market, given it is a market which is so heavily manipulated? Second, does it provide a reliable method for predicting future price action? And third, why is technical analysis so popular with forex traders?

In order to answer these three questions I want to consider the history of technical analysis which has its roots in the 16th and 17th century rice markets of Japan. However, it is Charles Dow who is generally credited with its introduction to Western financial markets in the late 19th century. At the same time Dow also developed a number of stock indices, all underpinned by his work which later became known as Dow Theory.

In essence, Dow Theory categorised market moves as primary trends or minor secondary trends, and this work formed the basis for a number of financial theorists who subsequently followed. These included Ralph Nelson Elliott, who developed the Elliott Wave Theory. The work of WD Gann and Richard Wyckoff was also heavily influenced by Charles Dow, with Richard Ney developing the ideas further in a series of books and publications in the 1960's.

All of these legendary traders and financial analysts had two things in common. First, their work was based either on the stock or commodities markets, but secondly, and of primary importance to us, is they all used volume as a key indicator in their theory and analysis. Moreover, it is in their original work you will come across the concepts of accumulation and distribution, as this refers to the buying and selling volumes by traders and market makers across the markets.

Here we have a group of iconic traders, who built their fortunes on one simple principle. That price, when validated using volume holds the key to forecasting future price action. These traders succeeded using pencils and graph paper, and a simple ticker tape which printed out the price movements and associated trading volumes. Using these simple tools, vast fortunes were built. Therefore, would it not make sense for us as traders to follow their lead?

Naturally, it goes without saying that the foreign exchange markets simply did not exist at the time, so technical analysis as an analytical tool was developed almost exclusively based on the price movements in equity and commodity markets. Price movements which, when coupled with volume, generally reflect the true balance of supply and demand. This analytical methodology was developed using the equity and commodity markets, with the price volume relationship at its heart. Furthermore, it was also premised on the belief that equities were bought and sold primarily as investments.

This is a world away from the complex foreign exchange model that exists in today's modern world, and perhaps also begs the question as to how this method fits into the forex market.

After all, there is no volume in forex as there is no central exchange - or is there? Second, whilst the forex market is changing with currencies now growing in popularity as an asset class, in general it is still primarily a market of speculation and corporate money flows. Third, the forex market is probably the most manipulated of all the capital markets, and most definitely not a level playing field.

The question therefore is whether this increasingly popular analytical approach, with no foundation in foreign exchange is suitable or even valid for such a dynamically changing market. For an answer to this question I would like to consider price and price action in a little more detail.

Just as I have tried to explain my own three dimensional approach to trading, price action itself is generally viewed by many traders in a one dimensional way. Indeed, some of you reading this may remember a popular game show in the 1980's which involved guessing the price of a well known item. The winner was the contestant who came closest to the actual retail price, without exceeding it. And in some ways, this is how many traders view price action on a chart. In reality, price is created through two parties agreeing to disagree, and I often make this point when I am contacted with regard to one of my market forecasts. This is my view, yours may be very different. We agree to disagree. Without it, there would be no market price action.

In other words, price is the fulcrum on which all market opinion is balanced, tilting backwards and forwards on each release of news, data, and geopolitical event which, are first absorbed, and then reflected in the price on a chart.

It could be said price is the basic building block of every chart. Without the price, there is no measure of market sentiment, and no sense of where the fulcrum of the market is at any given time. Price contains all this information in one simple bar, embracing, as it does, the views, news, hopes and aspirations of traders and speculators around the world, all of whom are driven by two primary emotions, namely fear and greed. Without the fulcrum of price, these twin emotions would simply wither and die. It is price which feeds a trader's emotional responses, which is displayed in one simple bar, on one simple chart. Price distils everything to one single fulcrum, where it balances for a split second, before moving on.

Price is the DNA of the market and contains all of this collective information in one single number. As Wyckoff himself used to tell his students".....prices are made by the minds of men...."

Each price bar on a chart is composed of four elements: the open, the high, the low and the close. Of these, one element is key when considering any analysis of price and that's the open, because it sets the fulcrum for the trading session ahead. The open represents the starting point, regardless of time frame. It is the benchmark against which all other price action is then measured, whether on a one minute chart or a yearly chart.

The high is the highest point the market traded during any session. It is the price at which the buyers were no longer prepared to go any higher, from which the price fulcrum began to tilt lower. The low is the lowest point the market traded during any trading session, and is the price at which the selling was exhausted with the buyers seeing an opportunity to profit from a bargain.

The close is the last price agreed between buyers and sellers, at the end of the trading session. It is an important piece of information as it defines the market's final evaluation of the session. It draws a line under the price action for the session, before moving on to repeat the process.

At its simplest, a single bar on a single chart will show the open, high, low and close with all these points clearly defined. In addition, this single bar is also revealing a history of market sentiment during a point in the trading session. In an up bar the closing price will be higher than the open as the balance of market sentiment throughout the session was positive. This single item of information will not, of course, reveal where the price is likely to go next as any subsequent bars could be either up or down.

Price alone can only reveal where the market has been at a particular point in time. Much like the rear view mirror in a car, it can show where it has been, but not where it's going.

In order to compensate for this many traders turn to technical indicators based on an historical view of price of what has gone before. Such indicators are known as 'lagging indicators' and this is where their problems start.

For example, imagine a chart where there have been ten consecutive, rising bars. Does this mean the next bar will also rise? The answer is no one can be sure. However, one thing is certain that any indicator based on historical price action will almost always suggest the next bar will be an up bar. The reason for this conclusion is straightforward, the indicator has nothing else on which to base its decision, other than what has already happened in the recent past. And the forecast will be that the price will rise. The indicator has arrived at this conclusion through no analysis. The conclusion is based solely on historical data.

In many ways, this type of indicator is no better than a system which claims to be able to predict where the little white ball on the roulette wheel will land, based on where it has been in the past. However, no one can ever know and no system or methodology can ever forecast such a thing. Moreover, any system which claims to be able to do so could simply not be taken seriously.

Yet, this is what traders are being asked to believe and place their faith in whenever they use 'lagging indicators', or systems which include these indicators. The clue is in the word 'lagging'. They are lagged, and will always lag the live market price action to a greater or lesser degree. As with the analogy mentioned earlier, driving a car using a rear view mirror can only have one outcome. Sooner or later the driver of the car will crash. It is not a question of if, but when.

Unfortunately for traders, there are literally hundreds of such indicators and most can be found, for free on all broker platforms.

Lagging Indicators

Lagging indicators fall into two broad categories, trend following and oscillating. The most popular are moving averages, MACD, Stochastics, Bollinger Bands, and Elliott Wave, to name but a few. And all, without exception, have two things in common. They lag the market and look great in hindsight.

It is one reason why so many traders struggle with trading and fail to achieve their potential. Furthermore, many traders do not appreciate their failure to succeed is not necessarily their fault. It is simply they are working with signals and indicators which are based on historic data and therefore virtually useless at predicting future price direction.

The above notwithstanding I firmly believe a technical trading approach in terms of pure price action is valid for the forex market, but only when the price action is validated. And not just for forex but also for stocks, bonds and commodities and for all instruments, because only price can reflect market sentiment at a given moment in time. It is the only indicator which can do so. Price action is price action, whether on a currency chart, a stock chart or a futures chart. It will always be a leading indicator, revealing as it does in real time the market's moods, hopes and fears millisecond by millisecond.

However, as to whether a technical approach can provide forex traders with a reliable method for predicting future price action - the second question - here the answer is most definitely no, unless that price can be validated. And this is the key.

First, when traders consider and scrutinise price charts what they are actually looking for is validation of the price action. Therefore, they try to use a variety of tools and techniques to achieve this, as price on its own reveals very little about the future direction of the market. It is only when price behaviour is validated can it then become a powerful predictor of the future direction of the market.

Second, as explained earlier validation of the price action cannot happen with 'lagging indicators' alone.

Third, validation of price can be done in many ways in terms of patterns, trends, price bar formation and from other indicators (which I will explain later). Only then can price become a powerful predictor for the future direction of the trend.

When analysing price action we can use a wide variety of techniques. These may include using indicators and price behaviour to confirm the analysis, which in turn will reveal significant price levels or price points which become trading targets. If these targets are met, they confirm the analysis, and from there the process starts all over again.

So, whilst technical analysis primarily focuses on price action, it is the interpretation of the price action that is key, and even more so in the forex market. This is why I have an issue with those who claim technical analysis is about forecasting price. It is not. Technical analysis is about understanding how to validate price action. If the price is validated, traders can forecast with confidence where the price is likely to go in the future. Without validation, there is no forecast.

My third question was why technical analysis is so popular with forex traders, and the answer is probably because of its simplicity. Walk onto any trading floor in New York, Tokyo, London or Singapore and the first thing most traders do is pull up a chart and start looking for trading opportunities. The same is true for retail traders.

The reason for this is straightforward. A price chart removes all the complexities of the market which can often appear random and chaotic. A further reason is a price chart provides a simple, visual image of the market and requires almost no effort on behalf of the trader. In addition, many retail traders may not have the time (or motivation) to learn the approach and techniques advocated in this book.

So what's the answer? And in case you hadn't guessed already, it's volume. There are only two leading indicators on a price chart. One is price, the other is volume. It really is that simple, and is the essence of technical analysis and forecasting price behaviour.

As I mentioned earlier, all the iconic traders of the past understood the power of volume and used it in their own trading. The great traders I am referring to here include W D Gann, R N Elliot, Jesse Livermore, Richard Wyckoff and Richard Ney. Richard Ney is a particular favourite of mine. His books are sadly out of print, but they still offer some great insights and quotes about the markets and trading. Fortunately, we can still buy secondhand copies.

However, just like price, volume on its own tells us little. In isolation, it is a weak indicator and reveals very little that is helpful. For example, if 1 million Google shares are traded during a session, this information fails to give any sense of what is happening to the price. There is no context and there is no clue as to where the price is heading in the future.

Let's suppose in the same session the Google share price rose $5 on the day, does this extra detail make any difference? The answer is still no.

However, what if over the previous 5 days the volume in each trading session had been averaging 500,000, and on each of these days, the price had been rising 50 cents on average? Now a picture starts to form which can be put into context and analysed. In other words, we have a benchmark against which to compare the volume against the price.

This is the power of the price volume relationship. Individually, price and volume reveal little about the future. Put them together, and they react like two chemicals, and from that chemical reaction the power of price and volume combine to give us the market's only true leading methodology which then reveals where the market is likely to be heading. For the iconic traders of the past, it was the ticker tape which printed price and volume, for us it is an electronic chart. But the two elements are identical.

This is what I meant when I said price has to be validated, and volume is the only indicator that can do this. For example, if the price moves higher with rising volume, this is a valid reaction, and traders can be confident in any analysis. It is at this point all the other analytical techniques of price patterns, price bars, trend and momentum can be applied to give a picture of how far and fast the price action is likely to run.

Volume and price are the twin pillars on which technical analysis is built. However, with no central exchange for the spot forex market, how can traders overcome this problem and still use volume and price for their trading?

The answer is simple. Traders can use tick data as a proxy for interpreting volume, which in various studies over the years has proved to be over 90% accurate in representing the volume activity in the market. After all, tick data is essentially activity in the form of a change in price, and if the price is changing rapidly, it is a perfectly valid argument to interpret this 'activity' of buying and selling as a representation of volume. So, until there is a central exchange this is the best there is. It works perfectly, even on the free platforms many forex traders use, such as the Metatrader MT4 and MT5, and freely available with most broker accounts.

In summary, price and volume co-exist together. Each is mutually dependent on the other. In isolation they are weak. Together they are strong with each validating and confirming the other. When combined with all our other technical indicators and analytical techniques, traders have the ultimate tool to analyse price action in the most complex market of all – foreign exchange.

Finally, there is one other element, and just like my own three dimensional approach to trading, the approach you will discover here for technical analysis, also has its own three tiered approach. After all volume and price work in tandem, and reveal the truth about market behaviour. Price is validated by volume, and volume validates the price, but there is a third, and equally important element, and that's time. The relationship that underpins all others in technical analysis is the Price/Volume/Time relationship, and it is one I will return to again and again in the next few chapters. To put this into context for you, it was Wyckoff, one of the greatest exponents of volume price analysis, who proposed in his second rule, the concept of 'cause and effect'. In other words, the greater the cause (the time element), the greater the effect (the associated price move). Put simply, the longer the time element the greater would be the associated price movement. Wyckoff was the first person to codify volume price analysis into his three classical laws.

To summarise all this for you.

Many forex traders struggle to succeed, as they have never appreciated the significance of volume, or its power. The forex market is the most manipulated of all, making it even more important to validate any price move. Without it, you will never know, and never be sure.

This is the only approach I believe works for all the reasons I have outlined in this introduction. Too many traders come to the market relying on lagging indicators which reveal little of value. Learning to interpret volume and price takes time and effort, but imagine the advantages we have over those iconic traders who only used used pencil and paper.

All the analysis is done for us. Volume appears instantly on our charts, and tells us immediately whether a move is genuine or false. It really is that simple. As I mentioned earlier I have recently written another book which explains this approach in detail, and if you would like to learn more, simply visit my personal site for further details - www.annacoulling.com - or take a quick look on Amazon, where all my latest books are published. You will also find all the details in the back of this book.

Here however, I propose to introduce the basic concepts to help you get started, and if you would like to take your knowledge to the next level, the second book and subsequent books with worked examples, will help you to understand more.

At this point I would like to take a closer look at how price action is represented on a chart, before moving on to consider all the other analytical techniques used to examine price behaviour.

Speak to any trader in any market and it is highly likely a candle chart will be the price chart of choice. Candle charts are becoming the 'de facto' standard for representing price action, with only the humble bar chart still in widespread use. Candle charts are now also dominating the retail market and it is these charts that I too use exclusively, in all my trading and market analysis. Hence the reason for devoting this section of the book to candle charts.

But there is one other, perhaps even more compelling reason, which is this. When candlestick charts are coupled with volume and price analysis, this brings the entire concept to life. Many exponents of volume and price analysis, use simple bar charts, which is a mystery to me. Bar charts, as you will see shortly, reveal very little about the price action. Candlesticks on the other hand, reveal everything in graphic and unequivocal terms, and when analysed with volume, reveal the truth behind the price action. I would not say this approach is unique to me, it probably isn't, but it was the way I started, and is the method I have used ever since.

Combining candlesticks, volume and price are equivalent to mixing Saltpeter, Charcoal and Sulphur, your charts will explode into life. And in case you didn't know, mix the above together in the correct quantities and you get - gunpowder. If the old time traders had been aware of candlesticks, they would have used them too, and no doubt made even more money. Which I guess also confirms the power of volume. After all, they were using bar charts. You have the additional power of candlestick charts. There really isn't any more I can say.

The components of a price candle are very simple. The upper and lower 'tails' are called wicks, with either an upper wick or a lower wick, and the solid, coloured part of the candle is called the body. This can be any colour. The open price, the high, the low and the close are clearly defined, and it is the colour of the body which defines whether the candle was an up candle, with prices closing higher, or a down candle, with prices closing lower. See Fig 17.10.

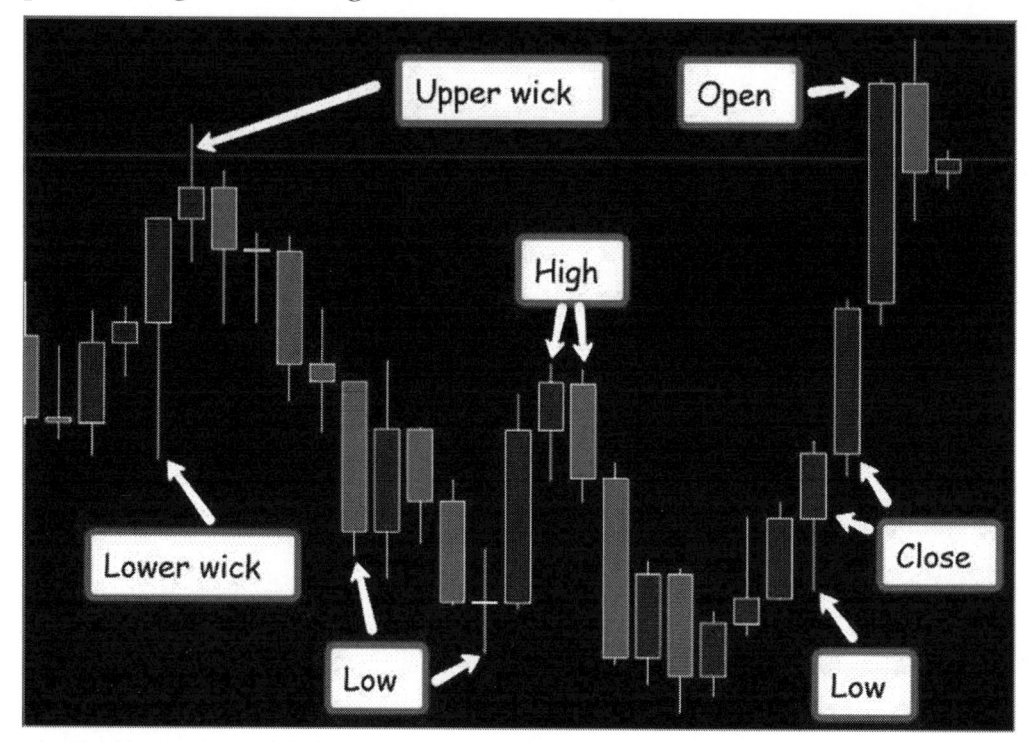

Fig 17.10 Typical Candle Chart

A bar chart is the simplest way to present price action and many forex traders use this style for their price plots as it is very clean and removes much of the noise from the market. The bar is often referred to as an 'ohlc' bar as this denotes the Open, High, Low and Close of the bar. The price action in the time period is created as a simple line or bar with the opening price designated by a small horizontal line to the left and the closing designated by a small horizontal line to the right.

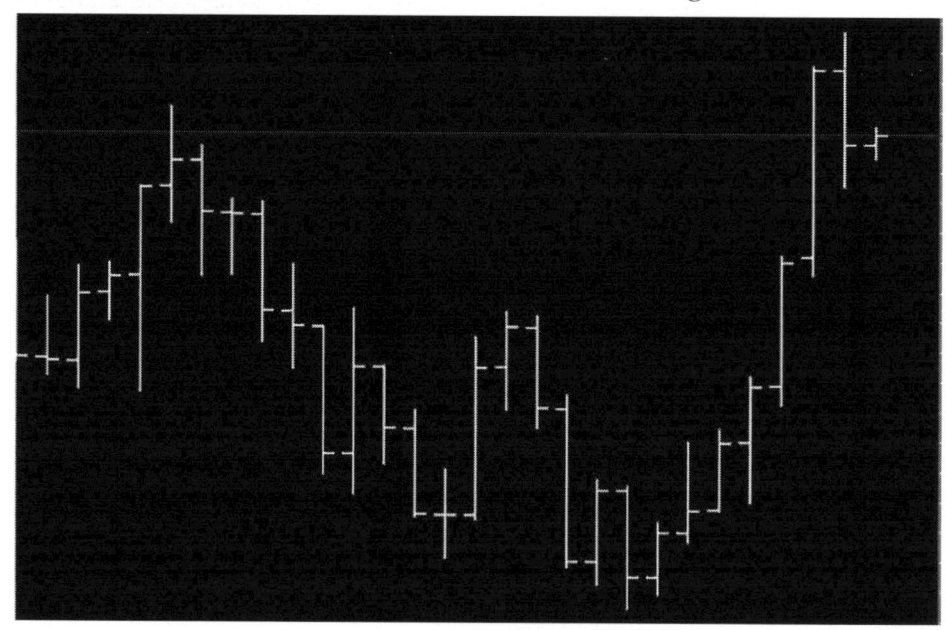

Fig 17.11 Bar Chart

Although many traders use bar charts, I prefer candlestick charts for reasons that will become obvious in the remainder of this chapter. I have used them for over 20 years and have never found any other representation of price that comes close to communicating so much and so quickly on a chart. For me, they are the lynch pin of price analysis and have served traders well for over 400 years.

Candlesticks originated from the Japanese rice traders of the seventeenth century, and have been widely adopted by Western chartists since the mid 1990's.

Most traders also consider price action easier and quicker to analyse on a candlestick chart. They are visually more appealing, and offer traders a plethora of different candle patterns, formations and types to signal market sentiment and potential changes in market direction. Many of these still retain their Japanese names. For me, they are the 'de facto' standard when analysing a chart using volume. There is no other representation of price that conveys the message of the volume price relationship more clearly.

The candle is formed with a solid body created by the opening and closing prices, and the high and low are then designated with 'wicks' or 'shadows' to the top and bottom of this solid body as shown in Fig 17.10. I prefer to call them wicks as shown in the annotated chart.

The body is then coloured red (generally) to represent price action that has closed lower during the period, and blue (generally) to show price action that has closed higher during the period. There are literally hundreds of different candles and candle patterns which have been developed over the last twenty years, but of these there are only a handful which I have found to work, and more importantly to work consistently in the forex markets. From my experience I know the candles to watch, and the ones to ignore, as well as the patterns which are important and those which have less significance.

In a moment I'm going to explain my three top candles, what they are, what they tell us and why they are so powerful. These are the candles traders can learn quickly and spot instantly on any chart and in any time frame so they become second nature. Furthermore, these candles are not based on some vague theoretical approach to trading, they are the ones I use and are based on my own trading experience. I know they work and work consistently, particularly when used in conjunction with the other analytical tools which I'll cover in the next chapter. Moreover, when the candles are used with relational and fundamental analysis they can provide powerful trigger signals for market positions.

The candle is the first step, it is the first signal of a potential change in price. The signal then has to be validated by other analytical tools and techniques.

One final point, before moving to the candles and candle patterns. The significance of a candle will change depending on where it appears in the price action or trend and there are always two factors to consider. The first is the candle shape itself, and the second is where the candle appears in the cycle or trend.

Finally, as we get started on our candlestick journey, remember candles and candle patterns work in all time frames from a tick chart to any time based chart. The signals they send are the same, whether, as a trader you are looking at a 1 minute chart, a daily chart, or a 500 tick chart. Their meaning and interpretation using volume and price analysis will be identical.

The following are my three top candles. They are not in order of importance, as they are all equally important.

The first is the 'hammer' which appears at the bottom of a bearish trend when prices have been falling in a series of down candles as the market moves lower. The hammer candle appears at the end of this 'waterfall'. Here is a classic example in Fig 17.12

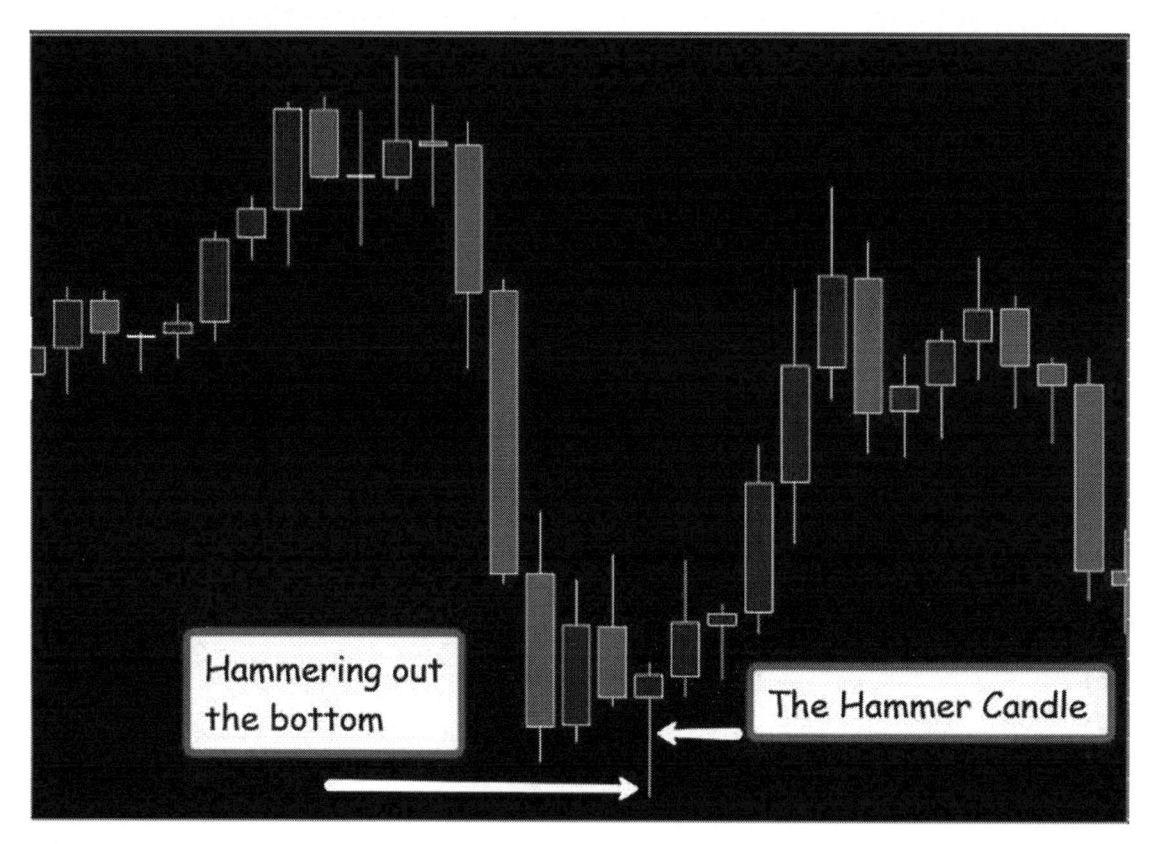

Fig 17.12 Hammer Candle

The price action in this example is obvious as downwards pressure continued, the price moved lower with sellers firmly in control.

Then something changed, buyers suddenly started to appear, preventing the price from falling further. It is their action which took the price back higher to recover close to the opening price of the candle. It is possible to visualise this action in the following way. Imagine every candle as a battle between the buyers and the sellers, rather like an old fashioned 'tug of war'. If the candle is a down candle, the sellers are in control. If the candle is an up candle the buyers are in control. If the candle is neither up nor down there is an equal battle for control. This is the fundamental principle of price action in the markets, ignoring the issue of price manipulation for the time being.

In the case of the hammer candle, initially the sellers are in control, pushing the price lower, but then the buyers come into the market and slowly they begin to outnumber the sellers with prices rising to close near the open. This simple candle is therefore signalling a potential change in market sentiment and direction.

However, please note the word 'potential' – because this is all it is at this stage. It is the first sign the downwards trend is possibly coming to an end and the first sign of a potentially new trend beginning. For traders it is an opportunity to enter the market, which is why this candle is so powerful.

The perfect hammer candle is one where the open and close are identical, or as close as possible, whilst the tail of the candle should be as long as possible, so here are my rules to help you define a true hammer candle. Many analysts become too focused on the depth of the body, suggesting it has to be a certain percentage of the overall price action, but I am not so pedantic. My rules are more relaxed.

First, if the hammer candle has a small body, this can be either blue or red. It doesn't matter. If the close is above the open with a blue body or the open is above the close with a red body, either is fine. Furthermore, in my opinion the colour of the body has no particular relevance.

However, what is important is the length of the lower wick. This should be at least three times as long as the body and, as a general rule, the longer the better.

Finally, the candle should have no, or only a very small upper wick to the top of the candle, as shown in the Fig 17.12 example.

No upper wick is better.

The hammer candle when formed, looks exactly like a hammer in profile, and the reason it is often referred to as a hammer is twofold. First it looks like a hammer and, second this candle is considered as 'hammering out' a bottom to the market. In other words a potential reversal from bearish to bullish.

However, the hammer candle says nothing about how long this reversal may last, or indeed whether it is a major or minor reversal. Indeed, the candle may simply be signalling a minor pull back in the longer term downwards trend. At this stage nothing is certain. What is known simply from the construction of the candle, is that bearish sentiment has dissipated, to be replaced with bullish sentiment, which could be a temporary change, or the start of a longer term trend reversal. This is where other techniques and indicators are deployed to confirm and validate the likely extent of any reversal of the trend.

The other key point is that when a hammer candle appears as the first signal of a possible change in sentiment and trend, it does not necessarily mean this will occur immediately. This was one of the first lessons I had to learn when I started trading. As a new trader I expected to see the price turn instantly and start to reverse higher. What I soon learnt was that patience is required, particularly when looking at longer term time frames.

The reason is simple. Markets take time to turn, they do not just turn on a dime. Typically, once a hammer candle appears, the market pauses and consolidates at this price level before moving higher.

To recap the hammer candle. The market has moved lower, with sellers in the ascendancy and the hammer candle appears as the buyers have decided the price is now cheap, so have entered the market, buying into the market and stopping the price from falling further. It is this action which results in the price starting to rise, forming our hammer candle. However, this initial rally from the buyers may not have absorbed all the selling, since the trend lower has been in place for several bars. As a result, there are sellers still in the market who continue to sell, only for the buyers to continue buying at this level and support the price as a result. This 'mopping up' operation of buyers may go on for several bars, until all the selling has been absorbed and the buyers are now in control, and can then take the market higher into the new trend.

At this point the market may not be ready to move higher as validation is required so patience is the watchword. The hammer is merely an early warning signal of a 'potential change' in sentiment and trend.

It's not an entry signal. Indeed, this applies to all the candles and candle patterns mentioned here. They are not entry or exit signals, but simply an early warning of a possible change in the price action.

Validation of the candle comes from other tools and techniques because price on its own tells us very little about the future. It is only when it is validated with volume that it becomes all powerful.

Of equal importance to the hammer is its opposite, sometimes called the upthrust or shooting star candle which gives traders a potential signal of the market turning from bullish to bearish.

In the case of the shooting star, this candle appears after a rally or up trend in prices, with the market having moved steadily higher with the buyers in control. However, within the shooting star candle the buyers continue to push the market higher, but at some point during the formation of the candle, the sellers enter the market, overcoming the buyers and taking control. As the price moves lower, the selling pressure increases, with the market finally closing at or near the opening price.

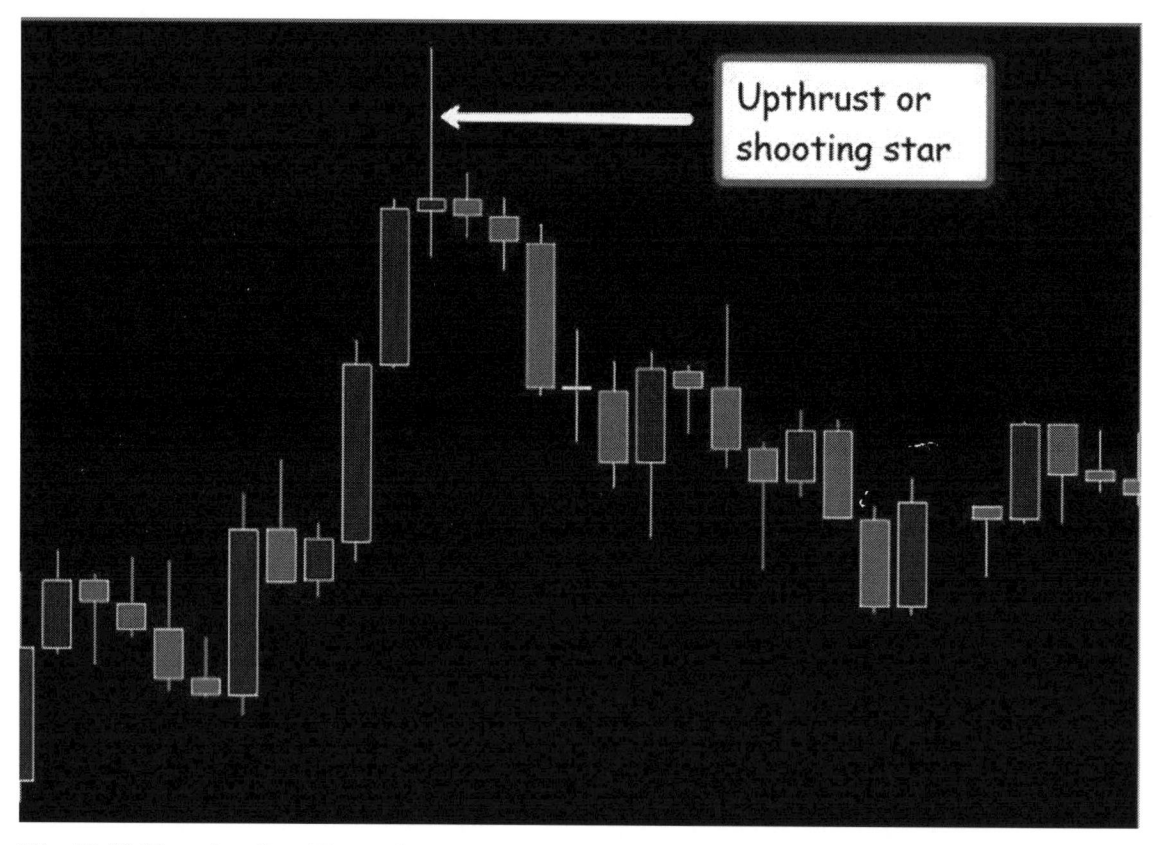

Fig 17.13 Shooting Star Example

The shooting star candle sits at the top of an uptrend, and is characterised by a long upper wick and no, or only a very small body. It is the exact opposite of the hammer. In the formation of a shooting star it is the bulls who have driven the market higher, to a point where it can no longer sustain higher prices. In the forex market this point is referred to 'overbought'. It is at this point that sellers appear. The analogy I like to use here is of a market stall.

In this example the stall holder sells watches, which retail at a higher price in the shopping arcade. The stall holder begins selling at a lower price, and there is demand from the buyers, who see this as a bargain. Every day the stall holder gradually increases the price, and buyers continue to see the price as attractive. However, as the price nears the shopping arcade price, buyers lose interest so the stall holder has to drop the price lower in order to continue to attract the buyers. In other words, the price has found a resistance point, at which buyers are no longer interested, so the price has to be lowered. This, in essence, is what is happening with the shooting star. The buyers have been overwhelmed by the sellers and the price has been forced lower and back to where it started.

Once again, as with the hammer, it is only the first signal of a *potential* change in trend and possible reversal in the price action. It does not say anything about how long any reversal may last, only that there is the potential for a change. Nothing more, nothing less at this stage.

The same rules apply as for the hammer candle. The body can be either red or blue, and the upper wick must be at least three times the length of the body. Finally, there should be no shadow, or very little to the lower body of the candle, and the longer the wick in relation to the upper body the stronger the signal.

The shooting star is an immensely powerful reversal signal of a market 'running out of steam' and possibly turning lower, and once validated by other indicators, is an excellent candle to watch for.

In all my years of trading these two candles have probably contributed the most to my trading and investing success. The hammer and shooting star candles are so powerful in giving traders an early warning to an impending change in sentiment or trend. Once they appear on a price chart they are saying 'sit up and take notice, there may be a change coming, so pay attention'.

The third candle I now want to consider is called the 'doji' which in Japanese means 'the same price level' and, in this case in particular the long legged doji.

The chief characteristic of the doji candle is that, irrespective of where it appears on the price chart, trend or cycle it is a visual representation of the battle between the buyers and the sellers. It represents a tug of war between these two groups or teams. Each team pulling on the price rope with a white marker in the middle. First, the rope is pulled one way, and then the other, before finally the white marker moves back to the middle as the referee blows the whistle and both teams stop pulling with the result declared as a draw.

In essence, this is what happens with a doji candle. First, one group is in control, then the other take control only to lose control once more before the first group take the initiative once again. All this 'to and fro' is reflected in the doji candle, with the opening and closing price ending virtually the same and with long deep wicks both above and below.

What the doji candle represents and, the long legged candle even more so, is market indecision or a lack of direction. Therefore once again it is warning traders of a potential turning point. In this case the candle is found in both up trends and down trends. Again, it is extremely powerful and in the example in Fig 17.14 there were two consecutive long legged dojis, as the markets waited for news which never came.

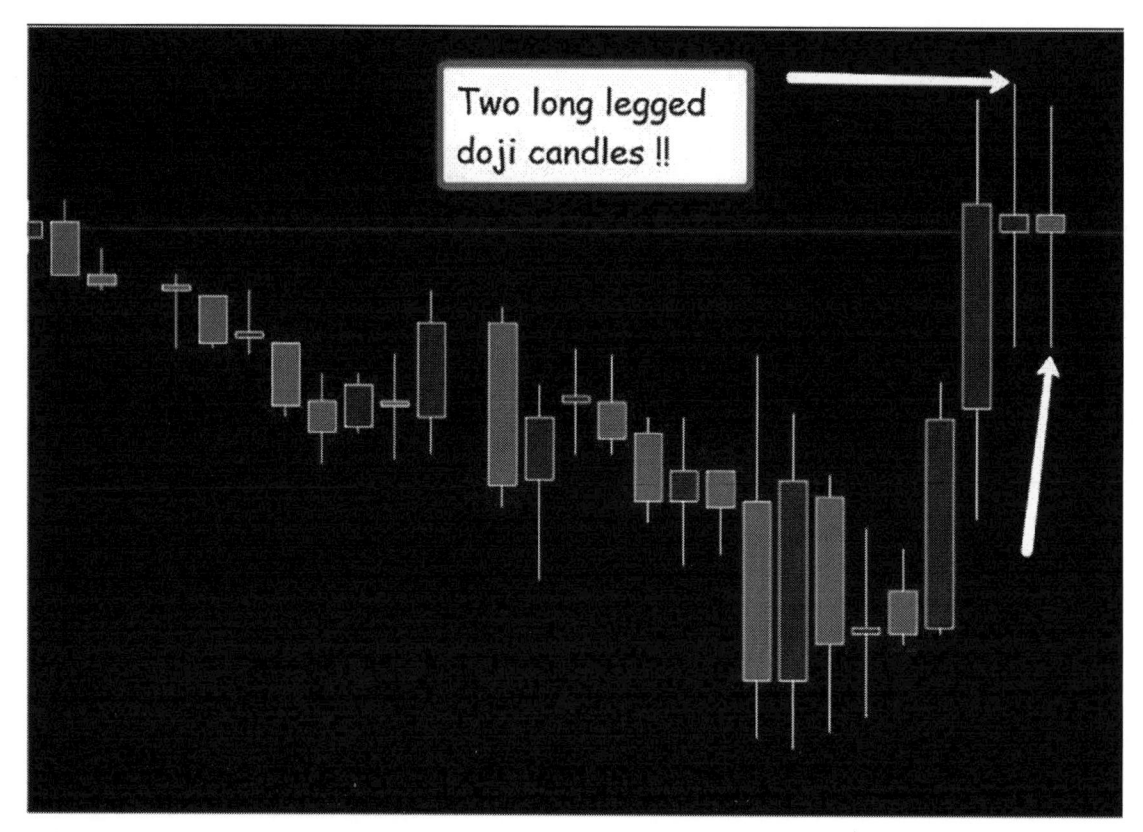

Fig 17.14 Doji Candle Example

The two candles represent the final price action on a Friday evening, as the markets closed waiting for news of a key piece of legislation to be agreed by the US Congress. When no agreement was forthcoming, and with no release to the market before the weekend, this indecision was captured by these two classic candles.

Doji candles are so descriptive, it is unbelievable so few forex traders pay attention to them on the chart. The market is clearly signalling indecision. This indecision may be the prelude to a reversal or simply warning of weakness to come and further indecision and a congestion phase. However, there is one certainty and that is the trend, in whichever direction it had been travelling in before the doji candle(s) appeared, has temporarily paused, and is waiting. The trend has run out of energy. The buyers and sellers are in the market in equal measure and traders now have to be patient, and wait for the market to signal its intent. Once again, this is an early warning signal of a potential change, as the trend has lost some of its momentum.

Doji candles come in all shapes and sizes. They appear in all time frames and many times during the trading day in the shorter term charts. However, the doji candle to look out for is the long legged doji which resembles a 'daddy long legs' - one of those creepy crawlies which fly around at night.

The reason the long legged doji is so much more powerful than regular doji candles, which appear all the time, is by virtue of the length of the wicks. And the rationale is this. In addition to indicating a market lacking in direction and therefore at a potential turning point, the long wicks to the upper and lower body are also clearly signalling extreme market volatility. This suggests a tug of war on a grand scale between the buyers and the sellers and, is therefore a much stronger signal of market indecision and a possible longer term pause point developing and the possibility of a reversal in due course. Furthermore, long legged doji candles often follow major economic news releases, announcements or statements as market participants absorb the news and battle for supremacy.

The rules for the construction of a long legged doji are much the same as for the hammer and shooting star. First, the body can be either positive or negative and in the example in Fig 17.14 there are both. However, the key is that the body of the doji should be as small as possible, ideally with the open and close identical or virtually identical, thereby creating a single horizontal line rather than any solid body. Again, this is not precise. As I said at the start of this chapter, technical analysis is an art, not a science. The two long legged doji candles in Fig 17.14 are perfect and would have alerted all traders.

Second, the length of the legs should be extreme and at least five times the length of any body. Third and finally the length of the leg or shadow to both top and bottom should be the same length, or as close as possible. If one is much shorter than the other, the signal strength is reduced accordingly. The examples I have chosen here are almost perfect.

The long legged doji is another early warning signal of a potential reversal which can appear in both an up trend or a down trend. Therefore, it can signal a reversal from bullish to bearish after a long rally higher, or a reversal from bearish to bullish after a long trend lower. In many ways, it signals the final battle between the buyers and the sellers for control of the market. This is why the length of the legs is so important as it marks the extent of the volatility in the market. The longer the legs the more volatile the price action and the more fierce the battle. The more fierce the battle, the stronger the signal of an impending change. This candle is also telling traders to pay attention. However, please note, patience is required, as this could simply be a pause point in the longer term trend. The long legged doji is not sending the same message as a hammer or a shooting star, and so we have to wait for confirming signals to follow. Remember, this may simply be associated with a news release, and once the dust has settled, 'normal service' has been resumed. So patience, patience, and more patience. Wait for price and volume to confirm the direction, once it is established or re-established.

These are the three most important candles in the forex world which appear across all charts and time frames. They warn all traders, from short term scalpers to position traders, market sentiment is about to change or is indecisive.

However, they are not trading signals to enter or exit the market. They are only red flag warnings of a *potential* change and as with all signals need to be validated by other analytical tools and methods.

Finally, two other important points before moving on.

First, the technical element from the three dimensional approach applies equally to all other markets. These candles are just as powerful and can signal possible reversals in equities, futures, commodities and bonds.

Second, the power of these candles becomes even more potent, once volume is added into any analysis.

Just as these candles appear on currency charts they are equally important in other markets and charts and can also be validated using relational analysis. For example, if a shooting star appears on a chart for a particular currency pair while a hammer candle appears in a related market which moves inversely, this is doubly powerful and a strong sign a reversal may be imminent. This is a simple example of using these primary candles across related markets to analyse and validate price action.

All the candles and candles patterns in this book are applicable to all the four capital markets and to all time frames. As soon as they appear they are strong signals which should prompt further attention and analysis.

Finally, I am often asked whether these three candles fall into any hierarchy of importance or reliability. My answer has always been the hammer and shooting star are on an equal footing for giving traders an early warning of a reversal, whilst the long legged doji may sometimes simply be signalling a pause, followed by a continuation of trend.

However, they are all strong signals in their own right and, if traders just focused on these three any price analysis would be easier, consistent and more successful. In addition, they force traders to be patient, a virtue which many lack.

There are, of course, many many other candles and candle patterns, but for the purposes of this book I wanted to highlight what I believe are the most powerful to get started.

There are also many excellent books on this topic and I mention my own personal favourites in the resource section of this book. It is a huge subject in its own right, and all I am attempting to teach here, are the 'major' candles and patterns to look out for. They are the strongest and most powerful. These are the candles and candle patterns to use to validate price action and which can help you achieve consistent trading success.

Now I would like to consider my top three reversal candle patterns. This is where two candles combine to give traders a potential reversal signal, and the first of these is the bearish engulfing candle pattern. This is created at the top of an up trend and is when an up candle is followed immediately afterward by a down candle, which 'engulfs' it completely, as shown in Fig 17.15

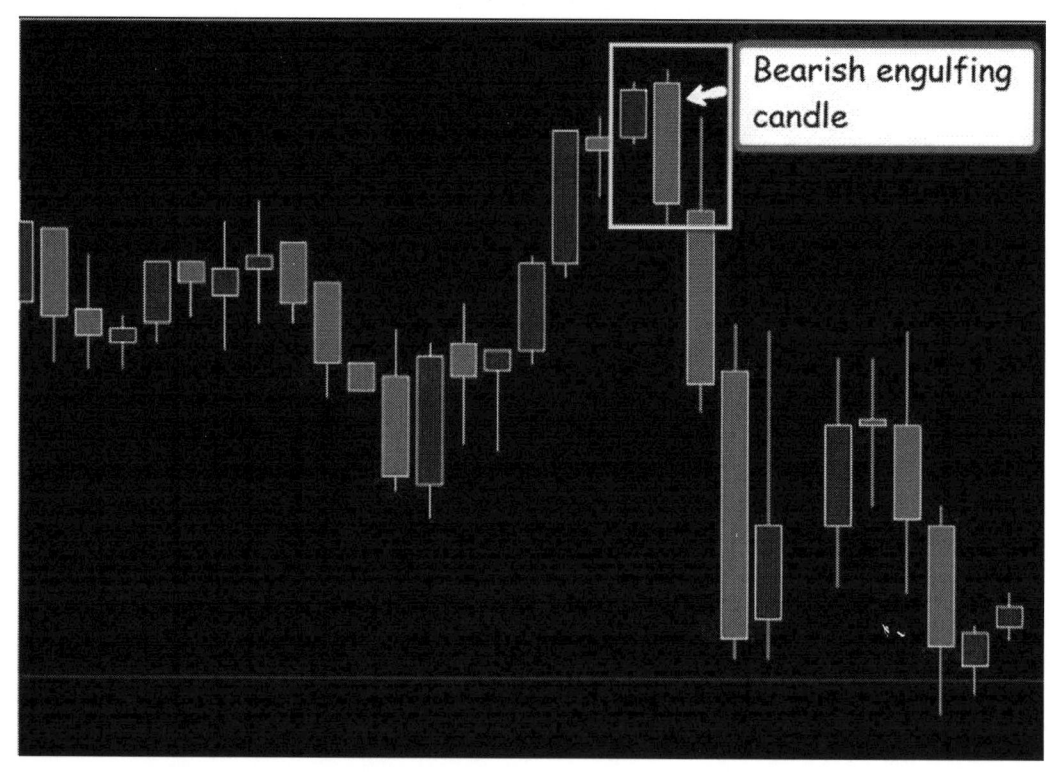

Fig 17.15 Bearish Engulfing Example

Fig 17.15 is a one minute currency chart and a good example. The important element here is the second candle which is a down candle, must engulf the preceding candle which is an up candle. In other words, the price action of the down candle must overwhelm entirely the price action in the up candle. This produces the 'bearish engulfing' signal which is again a red flag warning that the market may be about to turn lower after a bull rally.

The price action of a bearish engulfing candle pattern is in fact a shooting star. If the two candles were merged, the effect would create a shooting star, but spread over two candles. This pattern is also referred to as a two bar reversal for that reason and once again makes the case for using multiple timeframes. Overlaying two candles is easy as shown here. Overlaying several is almost impossible.

In the first candle, the buyers have been in control for some time with the market moving higher as a result. At some point the sellers come into the market, over powering the buyers and creating the second candle. This candle engulfs the buyers, and changes market sentiment from bullish to bearish, thus creating a potential reversal signal.

The difference here is the price action happens over two candles as opposed to the shooting star where the action is in one candle.

The key rules for this pattern are as follows. First, the down candle must engulf all of the price action of the previous candle, including any wicks to the top and bottom, so the whole of the previous price action is contained within the down candle, or as closely as possible.

Second, the down candle should have no wicks, or at least only very small wicks to the top and bottom of the body of the candle. The relative size of both the up and down candles is irrelevant. What is important is the up candle is completely swallowed up or engulfed by the second.

The price action which precedes this candle pattern is fairly straightforward. As we can see in Fig 17.15, following the reversal from bearish to bullish, the price action delivered two wide spread up candles, as the market moved firmly higher. Then a pause with the small doji candle, but still the market managed to struggle a little higher. The struggle higher is reflected in the spread of the up candle which is narrow. If the market were moving strongly this candle would be much wider and closer to the earlier ones.

At this point in the price action the market is looking a little weak, when it is suddenly engulfed by a wave of selling. It is like someone standing on a beach, knee deep, and being knocked over by a large wave. The narrow spread up candle was the last heave higher, and to return to the tug of war analogy with two teams pulling on a rope, this is equivalent to one team, the buyers, putting in one final big effort which just manages to pull the white marker in their direction, before they are hauled back by the sellers on the other end of the rope. Urged on by their coach, the sellers give an almighty, determined and prolonged heave, collapsing the buyers who capitulate exhausted in a heap. The sellers have won the battle and regained control or, at least for the time being, and until the next time.

For this candle pattern to have additional strength the last up candle should have a nice wide body, at least two to three times times the norm. The engulfing candle should, of course completely overwhelm it. In the example chart in Fig 17.15 I deliberately selected a pattern that was far from perfect as it helped to explain the price action.

However, for a bearish engulfing candle pattern to qualify as a two bar reversal both candles need to have a wide spread, and when merged, would result in a classic shooting star with a narrow body. Furthermore, if both candles have a wide spread this means there is momentum and volatility associated with the price action. In other words, what traders want to see is a sharp move up, followed by an equally sharp move down. This type of action increases the validity of the signal and increases the prospect of an extended move lower. In the example shown in Fig 17.15 a reversal did take place, and lasted for some time with the market drifting lower over the next hour. However, whilst the signal here was perfectly valid, the more volatile the two bar reversal the more likely an extended trend will develop, backed by momentum and based on a strong reversal in price.

Once again the bearish engulfing candle pattern can be found across all the capital markets. It appears in all time frames and is a powerful signal.

Its 'celestial twin' is the bullish engulfing candle, and occurs in reverse at the end of a trend lower.

The example I have selected to illustrate the bullish engulfing candle pattern is not perfect, but I have done so to reinforce the point technical analysis is not a science, but an art. In watching these candle patterns form, traders have to be flexible in any analysis, and even more so on currency charts, as gaps in the price action are rare. They do occur, but only infrequently.

Therefore, as one bar closes the next bar opens at the same price, so it is unusual to find perfect examples of 'engulfing' patterns. In other words, forex traders have to allow the engulfing candle a little leeway. In markets and instruments with gaps, textbook examples of engulfing candles are much easier to find.

As long as the engulfing candle encloses the preceding one this will be enough. In many ways a flexible attitude applies to all candlestick analysis and all markets.

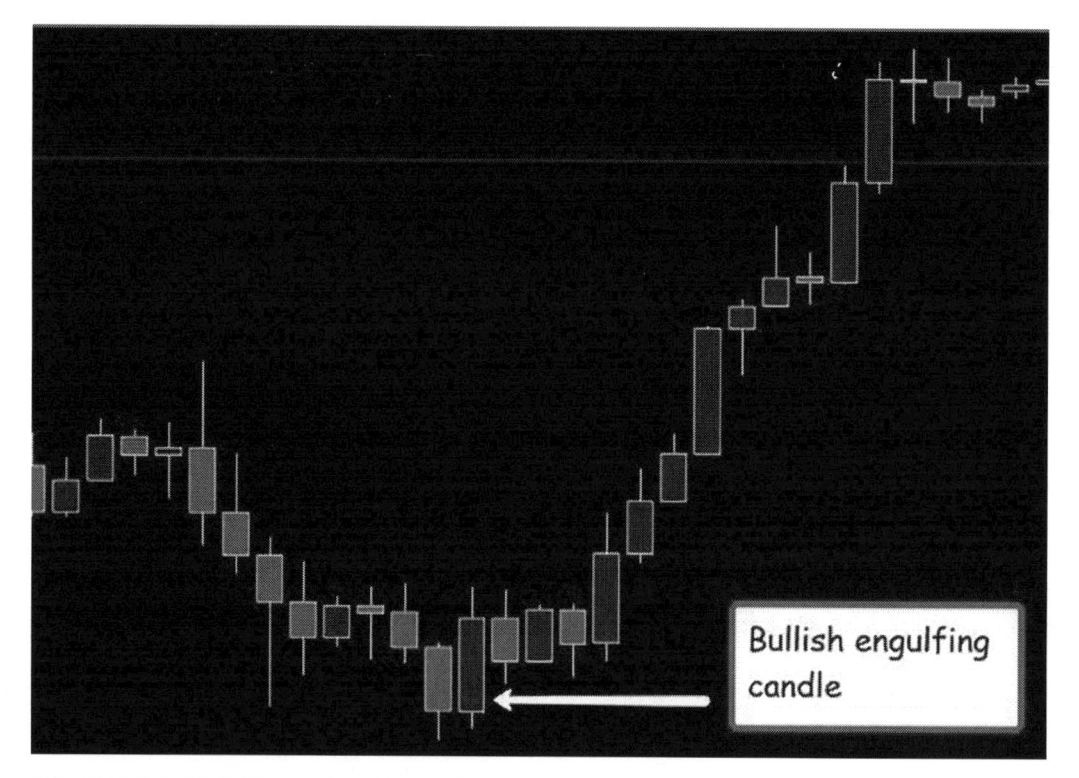

Fig 17.16 Bullish Engulfing Example

In Fig 17.16 the bullish engulfing candle has been taken from a four hour chart and, illustrates perfectly the momentum this price reversal can generate, as a result.

In this case, the market had been selling off over a couple of days, before the down candle is engulfed by the bullish up candle. The body of the up candle completely engulfs the body of the down candle, after which the price action moves sideways for three periods as the market consolidates at this level. During this consolidation period the market absorbs the remnants of selling, as it prepares to move higher.

In the tug of war example it is the sellers who have put in one last huge effort before being overcome by the buyers who respond, with their coach urging them on and heaving the rope back as the sellers collapse in a heap on the ground. Once again, this price action can be imagined as a hammer candle, which is created in two time frames with the sellers moving the price lower in the first time frame followed by the buyers moving the market higher in the second time frame. This would be the case if viewed on an eight hour chart.

An overlay of one candle on the other produces the familiar hammer candle which, in this case would have an up body.

The same rules apply to the bullish engulfing pattern as for the bearish engulfing. The primary rule is the up candle must engulf the preceding one down, but again these rules need to be applied with common sense. The key is the engulfing candle should swallow the body of the previous candle, which should have minimal wicks.

Bullish and bearish engulfing candle patterns are once again great signals, which traders should pay attention to. The market is speaking and indicating a potential reversal. Traders need to validate the signal with other tools and techniques before deciding to take a position in the market.

To complete this section on my top three reversal candle patterns I want to end with ones called tweezers. Like the engulfing candle patterns tweezers come in two varieties, namely tweezer tops and tweezer bottoms, and again they signal potential reversal points on the price chart.

However, there is one key difference which is they only apply to the forex markets and fast timeframes and the reason is as follows.

As the name suggests, tweezers are a 'precision tool' designed with precision in mind. They are the weapon of choice for ultra fast scalping in the market. I suspect (and this is purely my own opinion) their power comes from the rapid rise in HFT (high frequency trading) which triggers buy and sell orders based on short term support and resistance. The concept of support and resistance is explained later in this chapter.

Moreover, tweezers are not suitable for trading longer term. However, they are most definitely a pattern for the scalping trader and should only be used on very fast time or tick charts. Whilst it is impossible to give a hard and fast rule here, I would suggest that a 5 minute chart is the maximum timeframe in terms of 'time based' charts, and for tick charts, somewhere between 50 and 100 ticks. Tweezers are a precision tool, and this pattern is designed to identify fast scalping opportunities.

To reiterate, please don't use tweezers in other markets, but for forex they are a great candle pattern for short term trading.

The reason it is called a tweezer pattern is the name is derived from the shape they form on the chart. In the example in Fig 17.17 which is from a one minute chart it is easy to get a sense of the speed of the moves using these patterns.

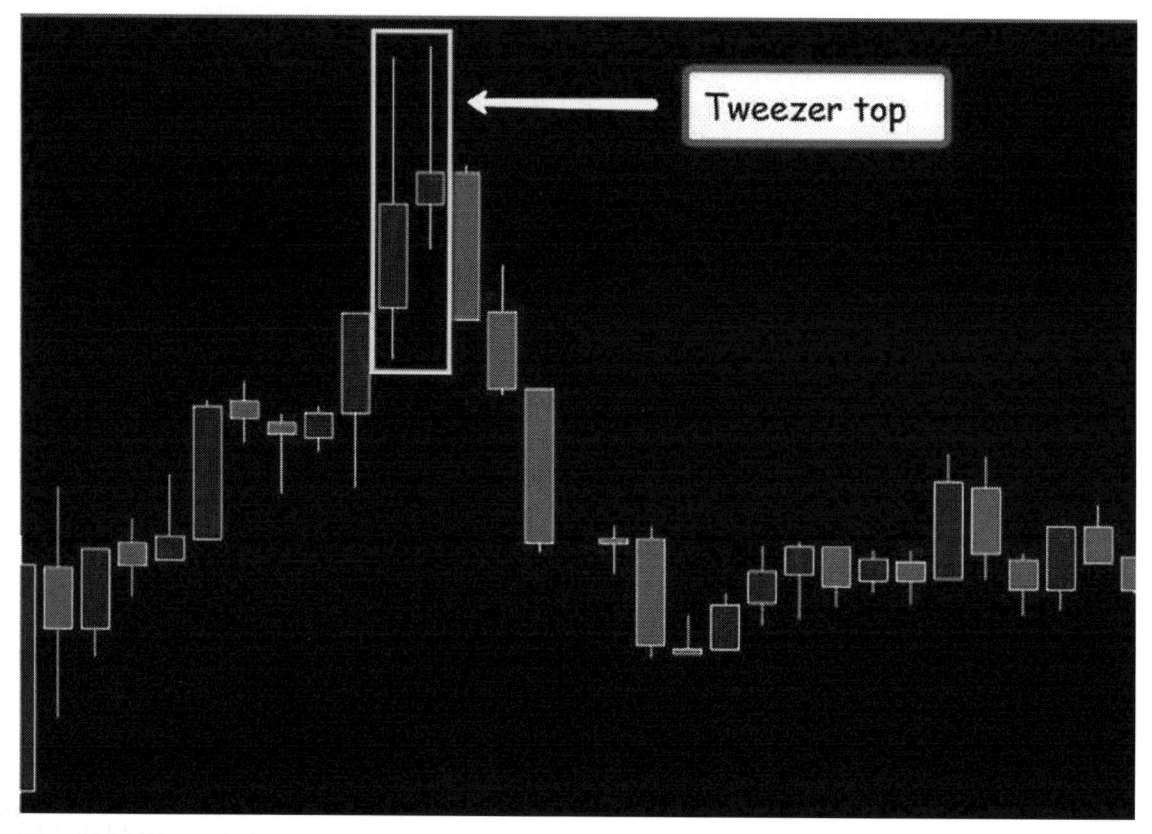

Fig 17.17 Tweezer Top Example

The term tweezer is derived from the appearance of the pattern, which resembles a pair of tweezers. There are always two candles, both with long upper wicks, which give the pattern this unique appearance.

The key point for this pattern is the high of the candle on each bar is identical, or as close to identical as possible, creating as it does a pair of tweezers. However, some flexibility is required. In this example the high of the second candle is marginally above the first, but that's fine, it is close enough to qualify as a tweezer top. What is also interesting in this example is the second candle is our old friend, the shooting star, so here we have a 'double confirmation' if you like. The tweezer pattern with the second leg of the tweezers being a shooting star, so adding a further element of confirmation to the pattern.

The significance of this pattern and what it reveals about market sentiment, is fairly straightforward. At a tweezer top the market has moved higher, with the buyers firmly in control. Ideally, the first candle in the tweezer top has to form with an up body and, preferably a long body with a nice wide wick to the top of the candle, as we have here.

The following candle in the pattern should also have a strong wick to the top of the candle and a long body as well, although this is not essential as we can see in this example. The reason for the deep wick is this is an additional sign of weakness. The market has run higher, but fallen back quickly. Then tried to run higher again before failing once more. All of this is signalled in the depth of the upper wick, and just like the shooting star and the hammer candle, the length of the wick is a key component to the strength of the signal. I cannot stress too strongly these patterns need to look like tweezers. Other candlestick books will suggest this is not important. This is not the case. The upper wicks must be long on both candles if traders are going to use this pattern for fast scalping.

What is interesting about tweezers is the second candle in the pattern can be either an up or a down candle, it doesn't matter. The important point is the price has stalled at the same level. In other words, the market has hit and stalled at a 'resistance level' as though there is an obstacle in the way.

The buyers are now struggling to break above this price point which the sellers are defending. The sellers have created a barrier or wall and there is now an obstacle to any further move higher. This is one of the many analytical techniques used when considering price in terms of price patterns, namely support and resistance areas created by previous price history. What is happening here, in a very short time frame, is the price action has reached a short term barrier, from which the market reverses, before taking another run at this level some time later.

The tweezer pattern so created suggests weakness and is therefore a potential reversal point, as a result. Therefore, whilst the rules for a tweezer top pattern are relatively flexible, the key points are as follows.

First, the high price of both candles must be identical or as close as possible that visually they look identical. Second, the candles must have deep wicks to the upper bodies in order to create a true tweezer top.

Third, the first candle must be the same colour as the trend, but the second candle can be either up or down. And finally, the bodies of both candles should be long if possible which adds strength to the signal.

This then is the tweezer top, and the tweezer bottom is identical except it appears at the bottom of a fall and marks a potential reversal from a bearish trend to a bullish trend. Once again, it is an early warning to traders to pay attention. The same rules apply, with the key being the low of the two candles which must be close or identical.

In addition, the candles should have long bodies and deep wicks to the lower body. In a tweezer bottom the first candle should have a body which reflects the trend, but the second candle can have either an up or down body.

Here is a typical example in Fig 17.18. As the rules for tweezer bottoms are exactly the same as for tweezer tops I won't repeat them. However, it is essential that the lower wicks to both candles must be long, otherwise the strength of the signal is diminished.

Once again, the example in Fig 17.18 is from a one minute currency chart, where as you can see reaction to the tweezer pattern lasted for over 20 minutes, so this gives a sense of the short term nature of this pattern

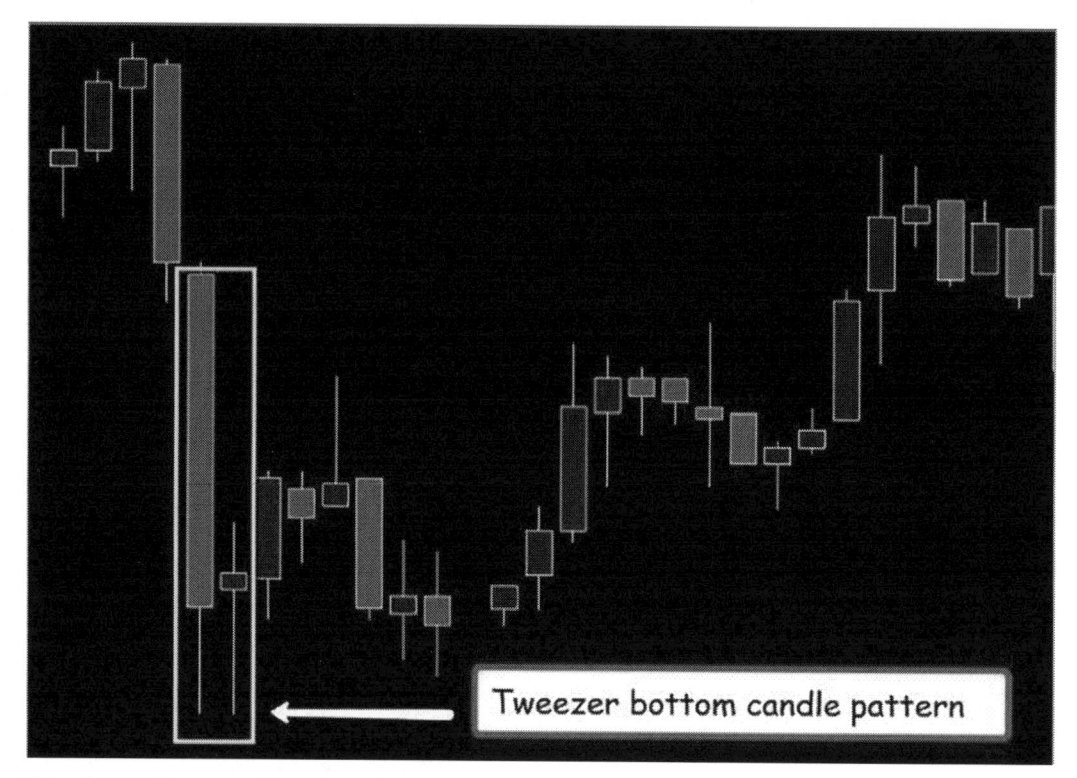

Fig 17.18 Tweezer Bottom Example

It is a great pattern for forex scalpers. It is immensely powerful, but only on very fast charts, and for scalping a few pips.

These are my three top candles and candle patterns – the premier patterns and signals to watch. However, there are many others and in the next section I am going to look at several more which I consider both valid and useful. There are many others but, in over 20 years of trading and investing, I have found trying to follow too many is simply counterproductive. These candles and patterns are the ones which can be relied on to work consistently. Now let's take a look at what I call secondary candles and patterns, which are less powerful, but work well in either validating those we have just looked at, or in providing alerts to pause points in trend.

The first one in this supplemental list is the 'hanging man'. It has the same shape as the hammer, and is only known as a hanging man when it does not appear at the bottom of a trend.

The hammer only appears at the bottom of a trend, following a fall in the market and is therefore a possible reversal from bearish to bullish. When the hanging man appears at the top of a trend it is signalling the opposite. It is a bearish signal and is a potential reversal from bullish to bearish sentiment.

This is one of the characteristics of candles. Two candles with identical shapes can have completely different significance depending on where they appear on the chart or in the context of its place in a trend.

Here in Fig 17.19 is an example of an hourly chart where we have the same candle appearing at different points of the price action. The first hanging man appeared and was followed by a second several bars later, confirming the weakness in the market at this price level.

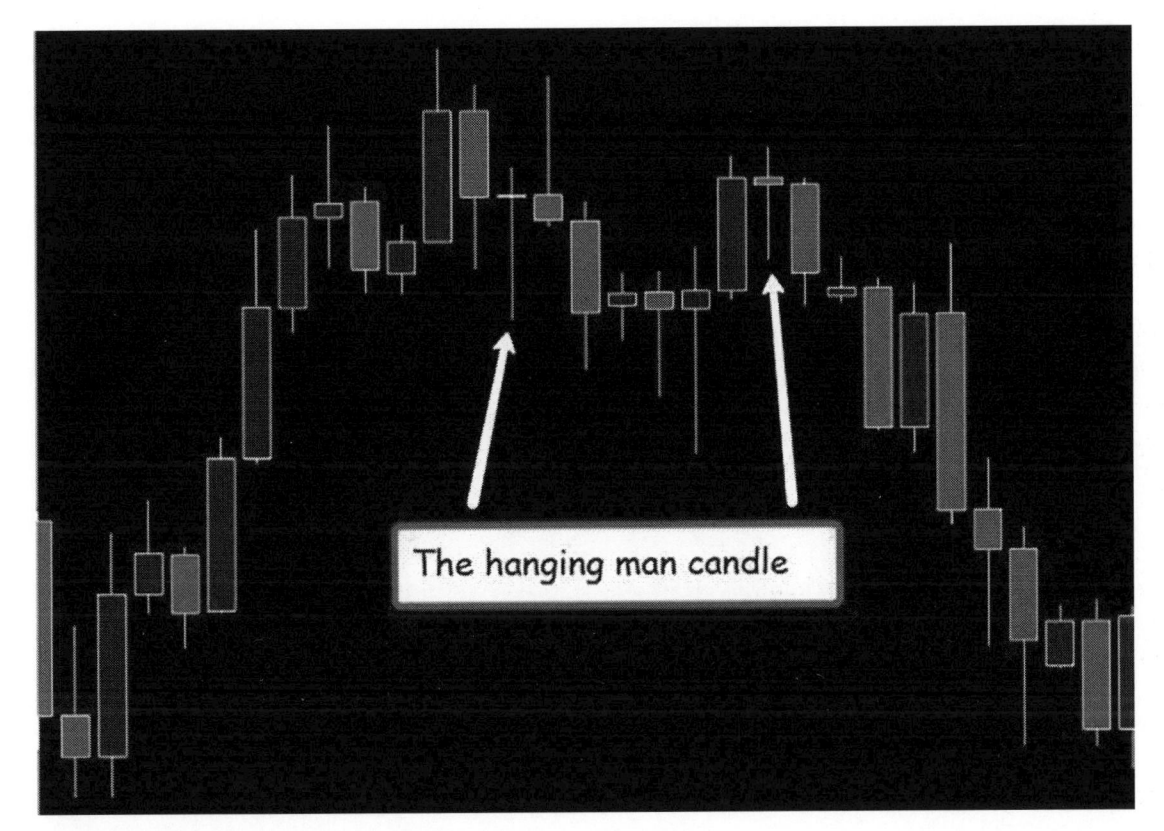

Fig 17.19 Hanging Man Example

The market had been rising steadily with the buyers in control and the hanging man candle begins to form as the sellers come into the market. This drives the market lower, but the buyers aren't finished yet and fight back pushing the market higher once more, before finally closing at or near the opening price. However, this is the first signal the sellers might be about to take control of the market. Despite having been repelled by the buyers on this occasion, it is a clear initial sign of potential weakness.

The sellers continue to build up strength, which may eventually overpower the buyers, thus ending the trend and creating a reversal in due course. In this particular example, immediately following the hanging man, comes another sign of weakness, namely, a shooting star. Now there are two consecutive signs of weakness, one after the other.

The price action moves sideways and remember what I said earlier, markets rarely turn on a dime, they take time to absorb any residual selling or buying pressure before changing trend. In this case, there were a further five candles of sideways price action, before finally on the sixth candle following the shooting star, a second hanging man candle appears, adding further negative sentiment at this level. Clearly the market is struggling at this price level, and following this third bearish signal, finally starts to trend lower and move into a bearish phase.

Although the hanging man is a secondary signal, when it is validated by a premier candle or candle pattern, its significance increases exponentially. It is only an early warning signal of a potential change in sentiment, but it has to be validated. In this case, part of the validation process was provided by the subsequent candles that developed on the chart.

The key points for this candle are the same as for the hammer. First, if the hanging man candle has a small body this can be either up or down, it doesn't matter. The close can either be above the open or below the close. In this case, the open and close were identical creating the 'perfect' hanging man.

Second, the lower wick or shadow to the underside of the candle should be at least three times as long as the body and, as a general rule the longer the better. Finally, the candle should have no upper wick or almost no wick for the candle to qualify as a hanging man.

Another pattern I look for on a chart is called an 'inside day', as it can be an early warning signal. However, unlike the other patterns mentioned, an inside day can also signal a pause before the continuation of the trend, or it can be a reversal. In addition, and just to clarify, although the candle pattern is referred to as 'inside day', the pattern is perfectly valid across all time frames.

The key as to whether the signal is a reversal or a continuation of the trend depends on how the candles immediately following are created and for novice traders I would suggest this pattern is only used to confirm the continuation of a trend.

In this example in Fig 17.20, the market reached a top several bars earlier, before starting to sell off, moving lower in even candles. However, following the formation of the fourth candle, buyers entered the market, as evidenced by a narrow spread up candle. This buying is all contained within the spread of the previous candle, creating the 'inside' price pattern, where the price action on the small up candle is completely contained within the price action of the previous down candle. This is followed by an even weaker signal of bullish intent, before the market breaks to the down side again, confirming the original trend.

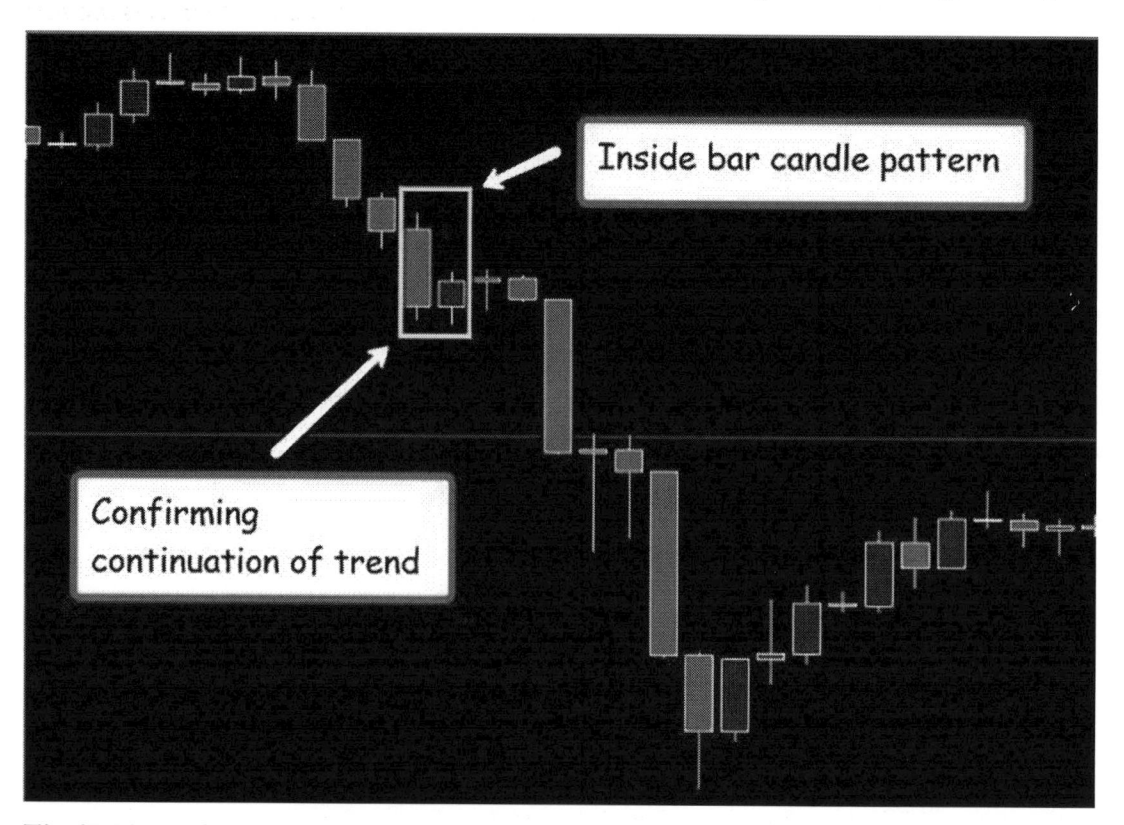

Fig 17.20 Inside Day Example

The inside bar here has merely confirmed the bearish nature of the market, with the trend continuing lower, following the pause point of the inside bar.

What is happening in this example is the market is in a strong down trend, but buyers have come into the market, attempting to take control. However, they have been swamped by the selling pressure. The initial bullish bar is weak with the buyers contained within the spread of the down candle. The buyers have been contained with the spread of the selling bar maintaining the integrity of the trend. The following bar is even weaker with a narrow spread up candle sending a clear signal. Finally the next candle breaks lower, and confirms the sellers are still in control.

This candle pattern has two uses. First, for traders who have not taken a position in the market, it is confirming the trend and is therefore an opportunity to enter a new position, once the market has broken below the inside day candle. Or, if a position has been taken in the market it is giving traders the confidence to hold that position and stay with the trend.

The principle of an 'inside' candle is that of market indecision. The market has paused and may reverse but, if it continues, as in this case, a move below the candle is confirming the trend remains strong. The key point here, like all candles, is to wait for validation and in this case, part of the validation process comes from the subsequent price action.

However, if the candle is not validated by a continuation of the trend, a potential reversal is in place. Just like the doji candle, this is signalling indecision and a possible turn in the market.

The chart in Fig 17.21 shows an example of both a continuation and reversal of trend. The market is moving lower and the first inside candle is validated as a continuation of the trend by the wide spread down candle which appears two candles later. However, after a further two candles, we see another inside day pattern, with the narrow spread bullish candle contained within the narrow spread down candle. The subsequent candle is a wide spread up candle, sending a strong signal this is a potential reversal of the trend, which duly develops into a strong move higher.

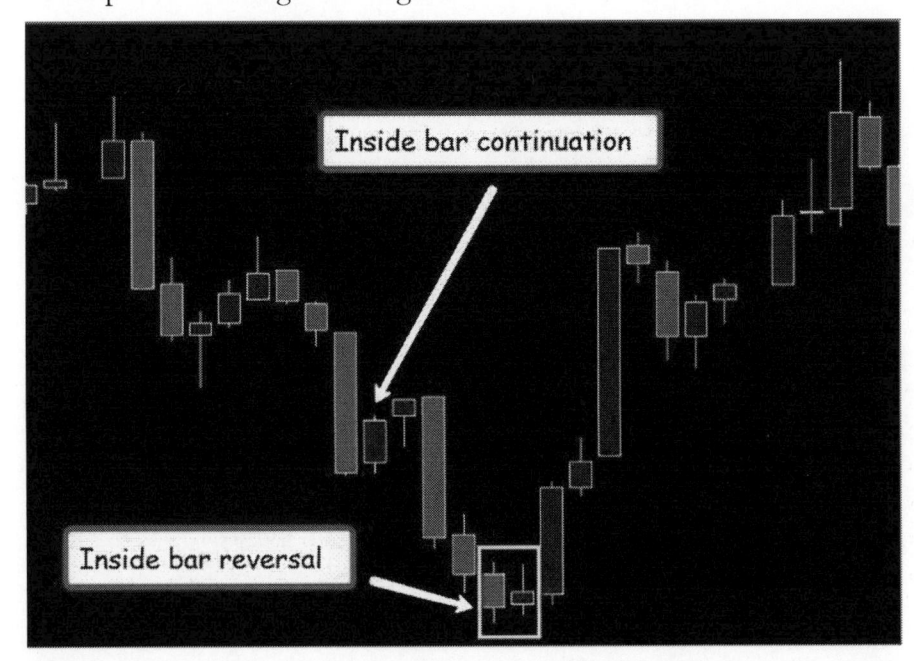

Fig 17.21 Inside Day Continuation & Reversal Examples

The opposite to the 'inside day' candle pattern is the 'outside day' candle' pattern. This pattern is extremely close to a bearish or bullish engulfing candle. In other words, the following candle engulfs the previous one.

There is a degree of controversy surrounding this candle pattern and a continuing debate between what is considered to be the 'Western' view of this pattern and the pure Japanese description. To be honest, my own view is I simply apply the bullish and bearish engulfing principles we looked at earlier which constitute an 'outside day' candle pattern arrangement.

These then are my top candle and candle patterns which I refer to all the time when trading. They have all become second nature to me. Each candle and candle pattern tells its own unique story which is validated in ways I am going to cover shortly. As I said earlier, there are literally hundreds of other candle and candle patterns but, for me, these are the ones I have found useful in all my trading and investing, regardless of the timeframe on the chart.

To round off this chapter, I would like to devote the next few paragraphs introducing you to the concept of time in trading, which may sound rather obvious and perhaps even irrelevant. However, please bear with me, as it is absolutely fundamental to the way I trade using a technical approach, and one I hope more traders will adopt, not only because it works, but also because it is so powerful and just makes sense.

Imagine for a moment the forex market is like a pond and a typical trader is sitting in a boat somewhere in the middle. The trader drops a pebble over the side, and the ripples gradually move out across the pond until they finally reach the edge. This simple analogy is how I explain the concept of price action in the market and how it ripples out across the price charts.

Now imagine having 5 charts open, starting with a 5 minute chart, followed by a 15 minute, then a 30 minute, a 60 minute and finally a four hour chart. Suppose one of the red flag economic indicators mentioned earlier is released to the markets which reacts with a change in trend. Where is this reaction likely to be seen first in terms of the trend change?

The first reaction will appear and be seen on the 5 minute chart. If a trend starts to develop it then gradually begins to appear on the 15 minute chart and, as the market absorbs the data further this soon starts to ripple through to the 30 minute and, ultimately to the hourly chart before finally appearing on the four hour chart. By the time this reaction has appeared on the four hour chart, the trend is extremely well developed in the faster time frames and is just starting to take effect in the four hour chart. At this point this trend may even develop further and move out into the daily chart and beyond.

In this scenario, if a trader's preferred time frame is the 15 min chart the change in sentiment will first appear on the five minute chart, before filtering onto the 15 minute chart, at which point a position can be taken in the market.

The change in sentiment then appears in the 30 minute chart and the trader continues to hold the position as the ripples extend further, finally reaching the 1 hour chart and, ultimately the four hour chart. By this time the trader is a holding a very strong position in the market, having ridden the trend higher, watching the lower time frame charts for signs of any pullbacks or reversals, and the higher time frame charts for signals the trend is continuing to build and extend in these slower charts.

What I have described here is the core principle full time traders adopt for trading any market. It is the approach I employ in every market either speculatively or for longer term investing. All that changes is the timeframes of the charts I consider. For speculative trading it's minutes and hours, for investing its days weeks and months.

The principles are very simple and based on the concept that if you are trading with the dominant trend in a slower time frame, the risk on the trade is that much lower and the probability of success that much higher. After all, a long position on a 15 minute chart, which coincides with a bullish dominant trend on the 30 minute charts means trading with the trend and not against it. In other words, swimming with the current. Of course, there is nothing wrong in trading against the dominant trend, it simply means the risk on the position is higher and any trade is unlikely to last very long.

In the same way that relational, fundamental and technical analysis gives you a three dimensional view of the market, so this approach to the charts, gives you a three dimensional view of the price action. Long gone are the days when a trader could simply watch one chart. This simply does not work. There are too many forces, too much volatility and too many complexities for such a simplistic approach to produce consistent profits week in and week out.

The combination I use is as described above. In other words, three charts, using the middle chart as my entry, and the two charts either side as my view on what is happening in the faster and slower time frames. If I have a position and the trend does not develop on my slower time frame chart, and my faster time frame chart seems to be confirming this view, I exit. If the trend does develop in the slower time frame chart, this gives me the confidence to hold the position. Even more so if I am trading in the direction of the dominant trend on the slower time frame. And, as I said earlier, I take exactly the same approach when trading using tick charts. The principle is identical with three charts, slow, medium and fast, taking any positions in the middle lane and watching for signals on either side.

Finally, this approach not only gives us a powerful methodology for trading, but also trading with increased confidence as we are trading with the trend and not against it.

Furthermore, it also gives us another powerful weapon to validate price action. After all, if a signal appears in one time frame, which is then validated with a confirming signal in a slower time frame, this is yet another powerful analytical tool. In this case, it is price validating price and, whilst there are many other tools and indicators, this is one of the simplest, yet under utilised of all trading techniques.

Consider this as a simple example.

On a fast time frame chart a shooting star candle appears suggesting a reversal which is duly confirmed on the medium time frame chart with a similar candle, and a position is taken. Finally, on the slow time frame chart, perhaps a bearish engulfing pattern appears, adding further confidence and confirmation the trade is with the trend and the market is now turning bearish. A simple example perhaps, but one which I hope starts to paint a picture for you. I cannot stress how powerful this approach is to understanding market behaviour.

If it is a technique you have never used before, it will revolutionise your trading. It is simple, powerful and effective and will give you that three dimensional view of price action. This is underpinned by using the relational and fundamental analysis explained earlier in the book. This gives us a complete picture of the market.

There is also one other immensely powerful reason for adopting this approach, and that's in exits. If there is one area of trading which virtually all traders struggle with, it is in getting out of the market once in. Getting in is the easy part, and as you will see in the next chapter, when we combine the power of the candles and candle patterns with volume I have described here, this is simple. But when to exit? This is always the problem and perhaps the one area of speculative trading that requires a great deal more research.

Full time traders like myself are generally discretionary traders in terms of exits, and these are often dictated by price congestion region, changes in the volume and price relationships at various levels, and sometimes just on trading experience and instinct. This is hard to teach and is only learnt through years of experience and studying charts and price behaviour. However, this is where multiple time frames help enormously and make the job easier.

Why?

Well put simply - they are once again giving you a three dimensional view of the world. A three dimensional view of the price action. If the market is perhaps running into resistance on a 30 minute chart and you are trading on a 15 minute chart, then perhaps this is time to close the position, and take your profit off the table.

This is what trading in multiple time frames gives you, not just the opportunity to see a trend developing, but also, and perhaps more importantly to see when a current trend is running out of steam. As I said earlier, getting in is easy, getting out is the hard part, and using multiple time frame charts will help you enormously.

In the next chapter I am going to consider technical indicators in more detail. In particular those that work and those that don't.

Chapter Eighteen
Technical Indicators

The market's personality. It is irrational and unsentimental. It is cantankerous and hostile. At times, it is forgiving and congenial.

John Neff (1931-)

Ever since the financial markets were created, traders, investors, mathematicians, and anyone fascinated by their never ending ebb and flow, have tried to create the ultimate mathematically generated indicators to forecast their future direction. The sole purpose has been to give traders (and investors) the confidence to open a new position in the market. These indicators are then displayed in graphical format on the trading screen in a variety of ways.

Some of these mechanisms or indicators are more useful than others. However, what this constant search for the ultimate indicator that always forecasts the market correctly has produced, is a vast and ever growing library of what are referred to as 'technical indicators'. In most cases, these are simply 'price indicators' since this is really all a technical trader is interested in.

Over the decades, some indicators have developed strong followings, whilst others have fallen by the wayside. The problem for inexperienced traders is knowing which ones provide useful information, and which are perhaps less useful.

Moreover, for novice traders the temptation is always to have as many indicators as possible on the screen, in the hope they will align, confirm any trading signals and help to reduce the risk of the trade. This is perfectly natural and is a cycle almost all traders follow, before they finally come to the realisation the most important aspect of technical trading is price behaviour, supported by some simple, uncomplicated indicators which provide information that would be difficult to produce manually, and at speed.

In other words, price action or price behaviour is primary and, technical indicators are secondary. Technical indicators can certainly be useful and helpful in providing an alternative view of complex markets, particularly the forex market which is the most complex of all and I use several myself, but ultimately trading is a discretionary business, and one where trading indicators can only ever play a supportive role. Technical indicators should only every support a trader's analysis, ***not*** replace it.

Unfortunately, many traders abrogate their trading decisions to a trading indicator through fear, which is entirely understandable when first starting out. In addition, it is also a lot easier to blame a bad or losing position on the market or indicator. Again this is perfectly normal and part of a trader's learning curve. In fact one of the things you will need to decide is whether you are suited to a discretionary approach or a systematic one, and this will be dictated by your personality traits. There is no right or wrong way to trade, just what suits you and works best.

Perhaps one of the hardest lessons for any trader to learn is to take a loss, move on and not to take the loss to heart. This is easier said than done and, although I'm straying into the world of trading psychology here, this is one of the reasons trading indicators are so popular. They have much more to do with the psychology of trading, as opposed to whether they work. As I mentioned in a previous chapter, learning to trade is a lot like learning to swim. The indicators can be supportive while a trader is learning. However, the problem for many traders is they never learn to trade unaided, and continue to add more and more indicators, in the mistaken belief this will help to build confidence.

Unfortunately, the opposite is more likely to be true. A trader's screen ends up filled with coloured lines and flashing symbols which simply confuse, leading to indecision and further confusion.

However, there is no reason why traders should not use trading indicators, and in this section I want to explain the better ones and how to use them. Trading indicators can be found on all good charting and brokerage platforms, and for the purposes of this chapter I am going to focus primarily on those which are freely available, plus a couple I have developed for my own trading. My approach, as with everything I do, is to keep things simple.

The first thing to note about trading indicators is their only role is to provide supportive analysis to the price action on a chart.

Second, trading indicators fall into five principle groups, under two main headings. These are leading and lagging. As these terms imply, a leading indicator is one that truly leads the price whilst a lagging indicator is one based on historic price action. In the leading category there are only, whilst under lagging there are hundreds.

In the leading indicator category I would only include price as one, and volume as the other. I have to stress this is my own view and I'm sure there are traders who disagree.

Every other technical indicator is lagging the market. It has to be, since every one of these indicators has one thing in common. They use price history to construct the indicator, so are all lagging the true price action to a great or lesser extent. As I explained in an earlier chapter, some are better than others and, some work well under certain conditions, but perform less well when market conditions change. For example, one type of indicator may work when a market is trending strongly, but breaks down when the market moves sideways. This lack of consistency is one issue. The second is many traders simply do not know which indicator to apply in different market conditions.

The first group of indicators can loosely be termed as trend indicators. Many traders will know the well worn trading motto of 'let the trend be your friend', and trend indicators have been designed to help identify when a trend has formed or is forming.

Furthermore, trend indicators should also help traders stay in a trade once the trend as developed.

However, as I stated earlier, all technical indicators have their strengths and weaknesses and, whilst this group performs well when the markets are trending nicely, they perform less well when markets are moving sideways and price action is confined to a narrow range. This, of course, is only to be expected.

As a general rule, these indicators smooth out the price action into more consistent lines or patterns. By far the most popular are simple moving averages, which plot an average of prior prices over a user defined period. This then produces a simple line on the chart to project likely future price behaviour.

From this simple concept has sprung a plethora of other moving average based indicators including, weighted, exponential and multiple moving averages.

In essence, all traders are only interested in predicting a future price move. So, in theory, if an indicator can help us do this, it is worth using and perhaps the simplest of all indicators is the Simple Moving Average.

This is an indicator which looks back over a user defined number of periods. In Fig 18.10 the SMA is looking back over the previous five price bars and taking the average closing price of each of these. It then plots the line accordingly, based on this historic price action to suggest where prices are likely to move next.

In simple terms for each new bar the SMA will take the previous 5 prices on close, sum them together and divide by 5. This figure will then be plotted on the chart and is recalculated at the end of each session, or whatever the time period of the chart.

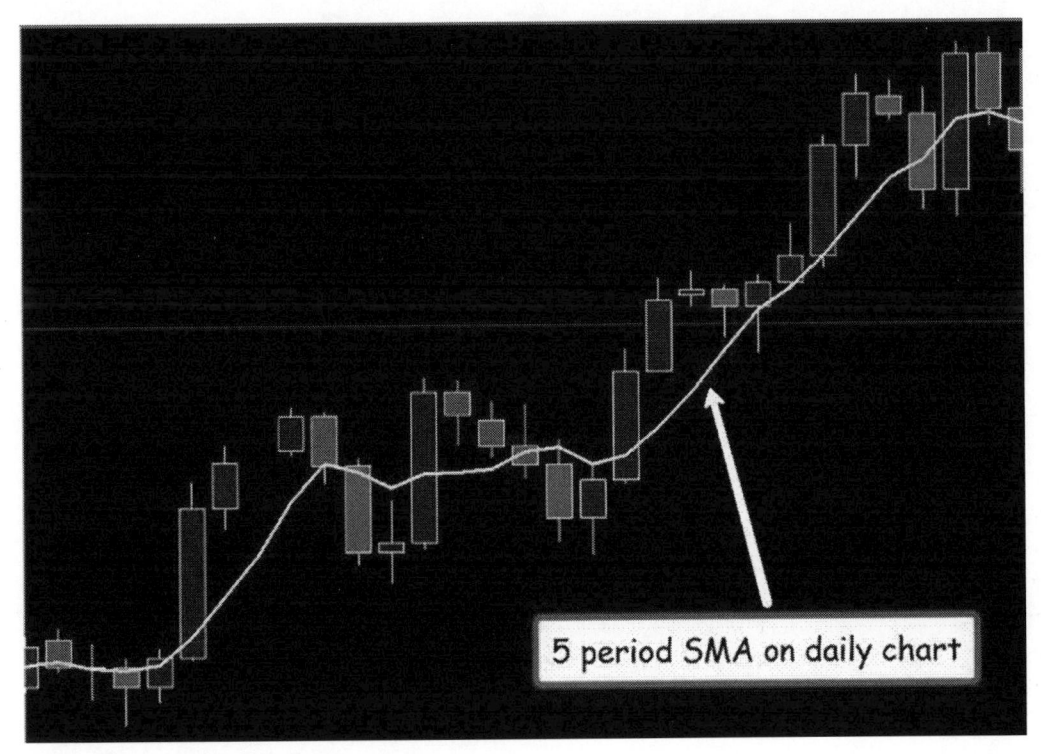

Fig 18.10 Simple Moving Average

This is the simplest form of indicator. A simple moving average can be calculated for any time period. For example a 10 minute SMA, a weekly SMA, or any user defined period which is then plotted on the chart accordingly. The simple moving average is based on the price and calculated on every price change.

There are a number of ways traders use moving averages to find and place trades. One of the simplest is to enter a long position when a price moves above the moving average, and exit when it moves back below. The theory with this strategy is the indicator is providing a good guide to the overall trend.

Therefore, a trader will place a trade when the price is trending up, and exit the trade when the price begins to trend down.

Another very popular strategy using moving averages is to enter and exit trades when two simple moving averages cross one another. The theory here is that when one moving average crosses the other, it indicates a change in trend and is therefore a trading opportunity. In the example in Fig 18.11 the 15 SMA has crossed above the 50 SMA, suggesting a bullish trend is about to start and in this case, it did. This is on a weekly chart.

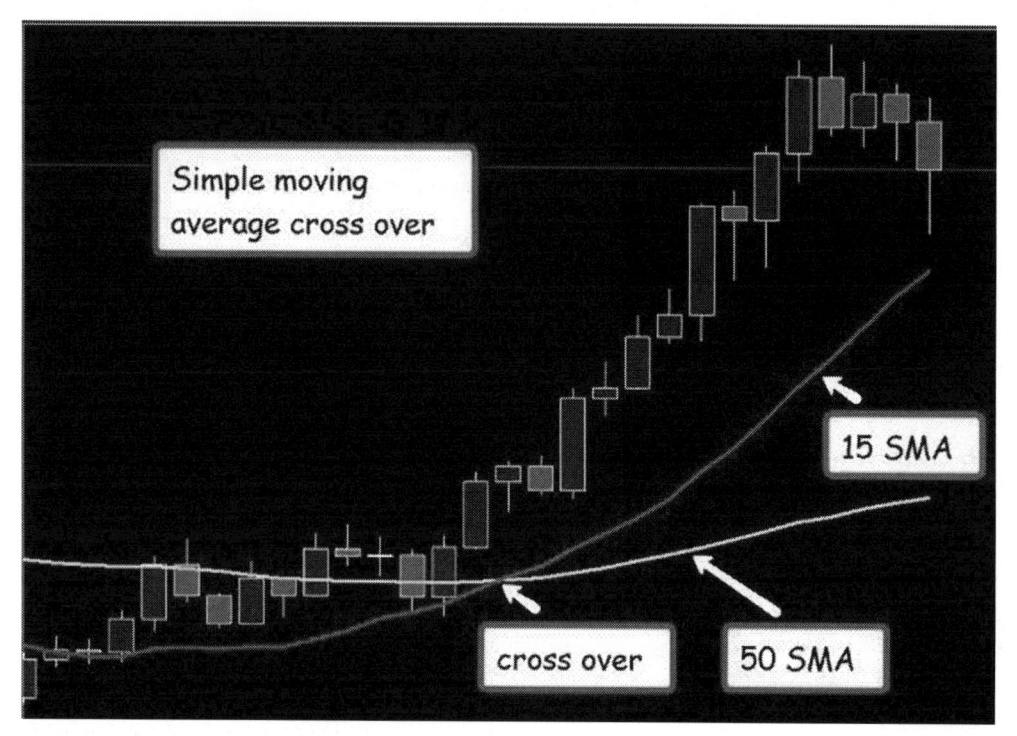

Fig 18.11 Moving Average Crossover Strategy

However, there is a problem with moving averages and it is this. The shorter the time frames used (such as 5, 10 or 15 periods) makes the SMA highly sensitive as it is very close to the price action of the market and therefore more likely to provide false signals.

Even the longer period moving averages, such as the iconic 100 or 200 moving averages, present their own problems. In this case, the averages are so far away from the price action traders may need significant capital to trade these moving averages.

There is also an entire philosophical debate about moving averages and in particular a debate surrounding the two averages mentioned above. I deliberately used the word 'iconic' to describe these, because they do exhibit some interesting characteristics, not least their almost 'mystical' quality in relation to price. The 200, in particular, is even quoted by the financial press whenever it approaches a key price point.

The question, however, as always is this. Is it the market reacting objectively to these price levels, or is it simply that with so many traders watching these indicators, they become a self fulfilling prophecy as a result?

After all, if all traders believe that a market is going to bounce higher off a 100 or 200 moving average, provided a sufficient number take positions on this expectation, the prophesy will be fulfilled. By the same token, if price breaks below one of these averages, many will enter short positions which will inevitably drive the price even lower.

Moving averages are incredibly easy to use and follow and in recent times have also been afforded a degree of validation by the financial media. This has further reinforced their authority and because they are seductive, they appear to work when applied to historic price action.

However, with so many traders looking at the same charts and having the same beliefs about this indicator there has to be an element of a self-fulfilling prophecy about them.

Over the years there have been many studies by leading academics, who have tested hundreds of different strategies using technical indicators, and in particular moving averages. All of these studies reached similar conclusions. The success rate of each strategy varied between 37% and 66%. The research suggests moving averages only give positive results about half the time, thereby making them a risky proposition for any effective market timing.

In other words they only work half the time, the problem is similar to the advertising conundrum. Which half and when. Generally of course, they will work well in trends, but then a trend is sometimes only obvious after the event, unless you understand volume and price, along with all the associated aspects of price behaviour such as congestion phases.

Nevertheless, they do have their place and I use them myself, albeit sparingly. I use them to give myself a perspective on price behaviour in different time frames. This is how they should be used. Giving traders a perspective, nothing more and nothing less.

Within this group there are many other indicators. Some have exotic and unusual names and these include: the Parabolic SAR, Rainbow 3D moving averages, and the KST indicator. They all have their fans in the trading world but, to be honest I have never used any of these so cannot comment on their validity or otherwise.

One indicator I have used for trading yen based currencies is the Ichimoku Cloud indicator for the same reason I watch the 100 and 200 period SMAs. Japanese currency traders use Ichimoku almost exclusively for trading, so it does have an element of a self fulfilling prophecy. I will be explaining Ichimoku in more detail later.

The second group of indicators I would like to examine is what I call strength type indicators, of which the most popular is of course volume. This is the fuel that drives the markets. This is the indicator I have been using consistently for more than 20 years. It was the indicator I started with as part of volume spread analysis in the futures market, in the days long before the internet.

Volume too is covered in detail later, within the concept of volume price analysis. Volume price analysis is my own methodology and the approach I use exclusively for my personal trading and investing, and in all my market analysis and forecasts. It is the approach I teach in my live webinars. I use it for all markets and instruments. I have recently written another book which explains this methodology in detailed, and is entitled: A Complete Guide To Volume Price Analysis. You can find further details on my site at http://www.annacoulling.com and since then I have added several other books with worked examples for all markets including stocks, cryptocurrencies and forex.

Volume (in my opinion) is the only indicator (other than price itself) that can be considered a leading indicator. Volume appears in real time at the live edge of the market, and the signals it delivers are then interpreted as part of the volume price relationship. It is because these signals are delivered in real time which makes volume and price so powerful.

However, in the spot forex market there is only tick volume, which is then used as a proxy for volume. Tick is activity and can be interpreted in exactly the same way using the same techniques.

It's not perfect, but when combined with all the other analytical techniques, price action analysis, and supporting technical indicators, provides a powerful way to interpret activity in the spot forex market. Furthermore, volume price analysis gives traders a huge advantage.

A second method of using volume is to consider related markets, such as the futures market or in equity markets. Price reversals can be seen in currency futures as well as in currency specific ETFs. The volume is there and at the live edge of the market, so can be harnessed and exploited. All other indicators based on historic price action are lagging whilst volume is leading because, like price, it is reported in real time.

The third group of technical indicators fall into the volatility grouping, and these indicators are designed to show fluctuations in price over a period of time. By far the most popular in this group are Bollinger bands, developed by John Bollinger. This is a series of lines creating a band which envelope the price on the chart. Bollinger bands utilise simple maths and standard deviation with the lines plotted as two standard deviations away from a simple moving average. Fig 18.12 is an example plotted on a monthly chart using a 20 period moving average.

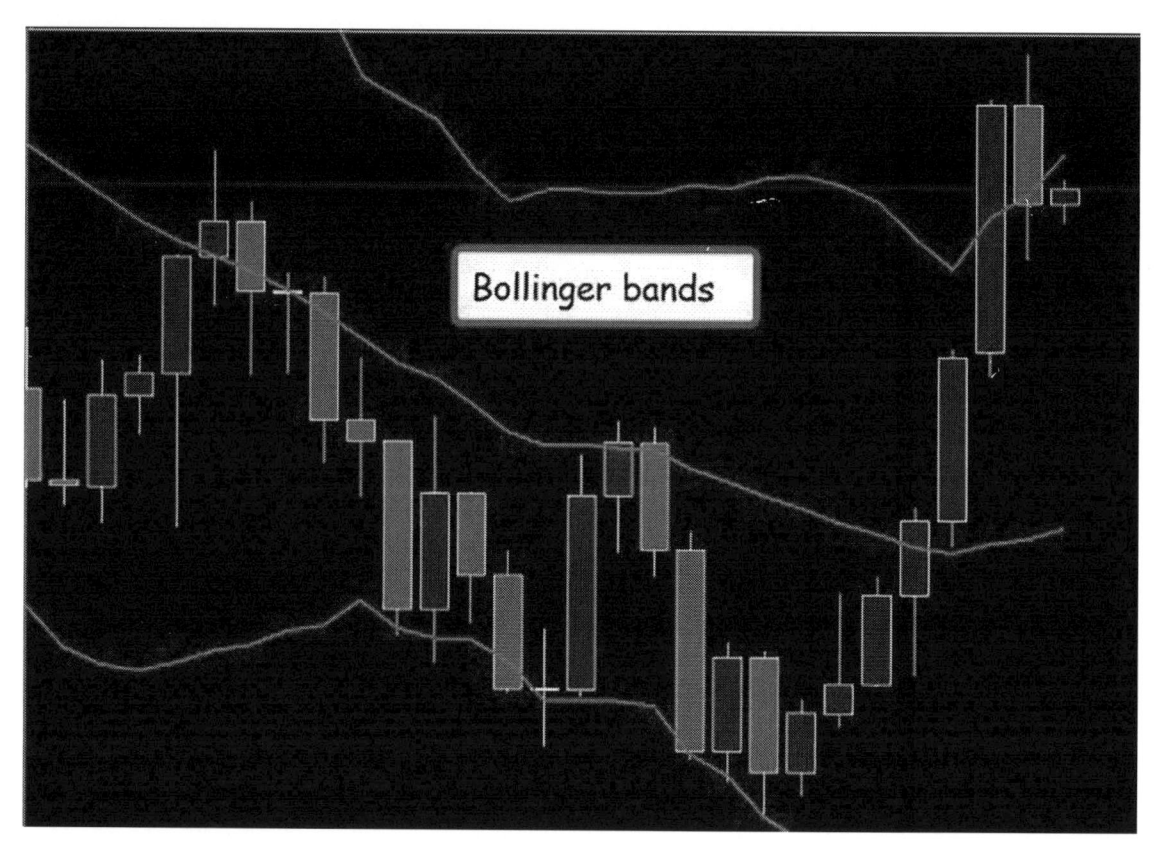

Fig 18.12 Bollinger Band

Looking at the chart, it would appear the Bollinger bands seem to know where the price is heading next. However, this is what Investopedia has to say about them.....the following is taken directly from the web site:

The problem with Bollinger bands

As John Bollinger is the first to acknowledge, "tags of the bands are just that - tags, not signals. A tag of the upper Bollinger band is not in and of itself a sell signal. A tag of the lower Bollinger band is not in and of itself a buy signal". Price often can and does "walk the band". In those markets, traders who continuously try to "sell the top" or "buy the bottom" are faced with an excruciating series of stop outs, or worse, an ever-mounting floating loss as price moves further and further away from the original entry."

A less than ringing endorsement from the originator.

I was introduced to this indicator many years ago when trading futures and reached the same conclusion. However, what the indicator was designed for and reveals simply and clearly is volatility. The squeeze describes when the bands narrow showing reducing volatility and then expanding as volatility increases.

There are several other indicators in this group, such as the volatility ratio, volatility, Chaikin volatility and many more. Again I have to confirm I have never used any of these, so cannot comment on their usefulness or otherwise.

The next group of indicators is what I call cyclical and, these are essentially indicators which look for patterns, or rather patterns of price action, that repeat or cycle. The two most popular in this group are Elliot wave and Fibonacci.

Fibonacci is based on the work of Leonardo of Pisa, who developed a number sequence based on the number series 1,2,3,5,8..... in which each number is added to the next in order to build the series. So, the next in the series here is 13. This number sequence also appears throughout the natural world, and has been developed into one of the most popular trading indicators, particularly for forex traders, with the Fibonacci retracement probably the most widely used application of the sequence. The most important retracement percentages are 23.6%, 38.2%, 61.8 % and 76.4% and, below is an example applied to a 5 minute chart. Traders also use the 50% level, even though this is not part of the Fibonacci sequence.

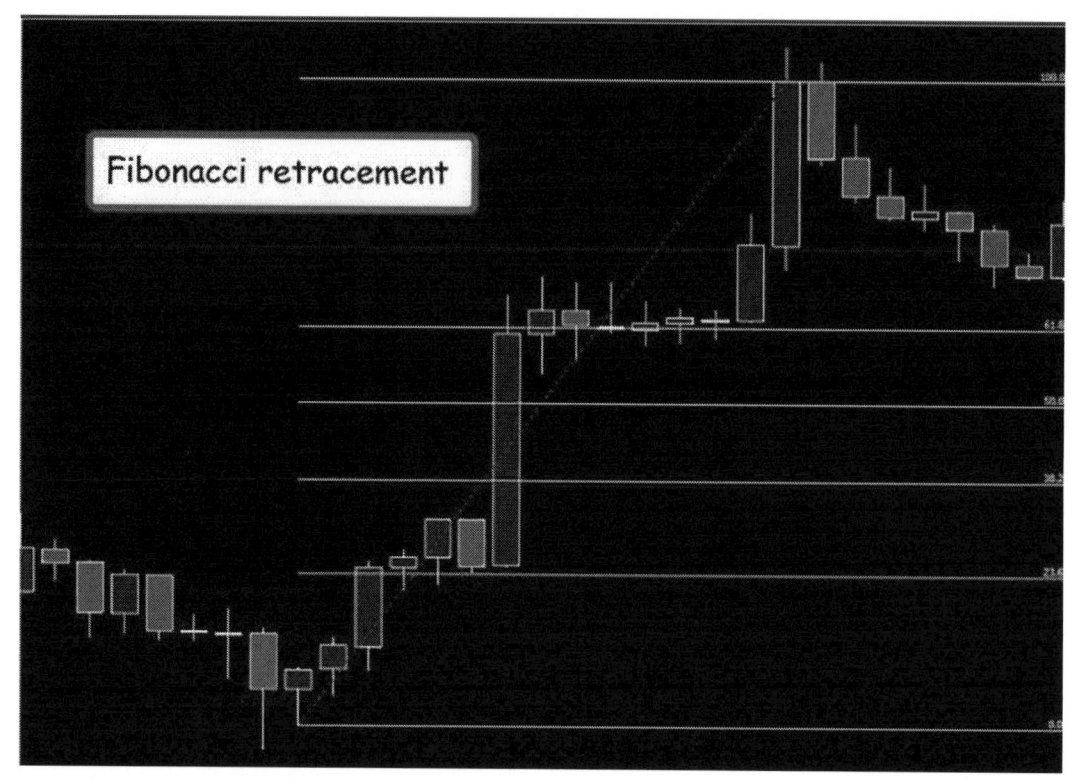

Fig 18.13 Fibonacci Levels

In the example in Fig 18.13 the market paused at the 61.8% where a large number of traders would have taken a short position based on this price action. However, the price simply consolidated at this level before pushing higher and eventually ran out of steam at the 100% level. This level too is not part of the Fibonacci sequence, but is related to Gann levels. However, traders have incorporated this percentage into Fibonacci. Fib levels are very popular but, once again I suspect there is also a strong element of a self fulfilling prophecy about them given the number of traders who use them. There is also some debate about where and to which levels to attach them to a chart. How far back? What is the high, and which is the low? All rather vague questions and to which there is no firm answer.

Another popular trading approach is Elliott Wave. Elliot Wave Theory was developed by Ralph Nelson Elliott, and is also premised on the principle markets move in waves or patterns, of higher highs and higher lows. This is certainly true, but for Elliott the key levels and patterns are all based around a cycle of three. Proponents of Elliot Wave will often add in some Fibonacci, and vice versa. A little Gann may also be included, just for good measure, so once again 50% and 100%, which are key Gann numbers become important. Once again, although I strongly believe there is an element of a self fulfilling prophecy surrounding these numbers, as traders we should at least be aware of them, even if we never use them (like me).

Finally, there is a large group of indicators which loosely come under the term momentum. These indicators generally sit at the bottom of a price chart and have been designed to determine and plot the strength and weakness of a trend. This group of indicators is also mapping the speed at which prices are moving over a given period of time with any divergence between the price and trend signalling strong or weak momentum, and therefore a potential change in market direction.

The two most popular are MACD (Moving Average Convergence Divergence) indicator and the RSI (Relative Strength) indicator. The MACD is a convergence and divergence indicator which uses moving averages. By contrast, the RSI indicator averages out the price history to try to forecast whether a market is over bought or over sold.

Many traders are taught to use MACD convergence and divergence to take trading positions. The theory is that where the price movement is at odds with the trend of the MACD indicator, the price is likely to turn.

Fig 18.14 shows a chart with the MACD indicator applied on a 5 minute chart.

The MACD is another hugely popular indicator, which while working well in trending markets, can give a huge number of false signals when markets are moving sideways. The problem is always trying to forecast when a market is going to break into a trend. However, my philosophy here is very simple. If you can understand price patterns, and when a trend is about to start, or is possibly coming to an end, why do you need the MACD. After all, as I explain later, and in my book on volume and price, it really is very simple, if you can just take a little time to learn and understand how to identify where trends are borne, simply from studying the price action and associated volume. It really is self evident once you begin to study volume price analysis or VPA.

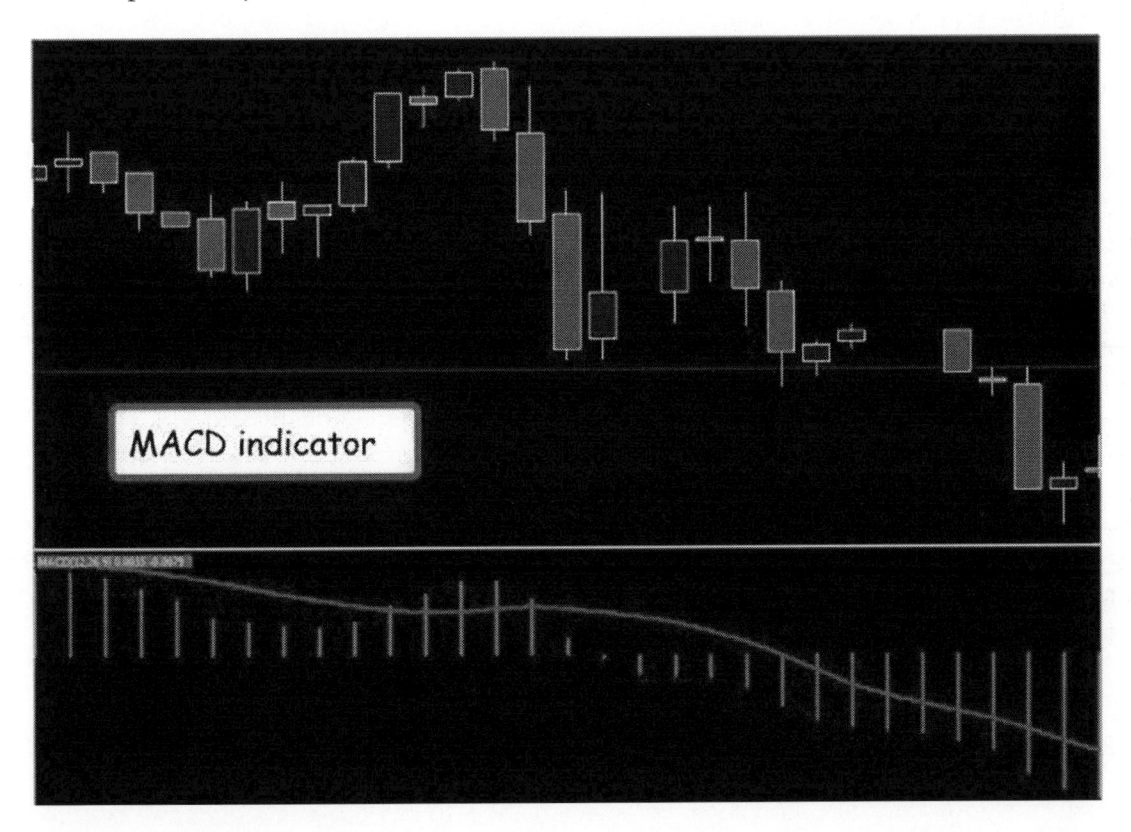

Fig 18.14 MACD Indicator

Finally, the RSI indicator which represents a key concept for forex trading, as currencies are constantly moving from oversold to overbought in every time frame. It is the nature of this market as a currency will never move to zero, so identifying these turning points is an important skill forex traders need to acquire.

In this respect the currency markets are unique. For example, when trading gold or gold futures there is only one instrument which is being bought or sold. However, when trading forex a currency can be bought and sold against any number of counter party currencies. For example, in the case of the US dollar, this can be bought against a host of other currencies, not just against the majors. So, when the US dollar is being bought, this may be against all other currencies, or just a few. This is one of the issues that makes forex trading unique and complex. Moreover, a bank or large institution wanting to sell euros and buy US dollars may not take the most obvious route through the EUR/USD pair. Instead, selling of a large volume of euros could be against the British pound, with the result they are now sitting on a quantity of British pounds. These could then be sold against the US dollar and the result would be the same. This is why understanding and identifying when a currency is strong or weak is the first step in any analysis. The next step is to identify where that strength or weakness is appearing and trade it accordingly.

This can be seen quite clearly on the charts where the US dollar may be rising against one currency, but falling against another. This is probably my most important forex trading tactic and is where I have developed my own personal proprietary indicator. This indicator identifies for me those currencies which are strong and those which are weak. Which are rising together or falling together and therefore not in a trend. And most importantly which are overbought and which are oversold and therefore likely to reverse. From there it is a simple task to check all the charts for that currency and identify possible trading opportunities. It is my own personal radar system on the forex market. Individual currency strength and weakness is displayed graphically and is so quick and easy to identify, thereby replacing hours of cross checking and comparing charts. This is where an indicator fits in. It delivers complex information quickly and easily and in an intuitive format, guiding you to those trading opportunities for further analysis.

In many ways this is the key to trading indicators. It is when they offer something of value, which can then help with any analysis and short cut the process. Unfortunately, most of the indicators I have examined in this chapter are promoted as providing entry and exit signals, which they do not. In addition indicators only work under certain market conditions. Some work in trending markets, whilst others only work in sideways or congested markets, and the problem for traders is often knowing what the market is doing at any one time. This is where it comes down to understanding price behaviour and having the skills to analyse what is happening on the chart which no automated system can do. The reason is that the interpretation of price action is, not only highly subjective, but also highly nuanced.

A further problem with technical indicators is often traders who use them have little or no idea of the algorithms driving them. Therefore, when traders apply them to their charts, the chances are many of these indicators will be executing similar calculations, but in slightly different ways. This can result in indicators giving conflicting signals, and rather than boosting confidence, adds further confusion and can lead to a loss of confidence.

My advice is, therefore very simple and amounts to a three step process. Step one, and the starting point for any trader, is understanding price action by way of candles and candle patterns. Step two, is to develop the analytical skills related to price behaviour. These skills include how to recognise the six phases of price behaviour. Finally, step three is to add in only those trading indicators which will act as support mechanisms. The trading indicators should be there to help and not to hinder or confuse. This is the approach that will ultimately lead to trading success.

Before moving on to consider volume in detail, I promised to explain one type of indicator which I've used when trading in the Japanese yen pairs, namely Ichimoku Cloud. The reason being the majority of Japanese currency traders also use this technical indicator. If you have ever seen the trading floor in a Japanese bank you'll know what I mean. It is extremely popular with forex traders and, in many ways, this indicator is testament to the concept of a 'self fulfilling prophecy', particularly for the yen pairs.

The first and most important point to make about Ichimoku is that this indicator should only be used with longer term time frame charts. It is particularly suited to daily charts and above and is not really suited to intraday trading.

At first glance, Ichimoku can appear very confusing, so let me try to explain the elements which make up the indicator before moving to a chart.

The indicator uses simple candles and candle patterns along with two moving averages, namely the 9 and 26 SMA. However, these moving averages are calculated using the mid point price which is why they appear as a spiky line on the chart.

These two moving averages can have a variety of names depending on the charting package or programme. The nine period SMA can be known as any of the following: Conversion Line, Turning Period or, by its Japanese name of Tenkan Sen. Meanwhile, the twenty six SMA can be referred to as Base Line, Standard Period or, by its Japanese name of Kijun Sen.

Finally, there is one more number that needs to be added to the charting package, before it will draw the chart and this is the number fifty two. This third time element is again called various things by different packages, but these are the ones I have come across. Leading Span B, Span B, or Period three. Its correct Japanese name is Senkou Span B.

Whichever name it has, this needs to be set at fifty two. Although, this line is similar to the two simple moving averages in that it is calculated by taking the average of the highest high and the lowest low for the last fifty two periods, it then takes this information and shifts the line forwards by twenty six periods, giving this indicator the unique ability to project forward into the future.

Therefore, the Senkou Span B line is 52 as it is based on a two month period of the twenty six day working month, but time shifted ahead to give a one month future view of the market.

So, to recap. When setting up Ichimoku on any charting package traders have to input three numbers, nine, twenty six and fifty two which create the three lines on the chart. The Tenkan Sen is the modified 9 period SMA, the Kijun Sen is the modified 26 period SMA, and the Senkou Span B is the one month simple moving average look ahead line shifted twenty six periods forward.

Finally, the chart has two other lines. The first is the Senkou Span A, also known as the Leading Span A. This line is the average of the 9 period SMA (the Tenkan Sen) and the 26 period SMA, (the Kijun Sen). In other words, an average of these two SMAs. The Senkou Span A is then plotted twenty six periods ahead and forms the envelope which appears as the cloud.

So, the cloud is formed between the two leading lines which are projected into the future, the Senkou Span A and the Senkou Span B and it is this construction which gives this indicator its unique appearance.

Last there is a fifth and final line which is a lagging line called the Chikou Span, which is the closing price of the period plotted twenty six periods behind.

Once the indicator appears on the chart it can be used in three ways. First, by taking the crossover signals of the 9 and 26 SMAs. So, if the 9 moves below the 26 SMA this gives a bearish signal, and moving above the 26 SMA gives a bullish signal.

Second, is the cloud itself which is the key feature of this indicator, and it is important to realise the clouds themselves reveal several things. First, the thickness of the cloud is important, and just like real clouds, the thicker they are the heavier the atmosphere or pressure. So, a deep thick cloud indicates the market is likely to struggle to break through this area. This is similar to support and resistance, which I am going to cover shortly.

Therefore, if the cloud is above the market this is a bearish signal and if the cloud is below the market, as it is shown in Fig 18.15, then this is a bullish signal.

If the cloud is thin the market could reverse and change direction, whilst a thick cloud suggests a strong trend and a barrier to any reversal in the trend.

With the forecasting element (the look ahead if you like) of the indicator, what traders are looking for is a cloud that is becoming steadily fatter and fatter, reducing the chances of a trend reversal and giving confidence the trend is likely to continue. If the cloud is very thin, or becoming thinner, as it seems to be in Fig 18.15, this suggests a possible reversal is in progress and traders need to be cautious in trading the longer term trend.

With regard to the Chikou Span (the lagging indicator) this is used in the following way. If the line is above today's candle then the market is considered to be bullish, but if it is below today's candle then the market is considered to be bearish in the longer term. On the chart in Fig 18.15 this line is below the last daily candle, so traders can expect a change in trend in due course.

Equally, if the Chikou Span is above the current cloud then the market is viewed as bullish, and if below the cloud it is bearish, so many things to consider with this interesting and little used indicator.

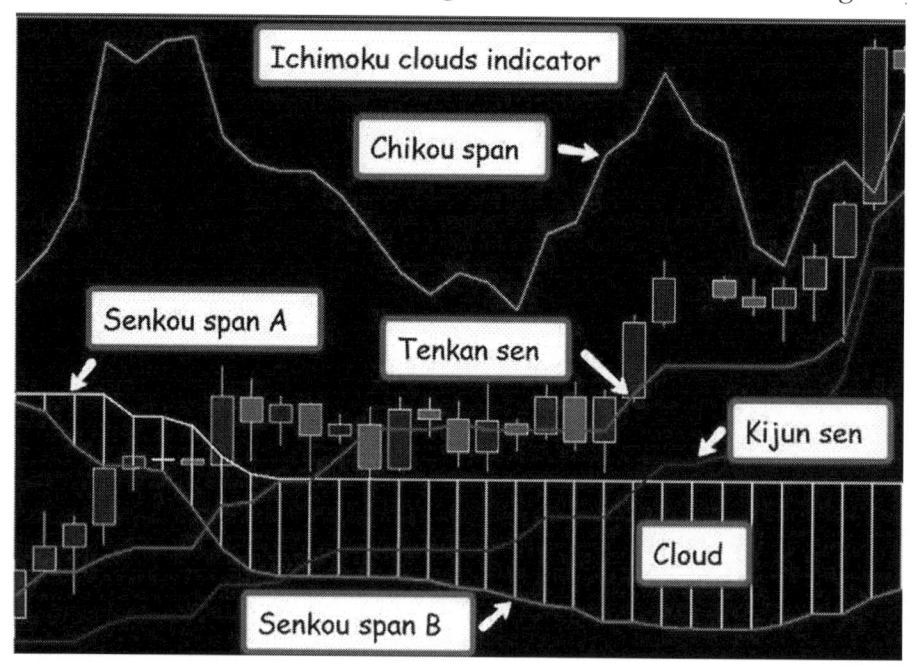

Fig 18.15 Ichimoku

Finally of course, this indicator is always used in conjunction with candle and candle pattern analysis and never in isolation.

As all forex traders know the forex market is unregulated and with no central exchange there is no reported volume. In other words, there is no equivalent to the volume reported in virtually all the other markets, either directly as in the cash markets such as equities or, indirectly in the futures market. However, this is not necessarily a drawback, not least because there are some exciting new developments in the use of tick volume. There are software applications that are increasingly able to mirror what is actually happening in the interbank forex market, by interpreting the tick volume and creating a volume chart to represent both the buying and selling. These applications are becoming increasingly common and as I mentioned in an earlier chapter, tick data is activity or flow and therefore volume. Furthermore, studies have shown using tick data as a proxy for volume can be extremely effective and a reflection of the buying and selling activity in the market.

Volume is therefore becoming ever more important in forex trading, and here I would like to outline in more detail the technique I use, namely volume price analysis. This is the analysis of volume and the associated price action on the chart which is most likely to reveal the future direction of the market. This is a big subject, and one which I cover in great detail in a separate book. However, I would like to cover the basics and explain why it is such an important concept. Not all traders are convinced of the power of volume and price but, I hope to provide sufficient and compelling evidence of its effectiveness.

There are many reasons why, in my humble opinion, I feel so passionately about volume and why it can be considered a true leading indicator, not least because it appears in real time and at the live edge of the market. Furthermore, volume is not a mathematical indicator based on historical price data which is then displayed after the market has moved on. Volume is real and reported every second throughout the day. It is also displayed live in the same way as price appears on the chart.

Moreover, when considering volume and analysing the price action associated with it, the net result is a unique indicator which tracks the market in real time and, perhaps more importantly, any analysis is trader based and not reliant on any external factor.

It has been said many times volume is the fuel that drives the market. Volume reveals activity and whether the buyers or sellers are out in force. Conversely, it also reveals whether there are few or even no buyers or sellers.

A way to imagine volume is to think what happens when the retail stores begin their sales. First, the sale signs go up, promising big discounts on prices. People start to queue to snap up the bargains and as the day approaches the crowds grow, until the doors of the store opens and the crowds rush in. This is volume at work.

There is a similar pattern of behaviour in the financial markets. The market moves lower and the buyers come out and start buying in volume, snapping up the bargains and eventually cleaning out the store.

However, it is linking this activity to the price which reveals what these buyers and sellers are thinking and more importantly what they are doing. A correct analysis of what is happening will not only validate the price action, but also forecast future price behaviour. This is why volume price analysis is so powerful.

After all, to return to the store example, if the sale attracts very few buyers this would be signalled by low volume and prices would have to fall, perhaps quickly, in order to attract the buyers into the store. On a price chart this would be illustrated as a narrow spread down candle (a hammer perhaps), with a high volume bar below, giving a clear signal the buyers are in the market and buying at this price point.

Therefore, in studying volume and its relationship to the associated price action, traders are only looking for two things.

First, confirmation that volume and price are in step with one another. In other words, does the price action reflect the volume and vice versa. If the answer is yes, the move higher or lower is genuine and the volume is confirming the price action on the chart. Volume validates price.

Second, anomalies where the price action does not reflect the associated volume or vice versa, which could be an early warning signal of a potential change in direction for the market

This, in very simple terms, is what to look for in terms of price and volume. In other words, is the volume validating and confirming the price move. If not, then it is question of 'trader beware'.

There are also one or two other factors surrounding volume which are often misunderstood by traders. One is the concept of high volume in terms of both rising and falling prices. The concept of something needing effort to rise is familiar and easy to grasp. Acceleration which increases the power of an engine to drive up hill is also easily understood. The same principle applies if price is to move higher. Volume is required and without it, price simply stalls.

Of equal importance, however, in the context of price is that power is also needed to move prices lower. Fuel is also needed because prices do not move lower simply on gravity. Without fuel, any move to the downside would also stall.

At this stage let me just write a few words about market manipulation. Market manipulation is a fact of trading life. It happens in virtually all markets, with the possible exception of the futures market which is considered a zero sum game. In other words, the exchange regulates and manages this market, and simply matches buyers with sellers. However, even here we have the appearance of the large operators who are able to move the markets, which is once again revealed in volume. Therefore, if a trader buys a futures contract another trader has sold a futures contract. When that contract is closed or expires the profit on one side of the contract will be matched by the loss on the other side of the contract. One trader's loss is another trader's gain.

Meanwhile, manipulation in the equity markets is by the market makers, who are responsible for making the market, and who also have a legal obligation to have stock when buyers want to buy, and accept stock when sellers want to sell. Market makers can best be described as 'wholesalers in stock' repeatedly buying and selling the same stock time and time again. And in order to ensure they have sufficient stock in their warehouse at any time, they use the news to move the markets up and down to either frighten investors into selling, or to encourage investors to buy. This is done using the twin levers of fear and greed.

However, the only activity market makers cannot hide is volume which reveals everything a trader needs to know and whether a market move is genuine or false.

Market manipulation also occurs in the forex market and it is the most manipulated of all for a number a reasons. First, there is no regulation and very little control. Second, the interbank market which sets the exchange rates, is dominated by a handful of major banks who between them control around eighty per cent of all the trading volume on a daily basis. Third, the central banks also play their part via overt and covert interventions. Moreover, it is further compounded by some brokers who trade against their own clients.

And the basic principle of understanding volume price analysis is this. We want to follow the insiders, the market makers. After all, they know where they are moving the market to next, so doesn't it make sense to follow them? So when we are considering volume, we view it from the perspective of the market makers as they cannot hide volume. We buy when they buy, we sell when the sell, and stay out when they are not participating. It is these simple principles which govern everything else.

Finally, just to round off this introduction to what I believe is the single most important indicator, let me include some additional concepts, and then I'll outline how to use volume and price to analyse the market.

Volume is also valid for longer term analysis using end of day data. A swing or longer term trader (or investor) can use an end of day chart with the volume reported to analyse risk appetite and money flow across all markets. This would help to reinforce, validate and confirm the trend in the instrument under consideration. In this case, volume on a longer term chart can give accurate signals as to the longer term trend. For forex traders looking to take longer term positions these trends can be found in markets and instruments such as ETFs and futures.

Intra day forex traders have the choice of using live tick data or the volume which appears in the currency ETFs or futures market. Whichever is used the principles of volume price analysis are identical.

I sincerely hope I have started to make a convincing case for the importance of volume. It really is a unique indicator which, when used correctly, is one of the very few indicators that can give traders a view of the market in real time.

Having looked at volume and its importance as an indicator across all the markets, I would now like to explain volume price analysis and how this technique can be used to identify and confirm signals as they arrive on the charts.

The first step is to set up the volume indicator. This is very easy. Simply select 'volume' from the add indicator tool menu and this will then appear in a separate section at the bottom of the chart. Beneath each candle will appear a vertical bar which is the volume for that particular time period. Fig 18.16 is an example from the MT4 platform.

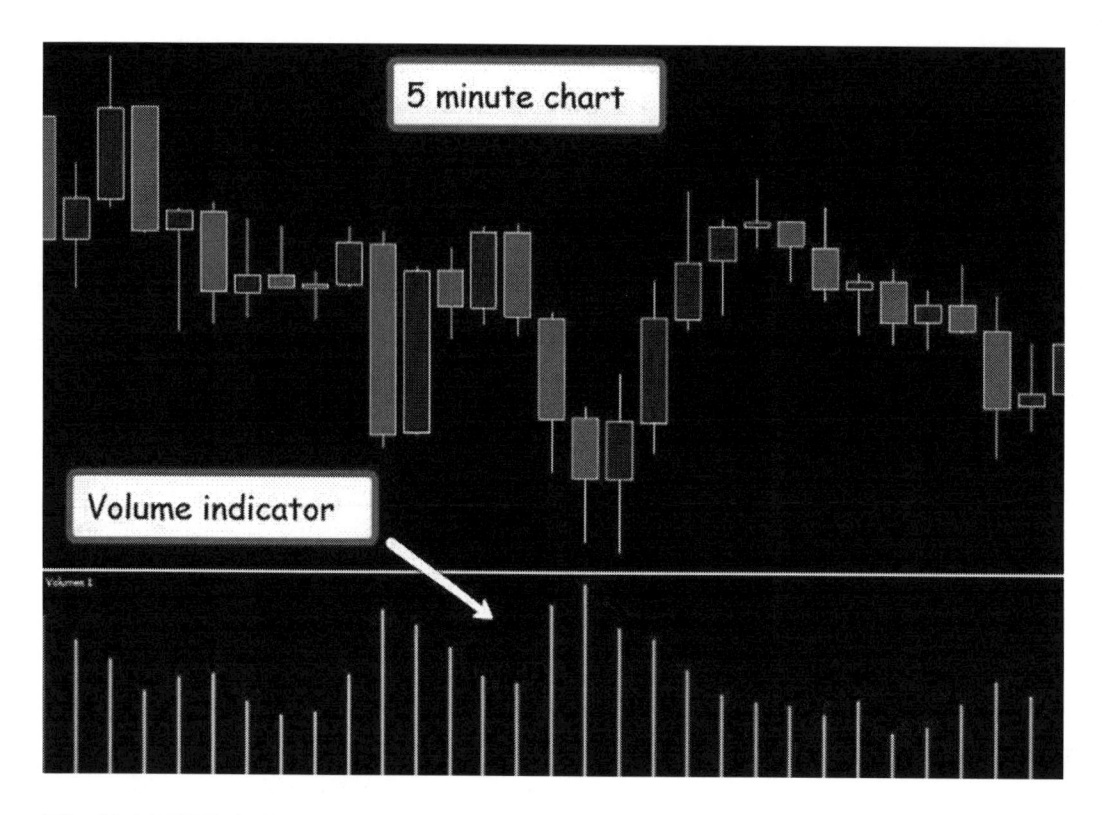

Fig 18.16 EUR/JPY - 5 Minute Chart

Fig 18.16 is a 5 minute chart from the spot forex market and displaying the standard volume indicator that comes with the platform.

The first thing the volume indicator confirms is the activity for the period in question. In equities it would be the number of shares traded, but in this case it is tick volume which is displayed.

Second, when compared to previous bars it is easy to see whether this volume was high, medium or low. This clear visual picture is one of the beauties of volume. The relationship between the volume bars is there to see, can be judged accordingly.

Traders can spot whether any volume bars are high, medium or low instantly. Of course, what these volume bars do not reveal is whether the volume displayed is buying volume, or selling volume. And the answer to this lies in the associated price action, the candles and candle patterns.

This is generally signalled by any anomalies between the volume and price and as such, the anomalies will signal potential trading opportunities and reversals in trend. They will also reveal whether the market makers are buying or selling, or perhaps just sitting on the sidelines and not participating.

The best way to explain this is with some simple examples and all of these are using the spot forex market on the MT4 platform. However, the same principles would apply on a futures chart for commodities or currencies, a cash chart for equities, or on an index chart. All have volume and this will help you when considering price action in related markets, using relational analysis.

The example in Fig 18.17 is a 1 minute candlestick chart with the volume indicator, and the area of the chart I would like to focus on is shown by the rectangular box.

Here the market has been moving sideways for a few bars prior to arriving at the region denoted by the box, with both the volume and price meandering along together and doing nothing of particular interest. The first volume bar appears in the box, and the price action is again narrow, but nothing unusual. However, on the next candle, the price breaks out from this narrow range and starts to move higher and, coupled with this move higher in price, the volume is increasing also.

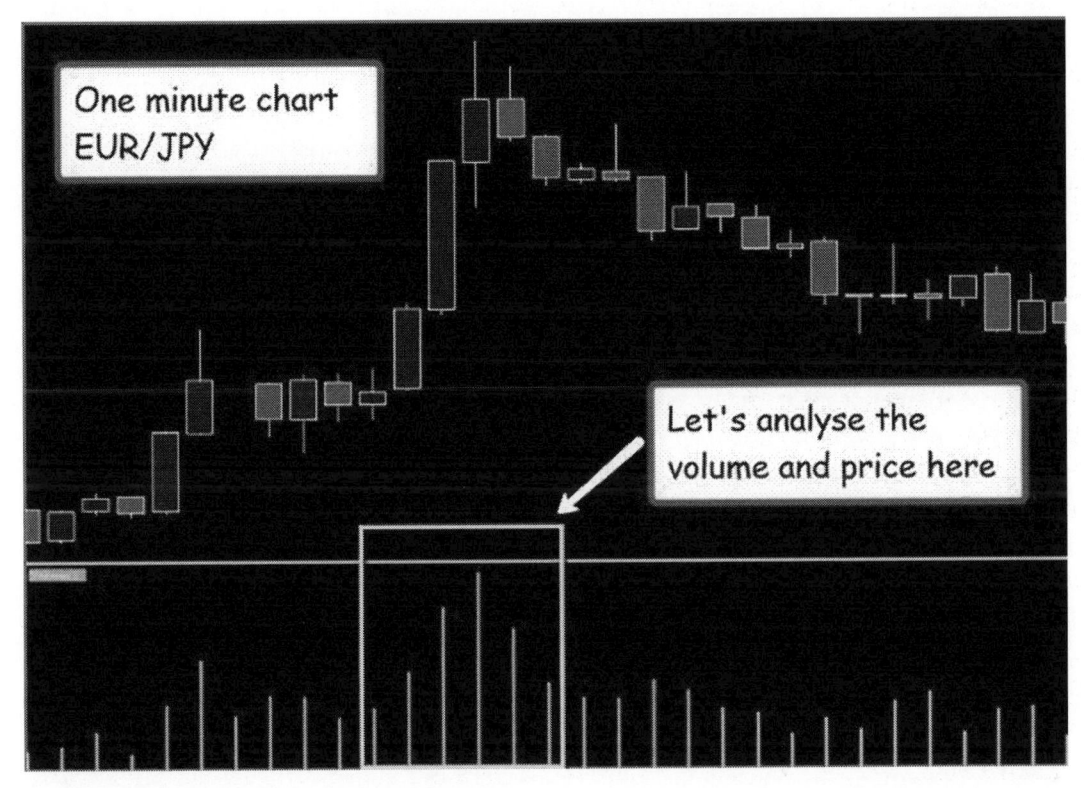

Fig 18.17 EUR/JPY - 1 Minute Chart

This is what traders should expect to see. There is a nice up candle, with no wicks either to the top or bottom, and rising volume accompanying the move higher. The moves in both price and volume are congruent as it takes effort for price to move higher (and lower). Effort is being used to take the price higher and all is well as the price continues to move up, fully supported by rising volume.

As the subsequent bars form, once again the price is rising with rising volume. This time, the volume is higher than the previous bar and the spread of the candle is also wider, which again is what is expected. After all, the wider the spread of the candle, the more volume will be required to push the price higher. So both the price action and the associated volume are in agreement. It also validates the previous candle and volume bar. So far all is well, with widening candles, supported by rising volume.

By the time the fourth volume bar is displayed, the first thing to note is once again it is higher than the previous three volume bars. Volume is clearly rising, but the associated price candle is not as expected. This candle has closed with a narrower spread than the previous three. The price spread on this candle is clearly not in line with the spread of the previous candles and, clearly not in agreement with the volume. If price and volume are directly related and price requires effort to rise, by closing with a narrow spread on rising volume can only signal one thing. This candle is signalling weakness because, if the market were strong this candle should have closed as a wide spread up candle, wider than the previous candle. In fact, it has closed with a narrow spread with wicks to both the top and bottom. Not a sign of strength but, a sign of weakness. This is what the price volume relationship is signalling here.

Therefore, in this instance the volume associated with the price action can only be selling because, had it been buying volume, the price would have risen higher on strong buying. It did not. The price stalled, so clearly much of the associated volume must have been selling volume. In other words, sellers have come into the market at this level and caused the market to stall. If this had been pure buying the candle would have been wide. The price has tried to rise, as shown by the wick on the top of the candle, but the sellers have knocked the price back down. The sellers have not necessarily won the battle, but they have certainly stopped the EUR/JPY in its tracks at this level. All this has been signalled by an analysis of the volume and price. Clearly the market makers are selling into short term weakness here.

This is a clear anomaly and once alerted, traders can now watch for a trading opportunity. The high volume should have seen the price continue higher – it did not, so traders can safely conclude much of this volume is selling volume, as the buyers are losing momentum, and the market makers are selling.

The next stage is the subsequent bar that forms as a narrow spread down candle with average to high volume. This is telling us the price attempted to rise but failed and closed lower. Furthermore, in doing so the resulting candle is an 'inside day' signalling indecision and a possible reversal. It is also important to remember an 'inside day' candle can also be a pause in a trend which may resume once the price breaks above the high of the candle. Alternatively, it could be signalling weakness, and a reversal of the trend.

In this example the subsequent candles fail to break above the high volume up candle at the top of the trend, and candlestick analysis confirms this bullish trend has come to an end with a bearish move likely to start. The question, of course, is whether this move lower is strong or weak, and once again it is volume which provides the answer.

As each subsequent bar forms two things become clear as the trend develops. First, the bars are accompanied by a series of volume bars which are falling and not rising. Remember, for price to move lower, it too requires effort so, if price is falling strongly, expect to see rising volume and not falling volume as shown here. Rising prices require rising volume and falling prices also require rising volume.

Second, over the next 10 to 12 bars, the price spreads on the candles are all quite narrow and price is bearish. So, in this time frame it would present an opportunity to scalp. However, what the price/volume relationships is also telling us is this move lower is lacking momentum, clearly signalled by the falling volume and the narrow price spreads. This chart is sending a very clear message.

First, the 'inside day' candle gave the signal of a possible reversal, and once confirmed presented a scalping opportunity. Second, with falling volumes and narrow price spreads, it is clear the price is not going far, so any short positions are not likely to last very long. The move lower is a pause point and likely to be characterised by low volumes and price consolidation.

This is the conversation I have with myself as I watch each candle form along with the associated volume. What I am attempting to do on every candle, is to interpret what I see in the price, and match this to the associated volume. If there is an anomaly between the two, what is this telling me? Is the volume likely to be buying or selling and is this a possible turning point in the market or merely a pullback?

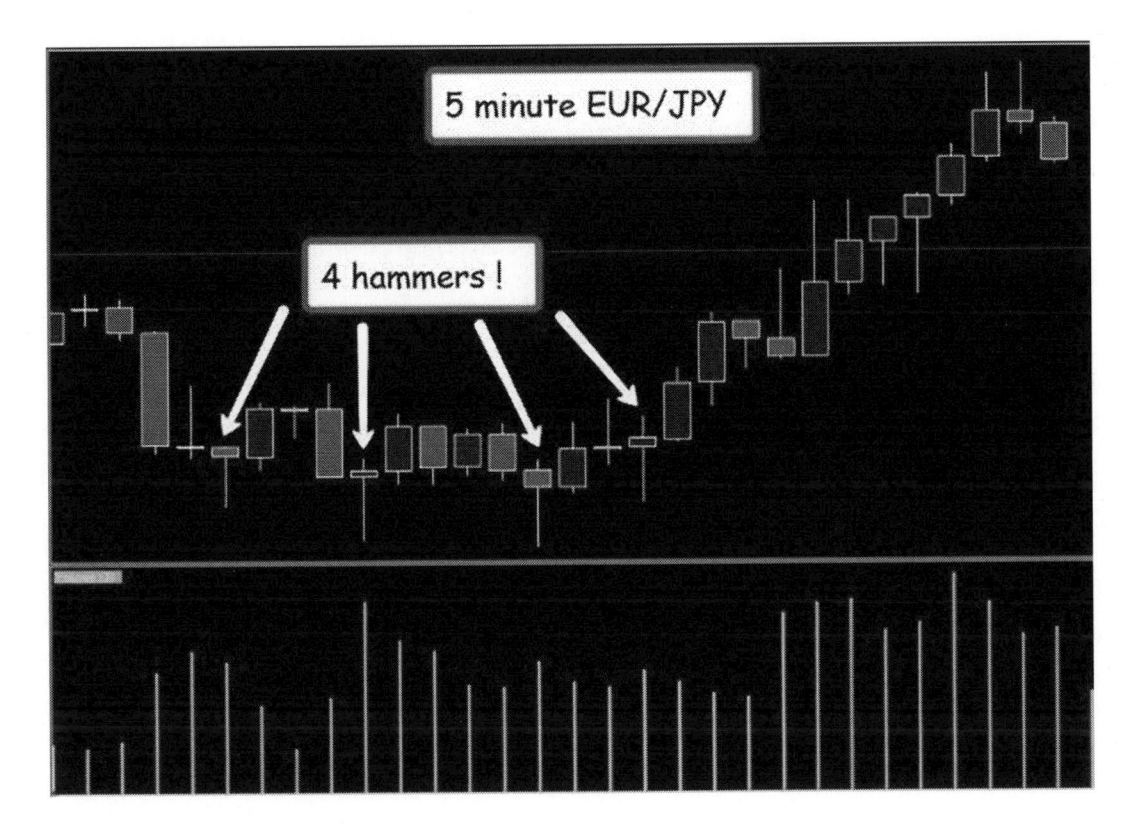

Fig 18.18 EUR/JPY - 5 Minute Chart

Fig 18.18 is a further example of the volume price relationship which yielded a nice long trade on a 5 minute chart, starting with the price action on the left before moving across to the right.

As can be seen on the left of the chart this currency pair has been moving sideways over three bars, on low volume. The price is going nowhere.

Then a wide spread down candle accompanied by rising volume appears on the chart. This is as expected so perhaps the currency pair is preparing to move into a bearish phase, but there is no anomaly here, because a wide spread down candle and rising volume is perfectly normal.

However, the subsequent candle is interesting, and is a shooting star candle in shape, but has appeared at the bottom of the trend. When this happens the candle is often referred to as a gravestone doji. Volume is rising, and the price action is the first signal buyers are coming into the market.

It is the buyers who have tried to stop the market moving lower, but on this occasion have been overcome by more sellers, and the price has been pushed back down to the open. However, the key point here is this is the first sign buyers have entered the market.

This is followed by the first of four hammer candles, all on high volume, a clear signal of buying by the market makers. After all, if this were selling the price would have fallen further. It hasn't. The hammer candles and the associated volume are sending another clear signal this is buying, and strong buying too by the market makers. The sellers have tried to move the market lower but the market makers have stepped in to prevent it falling further, and are simply absorbing the remaining sellers.

The price tries to rise, but the volume is falling on these next two candles, with the second having a very narrow spread. So, whilst there has been confirmation the price is preparing to rally, traders need to wait and be patient. Indeed, there is a further minor sell off in the next candle, but only on average volume. It is clear this is not a strong move lower. It could even be a move to take out stops.

This is immediately followed by the second hammer candle which is accompanied by even higher volume than on the first, sending a very clear signal. Once again the sellers have tried to take the price lower but, the market makers step in once more.

At this point, the price tries to rally on the next bar, but the spread of the candle is narrow, and the volume is above average. In this instance, whilst it is clear the buyers are taking control, there is still selling resistance to be 'mopped up' and this is a perfect example of the point I was making earlier about the power of the hammer candle. It is a strong and powerful candle, but traders need to patient and wait for validation. Markets do not turn on a dime. Selling pressure has to be absorbed by the market makers completely, before the price can move higher and, here is a classic example with four hammer candles of which this is the second.

The market then moves on for the next four candles, up and down in classic consolidation as the buyers and sellers struggle for control. After four of these candles the third hammer candle appears and, once again is accompanied with above average volume. However, the volume is not as high as on the second hammer, but is still buying volume - it cannot be anything else. Once again, the price has moved lower only to be pushed back higher to close near the open to form the classic hammer, and again the market makers are absorbing the selling pressure.

Price rallies once more and the fourth and last hammer candle makes its appearance, which finally confirms the market is preparing to move higher, as the candle is accompanied with above average volume.

Finally, the currency pair manages to break above this sideways price congestion (another key signal which I will explain shortly) and the trend starts to develop, with rising volume and rising prices until the move starts to peter out at the top of the rally, for two reasons.

The first sign of weakness in this rally is the narrow price spreads with high volume. After all, high volume should be associated with wide spread price action in the candle, and here this is not the case as the price approaches the top of the trend. Second, at the top of the trend there is a shooting star candle with above average volume which is validated with a bearish candle on the following bar along with rising volume. This trend appears to be coming to an end.

At this point in any long position, traders should be looking to tighten any stop loss to lock in some profits, or even close out a portion of the position.

Finally, to round off this section on volume and its role as the only leading indicator with price, I would like to finish with another simple, yet classic example in Fig 18.19 as confirmation of the power of this trading approach.

Once again it is an intraday chart, the 15 minute chart. This pair had initially been drifting lower, before picking up some bullish momentum as evidenced by nice wide up candles, supported by rising volume. However, what is clear on the two consecutive wide spread up candles, the volume on the second is lower than on the previous one, signalling perhaps the move is starting to run out of steam.

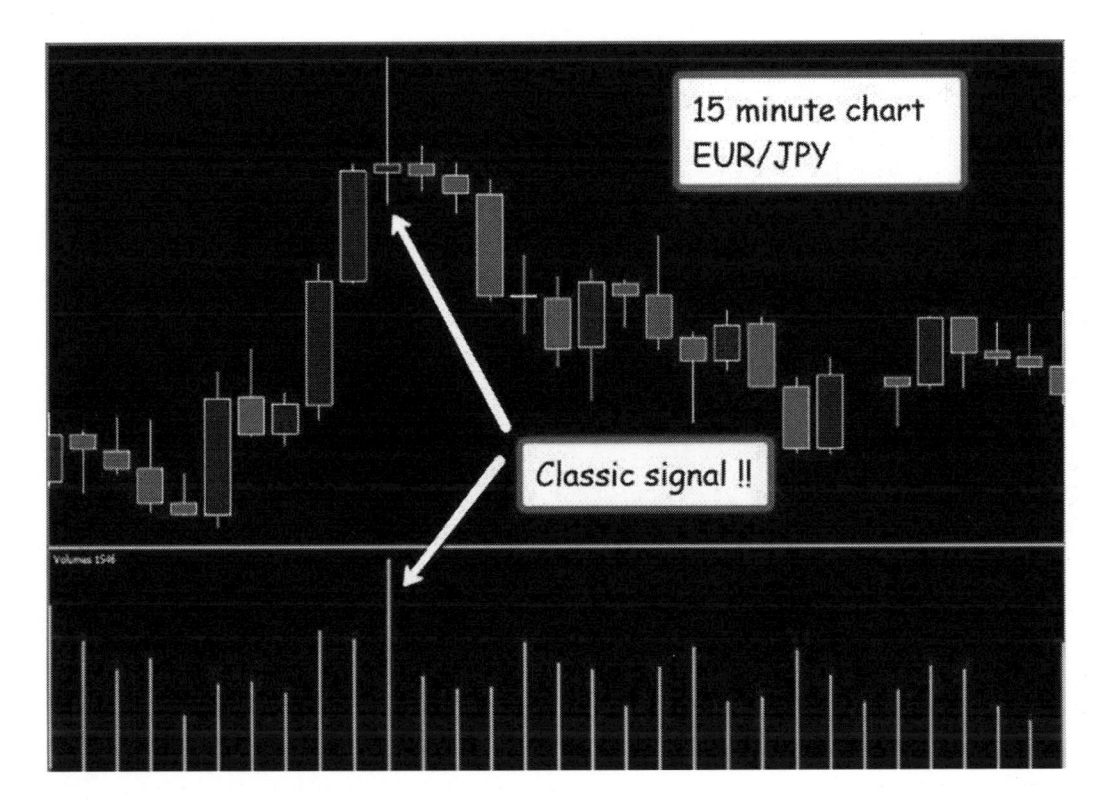

Fig 18.19 EUR/JPY - 15 Minute Chart

This is a purely subjective view and not a signal in itself – it is merely a possible early warning before the appearance of a premier candle, which in this case is a classic shooting star. On its own and in its own right, the shooting star always signals weakness and a potential reversal. The reason is straightforward.

The price has risen, pushed up by the buyers, but the sellers have come into the market and knocked the price back lower, to close near the open. What gives the candle such authority now is the significant volume associated with the price action and here is a classic example of a powerful reversal candle, with huge volume below. The volume here **must** be selling volume, and there is a lot of it.

What is clear is there has been a huge amount of effort to push the price higher but, all this effort has failed and the move is now looking very weak. The market makers are selling into weakness. Clearly, if all this volume had been buyers, the candle would have been wide and up, and not a reversal candle. In other words, the price would have continued higher, but it hasn't. The market is now resistant to higher prices and regardless of the effort put in by the buyers, they are immediately overwhelmed by the sellers.

This is the descriptive picture being presented by the combination of price and volume. The message is clear. Expect the market to move lower, and soon. The market makers are selling and selling strongly.

With this signal, traders are now ready and waiting. By checking other indicators, and using the analytical techniques I am going to cover in the next chapter, these will validate this price action. Trading success is all about quantifying risk. It's why I use a three dimensional approach in my trading.

Boil it all down to the essence of what we are trying to achieve, and its simply that - to quantify the risk. On the balance of the information I have from my relational analysis, weighted with the fundamental picture, and validated with volume price analysis, is the risk high, medium or low? That in a nutshell is all we are trying to achieve. Overlay this with multiple time frames and hey presto - risk is quantified.

It is the price volume relationship that gives traders the visual signals to prepare for a reversal. Price and volume leading the way once again.

As I mentioned earlier I have recently published a separate book which covers this subject in much more detail. Here I have just introduced you to the basics of volume price analysis, but if you are interested in discovering more, the book details are on my personal site www.annacoulling.com and you can find this one and many others on Amazon in both Kindle and paperback format.

So having covered the principle technical indicators, I now want to examine some other key analytical tools and techniques which are essential concepts in technical analysis.

Chapter Nineteen
Technical Analysis Techniques

The paradox is you have to listen to the market and yet form an independent opinion.

Kerr Neilson (1950-)

In the previous chapter I looked at some key technical indicators which can help to make sense of price behaviour. They are also the ones I use, with volume being the the most important.

I started my trading career as a student of price and volume and, it is the methodology I have used consistently in every market and instrument I have traded and invested in. I accept not all traders and investors will agree with this approach. However, there are, as they say, many roads to trading success. For me, using volume and price to determine market direction seems the most logical and continues to deliver consistent and profitable results. I explain the methodology in more detail in my book, A Complete Guide to Volume and Price Analysis.

In this chapter I would like to consider a number of simple techniques which traders can also use to determine changes in market direction. These techniques are rooted in an analysis of the chart itself and the patterns created by the candles themselves. The first of these is what traders refer to as 'support and resistance'. Support and resistance are price levels or zones created on a chart. They are points at which price pauses, stops and sometimes reverses.

Support & Resistance

Support and resistance is one of the cornerstones of technical charting, but here too with so many traders watching the same charts, the question is whether there is an element of a self fulling prophecy. However, regardless of the reasons why these levels or zones are created, it is still a powerful and important trading technique. Support and resistance works on all charts in all time frames, from tick to time charts. It is used in all trading strategies, from intra day scalping to longer term position trading and investing. Furthermore, as a technique it is simple and easy to use, and is one which also helps in any validation of price behaviour.

Support and resistance price levels and zones are created because markets primarily move in one of three ways: markets go up, markets go down and markets move sideways. It is when markets move sideways areas of price congestion (or consolidation) are created. These are zones where the price simply moves up and down within a relatively small price range, neither up nor down, but simply oscillating like a vibrating string. These levels are defined by price alone, nothing else.

Like other technical analysis techniques, these movements can be found in all time frames and in all markets and instruments. Price congestion is so important because it is when the market has paused and the bulls and the bears are battling for control of overall market direction. This battle can continue for some extended time. It could could be minutes, hours, days or even weeks as neither side is able to dominate the other. This results in this 'choppy' price action, with the market moving sideways creating a region of price congestion. Markets spend more time moving sideways than they do in trends, generally between 70% in congestion and 30% of the time in a trend, making it all the more important to identify any new trend as quickly as possible, which is why support and resistance is so important.

However, there is a far more significant reason to be able to identify and recognise when markets are in their congestion phase which is this. It is during these periods the market is preparing to either develop a new trend, or to continue an old one. It is in within these regions of price congestion, that trends are borne. The analogy I always use is that of the salmon, returning upstream to spawn their young. It really is that simple. Many traders become impatient when markets move sideways. Not me. And if you remember in the introduction to technical analysis, I mentioned Wyckoff's second rule, that of cause and effect. Price congestion is a classic example. In other words, the longer the market is in a congestion phase, the longer the trend will last once the market breaks away. And of course, one of the key signals we use to validate any breakout is volume. Now perhaps you can start to see how everything fits neatly into place in this three dimensional world. In addition volume also reveals the lack of participation in such phases of price action, and the classic example here is ahead of a major news release. Price action narrows, spreads become small, and volume drops away to low levels.

In Fig 19.10 I've highlighted what is referred to as the price 'congestion area' with two lines, one above and one below, which show how the market has remained contained within a narrow range for some time. Beginning with the lower or support line, what is happening here is the market has been bullish for some time, but starts to run out of steam, as all markets do. No price ever goes up in a straight line or down in a straight line, but in a series of steps, rather like the stairs and landings in an old fashioned house, first rising, pausing, then rising again.

On the chart I have drawn two lines, the upper line we call the resistance, and the lower line we call support. The market has moved higher and fallen back to the lower line before rising again, then falling back once more creating what we call an area of price support at the lower level.

In other words this price area on the chart is acting as invisible support, a platform or safety net, if you like, which prevents the price falling lower every time it arrives at this level and tests.

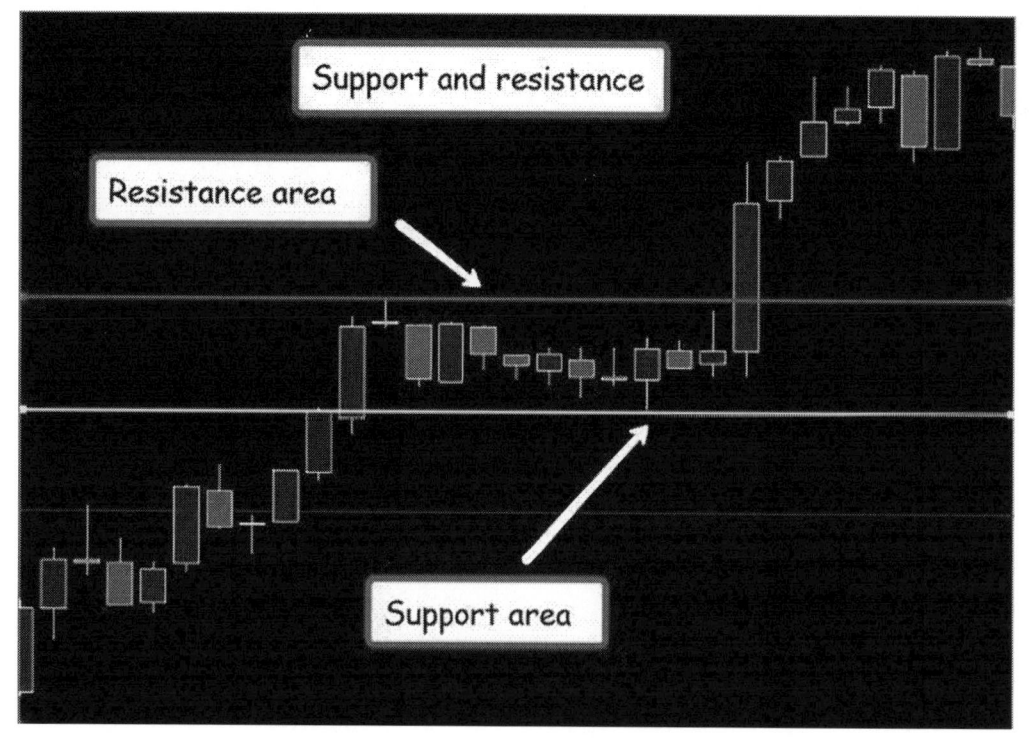

Fig 19.10 Support & Resistance

The longer the price continues to move higher and lower within this price region, the more defined becomes the area of support. In this case eleven candles have formed in this narrow range. So this lower level defines a level of price support, as each time the market looks as though it may be falling, the invisible support area comes to the rescue and helps the price recover once again.

The second line, above the price action, is referred to as a level of price resistance, since here it is the exact opposite of price support. Each time the market reaches this price level it bounces off just as if there were an invisible ceiling in place. This stops the market moving higher and creates the so called 'price resistance area' on the chart.

Traders will see this action happening in all time frames and in forex, the longer a currency pair is in sideways consolidation, the more important this price region becomes for reasons I will explain.

At some point, of course, the market does eventually break away from the price congestion area and develops into an important price trend. However, the price area left behind then becomes a key price region for future price action, and the best way to explain this is with the example annotated in Fig 19.11.

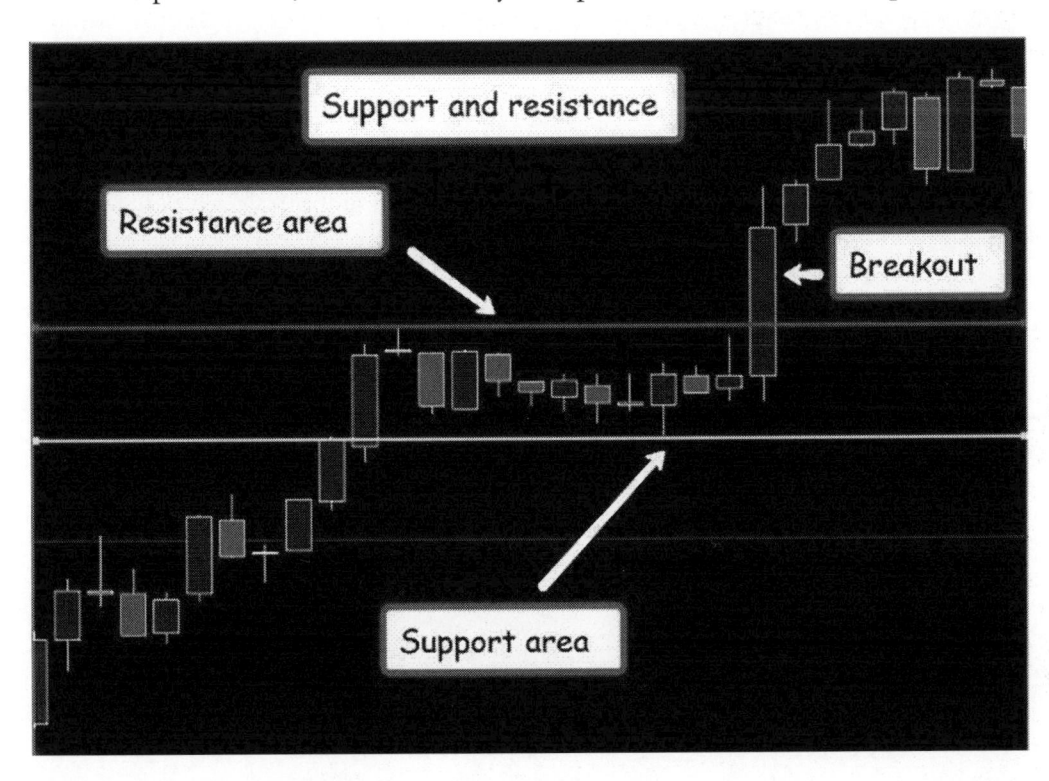

Fig 19.11 Support & Resistance - Breakout

On this chart the most important candle is the one annotated at the point where the price action has moved away to the upside of the price congestion with the 'breakout' candle.

In this case, the resistance level has now been breached, the glass ceiling broken, and the market is now moving firmly higher. However, at some point in the future the market may move back down to this price level to test the price congestion. The original area of price resistance has now become a potential area of price support. What was the 'ceiling' has now become the floor, and a new area of price support.

The easiest way to imagine support and resistance is to think of it in terms of standing in front of a house. If the front facade of the house were removed the house would be in cross section with all the floors and ceilings exposed.

If movement through this imaginary house were only through the floors and ceilings, it is easy to see how a ceiling would become a floor and vice versa. This is the principle on which historic price congestion works, creating these floors and ceilings in all time frames. In our example here, what was the ceiling has now become the floor and as a result provides a powerful platform of support to the move higher for two reasons.

First, it is a 'natural' area of protection if the market moves back to test this region in the future, as it takes additional effort to move back and through these deep areas of congested price action. So it provides traders with an additional 'comfort level', a natural place to position a stop loss for example. Second and more importantly, any breakout from such a trading range sends a powerful signal of a new trend starting to develop.

In other words, the market has moved higher, paused, built a platform of support for itself, before moving higher once again, with this solid platform now acting as support. This is the principle of a breakout and if this is accompanied by the requisite and associated volumes, gives traders a clear and unequivocal signal of a new trend and a valid entry signal, or continuation of an existing one.

In the example in Fig 19.11, the market had been bullish, it then paused, moving into sideways congestion, before breaking out and continuing higher. This is a powerful signal as the market is clearly not prepared to fall and even if it does reverse in the short term, there is a strong and natural platform of price support built into the chart. This is often the case, once a move away develops, the old region of price is often retested.

The opposite of this action is where a currency pair has started to sell off, but then pauses and moves into sideways congestion and as before, the resistance level is shown above and the support level is marked below. The pair remain in this tight range for some time and at this point, traders have to be patient and wait as the pair could reverse from this level bouncing off the developed platform of support and return to a bullish phase. Alternatively, the pair may continue with the current trend, but either way traders simply have to wait.

As we can see in Fig 19.12 the pair eventually breaks through the support line, which then becomes resistance to any attempt to reverse higher. Once the price has broken through the support, this is now a powerful signal the bearish trend is set to continue, and with a strong platform of price resistance now above, is adding further downwards pressure to the move lower, as well as providing protection to any reversal in the short term.

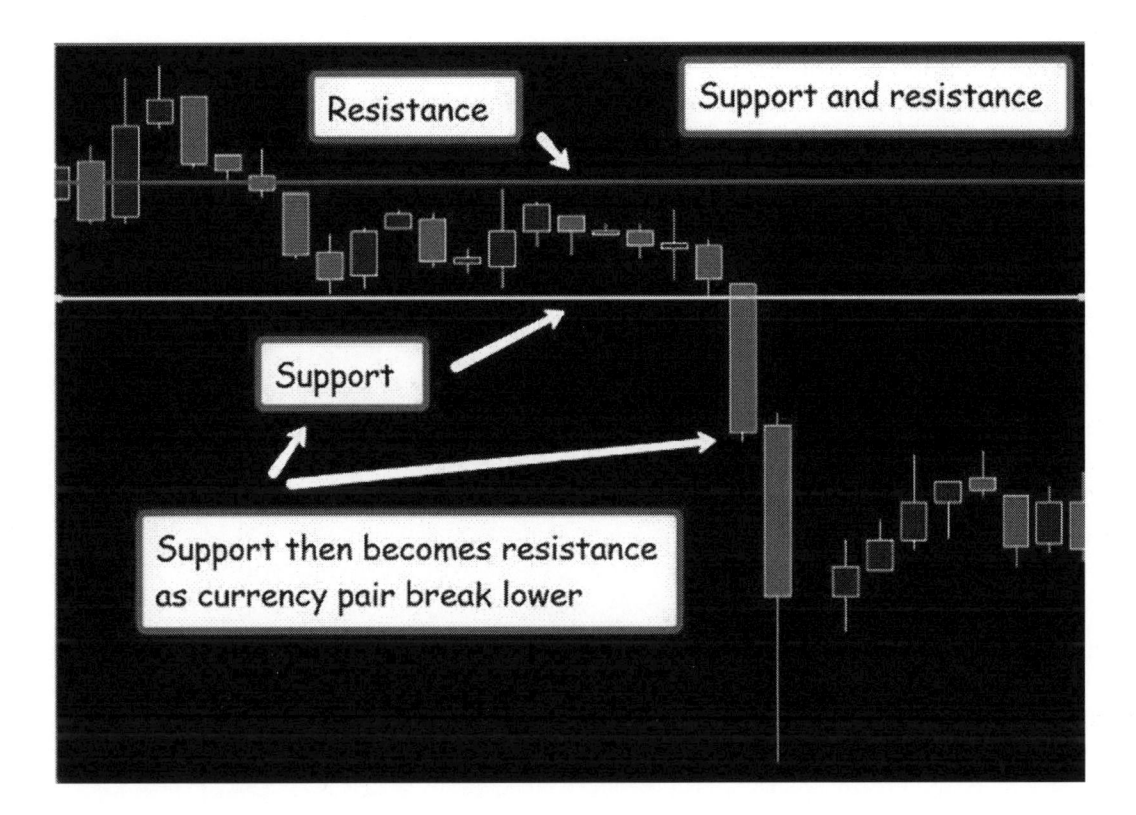

Fig 19.12 Support & Resistance - Bearish Breakout

Whenever a market starts to trade in a sideways congestion area, traders know at some point the market will eventually break either to the upside or downside. A breakout will occur, so patience is the order of the day.

Second, and following on from the first point, once a break occurs from this range, this is an excellent signal the market is now set to trend in the direction of the breakout. If the market breaks to the upside, the trend should continue higher with bullish momentum and conversely a break to the downside should see a bearish trend established in due course.

Finally, these areas of price congestion provide natural barriers to any retracement of the market should it return to re-test these areas of support or resistance. These price regions can also be good places for any stop loss. Areas of price congestion also offer an extra layer of protection, so if the break is to the upside and a long position is taken, any stop loss could initially be placed below the underside of the price congestion. Conversely, in any break to the downside and a short position is entered, the stop loss could initially be placed above the price congestion area.

In both cases, the price congestion acts as a natural price barrier to any minor change in direction of the market.

There is a further aspect of support and resistance in that not all areas of support and resistance areas are created equal. These areas or zones come in all shapes and sizes. However, as a general rule, the governing factor for their strength or weakness is time. Put simply, the longer the price congestion lasts, the greater the significance and strength of any breakout.

For example, any breach of support or resistance in a market or instrument that has been consolidating over a number of days or weeks, will be extremely significant. Plus, the impact and duration of the break is likely to result in a strong and positive trend. Moreover, this is a direct reflection of Wyckoff's second principle of cause and effect. In other words, the greater the cause (time it takes) the greater the effect (consequent price move).

By contrast, any break away from price consolidation on a short time frame chart may not be so dramatic and will simply be proportionate to the time frame in which it occurs.

This is also a reason why trading using multiple time frames is so powerful, since this gives traders an insight into the market's likely direction, not only on the intra day consolidation phases which constantly recur, but also on the price action in the slower time frames. By comparing and contrasting the price action across multiple time frames traders can become more confident in their trading decisions.

For example, if on a longer term chart the market has broken out of a recent, strong period of sideways consolidation, any trade taken in a lower time frame is likely to have some momentum and trend strongly, as a result. This not only gives traders confidence, but also helps to reduce the risk on the trade itself.

This is one of the many advantages of trading using three time frames. Here, it is not just about validating price and volume, but also includes support and resistance together with candles and candle patterns. After all, if a valid breakout occurs on an hourly, chart any trade taken in the same direction in a lower time frame is likely to be less risky, be more successful and deliver more profit. Trading multiple time frames is a technique I teach in all my online and live seminars. So please do consider using this approach. It's immensely powerful and will give you a very different perspective along with lowering the risk.

The further point I want to make about support and resistance levels and areas of price congestion relates to time, and in particular the number of times an area is tested before it is breached. As a general rule, the more times a level is tested before it is broken, the greater its significance and strength, if and when it is re-tested. In other words, if a support or resistance level is created with just two tests before breaking out, this is weaker than a level created with three tests or four and so on. The same principle applies when levels are re-tested in the future. So, if an area of support or resistance is tested in the future, the more times it holds and fails to break, the stronger it becomes and the more likely it will hold.

To summarise and to try to put it into context. First, support and resistance levels are not a guarantee nor are they a cast iron trading certainty. Instead, they are an extremely reliable analytical technique and more often than not they work, and work well.

However, traders should not think they are some form of concrete wall that will never be broken. You should consider them as elastic bands and build in some tolerance to the levels on the chart. This also applies to drawing the lines of support and resistance. As traders we need to adopt an element of 'poetic licence' when drawing these lines on a chart and remember that technical analysis is an art, and not a science.

Second, support and resistance is a fantastic tool for anticipating and planning trading opportunities in the future, provided traders are prepared to be patient. Whenever markets are trading in a narrow range it is easy to become impatient and try to second guess which way the market will break.

It is difficult to be patient, but once the break has occurred it generally heralds the start of a good trend, and is therefore worth the wait. Always remember, that drawing support and resistance lines is not an exact science. At best it can only ever be a 'best fit'. It is never possible to try get all the highs and lows of the candles to line up. Some candles will have their wicks above the line and others below. What is important is that most of the extremes are touching these lines. Not every single candle will line up, and the market is never that precise anyway. Therefore, a 'best fit' is good enough. Furthermore, it is important not try to create levels of support and resistance when they are not there.

Another feature of support and resistance is a 'fake out' which is where price appears to be breaking out, only to pull back into the congestion area once again. This can, and does happen and it is sometimes difficult to avoid being caught out. The solution is a combination of patience, judgment and experience. One solution is simply not to enter any trade until there has been a clean 'break and hold' away from the sideways congestion. However, it is a judgment call and one which is, again, more art than science. For volume traders however, this is not an issue as volume always confirms if the move is genuine or fake.

In summary, support and resistance is another of those essential tools for validating and identifying future price behaviour. And one last point. These areas are also excellent in terms of judging the return on any trading position. After all, if there is deep congestion overhead, the market is likely to struggle in any mover higher. If congestion is light or perhaps some distance away, then the market is likely to move higher easily. This is the best way to judge a trading opportunity - not some absurd risk/reward ratio of 2:1 or 3:1. This is nonsense. Use the charts to give you this information, and nothing else.

Chart Patterns

A similar and related tool to support and resistance also used for validating price is the use of patterns on a chart. These are specific patterns of price action which are created in all charts and in all time frames. What is remarkable about them is they are consistent and recur. However, one reason they recur could simply be the market's memory as it runs into old price areas where weak traders are looking to exit positions. Alternatively, these patterns could be the result of a self-fulfilling prophecy.

Indeed, there continues to be a heated debate as to whether all technical analysis is nothing more than a self-fulfilling prophecy, given the number of market participants who are all looking at the same charts and using the same tools. Suffice to say, traders need to know and understand certain patterns just recur and they should be monitored, not only on the chart being traded, but also in slower time frames to assess the risk of any trade.

There are many patterns which have been identified, but here are my top five and the ones I like to watch and use in my own trading and market analysis.

Triangle

The first of these patterns is in fact a group of three which are all related and form a triangle pattern on the chart. This pattern is similar to support and resistance in that the triangle represents a market which is consolidating in a tight trading range. On this occasion however, the price action is contained within a triangle formation which can be drawn around the price action generally in one of three ways.

It can be drawn as a pennant, a rising triangle and, finally a falling triangle

The pennant pattern is so called because the shape resembles a pennant or flag. This pattern is also referred to as a 'flag', but I prefer to call it a pennant. As always the best way to explain the pennant is with an example.

The example in Fig 19.13 is the hourly chart for the CAD/JPY (Canadian/Japanese Yen) currency pair. The pair is clearly moving sideways, but this time the highs and lows of each price candle are gradually moving in an ever smaller range within the trading period. What is happening is that the low of the session is rising each time, and the high of the session is falling each time. This ultimately results in a typical pennant formation, which is a falling sloping line bounding the price action to the upside, and a rising sloping line bounding the price action to the down side. This creates this unique pattern which resembles a pennant attached to a flagpole, as the price continues to move in an ever narrower range. As the price action moves it tightens towards the pennant.

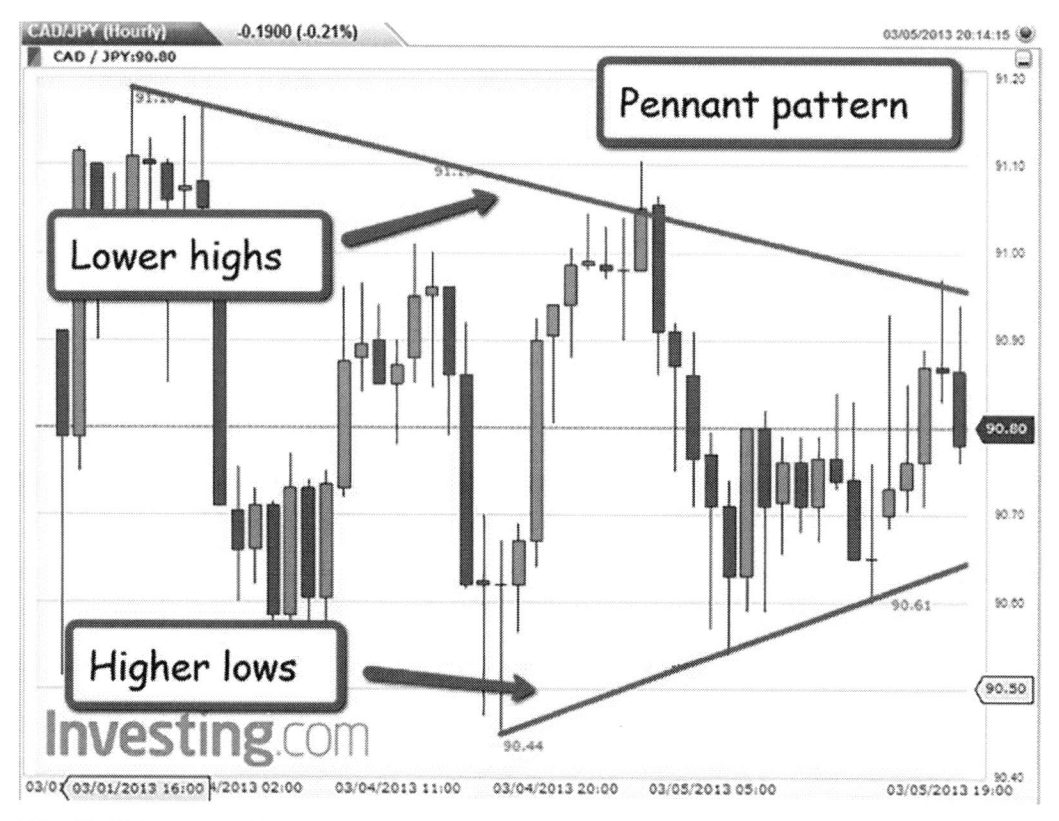

Fig 19.13 Pennant Pattern

In many ways this type of price action can be likened to a coiled spring, which is being wound tighter and tighter until eventually it releases all its energy in an explosive break, and this is typically what happens with a pennant formation.

The market winds itself up with the price action moving in an ever narrower range, as it moves toward the point of the pennant until suddenly, the coiled spring unwinds and all the pent up energy is released, generally resulting in a dramatic and rapid move away from the congestion area.

The issue with this pattern is traders never really know which direction the market will move on the breakout. However, this is not a problem as we are not in the business of guessing, so must simply wait for the market to reveal which way prices are likely to go. And, just like support and resistance patterns, once a pennant starts to form patient traders know once price breaks away, a sustained trend is likely to follow.

Again, as with support and resistance formations, time is also a key factor. In other words, the longer the price action continues, the more explosive the eventual breakout and the more weight this carries for the pattern. For example, a pennant on a five minute chart will have less weight than one on an hourly chart which, in turn will carry less weight than one on the daily chart. Therefore, it is vital traders check for these chart patterns across all time frames

There are two other triangular patterns which are variants of the pennant, and these are known as the rising triangle and the falling triangle.

Rising Triangle

The rising triangle which is shown in Fig 19.14 is an example of where, once again, prices are consolidating in a narrow range.

Fig 19.14 Rising Triangle Pattern

However, in a rising triangle the low of each candle is higher than the previous and results in a rising sloping line to the underside of the triangle. Meanwhile, the high of each candle tends to remain fairly flat, at much the same price level resulting in a horizontal line.

The key difference with both the rising and falling triangle pattern is that traders have a fairly good idea of the direction of the breakout. In the case of the rising triangle it is the line to the underside of the triangle which is significant. It is this line which holds the clue as to the likely breakout, which in this case is likely to be to the upside. In a rising triangle each candles closes with a higher low, suggesting upwards momentum. This is logical because if the lows were lower, this would suggest a weak market. Clearly on every candle, there is less desire to fall, since each low is higher than the last, which is why traders can expect to see this pattern break higher. This is what the price action is telling us.

However, with all price patterns traders have to be patient, wait and not second guess.

Falling Triangle

The opposite of the rising triangle is the falling triangle. In a falling triangle the high of each trading candle is lower, resulting in a downwards sloping line, and the low of each session creates the horizontal base of the triangle, as shown in Fig 19.15.

In the case of a falling triangle pattern, traders can expect to see a break to the downside signalled by the lower highs of each session. The price behaviour is clearly signalling weakness, since the highs of each candle are struggling to move beyond those in the recent past. A falling triangle is a signal of a bearish breakout once the floor of the triangle is breached.

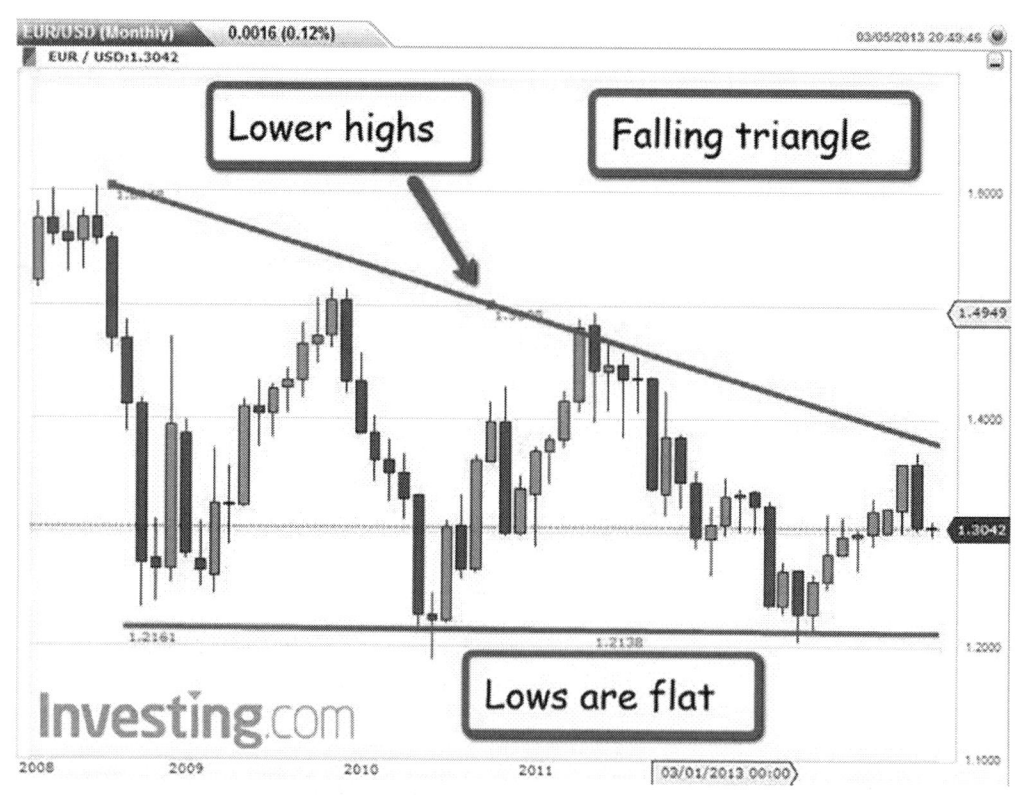

Fig 19.15 Falling Triangle Pattern

These are the three triangular patterns I am always looking for in forex (and other markets), simply because they provide some excellent clues as to future breakouts once a pair starts to consolidate. They are worth waiting for, but patience is key.

Any breakout from a consolidation pattern is, of course, only the start and there are strategies which traders can use to take advantage of this type of price action. These include using options. Whilst these can be complex and a topic for a separate book, nevertheless option strategies are becoming increasingly popular with retail forex traders. Currency options also include strategies for longer term trading as well as short term scalpers and in both cases, chart patterns play a big part of the trading strategy.

Triple Top

Finally, to round off this section on my top five chart patterns, the last two I always look for are, triple tops and triple bottoms. And the reason for including these two is that they are often the signal for a major turning point in a market or instrument.

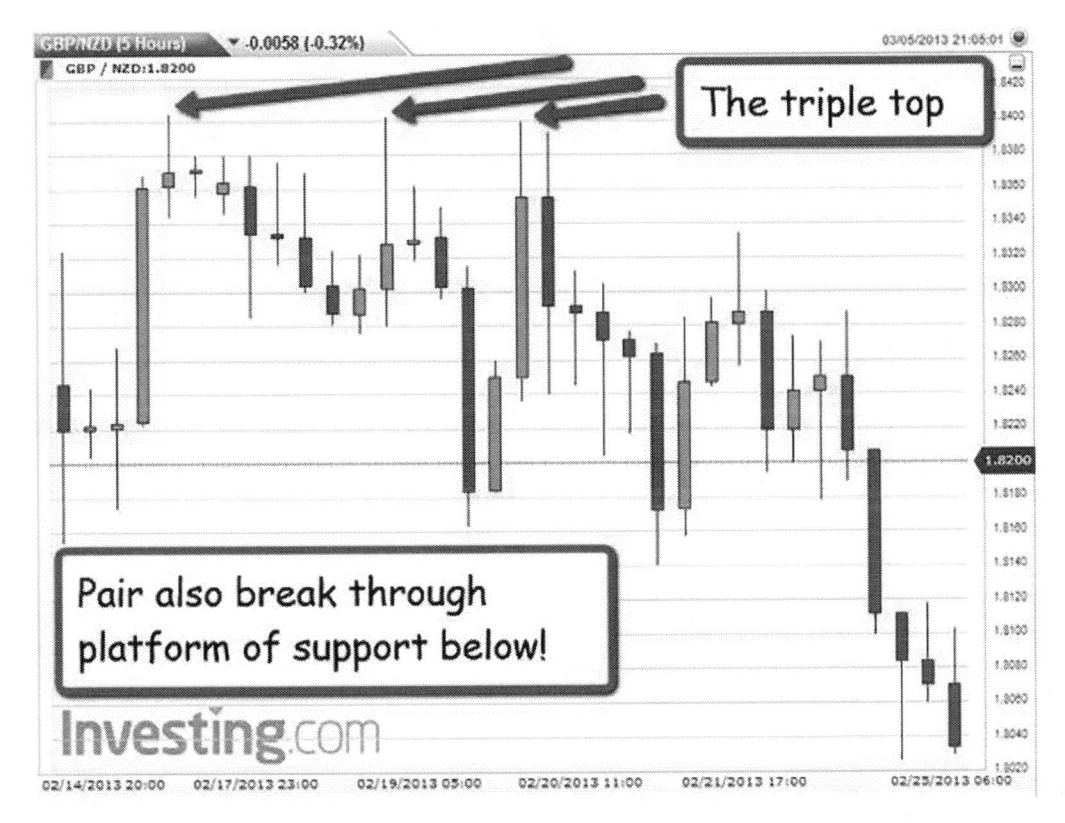

Fig 19.16 Triple Top Pattern

The triple top example in Fig 19.16 is a good one. A triple top occurs on a chart at the top of a rally, at a point when a market is beginning to struggle to move higher. Indeed, in this example a fourth top was almost formed.

In the price action associated with a triple top a market tries to break higher once, then a second time before trying for a third time. With this failure, prices are likely to start moving lower, simply because the market has failed to break this price level on three separate occasions which suggests weakness. Furthermore, any move lower from a triple top can also be fast and furious.

The triple top price action is a classic sign of weakness in a market, and with all these patterns, they can be seen in all time frames. Naturally, any triple top on a longer term chart such as a daily or weekly would also suggest any bearish trend lower is likely to last for some considerable time. What is also interesting from the example in Fig 19.16, was the break below the platform of potential support, which failed to hold the move lower, adding further bearish momentum to the price.

But once again traders have to be patient, and wait for the third failure to occur. The pattern is given additional weight if each top results in a strong reversal candle such as a shooting star or a bearish engulfing pattern. In this example there were two shooting star candles which would have been validated with the associated volume.

Triple Bottom

The triple bottom pattern is the mirror image of the triple top with traders expecting to see the market move higher and develop a longer term bullish trend.

In the case of a triple bottom the market has reached a price level which has subsequently created a strong level of support. At this level the market refuses to fall any further, and following a third attempt should then start to move away and develop a sustained and longer term trend higher using this support platform as the base.

Fig 19.17 Triple Bottom Pattern

What was also very nice in the example in Fig 19.17, was the break through the potential resistance, which then gave the break to the upside some additional momentum.

As with the triple top, the triple bottom will have added significance if the lows are accompanied with strong reversal candles such as a hammer, a bullish engulfing candle, or even the long legged doji candle, and the longer the timeframe the greater the significance and impact.

So, in summary these are the five candle patterns I look for across all the markets and instruments, both on the short and longer term charts. There are, of course, many, many other patterns such as the 'head and shoulders' and 'cup and handle'. However, in my years of watching charts and trading, the five listed here have been the most consistent. They are also straightforward and very easy to spot on a chart. You cannot miss them, and when these patterns reverse or break out, the resultant trends are generally strong and can last a reasonable length of time, regardless of the time frame being traded.

The advantage of these patterns is that once validated they can also give you the confidence to stay in a trade. However, as always as traders we must remember the creation of these patterns is not scientific. Price points will not always line up precisely, so there must always be a degree of leeway when drawing any lines or joining up the price points to mark up a pattern.

Flexibility in drawing lines and joining price points are also applicable to trend lines which I have already covered as part of support and resistance. The lines drawn on a chart to mark the areas of price consolidation for support and resistance are trend lines, but on a horizontal plane. Two parallel lines are drawn which define the upper and lower range of the oscillating sideways price action.

Trend Lines

The trend lines in this section refer to those which help to mark the price action as it moves higher or lower. However, the forex market, like all other markets and instruments, never moves in a straight line. Instead, markets move in a series of steps, creating a series of higher highs in an uptrend, and a series of lower lows in a downtrend.

From the example in Fig 19.18 here the market has been rising steadily and creating the classic pattern of series of higher highs, and higher lows, as the trend develops further. It is these price points which are joined together to form the trend line. The trend line is now a channel with an upper and lower line, as with the support and resistance channel.

Fig 19.18 Up Trend Pattern

In this case the channel is sloping upwards to define an upwards trend, and equally in the example in Fig 19.19 the trend is sloping downwards with a series of lower highs and lower lows creating a channel of price action.

From these examples some traders may question the use of these lines given the trend has already formed. However, the purpose of creating the trend lines is what they reveal about price support and resistance.

Fig 19.19 Down Trend Pattern

Trend lines are not simply there to state the obvious. In other words, that a trend has been created. Instead they are there to help identify the points at which the price may reverse. They help to identify points of price support and resistance which are one of the key building blocks of technical analysis.

These points of support and resistance are equally important once a trend has begun to develop. However, an important point to note is that traders should never try to create a trend where none exists. It is very easy to fall into this trap, and the easiest way to avoid it is to only draw a trend line when there are three or more price points which can be joined with a straight line. Then, and only then has a valid trend line been created. Some technical analysts consider two price points sufficient. I don't, for the simple reason that in using only two points a trend line can be made to fit what a trader wants to see, and not what is actually happening. So my advice is to always use at least three points.

The second reason for always using three points is this also suggests a stronger trend is in place. It relates back to classical support and resistance theory where the greater the number of times a price level is tested, the stronger that level becomes. The same applies with trend lines, and with three points in place traders can assume a strong trend is underway.

As I mentioned earlier, the key to trend lines is not that they necessarily reveal whether there is an up or down trend in place, but that the lines identify the potential areas of support and resistance in the trend as it moves higher or lower. And it does this in two ways.

Looking back at Fig 19.18 where there is an example of a rising trend, it is clear that, as the trend moves up, the market pulls back and tests the trend line. This then provides support to the upwards move higher and, as such, gives traders three signals.

First, the trend is likely to continue higher as the trend line has provided a level of support. This is important as it helps traders stay in any existing positions as the price moves higher and therefore are less likely to be panicked out of any trades.

Second, this can then provide traders with a potential entry signals, if not already in a trading position. Finally, the upper trend line acts in the same way and can provide traders with a possible exit point, particularly if entering a new position as the market could pull back once it hits the upper trend line, which is the resistance line.

Naturally, at some point, one or other of the trend lines will be broken, and the price action will break above or below the price channel. This could signal two things. First, the current trend has broken down, and secondly it could be the start of a reversal, and the subsequent creation of a new trend in due course.

The same is true for a downtrend which is detailed in Fig 19.20. In this example the market is moving lower in a series of lower highs and lower lows, and the trend lines are in place. Each touch and move lower from the upper trend line is a confirmation of the trend remaining in place, and as such is a potential entry point if no trade is already in place. Alternatively, it could also provide confirmation to stay with a trade already taken. The move lower is also suggesting a potential target for the trade as well as an exit point as the trend moves lower.

Fig 19.20 Down Trend Pattern Second Example

Ultimately the upper trend line will be breached, signalling a potential reversal and establishment of a new trend in due course.

As with all aspects of support and resistance and chart patterns, time is key. For example, a trend in a one day chart will have more significance than a trend on a one hour chart, which in turn will have more significance than a trend on a five minute chart.

Equally important is the number of times the trend lines are tested. Just like support and resistance in sideways moving markets, the greater the number of tests of an upper or lower trend line, the more strength this will give to the overall trend. Most good charting packages will have the option to create trend lines automatically simply by highlighting a particular price point on the chart.

Finally, to round off this chapter, and also to complete this introduction to price action and technical analysis, I would like to end with one of the most powerful techniques any trader will ever learn about price behaviour, and which really pulls together all these concepts and ideas.

This technique is the cornerstone of the price action methodology I teach in my seminars and live trading rooms.

As I wrote earlier in the book, markets really only move in three ways. Up, down or sideways, but spend the largest percentage of their time in congestion or consolidation, moving sideways. This is why the concept of support and resistance is so important in understanding price behaviour. But, how can we identify where the price is at any point in this cycle?

In order to identify what the price action is doing, and where it is in this endless cycle, it is necessary to break the price action down into the stages of this process. A process which is repeated over and over again in all time frames, and in all markets, and to explain the principle I want to use the example as shown in Fig 19.21

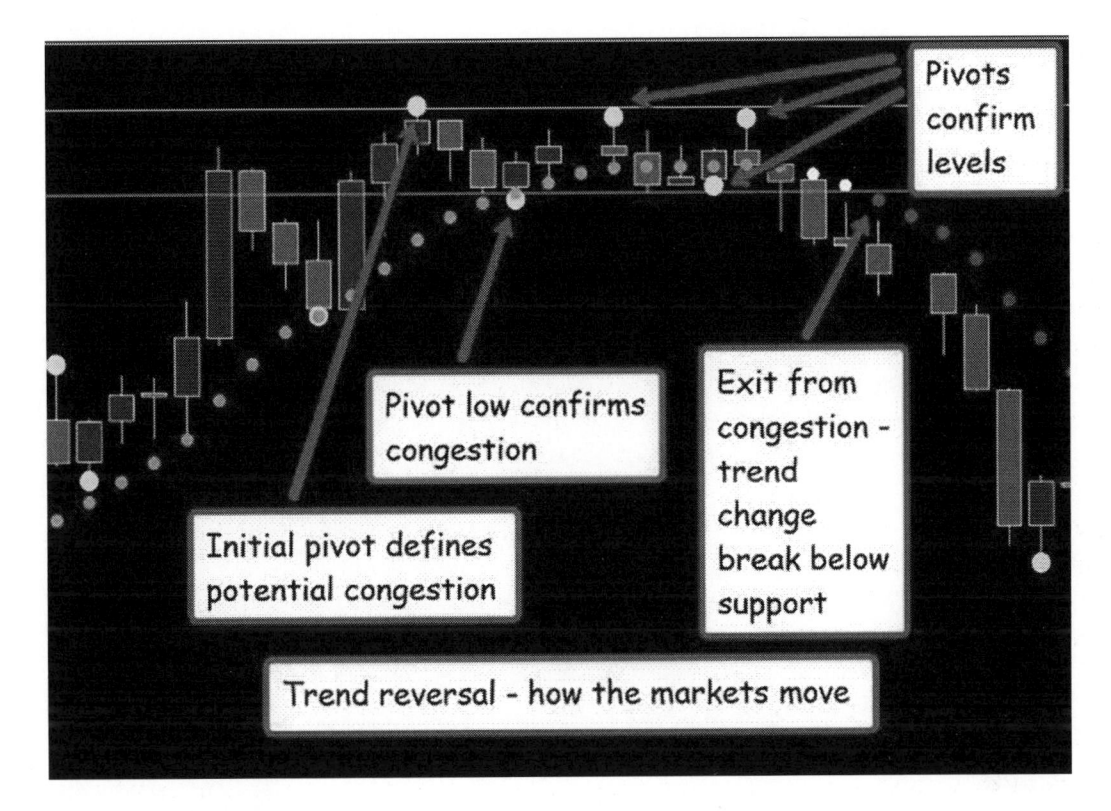

Fig 19.21 How The Markets Move

In this example it's clear the market has been rising steadily. Throughout this phase of price action, the market rises, pulls back but then rise again, and continues on its journey.

At some point however, a pivot high is formed as shown by the first dot which marks the start of a 'potential' congestion phase. At this point, it is not clear whether the price action is entering a congestion phase, or whether this is simply another minor pause point before the price action reverts higher once again.

However, on this occasion, the market pulls back for the first two bars, and then on the third candle a pivot low is posted. With the posting of this second pivot, two levels of a potential congestion area, have been defined. The pivot high to the upside and the pivot low to the downside. The next step is wait for either level to be confirmed, and two bars later, a second pivot high is posted, which confirms the upper region of price resistance as shown by the line above.

The market then moves back lower again, and a further pivot low is posted, confirming the lower support level, before moving higher once again to post a further pivot high. There is now an extremely well defined area of congestion, defined by the pivots to the support and resistance areas.

In addition, the trend dots have flattened, clearly signalling and confirming the price action is preparing to enter into a congestion phase of the trading cycle. The price action then breaks out of the congestion zone, defined by the two lines, and starts to move lower, confirming, that on this occasion we have the start of a trend reversal.

With deep resistance now overhead, this gives us a good, potential low risk entry position as the price moves away from the congestion phase.

This price behaviour is repeated endlessly in all markets and instruments. In forex it can be seen in every currency pair and in every time scale. It is the power of the simple pivots which help to define these areas so clearly, with the trend dots then adding further clarity to the overall picture. The first pivot to form gives an initial signal of the potential start of a congestion phase, and provided a subsequent pivot low is formed shortly after, this defines the upper level and lower level of the initial congestion phase.

It is important to note at this point the market may simply continue higher from the pivot low, and not post another pivot high, in which case this was simply the normal pattern of pull backs and reversals that are all part and parcel of price behaviour. Indeed, on the extreme left, there is an example of where the market posted a pivot high followed by a pivot low, but with no subsequent pivot high to confirm the congestion and set the levels in place, the market simply paused and moved on. The lack of a subsequent pivot high simply meant the trend remained firmly in place at this point.

A second example in Fig 19.22 is where the trend continued and did not reverse, but simply moved into congestion, before moving on again in extending the trend further. Here, the market had been moving lower, and the price action posted two congestion phases in the same trend here.

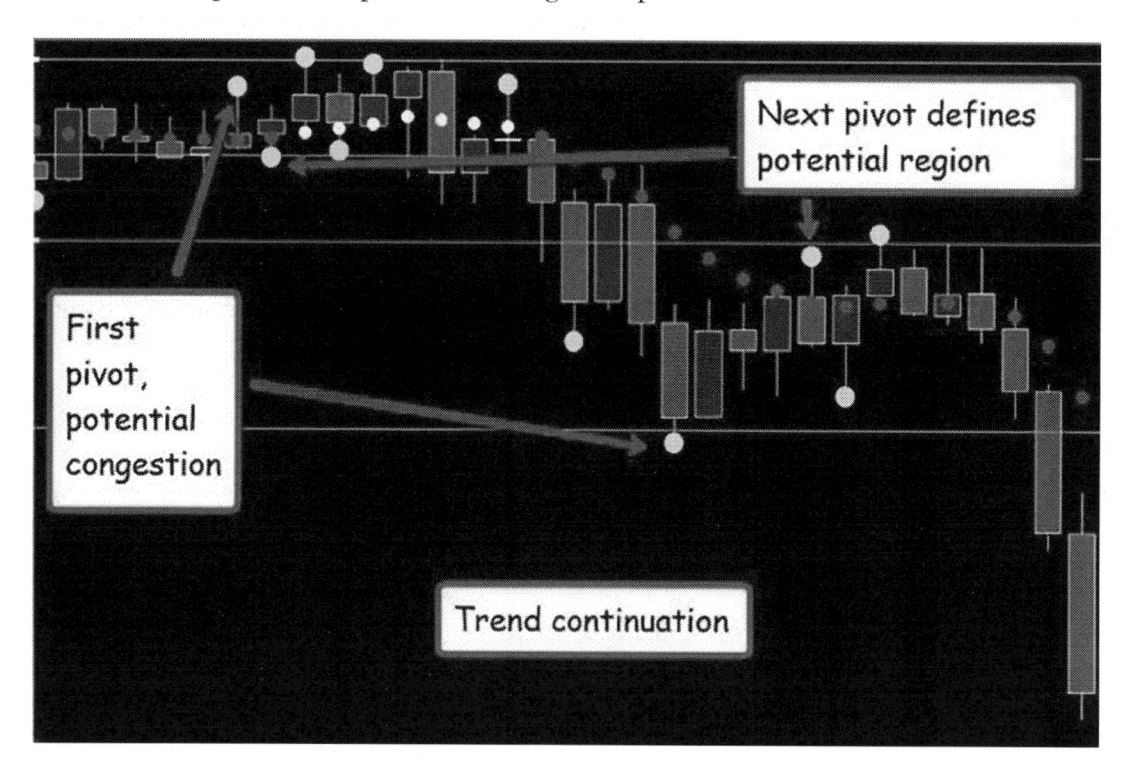

Fig 19.22 Trend Continuation

First, the price action moves into the initial congestion phase, and posts a pivot high and pivot low, which sets the potential level for the support region, followed shortly after by a pivot high, which sends a signal the price is potentially moving into a congestion phase. The next pivot low confirms the floor of support before two further pivots are posted to the resistance level. The trend dots flatten to confirm the price behaviour, before there is a break below the price support area, with the trend dots moving lower and also changing colour to confirm the trend remains in place.

This price action is then repeated at a lower level, with the pivot low forming first followed by the pivot high to define the resistance level once again, before the third pivot forms to confirm the support area once more. The trend dots go flat, but on this occasion, do not change colour, and ultimately the price breaks below the support floor once again, to confirm the bearish trend remains firmly in place for the time being.

This is the price behaviour the markets follow every day, and on every chart from tick based to time. It is the function of price behaviour, which once understood, is easy to interpret and follow, and using some simple tools, indicators and techniques, coupled with the power of price support and resistance, will truly give you an insight into market behaviour which will set you apart as a master forex trader.

This principle of price congestion is another I cover in detail in my book on Volume Price Analysis, as it is a key concept and goes hand in hand with volume and price analysis. The single reason price congestion areas are so important is this. The problem we all have as traders, whatever the instrument or market, is to identify when a trend is developing, and to take advantage accordingly. Easier said than done. However, this is the power of a congestion phase and being able to recognise this in real time at the live edge is key, and the same applies to trends and trend development.

Congestion phases are the spawning grounds for trends, and just like salmon returning up river to rear their young, is is here trends are created and borne. From there they develop and grow and eventually breakout, and just like the young salmon, return to the sea as fully grown fish. The salmon is the analogy I use all the time to explain congestion phases on charts. I cannot stress their importance too strongly. Many traders view them as 'lost' trading opportunities, and impatient to trade, they are then whipsawed out of the market time and time again.

Markets moves sideways for a reason. They are building strength for the next phase in a move, which may be a continuation or a reversal. It doesn't matter. One thing we can be sure of is this - when the market does break out, a trend will develop, and as traders, all we have to do is to validate that breakout using volume and price analysis.

Understanding where we are in the journey of price action, is what price congestion is all about, and using the simple process outlined above, the pivots give us simple signals of where we are in the journey. They are markers, signposts, street lamps if you like, marking the side of the road, and lighting our path ahead. Once we are in a congestion phase, all we have to do is wait, be patient and once the move away from this region occurs, to validate it using volume price analysis, which itself is then validated using multiple timeframes.

Technical analysis and VPA of course apply to all markets. When using our relational techniques they can be applied to charts for bonds, indices or equities. They work on futures, ETF's and spot markets. A chart is a chart, and provided there is volume displayed, we have the ultimate in analytical techniques. Not everyone of course is a believer. I started my own trading journey using volume and it has shaped my trading career over the years. I hope it will do the same for you.

When combined with my three dimensional approach to trading, I truly believe this is the only way to succeed as a forex trader. As I have said many times throughout this book, the forex market is the most complex of all the capital markets, but I hope that in reading so far, you will be able to take away, some if not all of the knowledge and experience I have tried to convey here. You may feel slightly overwhelmed, but trust me - learn a little every day, and you will slowly become that master forex trader we all desire to become.

In the final chapter I would like to round off this book by considering some of the characteristics of currencies and currency pairs, take a look at the majors, the cross pairs and some exotics, as well as explain the currency matrix.

Chapter Twenty
In The Currency Jungle

You have to learn the rules of the game. And then you have to play better than anyone else.

Albert Einstein (1879-1955)

In this, the final chapter, I wanted to try to leave you with a sense of the individual currencies and currency pairs you will be dealing with in your journey to become a master forex trader. I've deliberately used the term 'jungle' in the title, as the world of forex trading can be precisely that to those who simply jump straight in. Some of the dangers are more obvious than others, but I hope in reading this book, you will at least be aware of some of them, if not all.

My purpose in the final chapter is to try to explain the characteristics of the principle currencies and currency pairs, along with the cross pairs and some of the exotics. The good, the bad and the ugly in the jungle if you like. Each has a personality of it's own, but one which changes according to the counter currency of the pair. In addition, I also want to leave you with another important concept, which is rarely explained, but which is a key forex trading strategy and is what I call the 'currency matrix'. The currency matrix plays a crucial role in my own trading, and I hope it will also play a part in yours.

However, let's start by looking at each of the individual currencies, and then broaden out into the pairs themselves, but before I start, let me give you some general thoughts if I may, based on my own experience.

Many books on trading will suggest, and perhaps even advise that you only ever trade the major currency pairs. How wrong can they be. Yes, I fully accept the spreads on the major currency pairs will be tighter and generally more liquid. However, in ignoring the cross currency pairs, you will be missing out on some wonderful trading opportunities. In the last few years, and certainly since the start of the financial crisis, trading volumes in the cross currency pairs have increased dramatically, as speculators and investors have sought out alternative currencies, driven by a variety of factors. Not least by the problems with the US dollar and the euro. Artificial weakness with one, and political intervention with the other.

Trading both of these currencies has become something of a lottery in recent times, and the halcyon days of trending markets driven by 'free floating' exchange rates have long since disappeared. As I have tried to explain throughout the book, the rules of the forex market have changed, and changed forever, and we as forex traders have to adapt and change with it.

Those books written ten years ago, suggesting the majors were the only pairs to trade, are outdated and out of step. The currency wars have seen to that, and with these set to continue for some time to come, we have to change and change fast in order to survive. Remember, in the jungle it is survival of the fittest and as master forex traders we are guerrilla fighters now. Fast and agile. The old adage of the forex market being a strongly 'trending' market is gone, not forever perhaps, but certainly for the next few years. This is how dramatically the market has changed in just a short period.

We have to be aware of what is happening and change our approach and tactics accordingly. High frequency trading is also here to stay, another game changer, and another trend likely to get stronger, despite the authorities imposing 'speed limits' on such activities.

Therefore, I hope the above has given you some food for thought. It is what I believe and how I trade, and to become a master forex trader, it is how you will have to think in the future. The days of simply trading in the EUR/USD are long gone, and in fact this is now one of the most difficult pairs to trade. What a difference a decade makes.

I will be starting with the currencies themselves, before moving onto the major pairs, the cross pairs, and rounding off with some of the exotics. Then we'll look at the currency matrix.

US Dollar

Still a safe haven, and likely to remain so, although other currencies are starting to nibble away at this once traditional role. As forex traders understanding market sentiment towards the US dollar should be paramount. Therefore, the dollar index is always the first port of call, and I like to use the FXCM version as it gives me a much clearer picture, particularly for intraday trading. All the technical analysis techniques covered in this book can be applied to this chart.

Understanding the US dollar is key.

Euro

Political with a capital P. The problem with the euro is trading it without an opinion. Almost impossible, since the currency has been written off so many times, by so many people it is difficult to ignore the chatter. The euro, in its present format will go - eventually, but with the Chinese reducing their dollars in favour of euros, not just yet. Because it is such a political currency it is fiendish to trade with any certainty, and price action is often illogical.

In many ways the markets are now so inured to bad news in Europe, that as each subsequent crisis unfolds, the reactions become less and less volatile. Indeed, a minor crisis is often welcomed as 'good news'! In stark contrast to the US dollar the euro is increasingly seen as a high risk currency. When risk is on, the euro will often rise. However, with politics at the centre and with only one economy which keeps the euro alive, not easy or straightforward.

Yen

Safe haven and politics all rolled up in one neat package. The darling of the carry trade and another funding currency to match the US dollar. Protected and loved by the Bank of Japan, the yen will always come first when any decision has to be made. As interest rates start to rise, watch the yen weaken further and faster as the carry trade comes into play once again.

British Pound

In a state of flux right now due to Brexit. Extreme intraday volatility which looks set to continue should no divorce agreement be reached with Europe. Extremely difficult to trade with any certainty post Brexit. It will revert to its original character of staid and steady in the next few years, and become straightforward once again.

Australian Dollar

A solid and well managed currency, but which catches a cold each time China sneezes. Commodities hold the key, and in the last few years, the currency is increasingly seen as a safe haven, but with a 'risk' label due to the high interest rates and carry trade drivers. Expect to see the currency strengthen as interest rates rise globally, with hot money flowing in, provided the Chinese economy continues on track.

Canadian Dollar

Just as the Australian dollar is linked to its largest trading partner, China, so the Canadian dollar is heavily influenced by its next door neighbor, the US. Strength or weakness in the US economy will always impact Canada directly and quickly, which can make the USD/CAD a tricky pair to trade. In addition, commodities play their part with oil in particular, and if we throw the yen into the mix, trying to establish what is driving the currency can be difficult. Nevertheless, another solid currency representing a well managed economy. Remember the weekly oil stats release on a Wednesday, will impact the Canadian dollar more than the US dollar, even though the data is released in the US.

New Zealand Dollar

In the majors, the preferred currency of the carry trade, with subsequent flows of hot money, although in recent years this has become less of an issue, with the interest rate falling below that of the Australian dollar. However, once rates start to climb again, watch for buying of the currency, particularly against the yen. A great 'trending' currency as a result, but when the trend reverses, watch out - they can move equally fast in the opposite direction as money flows out again. The Australian economy also plays a part, as one of New Zealand's largest trading partners, and of course commodities are in the mix, although soft commodities are more significant. In fact, China has recently become New Zealand's largest export market for dairy based products, such as milk powder, butter and cheese. Indeed the NZD came under pressure recently following a problem with milk powder exports to China.

Norwegian Krone

A very tricky currency to 'put in a box' in any well defined way. Norway is certainly stable, and extremely wealthy, and in many ways similar to Switzerland in this respect, particularly given its huge oil fund. Yet the currency struggles to be accepted as a 'safe haven' by investors which is rather odd, given its huge current account surplus. Oil, of course, is one of the determining factors for the currency, but in a currency whose volumes can be light during the trading day, volatility can be an issue. One opportunity on the horizon with the Krone is the prospect of rising interest rates due to the housing market which has been booming recently. This may force the Norwegian central bank (Norges Bank) to step in and raise interest rates, much against global trends. With rates in Europe falling and a possible increase for the Krone, this could see the development of a longer term trend, particularly if coupled with any move higher for oil.

Swiss Franc

Two words sum up the Swiss franc - 'safety' and 'security'. Over the last few years Switzerland has increasingly been seen as another 'safe haven' country, under pinned by gold. Unlike Norway, overseas investors have been flooding in and buying the Swiss franc, particularly from Europe. The SNB has since given up supporting the currency having removed the floor. Swiss interest rates remain in negative territory and look set to do so for some time to come. Gold underpins everything.

South African Rand

Moving to some of the more exotic currencies which can offer excellent trading returns, but equally can be extremely volatile and fast moving. The South African Rand is a case in point and a currency influenced by a variety of factors. The first is commodities and gold, then comes demand from China, and finally we have the interest rate differentials. At the current rate of 6.5% this is attractive, but for how much longer? After all, as major currencies start to move higher, with Australia possibly leading the way, the decision is then between a 'risk safe haven' high yield currency vs a 'high risk' high yield currency.

The recent weakness in gold has also been a factor, and as with many other countries dependent on China, any slowdown in the economy will be reflected directly in the rand. As an exotic currency it is extremely volatile with wide spreads. Japanese investors have been increasingly dominant in this currency moving into higher yields, underpinned by gold, but with the resurgence in risk, these investors are now selling the currency and moving back into 'risk assets' in particular Japanese and US equities, with the rand being sold as a consequence. As an 'exotic' currency, this may not be available on regular trading platforms, but can be traded as a future through the CME.

Mexican Peso

The Mexican peso is one to watch, as it is poised to become a key currency for forex traders over the next few years. If this is not on your list - do consider it for the future. The Mexican economy is increasingly seen as stable, with a central bank that has managed the financial crisis well, and with the transition almost complete from a commodity driven export market to one built on technology, the peso is the one to watch. Overseas investors are flooding into the country for all the right reasons, and whilst the interest rates are attractive for the 'hot money' speculators at 8%, the flows here are manageable, and not purely speculative. As a result, the peso has been strengthening against most of the major currencies, and once again for investors and longer term speculators, a choice between a volatile currency offering high yields, against a stable currency with lower yields, it is really no contest. Expect to see further strength in the peso against the major currencies.

As with the rand, if this is not available on your trading platform, the CME offer futures and options under emerging markets.

Korean Won

The VIX of the currency world, which unlike the Japanese yen tends to weaken when the economy is weak, and strengthen when demand begins to pick up. Therefore, expect a return to strength once global markets begin to emerge from the carnage of the recent crisis. The currency is extremely volatile and indeed it is rare to see a candlestick with no wick. Generally they have wicks to both top and bottom. Very much a currency for longer term trading based on an analysis of the fundamentals and economic cycles initially.

The Major Currency Pairs

Having looked at some of the principle currencies, along with some of the more exotic currencies, which may become, 'majors' of the future, let's now look at the major currency pairs, followed by some of the cross currency pairs, and how these characteristics are reflected.

EUR/USD

This may be the most widely traded currency pair in the forex market, but it is one of the most difficult. On one side we have a political currency now considered high risk, and on the other we have the US dollar, safe haven, yet increasingly manipulated by the FED policies. This pair is always promoted by brokers as the one to trade, primarily because of highly competitive spreads. This may have been the case a few years ago, but in my view this is no longer a valid argument. It may be very liquid, and is generally the pair that has the tightest spreads in the market, but these are about the only benefits. This is a pair I rarely consider, and rarely trade. It is a wolf in sheep's clothing. Billions of dollars have been lost by speculators shorting this pair. Each time there is a new crisis in Europe, the latest being in Italy, the COT report shows the same patterns, with a massive build in short positions. The ECB step in with supporting rhetoric, the storm passes and the euro duly recovers.

Furthermore, the EUR/USD is a classic example of just how dramatically the forex market has changed over the last five years. As I said in the introduction to this book, the rule book has been torn up, and this is one of the casualties. Any book on trading forex, written before 2008, would have suggested the FX markets trend strongly, are driven by interest rate differentials, and that the EUR/USD was the place to start given the depth of liquidity and strength of the two currencies. None of this is true at present. It may change in the future, but not in the short term. So my advice, is to look elsewhere, and not start here. There are many others pairs to choose from, and the cross currency pairs in particular offer increasingly good trading opportunities.

USD/JPY

This is another currency pair where we can tear up the rule book. Once upon a time, this pair was considered almost impossible to trade, and certainly not a 'novice' pair with two 'safe haven' currencies battling for supremacy. Then along came QE, which both central banks have embraced with enthusiasm. In the case of the Japanese, rather too enthusiastically as the BOJ prepares to release its 9th and most aggressive version yet. The BOJ are desperate to weaken the yen further, and to date they have succeeded in grand style, making this one of the 'no decision' trades of the year. But remember, when global interest rates start moving higher once again, the yen will be sold even more strongly, with any counterbalance effect from the US dollar, only having a muted effect.

After all, if the carry trade explodes back in the market, which it will, the yen will be the prime candidate once again, with strong trends in this and other yen based pairs. Furthermore, with the yen, when risk on appetite is in the ascendancy, the Japanese will be selling the yen and moving into equities, and giving the BOJ a further helping hand. All good news for the Bank of Japan, moving forward. In contrast the Federal Reserve's attempts at QE seem restrained and almost amateurish.

The message is clear. Ignore the older forex trading books - the 'old rules' no longer apply. It is time to move away from a single currency pair. Start trading the USD/JPY, but if you prefer to trade the euro, simply move to the EUR/JPY as this correlates extremely closely with the USD/JPY, particularly on the hourly, daily and weekly timeframes. This is a positive correlation as you would expect.

GBP/USD

At present and following Brexit, this pair has changed, but will revert back to the it's original character. Before 2016, it was solid steady and reliable. It ticks along like Big Ben, rarely volatile and generally predictable, and whilst it does have periods of excitement, the reasons are generally clear and self evident (as is the case at present). There are no politics with the pound, and it is increasingly seen as a safe haven and an alternative to the euro. Before the financial crisis, the GBP/USD and the EUR/USD would generally have moved in lockstep together, with both moving higher or lower on US dollar strength and weakness. This relationship has long since broken down, and now the two react and move independently, with the primary driver for the EUR/USD being politics in Europe, whilst for Cable it is the UK economy. The good old British pound keeps plodding along, and despite the recent downgrade, confidence in the currency was only temporarily dented, before strength returned.

This is not an exciting pair to trade, but then trading success is not about excitement, it's about making money. The trading range typically is between 70 and 100 pips per day, and this is the currency which tends to set the tone for the London session following the open in Europe and from the overnight in Asia.

If you are a novice or inexperienced trader, I would urge you to consider starting with the GBP/USD, but only once any agreement has been reached with Brussels. Until then, it's not one for novice traders.

AUD/USD

The Aussie dollar is one of those currency pairs which gets a 'double boost' whenever the US dollar weakens or strengthens, given its association with commodities, and as result tends to develop strong trends. One only has to look back over the last few years and see how the extended bull run in commodities has been reflected in the pair. More recently, the pair has been in an extended phase of consolidation, with the bullish trend having run out of steam as the commodity super cycle begins to slow. China is the biggest influence on this pair. Next the interest rate differential is also playing its part, and with an economy that is stable and well managed, providing China does not implode, we can expect to see interest rates rising in Australia thereby increasing the differential between the two currencies. Hot money flows should see the pair continue higher in the longer term. Fundamental news has a major influence on the pair with Chinese data leading the way, not US data.

As you might expect the pair correlate positively with the NZD/USD, but only on the longer term timeframes of weekly and above.

USD/CAD

The biggest influence on the USD/CAD is the US, with the pair almost a mirror image of the AUD/USD on the longer term charts, and following the longer term cycle in commodities. Oil is the predominant commodity so once again a double whammy for the pair, with movements in the US dollar reflected in the oil price, as well as the Canadian dollar. As mentioned earlier, the weekly oil stats can have a significant impact mid-week, with any draw or build reflected in strength or weakness for the currency.

NZD/USD

A very similar picture to the AUD/USD pair. A well managed economy which has survived the worst of the financial crisis, but once again it is China which influences the pair strongly. Another commodity currency and in its relationship with the US dollar, any effect is magnified as commodity prices rise and fall with strength or weakness in the US dollar. In addition, with China now taking over the number one spot as New Zealand's primary export market, any bad fundamental news here, will instantly impact the currency, along with the Australian dollar. As you would expect correlation between the two pairs is relatively strong, particularly over the longer term time frames.

USD/CHF

Again, as with the USD/JPY, this is 'safe haven' meets 'safe haven', but in the case of the Swiss franc, underpinned by gold. This is one correlation that still holds good, with the USD/CHF moving inversely to the EUR/USD and maintaining this relationship across all the time frames, despite repeated interventions by the SNB (Swiss National Bank), which only goes to prove the greater power of the market.

As an aside, some traders believe they have stumbled on a magic hedge, when this relationship is first discovered, and that trading long (or short) in both provides the ideal 'safe bet'. I'm afraid this is completely wrong. This is simply constructing the EUR/CHF in another way, and using two pairs to do it, so an expensive way to trade a cross currency pair.

Over the longer term charts, the USD/CHF has reflected the strength in commodities, with strong buying on safe haven demand also moving the pair lower. However, as economies start to recover, and better returns become available elsewhere, then expect to see the Swiss franc being sold, as money is moved out of safe haven and into higher yielding assets. Does this mean the euro will weaken against the US dollar? To which the answer is yes, provided the correlation continues to hold. Further weakness in gold could speed this process along, and if the SNB gets its way and is able to sell off some of the gold reserves, this may be the trigger for investors to move elsewhere and into higher yielding assets. Moreover, as the current recession comes to an end, with inflationary pressure still some way off, demand for gold may fall.

One other tip with the USD/CHF and EUR/USD correlation. If you are trading the EUR/USD, using volume price analysis is a great way to validate the price action using an 'associated' market. After all, if the volume and price is confirming the trend higher for one currency pair, you should be seeing the exact opposite in the other.

USD/NOK

Another commodity currency pair with oil the defining commodity. Again the pair react to the twin forces of US dollar price movements, coupled with the associated movements in oil, so a double whammy effect. The problem with this pair is that, unlike the others in this list, it is relatively thinly traded and therefore can be very volatile. Furthermore, there is little liquidity in the Norwegian bond markets. Norway is certainly a safe haven, but to date the krone has failed to attract the inflows of currency to establish it in the markets with this tag.

The key here will be any interest rate changes which are likely to be triggered by the housing bubble. The housing bubble has been developing for some time, and this could provide the catalyst with oil and the US dollar adding a further boost.

The Cross Currency Pairs

As I mentioned at the start of this chapter, the old rules in forex trading have gone, and as result we have to adapt and change as well. No longer are the major currency pairs the 'de facto' standard for us as forex traders. The world has changed and so has the world order of currencies and currency pairs. It is ironic I have suggested you avoid trading the EUR/USD for the foreseeable future. This would have been unthinkable a few years ago.

Therefore, let me highlight some of the cross currency pairs which I hope you will investigate for yourself. I accept the spreads will be wider, and yes you may have to take a slightly longer term view in order to make the maths work in your favour, but nevertheless, you can find some great trading opportunities in these pairs. As a fellow trader once said: 'let the cross be your boss'. You just have to lift up your eyes, your time horizon and your perspective a little - not a lot, just a little.

In addition there is a further, perhaps self evident reason, which is this - you will no longer be at the mercy of the US dollar. Naturally, the market will always be dollar centric, but its effect on these pairs will simply be indirect. Here are my suggestions.

EUR/GBP

Move the euro to a different pair and its behavior changes almost completely. It's as though the influence of the slow and measured UK pound brings the political upstart into line. The pair moves in a controlled way, is rarely volatile (other than at present with Brexit), and driven more by genuine market sentiment and fundamental news, than by the eternal politics that dominates the price action in the major. Here is a pair of the old school, the way forex markets 'used to be'. Price action swings along at an even pace, supported by the economic releases and the technical picture. In many ways this is a great currency pair for 'learner traders'.

It will never set the world on fire, but neither will it frighten you to death. It is a currency pair many traders ignore, but is an excellent one, in my humble opinion, for gauging the true market sentiment for the euro, devoid of politics, and also disassociated from the US dollar. So a clear view of the euro in every sense of the word. It is not a pair that will make you a fortune quickly, but it is a reliable and solid currency pair that behaves in the way currency pairs used to behave. You will make money with it, as it is predictable and follows the 'rules', and I say hurrah for that.

The EUR/GBP has a very strong correlation with the GBP/CHF pair across all time frames, with an inverse relationship.

AUD/JPY

I've chosen the AUD/JPY pair here, but to be honest we could have chosen any of the yen currency pairs, as they all correlate very closely, driven by the Japanese yen which dominates the pairs. Therefore, get the direction for the yen correct, and you are spoilt for choice. Furthermore, with the FXCM yen index, you have the perfect chart to reveal yen strength and weakness against the four major currencies, so use it.

The reason I selected the AUD/JPY is simple. It is a proxy pair for risk, and is the currency pair which should be checked each day for an assessment of market mood and sentiment. The same could be said for the EUR/JPY which used to have a very strong positive correlation with the S&P500, but I prefer the AUD/JPY. Here we have a commodity currency with a high yield, balanced by the counter currency of safe haven and the funding currency for the carry trade. As with all yen pairs, the index to watch is the Nikkei 225. If the index is rising money will be flowing into high risk and out of low risk. The yen will therefore weaken as Japanese (and other investors) sell the yen and move into risk.

CAD/JPY

Another of the yen pairs, and if you remember this is one that has a relatively close correlation to the price of oil. Canada as a major exporter, and the Japanese as a major importer. If oil prices are rising, at the same time as the yen is being weakened by 'risk on' or politics, the pair will move quickly. The weekly oil stats release on the economic calendar will also play their part here, with any build in reserves, bad for the price of oil and any draw, generally good. So there are several influences here, but as always with the yen crosses, get the direction right and you make money very quickly.

AUD/NZD

I have included this pair as it is an interesting combination of 'commodity currency' vs 'commodity currency'. Near neighbour vs near neighbour. Australia and New Zealand are very similar in terms of exports and stability with similar risk profiles for their currencies. Surprisingly this pair trend extremely well, but only in the longer term timeframes, once you move beyond the hourly chart. Therefore, this is definitely a pair to consider for longer term swing or trend trading. And as I mentioned earlier, given the spreads on many of these pairs will be wider than the more usual one or two pips of the majors, a longer term approach is required.

In this pair the question is which commodities are dominating and why, and as I outlined earlier, the Australian dollar is closely connected to hard commodities whilst the New Zealand is more aligned to the 'softs'. In addition, both now have China as their largest export market, and both have comparable interest rates. Therefore, what are the likely drivers of this currency pair, and again the answer is very much China? So, even if the Chinese economy does slow down, the Chinese people still have to eat, this is likely to have a greater impact on the AUD rather than the NZD. This would then be reflected in the pair in a move lower.

EUR/CHF

There are, of course, many cross currency pairs and impossible to cover them all here, so to round off this section, I just wanted to end with one I would suggest you perhaps do not trade, unless you actively enjoy watching paint dry. And that is the EUR/CHF. If you are prepared to wait months, and I do mean months, for a trend to develop, this pair may offer some trading opportunities. However, it remains rangebound for extremely long periods, and more likely to bore you out of a position before it moves. That said, since the SNB removed the floor of support in 2015, this pair has seen more lively price action since, so perhaps one to consider.

The Currency Matrix

Finally to round of this chapter let me introduce you to the concept I call the 'currency matrix'. The forex markets are distinctive in many ways, but one aspect in particular stands out above all others. And it is this. The fact a currency can be bought or sold against many other currencies. There are over 1000 global currency pairs, so there is always plenty of choice. This makes it extremely difficult for us as forex traders, to be able to identify where the buying or selling is actually taking place. Is it in the major currency pairs, or is it perhaps in the cross currency pairs? For example a bank selling euros and wanting to buy US dollars, might choose to do so with the EUR/USD, but they might not. One option could be to sell euros using the EUR/GBP, and then to sell pounds against the US dollar. The result would be the same, but the route would be very different.

The Interbank market makers do this all the time as they like to cover their tracks as much as possible, not just from us, but more importantly from their competitors. In addition, in moving large flows, they may put the price up against themselves in the process. So the question is this. Whenever we see a currency pair strengthening or weakening, can we validate this strength or weakness in any way? And the answer is yes, using the currency matrix.

Trading in forex is really about one thing and one thing only. Identifying currency strength and currency weakness. This is made doubly difficult for us, as we have to deal with two complex issues. First, is the currency pair being driven by strength or weakness in the base currency or the counter currency. Second, is that strength or weakness universal, in other words it is across all the other related currency pairs. And this is where we turn to the currency matrix for an answer to these questions. Moreover, it is somewhat ironic that as we come to the end of a book on three dimensional forex trading, this concept of looking at the markets in 3D comes in once more. However, this time directly and just using our forex charts.

The easiest way to explain a currency matrix is with some examples.

Suppose you are trading the EUR/GBP and the pair is moving higher. Is this move the result of euro strength or pound weakness?

Now imagine. Instead of looking at one chart for the EUR/GBP you also had the following charts on your screen, and this is what I call my currency matrix:

- EUR/USD
- EUR/JPY
- EUR/CHF
- EUR/AUD
- EUR/CAD
- EUR/NZD

Suppose in all these pairs, the euro was also rising. What conclusion could we draw? Simply and clearly the EUR/GBP is being driven by euro strength and not pound weakness, since all the other euro pairs are rising along with the EUR/GBP. In other words, these other currency pairs are validating the move higher, and indicating in clear and simple terms the move higher is being driven by strength in the euro.

Next, what this matrix of charts will also tell you, is if this is not the case, in other words, if some pairs are rising and others are not, perhaps the move is lacking momentum and therefore unlikely to develop into a longer term trend. After all, if the market is buying euros across all the other pairs, this is a strong signal the euro is being bought everywhere, and other currencies are being sold. At the same time we can also check the GBP complex, and if the same is seen here with strong selling of the pound, we have the perfect combination. Buying of the euro across the complex, and selling the pound across its complex.

Finally, the currency matrix also reveals something else. It reveals the best currency pair to trade. If you are trading euro strength, for whatever reason, it will be instantly self evident from the matrix, which euro pairs offer the best trading opportunities based on your analysis. The move higher in the EUR/GBP may be sluggish compared to a move higher in the EUR/JPY or the EUR/CAD.

This is where a currency strength indicator can also help. The indicator can guide you to those currencies that are either overbought or oversold, and together with the currency matrix quickly and easily identify where the buying and selling is really taking place.

So in summary, a currency matrix does three key things for us.

First, a currency matrix helps us to identify the driving force in the currency pair. Is it the base currency, or the counter currency.

Second, the matrix helps us to validate the move, by confirming strength across all the related pairs.

Third, the matrix identifies the best pair to trade.

Setting up the currency matrix is very simple and I am always amazed forex traders rarely use this approach. To me it is common sense and yet few traders I have ever met use this simple technique. The charts are there, you simply need to set up a workspace with the six charts according to the main currencies you trade.

Therefore, you would have a yen workspace, a euro workspace, a pound workspace, a dollar workspace and so on, each with six charts for the primary currencies. For example, the yen workspace would be as follows :

- USD/JPY
- GBP/JPY
- AUD/JPY
- EUR/JPY
- CAD/JPY
- CHF/JPY

I will leave you to create the remainder. And whilst this can be done manually, I have since created an automated version which you can find on the Quantum Trading site.

And so we come to the end of the book.

I hope you have enjoyed reading it, and more importantly I fervently hope it is has changed the way you view the forex market, forever. My purpose has been to try to explain why I believe the forex market is the most important and powerful of the capital markets. And to explain some of the least understood linkages and relationships which exist between the four principle markets. As I have written many times, trading in isolation, without reference to any other market or instrument and focused on one chart, is doomed to failure. Yet this is how most traders trade, having been seduced into thinking it is simple, and an easy way to make money fast.

However, like every profitable endeavour, it takes time and effort, and a little hard work so I make no apology for the length or scope of this book. It explains, what I believe is rarely covered, and in my view is the only way to approach the forex market with any guarantee of long term success.

In applying the principles you have discovered here, you will be laying down the foundation stones of success in your own trading career. The forex market does not operate in a vacuum nor in isolation. Furthermore, it sits at the heart of all trading and investing and is the axis around which the other markets rotate. Whilst some of the linkages may be complex and take time to master, others are more straightforward. When you think about it logically, all the financial markets are signaling, second by second and day by day, is sentiment, risk, money flow and returns, and this is always reflected first in the forex market. And the reason, is simply because it is the quickest and easiest market in which to move from risk to safe haven, and back again. As Bernard Baruch said in relation to the stock market, but which applies equally to all markets:

'Above all else, in other words, the stock market is people. It is people trying to read the future. And it is this intensely human quality that makes the stock market so dramatic an arena in which men and women pit their conflicting judgements, their hopes and fears, strengths and weaknesses, greeds and ideals.'

I started my own trading journey in the futures markets trading indices many years ago, and came to the forex market last of all. I only wish someone had explained to me why market behavior is a three dimensional process, and its importance. The clues and signals are there in plain sight, so why ignore them. The reason most traders do, is this approach has never been fully explained, and that has been my purpose here. To explain, in what I hope has been a simple, clear and logical way, how and why these relationships exist and how to profit from this knowledge.

If I had been armed with this knowledge when I first started, it would have saved me a great deal of time and short cut my own learning curve. And I hope it will do the same for you in your own trading (and investing) career.

Finally, I would, of course, like to thank you for purchasing this book, and if you do have any comments, questions or suggestions I would be delighted to hear from you. You can contact me on my personal email at anna@annacoulling.com and I guarantee you will receive a reply. This book is based on my own personal trading experience, and from what I found has worked for me over the years. However, I am also conscious it is impossible to cover all aspects of trading in one book. The purpose here has been to demonstrate how a three dimensional view can provide the foundation and framework against which to make trading decisions.

If you have enjoyed the book, naturally I would be grateful if you could spread the word, to help other traders who may still be struggling to understand how and why the forex markets behave in the way they do. I would of course appreciate a review on Amazon, which will help others to find this book more easily. So thank you in advance.

You can find details on all my other books in the back of this one, or on Amazon where they are all available in Kindle format or paperback. You may also be interested to learn I have since developed The Complete Forex Trading Program which takes all the concepts and ideas to the next level, as well as integrating them with the complete suite of trading tools and indicators, some of which I have mentioned here. You can find all the details at https://www.quantumtradingeducation.com - The Complete Forex Trading Program

My purpose here has been to explain broad concepts, and not detail, but to provide a framework. All subsequent books will be premised on two simple concepts. First, all markets are interconnected and to succeed you need to understand the three dimensional approach I have explained in this book. And second, that volume price analysis underpins all technical analysis and trading.

Once again, thank you so much, and may I wish you every success in your own trading journey towards becoming a master forex trader.

Warmest regards, and many thanks again

Anna

PS - please do follow my market analysis on my personal site and check for the latest book, or join me on Twitter or Facebook - In addition I also run regular seminars, webinars and trading rooms where I explain the concepts and methodologies in more detail. I look forward to seeing you there, and thank you once again.

http://www.annacoulling.com

http://www.twitter.com/annacoull

http://facebook.com/learnforextrading

My Other Books & Acknowledgments

Appreciation is a wonderful thing. It makes what is excellent in others belong to us as well.

Voltaire (1694 - 1778)

My Other Books

A Complete Guide To Volume Price Analysis

With over 280 five star reviews, I'm proud to say this has now become the 'go to' book for traders and investors in all markets. For many, it has been the book which has turned their trading around.

Volume price analysis provides the bedrock methodology for trading all markets and all timeframes. It is the approach the iconic traders of the past used in building vast fortunes using nothing more than the humble ticker tape as it punched out its incessant stream of prices and volume. Trading greats such as Jesse Livermore, Charles Dow and the father of volume trading Richard Wyckoff who codified the underlying principles in his three laws.

Now you too can employ this powerful methodology which truly reveals the truth behind the price action. Whether you decide to blend it with your existing approach, or to use it supported with other tools and indicators, is a personal choice. But one thing is certain. Once you read the book, you will read the market with confidence you never thought possible.

Available on Amazon in Kindle and paperback

Forex For Beginners

As a trader and investor with over twenty years experience, I wrote Forex For Beginners with one clear objective in mind. To provide a clear, detailed and unequivocal guide to this market and how to trade it.

The marketing hype which embraces the forex world has two very simple messages. First, it's easy to get started and second, it's easy to make money with little effort. The first of these statements is certainly true. The second is not. Forex is a complex market which sits at the heart of all the financial markets, and to succeed requires a deeper understanding than would first appear. This is why so many struggle and ultimately fail.

From the many five star reviews on Amazon, it seems I have achieved my goal in providing new and novice forex traders with a foundation course for trading forex and on which to build.

Available on Amazon in Kindle and paperback

Forex Trading Using Volume Price Analysis

And if you're trading forex, either in the spot market or in futures, then this is the companion book for you.

Once again it's packed with worked examples in all timeframes from the slowest to the fastest. so whether you are an intraday speculative trader on the minute charts, or perhaps a slower swing or trend trader on the hourly or daily charts, all are covered in this book.

Every chart is fully annotated to illustrate and highlight key points in the associated text, and together provide a detailed and comprehensive study of the volume price relationship, giving clear signals as to where each currency pair is heading next. And perhaps most important of all, these examples reveal the power of volume price analysis in a market where there is no central exchange. Here we are using tick activity as a proxy for volume, and yet it works perfectly as you will discover.

Available on Amazon in Kindle and paperback

Stock Trading & Investing Using Volume Price Analysis

If you enjoyed reading A Complete Guide To Volume Price Analysis, then you'll love this one too, which is the perfect companion book, and one I wrote following hundreds of emails asking for a follow up to the first.

Stock Trading & Investing Using Volume Price Analysis, takes the VPA principles and builds into a comprehensive workbook of over 200 examples. The examples presented are drawn primarily from US stock markets, but also include others from the futures markets such as indices, commodities, currency futures and bonds. Each chart is fully annotated to illustrate and highlight key points in the associated text, and together provide a detailed and comprehensive study of the volume price relationship, giving clear signals as to where the stock is going next.

Available on Amazon in Kindle and paperback

Investing & Trading in Cryptocurrencies Using Volume Price Analysis

Finally in this trio of books comes the new kid on the block of cryptocurrencies, and another companion book for volume traders, Investing & Trading in Cryptocurrencies Using Volume Price Analysis.

Cryptocurrencies are the latest to join the digital revolution and given the volatility associated with these markets since their launch, volume price analysis is the perfect methodology to reveal the truth behind the price action. Here too, we have no central exchange, and indeed even less regulation than in spot forex markets. Yet as you will see, volume price analysis works perfectly in this market, just as for stocks and forex.

The book is packed with worked examples in all the major cryptocurrency pairs, starting with the most widely traded of all, Bitcoin. From there the book moves on to consider Ethereum, Litecoin, Ripple and many others. Each chart is fully annotated to illustrate and highlight key points in the associated text, and provide a detailed and comprehensive study of the volume price relationship when applied to this exciting and volatile newcomer.

If you're a trader or investor in cryptocurrencies, this is a must read book for you. It will give you the insights and understanding to make rational and logical decisions, and not ones driven by the emotional response of a fear of missing out, which has been so damaging to many in this market.

Available on Amazon in Kindle and paperback

Binary Options Unmasked

Are binary options for me? This is the question I hope will be answered for you in this book. in writing it, I have tried to provide a complete introduction to the subject, with practical examples of how to approach these innovative instruments. Every aspect of this market is explained - both the good and the not so good! Nothing is left unsaid.

Binary options have much to offer, and used with common sense and thought, are perfectly valid trading instruments. The book reveals the true characteristics of the market. It explains the current market participants, along with the product offering. Moreover, not only are binary options explained in detail, but their application as a trading instrument is also illustrated.

Trading strategies and approaches are also explored, along with an innovative and practical approach to interpreting volatility, a key component of any options trading. I hope this book will give you the confidence to consider these instruments in more detail for yourself, with an open mind and eyes wide open.

Available on Amazon in Kindle and paperback

Acknowledgements & Resources

I would like to acknowledge the following companies who have kindly allowed me to use their charts freely, and who have made this book possible.

www.investing.com

A free trader resource covering virtually every global market, and of course the 'old style' USD index is also here. Here you will also find live futures prices, and charts for over 1000 currency pairs. Many of the chart examples are from the site, and I would urge you to visit it, as they offer an array of tools for forex traders.

www.ninjatrader.com

Many of the chart examples in this book are from my NinjaTrader trading platform. The NinjaTrader platform with the Kinetick data feed is one of the most powerful combinations in the market, and is available on a FREE, end of day basis.

www.forexfactory.com

One of the best online resources for fundamental news and releases. Recently updated and revised with some of the fundamental news items being re-categorized. My thanks to them for allowing me to use images from their excellent site in this book.

www.annacoulling.com

My own site for regular market analysis across all the markets including commodities and stocks. You can also contact me there (or leave comments on posts which are much appreciated) or email me personally on anna@annacoulling.com

www.quantumtrading.com

Here you will find all the tools and indicators mentioned in the book such as the currency strength indicator and the currency matrix along with several others.

www.quantumtradingeducation

Here you will find details of The Complete Forex Trading Program which I developed with my husband and trading partner David.

www.cftc.gov

Here you will find the weekly Commitment of Traders Report. The data is not pretty, but it's there and freely available and will give you an insight into the big market operators.

www.cmegroup.com

The premier exchange for market analysis of all futures markets, and of course contract specifications. For currency traders the futures world is opening up as well, with the CME moving away from the once traditional large contracts, to offer micro and mini contracts for retail traders.

www.mataf.net

An excellent site for checking on the latest correlations between currency pairs. This is under the Tools/Charts section, and updated in real time.

www.freestockcharts.com

Here you can find free live charts for a variety of markets, in particular US stocks, US indices, ETFs and currencies.

www.research.stlouisfed.org

Here is where you can create your own charts for TIPS & the TED Spread using the FRED economic data. Again, not an easy site to use, but worth the effort for your TIPS and TED.

Printed in Germany
by Amazon
Distribution